D1423121

2590136. 27. 4. 79.

The Oratory School
* 0 0 0 0 3 8 3 3 *

ORATORY SCHOOL
LIBRARY

CLASS 946.08

BOOK No. 7836

Ronald Fraser

Blood of Spain

The Experience of Civil War, 1936–1939

Allen Lane

ALLEN LANE
Penguin Books Ltd
17 Grosvenor Gardens
London SW1W 0BD

First published 1979

Copyright © Ronald Fraser, 1979
All rights reserved

ISBN 0 7139 1085 2

Set in Monotype Ehrhardt and Bodoni

Printed in Great Britain by
Ebenezer Baylis and Son Ltd
The Trinity Press, Worcester, and London

Maps drawn by Reginald Piggott

FOR RvdB

Contents

AUTUMN 1936

WINTER 1936

SPRING 1937

SUMMER TO AUTUMN 1937

Acknowledgements

I wish to thank the more than 300 participants who have made this book possible. Over and above their help, their kindness made my task both easier and more pleasurable. With their agreement, the majority appear under their own names and I will not acknowledge them individually here. To those who participated and who do not appear in the book, I offer my apologies; the exigencies of space are alone responsible.

My task would have been impossible without the help of many dozens of other persons who gave of their time and energy to suggest and locate participants. As I have acknowledged them individually in the Spanish edition of this book, I will not repeat the list here.

Given the nature of the book, I wish to stress that appearance in it does not involve responsibility for the final product. Liability for any errors of fact or interpretation rests entirely with me.

I owe a very special debt of gratitude to Rosalind van der Beek, who has helped me see this project through from beginning to end, who has transcribed and typed many millions of words in the course of it, and has made invaluable editorial suggestions; and to Margarita Jiménez, who undertook the transcription and translation of a number of important interviews. I wish to thank Susan Harding for help with anarcho-syndicalist problems in Aragon, and Alastair Reid, to whom I owe the idea for this book.

Finally, I must acknowledge the help of those who read parts of or the entire draft of the book: Dr Michael Alpert, Mark Fraser, Susan Gyarmati, Fred Halliday, Miren Lopategui, Juan Martínez Alier, Maxime Molyneux and Gareth Stedman-Jones. All made invaluable critical comments which have improved the book; but here again I must stress that they are in no way responsible for any errors which remain.

List of political parties and organizations

The following are the major political parties, movements and trade unions mentioned in this book. Those marked * signed the Popular Front pact of 1936; those indicated with ** joined the counter-revolutionary or National Front in the same year's general elections.

CENTRE AND RIGHT-WING

**AP (Acción Popular) – the major party within the CEDA, founded in 1932

**CEDA (Confederación Española de Derechas Autónomas) – Catholic, founded in 1933

*Lliga Catalana – Catalan nationalist party of the large bourgeoisie, founded as successor to Lliga Regionalista in 1933

Partido Agrario – CEDA ally, representing mainly Castilian landowners

Partido Republicano Radical – oldest republican party (1908), major government party in 1933–5

PNV (Partido Nacionalista Vasco) – major Basque nationalist party, founded in 1895

EXTREME RIGHT-WING

**Comunión Tradicionalista – the political party of the Carlist movement from 1931

Falange Española – fascist, founded by José Antonio Primo de Rivera, 1933

JONS (Juntas de Ofensiva Nacional Sindicalista) – fascist, founded in 1931, fused with Falange in 1934

**Renovación Española – monarchist, founded in 1933

UME (Unión Militar Española) – unofficial right-wing officers' union

LEFT-WING

*ANV (Acción Nacionalista Vasco) – split from PNV, founded in 1930

*Esquerra Republicana de Catalunya – Catalan left republican nationalist party, founded in 1931

Estat Català – radical separatist Catalan party, one of the founders of the Esquerra Republicana de Catalunya; as a wing of the latter it became proto-fascist by 1934; elements from it broke away from the Esquerra to reform Estat Català before the war

*Izquierda Republicana – left republican party, formed under Azaña in 1934 from Acción Republicana (1925), Partido Republicano Radical-Socialista (1929) and MAOC (Milicias Anti-fascistas Obreras y Campesinas) – communist-organized workers' and peasants' anti-fascist militias

ORGA (Organización Republicana Gallega Autónoma)

*PCE (Partido Comunista de España) – official communist party, founded in 1921

*PSOE (Partido Socialista Obrero Español) – the Spanish socialist party, founded in 1879

PSUC (Partit Socialista Unificat de Catalunya) – formed on outbreak of war from *Unió Socialista, *Catalan federation of the PSOE, *Partit Comunista de Catalunya and *Partit Català Proletari. Affiliated to Comintern, thus effectively the communist party in Catalonia

UMRA (Unión Militar de Republicanos Anti-fascistas) – unofficial military union of anti-fascist republicans
*Unión Republicana – a split, led by Martínez Barrio, from the Partido Republicana Radical, founded in 1934

EXTREME LEFT-WING

BOC (Bloc Obrer i Camperol) – Workers and Peasants Bloc, dissident communist party in Catalonia, formed in 1931 from a split in the PCE and a fusion with the Partit Comunista Català; led by Joaquim Maurín
FAI (Federación Anarquista Ibérica) – militant federation of anarchist groups, founded in 1927
IC (Izquierda Comunista) – Trotskyist split from PCE, led by Andreu Nin
*POUM (Partido Obrero de Unificación Marxista) – dissident communist party, fusion of BOC and IC in 1935, led by Maurín and Nin

TRADE UNIONS

AET (Agrupación Escolar Tradicionalista) – Carlist student union
CNT (Confederación Nacional del Trabajo) – anarcho-syndicalist
FNTT (Federación Nacional de Trabajadores de la Tierra) – socialist-led Land-workers' Federation, part of UGT
FOUS (Federación Obrera de Unidad Sindical) – POUM-led trade union
FUE (Federación Universitaria de Estudiantes) – student union, founded in 1920s to combat the dictatorship, moved increasingly leftwards in 1930s
GEPCI (Gremis e Entitats de Petits Comerciants e Industrials) – PSUC-organized union for Catalan artisans, tradesmen and small manufacturers
SEU (Sindicato Español Universitario) – Falangist student union
STV (Solidaridad de Trabajadores Vascos) – Basque nationalist trade union
*UGT (Unión General de Trabajadores) – socialist

YOUTH ORGANIZATIONS

*JS (Juventudes Socialistas) – socialist youth
JC (Juventudes Comunistas) – communist youth
JSU (Juventudes Socialistas Unificadas) – unified socialist youth, formed in 1936 from fusion of JS and JC
JCI (Juventud Comunista Ibérica) – POUM youth movement
FIJL (Federación Ibérica de Juventudes Libertarias) – anarchist youth
JAP (Juventudes de Acción Popular) – Catholic

Glossary of Spanish words

abuelo, *abuela*, grandfather, grandmother
alférez provisional, provisional second lieutenant
amatxu (Basque), mother
bacalao, dried cod
bandera, Foreign Legion battalion
barrio, quarter or neighbourhood of town or village
buenas tardes, good afternoon, evening
butifarra (Catalan), sausage
cabezalero (Andalusian), foreman, manager of collectivized farm
cabrón (pej.), bastard
cacique, political boss
caciquismo, system of political bossism
canalla (pej.), scum
carabinero, frontier guard
carca (pej.), reactionary
casa del pueblo, workers' club, usually socialist, often also the latter party's and socialist trade unions' local headquarters
casino, club
caudillo, leader (Franco)
centinela, sentry
chamizo (Asturian), narrow coal shaft
checa, unofficial political court or prison
chico, *chica*, boy, girl
chirla, small clam
churro, fritter
compañero, *compañera*, companion
cojones (lit. testicles), courage, guts
coño (lit. cunt), hell! damn!
cortijo, large farm
denuncia, information or charge laid against a person
detente, small piece of cloth bearing image of the Heart of Jesus worn on the chest
dios mio, good lord!
doble (measure in Aragon), 12 kilos of olives
duro, five pesetas
fanega (Andalusian land measure), 0·6 hectares, approx. 1·5 acres
fueros, rights of self-government in Basque country and Navarre
gazpacho, soup of bread, oil, vinegar, tomatoes, garlic
generalísimo, supreme commander
gente de orden, law-abiding citizens
granuja (pej.), rogue
gudari (Basque), Basque nationalist soldier
guerrillero, guerilla
hidalgo, minor noble
hijo, son; *anda hijo*, come on, son; *hijo mío*, my son
hombre, man
labrador (Andalusian), large tenant farmer
Madrileño, native of Madrid
masía (Catalan), farmhouse
me cago en la leche (lit. shit in the milk), well I'm damned!
muchacho, lad
mujer, woman, wife
nada, nothing
¡no pasaran!, they shall not pass!
novio, *novia*, boyfriend, girlfriend intending to marry
obrada (Castilian land measure), 0·56 hectares, approx. 1·4 acres
paella, rice, meat, fish dish
paseo, to take for a ride, assassination
peque (from *pequeño*, small), lad, kid
por dios, for God's sake
practicante, medical assistant
pronunciamiento, military revolt to change political regime
pueblo, village or township
puta, whore
regulares, Moroccan troops
rejoneador, mounted bullfighter
reparto, division of large estates among landworkers
requeté, Carlist militia or militiaman
rojo (pej.), red
saca, taking out (of prison cell etc.) to execute
señorito, young gentleman
sindicato, trade union
sin novedad, nothing to report
tabor, battalion of Moroccan troops
tercio, Foreign Legion or Carlist regiment
tertulia, informal social group meeting to talk
torre (Catalan), villa
treintista, member of movement expelled from CNT in 1932 for holding that revolution could not be made by small, audacious groups
turrón, type of nougat

MAPS *(pages 16–23)*

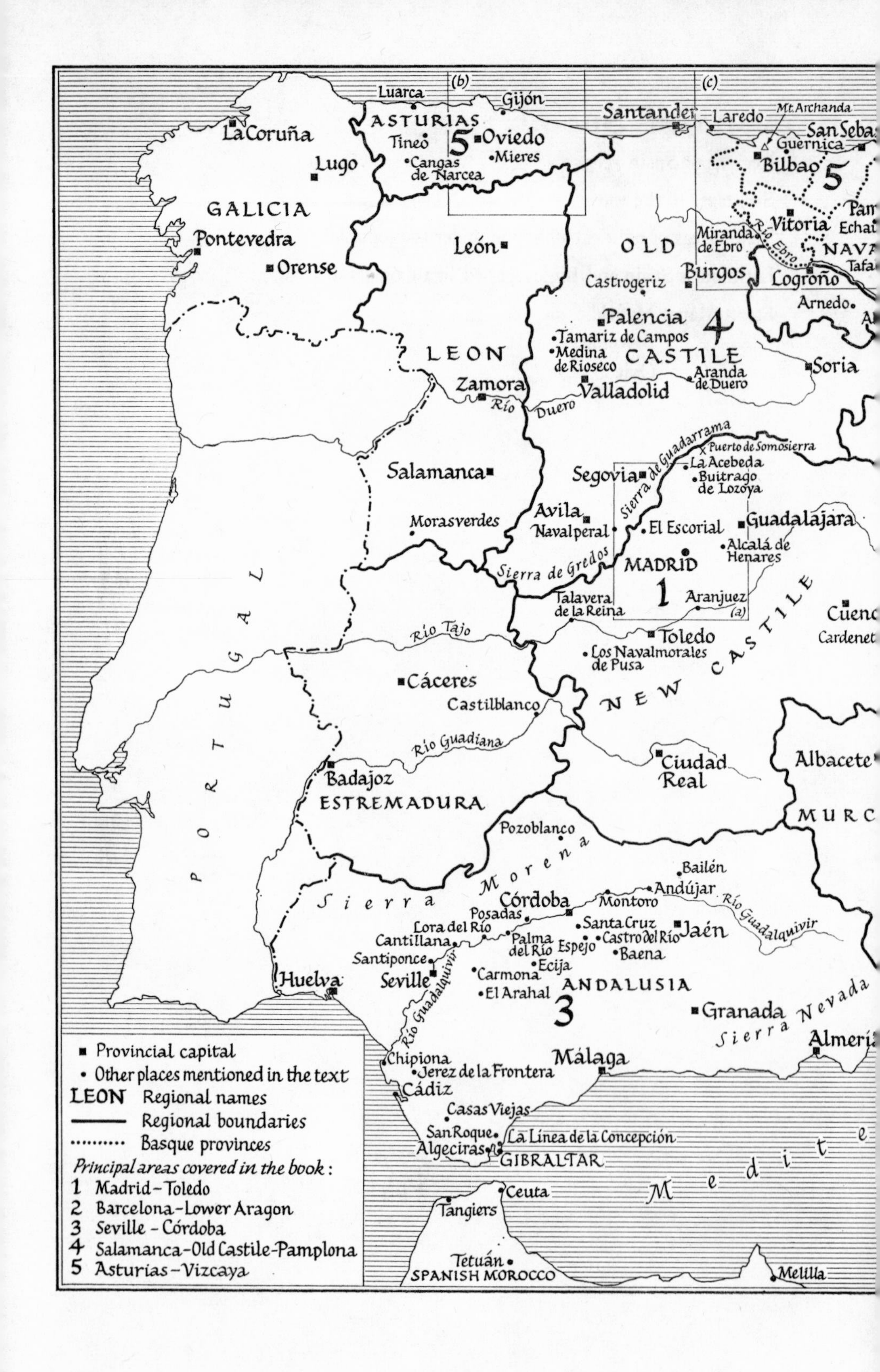

Luarca
Gijón
ASTURIAS
Tineo
Oviedo
Cangas de Narcea
Mieres
Santander
Laredo
Mt. Archanda
Guernica
Bilbao
Vitoria
Miranda de Ebro
Río Ebro
Burgos
Logroño
Arnedo
La Coruña
Lugo
GALICIA
Pontevedra
Orense
León
OLD
Castrogeriz
Palencia
Tamariz de Campos
Medina de Rioseco
CASTILE
Aranda de Duero
Soria
LEON
Zamora
Río Duero
Valladolid
Puerto de Somosierra
Sierra de Guadarrama
La Acebeda
Buitrago de Lozoya
Salamanca
Segovia
Morasverdes
Avila
Navalperal
El Escorial
Guadalajara
Alcalá de Henares
MADRID
Sierra de Gredos
Talavera de la Reina
Aranjuez
Toledo
Río Tajo
Los Navalmorales de Pusa
NEW CASTILE
PORTUGAL
Cáceres
Castilblanco
Río Guadiana
Ciudad Real
Albacete
Badajoz
ESTREMADURA
Pozoblanco
Sierra Morena
Bailén
Andújar
Montoro
Córdoba
Posadas
Lora del Río
Cantillana
Palma del Río
Santa Cruz
Castro del Río
Espejo
Baena
Jaén
Río Guadalquivir
Santiponce
Seville
Ecija
Carmona
El Arahal
Huelva
ANDALUSIA
Granada
Sierra Nevada
Chipiona
Jerez de la Frontera
Málaga
Cádiz
Casas Viejas
San Roque
La Linea de la Concepción
Algeciras
GIBRALTAR
Ceuta
Tangiers
Tetuán
SPANISH MOROCCO
Melilla
Provincial capital
Other places mentioned in the text
LEON Regional names
Regional boundaries
Basque provinces
Principal areas covered in the book:
1 Madrid-Toledo
2 Barcelona-Lower Aragon
3 Seville - Córdoba
4 Salamanca-Old Castile-Pamplona
5 Asturias-Vizcaya

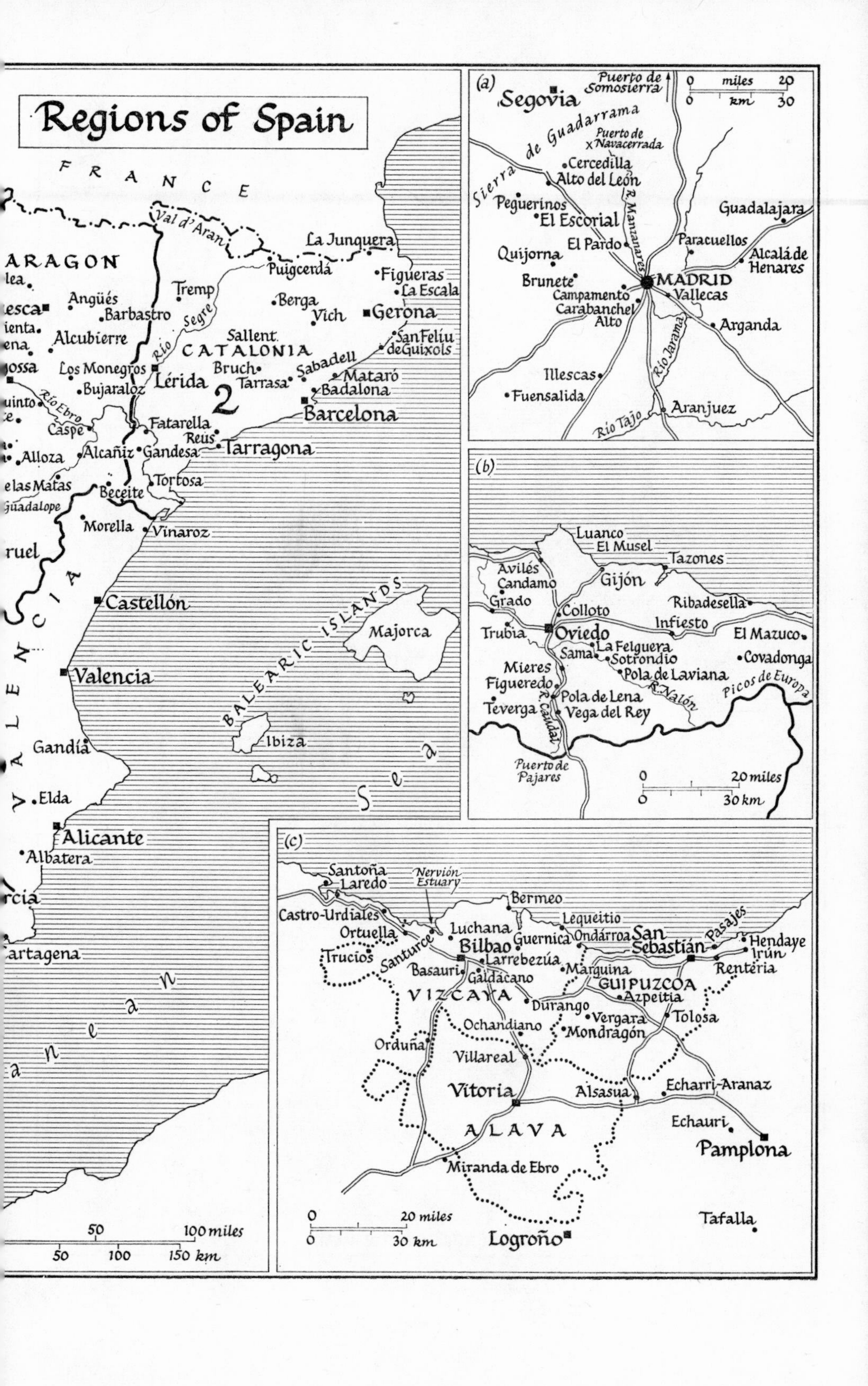
Regions of Spain
FRANCE
ARAGON
CATALONIA
VALENCIA
BALEARIC ISLANDS
Val d'Aran
La Junquera
Puigcerdá
Figueras
La Escala
Tremp
Berga
Vich
Gerona
Angüés
Barbastro
Río Segre
Sallent
Alcubierre
San Feliu de Guixols
Los Monegros
Lérida
Bruch
Tarrasa
Sabadell
Mataró
Bujaraloz
Badalona
Barcelona
Río Ebro
Caspe
Fatarella
Reus
Tarragona
Alloza
Alcañiz
Gandesa
Tortosa
Beceite
Morella
Vinaroz
Castellón
Majorca
Valencia
Ibiza
Gandía
Elda
Alicante
Albatera
Cartagena
Sea
50
100 miles
50
100
150 km
(a)
Segovia
Puerto de Somosierra
0 miles 20
0 km 30
Sierra de Guadarrama
Puerto de Navacerrada
Cercedilla
Alto del León
Peguerinos
El Escorial
R. Manzanares
Guadalajara
El Pardo
Paracuellos
Quijorna
Alcalá de Henares
Brunete
MADRID
Campamento
Vallecas
Carabanchel Alto
Río Jarama
Arganda
Illescas
Fuensalida
Río Tajo
Aranjuez
(b)
Luanco
El Musel
Tazones
Avilés
Candamo
Gijón
Grado
Colloto
Ribadesella
Infiesto
Trubia
Oviedo
El Mazuco
La Felguera
Sama
Sotrondio
Covadonga
Mieres
Pola de Laviana
Figueredo
R. Nalón
Picos de Europa
Pola de Lena
Teverga
Vega del Rey
R. Caudal
Puerto de Pajares
0
20 miles
0
30 km
(c)
Santoña
Laredo
Nervión Estuary
Bermeo
Castro-Urdiales
Lequeitio
Ortuella
Luchana
Guernica
Ondárroa
San Sebastián
Pasajes
Hendaye
Irún
Trucios
Santurce
Bilbao
Larrebezúa
Basauri
Marquina
Rentería
Galdácano
GUIPUZCOA
VIZCAYA
Azpeitia
Durango
Vergara
Tolosa
Ochandiano
Mondragón
Orduña
Villareal
Vitoria
Alsasua
Echarri-Aranaz
Echauri
ALAVA
Pamplona
Miranda de Ebro
0
20 miles
0
30 km
Logroño
Tafalla

Six stages of the war

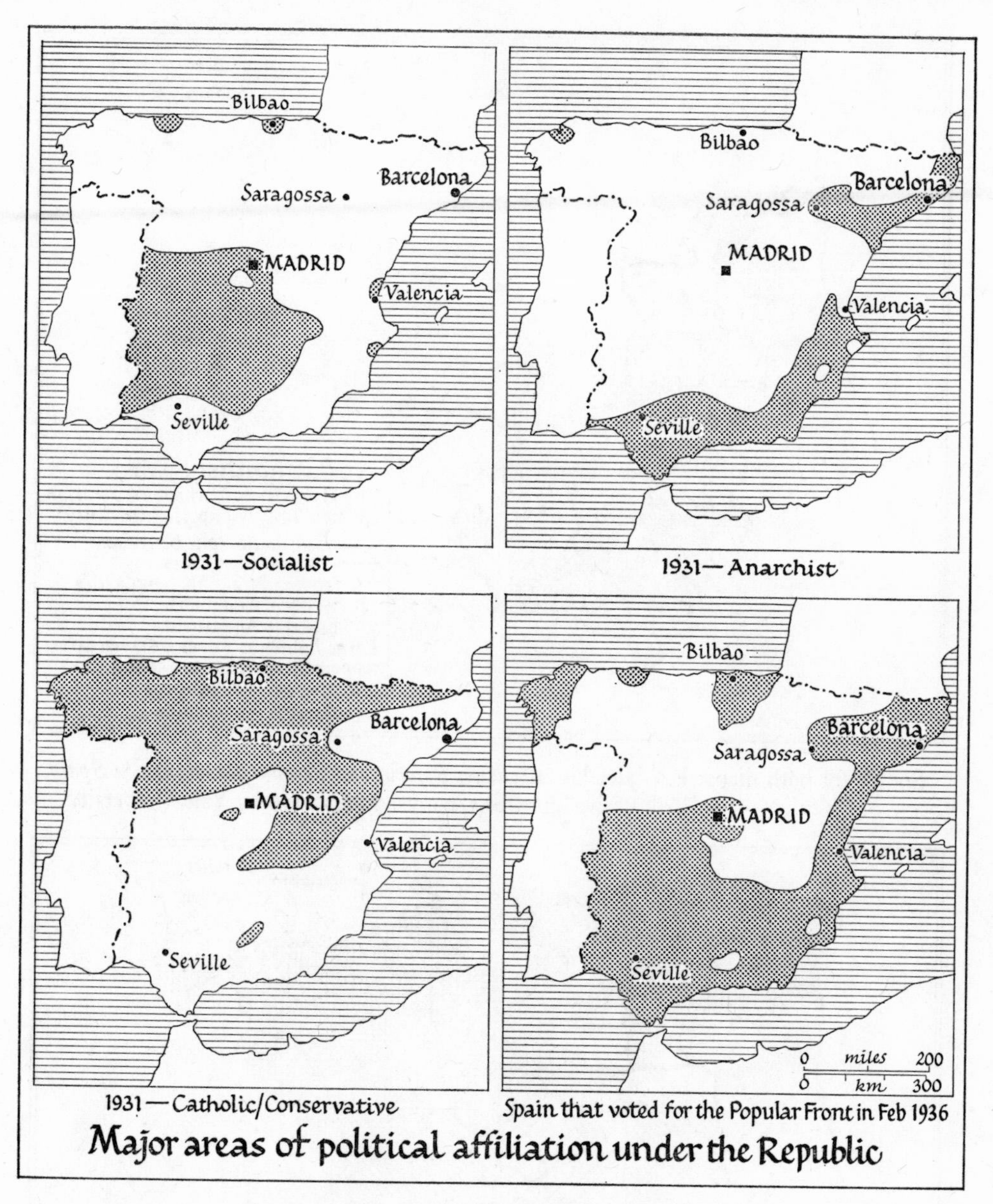

Source: G. Brenan, *The Spanish Labyrinth*, Cambridge University Press

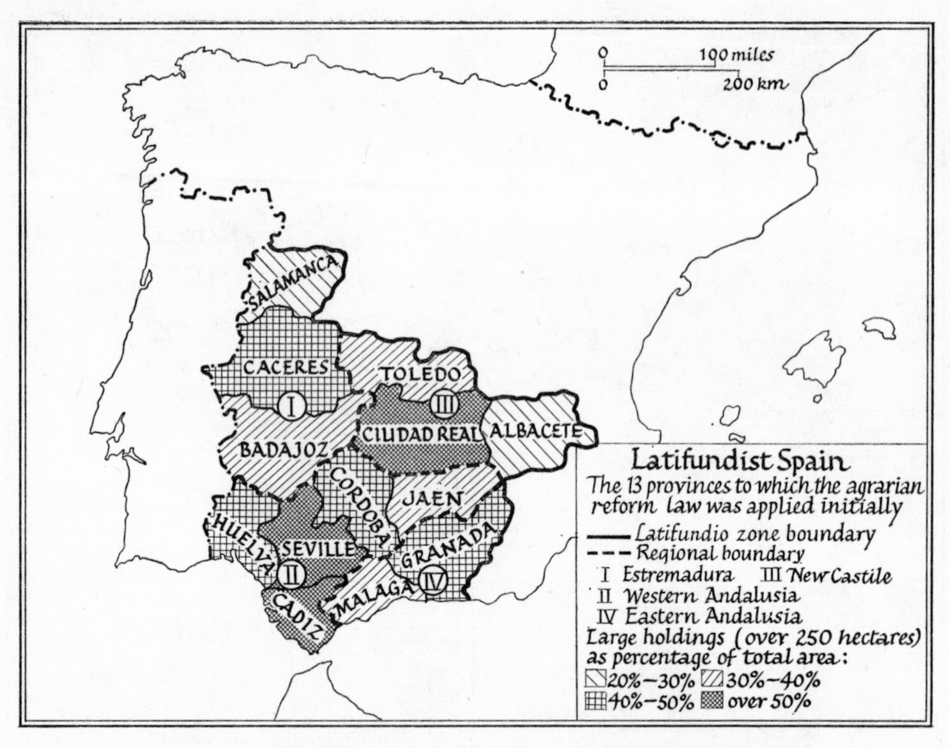

Source for both maps: E. Malefakis, *Agrarian Reform and Peasant Revolution in Spain*, Yale University Press, copyright © 1970 by Yale University

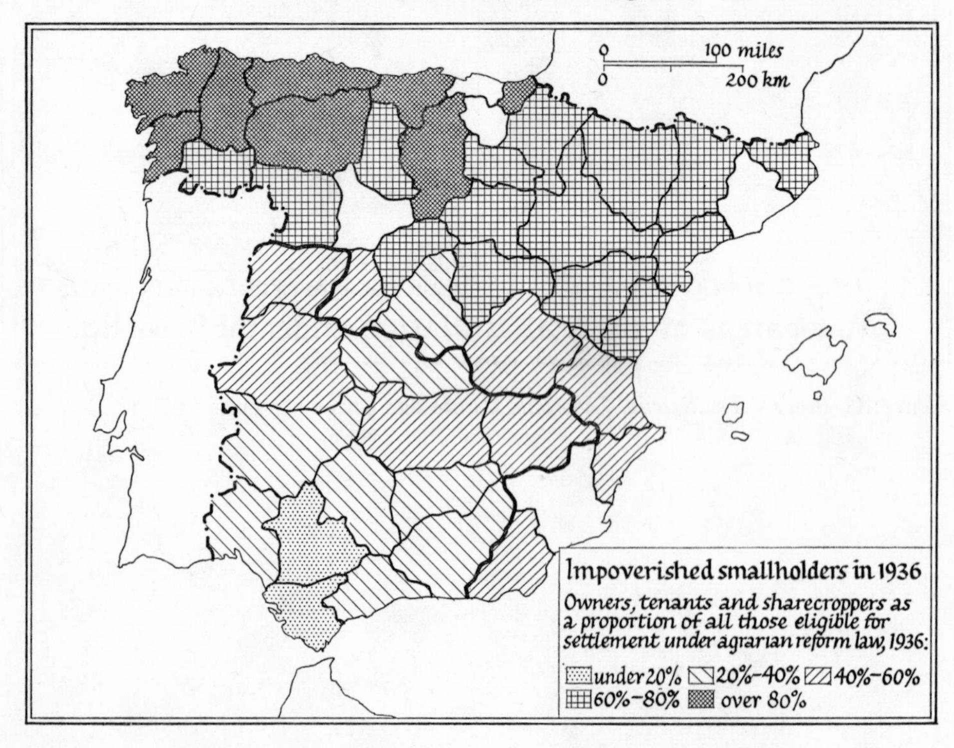

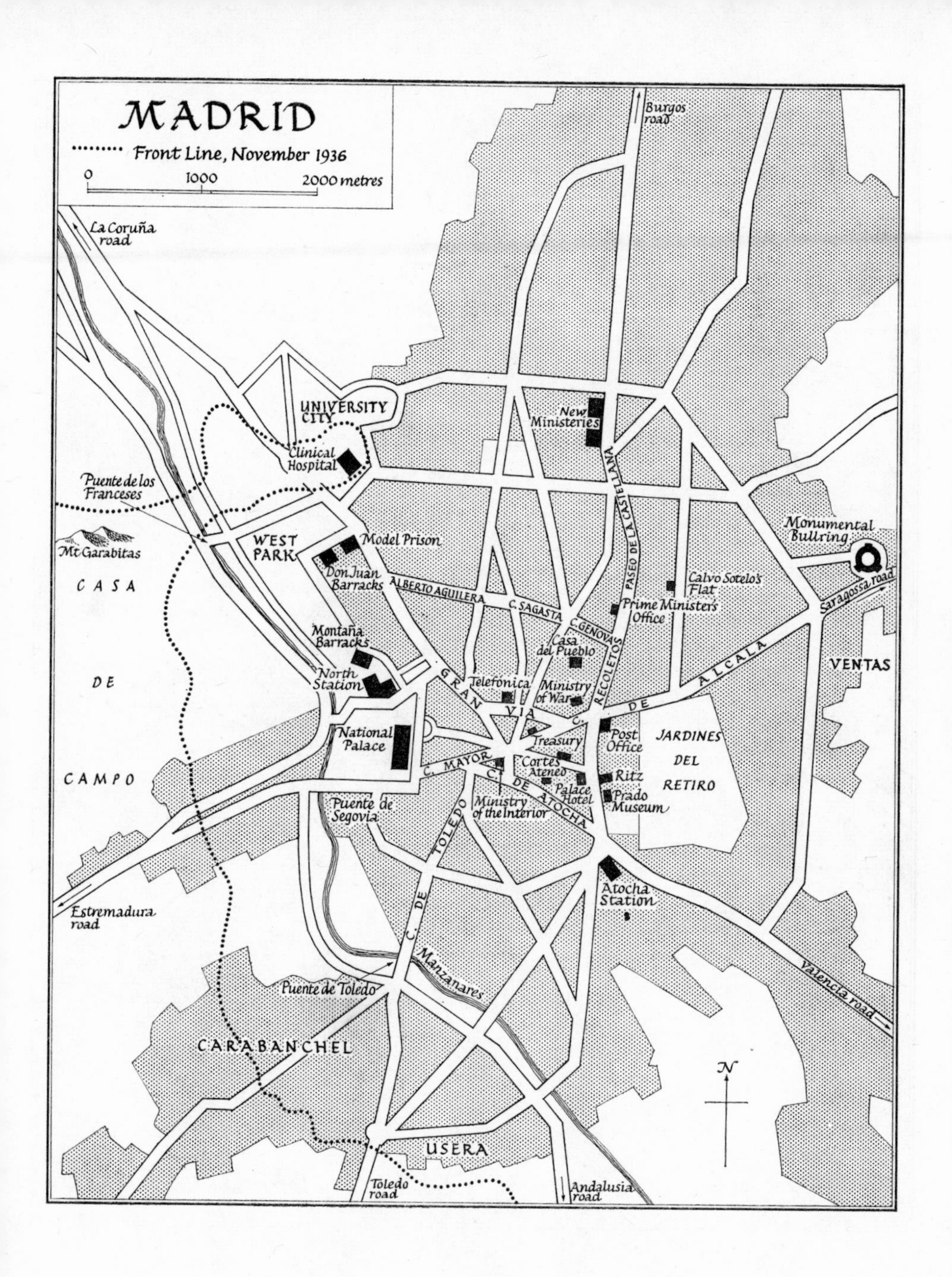
MADRID
Front Line, November 1936
0
1000
2000 metres
Burgos road
La Coruña road
UNIVERSITY CITY
New Ministeries
Clinical Hospital
Puente de los Franceses
PASEO DE LA CASTELLANA
Monumental Bullring
WEST PARK
Model Prison
Mt Garabitas
Don Juan Barracks
CASA
DE
CAMPO
ALBERTO AGUILERA
C. SAGASTA
C. GENOVA
Calvo Sotelo's Flat
Prime Minister's Office
Saragossa road
Montaña Barracks
Casa del Pueblo
RECOLETOS
VENTAS
North Station
GRAN VIA
Telefónica
Ministry of War
C. DE ALCALA
National Palace
Treasury
Post Office
JARDINES DEL RETIRO
C. MAYOR
Cortes
Ateneo
Ritz
Palace Hotel
Prado Museum
C. DE ATOCHA
Puente de Segovia
Ministry of the Interior
C. DE TOLEDO
Atocha Station
Estremadura road
Puente de Toledo
Manzanares
Valencia road
CARABANCHEL
N
USERA
Toledo road
Andalusia road

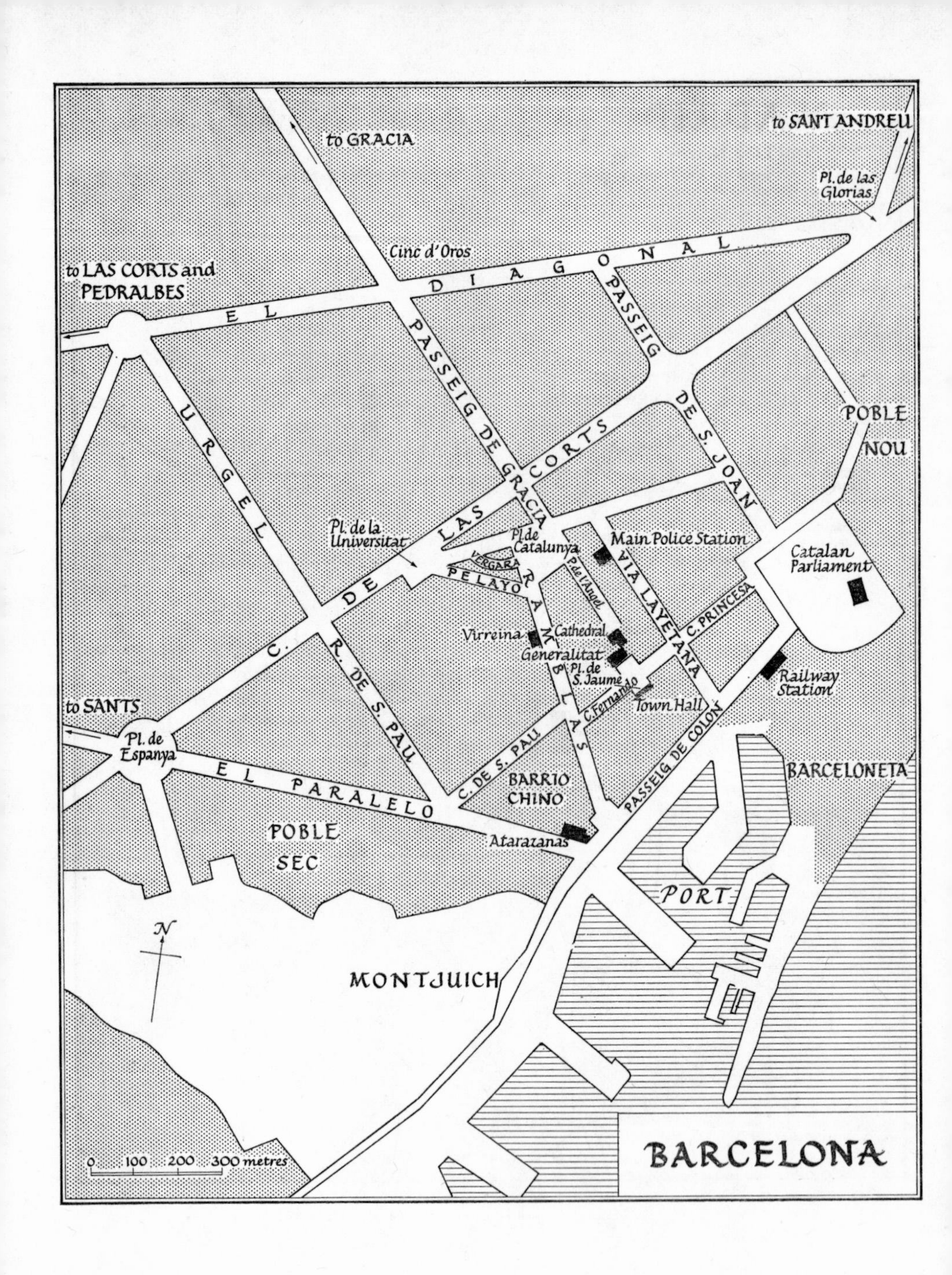

to GRACIA
to SANT ANDREU
Pl. de las Glorias
Cinc d'Oros
to LAS CORTS and PEDRALBES
EL DIAGONAL
PASSEIG DE GRACIA
PASSEIG DE S. JOAN
URGEL
C. DE LAS CORTS
POBLE NOU
Pl. de la Universitat
Pl. de Catalunya
VERGARA
PELAYO
Main Police Station
P. de l'Angel
VIA LAYETANA
Catalan Parliament
C. PRINCESA
Virreina
Cathedral
Generalitat
Pl. de S. Jaume
RAMBLAS
Railway Station
C. Fernando
Town Hall
to SANTS
R. DE S. PAU
Pl. de Espanya
C. DE S. PAU
BARRIO CHINO
PASSEIG DE COLON
BARCELONETA
EL PARALELO
POBLE SEC
Atarazanas
PORT
N
MONTJUICH
0 100 200 300 metres
BARCELONA

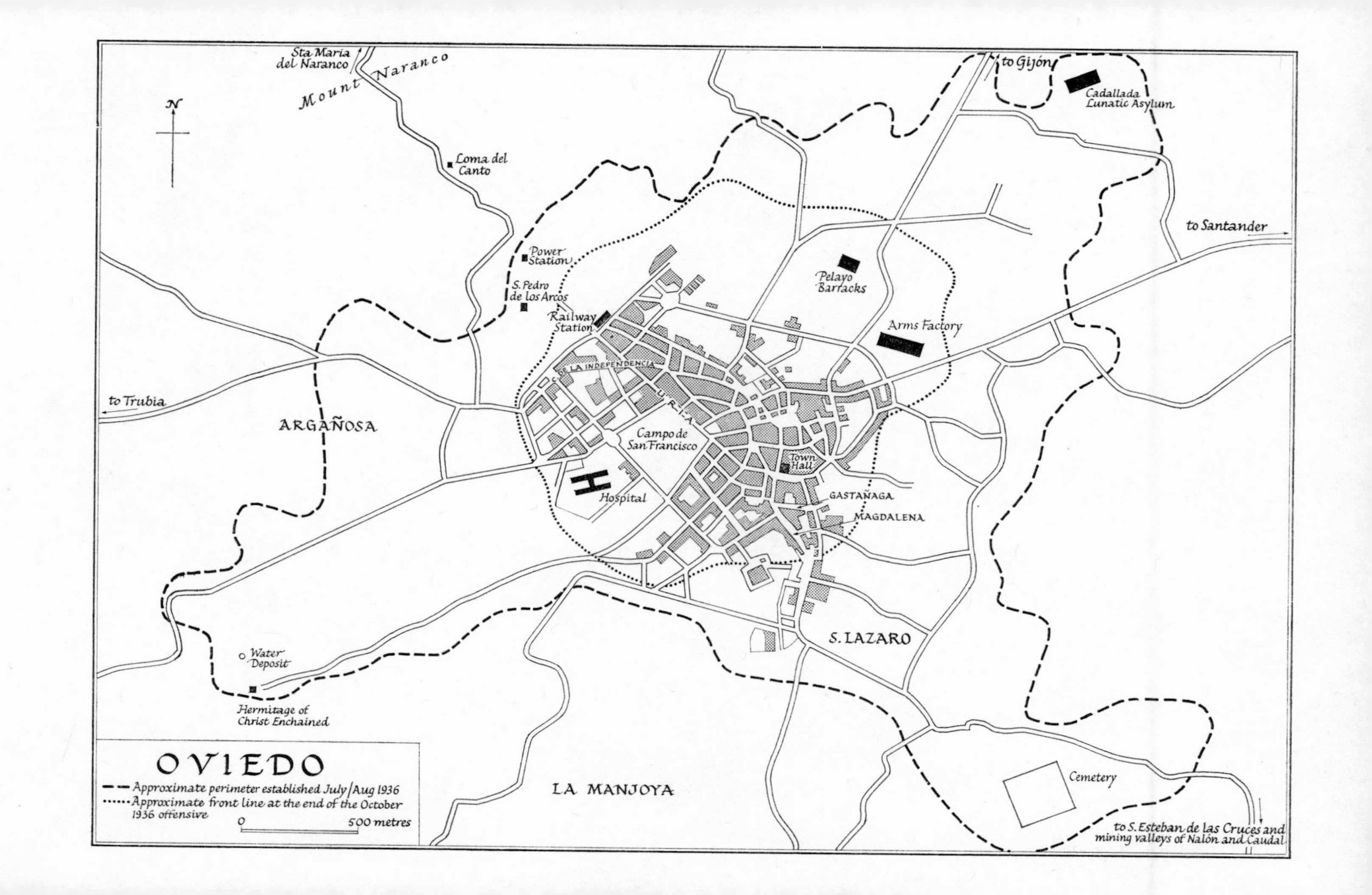

OVIEDO
Approximate perimeter established July/Aug 1936
Approximate front line at the end of the October 1936 offensive
0
500 metres
N
Sta Maria del Naranco
Mount Naranco
Loma del Canto
to Gijón
Cadallada Lunatic Asylum
to Santander
Power Station
S. Pedro de los Arcos
Railway Station
Pelayo Barracks
Arms Factory
C. DE LA INDEPENDENCIA
URIA
to Trubia
ARGAÑOSA
Campo de San Francisco
Town Hall
Hospital
GASTAÑAGA
MAGDALENA
S. LAZARO
Water Deposit
Hermitage of Christ Enchained
LA MANJOYA
Cemetery
to S. Esteban de las Cruces and mining valleys of Nalón and Caudal

Blood of Spain

The Experience of Civil War, 1936–1939

History proceeds in such a way that the final result always arises from conflicts between many individual wills, and every one of them is in turn made into what it is by a host of particular conditions of life. Thus there are innumerable intersecting forces, an infinite series of parallelograms of forces, which give rise to one resultant – the historical event. This may in its turn again be regarded as the product of a power which operates as a whole *unconsciously* and without volition. For what each individual wills is obstructed by everyone else and what emerges is something that no one intended.

Engels to Joseph Bloch,
London, September 1890

Who built Thebes of the seven gates?
In the books you will find the names of kings.
Did the kings haul up the lumps of rock?
And Babylon, many times demolished
Who raised it up so many times? In what houses
Of gold-glittering Lima did the builders live?
Where, the evening that the Wall of China was finished
Did the masons go? . . .

So many reports
So many questions.

Questions from a Worker who Reads
(Bertolt Brecht)

Foreword

'The subjective aspect of events, the "atmosphere" in which they took place, is also a condition of history . . . Indeed, can history be made real if (this aspect) is not resuscitated? Shall we leave the task solely to the novelist? . . .'

Pierre Vilar: 'La guerra de 1936 en la historia contemporánea de España'

The appearance of a book on the Spanish Civil War of 1936–9 today requires some explanation. Major historical works over the past fifteen years or so have charted most of the features of that conflict, and it would be vain to hope to add anything new to the overall map of the period. But within the general and even detailed knowledge, one area has remained unarticulated: the subjective, a spectrum of the lived experiences of people who participated in the events. This is the purpose of the present book.

Oral history, as conceived here, is an attempt to reveal the intangible 'atmosphere' of events; to discover the outlook and motivations of the participants, willing or unwilling; to describe what civil war, revolution and counter-revolution felt like from inside both camps. The cause of the civil war lay deep within the formations of Spanish society; though rapidly internationalized, the war was fought out very largely by classes and sectors of that society. This book is rooted, therefore, in the Spanish experience.

Never more than at a time of extreme social crisis does the atmosphere become a determining factor in the way people respond to events. For, however intangible, it is never abstract or distant. It is what people feel. And what people feel lays the ground for their actions.

This is especially observable in a civil war. Clausewitz's maxim on war can be reformulated for the circumstance: civil war is the continuation of politics – internal class politics – by other means. The political mobilization (or the broadening of a previous mobilization) of large masses of 'ordinary' people, brought on by a deepening social crisis, is a condition of it.

But it is often less in the unmediated articulation of these politics than in the (ideological) climate of the times that can be found many of the clues to social and individual behaviour in the conflict. It is in the latter that, seemingly, lie the sources which explain, for example, why individuals of the same class fought on opposing sides; why a man took up arms for the camp that was assassinating his relatives; why brother fought brother. The attempt to understand the atmosphere in which such events could occur can make accessible to us some of the realities and contradictions of the larger, impersonal movements of history. For the atmosphere does not hang above events like the ether; it is a social emanation, the result of very terrestrial struggles.

These observations have shaped the underlying pattern of the present work.

But the creation of an intelligible 'mosaic' of more than 300 personal accounts has necessarily extended beyond this sphere. The attempt has been made to describe the major contours of the war through eyewitness narration. This, in turn, has required a particular narrative and analytical structure. The limitations of this type of oral history – and more especially of this particular book – must therefore be stressed.

Let me enumerate the most important of these. Oral history, in the sense practised here, is not a substitute for, but an adjunct of, traditional historiography; it functions within the interstices of the latter.[1] The sum of micro experiences does not, of itself, make up an objective macro totality. The atmosphere, as I have indicated, does not explain the subsoil, but rather the reverse.

For this reason, in addition to that already advanced, the present book does not set out to provide a general history of the Spanish republic and civil war. It does, however, concentrate on what, forty years later, appear as some of the major issues. Within this framework there are further, specific limitations. The first is territorial. The personal accounts were deliberately sought in five regions: two on the republican side, two on the nationalist side, and one (which would be better stated as two) on both sides. These are, respectively: Madrid –rural Toledo and Barcelona–lower Aragon; Seville–Córdoba–surrounding countryside and Salamanca–Old Castile–Pamplona; finally, the 'north', Asturias and Vizcaya, which were captured by the nationalists halfway through the war. Excluded from the book, therefore, are two major areas: Galicia in the nationalist and the Levante in the republican rearguard.

Secondly, the book does not focus on the war at the front. After the first months, when direct civilian militia participation was all-important, it follows the fighting rather from the rearguard. In the circumstances this may seem a curious procedure. It is based on the conviction that the civil war was won as much in the rearguard as at the front and that the social and political issues at stake had their clearest expression in the former.

Thirdly, the international dimension is largely absent. The determination to present the war in its Spanish roots and as 'lived' by Spaniards is responsible. Apart from routine anathema of the fascist powers' intervention and Anglo-French non-intervention, popular recollections of the international situation on the republican side tended to be slight. Soviet aid, the Moscow show trials, occasionally Munich. The situation was not much different in the opposing nationalist camp despite the presence of Italians and Germans. Although international aspects could never be kept totally out of the mind – propaganda did not allow it – the war for most Spaniards was a matter for Spaniards to resolve.

Fourthly, it does not concentrate on politics at governmental or leadership level. In this sense it is grass-roots history. It does, however, focus on the major socio-political forces in each of the areas selected. For this reason it may seem an overly 'political' book. Let me repeat: the civil war was about deeply political issues and the crisis which preceded it had polarized and politicized very large sectors of public opinion.

1. The debt owed to it by this work is so pervasive that, apart from the prologue, where the reader will find the major sources, I have not burdened the text with repeated acknowledgements.

Oral history, I believe, should articulate the experiences of people who, historically speaking, would otherwise remain inarticulate (and in which sense alone the adjective 'ordinary' can be attached to them). In principle, therefore, I sought out people who had not occupied leadership posts, who had not written their memoirs, who did not have public or political reputations to defend. Rightly or wrongly, I believed such people would give a more direct and immediate feel of events. Usually, if they were members of a political or trade union organization, they were middle-level militants. Sometimes, tempted by the possibility, or led on by the reading of testimonial material, I ignored my own guidelines, as the reader will see. Almost invariably, I was glad to have done so. But by and large I preferred to adhere to the original concept.

I recorded some 2,750,000 words of interviews in just under two years. In collecting, and later selecting, material for this book (which uses less than 10 per cent of the original) I gave preference to concrete personal experience rather than to global opinion; struck out slander and – with a couple of exceptions – hearsay; and solicited political self-criticism rather than criticism of other parties or organizations. I mention the latter because it is the source of another deficiency. The acerbity of the tone in which political polemic was, only too frequently, conducted is not, I now believe, sufficiently reproduced. The reader has only to compare the newspaper and other quotations which are scattered through the book to verify this. In part this is because the sharpness of tone has diminished with the years; but also because at the time I believed there was little to be gained by reverting to a style of polemic which, hopefully, had been transcended. I still believe this, but I signal its absence from the book.

I have, however, often let stand participants' descriptions of the opposing side as 'red' or 'fascist'. Misleading and often deliberately provocative, these labels have been retained because they summon up contemporary perceptions of the enemy. The solution I have adopted to the problem of names is as follows: those who rose to overthrow the republican regime on 18 July 1936, I have called insurgents until, in October of the same year, they formed their own regime; thereafter they become, in their own nomenclature, nationalists. The republican regime was plainly transformed into something new by the outbreak of war. I have frequently used the term 'Popular Front' to describe it in an initial period, although recognizing that it is not strictly accurate: while fighting on this side, the anarcho-syndicalists did not form part of the Popular Front before or during the war. Later, as bourgeois democratic principles were re-asserted by the central government, I have tended again to use the title republican.

Another question with particular relevance to th s book is certain to arise in the reader's mind. And that is: how are we to know that what people say is the truth? It is a justifiable question and can be answered without impugning the good faith of any of the participants: we cannot *always* know. Memory can be notoriously tricky, a long time has elapsed. It was not possible to check each assertion, every experience, unless documentary evidence existed. Where there seemed to me doubt and I had some documentary source to support it, I went back to the witness; if the matter still seemed uncertain I tended to omit it. Sometimes, however, an assertion of fact that is demonstrably untrue constitutes part of the atmosphere; in this case it is left to stand but, in one way or another, its validity is challenged shortly afterwards. On other occasions I have let statements stand that fall into neither of these categories. I was guided then by a sense that, even if some doubt might exist, the statement corresponded to a general climate of feeling which it was important to capture. The aim of the book, as I have said, was not to write another history of the civil war but a book about how people lived that war. It was *their* truth I wished to record. And what people thought – or what they thought they thought – also constitutes an historical fact. Inevitably, memories of thirty-five and forty years past have been 'worked over' in the intervening years; but much less, I am convinced, than might have been the case in other circumstances. This is due, first, to the nature of the war itself; secondly, to the political immobilism imposed by the victors in the post-war years and, lastly, to the fact that many participants were very young. Memories have 'frozen' as a result. Certainly, some of the participants have changed their views (and sometimes political affiliations) over the years. Rather than detract from their evidence, it tended to enhance it for me by focusing on it a critical light. Again, because of the need to make a coherent totality, it may seem as though this book is saying: this is 'how it was'. But no. This is how it is remembered as having been.

Finally, the reader may well wonder whether a foreigner was best suited to inquire into matters so deeply Spanish. I often asked myself the same question; especially as much of the writing on the civil war has, perforce, been done by non-Spaniards. The answer, I believe, lies in uneven development: a Spanish publisher could not then afford the commercial and political risk of supporting a project which, after four and a half years' full-time work, might be refused publication. The more advanced economies of the US and Britain, and the willingness of my publishers in both countries to take a gamble, made it possible for me to carry out. I trust that in the Spain of today this situation would no longer exist; for in the intervening period one epoch has ended and a new one begun.

*

These interviews were recorded in the twilight of the Franquista era, between June 1973 and May 1975: 95 per cent of them in Spain, the rest in France. No problems were put in my way. Apart from caution in rural areas, especially in Andalusia where there was still fear, people talked openly. It was a privileged moment in which to capture memories of a period distant enough to be history and yet near enough to be vividly remembered by a representative cross-section of participants. Six months after the last interview, Franco was dead. The dictatorial regime created by the victor of the civil war began to be dismantled. A new era was opening for Spain.

Author's note

All Spanish regional names have been anglicized in this book, while all provinces and capitals retain their Spanish spelling. There are two exceptions to the latter: following accepted tradition, I have anglicized Sevilla (Seville) and Zaragoza (Saragossa).

Throughout the book I have used the word *libertarian* to indicate a member of one of the three anarchist or anarcho-syndicalist organizations (CNT, FAI and FIJL), or their social ideas and objectives.

All CAPITALIZED SURNAMES in the book are those of participants and appear shortly before or after a quotation. The latter is introduced by — if not by the usual quotation marks.

Prologue

UNEVEN DEVELOPMENT

The Spanish Civil War of 1936–9 was the fourth (some will say fifth) in a century. The struggles of the nineteenth century revolved around many of the same basic problems of Spanish society and state which led to the explosion of the 1930s. A brief survey of the former may, thus, assist an understanding of the last, and most total, of these civil wars.

The foremost of the underlying problems, indubitably, was the weakness of capitalist development. The nineteenth-century civil wars between Carlists and liberals were part of the long struggle in the overthrow of absolutism and the consolidation of a bourgeois state. The relative strengths of the two opposing social forces can be gauged by the fact that these wars stretched intermittently over more than forty years, of which some sixteen were consumed in actual fighting at different levels of intensity. In the name of a past Catholic unity of Spain (as opposed to a future capitalist unification of the national market) and of a traditional Catholic (as opposed to a constitutional) monarchy, a northern rural resistance fuelled the Carlist counter-revolution to the advance of liberalism. Significantly, the first of these wars, from 1833 to 1840, aroused the conscience of Europe which felt – as it was to do again in 1936 – that the great issues of European civilization were being fought out on Spanish battlefields. In the one case, as in the other, as Raymond Carr has pointed out, the projection distorted and over-simplified the issues at stake.[1]

Liberalism proved the stronger (initially in no little part thanks to British and French aid, which included volunteer forces) and the Carlist cause was overcome. But the underlying problems were not fully resolved. Resistance to the liberalizing concepts of a fully developed bourgeois democracy remained an important factor as was seen again in the 1930s when not only did the Carlists re-emerge in strength but other anti-democratic forces arose. This resistance, moreover, infected the victors of the wars, the new nineteenth-century ruling class.

The unevenness of capitalist development made the introduction of an advanced bourgeois democracy problematic at the best of times. It precluded, for example, the ascent of a *national* bourgeoisie to the helm of the nineteenth-century state. This, in turn, contributed to the failure to weld together a modern, bourgeois state from a nation which, since its inception in the fifteenth century, had been prone to centrifugal tendencies. The latter were reinforced by the advance of industrial development in the geographically peripheral north and north-eastern seaboards which coincided with a growth of local Catalan and Basque nationalist sentiment directed against an agrarian and centralist ruling class in Madrid.

Three 'national' Spanish institutions attempted to make good this developmental deficiency: all failed. The monarchy never succeeded in acquiring the

1. See R. Carr, *Spain 1808–1939* (Oxford, 1966), p. 155.

respect of the masses, never became a 'useful symbol of community', in Pierre Vilar's phrase.[1] Nor, by the end of the first third of the nineteenth century, was the church better placed to play this role. The identity between Catholic orthodoxy and Spanish national 'cohesiveness', which had been forged in the fifteenth-century reconquest of Moorish Spain, no longer held, except for the Carlists (although later the ruling class would refurbish it for lack of an alternative ideology). Having occupied a dominant position – economic but above all ideological – under the *ancien régime*, the church moved into an immobilist, reactionary posture in the face of liberalism which threatened it on both scores. From this period anti-clericalism became an overt and recurrent fact of Spanish history: 1835 marked the first massacres of clergy and church burnings, on rumours that monks had started a cholera epidemic by poisoning drinking water. (The persistence of anti-clericalism can be judged by the fact that one hundred years later a rumour that monks had given poisoned sweets to children was still capable of driving a mob to attack and burn churches.)

The last of the institutions, the army, started the nineteenth century as a liberal force, and owed much of its importance as a political power to its role in defeating the Carlist counter-revolution. But as the century progressed, it turned increasingly conservative. A 'state within a state', it came to see itself as the incarnation of the national will, the bulwark of moral and social order, the defender of territorial *unity*. As such, it expressed not the popular will but a centralizing force ready to substitute for an as yet uncertain ruling class; the presence of the army officer in politics reflected the absence of the businessman. When, in the last quarter of the century, the military withdrew from direct political intervention, it was in order to stand as the ultimate power behind the new political alliance of the old landowning class and upper bourgeoisie which took control of the state.

It was, indeed, a *pronunciamiento* which ushered in this new alliance, sweeping aside an unstable republic which lasted barely twelve months (1873–4). The army's previous overthrow of the Bourbon monarchy in 1868 had unleashed a revolutionary process. Attempts by General Prim to contain it by instituting a new constitutional monarchy failed; so too did the subsequent republican regime under petty bourgeois leadership. In the revolution's final stages, due in large part to anarchist influence, sovereign 'cantons' were established in a number of cities, threatening the nation's unity as well as ruling class domination. Frightened, the upper bourgeoisie sealed its pact with the old landowning class to put an end to it. The army restored the Bourbon monarchy in the person of Alfonso XII.

The opportunity of achieving a fully developed bourgeois democracy had been missed. The new ruling bloc, based essentially on agrarian interests, controlled the Spanish state for the next forty-eight years, from 1875 to 1923. In the course of the preceding liberal struggle against the economic foundations of the *ancien régime*, the pattern of land ownership had fundamentally changed. Church, noble and common lands had been disentailed, put on the market and, in the main, been purchased by the bourgeoisie and a part of the old landowning class. Many of the large estates (latifundia) of the south and south-west were created in this period. In the course of a century, the bourgeoisie continued to

1. P. Vilar, *Historia de España* (Paris, 1963), p. 86.

extend its holdings until, by the 1930s, approximately 90 per cent of Spain's farm land was in its hands, the rest being owned by the upper nobility. The liberals' mid-nineteenth-century hope (which was not alone in motivating their disentailment laws) that a new, small and prosperous peasantry could be created by these means was disappointed.

Given the bourgeoisie's extensive stake in the land, it was not surprising that the new ruling bloc should be dominated by an agrarian oligarchy. A manipulated electoral system kept it in power under the restored monarchy, while excluding peasantry and proletariat from representation. With parliament not even formally expressing the nation's will, the ruling class could not rely on even an attenuated form of political consensus to avert grave crises which involved those who were politically excluded; more direct police methods had to be used. Not surprisingly, it failed to produce an ideology which would 'incorporate' these excluded classes. Much of the widespread working class 'a-politicism' to which anarchism could appeal stemmed from, or was reinforced by, that exclusion.

This pseudo-parliamentary democracy bought a temporary social peace for the ruling class; but it was at a price. The dominance of agrarian interests and their refusal to 'modernize' agriculture placed obstacles in the way of industrial development. Adopting the mode of their predecessors, the new capitalist land-owners failed to invest in their estates. 'The psychology of feudalism outlived its juridical disappearance.'[1] Lack of investment and low wages on the estates of the south and south-west, where a mass of landless labourers was out of work for months at a time, could provide little expansion of the home market for domestic manufacture. Large estates and social unrest became synonymous. Outside the latifundist region, most peasant agriculture revolved in a secular and precarious quest for self-sufficiency. 'Favourable geographic and social conditions for agriculture existed only on the northern and Mediterranean peripheries of the peninsula . . . [which constituted] less than 10 per cent of the surface of the country.'[2]

Spain thus entered the twentieth century still a dominantly backward agrarian nation – a nation which had, moreover, lost its colonies and was, to no small degree, itself 'colonized' by foreign capital. Development remained uneven and weak. This was reflected in uneven social and cultural development between town and country, between regions, within classes.

The phenomenon, true of all development, was revealed with particular sharpness in the case of Spain. Among the more obvious socio-economic examples drawn from the 1930s was the continuing existence of a few thousand landowners in the south – less than 2 per cent of all owners there – who had over two thirds of the land, while 750,000 labourers eked out a living on near-starvation wages. These southern estates contrasted in turn with the plots of the north-west and elsewhere, which were too small to give a peasant a living. At the cultural level, while between 30 per cent and 50 per cent of the population – no one knew exactly – was illiterate in the 1930s, a handful of poets, novelists and playwrights was leading the country into a literary renaissance. Politically, a highly combative working class, on the one hand, encountered an

1. P. Vilar, op. cit., p. 92.
2. G. Jackson, *The Spanish Republic and the Civil War* (Princeton, 1965), p. 8.

almost total absence of revolutionary theoreticians, marxist or anarchist, on the other. While the differences between a landless anarcho-syndicalist Andalusian day-labourer and a Catholic, smallholding peasant in Old Castile were obvious, there were less obvious but also great differences between a middle-class left republican in one of the large cities and a provincial petty bourgeois who had become republican to protect his interests; or between the nationalist petty bourgeoisies of the two most advanced regions, Catalonia and the Basque country. Spain was not one country but a number of countries and regions marked by their uneven historical development.[1]

From the turn of the century, however, there had been a significant advance in industrial development. It was aided by an economic boom during the First World War, in which Spain remained neutral, and the world boom of the 1920s. 'By 1930 Spain was halfway on the road to capitalist development.'[2] A new factor began to make its political presence felt: the proletariat. Between 1910 and 1930, the industrial working class more than doubled to over 2,500,000. (It now represented just over 26 per cent of the working population in place of the 16 per cent it had occupied twenty years earlier. Those engaged in agriculture fell from 66 per cent to 45 per cent in the same period.) At the same time, the industrial bourgeoisie, concentrated especially in Catalonia, attempted to take over and 'renovate' the state, using the lever of Catalan nationalism to bring pressure to bear for its ends.

Under these different pressures the political system, forged in 1875 to keep in power an agrarian oligarchy, began to disintegrate. The monarchical ruling class was incapable of finding new political and social forms of incorporating the proletariat (as well as certain, mainly nationalist, sectors of the petty bourgeoisie) into a political system which would legitimize its power and ensure its continued domination: the continuance, in other words, of capitalism without threat of revolution (or nationalist secession).

1917 marked the opening of the crisis. Five months after the February revolution in Russia, a general revolutionary strike was declared by socialists and anarcho-syndicalists. Although it was crushed by the army, the old system could do no more than stagger from one crisis to the next for the following six years. During this period Andalusia was rocked by the 'Bolshevik Triennium' – three years of revolutionary anarcho-syndicalist agitation which appeared to threaten the existing social order in the south.

Anarchism, it may be recalled, had been introduced to Spain in 1868 before socialism. (In its origins, and for a number of years thereafter, the Spanish Federation of the First International *was* anarchist.) Its success in attracting recruits was immediate. From the start, the twin poles of recruitment were Catalonia and Andalusia – respectively the most advanced industrial and one of the most backward agrarian regions. In the rest of western Europe, with the

1. This uneven development impressed its particular imprint on the civil war from the start, in part explaining the success or failure of the military uprising in different regions (see P. Vilar, 'La guerra de 1936 en la historia contemporánea de España', *Historia internacional*, Madrid, April 1976).

2. Mª C. García-Nieto, 'La segunda república (1)' (*Bases documentales 8*, Madrid, 1974), p. 12. From 1900 to 1935 there was rapid demographic growth, the population increasing from 18·5 to 24 millions. But more than half the population (57 per cent) still lived in the countryside.

exception of Portugal, anarchism as a mass phenomenon disappeared after the First World War. In Spain it grew.[1] In 1911, the anarcho-syndicalist CNT (Confederación Nacional del Trabajo) was created in Barcelona. 'Emancipation of the workers must be the task of the workers themselves.' Syndicalism was 'the struggle between two antagonistic classes'. General strikes must be revolutionary. Eight years later, in 1919 – after bringing Barcelona to a halt for a fortnight with a general strike – the CNT came out openly for libertarian communism: the abolition of private property and the state, and the organization of production by free associations of producers. At this time it claimed 700,000 members, over half of them in Catalonia.

In a dominantly agrarian country, where the middle class enjoys little social weight and the ruling class is suffering a political crisis, even a numerically small proletariat, concentrated in specific nuclei, can play a decisive leadership role. 1917 had demonstrated this in Russia. Lenin saw Spain as a country destined for revolution.

The Spanish ruling class was not unaware of the parallels between its country and Russia. The response to the fear of revolution and the general political crisis was for the army to move decisively for the first time in fifty years. With the king's approval, General Primo de Rivera took power in 1923.

The fundamental problem being what it was, the general's social programme, not surprisingly, was based on 'the suppression of the class struggle'. The CNT was outlawed. The socialist-led trade union the UGT (Unión General de Trabajadores), with some 200,000 members, was tolerated, however, and its secretary general, Largo Caballero, collaborated (albeit briefly) with the dictatorship. The original schism between anarchism and socialism was reinforced, maintaining the split in the working class. It was in these circumstances that the FAI (Federación Anarquista Ibérica) was formed in 1927. Its founding aim was to federate the previously scattered anarchist groups in Spain. As an anarchist federation (whose existence as a clandestine organization was not announced for two years) it could have no general 'political line'. But in Catalonia, especially, in the 1930s it pursued an ultra-leftist and insurrectionist policy.

1. Traditional explanations which ascribe this persistence to a Mediterranean 'temperament' in search of a 'secular religion' (millenarianism) or subject to an aimless (if justified) 'irrational fury' at oppressive social forces – the state, the church, etc. – fail to see anarchism as a response to concrete socio-economic conditions and needs. To single out but a few of these: the need, at the beginning of a revolutionary period (1868–74), to provide the working class with a revolutionary organization; the intransigence of rural and urban (Catalan) employers and an oppressive state; the links in a semi-developed capitalist society between an urban working class and its rural antecedents; the proximity (in small-scale production and unmechanized agriculture) of employers and employed; the poverty of large cities like Barcelona. Anarchism answered these conditions in a specific manner, often reinforcing existing tendencies: its anti-state, a-political ideology buttressed, in the regions where it took root, an existing hatred of the state and politics; its federal aims and structure, its stress on local self-organization, worked in the same direction, reinforcing existing 'localisms'; its concept of producers' self-management strengthened the notion (within small-scale production) of the 'dispensability' of the bourgeoisie, satisfying artisans threatened by capitalist growth as well as the proletariat; finally, its loose, unbureaucratic structure allowed it to submerge and re-emerge in response to political repression. (For an extended discussion of this question, see particularly T. Kaplan, *Anarchists of Andalusia, 1868–1903*, Princeton, 1977.)

Buoyed by the boom of the 1920s, the Primo de Rivera dictatorship collapsed with it in 1930, dispatched in large part by the conservative forces it had set out to defend. For the next fifteen months, efforts were made to save the old system with the king at its head.

In the meanwhile, republicans of all shades of opinion met in the summer of 1930 and formed a revolutionary committee with the aim of overthrowing the monarchy. Two members of the PSOE (Partido Socialista Obrero Español) attended the San Sebastián meeting in a personal capacity; and two months later the socialist party executive agreed to participate in a future republican government. The largest working-class political party (the anarchist movement was *not* a party) prepared to hitch its fate to the petty bourgeois republicans.

In December 1930, a republican uprising failed; but general strikes took place in most major cities with the exception of Barcelona and Madrid where general strikes had occurred a month earlier.[1]

In the hope of being able to arrange a return to the pre-dictatorship constitution, municipal elections were held in April 1931, to test the wind. The large towns – but not the countryside – voted overwhelmingly for republican candidates. The elections were interpreted as a plebiscite against the monarchy. Two days later on 14 April the king – warned by the civil guard commander, General Sanjurjo, that his forces would not stand behind him – left the country, and the second republic was declared.

*

That evening the crowds gathered in the Puerta del Sol in the heart of Madrid. Among them was a fifteen-year-old secondary school student, Victoria ROMAN, who had come with many of her fellow pupils and teachers to witness the historic moment. Republican flags had appeared as though by magic all over the city; elsewhere the republic had already been declared, often to the strains of the *Marseillaise*. In the distance she saw the leaders approach the door of the interior ministry. There were Largo Caballero, Azaña, Alcalá Zamora. They went in. She saw the bearded figure of Fernando de los Ríos approach another door and strike it with his walking stick. The door swung open and he went in. Power, it seemed, was there to be taken by a knock on a door.

—'The republic has arrived without bloodshed,' one of my teachers said. 'Yes,' replied another, 'without bloodshed – and we shall live to regret it.' I was shocked to hear him talk like that; but later I came to wonder if he wasn't right . . .

In Barcelona similar crowds gathered in the Plaça de Sant Jaume. A new left republican Catalan party, the Esquerra Republicana de Catalunya, formed barely a month earlier, had won the elections. Its leader, Francesc Macià, proclaimed the Catalan republic.[2] In the square a prominent CNT militant

1. See M. Tuñón de Lara, *El movimiento obrero en la historia de España* (Madrid, 1972), pp. 844–5.

2. The 1930 San Sebastián meeting of republican leaders, attended by Macià and other Catalan nationalist politicians, agreed that a future republican government should find a constitutional solution to Catalan aspirations. The republican cause thus assured itself the backing of the petty bourgeois Catalan nationalists. It is worth noting that no similar identity of aims existed for the dominant Basque nationalist party, PNV (Partido Nacionalista Vasco), which

was encouraged to address the crowd. Climbing on to the shoulders of a couple of men, Josep ROBUSTE started to make a speech pointing out that the republic was no more than a word. No one listened to him.

—They were drunk with the idea of the republic. They thought it was a miracle, a panacea for all past problems – not least the dictatorship which had brought brutal repression to Barcelona. I got down. Had I attempted to go on talking I might easily have been physically assaulted . . .

The popular enthusiasm of the large urban centres was not repeated everywhere in the provinces. For example, at the college run by monks in Salamanca where he was studying, Juan CRESPO recalled that the proclamation of the republic was treated as a day of mourning. The headmaster of the school preached a sermon on the tragedy of the king's departure.

—He criticized the Spaniards' ingratitude to the king, praised the monarchy's service to the nation, recalled the example of the Catholic Kings who had united the nation. By the end he was nearly in tears, and so were we . . .

*

Public tears of joy mixed with private tears of sadness. Neither adequately measured the size of the task which confronted the new republican regime. This was nothing less than to bring into being what one hundred years of history had unsuccessfully striven to achieve: an advanced bourgeois democratic state. The bourgeoisie having failed (or rather, having failed to attempt) the task, this was now left to the political leadership of what one historian has called 'a thin but politically very active layer – the lower middle classes of the towns'.[1] The greater part of the urban professional classes, intellectuals, school teachers and journalists sympathized with the petty bourgeois republicans. It was the class which had taken the lead in all the revolutions of the past seventy-five years but had never, except for brief revolutionary periods, held power. On the advent of the republic, the liberal republicans were organized in loose political groupings which owed allegiance more to a particular political figure – Manuel Azaña, Alcalá Zamora, Marcelino Domingo – than to a defined ideological or political programme. Such definition was achieved only in April 1934, when the left republican party under Azaña's leadership was formed.

In essence, the republic's task was to reform the socio-economic structures of the Spanish state with the dual but complementary objectives of 'modernizing' capitalism while preventing proletarian revolution (or nationalist secession).

---

did not attend the San Sebastián meeting. Nor did the Basques follow Macià's move. Instead, they welcomed the republic and demanded an autonomous Basque regime within a federal republic which recognized 'the freedom and independence of the Catholic church'. Macià was soon persuaded by representatives of the new republican government in Madrid to rescind his declaration and await passage of a home rule statute by a new Constituent Cortes. The audacity of his move none the less ensured that Catalan autonomy was put on the immediate political agenda and assured the Esquerra of political hegemony in Catalonia until the outbreak of the civil war. See I. Molas, *El sistema de partidos políticos en Cataluña, 1931–1936* (Barcelona, 1974), p. 83, and A. Balcells, *Cataluña contemporánea II (1900–1936)* (Madrid, 1974), pp. 23–4.

1. G. Brenan, *The Spanish Labyrinth* (Cambridge, 1950), p. 231.

This entailed finding new forms of legitimizing the capitalist system which – thanks to the reforms involved – would serve to incorporate the proletariat (and the nationalist petty bourgeoisie) into the new political system. This the republican–socialist coalition hoped to do by concentrating its major reforms on three sectors: the 'latifundist aristocracy', the church and the army. Adding to the already considerable difficulties involved in this task was the fact that the attempt came at a moment of world economic crisis when, internationally, parliamentary democracy appeared on the retreat before fascism. What could be achieved in the circumstances, how much had been done?

From the very start the republican regime had made a crucial mistake, thought Juan ANDRADE. One of the founding members of the Spanish communist party and subsequently a leader of the dissident communist POUM (Partido Obrero de Unificación Marxista), he felt that the regime had failed to keep the initiative, to take advantage of the popular enthusiasm in order to consolidate itself.

—There is only one way a revolutionary movement, which comes to power through elections, and which is being pushed forward by the masses, can consolidate itself: by taking radical measures *immediately*. This it failed to do. The bourgeois forces were demoralized, measures to reform the basic structures of the state, the army, the land could have been taken straight away. Failure to do so allowed the bourgeoisie to reorganize, to begin the counter-attack . . .

While the coalition held political power, economic power escaped it. True, the constituent assembly adopted the classical measures of an advanced bourgeois revolution: separation of church and state, genuine universal suffrage (including women and soldiers), a cabinet responsible to a (single-chamber) parliament, a secular educational system. Significantly absent from the assembly, however, was the revolutionary working class, represented by the CNT, *and*, almost without exception, the former ruling class, the representatives of capital. The new constitution was unlikely to satisfy either, as a result. This was perhaps less important than the coalition's failure to achieve the basic reforms outlined above. Its agrarian reform programme frightened the important rural bourgeoisie, but did not in fact take its land – leaving the landless dissatisfied. Its religious policy attacked with unnecessary acerbity an important area of the bourgeoisie's ideological dominance – religious education – and made a gift to the reaction of a fertile terrain on which to recruit and regroup its forces. Its military reform allowed many officers to leave the army on full pay but did not fundamentally affect the military hierarchy or the position of monarchist (and later falangist) officers within it. Similarly, the coalition did little to change the old monarchical state apparatus through which it had to govern; and while it respected conservative financial orthodoxy it could do little or nothing to prevent the bourgeoisie exercising its economic power (flight of capital, refusal to invest). It temporarily incorporated half the working class, thanks to socialist collaboration, and effectively placed outside the law the other half, the CNT – which had decided to remain in 'open war' against the state and staged three insurrectionary uprisings in under two years. It gave an autonomy statute to Catalonia and failed to do the same for the Basque country. 'Like so many others before and since', in Hugh Thomas's words, it 'frightened the middle class without satisfying the workers'.[1] Finally, after two years in power, it split up in 1933.

The achievement of an advanced bourgeois democracy was, patently, going to have to be carried through without the bourgeoisie, if it were to be carried through at all. There was nothing unusual about this, perhaps. More unusual was that, seemingly, it would have to be carried through *against* the bourgeoisie.

The reaction did not take long to reorganize. Recovered from the shock of the monarchy's fall, reorganized in hostility to the coalition's 'anti-clerical and separatist' legislation, the right began its counter-attack. A wave of church burnings, which spread from Madrid to the south barely a month after the republic's proclamation, mobilized a large part of Catholic opinion. Less than a year later, however, an ill-supported army–monarchist uprising showed that 'extra-parliamentary' solutions were not yet the order of the day.

Rather, it was a newly formed mass Catholic organization, the CEDA (Confederación Españole de Derechas Autónomas), which for the next two years held the front line for the right within the existing contours of the parliamentary republic. Defence of religion, of the family, of property, of the social order at the service of Spain, were its guidelines.[2] Under the leadership of Gil Robles, a dynamic young lawyer, the CEDA scored a major victory in the general elections of November 1933, becoming the single largest parliamentary party. Its initial refusal to declare itself unambiguously republican, and its anti-left policies made it highly suspect to the forces of the republic's first ruling coalition. It did not immediately join the new centre government but supported it in parliament as it drove down wages and ignored, or put into reverse, reforms enacted during the republic's first two years.

The socialist party veered sharply leftwards. Mounting working-class militancy – 1933 was the hardest year of the depression in Spain – and disillusionment at their experience of power were among the domestic causes. Internationally, the recent fate of their fellow party in Austria at the hands of a corporative Catholic party that looked suspiciously like the CEDA was an important factor in leading the socialists to stage an ill-prepared uprising. Its timing was motivated by the desire to prevent the CEDA from joining the government. The rising took root only in Asturias where, for a fortnight, the working class held power in the mining valleys. October 1934 was a watershed. The unstable social equilibrium, underlying the monarchy's crisis and which the republic had given political expression to, broke. The right won a temporary victory over the left, which it misused, unable to produce coherent solutions to the country's problems. The left suffered a temporary, if bloody, setback which, very soon, it was able to use. The crisis had not been resolved, only foreshadowed.

The harsh repression unleashed, especially in Asturias, after October

1. H. Thomas, *The Spanish Civil War* (third edition, London, 1977), p. 107.

2. At the service of the 'anti-Spain' were: 'the mass who deny God and the principles of Christian morality, who proclaim the velleities of free love as compared to the sanctity of the family, who replace private property – base and drive of each person's well-being and the collective wealth – with a universal proletariat at the orders of the state which . . . enthrones the tyrannical empire of a class dictatorship'. From the 1931 founding manifesto of Acción Nacional, precursor of Acción Popular, the main party within the CEDA, led by Gil Robles (cited in A. Elorza, *La utopía anarquista bajo la segunda república española*, Madrid, 1973, p. 228).

radicalized the working class and the liberal petty bourgeoisie. Following the recent French example (and the Comintern's about-face), it led to the formation of the Popular Front, an alliance of working-class political parties and left republicans,[1] and to its victory at the polls. (Under the existing electoral law, only coalitions had any chance of success at the polls.)

The Popular Front pact was a republican-oriented minimal programme for continuing the reforms begun five years before at the start of the republic. It made no mention of socialism, and the left republicans explicitly rejected socialist calls for nationalization of the land and the banks, the establishment of unemployment benefits and workers' control in industry. Instead, they counterposed a republic directed not by 'social or economic class motives, but rather a regime of democratic freedom impelled by motives of public and social progress'.

The Popular Front electoral victory in February 1936, over the anti-revolutionary right-wing coalition led by the CEDA, was slender in terms of the popular vote;[2] five years of republican regime had polarized the country. Fear and anguish at their defeat spread among the right. Before them appeared the spectre of revolution.

—I can remember it still, though I was only six. My mother forced my father to vote. He was the manager of a dairy company in Madrid and he didn't agree with either the right or the left. But she said everyone had to vote, and he voted for the right, recalled Jesús DE POLANCO. When they lost, it was as though the world had fallen in on top of us . . .

For the other half of the electorate which supported the Popular Front, the victory gave hope that the problems which had confronted the republic since its inception would be seriously tackled at last.

While none of the left-wing organizations was planning revolution, the masses – in the view of Luis PORTELA, another founder-member of the Spanish communist party who had joined the POUM in Madrid – were distinctly heading that way.

—They wanted to go forward, they weren't satisfied simply with the release of political prisoners and the return to their jobs of all those who had been sacked as a result of the revolutionary insurrection of October 1934. Instinctively, they were pressing forward, not necessarily to take power, not to create Soviets,

1. Signatories to the pact were: the left republican party, the socialist party, the socialist-led trade union organization UGT, the communist party, the national federation of socialist youth, the syndicalist party and the dissident communist POUM.

2. The exact figures remain a matter of debate. They range (in the most recent estimate: J. Tusell, *Las elecciones del Frente Popular*, Madrid, 1971) from a Popular Front margin of 151,000 votes out of a total of 9,157,000 cast for both, to a margin of between 700,000 and 840,000 out of 8,800,000 votes polled by both. (To these totals must be added an additional 450,000 to 525,000 votes polled by the centre parties, including the Basque nationalist party, PNV.) M. Tuñón de Lara, in his *La España del siglo XX* (Barcelona, 1974), vol. 2, p. 483, resumes the different figures advanced. Because of the electoral system in force, however, the parliamentary representation did not reflect the closeness of the voting. When the new assembly met, the Popular Front seated 286 deputies (the major representations being: 99 socialists, 87 left republicans, 39 of Unión Republicana, 36 of Esquerra Republicana de Catalunya, and 17 communists, including one of the POUM); the right, 132 seats (of which the CEDA held 88), and the centre 42 (M. Tuñón de Lara, ibid., p. 488).

but to push forward the revolution which had begun with the republic's proclamation ...

And so it indeed appeared. Strikes broke out in almost every industry and trade. In the countryside the socialist-led Landworkers' Federation organized the mass seizure of large tracts of land to settle tens of thousands of farm workers. In the two and a half months immediately preceding the outbreak of the civil war on 17–18 July, the number of agricultural strikes reached almost half of those recorded in the heaviest year of 1933.[1] Street violence and political assassination in Madrid and the south became commonplace. The Falange, the Spanish variant of fascism, which had been founded in 1933, played a prominent role in these. The socialist and communist youth movements, which were in the process of fusing into the unified socialist youth, JSU (Juventudes Socialistas Unificadas), were the Falange's main antagonist in the streets.

The socialist party, under pressure from its left wing led by Largo Caballero, refused to renew its experience of governmental participation. This left the government solely in the hands of the left republicans, as it had been since the elections. Azaña became president of the republic. 'It seemed as though his presidency offered a double guarantee: against reaction, against revolution.'[2]

With the exception of a narrow spectrum of the urban and nationalist middle classes, the bourgeoisie had no faith in any guarantee; it doubted the government's ability to contain the working-class tide. It put its trust in the army, its constant defender for the past seventy-five years, and in the 'reserve army' of falangists, Carlists and monarchists. Large numbers of the CEDA's youth movement, JAP (Juventudes de Acción Popular), went over now to the Falange.

In the other camp, large sectors of the proletariat refused the strict limits of the Popular Front pact, pushing forward to achieve what five years of republican regime had denied them. The interests of neither camp were satisfied by the left republican government which tried vainly to contain both.

At the time of the Popular Front electoral victory, General Franco, chief of staff, had unsuccessfully urged the government to declare a state of siege. The new regime relieved him of his post, at the same time removing another potential threat, General Mola, from his command in Morocco. Franco was posted to the Canary Islands, where he was closer to the Army of Africa in which he had made his name; while Mola, in whose hands a number of generals secretly confided the planning of a military uprising, was sent to Pamplona, capital of Carlist Navarre and centre of fervent opposition to the regime. These inept moves were compounded by the government's refusal in the coming months to take any concrete measures against a military uprising, the imminence of which they were constantly being alerted to.

No *pronunciamiento* of the nineteenth century (nor General Primo de Rivera's in the twentieth) had resulted in civil war. The wars that were fought had other causes. But the situation had radically changed now. Given the balance of opposing forces a rising would almost inevitably lead to civil war. Momentarily, moreover, the initiative had passed to the reaction. Instead of an attempt to

1. See E. Malefakis, *Agrarian Reform and Peasant Revolution in Spain* (New Haven, 1970), p. 371.

2. P. Broué and E. Témime, *La Révolution et la guerre d'Espagne* (Paris, 1961), p. 64.

seize power, as in October 1934, the working class was defensively awaiting a pre-emptive counter-revolution which the Popular Front victory had virtually guaranteed. The working class was at a serious disadvantage; but things had gone too far to expect its passive acceptance of a coup. A socio-political crisis which could not be resolved *politically* would have to be settled by other means; class struggle by civil war.[1]

1. The complexity of the five years immediately prior to the civil war, and the shifts of popular feeling during them, cannot be adequately described in so few pages. The five-month period from the Popular Front electoral victory in February to the military uprising of July 1936 is described in more detail within the narrative of this book. A special section entitled 'Points of Rupture', pp. 513–74, attempts to deal with the earlier period in closer detail. It covers: A. The land. B. The petty bourgeoisie and the religious question. C. Two nationalisms. D. The libertarian movement and the republic. E. October 1934, Popular Front, orthodox and dissident communists. F. The army.

Every day there are street demonstrations. What do all these *vivas* shouted by the crowds mean? They mean *death!* Death to the adversary; outrage and persecution for the opponent.

ABC, monarchist editorial (Seville, 4 March 1936)

Trust no one. In the supreme moments of history, leaders always counsel moderation and discipline. Fascism is the systematized criminality of powerful castes. It can only be overcome by destroying the bases of capitalist society.

Solidaridad Obrera, CNT (Barcelona, 2 June 1936)

The civil governor told journalists he had no news to communicate. No information about military movements is authorized.

Defensor de Córdoba, Catholic (Córdoba, 17 July 1936)

July 1936

Friday, 17 July

MADRID

Just received from Tetuán, Spanish Morocco, the telegram, with its banal saint's day greetings, was signed *Fernando Gutiérrez.*

He counted the letters, seventeen, then hastened to pass the message on to General Mola in Pamplona: the army in Morocco would rise at 1700 hours.

MELILLA (Spanish Morocco)

Lt Julio DE LA TORRE, of the Spanish Foreign Legion, looked at his fellow officers; he saw that they, too, had seen the armed police outside. Lt Col. Seguí, the chief plotter in Morocco, who was giving his final orders, broke off in mid-sentence. In the momentary silence, the conspirators realized they had been betrayed.

The officers loaded their pistols, readied hand-grenades. While Col. Gazapo talked to the police lieutenant at the door of the map room, Lt DE LA TORRE leapt to the telephone.

—'Report immediately with some legionaries to the *Comisión de Límites,*' I told my sergeant at the post nearby. 'We're in danger.' . . .

Fear of betrayal had already made them advance the hour of the rising to that evening. But now?

Within minutes the sergeant and about eight legionaries burst into the courtyard where they saw only armed police. There was a moment of indecision.

—I leapt out, pushing past those in the door. My heart was beating wildly, my body trembling. 'Have faith in me! Load! Aim!' I shouted, looking at my men. At moments like that you command with the eyes more than the voice. The legionaries aimed their rifles at the policemen; my pistol pointed straight at the police lieutenant's heart. In our eyes they saw our determination. One of the policemen, with a look of terror, dropped his rifle. 'Lieutenant, don't shoot! We've got families!'

'Surrender! Drop your weapons!'

They did. Neither we nor they could imagine the full consequences of our first victory. After that, it didn't take long to capture the town. There was a bit of resistance, but the people fled when we brought in more troops . . .

MADRID

In the torrid afternoon heat, as oppressive as the political situation of the past week, parliamentary reporters gathered in the recessed Cortes, in search of news. While they were talking, the figure of Indalecio Prieto, the socialist leader, appeared unexpectedly. 'The garrison in Melilla has risen,' he said tersely. 'The workers are being slaughtered – ' The reporters ran to the phone booths. Some tried putting calls through to Melilla. 'The line is out of order,' came the reply.

In his office, Alfredo LUNA, a newspaper editor and moderate republican, heard his reporter's words with surprise. The seriousness of the situation had escaped him. 'How wrong! Worse, how wrong of the government not to have realized it, not to have taken adequate precautions!'

As work places closed, scores of communist and socialist youth, now fused into the unified socialist youth JSU (Juventudes Socialistas Unificadas), reported to their local branches. A 25-year-old clerk, Pedro SUAREZ, hadn't slept at home for many weeks. He and the other members of the workers' and peasants' anti-fascist militia, the MAOC (Milicias Anti-fascistas Obreras y Campesinas), were on active duty. 'Everyone knew the uprising was going to take place.' They had a few pistols, nothing more. But even unarmed they were ready, night after night, sleeping on benches in their local branches.

At the socialist *casa del pueblo*, Tomás MORA, national committee member of the UGT, broke the news to other trade union and socialist party leaders. But they decided not to announce it to the large cultural meeting MORA was about to open so as not to alarm the people.

Nor did the news appear in the papers the next day; the republican government slapped on total censorship. 'Our readers will think we're living in the best of all possible worlds,' grumbled a journalist. 'No one will believe that,' replied another. 'Lack of official news always means people will believe any rumour.'

Saturday, 18 July

SEVILLE

At dawn the heat lifted. A breeze from the east cooled the streets as Rafael MEDINA walked to the Sport café in the Calle Tetuán. His brother-in-law, an air force captain, had been sent home under house arrest a few hours earlier for firing at a plane sent from Madrid to bomb the insurgent military in Morocco; he and Capt. Vara del Rey had knocked it out on the ground. Prepared to die for his ideals, his brother-in-law had just escaped and returned to Tablada airfield.

The streets were almost deserted: the calm before the storm that must now break, he thought. Things couldn't go on like this. Calvo Sotelo's murder at the beginning of the week, 'in which the Popular Front government had had a hand', was the final blow.[1] The army wouldn't wait any longer.

Turning into the street, he remembered what his father had said as they passed a group of day labourers out in the country not long before. Seeing the rancour and contempt with which they looked at the car, his father commented: 'Rafael, unhappily there is no solution to all this.'

Nor was there. Those on top, the landowners, had failed to understand; they

1. The right-wing monarchist leader had been assassinated by members of the police forces acting on their own initiative the previous week (see pp. 102–3).

had refused to follow his father's example in setting up village industries, in distributing land among the village labourers. Those on the bottom were filled with envy. Understandably. The result was the greatest imaginable hatred among classes, a complete rupture between those who called themselves right- and left-wing. Nowhere were the social differences greater than here, in Andalusia. The left was preparing a revolution, foreign communist leaders were entering the country, he believed; while those with means on the other side were leaving. It was the brink of class war.

He walked into the café. His friend, the *rejoneador* Pepe 'El Algabeño', was waiting; the rising in Seville was to take place that evening or the next morning. General Queipo de Llano was to lead it.

—Queipo! A Republican, a man who had conspired against the king, who had fought José Antonio Primo de Rivera, founder of the Falange to which I had belonged since the Popular Front victory at the recent elections. What shape would the coup take under his leadership? I didn't like the sound of it, nor did Pepe . . .

SAN SEBASTIAN

The civil governor looked up as he walked into the office. 'What, you again!' 'Of course,' replied the CNT official, 'you're supposed to be the arbitrator of the fishermen's strike, and I've come to see what you're doing about it.'

Miguel GONZALEZ INESTAL, one of the few full-time paid anarcho-syndicalist union officials, was secretary of the northern regional federation of CNT fishermen's unions. His members at Pasajes, the large fishing port near San Sebastián, had been on strike since May for higher wages and better work conditions. For a moment he and Governor Artola, a left republican, discussed the strike; from the governor's expressions, GONZALEZ INESTAL began to realize that he didn't yet *know*.

—'I think you must be unaware of what has just happened.' 'What's that – what has happened?' 'The military have risen in Morocco. A state of emergency has been declared.' 'I don't believe it,' he cried. 'Why don't you get on the phone and find out? . . . '

As the governor reached for the telephone, the military commandant of San Sebastián was announced; the two conferred. A staff major, on holiday in the Basque city, arrived and urged the governor to take immediate measures to prevent the near-by Loyola barracks from rising. 'I am a right-winger, but I have sworn loyalty to the republic.'

—Then this officer, Major Garmendia, turned to me. 'Which side is the CNT on?' 'On the side of anyone opposed to the rising,' I replied. 'And the fishermen's strike – ?' 'It will be called off immediately. *Señor gobernador civil*,' I said, turning to Artola, 'the first thing you should do is to keep the military commandant here as a hostage.' I saw he didn't like the idea; he was a weak man. I turned away. His wife came up to me. 'You must encourage him to resist. Do everything you can, my husband is very passive, he doesn't realize the gravity of the situation.' She paused. 'You're a resolute man, I can see. Use his telephone, do whatever is necessary.' I went to the phone and rang up my union headquarters. I told the lads there to prepare for the trouble that was about to hit us. At the other end of the line the voices sounded pleased . . .

SEVILLE

The news went round the city in a flash. León MARTIN, a mechanic, heard it in the garage where he was at work. The atmosphere had been tense for weeks; everyone knew something was going to happen. 'But when it did, it happened so fast it took everyone by surprise.' He tried to get the ninety members of his local CNT section, of which he was the secretary, together; only a dozen or so turned up. Together they set off for the assault guard barracks in the Alameda.[1]

—'Arms! Arms!' the people were shouting. There were hundreds of us outside the barracks; but we didn't get any arms. A few patrols of assault guards were out in the streets, accompanied by a few civilians with pistols – but what could they do? . . .

After lunching at a hotel in the centre, General Queipo de Llano donned his uniform and drove to divisional headquarters. Meeting no more than verbal opposition, he arrested General Villa-Abrille and took command. He repeated the procedure at the infantry barracks next door. Ordering the regiment to be paraded, he found he had 130 men at his command; summer leave had depleted the army's effective strength in Seville as elsewhere. He detailed a captain to march into the city at the head of his men to proclaim a State of War.

In the Garden City suburb, Juan CAMPOS, a cabinet-maker, heard shooting; he wasn't sure who was firing or why. He set off for the centre. He had time on his hands, his furniture factory was on a three-day week. 'Like so many others, my employers were boycotting the republic; they gave work only when they wanted.' At the civil government building, he found a crowd clamouring for arms; but none were being handed out. A cry went up calling on people to make for the artillery depot in the Paseo de Colón, along the river.

—We set off, 2,000 of us at least. The divisions which had racked the working-class organizations in Seville no longer counted, recalled Francisco CABRERA, a sharecropper's son, who belonged to the communist youth. We weren't being armed because the republican authorities were more frightened of the working class than of the military. We communists didn't share the government's confidence that the rising could be put down in twenty-four hours. Party orders were for all militants to come to Seville . . .

Queipo had moved fast; an engineer captain with sixty men had been ordered to take the artillery depot where 25,000 rifles were stored. The workers were met by fire; men fell to the ground, wounded and dead. The rest scattered.

The cabinet-maker, a socialist party member, retreated to the *casa del pueblo*; he found the socialist headquarters deserted. An assault guard captain

1. Created by the republican regime as a loyal urban police force, the assault guards were a counter-balance to the *guardia civil*, the highly trained para-military rural police corps which had been in existence for nearly a century.

came looking for the two socialist parliamentary deputies. A general strike had been called, he said, they were needed. But they didn't show up.

—They stayed at home – and that's where the military found them. No party or union leader displayed the slightest sense of leadership when the moment came . . .

Returning to the Plaza Nueva in the centre, he found groups shouting: 'All workers back to their *barrios*.' What a mistake, he reflected. The people should stay to defend the city centre. But they took up the cry and started to leave for the working-class neighbourhoods to the west and over the river to the south.

—The Seville working class wasn't the organized proletariat of Barcelona, lamented León MARTIN. There was a lack of cohesion, a lack of consciousness. Seville was underdeveloped, the working class included an enormous number of sub-proletarians. If the pigmentation of our skins had been different, we would have been blacks . . .

Queipo's shortage of soldiers was made good with cannon; there was no difficulty in getting a field piece into the centre. A few rounds and the assault guards in the Telephone Exchange in the main square surrendered. Then the cannon was turned on the Hotel Inglaterra behind which stood the civil government building.

Ignacio CAÑAL, a falangist lawyer, advanced across the square towards the hotel. Very few civilians had joined the rising, he noticed; not more than twenty-five or thirty in the first six hours. Of course, most of his falangist comrades were still in gaol, but he had expected more volunteers. A shell whistled over his head, tearing through the screen of the outdoor cinema set up in the square, passed through a hotel window and exploded on the civil government building –

—Led by an artillery major we ran into the building. The governor and other authorities came down the stairs, their hands over their heads. In an extraordinary way, the events all seemed very ordinary, utterly provincial . . .

'From time to time I had to rub my eyes to convince myself I wasn't dreaming,' Queipo wrote later. Within a few hours, he had taken the centre of Spain's fourth largest city, 'red' Seville, in a coup which had had the prior support of only two majors and a handful of captains he had not even spoken to. Half an hour after the radio station was taken, Queipo was making his first broadcast.

'*Sevillanos*: To arms! The fatherland is in danger and, in order to save it, some men of spirit, some generals, have assumed the responsibility of placing themselves at the forefront of a movement of salvation which is triumphant everywhere.

The Army of Africa is preparing to cross to Spain to take part in the task of crushing this unworthy government which has resolved to destroy Spain in order to convert the country into a colony of Moscow.

Sevillanos: The die is cast, it is useless for the scum to resist. Legionaries and Moroccan troops are en route for Seville, and when they arrive they will hunt down these trouble-makers like wild animals. *¡Viva España! ¡Viva la República!*'

MADRID

During the day the government issued two communiqués calling for calm and assuring the nation that 'nobody, absolutely nobody' on the mainland had joined the uprising. There were rumours that the government was about to resign. The socialist and communist parties issued a joint statement supporting the liberal republican government, but calling on the working class to prepare to fight in the streets. With what? The government refused to arm the people.

Capt. Urbano ORAD DE LA TORRE, a retired artillery officer, went down to the artillery depot. There was no point in staying at the war ministry; the place was chaotic, he thought; Casares Quiroga, prime minister and war minister, was in a state of collapse, incapable of taking decisions. At the depot, he was talking to the commandant, Lt Col. Rodrigo Gil, a socialist like himself, when word was brought that the workers were preparing to take it by force in their search for arms.

—'What shall I do?' Rodrigo Gil asked. 'There are only 500 rifles left and no ammunition.' 'Hand out the rifles you've got and tell them to wait until the ammunition arrives.' I went out in a lorry to tell the workers to be patient, arms were coming. Then I fetched the rifles and, on the corner of the Calle Atocha, I handed them out to anyone who showed me a left-wing membership card. I didn't know who they were – they might have been bandits and assassins – but at that moment the people had to be armed . . .

More arms – another 4,500 rifles – had been handed out earlier that evening, mainly to members of the communist-led workers' and peasants' anti-fascist militia. There were ten times that number of rifles stored in the depot, all without bolts. For the past two years, due to fears of popular assault on military arsenals, rifles and bolts had been stored separately. Some 45,000 bolts were now stacked in the Montaña barracks close to the former Royal Palace. Only a few hours earlier, the officer commanding the infantry regiment in the barracks had refused to obey an order signed by the prime minister to hand over the bolts. The Montaña in the heart of Madrid was considered in consequence to have joined the uprising; it held the key to the widespread arming of the people.

NAVARRE

As the sun went down, four Carlist[1] peasant lads in shirt-sleeves lay in the ditch watching the road to Pamplona. It was hot. Three of them had pistols, the other a shotgun. Their leader, Antonio IZU, had been reaping wheat on the family farm that morning and hadn't heard of the rising until he got home. Turning the radio on, he learnt that the army revolt in Morocco had been crushed. Notwithstanding, Esteban Ezcura, a local landowner and *requeté* commander of the Echauri valley, had ordered Izu and the others to keep watch and stop any cars.

In the Carlist headquarters in Pamplona, Mario OZCOIDI, *requeté* captain,

1. The Carlists derived their name from don Carlos, whose claim to the throne in the early nineteenth century founded the movement in reaction to the introduction of liberalism. They remained staunchly traditionalist, Catholic, and anti-liberal in the twentieth century (see Prologue, p. 35). A *requeté* was a military body of about 250 Carlists and, by extension, a Carlist soldier.

waited. That morning, a message had arrived from General Mola and he, the only *requeté* officer available, had hurried to the general's HQ. As he waited for Mola, the chief planner of the uprising, to finish talking to the newly appointed *guardia civil* commanding officer in Pamplona, who was known for his loyalty to the republic, Mola himself came out and said: 'We've got to finish off this bastard.' OZCOIDI hurried back, planning to arrest, or kill if need be, the civil guard officer, who was about to take his men south to Tafalla on the Ebro river to resist the uprising.

—Suddenly, I heard shots from the *guardia civil* barracks. We didn't know what had happened. But soon the news went round like wildfire: the guards had shot down their commanding officer as he was attempting to get them to leave the barracks . . .

Not a single car had come along the road all evening. Before giving up his guard duty, IZU reported to his commander; Ezcura told him to have his men ready first thing in the morning and to make for Pamplona in the local bus.

—'We're at war now,' he told me. 'Ah, that's good,' I replied. And I went home very happy. I didn't sleep all that night, thinking of what a hell of a shindy we were going to kick up . . .

MADRID

In the evening the government resigned. A new government, under Martínez Barrio, leader of Unión Republicana, the party the farthest to the right within the Popular Front, was formed. The president of the republic, Manuel Azaña, had wanted the formation of a national government, from communists to right-wing republicans, to crush the military rising. The socialists, under pressure from Largo Caballero, leader of the party's left wing, refused to take part, calling instead for the people to be armed. The government which emerged in the late evening was composed exclusively of republicans, in general more to the right than those in the outgoing cabinet.

The Puerta del Sol was filled with people, who had been flooding in all afternoon and evening, shouting for arms. Suddenly, Julián VAZQUEZ, a communist tailor, saw a figure appear on a balcony of the interior ministry. There was silence, everyone waited. He began to read out the list of the new cabinet, and as he did so a cry went up, then a shout repeated from mouth to mouth.

—'Treachery! Treachery!' The atmosphere was explosive. If they'd given us arms at that moment we'd have been capable of conquering the world . . .

To a left republican schoolteacher, Régulo MARTINEZ, the new government seemed a prudent move. The military were rising to the cry of 'death to communism'; here was a government to show them that there was no such threat. But the people took the news badly.

—Even members of my own party – Azaña's party – began tearing up their membership cards. The masses wanted revenge, revolution. They threw caution to the wind; courage and resolution were the order of the day . . .

VALLADOLID

The rising was bound to succeed here, the heartland of Castilian Catholicism, birthplace of the fascistic JONS (Juntas de Ofensiva Nacional Sindicalista), scene of its unification with the Falange Española only two years before. The falangists, shut up in the cells that seemed like the pens where bulls are kept before being released into the ring, could hear the shouts of 'Fascists, assassins' from beyond the prison walls. Would the mob storm in? Would they be the first, unhappy martyrs of the uprising?

Tomás BULNES, a lawyer associate of Onésimo Redondo, co-founder of the JONS, had managed to persuade a warder to leave the cell door unlocked. But the precaution was proven unnecessary. The prison warders began to look more cheerful; one of them told the falangists that troops of the Farnesio cavalry regiment and assault guards were taking up positions in the streets. 'We knew then that the military had risen.'

Before dawn, the falangist militants were being released by a group of falangist youth, armed by the military. 'What's the point of your leaving?' the prison director asked Alberto PASTOR, a falangist farmer who had been imprisoned after a fight in his native village. 'Tomorrow, you'll be back in here anyway.'

—But I didn't stop to listen to any more. The moment we had been waiting for had come at last . . .

Sunday, 19 July

BURGOS

News of the Valladolid success had not reached the *requetés* who had been waiting all night in their headquarters. Under the traditional pictures of the Carlist kings, beneath the gaze of an eighty-year-old veteran of the last Carlist war, the *requetés* had been saying their rosary when fifteen-year-old José María CODON arrived, his raincoat bulging with the arms he had just dug up from his father's bakery. Carefully packed and greased, they had lain there under the very feet of the socialist workers. The veteran Carlist harangued them: 'My sons, you are about to set out, as I and 200 other Burgaleses set out in 1872 for the Cartuja (Charterhouse) and the war in the north – '

But were they going to set out? The night wore on without news. Was this another false alarm as in May? Only yesterday, the government had arrested General González de Lara and other officers who were to lead the rising in Burgos, he recalled. Suddenly he heard shouts of 'Aña' echoing in the stillness of the night.

—'Aña – ' 'What are they shouting? Is it *Viva Azaña* or *Viva España*?' We didn't wait to find out, we rushed into the streets. In the distance we heard the trumpets of the military detachment which had come out to proclaim a State of War. We unfurled the red and gold flag of Spain which we had longed in all those republican years to see flying again. What a mistake the republic made in changing the flag! One of my companion's sisters threw herself on her knees in front of the flag, tearing her stockings in order to kiss it . . .

Carrying the flag, they made for the cathedral where the bells began to toll a call to a thanksgiving service. Women in *mantillas*, wearing scapularies on their chests, men in blue falange shirts, army officers, *requetés* in their red berets, gathered to sing a *salve regina*.

—There were hundreds of people there; and yet it surprised me that the masses didn't join us immediately. This was a city which had always elected monarchist, Carlist, agrarian deputies to parliament under the republic. And this was a moment when, had there been any fighting to do, their support or lack of it would have been absolutely decisive . . . [1]

But their support was unnecessary. Burgos was taken almost without a shot. The small working class was disorganized and unprepared. The assault guards sided immediately with the military who took over, led by Brigadier General Dávila, a retired officer. The divisional commander, General Batet – to whom only two days earlier General Mola had given his word that he would not rise – was under arrest. So too were the commander of the civil guard and the civil governor.

BILBAO

They had spent all night listening to the radios installed in the party's newspaper offices. Juan AJURIAGUERRA, a young engineer from the Babcock and Wilcox plant and president of the Basque nationalist party in Vizcaya, had returned earlier from a party executive meeting in San Sebastián. It had reached no decision; there had been little definite news to base a decision on. All they knew was that the army had risen in Morocco.

—We had fought the recent elections alone, joining neither right- nor left-wing blocs. The right had been attacking us violently, the left was dragging its feet over getting our autonomy statute through parliament; we were quite alone . . .

He had driven back to Bilbao. The Basque nationalist party, PNV (Partido Nacionalista Vasco), was the largest party in the two northern Basque provinces. The military had risen nowhere in the Basque country yet, though in Alava – as in Navarre – it was a matter of hours. Some Basque nationalists were prepared to argue that the party should be neutral in the threatening conflict. Others, like the two parliamentary deputies Manuel Irujo and José María Lasarte, who had issued a declaration of loyalty to the republic, believed they must support the legal government.

Socialists, communists, anarcho-syndicalists and left republicans were patrolling the streets of Bilbao; miners poured into the city. No one was certain what the infantry regiment in the Garellano barracks would do.

As he kept watch, Ricardo VALGAÑON, a communist foundry worker, was

1. At about the same time, eighteen hours after Queipo had risen, Rafael MEDINA (later duke of Medinaceli) was surprised to find himself only the 187th volunteer to join the military in Seville. The provincial bourgeoisie preferred to leave it to the army to do what was needed

aware that the Popular Front parties were meeting in the civil government building. They didn't include the Basque nationalist party. 'We didn't count on the latter for anything, didn't even think about them, to tell the truth.'

In the newspaper office, AJURIAGUERRA continued to listen to the radio until the very last minute.

—Hoping that some news might come in which meant we didn't have to reach a decision: one side or the other might already have won. As the night wore on, one thing became clear: the military rising was the work of the right-wing oligarchy whose slogan was unity – an aggressive Spanish unity which was aimed at us. The right was ferociously hostile to any autonomy statute for the Basque country. The legal government, on the other hand, had promised it to us and we knew we would receive it in the end. At 6 a.m., after a sleepless night, we reached a unanimous decision. We issued a statement declaring our support of the republican government. We reached the decision without much joy but convinced that we had chosen the side which most favoured the interests of the Basque people; convinced also that, had we come to the opposite decision, our base would have opposed us . . . [1]

MADRID

At dawn Fulgencio DIEZ PASTOR, parliamentary deputy and secretary of Unión Republicana, drove to his party leader's house. He had to go out of his way to avoid a massive socialist demonstration sweeping down the Calle Fuencarral to protest against the new government being formed by his leader, Martínez Barrio. He understood the masses' feeling; such a government – possible four months earlier when it might have prevented all this – could now only mean surrender. An urgently summoned meeting of the Popular Front committee, which he had attended the previous afternoon, had unanimously called for the people to be armed. A few hours later, the prime minister-designate was telephoning General Mola in Pamplona in a vain attempt to secure his support. Mola refused it.[2]

When he reached the house, Martínez Barrio was in bed.

—I made him get up. 'You have announced on the radio that you are taking over as prime minister at 6 a.m. Where do you propose to do so? At the prime minister's office? It is surrounded by thousands of people. So is the navy ministry. The war ministry – you won't get near it. Never has there been a more unpopular government – '

He looked at us. He had accepted the premiership without consulting the

1. The PNV was a confederal party, and the decision affected only the party in Vizcaya (Biskai-Buru-Batzar). Later the same day, the Guipúzcoa PNV reached the same decision, as did delegates from Alava. Subsequently, following the military's triumph in Vitoria, provincial capital of Alava, the PNV there called on its members to put themselves at the disposal of the military authorities, expressing the hope thereby of avoiding a fratricidal war and of preventing anarchy.

2. Martínez Barrio subsequently denied having made such a call. DIEZ PASTOR: 'He never mentioned the phone conversation to me. But the new minister of communications mentioned it in a radio broadcast, saying he had spoken with the generals who had risen.' On Mola's side, several accounts have mentioned such a call and another from General Miaja, whom Martínez Barrio had appointed war minister in his ephemeral government.

party executive. He picked up the phone. 'Manolo, tell those gentlemen on my behalf that I am resigning. Yes, I can't lead a government which the Popular Front is demonstrating against in the streets – '

That was all. Without further explanation he quit. I hadn't washed or shaved or slept for three days. I went home . . .

The government which came in as the street lights went on vanished as the lights went out. With the dawn came yet another all-republican government, under José Giral.

—That was better news for all of us in the Puerta del Sol, recalled Julián VAZQUEZ, the communist tailor. We believed he would be tougher than the rest. And up to a point we were right, because he gave the order to arm the people . . .

*

His party had failed its historic mission; no party had been able to lead the masses forward, he thought. It was too late now, but it was going to cost them dear.

Sócrates GOMEZ, son of a leading socialist trade unionist, had fled Segovia where he was doing his military service. Seeing the preparations being made in the Artillery Academy he had taken off his private's uniform and asked a taxi-driver friend to take him to Madrid. As a prominent member himself of the unified socialist youth (JSU), he had no illusions about his fate if he remained. He was on the left wing of the socialist party, the largest working-class party in Spain.

Five months before, he thought, when the Popular Front won at the polls, the people had waited calmly, full of hope that this time, at the second attempt, their immediate demands were going to be met. After two years of reactionary government they had believed a new democratic period was opening before them. Instead, an all-republican government failed to produce a coherent social programme, an operative agrarian reform, the dismantling of the forces hostile to the regime, a solution to the country's many social problems. Disappointment had set in. The right staged constant provocations and street violence to sabotage attempts to create a democratic regime. In those months, the socialist party had made a big mistake; it should have joined the government, he saw that now, though then he had argued against.

—In government, the party could have crushed the plot, imprisoned the right-wing elements – the blindest and most passionately obtuse of any in the world – which were now rising. Without for a moment renouncing its aim of conquering power, the socialist party – the most marxist socialist party in Europe – could have shared governmental power in order to ensure, inasfar as such was possible in a capitalist regime, that the institutional and economic forces of coercion remained firmly in the government's hands . . .

There had been a chance; the left wing had blocked it. It was a serious error. The socialist party's failure to join the government and ensure the satisfaction of the people's demands increased fears that these demands would not be met. A pre-revolutionary ferment had begun. It was driven by fear; and fear, he reflected, did not make a clear-headed revolutionary counsellor. 'Rather it was the state of mind of a man in despair.' Divided, the socialist party had not been able to channel or lead this ferment. It had failed on both scores.

*

He had just had a lucky escape. Arrested by militiamen as he was trying to get into the Montaña barracks to join the military, he had been taken to the headquarters of a republican party for an identity check. Happily, the militiamen hadn't recognized him, David JATO, a founder of the falangist students' union, SEU (Sindicato Español Universitario). He waited. Ever since the Popular Front victory – no, from the time of the October 1934 revolution[1] – it had been clear to him that only violence would solve the country's problems. The republicans had come to power too soon, historically speaking, before they had a base in the country. Their traditional anti-clericalism, their refusal to allow the CEDA to govern when they won the elections three years before, exacerbated the fundamental problems. Liberalism everywhere was on the retreat. The choice lay between communism and fascism, the dominant ideologies which were deciding the fate of Europe.

—Both, especially in Spain, believed in violence. Both, given the international situation, enjoyed great influence, particularly among the youth. Increasingly disillusioned with the republic, the latter had gone over to extreme positions on either side . . .

Not that he feared that the communists were in a position to make their revolution; they were still too weak. But in conjunction with the left-wing socialists, who formed the bulk of the socialist party, under Largo Caballero, they might. It was this he feared. Since the Popular Front victory, the socialists had been increasing their militia strength. There were daily assassination attempts.

—Fourteen SEU members had been killed by the time the elections were held. And now Calvo Sotelo's murder. That was the final proof that only a violent solution could save Spain . . .

He heard a noise, some shouts. A lightning demonstration swept into the party headquarters protesting at the formation of the short-lived Martínez Barrio government. In the confusion, as people left, he walked out. It couldn't have been easier. He made for a cousin's house. A socialist, he would certainly give him shelter.

MADRID–BARCELONA TRAIN

The Popular Olympiad – a counter to the Nazi Olympics in Berlin – was due to open in Barcelona today, Sunday. A considerable number of Madrid youth had put their names down to attend. Despite the imminence of the uprising, the communist party had given its members permission to go because it was to be a large anti-fascist demonstration. Railwaymen – Narciso JULIAN, a communist party member among them – were well represented because they got free tickets on the trains.

1. The socialist-inspired rising against the centre-right government which had its epicentre in Asturias (see Prologue, p. 43, and Points of Rupture, E).

The threat of fascism, JULIAN knew, occupied the foreground of all attention now. Everything, even the need to push the bourgeois democratic revolution Spain had never made to its full completion under the Popular Front, had to be subordinated to the vital task of forging a solid anti-fascist alliance.

The country, since the 1936 elections, had been going through a period of great political and social effervescence; you could call it pre-revolutionary. The republic's failure to implement a thorough-going agrarian reform to solve the eternal land problem had led peasants to take over the land. Some had been killed by the landowners' traditional defence, the *guardia civil.* There were strikes and demands by the working class for better conditions; unions and political parties were increasing in strength as the struggle became more open.

—The communist party called for the creation of armed militia, and warned of the threat of a military uprising. Everyone could see that the republican government was displaying great weakness in the face of the threat. The Falange's gunmen were out in the streets, engaged in open warfare, assassinating well-known republican police officers. For the past fortnight, none of us communist militants had slept at home, knowing that the military were going to rise . . .

But none of this, he thought, could justify the military rising. It was not a revolutionary period that was leading to socialism. Not at all. That was the pretext the fascists used to justify their rising. It wasn't true – especially among the peasant masses; they weren't agitating for socialism. They wanted the republic to tackle the country's fundamental problems, and the land was one – if not *the* – major problem.

As the train passed through Valencia and began the long haul to Barcelona, he was unaware how lucky he had been to choose this, rather than the alternative route. Those who travelled via Saragossa would never reach their destination.

AGAINST FASCISM, YES. BUT ALSO AGAINST ANY TYPE OF DICTATORSHIP BECAUSE, WHOEVER EXERCISES IT, DICTATORSHIP IS ALSO FASCISM.

Solidaridad Obrera, CNT (Barcelona, 18 July 1936)

DECREE

By Agreement of the Council of Ministers and on the proposal of the War Minister, I decree as follows:

All troops whose commanders have risen against republican legality are herewith demobilized.

Madrid, the eighteenth of July, 1936. Manuel Azaña. The prime minister and minister of war, Santiago Casares Quiroga.

Gaceta de Madrid (19 July 1936)

Don Francisco Franco Bahamonde, Divisional General Chief of the Military Forces of Morocco and High Commissioner.

I proclaim:

Once more the Army, united with the other forces of the nation, has found itself obliged to respond to the wishes of the great majority of Spaniards who, with infinite bitterness, have seen disappear that which unites us in a common ideal:

SPAIN.

At stake is the need to restore the empire of ORDER within the REPUBLIC, not only in its external appearances but in its very essence; to achieve this, it will be necessary to labour with justice, taking no account of classes or social categories, to end the division of the country into two groups: those who dispose of power and those whose rights are trampled under foot . . . The re-establishment of the principle of AUTHORITY, forgotten in these past years, implacably demands that punishments be exemplary and are seen to be so by the seriousness and rapidity with which they are carried out . . .

To execute these tasks rapidly

I order and command:

Article 1. Martial law is declared in the whole territory and all armed forces in consequence are militarized . . .

Tetuán (Spanish Morocco, 18 July 1936)

BARCELONA

The factory clock showed a few minutes after 5 a.m. A CNT militant stepped from a car to give his companions the news. Almost simultaneously, sirens from the factories in Poble Nou began to wail in the still, clear air of the Sunday dawn the long awaited warning that the military rising had begun.

In his apartment near the Diagonal, Professor Josep TRUETA was awoken by the sirens, soon followed by shooting. It was as he feared: the military rising, of which he had heard the first news only the evening before when he and his wife went to the cinema, had spread.

He went to the window. Only a part of the Diagonal that cut a long swath through the city was visible. Some soldiers were coming from the direction of the Pedralbes barracks. He heard more shooting.

There was no excuse for this, the military had no cause to rise here. A confirmed liberal, he felt indignant. The violence which had swept some parts of Spain since the elections five months ago – and which a great number of people had a vested interest in fomenting, he thought – had been completely absent in Barcelona. Despite the growth of the anarcho-syndicalist movement, with its migrant base, which was a source of anxiety for people like himself, Barcelona had been peaceful. It was due to Catalonia's autonomy statute, he believed. He thought of a Spanish marchioness who had begged him recently to pretend that her son's fractured arm was serious, so that her husband would have an excuse for leaving Madrid. Newly appointed head surgeon of Santa Creu i Sant Pau, the city's largest hospital, he had hesitated. 'But in Madrid you can be gunned down in the streets by a car-load of falangists or communists,' she insisted. When her husband came to thank him, he used an expression TRUETA hadn't heard before: 'No wonder Barcelona is being called "an oasis of peace"; it is thanks to this police force of yours.'

*

All night, as every night in recent weeks, CNT and FAI militants had been on the alert. The CNT defence committee, centred round men like Durruti, Francisco Ascaso, García Oliver, Ricardo Sanz of the *Nosotros* group, had long been preparing for this moment.[1]

As soon as he heard the sirens, Ricardo SANZ picked up his parabellum pistol and set off. All night he and the others had been moving from one place to another in the city. Their weapons included a machine-gun, its tripod sawn off so as to fit into a suitcase, which had been smuggled out of the Asturias arms factory. They hadn't drawn up any concrete plan. 'We knew we had excellent CNT and FAI defence groups in all the districts; we were counting on them.'

In the main police station, Frederic Escofet, chief of police, heard the sirens' wail with mixed feelings. He and Lluis Companys, president of the Generalitat, the Catalan government, had agreed not to arm the people. The CNT, in their eyes, posed as serious a threat to the republican regime as did – from the opposing camp – the military revolt. And what, moreover, if the CNT's

1. Sometimes called anarcho-bolsheviks, this group was to provide the libertarians' leading military commanders on the Aragon front during the war (see Points of Rupture, D).

presence in the streets caused the *guardia civil*, whose attitude was uncertain, to join the rebellion?[1]

The distrust was reciprocated. The CNT had no faith in the Generalitat's ability to deal with the rising. Had not the Catalan authorities capitulated to a small military force in a few hours during the abortive uprising in October 1934? Had they not, just the evening before, tried to disarm CNT militants who had managed to seize arms from a ship in the port? The 200-odd CNT and FAI defence groups, some 2,000 men, were determined to prevent a repetition of the October defeat; then they had not fought in the streets, but now they would.

The number 22 all-night tram rattled up the Passeig de Gràcia; the sky was lightening for another hot day. Josep CERCOS, a CNT metalworker and libertarian youth member, had left the small pistol they shared with his friend after the night's vigil; nothing seemed to be happening. As the tram passed the Cinc d'Oros, the junction of the Passeig and the Diagonal, he saw a company of assault guards moving out from the Café Vienès, shouting '*¡ Visca la República!*' He looked up the Diagonal, saw the soldiers, heard a shot and leapt off the tram.

—I rushed back to find my companion. 'Come on, it's my turn. Give me the *pipa* [pistol]. You go for the dynamite – ' He had expropriated some sticks from a quarry, and we had put them aside for the day the fascists rose. Not that we thought they'd dare, because we were going to crush them if they did . . .

In the Ramblas, a young man with red hair standing on end as though each hair were an antenna, pedalled his bicycle furiously, shouting in Catalan: 'The soldiers are in the University square!' José ROBUSTE, a book-keeper who belonged to the syndicalist party, saw the people beginning to run. 'It was as if the lad had an enormous broom on the front of his bicycle which swept the people out of the Ramblas towards the University – '

From a rooftop, Ramón FERNANDEZ saw the soldiers coming into the square, shouting '*¡ Viva la República!*' He didn't catch on. The troops, accompanied by falangists in civilian trousers and army tunics, continued to advance to the same cry. CNT and POUM militants left their rooftop positions to join the soldiers as they marched into the Plaça de Catalunya. Even though the POUM carpenter had just come out of the army, he was taken in like the rest. In the middle of the Plaça, an old, fat officer suddenly shouted: 'Disarm all the civilians!' FERNANDEZ ran.

—The bullets whistled round me and I took a flying leap and landed headlong next to the small marble statue of a woman on the Ramblas side of the Plaça. Assault guards began shooting at the troops. I got behind a newspaper kiosk and fired my little pistol at the soldiers . . .

By the time he got back to the Cinc d'Oros, where he had jumped off the tram, Josep CERCOS found heavy shooting in progress. The assault guards, armed with carbines, were doing most of the firing; but behind every group there were half a dozen CNT militants, to whom, if they had no weapons, the guards had given their pistols.

1. See F. Escofet, *Al servei de Catalunya i de la república* (Paris, 1973), pp. 184, 189.

Barricades of cobblestones were already being raised as sixteen-year-old Eduardo PONS PRADES ran through the streets to the CNT wood-workers' union in Poble Sec. A young union militant, who lived opposite the Pedralbes infantry barracks, had been telephoning every hour to inform union leaders of the troop movements within, and had sounded the alert as the soldiers sallied forth.

—'Now that the CNT has brought out its men, there won't be another defeat like in October,' everyone at union headquarters was saying. There was complete confidence everywhere that the military rising in Barcelona was going to be crushed . . .

At the Cinc d'Oros, in the first decisive engagement of the day, the Santiago cavalry regiment, its colonel at its head, was driven back with heavy losses. But a new danger loomed: three batteries of the 1st mountain artillery were advancing on the docks. If they reached them, they would swing up into the old town while the infantry in the Plaça de Catalunya pressed down from the other side to capture the Generalitat, the Catalan government building.

By the docks, the solidly working-class Barceloneta district mobilized. 'Arms! Arms! Not another 6 October!' A police major began handing out rifles in exchange for trade union and party membership cards. Suddenly – whose idea was it? No one knew – dockworkers began shifting bales of recently unloaded paper to form a barricade. Electric trucks shuttled back and forth until 500 tons of paper formed a two-metre high barricade across the Icaria avenue. Police Commissioner Escofet noted that his forces were being aided by civilians, whose unexpected reinforcement 'was appreciated by the guards and contributed to sapping the enemy's morale'.[1]

The air force, which remained loyal, bombed and strafed the artillery barracks, demoralizing the rebels and cheering the defenders. By 10 a.m., the artillery batteries were defeated. In the final assault, civilians rushed forward, many without arms, to capture the field pieces. In an outburst of popular jubilation, men, women and children dragged the cannon along the avenue.

PAMPLONA

Wearing their red Carlist berets, the people streamed towards the Plaza del Castillo. At the entrance to the town the *guardia civil* had stopped the car and Dolores BALEZTENA's nineteen-year-old nephew, rather cautiously, had pulled out his red beret. 'Ah, very good,' the *guardia* had said, saluting. 'Forward . . . ' At last – the red beret was a passport.

As she drove into the square, tears came to Baleztena's eyes. Recognizing her, sister of the president of the Navarre regional Carlist junta, people stretched out their hands. She let go the steering wheel to grasp the hands. People were shouting, 'Long live Religion! Long live the King! Long live brave Navarre!' The people seemed delirious.

—Shouts of joy, happy faces. The population was sweeping in off the land. Lorries, tractors, farm carts bringing red berets from every side street into the

1. Escofet, op. cit., pp. 213, 426.

square. Most of the people in their Sunday best. A man in shirt-sleeves leapt from a lorry crying: 'Here we've come, confessed and communed, for whatever God demands.' These were the real, authentic people determined to defend their ideals. The people who loved their land, their farms, who had a pride in their race, even if pride was no virtue . . .

Amongst those who had arrived was Antonio IZU, the Carlist peasant lad who hadn't slept all night for joy that the shindy was about to begin. At dawn he had leapt out of bed; there was still a field of wheat to be reaped. After that – 'like good peasants' – he and his brothers returned home, had breakfast, washed, shaved and put on their Sunday suits. His youngest brother was to stay at home to look after the farm, for their mother and father had died by then. Had his father been alive, he thought, he would certainly have gone with them, for he had been a fervent Carlist. Little did he think, as he left the farm, that it would be three years before he would again be working the land.

In the Plaza del Castillo, the *requetés* were ordered to form up. The red and gold flag, which the republic had done away with, was hoisted on the provincial government building and the town hall to the frantic cheers of the crowds; and soon afterwards was ordered removed by General Mola. Izu had sent word to twelve men in his village to come to Pamplona; but only seven had joined him. The others made varying excuses. Then the *requetés* were ordered to report to army barracks in the town where they were equipped with army uniforms and rifles and sent out to lunch because there was not enough food for them in the army canteens.

SAN ROQUE (CADIZ)

It was noon. The thirteen-year-old boy looked out of the window of his house in the main square of the small town, some 8 km from Gibraltar and twice that from Algeciras, and saw Moroccan troops. They ran past the house and towards the infantry barracks at the end of the square. Wearing khaki trousers tied at the ankles and turbans, they took cover behind the trees, dropping on one knee and taking aim. After a moment's parley, Carlos CASTILLA DEL PINO saw, they entered the barracks. Not a shot had been fired.

Two days before, on a trip to La Linea to buy an anatomy book, he had heard that the Moors had risen in Morocco. 'Will they invade Spain like the Moors twelve centuries ago?' 'No, no, it's nothing important,' his friend's father had replied. And now they were here! They had landed at Algeciras that morning.[1]

—They didn't stay long. A new town council was appointed. My uncle Pepe, a monarchist like all my family, was made a member. Once the Moors had gone, the uprising seemed a passing event. My private tutor told me lessons would start again in a few days. Everything seemed to have returned to normal . . .

BARCELONA

In the Plaça de Catalunya, the military were still holding out. Their capture of

1. Part of a small contingent which the Army of Africa, the only professional fighting force in the Spanish army, had managed to ferry across by sea before the republican fleet blocked the strait of Gibraltar.

the Telephone Exchange building meant communications between Police Commissioner Escofet and some of his units, including those in the Plaça de Espanya to the west, had been cut. Assault guards had earlier allowed insurgent cavalry to take over the square. Workers threw up a barricade at the entrance to the working-class district of Sants and started shooting.

Miquel COLL, a POUM textile worker, saw a detachment of dismounted cavalry making down the Paralelo, and set off; if they were allowed to get through they could reach the docks and the old town. With his hands up, he crossed the square, telling the soldiers who stopped him that he was going for a swim. He ran towards the Ramblas; on the corner of the Carrer Fernando, he saw that Beristaín, a sports and gunshop, was being ransacked for arms. He rushed in and grabbed a shotgun. A CNT man broke open the safe and pulled out wads of banknotes.

—Then he struck a match and set fire to the lot. He burnt every note. It was amazing – true proof of the honour that so many CNT militants like him displayed. I grabbed two bandoliers and strapped them across my chest, stuffed full of cartridges, and went out of there looking like one of those Mexican bandits you see in films. I was only twenty . . .

In the Ramblas they saw a man carrying piles of looted objects, and they nearly shot him on the spot. Instead, they decided to throw the lot down a sewer. As COLL ran towards the Plaça del Teatre, snipers opened up. He raised his shotgun and fired; the recoil spun the gun from his hands and knocked him down. As he was picking himself up, he heard a man shout 'Atarazanas!' and he ran towards the barracks of that name. There he saw Durruti coming out with a sergeant carrying several machine-guns. He pushed his way in – there were only a corporal and a few soldiers in that part – grabbed a couple of muskets and ran to the POUM headquarters in the Ramblas.

The troops from the Plaça de Espanya had advanced three quarters of the way down the Paralelo, Barcelona's Montmartre. No police forces were positioned to stop them. Realizing the danger, Durruti, García Oliver, Ascaso and other CNT–FAI leaders gathered their defence groups and set off. García Oliver's group took the women's prison, a useful position to fall back on if the attack failed, and released all the prisoners, who left crying – elated, or hysterical, no one knew. The CNT defence groups forced the cavalry squadron to retreat to the Moulin Rouge bar; an insurgent machine-gun drove the anarcho-syndicalists back with heavy losses as they charged across the great width of the Paralelo. Breaking into the Chicago bar, the CNT militants set up their own machine-gun and, under cover of its fire, charged again. Already decimated, the troops surrendered with their weapons which included three machine-guns.

José ROBUSTE heard a voice shout: 'They're shooting from the top of the Santa Madrona church.' The syndicalist party book-keeper set off. His wife was with him. When he had gone home for his pistol, she had flung her arms round him.

—'I'm coming with you.' 'What, *mujer*?' 'Wherever you go – ' I had no choice but to take her. When we got to the church, we found men dragging out pews and trying to set fire to them. They poured petrol over them twice and each time only the petrol burned, though the wood was old and dry. A priest, dressed in civilian clothes, arrived. '*Muchachos*, why are you trying to set fire to these? They may come in useful to you – ' I turned to my companion. 'That man is right, let's have nothing to do with this,' and we set off up the Ramblas . . .

Police Commissioner Escofet had laid his plans carefully; tapped telephones had kept him advised of the rebels' plans. Madrid had been informed but had taken no action. Despite his efforts, however, the insurgents were holding on to the Plaça de Catalunya; attempts to dislodge them had failed. He decided on a bold step. He ordered two companies of assault guards to make their way underground along the Metro tunnels. At 1 p.m., they burst into the plaça; the rebels had not taken the precaution of occupying the underground entrances. Alejandro VITORIA, a socialist Treasury official, saw them emerging. From his position in the bank employees' union premises in the Carrer Vergara, where he had been trapped all morning by the hail of fire from the square, he could hardly believe his eyes as he saw an assault guard officer leading his men forward with only a riding crop in his hand. 'I began to realize how decisive it was that the police forces had remained loyal.'

Not decisive enough, however, to bring victory yet. The battle for the square had been raging for close on eight hours; the centre was littered with dead soldiers and civilians, dead horses and abandoned material under the harsh sunlight. Lying behind a low cobblestone parapet in the Porta de l'Angel a Catalan nationalist university student began to think that neither side could win. The assault guards made some progress, but the rebels were still ensconced in the Hotel Colón and the Military Club on the opposite side.

As soon as he had heard shooting, Manuel CRUELLS had jumped out of a window at home to evade his mother and run to the university. 'Get that one with long hair!' he heard someone shout. He began to run for his life towards the Ramblas as the shots whistled behind him from the insurgents who had taken the university. At the top of the Ramblas he ran into two youths, one a communist, the other a libertarian, and joined them. They had pistols, he was unarmed. Behind them, the width of the Ramblas led down to the port, opened the way to the heart of the old town, to the Generalitat. Just a few paces away was one of the city's two radio stations. They were the only defence! 'It seemed somehow symbolic that we three should be together there: a communist, an anarchist and a young Catalan nationalist with not very clear revolutionary ideas – '

After a time he had got a rifle from the police station and joined an assault guard and another youth in his position. Soldiers, sheltering behind a donkey, were crossing the square heading for the Telephone Exchange building. The assault guard scrambled to change places with CRUELLS to get a clearer shot; the donkey fell to the ground and the soldiers retreated. Almost immediately, a shot rang out and the guard doubled up, wounded in the stomach. A sniper had got him.

He tried to follow the assault guards' progress in the square, feeling that both sides were on the defensive now, fearing that somehow they were going to be caught. He started at the sudden sound of movement behind him, changing position to see what it was. A large formation of civil guards was marching up the Vía Layetana in battle order. The sun caught their tricorns. They stretched as far as he could see down the street. They advanced with military precision, in perfect step.

—'What's going to happen now?' I thought. All morning I'd been fearing a trap. The *guardia* – the people's historic enemy! If they came out against us . . .

Expecting the worst, he watched. The green uniforms continued to advance. At their head marched their colonel. They reached the main police station; he saw them halt. The colonel turned towards the balcony, where President Companys was standing, saluted and shouted: 'At your orders, *señor presidente*!'

—Then we knew they had come out on our side. It was unforgettable. Anyone who hasn't lived that moment can't imagine what it was like. The apotheosis of 19 July: the *guardia civil* on the people's side! We knew we must win now . . .

All morning, as throughout the past days, Commissioner Escofet had been uncertain about which way the *guardia civil* would swing. Their commanders were loyal; but what of the captains and majors? It was this officer rank which formed the backbone of the rising amongst the military. Despite some defections, the bulk of the force had remained loyal.

Hundreds of civilians rushed into the Plaça de Catalunya as the guards crushed the last resistance. Filled with joy, CRUELLS went off with a couple of CNT lads who invited him to a meal in the Barceloneta where, earlier, they had won a great victory behind their paper barricade. In the narrow working-class street, a table was brought out and piled with food and drink.

—They treated me like a hero – simply because, as a student, I must come from a 'good' family, and yet had taken up arms on their side. It was a moment of great fraternity. From that moment, it became a question of making the revolution . . .

Josep CERCOS, CNT metalworker, hurried to his union branch in Gràcia from the Cinc d'Oros where he had been fighting. The colonel and other survivors of the insurgent cavalry regiment had taken refuge in a Carmelite convent in the Carrer Lauria; they were surrounded and wouldn't escape. In the union office he saw a group of men, evidently under arrest. They looked like monks or seminarists. Women were laughing at them, making jokes. He told them it was wrong; the men would be tried in due course and sentenced if found guilty. Meanwhile they should be left alone. As he was talking, they heard shooting from the direction of the Plaça Bonanova and he set out. Some men there had caught a priest dressed in his vestments and were taking him to a CNT office. Well, he thought, you couldn't take suspects to a police station at a moment like this, especially when you knew that these people were your enemy. Now you had to defend yourself or run the risk of being killed.

—Because it wasn't only the military, the clergy, the large landowners who were our enemies; it was the very people who had brought in the republic, the representatives of capital . . .

He and a companion decided to 'expropriate' a car. As they were driving from the Plaça Bonanova, they saw some young women. 'Stop the car.' The women looked to CERCOS like nuns in civilian clothes; each was carrying a small suitcase. He jumped out. The women started to run.

—'Stop! Stop! I want to see what's in your suitcases.' 'We've got nothing – nothing at all.' They opened them to show us. Bras, sanitary towels, a bit of make-up, that was all. Seeing they weren't carrying arms, we let them go. They were very frightened. And then we drove on, making for where we could hear shooting . . .

The military were not yet defeated. At midday, General Goded had flown in from the Balearic Islands to take command. It was late. The insurgents had captured none of their strategic objectives – not even the two radio stations, each within a few hundred metres of the Plaça de Catalunya. All morning the radio had broadcast news encouraging the defenders. Artillery units had risen without infantry support and been defeated before they could be properly positioned; insurgent units had failed to link up; no satisfactory overall direction had been given. The *guardia civil* had entered the battle, on the wrong side; and now Divisional HQ was under attack.

A captured field piece was being manhandled by workers to fire on the HQ where Goded had established himself. Each time the cannon fired, it careered violently back across the pavement; there was nothing to hold it in position. Other workers, including Ramón FERNANDEZ, the carpenter and POUM militant, crept along behind an iron fence until they were directly in front of the massive building on the Passeig de Colón. After keeping it under steady fire for an hour, a white sheet appeared, and they leapt over the fence and charged.

Protected from the enraged civilians by police forces, the officers were brought out. General Goded was taken to see President Companys who persuaded him to broadcast a statement admitting his defeat. Though the military still held out in three isolated points, the rising in Barcelona was crushed.

OVIEDO

Standing on the pavement of the Calle Uría, the city's main street, the grocer's lad saw lorry-loads of civil guards approaching. They were giving the clenched fist salute and shouting, '*¡Viva la República!*' An old middle-class man next to him began angrily expostulating: 'It's intolerable, this is treachery. When has anything like this happened before?' Alarmed and outraged, he walked away. The lad could hardly believe his eyes. The *guardia civil*, only eighteen months after the October revolution, giving the clenched fist salute here, in Oviedo! 'What a change has come over them,' he heard a passer-by say.

In the civil government building, close to the Campo de San Francisco, Popular Front politicians were in meeting with the recently appointed civil governor. Dr Carlos MARTINEZ, former radical socialist deputy to the Cortes, was driving into the city from Gijón, his home town 27 km away on the coast, to attend the meeting. Outside the La Vega arms factory he noticed that the guard were wearing steel helmets instead of caps, as they had been yesterday. Then the atmosphere had been relatively calm. In the civil government building, he had found socialist deputies and leaders of the powerful Asturian mineworkers' union gathered with republicans around Col. Aranda, the military commandant of Asturias. Aranda was pointing at a large map, indicating the routes by which contingents of miners could be sent southwards to cut off the rebel military forces that might march on Madrid. From the capital, Prieto, the socialist leader, was urging their dispatch; with Aranda's approval, a column of miners had set off for Madrid.

While they had been meeting, a young republican opened the door, beckoned to one of the politicians and whispered that Aranda should be arrested immediately because he was a traitor.

—No one was prepared to believe it. I remembered a conversation I had had with Aranda only a couple of months earlier when I had been interim civil governor for a few weeks. He had protested most vehemently when I asked if he didn't expect a military rising. 'That would be a catastrophe too bloody to consider,' he answered. Aranda was an intelligent, calm, cultivated man who had made a good impression on me . . .

The young republican repeated his gesture several times to no avail. After midnight, Col. Aranda returned to the military commandant's building, despite protests from CNT and communist party representatives, who argued that he should not be allowed to leave the civil government offices. They had also protested at the dispatch by train and lorry of over 2,000 workers, the majority of them unarmed, who were heading south from Oviedo and the mining villages for Madrid. Meanwhile, Dr MARTINEZ drove home to Gijón, determined to return later in the day, a promise he was now fulfilling.

—When I reached the civil government building I saw people running back and forth, holding hurried discussions. Aranda had risen. Were the military about to make a sortie on the civil government? No one knew . . .

PAMPLONA

Carmen GARCIA-FALCES had gone to say farewell to her *novio*, *requeté* Captain Mario Ozcoidi. The column was about to set off.

—He said they were all off to Madrid, said it as though they were going on an outing. One of his friends was dressed in his ordinary clothes and white shoes. None of us gave it a second thought, they'd all be back soon . . .

General Mola had reviewed the column of troops, *requetés* and falangists. '*Ala*, lads, we're going to save Spain,' Antonio IZU, peasant *requeté*, heard him say as he passed down the ranks smiling, with his hand in the air.

—'Neither draw your sword without reason nor sheath it without honour,' he added, referring to an old Spanish army maxim, recalled Rafael GARCIA SERRANO, a falangist volunteer. Then he told us we were setting out for Madrid. That had always been the idea for us falangists – the decisive moment. We were much influenced by Mussolini's March on Rome . . .

Mario OZCOIDI didn't share his *novia*'s optimism that they would be returning so soon. Even if they took Madrid in a couple of days, it would take a lot longer to organize the new regime. The Carlists had risen to defend religion; there would have been no rising if the republic had not persecuted religion, he thought.

—Neither political, economic nor dynastic questions carried sufficient weight to justify starting a war. Law and order, the unity of the fatherland, the threat of a communist rising – which was due to take place a fortnight later, I had seen the plans – were factors. But religion was the crux of the matter; the war in Navarre was a crusade . . .

As the column set out, mothers attached crucifixes around their sons' necks. 'Don't stain your hands in blood if you can help it, don't steal, be good . . . ' As it was Sunday, most of the career officers were in dress uniform. OZCOIDI's commander was shortly in such pain from his dress boots that they had to be cut from his feet. Every lorry and bus had been requisitioned to carry the men. Dubious of the reliability of the ordinary conscripts, Asturian in the main, General Mola was glad of the *requeté* and falangist strength.

BARCELONA

As night fell, the euphoria of victory turned into a festival – a festival of the masses in the streets of the city. Expropriated cars, painted with the initials CNT–FAI, careered through the streets hooting horns – *da-da-da-daah* – in imitation of the hastily painted initials. Here and there an assault guard, even a civil guard, could be seen in a car, tunic unbuttoned, in shirt-sleeves, giving the clenched fist salute.

Commissioner Escofet saw the danger looming. Fearful that the situation was escaping his control, he sent a company of civil guards to the artillery depot of Sant Andreu where 30,000 rifles, as well as other war material, were stored. A short while later the captain in command of the company returned to report, tears in his eyes: it was too late.

Andreu CAPDEVILA, a CNT militant textile worker, and other libertarians had stormed the artillery barracks next to the depot, which they had been harassing all day and which had been bombed by loyal planes. Most of the officers in the depot had managed to escape when they heard General Goded's surrender broadcast. As the libertarians charged in, they were followed by a mass of people.

—They started taking whatever arms they could lay their hands on. More and more began to arrive from all over the city, in cars, lorries, any form of transport. Everyone was mad to get arms . . .

When Josep CERCOS, the libertarian metalworker, arrived, the ransacking was in full swing. A man came staggering out with a box which he put into a very small car. Then another.

—'These are all mine,' he told us. At that moment, the weight broke the bottom of the car and the boxes fell through. One smashed and we saw what it contained: rifle bolts! That's what he was so carefully taking away – bolts for rifles he didn't have. I didn't know much about weapons myself but I had a good look at what I was taking. Five rifles. I set off for Aragon with one of them three days later . . .

The situation was getting out of hand, thought CAPDEVILA.

—'We don't know who these people are,' I said to my companions. 'They may be fascists for all we know.' By now they were taking not only arms but typewriters and anything else they could move. There was total disorder. We formed a commission, and thereafter all arms were handed out only to revolutionary organizations.

Ten thousand rifles, I calculate, as well as some machine-guns, were taken. That was the moment when the people of Barcelona were armed; that was the moment, in consequence, when power fell into the masses' hands. We of the CNT hadn't set out to make the revolution but to defend ourselves, to defend the working class. To make the social revolution, which needed to have the whole of the Spanish proletariat behind it, would take another ten years at least, we believed. But the Catalan proletariat had been thoroughly inculcated with anarcho-syndicalist revolutionary propaganda. For so many decades had it been ingrained in the workers that any possible chance to make the revolution must be seized, that when the chance came they seized it. But it wasn't we who chose the moment; it was forced on us by the military who *were* making the revolution, who wanted to finish off the CNT once and for all . . .

MADRID

Capt. ORAD DE LA TORRE, retired artillery officer, had set up the two 75mm field pieces in the Calle Bailén. Less than 500 metres away, the rectangular pile of the Montaña barracks, on a slight prominence, stood out in the dark. At the same time last evening as the radio was broadcasting Goded's surrender statement from Barcelona to the jubilation of the Madrid crowds, his brother and an army officer had come to fetch him from home. They had given him news of the uprising, its successes and failures. Seville, Córdoba, Cádiz in insurgent hands; Pamplona, Burgos, Valladolid also – as was to be expected. Saragossa, the CNT stronghold, as well – that was a surprise; and now Oviedo where Aranda had risen. But Barcelona was safe, there was no fighting in Bilbao, Valencia was uncertain but the troops had not moved. In the Montaña barracks in front of him there were 45,000 rifle bolts which the military had refused to hand over.

There had been problems in getting war ministry permission to bring out the field pieces. He had to go to the National Palace – just behind him and the emplaced cannon now – to secure President Azaña's permission.

—'But what batteries?' Azaña asked. 'I've been told there are no field pieces equipped with range finders.'

'*Mi presidente*,' I replied, 'that's no problem. I am going to set the cannon up here in the Calle Bailén and I shall aim direct. I can't miss. Moreover, that will put heart into the people.'

'And the people?' he asked. 'What state are they in? What are they doing? What will happen if the military rise in Campamento?'[1]

1. A cluster of barracks on the south-western outskirts of the capital.

I reassured him; Col. Mangada already had militiamen posted behind trees. 'Everyone will resist for as long as possible.'

'Very good then,' he replied, shaking my hand. He didn't appear shattered, though he was obviously worried. So were we all; everyone felt that we had already lost . . .

Militancies I

REGULO MARTINEZ

Left republican schoolmaster

Some hours earlier, President Azaña, founder of the left republican party, had received him and a delegation of Madrid party members in the National Palace; there had been no protocol, it had been like a family visit. Thanking them for coming, expressing confidence in their opinion as left republicans, Azaña had not hesitated to tell them immediately that the thought of war appalled him. He did not want to arm the people; instead, he proposed that loyal officers and troops be given the task of fighting the enemy, while those civilians who wished could volunteer to join them. He was frightened that arming the people would lead to assassinations and pillaging.

—'Remember, the Spanish people have great virtues but also great defects. Since the time of the Romans they have been known as people who, when they weren't at war, in Pliny's words, invented wars in order to fight them. Don't forget that, with nations frightened of both communism and fascism, propaganda about crimes committed here will do untold harm to the republic. I am convinced that by now many republicans have fallen where the military have triumphed. But it will have been done coldly, methodically, with an air of legality.' He had already received a telephone call informing him of what was happening in a certain city taken by the insurgents. 'There are some things that are better not said,' he continued. 'The people will find out, of course, but if they learn of it now it will only inflame passions and they may respond criminally' . . .

He saw tears coming to Azaña's eyes.

—Normally a cold intellectual, he was unable to restrain the tears, couldn't hide them, as he surveyed the nation's prospects. He wasn't frightened, he was simply appalled. A war would be long and bitter; the uprising would not be put down amidst scenes of popular joy by the storming of a few barracks. He knew only too well the strength the military enjoyed in certain regions of the country and the support it would receive from the church. His whole preoccupation was with the nation – he even went so far as to say: 'If the solution lies in installing a democracy without a republic, I will not stand in the way; and that despite the fact that it is my duty and obligation to defend the republic. Had I not believed that democracy in Spain under a monarchy was an impossibility, I would not have struggled to bring in a republic.' He foresaw the likelihood of foreign intervention. 'That is what I fear, they will intervene in *their* favour. And all the more readily if crimes are committed on this side. That is why I oppose arming the people.'

'There is no other solution,' I said. 'Don Manuel, you no longer carry the responsibility of the republic on your shoulders. The republic's enemies, those who have refused to await their chance at the polls, have torn it from you. It is they who bear the historic responsibility for whatever happens now. The republic's only friends are the people. And you are their representative – the representative of the people who elected you to your position of responsibility. You have never deceived them, never attempted demagogically to pull the wool over their eyes. Your popularity obliges you at this moment – '

'You're probably right,' he replied, bowing his head. We too, I continued, feared that in arming the people there would be cases of personal vengeance and crimes – but had not the enemy merited it? The repressive measures might not, in the strictest sense of the word, be legal, but they would represent an historic justice. 'Let time pass and we shall see . . . '

They took their leave of the president. The country had its back to the wall, he thought; the only hope lay in the people. They had reacted heroically so far. He wasn't frightened, he had always been on the people's side. He remembered his father, a doctor in a small Toledo village, and one of his phrases which had made such an impression on him as a youth: 'I should be writing out prescriptions for the bakery and the butchers instead of for medicines.' The peasants lived on a few olives and a bit of bread. When he, Régulo, was ordained and sent to a rural parish in Guadalajara province in 1918, his first act had been to set up a Catholic agrarian trade union to help the peasantry, whose exploitation by usurous money lenders and *caciques* angered him. Soon his house, with its large living-room, became something like a *casa del pueblo* where peasants came to smoke a cigarette and chat after their work in the fields.

Although his faith in the priesthood had weakened while still a theology student, he had remained in Guadalajara for four years, believing that he was carrying out a useful Christian task. But when the opportunity arose of becoming a schoolmaster in a Madrid school for doctors' orphans, which his father was active in setting up, and his parents returned to the capital, he seized the opportunity to leave. Cardinal Segura, primate of Spain and archbishop of Toledo, ordered him to return to his parish; he refused. The cardinal threatened to defrock him; he argued face to face with the prelate that St Thomas Aquinas asserted that natural law took precedence over ecclesiastical and divine law, and natural law required that he be with his parents. Moreover, his spiritual state did not advise him to return to his parish. Despite further threats, the cardinal took no definitive action against him.

Politics replaced the priesthood. First, the organization called 'Agrupación al servicio de la república' (At the Service of the Republic), which prestigious intellectuals and writers like Ortega y Gasset, Dr Marañon and Pérez de Ayala had founded before the advent of the republic. But when the republic was proclaimed he came to believe that their interest in the new regime was too platonic; after hearing Manuel Azaña speak, he realized that here was a great politician and Spaniard, and joined his party. He did not regret his decision, despite the events he came to witness. There had been mistakes, committed by the party, not least on the religious question.[1] But other parties – the socialists, for example – had made their full share of errors too. The October 1934 rising, for instance: violence could only lend support to the enemies of the people. Sincere democrats had to be willing to wait to win back at the polls what they had lost at the polls. Had not Azaña himself, during the recent Popular Front electoral campaign, told the mass rally at Comillas that if people hoped to advance to power through violence he would be the first to oppose them?

Ever since the elections, the left wing of the socialist party, under Largo Caballero, had come out for revolution; it had only served to inflame the atmosphere. The 'Spanish Lenin', Caballero was called. Moreover, the UGT and CNT, the socialist and anarcho-syndicalist trade unions, were at loggerheads, with militants of each gunning down the other. The Falange had been responsible for political assassinations which had been replied to in kind. The world was becoming increasingly divided between fear of fascism on the one hand, fear of communism on the other. Although there were few communists in Spain, the atmosphere since the Popular Front elections, he thought, had become communistic, fellow-travelling. In the disorder precipitated by the military rising, the people had shown their eagerness for revolution and revenge. They were being led along by the parties and unions which were promising them the moon. Who, if not the communists, were most likely to benefit from all this?

Back at party headquarters – he was *de facto* president of the Madrid party now – he heard that the new left republican prime minister, José Giral, had ordered the people to be armed.

Monday, 20 July

MADRID

Inside the Montaña barracks there was a certain confusion. The insurgents' planning and coordination had been deficient in Madrid. Mola's plans did not envisage the possibility of immediate success in the capital: the Madrid garrison was to remain on the defensive until, in a lightning offensive, columns from outside relieved it. At virtually the last moment – yesterday noon – General Fanjul, a leading conspirator, had gone to the barracks to take command of the 1,200 officers and men of the infantry and engineers' regiments and a specialist unit quartered separately at the back. In addition, some 250 falangists had managed to reach the Montaña, and had been armed and given uniforms.

As the night wore on, some of the falangists became increasingly worried: why weren't they sallying forth to capture the city? The groups of militiamen, who had made access to the barracks so difficult for them earlier, appeared to have disappeared. 'What are we doing cooped up in here?' Eugenio LORTAN, a falangist student, asked.

1. See Points of Rupture, B.

—The majority of us had never handled a rifle before, recalled Mario REY, a carpenter who had been a member of the JONS before its fusion with the Falange. But our morale was so high we'd have made a sortie as soon as we received the order. We couldn't understand what we were waiting for. But that was how we'd felt ever since the Popular Front elections . . .

Not all those in the Montaña were prepared to support the rising. A soldiers' and corporals' organization, with its own clandestine paper *Soldado Rojo* (Red Soldier), had been growing in strength; it claimed more than 200 members in the Montaña's infantry regiment. A number of NCOs, as well as some officers, had been arrested by the insurgents in the barracks. Francisco SANPEDRO, a left republican student sapper, didn't sleep in his bed that night, fearing arrest, although he belonged to no soldiers' organization. Like other republican supporters he feared that the right-wingers knew where his sympathies lay.

—At dawn, shooting broke out. But we received no orders; none of the company was paraded or posted to defensive positions. We were completely at sea . . .

His arm in a sling from having fallen downstairs four days before and broken a finger, Capt. ORAD DE LA TORRE set his cannon at 400 metres range. Then he looked down the barrel. The barracks were so enormous he could hardly miss. He had wanted to begin firing three hours before but no order had come. At first light air force planes had flown over, dropping leaflets on the barracks calling for surrender; loudspeakers on houses all round repeated the call. Soon the planes would return with bombs. Thousands of civilians, most of them unarmed, were milling about amongst assault and civil guards. An emissary was sent to the barracks demanding surrender within twenty minutes; the man returned with the message that the military would never surrender.

—At 7 a.m. I gave the order to fire. The first round, in memory of Capt. Faraudo, fascism's first victim, assassinated in the streets of Madrid only a month before. The second round in memory of Lt Castillo, gunned down but a week before . . . The third in the name of the Spanish republic. All fired straight at the barracks. I had only 138 rounds, and I couldn't afford to waste any . . .

The first round hit the main gate. The barrack walls were so thick that unless a round went through a window or door it made no impact. ORAD DE LA TORRE ordered rapid fire to make it seem there were double the number of field pieces. Volunteers from the auxiliary technicians' corps and ex-artillerymen in the crowd served the guns. When he wanted the guns moved, civilians manhandled them through the streets.

—The people were heroic. Not many had arms. The evening before when I brought the cannon out I ordered the lorry to pass through the Puerta del Sol, and there I addressed the crowds, urging them to accompany me to lay siege to the barracks. A mass of people ran behind the lorry, shouting '*¡Viva la República!*' and 'Long live honest army officers!' . . .

From first light the defenders inside the barracks were aware that they were besieged. Eugenio LORTAN could see assault guards in the houses along the

Calle Ferraz preparing positions on the rooftops, placing mattresses on the balconies. He thought they ought to fire on them. But no orders came. Not that he had ever fired a rifle in his life. His ignorance of military matters was so great that when he put on his battledress top he tucked it into his trousers like a shirt instead of letting it hang. 'There was a lot of enthusiasm, a lot of determination, but little experience.'

Amongst the besiegers, he could see civil guards. 'With them and the assault guards and the civilian militias there's not much hope of being able to win,' he thought. But why didn't they attempt a sortie?

Barely 200 metres from the barracks, Lt Vidal set up a 155mm field piece.

—A pair of balls he had! He could nearly have been shot with a pistol at that range, thought Capt. ORAD DE LA TORRE. It caused them real panic in the barracks . . .

A shell passed through an opening and wounded General Fanjul and the infantry colonel inside the barracks. Still having received no orders, the republican sapper, Francisco SANPEDRO, found himself by the main gate of the engineers' barracks when, to his surprise, it suddenly opened. Without hesitation, he ran.

—My only thought was to escape. I jumped down the four-metre-high retaining wall into the street. As I did, they opened fire on me from inside the barracks. But even so I glimpsed a white sheet that had been hung out . . .

The cry went up amongst the attackers. 'The white flag! They're surrendering!' Capt. ORAD DE LA TORRE heard Lt Moreno of the assault guards shouting at the people not to move; heedless, they began running forward.

—There was a sudden lull in the firing from the barracks – a coincidence, no doubt, but one that was to become tragic for the defenders . . .

Running like a hare towards the barracks went fifteen-year-old libertarian youth member, Manuel CARABAÑO; he was unarmed. Bullets began to whistle past him. He got to the retaining wall before a machine-gun opened up from inside the barracks. The people running forward from the Plaza de España stopped, then retreated. He could see dead and wounded lying on the ground. An assault guard pushed him back, asked what he was doing there. Another told him to leave the lad alone, he'd risked his life getting that far. Manuel stuck to them, they were in the front line of attack, they were the ones who had arms. Pedro SUAREZ, of the workers' and peasants' anti-fascist militia, also ran forward.

—Everyone had seen the white flag. Then I saw Manías lying on the ground. He was dead. A communist youth member, he got his nickname because of his mania for crying out: 'Down with the *carcas* and the clergy!' when he sold left-wing newspapers. And now they'd killed him. I threw myself on the ground and got behind a soft drinks kiosk and there I stayed until the final assault half an hour or so later . . .

At noon, officers ordered the falangists to withdraw to the interior of the barracks. Eugenio LORTAN had seen or heard nothing of the white sheet.

—It had to be an attempt by those opposed to the rising to stage a counter-coup, he reflected later. As we withdrew to the interior, some military cadets were ordered to dismount a machine-gun they had been firing. Then we were ordered to abandon our arms; it seemed absurd . . .

—'The barracks are lost, you'd better make off,' Mario REY heard someone shout. In the distance he could hear a hullabaloo. I took my battledress top off and walked out through the crowd. People had poured into the barracks after the assault and civil guards had taken it. Men were putting on soldiers' helmets and grabbing rifles and shouting childishly. No one noticed me . . .

Manuel CARABAÑO had followed the assault guards in. The first thing he saw was a rifle and he grabbed it. He was armed at last! He went outside and saw a group of men in shirt-sleeves who were trying to hide the fact that they were officers by crying '*¡Viva la República!*' A group of militiamen surrounded them shouting 'Fascists!'

—Then I saw an unpleasant looking woman, who was with a wounded boy, point a pistol at the officers and fire. Shots rang out on all sides and that group of men was mown down like a field of wheat. It was the first time I'd seen people die – it remains the worst experience of the whole war for me . . .

'By divine providence' Eugenio LORTAN had managed to get out of the barracks unnoticed. The radio had announced that all soldiers were demobilized, so it surprised no one to see youths without uniform coming out of the Montaña. He made for home. Twice militia patrols stopped him, the second one of women with pistols. Where had he been?

—'In the Montaña.' 'What happened?' 'We killed all the fascists.' I was still wearing army trousers. But happily they didn't notice the moccasins I was wearing; they were hardly an ordinary soldier's footwear . . .

Capt. ORAD DE LA TORRE walked into the barracks. The courtyard was strewn with corpses. Defenders had been slaughtered. They had deserved their fate, he thought, because of what had happened with the white sheet. He walked on, passing an NCOs' room where he saw a number of officers around the table.

—I went in. At the head was a major with a bullet-hole through his heart; all the others were slumped with similar bullet-holes. They had sat down there, I supposed, when they knew all was lost, and the major had taken his revolver and committed suicide; his junior officers had followed his example. Among them were some I knew, brother-officers of mine . . .

In all, of the 145 officers in the Montaña, ninety-eight died in action, before firing squads, massacred, or at their own hands.

After the barracks's fall, neither Campamento in Carabanchel, where a regiment of horse artillery and a battalion of sappers was stationed, nor the No. 1 infantry regiment in a barracks on the south side of the Retiro park, put up much resistance. Among the fatal casualties in the attack on Campamento were Capt. Orad de la Torre's brother and fifteen-year-old nephew, both – like him – members of the socialist party.

*

The sound of cannon and machine-gun fire had been heard all over the city. Fernando TAFALLA, an architectural student, got up hurriedly, dressed in his normal clothes and went out to watch. The people's enthusiasm, spontaneity and bravery were incredible; so, too, was their lack of expertise. He pointed out to a worker that he was mishandling his rifle, and the man looked him up and down, in his *señorito*'s clothes, as though to say – what's this sort of person doing here?

A communist party sympathizer, he understood the man's attitude. The bourgeoisie had been doing everything possible to force the army to rise. They had been boycotting the republic. They would tell workers who had to go out to defend their legitimate interests to 'Let the republic find you work.' Faced with a boycott or lock-out, workers sometimes had to take over their work places. But that was a long way from pressing for revolution.

Across the city, Marquess PUEBLA DE PARGA, a young monarchist, was also awoken by the sound of gunfire. He was not surprised. The day before, after going to mass, he had been sitting with friends at the café Roma when a car packed with militiamen armed with sub-machine-guns roared past. '*¡UHP!*'[1] they shouted at the young bloods sitting there. 'It's started,' he said to the others.

Ever since the elections there had been a feeling of doom, a sensation that a catastrophe was about to occur. In the business and financial circles he frequented, dismay had turned to despair, not simply at the economic situation but because of the increasing social unrest. '*Une certaine idée de la patrie*', as the French say, was threatened: religion had been under attack since the republic was proclaimed; patriotism, the unity of Spain, endangered by Catalan and Basque nationalism. To all intents and purposes, he thought, the war had begun as long ago as 1932. Constitutional legality had not been respected, law and order had become a problem almost immediately, convents had been fired and religious education suppressed. Both sides had soon become convinced that the situation could only end in war. Recently, the British attaché, with whom he shared a flat, had told him, in the strictest confidence, that the embassy had information that a left-wing revolution was about to break out. The UGT and CNT were gathering arms. His friend urged him to go with him to Pamplona but, occupied with his father's inheritance, he had been unable to leave Madrid.

With the gunfire still in his ears, he set off for the British embassy to secure authorization to put out the Union Jack and a notice on the door proclaiming that the flat belonged to a British diplomat.

*

In the Puerta del Sol, the military buses were having difficulty getting through the crowds. Andrés MARQUEZ, a civil servant and leading member of the left republican youth, had just left party headquarters in the Calle Mayor for the first time in two days. He saw the pale-faced rebel army officers being brought prisoner in the buses, heard the crowd shouting, 'Traitors! Traitors!' The scene was tumultuous. He feared the crowd would take the law into its own hands. Five years before he had stood on this very spot and watched the people

1. The initials of 'Unite, Brother Proletarians!' – a slogan made famous during the October 1934 rising in Asturias.

display their joy at the proclamation of the republic. Now this! But, once again, the crowd showed its civic spirit; the buses were allowed to pass.

—What would have happened if at that moment the crowd had known that republicans, whose only crime was to have wanted to be free, were being hunted down like wild animals in towns where the military had triumphed? In the name of fatherland and religion, the Spanish right was prepared to commit any crime to save its privileges. Its false sense of religion imbued it with a heartless indifference. More than a military, financial or political oligarchy, the Spanish right was rooted in clericalism. A religion that had nothing to do with Christianity . . .

The republic's attempt to introduce a new, modern political mentality to the country was what the right feared most, he thought; if the evolutionary process were allowed to continue another year it would be irreversible. Unfortunately, the socialist left had tried to turn the workers away from this process; the best-organized, numerically largest party in the country, which had been the republic's firmest support at the beginning, had made a grievous error.

Was it not rather the petty bourgeois liberal republicans, by their failure to satisfy the most elementary needs of the people, who had made the most serious errors, reflected Antonio PEREZ, a left socialist youth student. 'A regime which, in its constitution, had declared itself a "republic of all the workers", had left the Andalusian day-labourer to live without work six months of the year on bread and vinegar.' The Spanish people were going hungry. This was the situation that had to be remedied. Constant pressure had to be kept on the republicans to ensure that they took action. It wasn't a question of revolution: the socialist youth had no clearly thought out revolutionary programme; it was a matter of meeting elemental needs, of combating the violence which was on the increase. There was permanent fighting between members of the FUE, the university students' federation, and the Falange at the commercial school where he was studying. What started as fist fights turned into stone-throwing, the use of clubs and finally of pistols. Two falangist students at the school were killed in a shoot-out while trying, it seemed, to attack the communist party newspaper building. 'Ever since the elections the coming struggle was plainly visible; there was no going back.'

Violence had been in the air even longer, since the October 1934 insurrection; it had begun at the verbal level and had taken over Spanish politics, official and personal, thought Paulino AGUIRRE. A liberal arts student at Madrid university, son of a politician under the monarchy, he had not been involved in the frequent clashes at the university; but he had no illusions about the depths of the violence.

—The idea that it was necessary to kill, to destroy in order to defend oneself was constantly expressed by ordinary people on both sides. It stemmed from the type of mentality that refuses dialogue and compromise. Verbal violence was a social fact. However, to the majority, it seemed inconceivable that the barrier between words and acts should be crossed. When a small minority did so – when things that had been said were actually done – a new situation arose. Verbal violence prefigured a war which was not generally expected, conditioned its outbreak, even hastened it . . .

SPANIARDS

100,000 MILLION PESETAS WORTH OF AGRICULTURAL PROPERTY AND LIVESTOCK

50,000 MILLIONS OF URBAN PROPERTY

25,000 MILLIONS OF PRIVATE INVESTMENTS

20,000 MILLIONS OF STATE INVESTMENTS

50,000 MILLIONS IN INDUSTRIAL AND COMMERCIAL FIXED INVESTMENTS

15,000 MILLIONS OF BANKING CAPITAL, DEPOSITS AND CURRENT ACCOUNTS

5,000 MILLIONS OF RAILWAY INVESTMENT

3,500 MILLIONS IN SAVINGS BANKS, ETC.

The fortune of Spain, 300,000 million pesetas, will be nationalized and taken over or destroyed by soviet communism. Those who haven't lost their lives, will be out of work – in the street with only the clothes on their backs.

Workers, employees, civil servants: if you vote for the communist-socialist-leftist revolutionary bloc, you will be slaves, working only for bad food and poor clothing!

Spaniards: if you have an ounce of sense, an atom of self-preservation, vote with iron discipline for the candidates of the anti-revolutionary front!

For the Salvation of Spain

La Nación, right-wing monarchist (Madrid, 15 February 1936)

WORKERS, DEMOCRATIC CITIZENS

The CEDA and its accomplices are asking you for your votes in order to continue their work of terror, injustice and theft of the past two years.

The Popular Front asks for your help and your votes to free 30,000 men from gaol, to make sure 70,000 return to their work places, and to demand retribution of the torturers and thieves.

VOTE FOR THE POPULAR FRONT

The Problem of Spain is not one of Political Change but of Transforming the Economy.

In the elections, the proletariat is aligning with the bourgeois parties, forgetting its essential mission of preparing and organizing itself to transform society.

Solidaridad Obrera, CNT (Barcelona, 14 February 1936)

February to July 1936

In February the Popular Front had won a narrow victory in the general elections in terms of the popular vote.[1] Immediately afterwards the uneven development of Spain began to show in the uneven spread of agitation and violence. In the advanced seaboard peripheries of Catalonia and the Basque country – engaged respectively in the primary (textiles) and secondary (metalworking) phases of industrialization – there was relative calm. In Catalonia, the Left Front had won 59 per cent of the popular vote. The Lliga Catalana, representing the bourgeoisie, had accepted its defeat and the role of loyal opposition. The Esquerra, the left republican petty bourgeois party, and principal victor, had become more moderate. Tomás ROIG LLOP, a Catalan nationalist lawyer and a prominent member of the Lliga, believed there was no reason for anyone in Catalonia to favour a military uprising, least of all fear of a proletarian revolution. 'A military coup could only threaten us with the loss of what it had cost us so much effort to win – our autonomy statute.'

Catalonia's relative calm – 'oasis of peace' – did not mean that the working class was necessarily satisfied with the state of affairs. CNT militants, in particular, railed at the republic for its failure to satisfy working-class needs. None the less, the CNT had refrained from calling on its members to abstain in the recent elections as it had done in 1933. Their votes, to free the thousands of political prisoners being held since October 1934, had contributed to the Popular Front victory. In the opinion of Andreu CAPDEVILA, CNT textile worker, the people voted to give the republican government *carte blanche* to put down the threat of fascism.

—Everyone knew the officer corps was conspiring. Why didn't the government take action, create a new army loyal to the republic? Failing that, call on the working class to throw up barricades around all the barracks in Spain under the leadership of trusted officers. Encountering the working class face to face, there was an 80 per cent chance that the troops would not have risen. But the republicans were more frightened of the working class than of the military . . .

*

In the regions of the predominantly medium and small landholding peasantry, stretching in a wide arc east and west above Madrid, there was no particular violence, but a generalized feeling of hostility. The republic had done nothing to ease the difficulties of these people: indeed, the right could argue that the republic had worsened their plight. Wheat producers, their production permitted only a slender and fluctuating surplus at the best of times. Two excellent wheat harvests, foreign imports and the depression had pushed down prices. Amongst this largely Catholic peasantry, the view that the 'republic represented disorder' was widespread. 'What we needed was law and order, peace and well-being. Those who supported the republican regime were constantly declaring

1. For the figures, see Prologue, p. 44, n. 2.

strikes and stopping people from working,' recalled the son of a largeholding peasant in the Castilian village of Castrogeriz.

Antonio GINER belonged to no political party. An employer of labour, he supported the workers' right to a union to defend their interests, but not when its leaders demanded that members abjure their Catholicism, 'a faith dear and traditional to us', which denigrated the very concept of union. He wanted a fair price for wheat: on the farm they had two years' crops stored in the hope that they could be sold at a reasonable price. 'We were lucky to have the space and the money. Most of the smaller farmers had to sell at the ridiculous prices being offered.' But his real needs, he felt, could be summed up succinctly. 'I was a farmer and wanted only three things: family, religion and work. Nothing else.' Supporting this view, a local ploughman, Fernando SANCHEZ, put his reasons for being on the right.

—I liked order. I liked to work honourably. We received little in wages, we ate garlic and a small piece of bread, and on that we worked all day – and we lived on what we earned. I belonged to no political party, I belonged to the land . . .

Castrogeriz[1] had voted for the right by a 570 to 270 majority, a proportion even higher than in Burgos province as a whole. The left's failure to organize the Castilian peasantry was not only self-evident but would have dramatic consequences in the future, thought a mechanic and CNT sympathizer in the provincial capital. The working class, José BESAIBAR could see, needed the peasantry on its side to prevent a successful capitalist counter-revolution. If the peasantry went over to the capitalists – as it was almost certain to do if left unorganized – it would provide the bulk of the capitalists' cannon fodder. The left's failure was due above all, in his view, to one reason.

—The working-class organizations refused to leave the religious question alone. Instead of uniting around their real interests – to make the revolution – they concerned themselves with whether people went to church. It was a fatal mistake as far as the peasantry was concerned . . .

The electoral defeat of the right, particularly of the CEDA, the mass Catholic party, left many of the latter's supporters disillusioned: the parliamentary road to the corporative authoritarian state had been blocked. The disillusionment was particularly strong in the largest right-wing Catholic youth movement, the JAP, many of whose members deserted to the Falange. A Burgos working-class JAP member felt that Gil Robles, the CEDA leader, had made a fatal mistake in not seizing power when he was in the government a few months earlier. Ever since the convent burnings of May 1931,[2] it had been evident to Maximiano PRADA, printworker and member of the Burgos Catholic Workers' Circle, that things were going badly. The Popular Front victory only confirmed it. He had believed, even hoped, that the beating the Asturian miners had taken after their insurrection in October 1934 would quieten things; instead, they appeared to have worsened. 'We wanted a strong republic, one that would bring law and order to the country, one that allowed political

1. In one respect Castrogeriz was an a-typical Castilian village in having a large proportion of landless labourers which tended, as everywhere, to increase social conflicts (see pp. 281–3).

2. See Points of Rupture, B.

parties but that forbade religious persecution. Gil Robles was too soft.' PRADA's view of the situation was sharpened by the increased unemployment after the elections which resulted from capital's investment boycott.

—The capitalists boycotted labour, refusing to give workers jobs, and the left-wing unions boycotted us Catholic workers. Things got so bad we had to be paid at midday on Saturday; if we got our wages in the evening, they might be stolen by out-of-work left-wingers . . .

The radicalization of the country's youth, right and left, was a distinctive phenomenon of the political crisis, the flight of JAP members into the Falange foreshadowing the parent party's future during the war. In Valladolid, Old Castile's major city, Mariano ESCUDERO, a leading CEDA member, tried unsuccessfully to staunch the flow to the Falange. A lawyer and local secretary of the Valladolid branch of the National Catholic Association of Propagandists, as well as former deputy mayor, he understood the reasons for his failure: 'Everyone was convinced there was going to be a communist revolution; the JAP militants believed we were all acting like cowards in the face of the threat.' The Falange, with its local strength, was the only organization prepared to confront it. Even he, to his regret, had come to believe that republican legality, shattered first by the socialists in the October insurrection, could no longer be restored by parliamentary means. The real cause of the regime's breakdown lay in the failure to develop a dialogue between the CEDA and the socialist party. The CEDA must take its share of the blame. It had attracted people who had joined simply out of fear, who had become sufficiently strong within the party to block reforms such as those proposed by their own agricultural minister.[1] Catholics, he believed, had an obligation to practise a social justice which would keep people 'from thinking of extreme left-wing solutions'. Dollfuss in Austria came the closest to the ideal. But the CEDA had often been retrograde. The socialists had turned to violence. No dialogue had been possible. And now he saw violence coming.

—I laughed, but I didn't feel any laughter within me. Whatever was going to happen, the outcome was certain to be very cruel . . .

His colleague, Ernesto CASTAÑO, had come to Valladolid to talk to members of the garrison about rising. One of the chief organizers of the Salamanca Agrarian Bloc,[2] he had been re-elected as a CEDA deputy to parliament in the elections and, with two others from his home province, unseated on dubious grounds of electoral malpractice. CASTAÑO believed that the republic had irremediably failed, and for much the same reasons as the monarchy before it: the refusal to permit the political spectrum to be expanded to its limits, right and left. The left republicans would tolerate no competing influence and maintained that Gil Robles was dominated by the church, and wanted to 'join the republic only to sink it'. Nothing was farther from the truth. 'If the CEDA had won the 1936 elections we would not have changed an iota of the republic. Gil Robles never dreamt of doing what his enemies accused him of: seeking to

1. See Points of Rupture, A.
2. See Points of Rupture, A.

gain power to install a fascist regime. No one was a greater enemy of fascism'...[1]

CASTAÑO found the Valladolid garrison indifferent to the idea of rising – something that would not change until May. As to the local falangist leadership, they were maintaining the 'absurd position' that a rising should take place without military participation. Acting without the knowledge of Gil Robles or any of the CEDA leadership, CASTAÑO continued to make soundings in different parts of the country for the rising which he considered the only solution.

Valladolid was the birthplace of the JONS, the national syndicalist movement which, in 1934, had merged with the recently created Falange in the same city. It recruited mainly among university students, service employees (waiters, taxi-drivers), artisans and small farmers. Onésimo Redondo, co-founder of the JONS, ran a sugar-beet growers' union, which had been able to improve the lot of the small peasantry in this sector. His close collaborator, Tomás BULNES, believed that the peasantry was anti-republican, not *a priori* 'but because of what the republic had turned out to be: anti-religious, tolerating if not fostering a nation-wide anarchy, ruinous for the farmer. Castile, above all, was religious, patriarchal. It was not for nothing that the Castilian peasantry provided the bulk of Spain's priests, friars and nuns.'

Militancies 2

ALBERTO PASTOR

Falangist farmer

In the small village of Tamariz de Campos, north-west of Valladolid, Alberto PASTOR, a member of the JONS since 1932, helped his uncle work the family 400-*obrada* (just over 200 hectare) farm. Tamariz – 'a village of a few who owned a lot' – boasted 100 pairs of mules (and, in consequence, the same number of day-labourers to work them), but its population of between 800 and 900 did not enjoy paved streets or running water in their houses, many of which were built of adobe. None the less, it was a place of prosperous wheat-growing farmers, two or three of whom owned twice as much land as PASTOR. The Tierra de Campos was good cereal-growing land.

For the past couple of months PASTOR had been languishing in Valladolid gaol. Ever since the republic came in, things had changed. Before, there had been, he remembered, a sense of camaraderie between the labourers and the farmers. Although he was the owner's son, he worked alongside the labourers

1. After its initial refusal to declare itself unambiguously republican, the CEDA leadership had, for the past two years, agreed 'to serve and defend the republic in order to serve and defend Spain'. The 1936 election campaign sharpened its enemies' fears that, if victorious, it would at worst impose a totalitarian fascist regime, at best drastically reform the constitution. Gil Robles publicly advocated the latter. At the same time, its electioneering slogans of 'All Power to the Chief', the semi-fascist salute, its brown-shirted youth movement mouthing anti-semitic slogans led its opponents to believe that its real aims went even further. It was not forgotten that Hitler had come to power through elections. (See also Points of Rupture, E.)

in the fields, ate the same food, sat and smoked and talked about anything during the rest breaks. 'There really had been no difference between us.' But the republic had spoilt all that. The labourers had changed, agitators came to stir them up, it became dangerous to go out to the fields. He carried a pistol in his pocket when he went to work; men who had been like brothers to him before the republic would now barely talk to him. But they knew him, knew he went armed.

He had always preferred being with workers to being with people of his own class. His father (a doctor) and mother had brought him up like that; his best friends as a child had been the poorest kids. One of his brothers was among the first to join the JONS. Less than a year after its creation, he, too, had joined. He was attracted to it by the social injustice he saw around him and the battle against terrorism and subversion it waged. Other nations might be ready for democracy but, he was firmly convinced, 'the latin race could live only under dictatorship'. Democracy was an ideal, but in Spain liberty immediately became libertinism. The national-syndicalist revolution the JONS proposed would be different.

—It meant redistributing part of the wealth of the country in a new, more just manner; it meant that everyone would have to work – but work in harmony together; it was pure evangelism, the doctrine of Jesus Christ that everyone should live better, not that some should be well-off and others poor . . .

This did not mean that everyone who owned wealth was to be expropriated. It meant that the rich must sacrifice a part of their wealth in order that the poor should live better. A landowner with 2,000 hectares who refused to farm the land properly had no right to so much while there were 2 million Spaniards crying out for land; the latifundist would be taken over and compensated – though at not very high prices. But a landowner who paid decent wages would not be expropriated, even though it might be necessary to ask him to make a profit of 7 per cent instead of 10 per cent so that others could live better.

—Our ideas were revolutionary – not evolutionary. But we offered not a bloody, destructive revolution but a constructive one. We were neither of the left nor right nor centre. We were a movement with our own spirit, out not to defend the rich but also not to put the poor above the rich. In many points we agreed with the socialists. But they were materialist revolutionaries, and we were spiritual ones. What differentiated us most was that we lacked the hatred of capitalism which they exhibited. The marxists declared war on anyone with wealth; our idea was that the right must give up a part in order to allow others to live better . . .

In March 1934, he attended the meeting in Valladolid at which José Antonio Primo de Rivera's Falange Española and the JONS were unified. The latter, he believed, was more revolutionary, the Falange 'less dictatorial, more philosophical'.[1] Not for nothing did the JONS call itself syndicalist; 'on occasions

1. The fundamental similarities were greater than the differences: both were fascist movements overlaid with Catholicism. 'Authority, discipline, the subjection of the masses, control but not liquidation of capitalism, a corporative state, were common elements,' in the words of Tomás BULNES, associate of the JONS co-founder, O. Redondo. The attempt to differentiate

we were capable of using the same tactics as the anarcho-syndicalists'. The meeting ended with shooting in the streets of Valladolid.

Back in his own village, where he was the only falangist, and virtually unable to leave his house at night, he attempted to blow up the local socialist *casa del pueblo* with a stick of dynamite; the labourers' threats were becoming intolerable to him.[1] If anything, the women were the worst. On one occasion, they broke up a religious procession by dancing and shouting around it in the streets. One man publicly urinated against the church door. Justice saw to it that he died a year later of cancer of the anus. The stick of dynamite exploded; but lacking experience in these matters, he failed to place it correctly to cause serious damage.

His *novia* sometimes had to carry his pistol in her bosom when they went out into the village because the *guardia civil* were always searching for arms. Not that he had much free time for going out; with the eight-hour day that the republic had introduced for agricultural labourers, farming was becoming impossible. He had to sleep in the stables to get the five pairs of mules fed and ready to be out in the fields by 8 a.m., and bring them back in the evening, to make the most of the labourers' work day, which had been previously from sunrise to sunset.

If things had been bad before, after the Popular Front victory at the polls they got even worse. One of the labourers pulled a pistol on his uncle in the fields. '*¡Me cago en la leche!* We're going to finish off all these *carcas*,' the man cried. His fat and cowardly uncle, who hadn't dared get off his horse in the fields since the republic was proclaimed, rode home in a sorry state.

—My blood boiled. I remember I was sewing headgear for the mules. When the workers came in from the fields, I disarmed the man and handed his pistol over to the justice of the peace. The next morning, when my uncle opened the door to let the labourers in, one of them again threatened to kill him . . .

Pistol in pocket, he set out to accompany his uncle to the townhall. The village square was packed – the labourers had gone on strike. 'Don't run,' he warned his uncle. He took cover behind a pillar; at that moment the people started to surge towards them. Frightened, his uncle ran, pursued by a labourer in whose hand PASTOR saw a gleaming knife. His uncle tripped and fell.

—I pulled out my pistol. 'Let's see if they can kill me,' I thought. I started to fire. The people fled. My uncle was scared out of his wits but unhurt. I walked into the townhall where the socialist council was meeting. 'Hands up!' At gun point I made them get out. 'Give me that pistol,' the justice of the peace said.

---

themselves from fascism stemmed from the fact that 'as a very national movement, we did not want people to think we were imitating any foreign model. We had to look back to our own Golden Age, follow the example set by the Catholic Kings of the fifteenth century.' (For further discussion of the Falange, see Militancies 10, p. 313.)

1. Socialist influence spread from the nearest town, Medina de Rioseco, which had a nucleus of socialist railway workers and was one of the few Old Castilian centres where the October 1934 insurrection had repercussions (see D. Ruiz, 'Aproximación a octubre de 1934', *Sociedad, política y cultura en la España de los siglos XIX–XX*, Madrid, 1973). In Tamariz, twenty-two people were arrested during the October events, charged with being in possession of illegal arms and petrol bombs, according to PASTOR.

'Grab hold of it by the barrel, then,' I replied. I wasn't handing it over with a hundred men outside in the square waiting to kill me . . .

Looking round the council room, he discovered the labourer's pistol he had handed in the evening before. He was going to need two to get out of there alive. In the square he could see men armed with wooden pitchforks and shotguns ready to come for him. Meanwhile, searching through some papers, he found 'the black lists of all of us who were to be assassinated'. It wasn't just his uncle they were out to kill. He looked out of the window again and saw that the *guardia civil* had arrived from Medina de Rioseco. There would be no more shooting. Before leaving the townhall, he sent out for the best cigar to be found in the village tobacconist shop.

—I came out and raised the cigar in my manacled hands above my head and shouted '*¡Arriba España!*' There was a tremendous uproar. They'd have lynched me if I hadn't been protected by the *guardia*. There wasn't a single landowning farmer to be seen; all of them, though they thought like us, had shut themselves up in their homes . . .

His counsel wanted to turn the trial into a non-political case. Opposed to this defence, PASTOR arrived in court wearing his blue falangist shirt and red and black tie, and gave the fascist salute. '*¡Arriba España!*' he cried. Sentenced to several months' imprisonment, he soon found himself in gaol with the bulk of the local falangist leadership who were under preventive detention.

After an assassination attempt on a leading socialist professor and deputy in Madrid, the Falange leadership in the capital had been arrested and its headquarters closed. José Antonio Primo de Rivera continued to direct the movement from prison. In Segovia, the local Falange chief, Dionisio RIDRUEJO, a student, remained at liberty. Convinced that the February general elections had been the last, he was equally sure that if the Popular Front established itself in power, there was going to be revolution: the socialists would take power.

—That was certainly what the bourgeoisie felt, rightly, I thought. The socialists kept continuous pressure on the government from the streets. The masses were taking the initiative, even if they weren't intentionally heading for revolution. The bourgeoisie was frightened. Never having made its own revolution, it was much more frightened of revolution than its French counterpart. A revolution was the end of the world as far as it was concerned. The Spanish bourgeoisie never had any confidence in itself, and throughout its history relied on armed force to sustain it . . .

After the elections, street fights, assassination attempts, funerals which turned into riots and generated new clashes, new funerals, were frequent. Whereas before the elections, he observed, the left had usually provoked such fights, falangists now instinctively understood that they needed to draw out the struggle to achieve their aims. If the military suddenly rose they were unlikely to hand power over to the Falange.

—But, by and large, the bourgeoisie didn't show much enthusiasm for the falangist riposte. They were waiting for the military to rise; they didn't want the struggle, the disorder, to continue: they wanted it ended. 'Things can't be allowed to continue like this,' was a phrase interminably repeated. Officers were publicly insulted, called cowards for not rising. The mounting lack of law and order was the apparent cause. (In truth, the disorder was about what one might expect in a democratic country during a critical moment of strikes and student agitation.) The real cause was the fear that the working-class organizations were going to make their revolution. The proof is that the military plot did not really begin to take firm shape until after the elections. They had tried before – ever since the republic was proclaimed – but without success. Now it became a bet to see who would rise first . . .

Various generals planned risings in April and again in May; the Falange was to take part in one of the latter. Carlists, who had uprisings 'in their guts' and had been training their *requetés* for the past two years, also planned to rise on their own – in Andalusia. Unluckily for the republic, all these attempts were called off at the last moment, their success being dubious.

Let us not deceive ourselves! A country can live under a monarchy or a republic, with a parliamentary or a presidential system, under communism or fascism. But it cannot live in anarchy. Now, alas, Spain is in anarchy. And we are today present at the funeral service of democracy.

Gil Robles, CEDA leader (Parliamentary speech, 16 June 1936)

There are strikes in Spain. That is natural, logical . . . We know that the proletariat's spirit of innovation cannot be reconciled with the interests of a republic which aims to preserve itself and the institutions which shape it.

***Solidaridad Obrera*, CNT (Barcelona, 2 June 1936)**

What no country can endure is constant bloodletting and public disorder without an immediate revolutionary end . . . I tell you, this is not revolution . . . it is the climate which fascism requires . . .

Indalecio Prieto, socialist leader (May Day speech, Cuenca, 1936)

No more strikes, no more lock-outs, no more usurious interest, no more of capitalism's abusive financial formulae, no more starvation wages, no more political salaries gained by happy accident, no more anarchic liberty, no more criminal loss of production, for national production is above all classes, all parties, and all interests.

Many call that the fascist state. If it is, then I who share that idea of the (integrative) state and believe in it, declare myself fascist.

Calvo Sotelo, monarchist leader (Parliamentary speech, 16 June 1936)

The proletariat must not limit itself to defending bourgeois democracy, but must ensure by every means the conquest of political power in order to make the social revolution. The form of government in the period of transition between capitalist and socialist society will be the dictatorship of the proletariat.

Resolution of the Madrid socialist party group,
Caballero-wing (21 May 1936)

In the barely industrialized capital of Madrid and southwards into the latifundist region of New Castile, Estremadura and Andalusia, with its high concentration of landless labourers, the level of agitation and violence began to rise. To the urban street violence between the Falange, reinforced by the influx of JAP members, and the socialist youth, now fused with the young communists in the unified socialist youth (JSU), was added renewed rural agitation. The left republicans in power were (as they had been throughout the republic) dependent on working-class support and this was being largely denied them; the revolutionary proletariat was not to be contained within the moderate Popular Front programme. From right to left, the bourgeois republican parties saw the danger and momentarily attempted to overcome their previous antagonism and close ranks;[1] it was too late.

Though scores of small towns and villages were trouble-free, in others the accumulated hostility of years erupted as soon as the election results were known. Such was the case in Fuensalida, a small village not far from Toledo. Looking out of the window of his house, the local vet's son, Pedro GARCIA, saw a man, shotgun in hand, holding off a crowd surging towards him in the little square, hurling stones. The man was a rich, right-wing landlord, the only one who had dared show his face. It was like something out of the wild west, he thought. Tension in the village had been rising for years. The labourers, who formed the bulk of the village, had become more and more violent, and the landlords responded in kind. In 1932, the *guardia civil* fired into a peasant demonstration, killing a father and his infant, and wounding several others.[2] He could remember how the labourers had traced a large cross in the earth of the main square.

—The tension affected even us children. The Pioneers, the socialist youth organization, terrorized us at school. They called us the sons of parasites – the word fascist wasn't yet fashionable – the *señoritos* who ate chops. There was an unbridgeable gulf between 'them' and 'us', between those who ate, and those who couldn't afford to eat, chops . . .

The Popular Front victory galvanized the peasantry in the latifundist regions. Barely a month after the election, 60,000 peasants in Badajoz, organized by the socialist-led Landworkers' Federation, took over 3,000 previously selected farms and began to plough them. In a single stroke, the peasantry occupied more land than the agrarian reform of the previous three and a half years had granted them.

1. Gil Robles, CEDA leader, wanted to reinforce Azaña's authority, hoping that the latter would turn the government towards the centre. The CEDA leader wanted a 'government of material understanding, strong and authoritarian', which could have been led by Prieto. The manoeuvre failed when the socialist party prevented Prieto from becoming prime minister in May (see R. Robinson, 'The Parties of the Right and the Republic', in *The Republic and the Civil War in Spain* (ed. R. Carr), London, 1971). The electoral failure had, moreover, weakened Gil Robles's position; Calvo Sotelo, monarchist finance minister under the Primo de Rivera dictatorship which preceded the republic, now took over the leadership of the right.

2. This was not a year after the massacres of Castilblanco, in which peasants slaughtered four civil guards, and Arnedo, where the *guardia* shot down seven peaceful demonstrators, including four women and a child, and wounded thirty more. Only a few months after the Fuensalida shootings, in what became an immediate *cause célèbre*, some twenty peasants were massacred by assault guards in Casas Viejas.

José VERGARA, a liberal republican agronomist, who had served as the Agrarian Reform Institute's delegate in Toledo province, believed that the situation had dramatically changed in the two years since he had left there.

—A revolution was brewing in the countryside, the bourgeoisie was frightened. There was no way the republic could solve the problem. The agrarian reform law as such was unworkable.[1] In its absence, the peasants were taking over the land themselves . . .

The communist party, the most determined of the working-class parties in its support of the Popular Front, participated actively in the land take-overs. According to the party, it was the Popular Front's task to carry the bourgeois-democratic revolution – 'which had never been made in Spain' – to its conclusion.[2] The expropriation of large estates fell within the confines of this revolution, whose historic task was to abolish 'semi-feudal' vestiges in the countryside.

Trinidad GARCIA, a day-labourer's son and member of the communist party's Toledo provincial committee, had been telling the peasantry during the election campaign that if 'those in charge' didn't make the agrarian reform, 'we'll make it ourselves'. The land was the key problem. In some villages, the peasants went out even before the elections and took over big landowners' farms and formed cooperatives or collectives on their own account. In others, like La Villa de don Fadrique, a communist stronghold, it took the elections to set the take-over process in motion. The communist mayor called an assembly of the township's 10,000 inhabitants and explained party policy: wherever possible, the poor peasantry and landless labourers should carry out the agrarian reform without waiting for the Agrarian Reform Institute.

—Then he went on to propose that all the local large estates should be taken over and worked collectively by the labourers; smallholders should get extra land from the estates, so that their holdings became viable family-operated units. But he urged the smallholders to work all their land collectively, stressing the social and economic advantages of this, recalled Julián VAZQUEZ, a communist garment worker who had been sent by a party weekly from Madrid to cover the event. The proposal was overwhelmingly approved. The three largest owners were brothers, each of whom, I remember, belonged to a different republican party; the political cleverness of the rich! It did them no good, they were all expropriated, including the one who had joined the left republicans! . . .

'Semi-feudal' vestiges in the countryside were being liquidated not only at the aristocracy's but also at the bourgeoisie's expense. This was inevitable, for the nobility owned little more than 10 per cent of the arable land – a fact that was little remarked at the time, but which was to have its repercussions on the rural bourgeoisie.

Month after month agricultural strikes increased; in the two and a half months leading up to the war, there were almost as many as in the most con-

1. See Points of Rupture, A.

2. For discussion of the communist party's positions on the need to complete the bourgeois democratic revolution under the leadership of the working class and peasantry before moving on to the next historic stage – the socialist revolution – see Points of Rupture, E.

flictive year of 1933. Harvest wages doubled, real labour costs on the land probably tripled.[1]

Things had got bad enough for José AVILA, a *labrador* in Espejo, an agro-township in Córdoba province, not to know whether it was worth sowing the land because he couldn't be sure whether the harvest would be brought in. Most of the *labradores* were in his position. He had given up planting crops which could not be left standing in the fields when ripe. Wages were the apparent cause of the strife, but when it came to claims they had always reached agreement in the end. What was it these labourers really wanted? What was it that caused these frequent lightning strikes?

—Politics, that was where the trouble lay. Everyone read a lot, everyone had his own point of view, everyone went his own way. If there had been just two sorts of politics, left and right, things would have been better. But there were so many ideologies, especially on the left: republicans, socialists, communists, anarchists. I don't know what the labourers really wanted. I don't think they knew themselves. But whatever it was, it wasn't good for us farmers.

At work they began to make remarks to our faces. 'Not a single fascist must be allowed to live.' It became risky for us to live on the *cortijos*. The labourers talked of the *reparto* but was that what they really wanted? When the republic took over the duke of Medinaceli's three estates near here,[2] the people didn't seem satisfied with the land they got. They wanted something else.

If only there had been a strong political organization, left or right, republican or non-republican, things wouldn't have reached the stage they did. Guarantees, rights – fine! But law and order as well. That was what was missing . . .

Militancies 3

JUAN MORENO

CNT day-labourer

—What did we want? Not the sort of agrarian reform the republic was trying to make. The state and capitalism are the worker's two worst enemies. What we wanted was the land – for the workers to take it over and work it collectively without the state intervening . . .

1. E. Malefakis, op. cit., p. 373. Press censorship makes it impossible to judge the exact dimensions of rural agitation. Moreover, new mayors appear to have been reluctant to report land invasions. In April, the left republican civil governor of Córdoba issued an order to them to do so, given the 'repeated denunciations' by landlords of various abuses (*Defensor de Córdoba*, 7 April 1936). The situation in Andalusia and elsewhere was worsened by the heaviest rains for a century which prevented landwork. Meanwhile, the foreign communist press published glowing accounts of land take-overs. The peasantry's 'revolutionary action' was causing 'absolute panic in government circles' wrote the Comintern's delegate, Cesar Falcón, in May (cited by B. Bolloten, *The Grand Camouflage*, London, 1968, p. 22).

2. For a description of the take-over, see Points of Rupture, A.

Forty-three years old, MORENO had been a syndicalist militant in his native township of Castro del Río for the past twenty years or more, including the 'Three Bolshevik Years' of 1918–20 when, in the space of eighteen months, he and his companions had declared six general strikes. They had won some notable gains, even if they had overthrown neither the state nor capitalism. Castro, with a population of over 10,000, had become one of the leading anarcho-syndicalist centres of western Andalusia.

Unlike the neighbouring township of Espejo, where the workers participated in the Agrarian Reform Institute's take-over of the duke of Medinaceli's estates, the anarcho-syndicalists of Castro refused to have anything to do with agrarian reform. The attitude of the Castro militants had been determined many years before during the 'Bolshevik Years' when a syndicalist congress had decided 'not to beg land from the ruling classes, since we are irreconcilable enemies of authority and property; if we want land we should follow the Bolsheviks' example'.[1]

More recently, at its first National Congress under the republic, the anarcho-syndicalist CNT had declared its hostility to agrarian reform: the rural unions' task was not to obtain land by cooperating with the government's agrarian reform, but to work for the 'revolutionary preparation of the rural masses' and the day when, in collaboration with the proletariat, they would overthrow capitalism and take the land. The Congress had gone on to declare that the CNT remained in 'open war' with the state, and that the republican regime, then two months old, was to all intents and purposes as 'oppressive' a power as any other.

—The reformists, the state socialists, wanted agrarian reform, wanted everything controlled by the state. When the state said 'stop' – stop; when it said 'render accounts' – render accounts; when the harvest was in – it would be there demanding its share. We didn't want that. The land must be in the workers' hands, worked and managed collectively by them. That was the only way the workers could control their own affairs, ensure that the produce which resulted from their work remained theirs to deal with as they freely decided. Not that each collective could remain isolated, a unit on its own. No! Each would be responsible to the local CNT organization, the local to the regional, the regional to the national. But each would be managed by a committee elected by the collectivists themselves, each at the end of the year would divide up the surplus produced among the collectivists . . .

Fear that the distribution of land to individual workers, even if they decided to work their plots collectively, meant the continuation of 'private property' and the eventual recreation of inequalities of wealth, was another factor militating against the reform, in Moreno's view. 'We'd be back where we started from;

1. J. Díaz del Moral, *Historia de las agitaciones campesinas andaluzas – Córdoba* (Madrid, 1929, 1967), p. 329. A majority of the same congress also adopted a resolution stating that 'we must demand of the powers that be that they hand over the poorly cultivated lands to the unions at their present taxable rates'. The contradiction between the two resolutions was symptomatic of the anarchist and syndicalist tendencies within the movement. (For further examination of these two tendencies, and their importance to the anarcho-syndicalist concept of the revolution, see Points of Rupture, D.

tomorrow we'd have the bourgeoisie again. And if there was one thing we didn't need, it was the bourgeoisie.'[1]

The bourgeoisie formed the bulk of the 200 landowners and all the *labradores* – the latter outnumbering the former – in Castro. Absentee aristocrats owned a few estates, but leased these to large tenant farmers on easy terms, as tended to be the nobility's custom. The average size of the estates was some 300 hectares; few reached 550. (In the latifundist south, an estate of 100 hectares was considered large; 250 hectares was a *latifundium*, and over 500 hectares was a giant holding.) Below this bourgeoisie there was, in Castro, a fairly large 'middle class' of small market-gardeners on irrigated plots along the river, artisans, muleteers. The landless day-labourers made up the bulk of the township.

After the death from TB of his father, a labourer, Juan MORENO began work on an estate at the age of ten. His first memory was of losing one of the pigs he had been set to herd and of returning in tears. The foreman docked his 'ration' – the little piece of bacon fat which the labourers got in their stew and which was 'about the only nourishment in it'. He had begun his apprenticeship.

Soon he was working in the fields, ploughing, sowing, reaping with the sickle on the estates where the hired hands spent fixed periods of time, 'always hungry on the little food they gave us, thin as rakes', sleeping on straw in earth-floored sheds, 'all together as though in a barracks'. The straw was the rougher stuff the oxen and mules refused as fodder. The men took off their boots and waistcoats to sleep. 'In spring we went to the animal stalls, you couldn't sleep in the dormitory for the fleas.' In a good year, employment might last eight months, in a bad year perhaps not even six. There was no unemployment pay.

The problem, declared a Castro anarchist in 1919, was 'not only one of bread, but of hatred'.[2] The problem had not changed a decade and a half later.

—We hated the bourgeoisie, they treated us like animals. They were our worst enemies. When we looked at them we thought we were looking at the devil himself. And they thought the same of us. There was a hatred between us – a hatred so great it couldn't have been greater. They were bourgeois, they didn't have to work to earn a living, they had comfortable lives. We knew we were workers and that we had to work – but we wanted them to pay us a decent wage and to treat us like human beings, with respect. There was only one way to achieve that – by fighting them . . .

They fought to abolish piece-work which was 'amoral' because it obliged a man to work like a brute to earn another peseta; to end the practice of children having to get up in the middle of the night on the estates to feed the mules; to win better food. They fought for more money. But nothing would lessen their hatred of the bourgeoisie and capitalism until the exploitation of man by man was abolished. 'The bourgeoisie was not needed. Let the workers take over the estates and you'd soon see the truth of that.' When property was collectivized

1. In fact, the agrarian reform law gave not the property of the land but its use to the recipient, who could not sell, mortgage or lease it. The property was retained by the state. The militant anarcho-syndicalists were opposed to both.

2. Díaz del Moral, op. cit., p. 355.

and everything belonged to the workers, there'd be no capitalism, no need for the state, no necessity for money to exist.

—Everyone would do his usual job, everyone would work. If you needed something, a pair of trousers or a pair of shoes, the collective would procure it from another collective by exchanging its goods. Money wasn't necessary for anything. Money is the rope round our necks, the greatest danger a people can face. If they need money, there'll be nothing but slavery, misery on all sides. Look at the large landowner with his millions: he commands more than the state or the *guardia civil* or anyone. No, we didn't need money, all that we needed was the wherewithal to be able to live . . .

The hatred of the bourgeoisie had not abated by 1936. The republic had, if anything, sharpened it. 'More and more bourgeois were joining the Falange, becoming fascists.' Nor had the republic brought any benefits for the workers as some republicans believed.

—Those of us who didn't believe in politics simply laughed. We knew that politics was nothing more than that – politics. Under the republic, under any political system, we workers would remain slaves of our bit of earth, of our work. When it comes down to it, politicians don't give a damn whether the common lot eat or not. Of course, one regime can give a bit more liberty than another, a little more freedom of expression; but most things it can't change. In many ways we were worse off under the republic than under the monarchy; the right became even more aggressive and reactionary, and we had to defend ourselves . . .

For large sectors of the provincial bourgeoisie beyond the 'advanced seaboards' law and order had almost supplanted the religious issue as the major rallying cry. Implicitly, if not explicitly, the cry expressed the demand to defend a traditional way of life, the privileges and material interests of those who thought fit to call themselves, as they always had, '*la gente de orden*'. It was a class which, ideologically, felt itself united by religion, especially the struggle to defend the church.[1] In the eyes of this bourgeoisie, the republic had 'attacked religion'; now it was showing itself incapable of ensuring the safety of bourgeois citizens or the integrity of their property.

The republic had become, in short, a symbol of disorder. 'So infamous a word among the middle classes,' recalled the son of a liberal schoolteacher in Córdoba, 'that any disorder or confusion was simply described as "a republic".'

Roberto SOLIS, a law student, had welcomed the republic and, within a month, after the convent burnings, had turned against it. The 'naïve anti-clericalism' of much of the left struck him as hellish. He had become a CEDA supporter. On the night of the 1936 elections he had gone round Córdoba polling stations; young girls in a working-class district had put him to flight, insulting him in the grossest imaginable terms. The fact of wearing a tie was enough to identify him.

1. For further discussion of this theme, see Points of Rupture, B.

—There was a simple social distinction: those who wore ties and those who didn't. It was a symbol, the uniform of the middle class . . .

In fact, he reflected, it was a petty bourgeoisie which knew few luxuries – at home his family didn't have a bathroom, amongst other things – but which enjoyed one overwhelming privilege: 'the working class was there to serve us'. Because that was how it had always been, the middle class believed that was how it should remain. Any deviation from the norm was termed 'communist'.

It was of small consolation that the bourgeoisie's 'bogy' – the communist party – did not share the view that the republic was foundering in disorder, threatening its property. Like most communist militants, Pedro CLAVIJO, secretary-general of the Andalusian communist youth federation, was convinced that the situation was well within limits tolerable to a democratic republic. There was no generalized sense of 'going out to take over the bourgeoisie's land'; the land invasions in Andalusia were far less extensive than was often alleged. The peasants – small tenants, for example, who had been unjustly thrown off their land during the two years of centre-right government – were correcting injustices done to them. People were confident that the republic could advance towards social reform within the framework of bourgeois democracy – 'and simultaneously doubtful about the manner in which it was advancing'. The socialist and communist parties kept the government under constant pressure to achieve the widest possible democratization: 'The sort of thing, to take a contemporary example, that Allende was attempting in Chile.'

A conservative republican parliamentary deputy for Córdoba agreed. Federico FERNANDEZ DE CASTILLEJO, co-founder with Alcalá Zamora (who had been deposed as president of the republic after the Popular Front victory) of the right liberal republican party, DLR (Derecha Liberal Republicana), viewed the Popular Front programme as 'extremely conservative' and a clear expression of the electorate's desire to prevent the republic's enemies from taking over.

—There was no threat of a communist attempt to take power; the party was, apart from anything else, much too small. Indisputably, the working class and peasant masses put their class interests before other loyalties. This made it difficult, if not impossible, to convince them to 'wait and put up with their hunger' and not to make things difficult for a government which was trying to help them. All the more so when the proletariat knew from long experience that economic concessions could only be torn by force from the capitalists . . .

He had seen how, from the very first day of the republic, the reactionary oligarchy had used economic boycott, flight of capital, closure of factories, refusal to invest and to work the land as terrible weapons to bring down the regime. 'And when the workers, especially in the infamous latifundist zones of Andalusia, invaded estates to get food or till the land, they were met sometimes with bullets, not bread. The republic defended private property, law and order.'

Only too well, thought Juan MARIN, a FAI building worker in Seville. But the Popular Front victory endangered the privileges of the ruling class, of capitalism itself.

—The people felt that socialist reforms would have to be made to solve the problems that the republic had proven it could not solve: the agrarian problem in particular. It was a pre-revolutionary situation . . .

Under constant pressure and threats of further mass land invasions (in fact, after the take-over of the 3,000 farms in Estremadura, there were no more), the government took over nearly 600,000 hectares of arable land and settled 100,000 landworkers in four months. Whether the agrarian problem was solved by a 'democratic' or a 'socialist' revolution was of academic interest to the rural bourgeoisie which stood to lose a great deal of land either way – if not, as many feared, their lives as well. Democracy had never been *their* solution; the latter would have to be sought in those forces prepared to put an end to the threat.

Agitation increased; strike after strike hit almost every industry and trade, culminating in the Madrid building strike which was still in progress at the start of the war. Street violence in Madrid, Seville and Málaga included inter-union assassinations of UGT and CNT militants.

On 1 May, Indalecio Prieto, the centrist socialist leader, warned the country that violence was paving the way for fascism and pointed to General Franco as the likely leader of a military uprising. On the same day mass demonstrations took place in cities throughout Spain.

SALAMANCA

—The marchers came down the street towards the town hall; at their head were about a hundred women wearing red scarves. One of them knew my friend, a tall, strong falangist who was standing next to me; he'd fucked her or something. She shook her fist in his face and shouted, '*¡Viva Rusia, fascista!*' He shouted back at her: '*¡Viva España, puta!*' The whole lot of them trampled over us until we had blood pouring from our noses and ears. All for crying, 'Long live Spain!' That had become a subversive shout . . .

Juan CRESPO, the monarchist student with falangist sympathies, nursed his wounds. 'We all longed for the military to rise, longed for a dictatorship to put an end to this chaos. Not that we thought the army would . . . '

MADRID

—We members of the workers' and peasants' anti-fascist militia marched at the head in our uniforms and leather belting, giving the clenched fist salute. The bourgeoisie, the aristocracy, watching from the balconies of their houses along the Castellana, got a good fright.

Our militia's task was to defend the republic from the fascist attack everyone could see was coming, not to organize for revolution, maintained the communist youth clerk, Pedro SUAREZ, in line with his party's strategy. In fact, had we tried to make the revolution there would have been a fine mess: the military would have simply risen even earlier. The post-election period was one of consolidating the democratic republic that had just been reconquered at the polls . . .

None the less, the new unified socialist youth, to which he belonged, had raised the slogans of a 'workers' government', a 'Red Army' at the May Day demonstration which Largo Caballero's paper *Claridad* described as a 'great army of workers on its march to the summit close to power'. Caballero, the left-wing socialist leader, now dubbed the 'Spanish Lenin', called insistently for revolution, the dictatorship of the proletariat, telling the workers not to hold back their revolutionary actions for fear of a military coup. In June, he *invited* the left republicans in government to 'leave their place to the working class', and *asked* President Azaña to arm the workers. Not surprisingly, neither happened. In fact, the socialist party, by far and away the largest working-class party, was paralysed. Largo Caballero's revolutionary postures, Prieto's desire to re-establish the republican–socialist coalition of the first two years, Besteiro's attacks on the 'bolshevizers', had torn the party open ideologically, tactically and even personally. The revolution the socialist left wing had been preaching for the past two years and more was, apparently, not to culminate in a seizure of power. The party remained firmly within the Popular Front policy.

ASTURIAS

From the time of the 1936 electoral victory, reflected a socialist miner, José MATA, veteran of the October revolutionary insurrection which held power in the mining villages for a fortnight, the working class was on the defensive.

—Waiting for the others to rise. I remember one of our union leaders, Antuña, saying that twenty-three out of the twenty-five garrisons were hostile to the republic. 'You mean, you know they're going to rise?' I asked. 'Yes . . . '

But nothing had been done about it. The government sent Franco to the Canaries where he was closer to Morocco and the Army of Africa; and Mola to Pamplona where he could conspire amidst known opponents of the republic – the Carlists. It wasn't the socialists' fault, he thought: Prieto had warned the government several times. The blame lay with the petty bourgeois republicans.

Another veteran of the October rising, Alberto FERNANDEZ, a socialist baker, believed that his party had made a big mistake in leaving the government solely in the hands of the left republicans. Faced with the threat of fascism, the Popular Front policy was the correct one; the revolutionary phase of October 1934 was over. With socialist participation, the government might not have been able to prevent the uprising, 'but might have been able to take the necessary precautions to snuff it out before it could spread'.

MADRID

The communist party insistently warned of the danger of a military coup. The whole thrust of its policies was to sustain the Popular Front with the petty bourgeoisie as the only effective anti-fascist alliance. The party had grown rapidly since the October insurrection which it had joined at the last minute and in which its militants had played a significant role. Unity in action with the other working-class organizations was bringing it an influence in working-class politics which a previous sectarian isolation had prevented. In the party's view the need for unity between the working class and all 'anti-fascist social classes and strata' who were willing to seek a democratic solution to the country's problems, meant that the anti-fascist alliance and the pursuit of the bourgeois democratic revolution were linked. But of the two there was no doubt which must take priority. Pressure from the masses, especially in the countryside, must be kept on the government to proceed with the revolution, but nothing must be allowed to jeopardize the Popular Front.

'The struggle of democracy against fascism must come first,' said José Diaz, the communist party's secretary-general.

The dissident communist POUM, whose main strength was in Catalonia, believed in exactly the opposite policy. 'The only anti-fascist struggle is the working-class revolutionary struggle to seize power and introduce socialism,' wrote Andreu Nin, the POUM leader, at this time.

Wilebaldo SOLANO, twenty-year-old medical student soon to become secretary of the POUM's youth movement, JCI (Juventud Comunista Ibérica), charted his party's view of events from the Popular Front victory: the people had voted for the left because they saw the elections as one battle amongst many to come; they were prepared to vote one day and fight arms in hand the next. The masses were moving forward, the revolutionary process was given a new impetus by the electoral victory.

—And as it happened – you could almost plot it on a graph – as the masses advanced the socialist party and unified youth, under communist pressure, went backwards. Into the shelter of an exclusively Popular Front, petty bourgeois programme, leaving power in the hands of the left republicans . . .

But, as Nin recognized, in the absence of a mass revolutionary party and of organizations to ensure working-class unity in action, the moment was not ripe for the seizure of power.[1] The pre-revolutionary situation had to be used to the maximum to create these necessary instruments.

The CNT, elements of which had made three insurrectionary bids to establish libertarian communism in 1932 and 1933, was now engaged in healing the split between the anarchist and syndicalist tendencies which had riven it for the past four years. At its Extraordinary Congress, which opened in Saragossa on 1 May, the proposal to create a libertarian militia to crush a military uprising was rejected almost scornfully, in the name of a traditional anti-militarism. Instead, much time was devoted to outlining what life would be like under libertarian communism.[2]

Thus, less than two years after the October 1934 rising, no working-class organization was ready to take pre-emptive action to prevent the enemy from seizing power even though it was evident that the unstable social equilibrium (which had underlain the monarchy's crisis, and which in turn was the cause of the relatively weak republican governments) could not remain much longer unresolved. The hesitation of the working-class organizations reflected a

1. See A. Nin, 'Después de las elecciones del 16 de febrero', in *Los problemas de la revolución española* (Paris, 1971).

2. The trajectory of the anarcho-syndicalist movement, of crucial importance to the revolution, is outlined in Points of Rupture, D.

dominant reality: it was not a revolutionary situation.[1] One of the two fundamental conditions was absent. While the 'lower classes' (especially rural) did not want to continue 'living in the old way', the 'upper classes' were not yet unable to carry on in the 'old way'. Fear that their power to do so was being threatened led them to take measures fully to restore – not the 'way' of the past five years but of the dictatorship which had preceded them: an authoritarian state which would render the working-class forces impotent. Means of restoring the 'old way' were at hand. In place of the parliamentary forces which had failed, there was the army. Alongside this was the 'reserve army' of falangists, Carlists and monarchists who were united in their determination to crush the threat of socialist revolution and separatism (united as well, in varying degrees, by their adherence to the concept of organic democracy[2]), if disunited in other spheres. The failure of five years of pre-revolutionary process to crystallize into a revolutionary situation was to be the measure of the counter-revolution's success.

*

In Pamplona, General Mola planned the definitive operation. By June, the plans were well advanced. Many of the conspirators at his headquarters firmly believed that a Comintern-planned coup to install a Soviet regime under Largo Caballero was due to take place.[3] Mola set the date for 12 July, but a serious stumbling-block arose. The Carlist leadership broke off relations with him because their minimal demands for joining the uprising had not been met: that they have political responsibility for the new state's 'organic and corporative' reconstruction, and that the rising take place under the monarchist, not republican flag. Mola, whose plans were to retain a republican regime under a military directorate, could not afford to jeopardize other right-wing alliances by politically mortgaging the uprising to Carlism. On 12 July, still without agreement, he sent a legionary officer to Morocco with the message: 'From 1700 hours on the 17th.' The plan was now for the Army of Africa to rise first, followed by risings on the mainland, staggered from twenty-four to thirty-six hours later.

On the same day, in Madrid, Lt José Castillo, a left-wing assault guard officer, was assassinated. The riposte was immediate. Calvo Sotelo, the leading

1. 'For a revolution to take place', wrote Lenin, 'it is not enough for the exploited and oppressed masses to realize the impossibility of living in the old way, and demand changes; for a revolution to take place, it is essential that the exploiters should not be able to live and rule in the old way. It is only when the "lower classes" do not want to live in the old way and the "upper classes" cannot carry on in the old way that the revolution can triumph' ('Leftwing Communism – An Infantile Disorder', *Collected Works*, vol. 31, Moscow, 1966, p. 85).

2. For a consideration of this concept see n. 1, pp. 319–20.

3. The plot, ridiculed at the time by *Claridad*, Largo Caballero's newspaper, is still given credence (see F. Maíz, *Mola, aquél hombre* (Barcelona, 1976); also J. del Burgo, *Conspiración y guerra civil* (Madrid, 1970)). Eduardo Comín Colomer, who was responsible for keeping the 'plot' alive in his history of the Spanish communist party (1965), retracted his earlier position. 'I know that the plot was the work of right-wing people. Believing that Spain was going to fall into communist hands, they drew up the plan, basing themselves on the schema outlined by the 7th Comintern Congress, as a warning to the country. Caballero was already being called the "Spanish Lenin". When I subscribed to the plot's authenticity, I did so knowingly, believing that the time had not yet come to reveal the truth.' (Statement to author, 26 September 1974.)

right-wing monarchist politician, was taken from his home by companions of the assassinated officer and murdered.

Responsibility for Sotelo's murder rested with the republican anti-fascist military union, UMRA (Unión Militar de Republicanos Anti-fascistas). Two months earlier, Capt. Faraudo had been gunned down in the street on the pretext that he had been training socialist militia. In response Capt. ORAD DE LA TORRE, a retired artillery officer, drew up a statement on behalf of the anti-fascist military.

—The statement expressed our shock and warned that in the event of another such attempt we would reply in kind – but not on the person of an army officer, but on that of a politician. For it was the politicians who were responsible for this state of affairs. We sent the statement to the right-wing Spanish military union, UME (Unión Militar Española) . . .

When Lt Castillo was killed, the threat was carried out. A light assault guard truck set out with about fifteen men to look for Goicoechea, the monarchist leader, or Gil Robles. Unable to find either, they were passing down the Calle Velázquez when someone remarked that Calvo Sotelo lived there.

—The government was in no way involved – it was we of the UMRA[1] . . .

Capt. ORAD DE LA TORRE, who had recently got married, played no role in the assassination; but he did not believe it was wrong, for had not the right murdered two left-wing officers?

Condemned immediately by the government, the assassination aroused a wave of stunned indignation on the right and amongst moderate republicans.

Alfredo LUNA, newspaper editor (UR): It was horrible. It shook the government. To retaliate for one murder by another, for Castillo's by that of a leading politician – what justification could there be for it?

Father Alejandro MARTINEZ: A passer-by came up as I was on my way to the seminary where I taught. 'It's a good job he's been killed, say what you will, all the right should be killed,' he shouted at me. 'Good, *hijo*,' I replied, 'each of us administers his own pocket and his conscience,' and I walked on.

David JATO, falangist student leader (SEU): One assassination more or less at that moment wouldn't have made much impact. But the fact that it was Calvo Sotelo and that he had been assassinated by the government's police forces made people take a stand finally against the government. Many garrisons, many people who a week before had been doubtful or even opposed, now saw the need for a violent solution. Without the assassination, the military rising, I'm convinced, would have failed.

Antonio PEREZ, student, unified socialist youth (JSU): It seemed to us just one more of a long list of assassinations. The political implications appeared unimportant – it was another death.

*

1. 'When Major Díaz Varela, one of the prime minister's military aides, informed the latter of the assassination, Casares Quiroga replied: "What a mess they've got us into" (*En menudo lío nos han metido*) – his literal words, often repeated to me by Díaz Varela' (ORAD DE LA TORRE).

Had it not been for Carlist intransigence, the rising would have already taken place. The assassination made agreement with the Carlists easier to reach. A pious letter from General Sanjurjo, who was due to take over the leadership of the uprising once he was able to return from exile in Lisbon, suggested a compromise which both Mola and the Carlists accepted. Dolores BALEZTENA drove with her brother Joaquín, president of the Carlist junta of Navarre, to San Juan de Luz in France. There Fal Conde, the Carlist leader, gave her some papers. 'Hide them where you think best. They must not be found at the frontier.' She hid them in her sandals. As they started back for Pamplona, her brother told her that they were the king's instructions for the *requetés* to join the uprising.

Las fiestas están alegres
Y las chicas guapas son
Mas yo me voy pues me llama
Alfonso Carlos Borbón.

The fiestas are joyful
And the girls pretty
But I shall have to leave
Because I'm called by Alfonso Carlos Borbón.[1]

—When I heard a Carlist group singing this song in the streets on my return to Pamplona, I felt a tremendous sense of anguish, and I went into a doorway to cry . . .

In the Pamplona cinema, the announcement of a Paramount week beginning on 19 July was flashed on the screen. Half a dozen of the best Paramount films of the year. Rafael GARCIA SERRANO, a falangist student, felt an anticipatory pleasure. One of the films was *The Bengal Lancers.*

—A film of heroism, imperial adventure, fighting – a film our founder, José Antonio Primo de Rivera, particularly liked and recommended to us. '*Coño*, what a great film!' I said to my companion. 'Wonderful fighting – ' 'It won't be a bad film of fighting we're going to have on the nineteenth ourselves,' he replied in the dark . . .

1. King of the Carlists and pretender to the Spanish throne, Alfonso Carlos was the last direct descendant of don Carlos. He died in September 1936, and was succeeded as regent by Prince Xavier.

ALEA JACTA EST!

THE ARMY RISES AGAINST THE POPULAR FRONT GOVERNMENT

DECLARES ITS PROGRAMME IS TO SAVE SPAIN FROM ANARCHY

GEN. FRANCO IS THE MILITARY LEADER OF THE MOVEMENT

Defensor de Córdoba, headlines (Córdoba, 20 July 1936)

¡VIVA
LA
REPUBLICA!

ABC, headline (Madrid, 21 July 1936)

The Victory Belongs to the Workers

The mortuaries are full of the corpses of proletarians mown down by the militarist scum . . . But there is no minister's nor ex-minister's, no former city councillor's among them. Only proletarian flesh and blood . . .

Will the ministers and ex-ministers, the collaborators of the treacherous army, try to administer the victory won by the proletariat?

They had better not try. The proletariat is in the streets, arms in hand. The proletariat knows how to retain the conquests it has cost so much blood to win. The CNT will never surrender while an enemy of freedom remains before the proletariat.

Solidaridad Obrera, CNT (Barcelona, 24 July 1936)

July 1936

Monday, 20 July

By evening the situation was growing clearer. Industrial and urban Spain – five of the country's seven largest cities – were in republican hands: Madrid, Barcelona, Valencia (where, with troops confined to barracks, the government's victory was not yet definite), Málaga and Bilbao. Seville and Saragossa (in both of which resistance was continuing) were the exceptions.

Peasant Spain was in insurgent hands. The wide arc, stretching east and west above Madrid from Saragossa to Salamanca and passing through the heartland of the medium and small Catholic peasantry, had risen against the republic. The insurgents' reach stretched north-westwards into Galicia.

Latifundist Spain was divided. In the fourteen provinces where agrarian reform was to be applied first, seven provincial capitals (although not yet the surrounding countryside), four of them Andalusian,[1] had fallen to the military.

Fighting continued everywhere; the position of the northern seaboard remained uncertain while military resistance continued in San Sebastián and Gijón. Beneath the fluid situation, the outlines of the two opposing camps could, none the less, be discerned: the landowning class and provincial petty bourgeoisie on the one hand (joined by the industrial bourgeoisie if it chanced to be in – or could reach – the insurgent zone); the industrial and rural proletariat, allied with the urban petty bourgeoisie, on the other. The fracture paralleled the previous social line of division. Of little import in a rapid coup, its correspondence to an urban/rural split was to have a significant consequence in a long war: the supply of food in the opposing camps.

The coup had fissured the republican regime, not crushed it. In that sense, it had failed. With a couple of notable exceptions, it had captured only what it could hope to capture and left itself the task of taking the rest. That meant war.

Civilian resistance had played a large part. But – contrary to popular belief – in no major town had the people *alone* crushed the military revolt. The loyalty of the security forces was essential to victory. Equally, however, the police forces had nowhere fought *successfully* without strong civilian support. The fusion of the two in *attack* brought victory in Barcelona, Madrid, Málaga, Gijón and – shortly – Valencia and San Sebastián.[2] This was clear to working-class militants in most of the towns, particularly Barcelona.

1. Seville, Córdoba, Granada and Cádiz. The other three were Salamanca, Cáceres and, briefly, Albacete. The republicans' recapture of the latter was balanced by the rapid loss of Huelva in Andalusia.

2. Other factors on both sides certainly contributed to victory or defeat. The failure to manoeuvre offensively, the retreat to isolated 'strongholds' or *barrios*, divisions in the working-class organizations, lack of decisiveness in the military, were among these. But where the *offensive fusion* was lacking the military triumphed. The assault guards might remain temporarily loyal as in Seville and Córdoba but on the defensive and separate from the people; or go over immediately to the military as in Saragossa and Oviedo. The end result was the same. Unarmed, isolated, disorganized, the masses were in no position to do more than stage a desperate resistance. The military, their task made easier by being able to bring out cannon to force the surrender of official buildings, took the offensive. It should be noted, moreover, that the totality of the Barcelona and Madrid garrisons did not rise.

—The combination was decisive. For all its combativeness, its revolutionary spirit, the CNT alone could not have fought off the army *and* the police forces, thought Jacinto BORRAS, a CNT journalist on *Solidaridad Obrera*. There wouldn't have been one of us left within a few hours . . .

Pere ARDIACA, communist party representative on the Barcelona Popular Front committee and soon to be editor of the newly formed PSUC's (Partit Socialista Unificat de Catalunya) paper *Treball*, saw that more than collaboration had been involved. In the action of assault guards and masses a dynamic had developed, which had produced the decisive result.

—The masses impelled the guards to defend their positions; and the guards gave the masses the organized support that was needed. Within this dialectic however, the attitude of the CNT and its leaders was extraordinary, virtually decisive when fused with that of the police forces . . .

Not that, in truth, thought Manuel CRUELLS, the Catalan nationalist student, it was accurate to speak of the 'masses'. Civilians fought and died heroically; but, from what he saw, it was the *militants* of the different organizations – the FAI and CNT defence groups especially, the POUM, the few communists, socialists and members of Estat Català like himself, the republican parties – who engaged in the actual fighting. The masses had not appeared until the evening when victory was assured; 'then the masses seized the victory for themselves'.

An FAI militant, Felix CARRASQUER, whose defence group had encircled the Pedralbes barracks and forced its surrender, agreed.

—Where there were 2,000 of us libertarians who rallied to put down a fascist coup – not, let me stress, to make a libertarian revolution – by 8 a.m. the next day there were 100,000 in the streets . . .

In Madrid, Juan ANDRADE, soon to be called to Barcelona to serve on the POUM's executive committee, drew certain revolutionary lessons from the events.

—The left would never have destroyed army discipline if the masses hadn't *attacked*. Only when a regiment was in real danger – as in the Montaña barracks in Madrid or in the streets of Barcelona – were there signs of refusal among the soldiers to fight their own working class. Until that moment, military discipline remained effective. But when soldiers and NCOs found themselves attacked on all sides they became demoralized, discipline collapsed, they would no longer obey their officers. Then the military units became ineffective fighting forces, and it was impossible for the officers to order out new units. For all that, it must be said that the assault guards played an absolutely crucial role, which was almost always overlooked. The guards were the only efficient police corps created by the republic, and in Madrid they were a revolutionary force made up almost exclusively of socialist youth or other left wingers. Their importance in the fighting that was about to come was equally decisive; it was they who, in the first couple of months, virtually saved Madrid . . .

*

Three decisive events took place on 20 July 1936 which were to condition the future course of events. The first was the landing that morning in Seville of two Fokker bombers from Morocco carrying twenty legionaries; in the afternoon, a further twenty-four legionaries and twenty Moroccan troops were ferried across. It was the beginning of the first major 'air lift' in history.

—As soon as the troops arrived, Queipo de Llano had them driven round and round the city to make people think far greater numbers had reached Seville, recalled Rafael MEDINA, falangist businessman. The Moorish troops arrived feeling very air-sick . . .

The 25,000-strong Army of Africa, the only professional fighting force in the Spanish army, was blocked in its bases by several warships whose sailors had risen and killed their officers who had been trying to rally to the uprising. Only two *tabores* of Moroccan troops had been able to cross by sea before the strait of Gibraltar was blockaded. But the rest of this crack army, composed of legionaries and Moroccan *regulares*, was desperately needed on the mainland to spearhead the march on Madrid. They would be ferried across, thanks largely to German and Italian planes, in the next two months.[1]

The following day, Rafael MEDINA, later to become duke of Medinaceli, participated alongside a group of legionaries in the attack on the Seville working-class district of San Julián.

—I quickly saw their combat spirit. After a couple of cannon rounds from a field piece emplaced by the famous Macarena arch, we advanced. The revolutionaries started firing. We suffered casualties. A legionary was killed. The man behind him jumped over his body shouting, 'Long Live Death!' and advanced down the street. We reached our objective, but as night was coming on the order came to withdraw. Shouting their battle cries, the legionaries led our withdrawal to safety. They were magnificent. The next day the red *barrio* fell . . .

It was the end of working-class resistance in Seville.

BURGOS

Leading monarchists had gathered at Gamonal aerodrome outside Burgos to welcome General Sanjurjo, the uprising's national leader, from his exile in Lisbon. Two days before the rising, the monarchists had received warning to leave Madrid for the safety of Burgos and Vitoria. Eugenio VEGAS LATAPIE,

1. Without the twenty Junkers 52 transport planes provided by Hitler and the nine Savoia 81s which reached Morocco from Italy, it would have taken nine months to airlift the Army of Africa to the mainland. As it was, just under 14,000 troops, eleven field batteries and 500 tons of war material were ferried from Morocco in two months (see Col. J. M. Martínez Bande, *La campaña de Andalucía*, Madrid, 1969). Britain played its part in refusing to allow republican ships to refuel in Gibraltar and ensuring that the International Commission which governed Tangier forced the navy to stop using the harbour. From 5 August, the republican naval blockade had been broken by the insurgents, although complete freedom of passage was not achieved until the end of September when the republican government ordered the fleet to the north.

editor of the monarchists' theoretical magazine *Acción Española*,[1] believed that the uprising had taken place without sufficient ideological preparation.

—It was like being in a house on fire without means of escape. You throw yourself from the window, without knowing whether you'll fall on your head or your feet . . .

The military, he feared, lacked a clear idea of the type of political regime the country needed. Not that this was by any means a purely militarist uprising, but rather a 'typical national movement' which transcended any one particular class.

—The army, the few members of the aristocracy who remained in Spain (most left the country after the republic was proclaimed), and the middle class – those were the components of the movement. The middle class, through its representation in the army and its readiness to leave home and fields to fight for ideological reasons, dominated. Its ideas had been shaped and hardened through five years of republican persecution, especially since the Popular Front elections. Calvo Sotelo's assassination was the spark that produced the explosion . . .

Scanning the sky for the light aeroplane, Pedro SAINZ RODRIGUEZ, monarchist parliamentary deputy, recalled General Sanjurjo's political plans for the nation. At first, a military junta would rule, its period in office depending on how quickly the rising was successful. Then there would be a plebiscite to determine whether the nation wanted a monarchy or a republic.

—Sanjurjo had spoken to me of these ideas, and the notes of a proclamation on the plebiscite had been sent to Burgos with a close friend of his. It was hoped, of course, that coming after a successful military coup, the plebiscite would favour the monarchy's return. A Constituent Cortes would have to decide what form the monarchy should take. As anti-parliamentarianism was in vogue, as we were all much influenced by the examples of Germany and Italy, it might well have taken the form of 'organic' democracy, instead of the 'pure' democracy which had been discredited by the republic . . .

All afternoon they waited in vain. That night, to their consternation, they heard on Madrid radio that the plane had crashed on take-off and Sanjurjo had been killed. It was the second decisive event of the day, and a bitter blow to the monarchists. Whether the Sanjurjo 'plan' would have been put into effect or not,[2] the monarchists had lost the main hope of a monarchist outcome to the civil war. More importantly, the movement had lost its leader.

1. Founded at the end of 1931, the magazine crystallized a new-style monarchist reaction to the republic. It was, in its editor's words, 'anti-democratic', believing not in the virtues of universal suffrage but rather in the principle of heredity. In its pages, he propounded the right to rise against 'an illegitimate power'. Other contributors preached the need for an all-embracing, hierarchical corporative state as the surest guarantee against proletarian revolution (see P. Preston, 'Alfonsist Monarchism and the Coming of the Spanish Civil War', *Journal of Contemporary History*, vol. 7, 1972).

2. Sáinz Rodríguez was never able to find the notes concerning the plebiscite's proclamation; and Vegas Latapie frankly doubted that they existed. Sanjurjo, who had won his military reputation in the Moroccan wars, led an abortive monarchist-military revolt against the republic in 1932.

BARCELONA

The day's third decisive event took place in Barcelona.

Jordi ARQUER, POUM executive committee member, went into the Generalitat, seeking news. He had returned to Barcelona only late the previous evening. He encountered a number of Generalitat councillors who asked him for news. He told them he had none. Had he seen Durruti, they asked. No. 'Well, if you do, tell him we want to have a talk.' As he went out of the building, he saw Durruti, García Oliver and Ricardo Sanz, three of the anarchists who had led the CNT–FAI defence groups in crushing the rebellion.

—I went up to Sanz. I knew him best because we had been members of the same union when I was in the CNT. Relations between the POUM and the CNT weren't over friendly. The FAI had expelled a whole series of people from the CNT and made our lives impossible. Anyway, I told him the councillors were looking for Durruti. 'If they want to say anything to us, let them come direct,' he replied haughtily, as though telling me not to meddle in these matters. Then they went into the Generalitat, which is where they had probably been going anyway . . .

That morning the last rebel bastion, Atarazanas barracks, had been stormed; in fact taken by an audacious assault over the side walls by a small group of libertarians. The assault had been costly in lives. Francisco Ascaso, one of the best known libertarians, had paid with his life. Ricardo SANZ had lifted his body off the hood of the ice lorry from which he had been firing at the barracks. Before the assault a company of civil guards had marched down the Ramblas, and Durruti had stopped them to ask what their orders were. 'We thank you,' he told the captain, 'but there are enough of us to take Atarazanas. Please inform your commander that Durruti has asked you to return.'

'Don't be so stupid, they're *guardia civil*,' a POUM militant said to Durruti. 'Let them attack first – ' But the CNT leaders had wanted the honour for themselves.

A few hours later, carrying their arms and still covered in the dust of battle, the small group of libertarian leaders went into the Generalitat for a meeting with President Companys. The latter had already been informed by Commissioner Escofet that the commanders of the civil and assault guards could no longer rely on their men to restore order in the streets. Even if the attempt were made it would mean fighting the libertarians, and the ensuing battle would be as heavy as, if not heavier than, the one which had just been fought in the streets. The chances of 'restoring order' were virtually nil.

The limits placed on the state's coercive power were the true measure of the depth of the revolution: the police, even the disciplined *guardia civil*, had abandoned their masters.

—When I saw a *guardia* sitting in a car in the Plaça de Catalunya, his tunic unbuttoned, his tricorn pushed to the back of his head and smoking a cigar, I knew there was no law and order any more, knew that the *guardia civil* had become infected by the populace, recalled Juana ALIER, a mill-owner's wife . . .

Escofet advised Companys that the only solution was to contain the situation politically. On leaving, the police commissioner reflected that he had never seen Companys look so profoundly concerned, so anxious.[1]

When the libertarian leaders were shown into the Generalitat, Companys shook them by the hand. The CNT and FAI had always been harshly treated, he told them, even by those who, in the past, had defended them (as he had frequently done) as a lawyer in the courts. 'Today you are the masters of the city and of Catalonia . . . You have conquered and everything is in your power; if you do not need or want me as president of Catalonia, tell me now. If, on the other hand, you believe that in my post, with the men of my party, my name and my prestige, I can be useful in the struggle . . . you can count on me and on my loyalty as a man and a politician; a man who sincerely desires Catalonia to march at the head of the socially most advanced countries . . .'

—His speech took us by surprise. He saw the situation more clearly than us because he hadn't been in the thick of the street fighting, recalled Ricardo SANZ. One of us replied: 'We have come to no decision about this, consequently we cannot give an answer.' We would have to return and report to the CNT. This was a new turn of events. Then another one of us – I don't remember who, it could have been any of us three because in the *Nosotros* group no one tried to piss outside the pot – said that Companys enjoyed the confidence of Catalonia and the CNT, and we hoped he would continue as president of the Generalitat. This was a purely conditional answer; it didn't for a moment preclude our returning in a couple of hours and telling him we were taking over. That was what the three of us, our group, were in favour of doing. But the organization had to make the decision . . .

Outside, in another room, representatives of the Popular Front – to which the libertarian movement did not belong – waited. At Companys's suggestion, the libertarian leaders met the latter and agreed to set up a militia committee which would not only organize armed forces but be a 'suitable organization for continuing the revolution until final victory'.

Meanwhile, the CNT local federation was discussing its position. Anti-authoritarian, anti-state and government, a-political if not anti-political, would the libertarian movement, which had preached and attempted revolution to free the working masses from all forms of coercion, take power? Make the revolution?

Appointed that day to the FAI peninsular committee – the leading body of that organization – Félix CARRASQUER, anarchist schoolmaster, was attending the discussions. Only the previous Friday, the day the uprising began in Morocco, he was proposing to the Catalan CNT regional committee the need to set up a Popular School or University to train CNT revolutionary cadres. Violence, so long preached in the movement, was no substitute for revolutionary leadership. Where were the trained militants who could sustain the revolution? The movement's most influential leaders, the most spirited and determined revolutionaries, lacked the training and preparation necessary to run a revolutionary society. And if that was true in Catalonia, vanguard of the movement, and Aragon, what of the less-developed regions? In Catalonia, with its three and a half million inhabitants, he had argued, it would need a thousand trained

1. See Escofet, *Al servei de Catalunya i de la república*, p. 403.

militants to take over strategic posts in factories, businesses, town halls, the university. These militants would have to have the necessary imagination and capacity to lead, organize and administer; if not, it was impossible to make a successful revolution. And where were those one thousand militants? At best, in his view, there were probably no more than two dozen.

Now, when García Oliver and the others returned from the Generalitat and informed the meeting of Companys's remarks, the perspective of revolution opened before them.

—We realized our strength. We could establish libertarian communism in Catalonia. But Catalonia wasn't the whole of Spain. García Oliver argued that the movement should take power, should impose libertarian communism as a dictatorship: it was the position he had defended for a long time. He was supported by a companion who had spent many years in the Soviet Union, who had always fought the Bolshevik dictatorship, and now defended the imposition of libertarian communism. What a contradiction! Libertarian communism could not be imposed! Dictatorship was the antithesis of libertarianism! . . .

CARRASQUER opposed García Oliver. While they were in a minority in the whole of Spain, a libertarian revolution could not be made. A civil war was certainly beginning. If the libertarian movement did not collaborate at all levels with the other forces opposed to the uprising, it would be crushed 'as had been the anarchists in Russia – crushed by those fighting on our side'. The movement had to cooperate in the defence of the republic – in the streets, town halls, factories and workplaces, wherever it was necessary: even in politics.

Abad de Santillán, the influential libertarian writer, argued along similar lines. Dictatorship was the liquidation of libertarian communism which could be achieved only by the liberty and spontaneity of the masses. To impose it would mean forcibly enrolling the petty bourgeoisie and exercising an implacable authority over it, as well as over the political parties, which would end up attacking the CNT, their *bête noire*. Nothing could be further from anarchism than to impose its will by force, it would be moral suicide. Moreover, if the rest of the country did not follow the Catalan CNT in making total revolution, Catalonia would be isolated, international capital would apply a pitiless boycott, and unless there were an international revolution, the libertarian movement would be crushed.

—As a group, recalled Ricardo SANZ, we didn't press the issue. We knew that the organization was opposed to dictatorship. And that's what it would have been if our position had been accepted. From the moment the movement took over responsibility for everything, everyone would have had to do what we ordered. What is that if not dictatorship? Certainly, dictatorship wasn't part of the anarchist programme, but our proposal was dictated by force of circumstance; we saw it as a way out at that moment. But it couldn't be done. Why not? The CNT was opposed. I believe – it's a hypothesis only – that they were frightened of us, of the *Nosotros* group. Frightened that if we imposed a dictatorship they wouldn't be in a position to take decisions; frightened that sooner or later some of them might be eliminated as traitors to the revolution, that Stalinist methods might be imposed. Stalin was just then beginning to eliminate a whole series of revolutionaries who weren't traitors, as we all knew. But in any case we didn't try to force the issue because there were other urgent matters: Companys had suggested that Durruti lead a militia force to take Saragossa which was in enemy hands . . .

The collaborationist option won the day. The discussion, if sometimes violent in tone, did not last long. The majority were in favour, no vote had to be taken. There would be no talk of attaining libertarian communism until the war was won.

Who has the greater possibility of victory in war? Whoever has the greater means at their disposal. That is evident . . . Well, all Spain's gold, all the monetary resources valid abroad, are in the government's hands . . .

War nowadays is principally a war of industry. Well, all Spain's industrial might, everything that can effectively contribute to maintaining the struggle, is, without exaggeration, in our hands.

With the nation's financial and industrial resources in the government's power . . . those who have impetuously launched themselves into armed struggle against the republic . . . will inevitably, inexorably, fatally be conquered.

Indalecio Prieto, socialist leader
(Broadcast over Madrid radio, 8 August 1936)

The movement we have launched has been fervently supported by honest working people to free our country from the anarchy and chaos which has been under detailed preparation since the Popular Front came to power . . .

Only a monster, and a monster of the complicated psychological constitution of Azaña, could have encouraged such a catastrophe. A monster who appears more like the absurd experiment of a new and fantastic Frankenstein than the fruit of a woman's love. When we triumph, it will be unjust to demand his disappearance. Azaña must be shut up, so that phrenologists can study his case, perhaps the most interesting case of mental degeneration known since Krostand, the primitive man of our time . . .

General Emilio Mola
(Broadcast over Burgos radio, 15 August 1936)

We know exactly what the fatherland must recover in these moments – nothing less than itself . . . We were no more than the humiliated depository, the dregs of crass, failed ideologies, a colony of Russia, that's to say, a colony of organized barbarity . . .

The Falange's profound preoccupation is to redeem the proletariat . . . Spain is virtually divided; one half, made up of the vast army of those who earn their daily bread by manual labour, who do not love Spain, who receive no pleasure from belonging to this illustrious nation . . . We must assure the workers of the spiritual patrimony which they have lost, winning for them, above all, the satisfaction and certainty of their daily bread.

Spain must be proletarianized. It must become a people of workers . . . The capitalists, the rich will be traitors to the fatherland, unworthy members of the state if . . . they continue as they have done up to now with their incorrigible egoism, their refusal to look about them at the trail of hunger, scarcity and pain they leave in their wake.

Bread for all, justice for all – these are our slogans and will shortly be put into practice. *¡España, Una! ¡España, Grande! ¡España, Libre! ¡Arriba España!*

Onésimo Redondo, Falange leader
(Broadcast over Valladolid radio, 19 July 1936)

July to September 1936

GUADARRAMA

On both sides, militiamen and troops rushed to the strategic passes of the Guadarrama mountains which held the key to the advance on Madrid from Old Castile.

Riding in one of Madrid's red, double-decker buses, which had been taken over, Pedro SUAREZ, young communist MAOC member, was heading for the Alto del León, the pass through which the main Madrid-Valladolid road ran. From the latter city, a young falangist, Francisco GUTIERREZ DEL CASTILLO, who had just been released from prison, was making in the same direction.

SUAREZ's wife was with him in the bus; she had insisted on going to the front. When they reached a point just below the pass and got out of the bus, he told her to join the militia to the right, while he went with the one to the left.

—So she joined El Campesino's forces, while I was with Col. Mangada's column. I didn't want us to be in the same lot together. Then we advanced up the pass . . .

By the time GUTIERREZ reached the pass from the other side, it had already been taken once by his side and lost.

—We reconquered it in a tremendous battle, with artillery firing at point-blank range. A Jesuit priest advanced in front of us, carrying the cross, and urging us on. Like madmen we followed him. What bravery he displayed – without touching a rifle! I'm convinced that it was his example that gave us our victory . . .

Arriving from Salamanca, Juan CRESPO, monarchist student, reached the pass at the height of the battle. He had been doing guard duty in his home town when he bumped into his army cousin who shouted at him to jump into the lorry. 'Where are you going?' 'To have a cup of coffee in Madrid. We'll be there for the feast day of St James.' Spain's patron saint's feast day was two days away, 25 July. He got into the lorry. When he reached the bottom of the pass, Col. Serrador, the military commander, was being brought down wounded: a stray bullet killed the new commander before they reached the top.

—Imagine how we raw militiamen felt! The Valladolid artillery was firing point-blank. There were no trenches, only rocks. I was terrified. The noise of my rifle firing produced an acute sense of physical discomfort. I couldn't see the enemy. Instinctively, my head shrank into my shoulders . . .

His side was lucky, thought GUTIERREZ, some of the republican army units deserted and crossed to their lines. 'Very few of our soldiers did the same.'

—So we took the pass and held it, recalled CRESPO. But after three or four days, I got fed up. Most of us militiamen attached to the infantry battalion felt the same. The outing was over. We had fleas. We were cold. We missed our evening beer. A supply lorry arrived from Salamanca. We got on it and rode home. My mother was very happy to see me. 'So you've got over all that business, have you?' she said . . .

Early every morning the Madrid militiamen, organized by parties, trade unions and local groups, left the capital and returned late in the evening from their day spent in the Guadarrama mountains. A fourteen-year-old boy in the working-class *barrio* of Lavapies had the daily scene engraved on his memory.

—In the morning there'd be shouts. 'Pablo! Pedro! Manolo!' and the men came out of their houses with their rifles in their hands. Under the other arm they had the lunches their wives had prepared. They set off for the sierra as though they were going on a Sunday outing, to shoot rabbits. Often they were accompanied by women, some of them political, but more often not. Whores, that particular type of Madrid prostitute of the time with enormous breasts and buttocks, Alvaro DELGADO remembered. How amazing it seemed when in the evening they all came to spend the night at home. The next morning the scene was repeated . . .

Once again, it was the *fusion* of police and popular forces on the offensive which, if not always victorious, held the enemy at bay. With great rapidity they had taken the initiative in rushing out from the capital to conquer and hold not only the passes but the neighbouring provinces: Guadalajara, Cuenca, Toledo, Ciudad Real.

—In the actual fighting it was the assault guards who again took the brunt, so much so that I can truthfully say that virtually not one Madrid assault guard or officer remained alive after six months, recollected Juan ANDRADE of the POUM. Militarily speaking, the militia were chaotic at the beginning . . .

Heterogeneous, untrained, often disorganized, the militia none the less served the immediate purpose of reinforcing the fighting units. On the opposing side a somewhat similar fusion of army units with falangist and *requeté* civilians was also operating, although here the army units were properly organized and led by their regular officers. The matter changed when the professional Army of Africa entered the scene.

The Madrid garrison, moreover, had not been completely dismembered in the wake of the uprising. Due to summer leaves, deliberately encouraged by the government, it had not been at full strength on 20 July; and the government's subsequent decree demobilizing soldiers meant that many conscripts simply vanished. None the less, several thousand soldiers and NCOs were sent out to fight. Francisco ABAD, communist soldier-organizer of the clandestine soldiers' and corporals' organization in the only infantry regiment not to rise in Madrid, helped to send the remnants of the other regiments to the front under officers from his regiment or otherwise known loyal officers.

—However, there weren't many trusted officers available for the 6,000 men we sent out. In my own regiment, the majority were arrested after the fall of the Montaña, which was a mistake. A great number of the junior officers could have served the republic. Suspicion and distrust combined to make us lose a potentially useful force. Career officers weren't treated justly nor used properly in those first months . . .

Major Jaime SOLERA, a staff officer at the war ministry, was one of these. A self-styled liberal democrat without political affiliation, he believed that an army officer's duty was to serve the legally constituted government. At the same time, he knew that his brother, a serving officer, was in the insurgent zone.

The majority of officers in Madrid, he thought, shared his view. But the people, fearing that their loyalty was merely a trick, were suspicious of all officers.

—It was natural enough. Those were days of terrible confusion and no one could be blamed; but many officers were not only in danger of their lives, they were killed. Living in fear, they tried to escape . . .[1]

While Major SOLERA waited in vain in the war ministry for orders that never came – 'no planning was undertaken to deal with the uprising on a national level; the general staff couldn't make any plans because it had no executive arm – the army itself' – other officers went to the sierra as military advisers to the hastily formed columns. An infantry colonel, who had arrested disloyal officers in his regiment, was among them. Standing with his own men, he saw their faces turn pale. A shot rang out. The colonel turned round. 'Shoot me from the front, not like a coward from the back,' he said.

NO-MAN'S-LAND

In a spa hotel on the banks of the river Ebro where it flows along the borders of Burgos and Alava provinces, a twenty-year-old Madrid philosophy student, Paulino AGUIRRE, was holidaying with his parents. His father, a liberal politician under the monarchy, had refused to believe war was inevitable; this was another *pronunciamiento* – the typical nineteenth-century bloodless Spanish military coup – which would be over in a matter of days or weeks at the most.

Marooned in the hotel, not knowing what was happening, Paulino AGUIRRE came to realize that it was essential to take a stand.

1. The belief that the 'army en bloc' rose against the republican government does not withstand examination. Of the two dozen active divisional generals, four (and only one of these with troop command in the peninsula) rose. Four out of five *guardia civil* generals and the general commanding the air force remained loyal. Of nearly sixty brigadier generals, less than one third joined the rising. This does not mean that the rest were all loyal; many were dismissed by the republic, no doubt with good reason. However, it was captains, majors and – to a much lesser extent – colonels who provided the bulk of the rebel officer corps. Possibly as many as half the men actually serving in the army at the time remained in the republican zone, and between one third and one half of the active service army officers. However, three factors reduced their *effective combat strength*: 1. The republican government's grave error in demobilizing soldiers (who refused to heed subsequent call-up orders and often joined the militia instead). 2. Working-class anti-militarism, particularly strong amongst the anarcho-syndicalists, but also in evidence amongst socialists. Combined with a general distrust of all army officers as a result of the rising – a distrust which was not unfounded as many deserted when the opportunity arose – this meant that the officers were not used. 3. The resulting lack of hierarchical chains of command, bureaucratic coherence and disciplinary coercion meant that while military units might still exist an army had ceased to. Despite these disadvantages, the Popular Front forces rapidly fought the insurgents to a stalemate in the Guadarrama, suggestive of the Spanish peninsular army's material unpreparedness for war. Mola had two divisional commands, Burgos and Valladolid (the 6th and 7th), to use immediately against the Madrid 1st. He was soon expecting to have to withdraw northwards because of shortage of rifle ammunition. The *combat capacity* of the peninsular army alone was probably not high enough to make possible a decisive breakthrough on either side; the Army of Africa alone had such capacity.

—Little did I realize the role geography was to play, how the chance of *where* one happened to be was going to define one's position for one. I saw people leaving the hotel to join relatives in near-by towns. I didn't know that, in effect, they were crossing from one zone to another – and that it cost some of them their lives . . .

The zones lacked definite frontiers, front lines; everything was fluid, ambiguous; and yet – who could imagine it? – it was going to be years before the frontiers which were being invisibly created could again be crossed. The isolation was heightened by the radio news from both sides, so evidently propagandist as to be unbelievable.

One day, bodies were floating in the river. They were weighted with stones and floated below the surface, but as the water was clear they were plainly visible. They came from Miranda del Ebro, the near-by railway centre, where the socialists had had considerable strength, and which the insurgents were purging.

—The horror of war was now evident; but life in the hotel continued with a sort of unnatural lack of tension. Everybody seemed determined to prevent tension rising, camouflaging their real feelings. We listened with fascination to Queipo de Llano's broadcasts from Seville; in their brutality, coarseness and violence, they expressed better than any the true nature of war.

Only when we heard a town had changed hands, when one side or the other advanced and took territory they had not initially held, did we feel psychologically caught in one of the two zones. Only when the front line moved – as it soon did when the Navarrese *requetés* began invading Guipúzcoa – were we aware that there *was* a line, that we were definitely in the insurgent zone . . .

BARCELONA

Coming down the Passeig de Gràcia, Josep CERCOS, libertarian youth metalworker, saw lorries and men assembling, accompanied by a few military. It was the Durruti column about to set off to capture Saragossa.

He had known nothing about it, hadn't dreamt of going to the front that day. The lorries were already full. On the spot he decided to go to the station, certain there would be another column leaving by train. He had the rifle he'd got from the Sant Andreu artillery depot, and twenty-five or thirty rounds left. Within a short time, as he'd imagined, a train pulled in and everyone piled aboard, without being formed into groups or anything. Antonio Ortiz, of the *Nosotros* group, was the commander, it appeared, with an army major and a couple of captains as advisers. CERCOS made friends with an Asturian who had no firearm and only got one when a companion was killed in Aragon.

—We were all workers. There was a tremendous fever to reach Saragossa, to take it – the CNT had always been strong there, and so too had the military . . .

In improvised transport, thousands of men headed westwards from Barcelona. Men who as often as not had never handled a rifle in their lives and who, with or without arms, were setting out to 'liberate' Saragossa, Huesca and Teruel, the three Aragonese provincial capitals which had fallen to the military. 'We didn't have any maps, and I'm not talking of military maps, I mean we didn't have even a Michelin road map with us,' Jordi ARQUER, one of the POUM column leaders, recalled.

—The people's revolutionary instinct was amazing, thought Wilebaldo SOLANO, another POUM member. They knew they had to inflict one defeat after another, move ahead every minute. There wasn't a moment to lose. The cry went up – 'To Saragossa'. I remember Sgt Manzana, who later became famous alongside Durruti in the latter's column, saying to me: 'To Saragossa? But we're still surrounded by fascists here. We've got to consolidate first – ' He was right, of course; but the people were even more right. They realized that Barcelona now wasn't the over-riding concern in this life-and-death struggle. Saragossa had to be taken. The movement to set off – and which was such madness in military eyes – came from the streets, from the revolutionary turmoil, no one knew from whom or how. No one even knew what the situation was in the towns en route. The cry became general: 'To Saragossa!' . . .

The columns drove into Aragon in search of the enemy. The right had taken over in most villages and the left had fled into the countryside. But under the weight of the advance, the insurgents began, in the main, to retreat towards the cities. The closer the columns advanced, the stiffer became the resistance they encountered. Saragossa was the pivot of the defence, prime target of the offensive. Militarily, its capture would poise the predominantly Catalan attackers on the roads to Madrid and the Basque country, threatening Mola's flank in Navarre and linking up the two major industrial areas of the Popular Front zone. Politically, victory over Saragossa would confirm the overwhelming strength of the CNT (deeply concerned at the loss of one of its strongholds) and poise the libertarians on the road to carrying their revolution triumphantly beyond the confines of Catalonia and Aragon.

Josep CERCOS emerged from the station at Caspe, in lower Aragon. The train had reached there without meeting resistance. In the station square CERCOS saw, to his great surprise, a company of civil guards. Each guard wore a red neckerchief.

—'What's going on here?' I said to the Asturian. One of the guards came up to me. 'Ah, my friend, when you see a civil guard without one of these round his neck, shoot him. Only those wearing them are on the republic's side.' That didn't impress me much. We didn't give a damn about the republic, we were concerned only about the revolution. I wouldn't have gone to the front if not to make the revolution. We had come out to fight in the streets of Barcelona because we had no option; but to go and fight the military in Aragon – no, I wouldn't have gone simply for that. It was the fever of revolution which carried us forward. We had preached anti-militarism for so long, we were so fundamentally anti-militaristic, that we wouldn't have gone simply to wage war. That was something we couldn't envisage. Today, without for a moment regretting it, I can see we wanted to go too fast, wanted to leap from one century to the future in a matter of days . . .

Not all the columns originated in Barcelona. One, swinging up from Tortosa, close to the mouth of the Ebro, was led by a Saragossa CNT leader, Saturnino

CAROD, who had escaped from the city soon after dawn on 19 July. Meeting in a wood on the banks of the Ebro outside the city the night before, members of the CNT local federation and regional committee had agreed that delegates should be sent out to raise the rural masses. CAROD, propaganda secretary of the regional committee for Aragon, Rioja and Navarre, had been delegated to raise lower Aragon, his native area, where he had spent much of the previous month on a speaking tour.

His absence from the city made him feel out of touch. But the other regional committee members seemed ill-informed, uncertain of what was planned to confront the military uprising when he hurriedly returned to Saragossa. Contrary to what was often thought, the libertarian movement in the city, he reflected, was not as strong, did not have the revolutionary consciousness it was credited with. A joint CNT–UGT delegation went to the civil governor to ask for arms: 10,000 rifles were promised, never arrived. Masses of CNT members, building workers in the main, gathered in the Plaza de San Miguel, waiting. When he went to summon the republicans to take action, he found them playing cards in their Ateneo; by the time he returned to insist more forcefully, he saw them being led away under arrest by assault guards who had joined the military. The masses began to break up and disappear. 'The republicans were more frightened of arming the CNT masses than of the military . . . ' As he left the city, he walked past military and civilian patrols which had taken over the streets.

On an improvised stage in front of the CNT branch office in Tortosa, he gave a speech calling for volunteers. Between 3,000 and 4,000 responded, the majority peasants.

—I told them quite plainly what the objectives were: to defeat the enemy in open country, to crush the military uprising, to fight for the republic – not to make the revolution, let me stress that . . .

No llores, madre, no llores
Porque a la guerra tus hijos van,
¡Qué importa que el cuerpo muera
Si al fin el alma triunfará
en la Eternidad!

Don't cry, mother, don't cry
Because your sons are going to war,
What matter that the body perish
When the soul triumphs at last
in Eternity.

Old Carlist song

SOMOSIERRA

Four field pieces fired from the lorries on which they had been roped down, the barrels resting on the cabin roofs. Another four had been unloaded and were firing from the ground at Somosierra, the main pass through the Guadarrama between Burgos and Madrid. The column which had left Pamplona six days before for Madrid had turned back to take the pass. Antonio IZU's spirits had dropped; turning back? All he and his fellow *requetés* wanted was to go forward, ever forward. What did it matter if Guadalajara on the column's route had been taken by the reds? They'd storm it! But General Mola thought differently.

They had spent a day in Aranda de Duero. Rafael GARCIA SERRANO and his falangist comrades had been sent to a convent for food. 'Eat all you want, my son,' a friar had said to him, 'for you are going to die for religion and us poor friars.' 'Yes, father, and for the revolution.' The friar hadn't liked that, they'd had a bit of an argument. He wouldn't deny the falangist revolution. The sight of a group of CNT workers and peasants being brought prisoner to the barracks in Logroño, where the column had met some shooting, had saddened him. Why weren't these workers on their side, like the Navarrese peasantry, he wondered. The Falange stood for them, not for those bourgeois CEDA supporters who stood on their balconies and cheered the column's arrival. But the workers hadn't understood, some of them even had the guts to shout '*¡Viva la República!*' as they were brought in; the falangists grabbed their rifles then and made sure they shouted '*¡Arriba España!*'

IZU had slept in the coal lorry in which he had left Pamplona. After mass, he and his companions made for a local bar which he saw, as they approached, was being sacked. By now such sights surprised him less than a week before. 'It's the blue shirts again,' he thought, remembering a nasty scene in Alfaro, a socialist stronghold in Logroño, which the column took without loss, on its second day out. Two right-wingers had been killed there the day before. He had been ordered to escort the local *guardia civil* corporal to bring in a man, and as they took him through the streets under arrest the villagers cried, 'Kill him, he's the worst.' In the plaza, the *guardia* corporal took a stick from an officer's hand and hit the man a tremendous blow over the head from behind. The man crumpled up dead. 'The things that happened there were shameful. The blue shirts were mainly responsible, going from house to house looking for people.' Twelve villagers had been shot.

The cannon boomed. Forces from Burgos – falangists, *requetés* and infantry – were sharing the attack with the Pamplona column. Among the *requetés* were youths of fourteen and grandfathers of sixty. The order came to advance.

Rafael GARCIA SERRANO heard strange whistling sounds.

—'Rafael, how the goldfinches are singing this morning,' said a friendly *requeté*. 'Goldfinches?' The noise did sound a bit like that. 'Are there goldfinches here?' The *requeté* began to laugh. I realized then what it was. Almost immediately, a soldier advancing beside me was shot in the stomach. We gathered round as a *requeté* doctor gave him first aid. Would he be all right, we asked; he was the first casualty and it impressed us. He died. We continued to advance . . .

Militancies 4

ANTONIO IZU

Carlist peasant

The grey barrier of the Guadarrama loomed before him. Even Napoleon, they said, hadn't been able to take the pass in a frontal attack. He heard the stray bullets whistle, remembered the Carlist veterans' tales; he'd been dreaming of nothing else since he was old enough to remember. His grandfather had fought in the last Carlist war, had told him how he'd made the liberals run. That war had been lost, all three Carlist wars had ended in defeat. Now, at last, the chance for revenge had come. They had been waiting a long time.

—Carrying the need in our hearts and souls, waiting for the opportunity. When it came, we grabbed a rifle and shouted, 'Let's get on with it.' . . .

Carlism was in his blood, he was conceived a Carlist, born one. You could ask most people why they were Carlists and they'd reply, 'Because I am.' It was the ordinary people, the lower classes in Navarre, who were Carlists. The rich and the intelligentsia didn't belong; Carlism was a popular movement.

His father had been a fervent believer in the cause, one of those who thought that everyone above a sergeant in the army, a canon in the church, should be swept out of office as a parasite. A bit of an anarchist at heart, he thought. In his native village of Echauri, 14 km from Pamplona, the family had 45 hectares of land, a pair of oxen, a couple of horses, a cow; they were comfortably off. The majority of the 540 villagers were smallholders with 6 to 10 hectares. There was only one republican, the local vet, and he soon became disillusioned. The village was almost solidly Carlist . . .

Ahead of him, on the road, a squadron of insurgent cavalry appeared, galloping along the verge towards Somosierra. At the head of the pass he could hear the artillery pounding; the going was beginning to get rough. It seemed like the Carlist wars all over again.

¡Viva el follón!
¡Viva el follón!
¡Viva el follón!
Bien organizado
Porque con él
Pide justicia todo el requeté.

Long Live the shindy . . .
That's well organized
Because that's the way
All the *requetés* demand justice.

That was the way they were going to make the Carlist revolution. People said Carlism, with its motto *Dios, Patria y Rey* (God, Fatherland and King), was ultra right wing. What a mistake! Carlism was neither of left nor right, it was simply Carlist, Catholic, and revolutionary. They were going to stir things up, kick up a shindy. Not to make a revolution of left or right, not to make a political revolution, no. But a revolution which, after a century's oppression, satisfied the innate need all Carlists felt to explode. They'd set off for war with the ideals of a religious crusade. The peasantry expected no other benefit from the cause.[1]

—What we saw was the harm others would do us if Carlism didn't exist. Defensive, it was a movement of indignation and displeasure with the way politics were being conducted. A matter of tradition. But not of going back, enthroning an absolute monarch. Far from it! . . .

The king he would restore would be like a manager; the people would decide the laws. The king would represent a stable executive while the people elected a Cortes which would legislate and demarcate his powers. 'I want a king who will drink from the wineskin with me,' the *requetés* said. None of this protocol and riding round in a carriage. 'A king must be like one of us villagers . . .'

The people had to be free; that was the essence, the popular meaning of the *fueros*[2] of Navarre. They expressed the people's innate refusal to submit; freedom from Spanish centralism, but not freedom from Spain.

Carlist social policy was a healthy one, IZU thought; the trouble was, hardly anyone knew much about it. In essence, it considered that there were two fundamental factors to production: capital and labour. The capitalist provided the former, the worker the latter. As production was shared, so the profits (after deduction for depreciation and interest on capital) should be equally shared. The shame was that no one attempted to practise the doctrine –

In front of him a cavalry man fell wounded, there were several dead horses. Things were beginning to look tough; the advance continued without pause.

It was curious, the republic he was fighting had been welcomed with widespread joy in Navarre. The Alfonsine monarchy had fallen at last! But within a month the republic had failed; when the churches and convents were burnt in Madrid and the south it was the end as far as they were concerned. The Navarrese were profoundly religious; it was a rare family which hadn't at least one, if not more, of its members in the church or a religious order. No churches had been fired in Navarre; yet, not infrequently, priests and friars were insulted in the streets. Not so long ago, the parish priest of Alsasua was bearing the *viaticum* to a dying parishioner when a group started to insult him. He handed

1. The Carlist revolution was outlined by Jaime del Burgo, president of the Carlist student association AET (Agrupación Escolar Tradicionalista) in Pamplona: 'Reaction is to return to the situation immediately anterior to the present. Revolution tends to restore a situation much more ancient, which we mean to be the traditional regime . . . the 16th century . . . For nothing in the world do we wish to return to what existed before 14 April (1931). Neither its principles nor its men; neither constitutional monarchy nor anti-foral centralism; neither dictatorial tyranny nor irresponsible governments which make pacts with the enemy. Thus, we are not reactionaries. We seek other, more Spanish, more Christian principles which accord better with the class spirit . . . These principles are old ones: a corporative, guild organization, which is Spanish . . .' (from an article of 16 February 1934 in *a.e.t.*, cited in the same author's *Requetés en Navarra antes del alzamiento*, San Sebastian, 1939).

2. The self-governing rights which Navarre retained when its kingdom joined the Spanish monarchy in the sixteenth century, and which, in modified form, were recognized by treaty at the end of the first Carlist war in 1841 when Navarre lost its status of kingdom.

the eucharist to the sacristan and said: 'You look after these, I'm going to look after them.' He soon put them to flight.

—Not that Carlists defended the clergy because they were clergy. Oh no! Carlists were capable of stoning priests out of their villages if they became friendly with the rich and didn't carry out their obligations to their parishioners. The Carlist defended religion, not the priest because he wore a cassock . . .

It wasn't like that elsewhere, he was soon to learn. The hatred of the church in other regions might be engendered in part by the local intelligentsia, but in greater part the clergy itself was to blame.

—There wasn't merely a difference between the Basque and Navarrese clergy and the clergy in the rest of Spain; the gulf was so wide it went beyond being a difference. The communists in Navarre were more religious than the priests in Castile. Does that seem a joke? It was the truth. In Navarre, a communist would go to mass, confess and take communion at least once a year which is what the church demands. In Castile, as we saw during the war, the person who didn't go to mass was the priest . . .

It became a matter for comment among the *requetés* stationed in Old and New Castile. When they talked to a local priest, as they often did, they were always struck by one thing: he never boasted about his church, never displayed pride in how well it was kept up. And with reason: the churches were generally run-down, poor, dirty, badly looked after.

—But almost everywhere, the priest had his house and his irrigated garden. It was the latter he boasted about: the crops he was growing and harvesting. Of spiritual matters priests didn't speak; of their plots they had plenty to say . . .

In such circumstances, where the priest made no effort to attract people to church, all you could expect was indifference. And that was what he found. The villagers' lack of education was another cause. In his own village there was only one illiterate youth; in Castile it was a different matter. In education, in farming, in everything, Castile seemed to him fifty to a hundred years behind Navarre. Though the people might be indifferent to the church, they could very well hate the clergy. 'The priesthood, from what I was to see in Castile during the war, completely failed in its task of providing spiritual leadership.' But these depressing discoveries still lay in the future.

The roar of artillery was closer, louder. He gripped his rifle, they were nearly at the top. He had not fired a shot. Exhausted, thirsty, he looked for water, digging his hempsoled sandal into the rushes to drink the muddy water that oozed out. The reds had made a big mistake in defending only the road through the pass and a couple of heights instead of the whole range. They reached the top.

Quickly realizing their error, the enemy began to attack. Taking cover behind outcrops of rock, the *requetés* held them off. Their captain waved; leaping up, they ran forward, chasing the dozen enemy militiamen for a couple of kilometres towards the pass. Dark stopped further advance, and they settled down to sleep on the open ground. His company had suffered not a single casualty in the attack.

The pass was captured; the following day the insurgents consolidated their victory by an advance on the Madrid flank of the mountain range, in which several villages were captured. In one, La Acebeda, Antonio IZU was depressed by the poverty he saw when he was ordered to search the houses. Beds without sheets, covered only with old blankets, doorways so low he had to stoop to get inside; the relative prosperity of Navarre seemed a painfully long way away. As though scourged by the poverty, the *requetés* came down with diarrhoea and a doctor diagnosed incipient scurvy. For nearly ten days since leaving Pamplona they had lived on cold rations, sardines and bread. Now hot food and supplies of lemon juice were brought up to the front.

The insurgents pushed to within 300 metres of the reservoir supplying Madrid's water before being held; any further approach drew heavy fire from the opposite side.

—A year later, on warm nights, I used to go down to the reservoir and swim. As far as I could see it would have been possible to cut off the water supplies or to have poisoned them, but nothing of the sort was ever attempted . . .

*

The insurgents held two of the three major passes in the Guadarrama; but they could not move their line forward towards Madrid. The lightning strike had failed; now it was necessary to envisage a longer offensive. Three days after the uprising, General Mola warned monarchists in Burgos that there was sufficient rifle ammunition for only a few weeks' fighting. The smallest aid from France to the republic would be sufficient to swing the balance, he said.[1] Mola needed 10 million rounds urgently. Monarchist emissaries were dispatched to Germany and Italy; meanwhile, he ordered his staff to draw up plans for a possible withdrawal north.

Franco, who had flown from the Canaries to Morocco to take command of the Army of Africa, had moved faster and higher. Within a few hours of his reaching Morocco on 19 July, an emissary had left for Italy; and on 23 July, while Mola's emissaries set off by road from Burgos, Franco's mission departed by air for Germany in a requisitioned Lufthansa airliner. Mola's men, after a stop-over in Paris, reached Berlin on 28 July and got stuck in the unhelpful bureaucracy of the German Foreign Office; Franco's mission went through the Nazi party and by the night of 25 July, barely a day and a half after leaving Morocco, was talking to Hitler. A little known German businessman and the chief of the diminutive Nazi party in Spanish Morocco – no Spaniard was present – presented Franco's petition to the Führer. After short reflection Hitler agreed; aid – more than Franco's limited requests – would be dispatched secretly to Franco alone, in the probable belief that he would be the final leader. By 28 July, Franco knew he was assured of German aid; two days later the first Italian assistance arrived.[2]

In Rome, Franco's emissary had been less successful; it required the arrival of Mola's two representatives, the monarchists Antonio Goicoechea and Pedro

1. See J. I. Escobar, *Asi empezó* (Madrid, 1974), pp. 56–7.
2. See A. Viñas, *La Alemania nazi y el 18 de julio* (Madrid, 1974).

SAINZ RODRIGUEZ, to clinch matters. It was they who, with Carlist representatives, had secured promises of arms and cash from Mussolini for an uprising two years earlier. The promises were now to be made good.

The only problem which SAINZ RODRIGUEZ, who was left in Rome to negotiate, encountered was that of finding a legal method for the Italians to provide military aid. While perfectly prepared to supply arms and planes, they were concerned lest this appear to contravene the Non-Intervention pact which had just been agreed on between the major European nations and the Soviet Union.

—If they were seen to break the pact, they feared the open intervention of France and Britain. That would be detrimental to our cause, they insisted. For that reason it was necessary to find some way of camouflaging the aid – although everyone knew it was being given . . .

As part of the camouflage, the Italian foreign minister, Count Ciano, initiated a curious procedure. SAINZ RODRIGUEZ had to visit him at his office in the greatest secrecy at 7 a.m. to discuss the war in Spain.

—But when, in the evening, I went to dine at the Casino, he would come in with a great number of friends and sit down openly with me and drink champagne. One day I asked him to explain. Ah, he said, people thought I was just a visiting Spanish professor and paid me no attention. 'Well,' I said, 'that's a strange idea of secrecy' . . .

The Italians immediately dispatched twelve Savoia 81s to Morocco to help airlift the Army of Africa to Seville, nine of which arrived safely. Franco meanwhile sent a freighter, the *Montecillo*, which succeeded in running the republican fleet's blockade, to Vigo with rifle ammunition for Mola.

The republican government had appealed to the French Popular Front government for aid almost at the same time. The final outcome was very different. Initially, the French – both government and private arms dealers – provided some seventy planes; but then, fearful of splitting the Popular Front and alienating Britain, the French government on 2 August proposed a Non-Intervention pact. Faced with German rearmament – Hitler had marched unopposed into the Rhineland but four months earlier – the French socialist prime minister, Léon Blum, feared the prospect of France's isolation. At the same time he could not afford an ally of Italy and Germany on his south-western flank. Britain had already unilaterally banned the sale of arms to Spain on 31 July; on 8 August, without waiting to determine the intentions of Germany, Italy or Portugal, France closed her frontier with Spain to military traffic. The effect was to deny the Spanish government its right under international law to purchase arms abroad for its self-defence. The capitalist order – the USA preaching non-involvement but permitting large quantities of oil (a 'non-war' material under the Neutrality Act) to reach the insurgents – had made its choice: 'fascist' counter-revolution was, for the moment, less dangerous to it than 'communist' revolution. Parliamentary democracy would not confront international fascism for the sake of an unstable member whose bourgeois order was threatened from below.

In various villages of which I have heard, right-wing people are being held prisoner and threatened with barbarous fates. I want to make known my system with regard to this. For every person killed I shall kill ten and perhaps even exceed this proportion.

The leaders of these village movements may believe that they can flee; they are wrong. Even if they hide beneath the earth, I shall dig them out; even if they're already dead, I shall kill them again.

General Queipo de Llano
(Broadcast over Seville radio, 25 July 1936)

The movement we are proclaiming has nothing in common with petty politics; it is a nationalist Spanish movement with the sole aim of saving Spain. It is said that the movement is against the working class; precisely the opposite is the case. We are in favour of the humble class and the middle class . . . Fear nothing, Spanish working people. Our movement is dangerous only for those who live like princes, for those who use trade union funds without rendering accounts, for those who do nothing but attack the republic. Something has to be done rapidly to save the republic.

General Franco
(Broadcast over the *guardia civil* radio, Tetuán, 22 July 1936)

I order and command that anyone caught inciting others to strike, or striking himself, shall be shot immediately.

Don't be frightened.

If someone tries to compel you, I authorize you to kill him like a dog and you will be free of all responsibility . . .

General Queipo de Llano
(Broadcast over Seville radio, 22 July 1936)

ANDALUSIA

The insurgents held the cities of Seville, Córdoba, Cádiz, and Granada, but not the villages and townships in the surrounding countryside where the situation was still more than uncertain for their cause. In some *pueblos*, a secret civil war, unknown and unheard of by the forces of either camp, was being waged.

BAENA Córdoba province

Its whitewashed houses rising up the side of a hill, Baena was a large agro-township, some 20 km from Castro del Río[1] on the same road between Córdoba and Granada. Its topography, rising from the lower flanks of the hill, where the 8,000-odd day-labourers lived, to the main square at the top where, beneath the ruins of a castle and the main church, the well-to-do landowners had their houses, represented a social pyramid of its 21,000 inhabitants. It was, in many ways, typical of latifundist Andalusia.

On 19 July, the *guardia civil* lieutenant, on orders from the military governor of Córdoba, proclaimed martial law. The town was already paralysed by its second labourers' strike since April which was now in its fourth week. The wheat harvest stood unreaped in the fields. Soon news came that labourers were assaulting the *cortijos* looking for arms, and inciting all the permanent hired hands to join them.

—They told us, 'The fascists have taken the town. We have to attack them by surprise,' Miguel CARAVACA, a permanent hand who had been forced to join, recalled. Anyone who had any sort of work implement, a sickle, a hoe, a wooden pitchfork was to stay in the countryside. Those who had nothing were to slip into the town, get an axe, a stick, anything and return . . .

As they were setting out, a lorry and a couple of cars appeared with *guardias* and civilian volunteers. The confrontation was immediate and bloody. Three workers were killed, and three *guardias*, including the lieutenant, wounded. Miguel CARAVACA fled: 'I wanted nothing to do with all this.'

That night, the ninety civil guards and civilian supporters of the uprising took up armed positions in the Telephone Exchange building, *guardia civil* barracks, castle and hospital at the top of the town, as well as in one or two outposts on its western flanks. In the preceding months, the *guardia civil* lieutenant, a former Foreign Legion officer, in collaboration with the land-owners' and farmers' association, had been arming as many people of 'law and order' as he could. Recently, the association, on his advice, had purchased 4,000 rounds of rifle ammunition.

It was not long before they were under attack. When the labourers couldn't advance up the streets because of the defenders' fire, they broke holes through the inside walls of the terraced houses and tunnelled their way to the top. Very few had firearms.

—And those they had were so old they must have come from the Cuban war of 1898. Most of them had bamboo canes with a metal point at the end, axes,

1. See Militancies 3, pp. 94–7.

sickles, wooden pitchforks, weeding hoes. When one of them found an old sabre he came out with it as though he were going to conquer the world . . .

As soon as he had heard the first shooting, Manuel CASTRO, a baker's son, had hurried home from the family's smallholding and bolted the door of his house. He knew things were going to be bad. It was the workers against the bosses. Hatred had reached boiling point. For the past eighteen months the labourers had been demanding higher wages, and many landowners had stopped working their land, saying life was impossible. That, he remembered, was when people started to have arguments from which violence sprang. Wearing a tie was enough to arouse hatred; it was a symbol of someone who didn't have to earn a day-wage. The labourers thought that everyone ought to have to work for a living, ought to be equal. That's what they were fighting for.

—For three days they tunnelled their way up. They were wild, they were gaining ground, they thought they would win. The women were the worst. They shouted at the men to get to the top. 'Let's get the fascists, *granujas*, they've killed one of ours.' On the fourth day they reached our home . . .

The family was ordered out, hands in air; a shot was fired which ripped through his mother's dress but didn't hit her. They were marched off between ranks of men and women carrying every imaginable sort of weapon. Red flags were everywhere, on bits of cane stuck out of windows and balconies. 'More red than the anarchists' red and black', he observed. His father wasn't on the left, belonged to no trade union, but neither was he a known right-winger. The crowd wanted to take them to the eighteenth-century convent of San Francisco, which they had made their headquarters and where they were keeping hostage many of the wives, children and relatives of the besieged right-wingers.

—'To San Francisco,' shouted some in the crowd. 'She's a good woman,' shouted others who knew my mother, 'let her go where she wants.' A swineherd, whom later I learnt was on the revolutionary committee, intervened in our favour. Finally, we were allowed to go free . . .

After five days of fighting, the labourers reached the heights and set fire to the church, only to be driven back by a hand-grenade attack. But the right-wingers' situation was desperate. Water, electricity and the telephone had been cut off by the besiegers; morale was affected by knowing that wives and children were in the attackers' hands. The lieutenant tried to get a message out; it was captured. The attackers sent a note demanding the defenders' surrender. In vain. They dispatched a group of women hostages, followed by armed men, towards the square. Before the women could open their mouths, the lieutenant fired his revolver, the bullets ricocheting at their feet. Screaming, the women fled back to the San Francisco convent.

A priest was dragged down the street, a halter round his neck, by men who were insulting him. A few minutes later, Manuel CASTRO, who witnessed the scene, heard the sound of a shot. One of the men had fired his shotgun in the priest's face, blinding him. He was taken to San Francisco, shot again and burnt.

—Why kill a priest? Because they were close to the rich, if only because they had to get money from the rich to be able to give alms to the poor. But the poor always believed that a part of the money, the best part perhaps, remained in the priest's hands. There were many priests who knew nothing of the labourers' lives, who lived aloof from the people . . .

But the majority of the workers didn't want priests killed, he was sure. In the first couple of days of fighting, the labourers killed only a dozen of the town's rich.

—And there was every justification for killing them, they were the harshest of the right-wing ruling-class landowners, the forty or fifty to whom the labourers had to go, cap in hand, to ask for work. And there would have been no more deaths, I'm convinced, if the *guardias* and the gentry hadn't resisted. It was this which drove the labourers wild. They were determined to take the town and make it their own . . .

At dawn on 28 July, after nine days of fighting, the attackers reached the heights, capturing the hospital from which they could fire down on the defenders. The lieutenant summoned a meeting of the most influential among them: to resist was to meet an honourable death, to surrender was to be put to death vilely. He spoke of patriotism, bravery, asked who would stand by his side. All those present agreed; with tears in his eyes, the officer embraced them.

While selecting positions to renew their offensive, the attackers did not immediately press home their advantage. It was noon. Looking up at the sierra from the Telephone Exchange, the defenders saw Moroccan troops, legionaries and civil guards on the heights. It was an expeditionary force from Córdoba, sent not to relieve the town but to take it, for they believed, having no news, that it was in the hands of the left. Seeing that fighting was in progress, Col. Sáenz de Buruaga ordered two cannons to fire over the town. Shooting stopped and the attackers, now suddenly become defenders, began to withdraw. As the Moroccan troops entered they began rounding up labourers and taking them to the square at the top.

—Our landowner's son vouched for us, recalled Miguel CARAVACA, and the lieutenant stamped our handkerchiefs and we tied them round our arms to show we were free . . .

Not all were as lucky. According to one account, thirty-eight men were executed in the square that afternoon.[1]

—The Moors shot the men; some of them were eating tins of sardines when they were given the order to fire. Not that many men were shot in the square, perhaps a dozen or so. The rest were taken down to the cemetery wall, CASTRO remembered. I counted seven lorry-loads, each of about eight or ten men. In all, close on 100 were executed . . .

1. Lt F. Rivas Gómez, 'La defensa de Baena', *Revista de Estudios históricos de la guardia civil*, no. 9, 1972. The author, a native of the town and a *guardia civil* officer, drew his researches from both sides. 'There can be no doubt that injustices were committed (in the summary executions), for the slightest accusation on the part of a defender was sufficient for a man to be shot.' Many inhabitants continue to believe that the repression was even costlier in lives.

That night, knowing that all was lost, the remaining defenders in San Francisco, which darkness had obliged the military to postpone taking, slaughtered their hostages. It was an indescribable massacre; eighty-one people, including women and children, were killed.

—Massacred not by the mass of local labourers, but by a few men, possibly outsiders, who managed to escape during the night . . .

Shattered by the tragedy, the insurgents, their sympathizers and the uncommitted tried to recover. The column returned to Córdoba, leaving a reinforcement of twenty-seven *guardias* in the town. For a week Baena seemed safe.

—Then, at dawn on 5 August, we woke to find the *pueblo* surrounded and under attack by republican militia. General Miaja's forces had advanced from Jaén, consolidated positions in neighbouring Castro del Río, and were now on the heights above us. Very rapidly, they took the castle ruins from which they could fire on the defenders who were again concentrated in the main square. One of them asked a friend to shoot him rather than let him fall into the hands of the 'reds' . . .

There was desperate hand-to-hand fighting in which the republicans were temporarily held off. The next morning, as the besieged prepared to die fighting, the republican bugles were heard sounding the order to withdraw. An attack had been launched on Castro by the insurgents from Córdoba, and the militia hurried to its defence. Baena was saved a second time. Although the front was never more than a few kilometres away for the rest of the war, from 6 August the town remained in insurgent hands.

The human cost of the three weeks fighting was twenty-two right-wing besieged and fifty-nine left-wing besiegers killed. The total of eighty-one combat deaths compared with a minimum of 119, and possible maximum of 180 people, killed by both sides in the repression.

ARAGON

At the same time as the second attack was made on Baena, Saturnino CAROD's column was engaging in its first hard battle in Muniesa, 80 km by road from Saragossa. Throughout the blazing hot summer days the column had advanced through lower Aragon, gathering new members in each liberated village, skirmishing with an enemy who, rather than defend isolated villages, preferred to withdraw towards Saragossa. Progress was marked by a number of incidents. In the village of Calaceite, the church was fired after CAROD had placed the keys in the townhall, saying that the church now belonged to the people. The CNT leader gathered the column and villagers in the square.

—'You are burning the churches without thinking of the grief you are causing your mothers, sisters, daughters, parents, in whose veins flows Christian, Catholic blood. Do not believe that by burning churches you are going to change that blood and that tomorrow everyone will feel himself, herself an atheist. On the contrary! The more you violate their consciences, the more they will side with the church. Moreover, the immense majority of you are believers at heart' . . .

He demanded that all lives and all property – not only religious – be respected. The column's task was to fight the enemy in open combat, not take justice into its hands.

Alcañiz, Calanda, Alcorisa – taken with a phone call ordering the right-wingers to come out of the village with republican flags – Montalbán, the progress was steady. In honour of a *guardia civil* lieutenant who had joined the column with some eighty guards and who had become his military adviser, CAROD re-named his force the Carod-Ferrer column. In Montalbán he was on the point of executing two of the column's men – common prisoners released from gaol with political prisoners – for theft. They were saved by the pleas of the women who had been robbed. Turning northwards, the column headed directly for Saragossa. In the township of Muniesa the situation changed. A two-day battle cost the column heavy casualties.

—It made me aware that we couldn't go on fighting like this. There had to be more organization. The column was very poorly armed – shotguns, a few hunting rifles, pistols, knives – but the enemy wasn't that much better armed either. In all truth, the rich, the right-wingers defended their positions in Muniesa with great courage, retreating only when we had inflicted heavy casualties. On both sides we were Spanish, had the same pride and arrogance, the same determination to defend honour with lives . . .

He started to re-organize the column, to 'militarize' it into smaller units with a command structure. The result was a near disaster; the militiamen abandoned the column and he was left with almost the *guardia civil* alone.

—It was understandable. For many years I had spoken to the peasants of Aragon not only about their problems – problems I knew because I had lived them – but of ideas. Opposition to capitalism, the state, the church, the military. They drank in these ideas; and now, when the revolution was happening, they couldn't understand when I spoke of the need for militarization, of the need to respect republican institutions and political parties, the need to organize new town councils, new organs of authority. They simply left the column. But in their home villages great pressure was put on them to return. Many came back. I addressed them: 'You can rejoin the column, but first you will have to do a fortnight's training. And your instructors will be the *guardia civil*.' Imagine telling a CNT militant he had to accept orders from a *guardia*! But I wasn't going to back down. 'In accepting, you will be demonstrating your willingness to become good combatants.' They accepted the training . . .

After the hard-won victory at Muniesa, the column was able to advance only some 30 km further north before being halted close to Belchite. In front of them the militiamen now found an army which had fortified a series of strategic townships barring the routes to Saragossa. Belchite was one of them. Consulting the rearguard, CAROD was told to establish a front, to dig in. He had great trouble persuading the militiamen to dig trenches on the 100 km of front he had to defend; the prospect of not advancing irritated them and they often organized their own assaults on the enemy fortifications which were – on both sides – a series of discontinuous strongpoints covering the rough terrain as adequately as possible. Through binoculars, from advanced positions, CAROD could see his house on the outskirts of the city, where his wife and two young sons were in hiding.[1]

Lack of military experience was bound to tell against the militiamen, most of them fighting for the first time in their lives, in open battle.

—'Come on – forward!' we shouted, and tried to advance without cover, in groups, Josep CERCOS remembered of his first major attack on the village of Azaila. Pinned down by a machine-gun in the church tower, I quickly came to realize the need of organization and tactics . . .

More than set-backs on the ground, however, it was air raids which demoralized the militiamen, as Narciso JULIAN, the Madrid communist railwayman who had enrolled in a Catalan communist-led column, discovered.

—We were so naïve that when the planes came over we thought they must be ours and stood up to wave. The bombs started to fall. We were on railway flat cars loaded with dynamite. Everyone, including the anarchist machine-gunner, leapt for cover; I never saw him again. The engine driver was the only one to show any control; he shouted at me to lie on my back and fire at the planes while he held the machine-gun's tripod. The planes veered away . . .

So many militiamen left the column after the raid that they had to remain in the township of Grañén to reorganize. Del Barrio, the column leader, announced that many of the anarchists amongst the militiamen wanted to leave. JULIAN, who had been caught by the uprising in Barcelona where he had gone to attend the Popular Olympiad, was given the invidious task of telling them they could not leave with their arms. He set up two machine-guns in a house facing the townhall.

—The heart went out of us all when we saw the numbers coming to hand in their names to leave. They weren't only anarchists by any means, nor did all anarchists leave. Without exception, those who wanted to go refused to surrender their arms, even when told that hundreds upon hundreds of peasants were waiting to use them. Finally, I pointed at the two machine-guns. One of the men threatened to shoot me all the same. 'Go ahead, not one of you will be left alive.' Trueba, the political commissar, harangued them and at last they handed in their weapons. Then they were put on two trains and sent back to Barcelona . . .

It was an air-raid also that apparently stopped the most direct and closest threat to Saragossa – Durruti's column, advancing along the main road from Barcelona, the vanguard of which reached to within 20 km of the city.[2]

1. In October, he was able to arrange their escape across the lines. The discontinuous front made it relatively easy to cross, and the CNT organized the escape of considerable numbers of left-wing militants from the city.

2. The raids, minor affairs by later standards, were the work of a few insurgent planes from Logroño; some of the first bombs on both sides were dropped by hand. Although the republic retained the best part of the antiquated air force, insurgent use of their few planes was effective against militiamen who crowded on roads at the beginning. On 20 August the insurgents on the Córdoba front stopped the republic's first major offensive by bombing and machine-gunning one of the attacking columns on the road not far from Castro del Río. Italian Savoias took part in the raid (see J. M. Martínez Bande, *La campaña de Andalucía*, p. 62).

All the columns, organized by the different political organizations, were brought to a halt by the stiffening opposition. In Barcelona, Ricardo SANZ, Durruti's companion, was in charge of supplying the Aragon front. Every night the column leaders telephoned him.

—All of them had more men than arms, more wounded than ambulances, more shortages than supplies. Arms, ammunition and supply waggons – everything needed for waging war – was scarce. We started to collect up the arms that remained in the rear. Arms, arms, arms! Those *cabrones*, the French, with their Non-Intervention that kept the arms from reaching us . . .

The POUM and CAROD's column received a consignment of Russian Crimean war rifles whose barrels, after two or three rounds, split open; armourers sawed off the ends, leaving the rifle 5 or 10 cm shorter. Were important stocks of arms being kept in the rear while men fought and died at the front with these antiquated weapons? The Durruti column dispatched a group to Sabadell, the Manchester of Spain, close to Barcelona, where they took 400 to 500 rifles and two machine-guns,[1] from trade union headquarters and political offices. Neither CAROD nor Jordi ARQUER, political commissar of the POUM column in the Sierra de Alcubierre, believed that significant quantities of arms were being held back. There was a general shortage of all weapons.

—That was the main reason for not being able to launch a major offensive. But it wasn't the only one. There was no overall plan – I don't believe there was a military officer in Catalonia capable of drawing one up; there was no proper coordination between the columns, and sometimes there wasn't even communication between us, ARQUER recalled. Unless Col. Villalba called all the column chiefs to a meeting, no one knew what the other was up to . . .

Worse, there were rivalries between the columns. A middle-aged CNT peasant, Fernando ARAGON, in the village of Angüés, only a few kilometres behind the line on the Huesca front, wryly observed them. The anarchist *Roja y Negra* column was on one side of the village, the POUM militia on the other.

—When the former went into action, the latter sat back with their hands in their pockets, laughing. When the POUM was in combat the anarchists, I have to admit, did the same. That's no way to fight a war, let alone win it. They should have got together to fight the common enemy . . .

Although they had failed to capture their major objectives – Aragon's provincial capitals – the columns had taken nearly three quarters of the region and advanced 100 km beyond the borders of Catalonia. This was a greater achievement than any other militia forces managed in a few weeks. But now,

1. According to a libertarian youth member who was in the group, the choice of Sabadell was not accidental: the *treintista* union was the only one in Catalonia not to return to the CNT fold at the start of the war, joining the UGT. The estimate by Abad de Santillán, the libertarian writer and member of the anti-fascist militia committee, that 60,000 rifles were kept in the rear, seems exaggerated. It is doubtful whether that many rifles had been seized in the first place; the anarchists, moreover, preferred pistols and hand-grenades for street-fighting as was demonstrated in Barcelona in May 1937.

as though the momentum were spent, the columns dug in, took root and remained. For nearly a year there was no major offensive on the 600-km front running from the Pyrenees to Teruel. The same could be said of some other fronts; but it was here that the CNT's greatest weight lay, backed by the resources (such as they were) of Catalan industry. Were the militiamen who rebelled against 'digging in' not instinctively right? Would not the 'people in arms' lose the initiative by adopting the enemy's strategy? Would a war of position not inevitably fail to develop an alternative, perforce revolutionary, strategy which would rely on mobility, harassment, erosion – *irregular warfare*? The example of their Ukrainian hero, Nestor Makhno, whose partisans fought white and red armies separately and sometimes simultaneously for three years, appeared to have been forgotten. Though it was the libertarians' only hope, they failed to seize it. In practice, the priorities of revolution and war were settled – even before they became the subject of polemic – in favour of 'war first' by the Aragon columns. To say this is to say no more than that revolution and war remained, if not two separate concepts, then two separate practices. At the front 'war', in the rear 'revolution', such was the paradox, as we shall see.

ONLY BY MAKING THE SOCIAL REVOLUTION WILL FASCISM BE CRUSHED

Solidaridad Obrera, CNT, headline
(Barcelona, 17 July 1936)

The Revolution, companions, is triumphing. We must be on the alert, however, not to be tricked out of the conquests won with our blood and sacrifice . . .

This is not the time to respect classic law, classic justice. The law, justice and history must be structured by the ongoing revolution. Almost nothing of what exists today is worthy of respect . . . That is why [the working class] must administer the triumphant revolution, a right it will not renounce, that it is prepared to defend arms in hand . . .

Statement of the newly formed PSUC,
unified socialist party of Catalonia – affiliated to the Comintern
(28 July 1936)

BARCELONA

In the streets, the revolutionary ferment was ceaseless, 'dreamlike, hallucinating', in the memory of a socialist youth treasury official, Alejandro VITORIA.

—All of us, whatever organization we belonged to, had a tremendous urge to participate. Somehow – I can't remember how – I found myself in an office in the Vía Layetana redeeming pawn tickets. The working-class women were streaming in, and we stamped their tickets and they went out to get back their goods – sewing-machines, mainly. It was a great moment in my life, I was very happy. We were overthrowing bourgeois capitalist values . . .

At the CNT woodworkers' union headquarters they were saying that the people were masters of the situation, the proletarian cause was certain to win now. To sixteen-year-old Eduardo PONS PRADES, listening to his elders, it seemed easy all of a sudden to reach that new world, that terrestrial paradise his libertarian father had so often told him about. It would be enough to change the flags, sing new revolutionary songs, abolish money, hierarchy, egoism, pride – the pillars on which the empire of money was built. 'It wasn't just I, a raw youth, who felt like that; it was the men, the CNT militants who had fought so long and hard in their lives.'

Nor was it only the anarcho-syndicalists who experienced the sense of revolutionary upheaval. Narciso JULIAN, the Madrid communist railwayman, was swept up by the tidal wave.

—It was incredible, the proof in practice of what one knows in theory: the power and strength of the masses when they take to the streets. All one's doubts are suddenly stripped away, doubts about how the working class and the masses are to be organized, how they can make the revolution until they are organized. Suddenly you feel their creative power; you can't imagine how rapidly the masses are capable of organizing themselves. The forms they invent go far beyond anything you've dreamt of, read in books. What was needed now was to seize this initiative, channel it, give it shape . . .

The city blossomed red and black flags, red and black neckerchiefs, banners and slogans. Almost no one wore hats or ties, the bourgeoisie went out in old clothes; overalls were the dress of the day. To move from one working-class *barrio* to another, different passes were needed; the anarcho-syndicalist militants who had taken over their districts accepted none but their own. In the woodworkers' union headquarters just off the Paralelo, with its music-halls, nightclubs and bars, PONS PRADES heard the men discussing what had to be done.

—'Listen, what about all the people who work in these dens of iniquity?' 'We've got to redeem them, educate them so they can have the chance of doing something more worthy.' 'Have you asked them if they want to be redeemed?' 'How can you be so stupid? Would you like to be exploited in that sort of den?' 'No, of course not. But after years at the same thing, it's hard to change.' 'Well, they'll have to. The revolution's first duty is to clean up the place, clean up the people's consciousness – ' 'And what about the customers?' 'Listen, do you think I'm the prophet Isaiah? Or are you trying to take issue with me?' . . .

*

The Catalan libertarian leaders (the CNT local federation, the regional committee) had decided, after President Companys's offer of power, that the libertarian revolution must stand aside for collaboration with the Popular Front forces to defeat the enemy. The dilemma confronting them (as García Oliver later wrote, justifying an outcome which he had forcefully argued against) was of 'collaboration and democracy' on the one hand, or 'totalitarian revolution, a CNT dictatorship' on the other. The former had been elected. Their own newspaper's injunction on the eve of the uprising – that only social revolution could crush fascism – was forgotten or passed off as journalistic rhetoric. Though it was not immediately apparent, the Catalan libertarian leadership had, in effect, taken the same course as the communist party: collaboration, victory in the war first, then 'revolution'. The real – revolutionary – dilemma, as was soon to be revealed, was the libertarians' misconception of the 'dilemma' confronting them.

Outside, in the streets, workplaces and factories, the revolution was being made. Fresh from the local federation meeting which had determined the libertarian choice, Félix CARRASQUER, newly appointed member of the FAI peninsular committee, returned to his *barrio* of Las Corts to find the CNT in control.

—Although we were anti-authoritarian, we were suddenly the only authority there. The local CNT committee had to take over the administration, transport, food supplies, health – in short we were running the *barrio* . . .

Rapidly he found himself involved. The city's main maternity hospital was in his *barrio*, and the Generalitat sent assault guards to remove the nursing nuns to safety. CARRASQUER rushed to the hospital; he had called out all the local armed CNT militants and told them to get the nuns off the buses at gunpoint and back into the hospital.

—I wasn't going to allow 2,000 newborn babies to be left without care. 'These nuns will only leave here when there are nurses to replace them.' They might be falangists for all I knew, but they had to continue working . . .

He took over the hospital administration, not unhappy to leave the FAI peninsular committee where 'everybody seemed to be doing whatever came into their heads, without direction – the same fault as always'. Teacher at a libertarian school in his *barrio*, he now found himself sleeping in what had been the priest's room in the hospital from which, at night, he could hear the nuns praying. He laughed. A libertarian of a different temperament might have ordered them shot, he reflected, but he knew they were just unhappy women.

With every day, the city moved deeper into working-class control. Public transport was running, factories were working, shops were open, food supplies arriving, the telephone operating, gas and water supplies functioning – all to one extent or another organized and run by their respective workers. How had this happened? The leading CNT committees had put out no such order.

Luis SANTACANA, a CNT militant, worked at España Industrial, which, with 2,500 workers, was one of the largest textile factories in Catalonia. The day after the fighting was over, his union told him and a few other militants to return to the factory. When they arrived they found the management and directors were not there; only a few clerks and book-keepers had turned up.

—We were confronted with the problem of getting the factory working again. We put out a call to the work force – the majority women – to return and, within four or five days, production had started up. Soon we had to take more drastic measures . . .

The same day, Manuel Hernández, of the CNT woodworkers' union, sent young Eduardo PONS PRADES off on his bicycle to reconnoitre the offices of the Wood Manufacturers' Association – the employers' organization – and report back immediately.

—'You're sure there's no one there, *peque*?' 'Not a fly.' 'All right then, let's go up and take it over officially.' And so we did. That was the beginning of the CNT Socialized Wood Industry which, though it wasn't yet called that, was soon to be reorganizing and controlling the industry from felling the timber to the finished product . . .

By that Tuesday Joan ROIG, the sole manager to turn up at the largest locomotive and engineering factory in Spain, La Maquinista Terrestre y Marítima, found workers already there assembling steel sheeting around lorries as a form of crude armour-plating for the Durruti column which was setting out for Aragon.

Even the large department stores were open – under CNT control. Joan FERRER, a book-keeper who was shortly to become secretary of the CNT commercial employees' union, knew that the CNT sent armed men to guard them, especially El Siglo and El Aguila, the two largest, for in the first revolutionary moments there had been attempts to loot them. When the CNT called for a return to work, the staff found that the owners had fled. 'The commercial employees' union, which included everyone from shop assistants to book-keepers, took over the stores and appointed a manager to run them . . .'

The revolutionary initiative had sprung not from the CNT's leading committees – how could it when the libertarian revolution had been officially 'postponed'? – but from individual CNT unions impelled by the most advanced syndicalist militants. Even then it might have gone no further than the workers controlling management's activities; the large-scale defection of owners, directors and managers in fear of their fate led in many factories to the next step.

—Shortly we received union instructions to take charge of our respective factories in the textile industry, recalled SANTACANA of España Industrial. We called a general assembly of the 2,500 company workers in a local cinema. The couple of dozen CNT militants among us met beforehand to draw up a plan of what we were going to propose . . .

The factory, he told the assembly, must be taken over because the directors and managers had fled. None of the many speakers opposed the proposal. About 80 per cent of the workers belonged to the CNT, 20 per cent to the UGT. The company accountant, who was not part of management, informed the assembly that there was no more than 300,000 pesetas in the company's bank accounts – barely enough to cover two weeks' wages. It was a derisory amount, the assembly agreed, for a company of that size to hold in cash reserves; but there was nothing that could be done about it.

The assembly, by a show of hands, elected twelve members to a committee to run the factory; they represented the workers, technicians and administrative staff and included two women from the spinning and weaving sections where the majority of the women worked. All the committee members belonged to the CNT; later the UGT approached them to ask for representation, to which they agreed.

—'Union brings strength,' I said. They were workers like us. 'The most important task is to face the common enemy together.' So they received a proportional representation of two members . . .

At the CNT glassworkers' union, Joan DOMENECH, the union secretary, was taking part in a discussion among the militants.

—'We should put in for a wage rise and a shorter working week. Now's the time,' one of them said. 'Don't you know we've made the revolution?' I asked. 'Yes, that's why we want to make these demands.' 'No, *hombre*, no. What we've got to do is to get rid of the employers and keep the workshops for the workers,' I replied. 'Ah – and how are we going to do that?' 'Wait a minute and I'll tell you' . . .

DOMENECH was taking time off from serving on the supplies committee which had the task of provisioning Barcelona.[1] But as a glassworker and union secretary he was concerned about his industry 'now that the revolution was staring us in the face'. He told the militants to call a meeting with the employers. Beforehand, he arranged to have two toughs with rifles standing behind him at the table where he would preside.

—The idea was, well, not that they should do anything but because, *coño*, this was the revolution!

'Well, *señores*,' I said, opening the meeting, 'you are the employers and we, at the moment, are in the full spate of revolution. Right now, if we felt like it, we could load you all into a lorry and that would be the end of it.' You should have seen their backsides wriggling on their chairs! 'But no, what we have to do right now is set about protecting your interests and ours.'

'Yes, oh yes,' they all replied. 'Of course.'

'Well now, it's clear that you employers really compete in an unfair and disloyal manner amongst yourselves. You try to undercut each other with unstated discounts, you buy large quantities of glass to get the factory discount and then often undertake work you don't need. All this can't continue. You should have formed an employers' association a long time ago.'

'Yes, yes,' some of them said, nodding.

'All right,' I continued, 'we'll do something straight away. We'll draw up a document creating an association: *The Mirror and Plate Glass Employers' Society*.' We drew up the document; one by one they signed it. They were silent.

1. See below, pp. 143–5.

'Now we're going to draw up another document which cedes all the Society's rights to the union.'

'*¡Hombre, no! ¡Hombre!*' They were all shouting now.

'Yes, yes,' I said very insistently; given the situation, they ended up signing. 'Don't get upset,' I went on. 'The first thing we're going to do is to make an inventory of all stocks held in each of your workshops, and ascertain the financial balance of each. To those showing a profit, we'll pay 10 per cent of the surplus shown every three months; for those showing a loss – bad luck! Moreover, each one of you will stay on as a union member and be employed as a technician with the corresponding wage.'

By now they were beginning to get a bit more enthusiastic. I encouraged them even more with a fantasy of the future in which I told them we would soon be building houses of glass, all the street signs would be of glass, and so on. 'You've never thought of things like that, but this is what we're going to do.'

'*Hombre*, yes, yes.' They left the meeting quite content in the end. And that's how we collectivized the plate glass business . . .

*

Revolutions move fast: 'Time is as different as when you've got a toothache; you don't eat, hardly sleep, you forget where you've been, what you've been doing. Days are like hours, and months like days . . .' a POUM militant recalled. The rush of the present into the future does not shed the weight of the past: half a century of anarchist anti-state ideology did not disappear overnight. The bourgeois Catalan state had virtually disappeared, the central Madrid state also.[1] Everywhere in the Popular Front zone, committees had taken the organization of local affairs into their own hands. Fragmented, differentiated, localized, the revolutionary committees ignored state power, drove past it as though it were a corpse; lifeless it indeed appeared, but it was still breathing.

—In forty-eight hours, the relation of forces in Catalonia, in particular Barcelona, changed completely. The state disappeared. President Companys expressed the predicament: to be able to carry out his functions he needed people who functioned. He pressed a button to call his secretary; the bell didn't ring, the electricity wasn't working. He went to the door to speak to his secretary; he wasn't there. Then he discovered that even had the bell worked, even had his secretary been there to call the head of department he wanted to see, the order would have been meaningless: the departmental head wasn't there. The whole administration had crumbled . . .

Jaume MIRAVITLLES, an ex-member of the dissident communist workers' and peasants' bloc, BOC (Bloc Obrer i Camperol), was now a member of the Esquerra, the republican party of the petty bourgeoisie which had dominated Catalan politics under the republic. The sight of the 'human fauna' which had suddenly appeared on the streets of Barcelona, which didn't speak Catalan, which was armed, astounded him. Where had it come from? He saw a man

1. Both had lost the use of their coercive instruments (the security forces) and the credibility of their institutions (parliament, the legal system, etc.) on which state power, as the expression of class rule, rests. But neither had lost the actual institutions or the coercive instruments – for they had not been destroyed – only the effective deployment of them.

with a cannon, the red and black anarchist flag attached, which he paraded behind a horse through the streets as though it were his own, shouting 'Long live anarchy!' Barcelona was not only a major industrial city but also a Mediterranean port.

—It bred a lumpen proletariat which now suddenly appeared and overwhelmed the CNT and even the FAI. The latter couldn't disavow these people because they represented the anarchists' very philosophy: the spontaneity of the masses. The Madrid government had made the fatal mistake of discharging all soldiers, and there was no way of getting them back to the barracks. The anarchists prevented them when they tried. What could be done? . . .

An idea was mooted to bring in all the *guardia civil* units which remained in the villages. The anarchists had got wind of the plan: he and Tarradellas for the Generalitat met Durruti, García Oliver, Mariano Vázquez of the CNT; they came armed.

—'If you try bringing in the *guardia civil* we shall call a general strike immediately; there will be a massacre of the Generalitat and Esquerra leaders.' They were well aware that the plan was aimed at them, that the force would be used to fight them, to win back control of the situation, and they were prepared to carry out their threat. Naturally, the order to the *guardia civil* was never given . . .

MIRAVITLLES was appointed one of his party's three representatives on the Central Committee of the Anti-Fascist Militias of Catalonia. This was the committee the libertarian leaders had agreed to join during their famous conversation with Companys on 20 July 1936 when he offered them power. A day after that meeting, he decreed the committee into existence, asserting thereby a power the Generalitat did not currently exercise but which it had not abdicated either.[1]

The anti-fascist militia committee was installed in the bullet-scarred Nautical Institute by the port, whose windows had been smashed in the street fighting of 19 July. Five libertarians, five republicans, five 'marxists'[2] took their seats, all appointed by their respective organizations. MIRAVITLLES was appointed the committee's secretary-general.

—The title meant very little; my role was that of coordinator. Regrettably, there was very little I could coordinate . . .

In almost permanent session, the committee controlled virtually everything in Barcelona (though by no means the whole of Catalonia): transport, communications, hospitals, supplies, the militias, security.

1. As it was to decree a whole series of measures, including the appointment of a defence commissioner, the reduction of the work week to forty hours, a general 15 per cent increase in wages, the reduction of most rents by 25 per cent, the control of the banks, etc.

2. As viewed by the libertarians: one representative of the newly formed PSUC, one of the POUM and three of the UGT. It is worth noting that the libertarians, who determined the representation, allowed the largest working-class party in Catalonia at that moment, the POUM, only one seat, the same as the then diminutive PSUC, effectively the new communist party of Catalonia. The libertarians, while technically representing the CNT and FAI, were all FAI members, with the *Nosotros* group providing three of them. Numerical equality between the political forces was seen by the libertarians as ensuring them the same rights in regions where they were in a minority.

—From an organizational point of view it was chaotic – it couldn't not be. Each 'secretary' did more or less what he liked; although we were in constant session, we were never all there at the same time. Very few agreements were reached in committee, the latter being simply presented with *faits accomplis*.

The building we were in was a sort of barricade with walls – the authentic atmosphere the libertarians liked. I don't remember when I ate or slept, and I certainly don't have the impression that I ever left the building to go home. I slept on a mattress on the floor or in a chair, and the same was true of the others. We were all sleep-walkers . . .

The libertarians, he thought, believed they *had* taken power through the committee – and from within that was how it appeared. They came to the meetings wearing bandoliers stuffed full of cartridges and laid their pistols or sub-machine-guns out in front of them. Thumping the table, they'd shout: 'This is how things are going to be done now – with *cojones*! – You're a lot of petty bourgeois. You're trying to hold back the revolution instead of giving it impetus. Everything is working fine without any bourgeois at all, the factories are running as normal.'

—They initiated a series of reforms which appeared infantile – I'd always doubted the possibility of anarchist society functioning – and it astonished us when it then seemed to function. It was all being done in a mood of hallucinatory exaltation. The libertarians controlled the most important 'secretariats' – but in reality power lay still in the streets. The committee functioned spontaneously, dealing with problems as they arose. It would give me pleasure to say that it represented a new form of organization through which the masses – such an abstract concept – were able to express themselves; but it didn't. It was an expedient to fill a gap; regrettably, it was not up to the historical demands made of it . . .

The committee realized it was unable to handle all the calls made on it and set up a supplies committee to provision the city. The CNT chose Joan DOMENECH, the glassworkers' union secretary, as one of its representatives. 'But I don't know anything about supplies. I'm a glassworker.' 'That doesn't matter, get over to the committee that's being set up,' replied 'Marianet', the CNT regional committee secretary.

He was shown into a small room, with benches and pupils' desks. Representatives from the other parties and organizations – the new committee was to have the same representation as the militia committee – were already waiting. After some time the door opened, and Abad de Santillán, FAI representative on the main committee, came in. Leaning against the teacher's desk, he announced that they were the supplies committee.

—'From now on you have got to provision the militia columns, the hospitals, the entire population. Good evening. Oh yes,' he added, as an afterthought, 'by the day after tomorrow, before noon, we need 5,000 cold rations for the militia column which is going to launch an attack on the Aragon front. You'll organize that. *Buenas tardes*' . . .

The men looked at each other; they had twenty-four hours. Where to start?

A man sitting at the teacher's desk pulled a piece of paper from his pocket and began to read out a series of instructions.

—'Where do you come from?' I asked. I've always been a bit strange in my ways, and the one thing none of us had come there expecting was that anyone was going to give us orders on how to carry out our task, even if we hadn't the slightest idea ourselves. 'I'm from the POUM,' he said. 'Well, you know the first thing you're going to do? No! Then I'll tell you. You're going to come and sit here with the rest of us and then we'll decide who's going to head this committee' . . .

DOMENECH found himself elected to the post. Since it was already 10 p.m. they decided to adjourn until early the next morning when they went to find the man appointed by the Esquerra to take charge of the Barcelona food markets.

—'We're the revolutionary supplies committee,' I told him. He looked rather frightened. People were being taken for *paseos* by then. 'Oh, oh – But I've been appointed by the town hall.' 'That's all right,' I replied. 'You can be our committee's president, if you like, and I'll be your secretary, and these companions will help us.' He was happy with the arrangement and turned up, in suit and tie, at 9 a.m. or 10 a.m. By then, dressed in overalls, I'd been at work for two or three hours. After a fortnight he hadn't the faintest idea of what was going on and said there wasn't much point in his continuing. I told him he could go to France to organize food purchases for us, and he went – never to return . . .

DOMENECH's first major problem was to control the available stocks of food. The revolution provided him with the means. When the armed workers' patrols, which had been set up by the militia committee, 'expropriated' a shop full of hams – '*coño*, it was they who had made the revolution after all' – the owner would in despair report to the supplies committee; and the latter would send out men to put a sign on the shop: 'Requisitioned by the Supplies Committee' or 'Taken Over by the CNT'. This prevented further looting of the shop, and kept it functioning with foodstuffs provided by the committee. A special warehouse was set up to provision the workers' patrols so that they should no longer 'confiscate' food, as were other warehouses for the militia, the hospitals, the poor. None the less, large queues formed outside the committee offices. DOMENECH took charge, posting a man at the door with strict instructions to allow only one person in at a time.

—As soon as each one came in he or she would start off on a long, involved story. A man whose wife had just given birth was asking for a chicken, but he couldn't get to the point. 'Tell me only what you want,' I'd shout at him, like a general. 'A chicken.' 'Take this bit of paper. Go to window so-and-so. They'll give you one. Next!' And so it went on until in an hour or so I'd got through the whole queue . . .

The supplies committee abolished money – 'a very anarchist idea' – and in its place organized a barter system: food supplies from the villages in exchange for manufactured goods from the city. Lists were sent out from Barcelona showing the surpluses of shirts, sandals, silk stockings, etc., that were available in exchange for chick-peas, olive oil, wheat or whatever surplus agricultural produce existed. Wheat and meat were DOMENECH's two major concerns, for Catalonia was self-sufficient in neither, and much of the wheat had to come from outside, especially from Aragon. But exchanges were arranged with villages as far distant as Andalusia.

—They'd say they wanted shoes. We'd get hold of the respective CNT delegate for the shoe industry and say: 'Tomorrow, we need 700 pairs of shoes.' And tomorrow they'd be there. We had confidence in the delegates who were running the industries they had taken over; we didn't need reports, stock lists, statistics. Good faith guided the people, that was what counted. In those first months there wasn't this whole state apparatus that could have provided such figures anyway – it was a revolutionary situation. And even if we had tried to get accounts and that sort of thing, our people in the factories probably wouldn't have known how to make them out. Good faith was worth a lot more . . .

The exchanges were based on the different products' market value pre-war. So many pairs of shoes were worth so much, that much would buy a certain quantity of wheat, so many pairs of shoes equalled so much wheat. The circulation of money, not money as the expression of exchange value, was abolished.

—In two to three months, we had exchanged about 60 million pesetas' [about £1,500,000] worth of goods without anyone touching any money. We organized foreign trade in the same way. We needed more wheat. We packed up all the surplus onions, champagne – which was of no use to us in war – Valencia oranges and other products and dispatched a freighter to Odessa with them. I put the consignment in the hands of one of those adventurers who always appear in time of war and whom I thought capable of organizing it. He took over a freighter that was in the port and sailed down the coast as far as Andalusia, buying whatever we knew the USSR could use; when the ship was well laden, he set sail.

By this time Antonov-Ovsëenko, the old Bolshevik who led the storming of the Winter Palace, had been sent as Soviet consul here. He viewed our experiment favourably, I believe. 'Catalonia will become the new Ukraine of Spain,' I said in a speech in his presence; to be truthful, I didn't know what the Ukraine really was, but it impressed him. Thereafter we used to exchange views, and he told me what produce the USSR needed and I what we needed, and it was on this basis that the first consignments of supplies were exchanged. We got seven ships loaded with excellent wheat, meat, condensed milk and other foodstuffs in return. The first to arrive, in October, was given a monumental welcome. The transactions for all seven were arranged by me; I kept the receipts made out in Russian and French. But the credit for the other six ships went to the communists, as I'll explain . . .

Jaume MIRAVITLLES continued to be amazed that such a system could work at all. Prices were controlled, people had money to buy things. 'This system functions,' he said to Josep Tarradellas, his Esquerra colleague on the militia committee.

—What we didn't realize was that the stocks which the bourgeoisie had left were being consumed in making it work. As soon as they were used up the situation became tragic, the dream began to fail . . .

But this was still in the future; at that moment his and his colleagues' attention was focused on a more immediately dramatic situation: the assassinations that were taking place.

—Day after day, we found ourselves on the committee repeating: 'Why these assassinations? A man was killed last night who belonged to the Esquerra. Why? Another man has been assassinated simply because his sister was a nun. Why?' It was a terrible mistake they were making. They saw the bourgeoisie as their main enemy. They called a man a fascist simply because he went to mass. President Companys told them they were drowning the revolution in blood. 'We shall lose the war for this reason.' The libertarians went pale. When Companys from time to time put in an appearance at the committee, we of his party stood up; the communists half rose, the libertarians remained solidly seated. 'Tell Companys not to come here again,' Durruti said to me and Tarradellas. 'If he does, I'll fill him full of bullets . . .'

An Eye for an Eye, a Tooth for a Tooth!

If it is true that our comrades have been shot in Saragossa on the orders of that uniformed bandit Cabanellas, Goded and all the fascist scum will pay with their lives . . .

Solidaridad Obrera, CNT (Barcelona, 24 July 1936)

COMRADES . . . The revolution must not be allowed to drown us in blood! Conscious justice, yes! Assassins, never.

CNT statement (Barcelona, end of July 1936)

The most original aspect of the revolution we are making is the role assigned to the petty bourgeoisie . . . This modest social stratum, which at the beginning of the proletarian revolution felt itself seriously threatened, has been calmed by our display of understanding and respect.

Solidaridad Obrera, CNT (Barcelona, 15 November 1936)

BARCELONA

Walking down the Carrer Princesa, the mill-owner's wife saw a house at some distance still, its windows, shutters and doors open, and a pile of furniture in the street. Had it been sacked? So many terrible things had been happening. Only a few days before, walking down the Ramblas where the church of Belén had been burnt, a crowd of people surged into the door of a house, and almost immediately a man appeared on a balcony. Did he jump, was he pushed? – whatever it was, he had fallen on the pavement almost in front of her and been killed. The scene still haunted her as she walked down the street. Approaching the house, Juana ALIER saw a magnificent grand piano on top of the piled-up furniture; smashed into the middle of the lid was an axe, its haft sticking out. She hurried on, overwhelmed with anxiety.

—Things were being destroyed for the sake of destruction. Why? The burnt churches, those marvellous stained-glass windows in the church of Santa María del Mar which could never be replaced. Every time I passed by I felt my anguish return . . .

Memories of an engraving of a French revolutionary tumbril came to Joan ROIG's mind as he watched the small lorry, decorated with red flags, being brought up to the gates of La Maquinista, the large engineering and locomotive works. In the back the workers had put a single chair on which the managing director was to be seated. ROIG, the only manager to turn up at the works where he had found the workers armour-plating lorries for the Durruti column, had rapidly foreseen the drama of the coming Saturday if there was no money to pay the men's wages, and after considerable effort had persuaded the managing director to come to the factory. Now he was being taken under armed escort to the bank.

—'Don't leave me,' he begged. 'Put another chair in the back,' I said to the committee, 'I'm coming, too.' I had no idea what might happen. We got to the Hispano-Americano bank and withdrew the necessary money. There was no problem about that. Then the armed workers started to surround us; I didn't know what the problem was when suddenly I found myself, with the managing director and a couple of committee members, bundled into a taxi on our way back to the works. Only later did I learn what our fate had nearly been . . .

Some of the committee had taken the position that their lives served no further purpose once the money had been collected. They were saved, he believed, by the fact that, due to the economic depression of the previous years, no new workers had been taken on, which meant that all the committee members knew the managers. 'Had there been new workers, some of them would undoubtedly have been extremists and taken the matter into their own hands.' Notwithstanding, a few days later one of the board of directors was found assassinated – the work of railwaymen, it appeared, for the dead man had been a railway company director.

ROIG, a practising Catholic, a man of the centre and a staunch Catalan nationalist who believed that the military uprising against a popularly elected government was totally unjustifiable, rapidly began to feel that the reaction to the uprising was equally unjustifiable. Particularly the assassinations. At the barber's one day, he heard a man who was being shaved telling the barber about the 'canaries' he and others took out every night and shot. ROIG turned away in disgust at the look of pleasure on his face as he described in detail how the prisoners pleaded for their lives, how he pretended they were going to be set free and then shot them in the back. 'The worst was when he invited the barber to accompany him that night to witness the spectacle.'

Church-burnings and assassinations had begun almost immediately. In the city's largest hospital, Prof. Josep TRUETA was still treating the wounded from the street fighting with an innovatory method he had evolved,[1] when he was called to see something. By a wall outside the ward three corpses were lying. 'It's the work of the FAI,' he was told.[2]

Soon afterwards the brother of a leading anarchist died in his hospital; eleven of the dead man's companions turned up and arrested Prof. TRUETA and a nurse, accusing him of ordering the latter to administer an injection which had been the cause of death.

—'He must be a fascist,' they said of me, 'and she must be working with him.' Then someone said, 'But she's a nun.' 'Ah, so you're protecting nuns as well.' We were put on trial there and then . . .

Extremely frightened, Prof. TRUETA could not help wondering at the fact that the head of the anarchist group was a surgeon who, before the war, had used a number of not so veiled threats, which included showing him a dedicated photograph of Alfonso XIII, to extort employment from him.

—'I'm in charge here,' he said to me now. 'You're going to be tried. Fairly. If it's proven that the injection you gave was tampered with, you'll be executed . . .'

The 'trial' was beginning when eleven UGT men, armed with rifles, burst into the clinic. A socialist orderly had managed to slip out of the hospital and explain at his union branch what was happening. The head of the socialist group, also an orderly, launched into a speech saying that if the charge were proven TRUETA must be executed as an example; if not, it would be a heinous crime to lay a hand on him – 'a surgeon whose hands have contributed to saving the lives of so many people.' The 'anarchist' surgeon began to look fearful. A sample injection was taken from a box to a municipal laboratory for testing. No one could be sure the injection had come from that particular box; but someone took the precaution of ringing TRUETA's friend at the laboratories to tell him what was at stake. 'We were kept under arrest until at last the report came back: the injections were uncontaminated.'

Many of Prof. TRUETA's fears appeared to him to be coming true. The growth

1. See p. 442, n. 1.

2. The CNT–FAI bulletin in Barcelona reported on 25 July 1936 that a priest in the hospital had a heated argument with a doctor, pulled out a revolver and fired a magazine not at the doctor but at the wounded. 'Bystanders were so infuriated that they picked out four of the most priestly and fascist of the brethren and shot them out of hand.' (Cited in Thomas, *The Spanish Civil War*, p. 269.) It should also be noted that in Barcelona and elsewhere the FAI was automatically blamed for assassinations and crimes.

of anarcho-syndicalism in Barcelona had long been a source of anxiety for liberal Catalans like him. It contained an explosive mixture, in his view: the ex-rural 'serf' who could see the myth of liberty now apparently realizable before him, and the Catalan individualist anarchist.

—The rural migrants' situation was rather similar to that of the Irish in England, as I was to see later; both had the worst jobs, the lowest pay and formed the most depressed sector of society. Individually splendid people – but imagine a situation in which Irish immigrants were in power in London. That was the situation which faced us here . . .

The Catalan petty bourgeoisie, which for the past five republican years had held political power in its country, was suffering the loss not only of its political dominance but of its economic livelihood – as well, in some cases, as loss of life. More than any other part of the Spanish state, Catalonia was the land of the small family business, passed on from father to son or newly created by skilled workmen and artisans, where upward mobility had some meaning. The joint-stock company was a comparative rarity. The urban petty bourgeoisie was politically supported by a relatively prosperous peasantry farming fairly equitably distributed land. It was these middle classes which formed the backbone of Catalan nationalist sentiment. Although not revolutionary, the bulk of this class was 'anti-fascist'. Clearly not because it was petty bourgeois, for that very class elsewhere formed the base of fascism, but because it was Catalan and nationalist. The triumph of military reaction in the name of the indivisible unity of Spain could only threaten it by threatening Catalan autonomy, within which it had established its political dominance.

But rapidly, the revolution became an even greater threat. The petty bourgeoisie's businesses and enterprises, its retail outlets, its textile, wood and metalworking shops, its taxis and its barbers' shops were taken over by the workers. As an employer of labour, if only of a handful of men, this petty bourgeoisie was identified as the capitalist class, and its representatives, whether hated personally or not as exploiters, had to be expropriated, harassed, even assassinated.[1] Little did it matter that leading CNT militants, like Joan Peiró, fulminated openly against such actions; nor that both the CNT and FAI issued statements categorically condemning assassinations. 'We must put an end to these excesses,' the latter declared. Anyone proven to have infringed people's rights would be shot – a threat which was carried out when some anarcho-syndicalist militants were executed.

Revolutions inevitably breed 'excesses'; revolution by definition is an 'excess' for those who yesterday held power. To ensure the rearguard from the class enemy's return to power was an urgent revolutionary task. But the excesses of repression and expropriation were spilling over randomly, arbitrarily, without thought of the revolutionary consequences. Who was the class enemy? The petty bourgeoisie? Evidently not, for its representatives, Jaume MIRAVITLLES among them, were sitting on the militia committee by the libertarians' choice.

1. The fact that the petty bourgeoisie in town and country was, everywhere, a frequent employer of small amounts of labour, explains in part the violence of both the industrial and rural proletariat's response to this class, which was automatically identified with the big bourgeoisie.

—Their leaders on the committee said the libertarian movement was not responsible for the assassinations. 'It's the armed workers' patrols.[1] Some of the members are assassins.' But in my view, they couldn't confront this type of people who represented for them their own ideology. With the notable exception of Durruti at the front, the CNT was always plagued with indiscipline within its own ranks and didn't know how to deal with it . . .

Eduardo PONS PRADES, of the libertarian youth, was in the CNT woodworkers' union when an employer's family came to see if the union leaders knew where he was. He and another man owned the firm. The latter, a merciless employer, had managed to flee to France immediately; but the former, well known for his kindness, and having nothing to fear, had remained. The union leader, Hernández, set inquiries in motion; three workers were soon arrested. It turned out that they had assassinated the man, mistaking him for his hated partner. Hernández questioned one of them, a young Cordoban.

—'How many times had you seen this man?' he asked harshly. 'Only once – ' 'You mean – you dared kill a man you'd only seen once. Like a dog! He was one of our best employers. Everybody knew he was a good man.'

'He couldn't have been good, I tell you,' the Cordoban replied. 'That's the end. How do you know?' The Cordoban hesitated, as though looking for words. At last, he said: 'Because he looked like the *señor* of our village – the scoundrel who ruined my father's health, led him to his grave, forced us to emigrate to Catalonia – '

The world suddenly shattered for me. What could have happened in that Cordoban *pueblo*? He was only twenty, had been living in Barcelona ten years. What could have happened that, from the age of ten, he had kept alive such hatred, such rancour for a man, that he could kill, kill another merely for looking like him?

In the end Hernández offered him only one possibility: to join the militia on the Aragon front where in all probability he would be shot – by an enemy bullet . . .

Too many of the anarcho-syndicalist revolutionary solutions appeared primitive, naïve, thought Manuel CRUELLS, the Catalan nationalist student who had set out to 'make the revolution' himself after the military were crushed. But the revolution that was being made, due to the anarchist as opposed to syndicalist influence, was more rural than industrial, more suited to an Andalusian *pueblo* than to an industrial city with a large middle class that had been influenced by European culture. At the university, where he was a leading member of the revolutionary committee which the Catalan students' federation had set up, they had recently had an unexpected visit. A commission of anarchist intellectuals and students, whom they had never seen before, arrived with an enormous package which they laid on the table; then they drew their pistols and laid them next to the package.

1. These acted as a revolutionary police force and were made up of 700 men – 325 of the CNT, 185 of the Esquerra, 145 of the UGT and 45 of the POUM (see C. Lorenzo, *Los anarquistas españoles y el poder*, Paris, 1972, p. 92).

—'We've come here to raise the anarchist flag over the university of Barcelona,' they announced. At that time, of course, the university was a bourgeois and petty bourgeois preserve: the majority of students belonged to Catalan nationalist parties or groups. I pulled out my pistol – as a rule none of us went armed – and laid it on the table. 'All right, when we can fly our university flag on your buildings' . . .

The scene started to become violent, but the students succeeded in calming things down, and it ended in embraces and glasses of vermouth. But it had a certain effect. A few days later, the Catalan students' federation decided to affiliate to the UGT. Later again it dis-affiliated, 'but the point is that ours was not an isolated reaction. Confronted by the irresponsibility and apparent violence of so many anarcho-syndicalists, it was the way most of the middle class in Barcelona reacted.'

The middle classes usually feared the non-Catalan anarchist – Murcian, Aragonese, Andalusian – more than the indigenous libertarian. Providing the labour force necessary to create the bourgeoisie's prosperity, the rural migrant to the city became also the spectre of an agrarian violence that would overthrow the bourgeois order.[1] But the CNT policy of admitting all and sundry to membership, the freeing of many common criminals along with political prisoners from gaol, the 'danger of giving a man a pistol in one hand and a certificate of impunity in the other', in the words of Jacinto BORRAS, a CNT journalist, made it difficult, if not impossible, to ensure the revolutionary order which the anarcho-syndicalist leadership called for.[2]

—There was a deep, very deep wave of popular fury as a result of the military uprising which followed on so many years of oppression and provocation. In order to save lives, as I and so many others did, you had to be prepared to stake your own. But it must be said that many people who, had they been arrested six or nine months later, would have been sentenced to a year or two in gaol, were shot in those first days . . .

Of the depth of hatred for the church, especially of the regular clergy, which

1. The following story was indicative. The house of a very wealthy, conservative, religious Barcelona family was being searched by an anarchist patrol, one of whose members went out into the garden and began poking about. When he came in empty-handed the family believed a miracle had happened. The rosaries they had buried had not been discovered. A few minutes after the patrol left the anarchist who had been in the garden returned. 'Idiots,' he said in Catalan, 'if *they* had found these they would have killed the lot of you.' He threw the rosaries on the table and walked out. 'He was a Catalan, that was the difference; not that Catalans are better people, simply that they have been Catalans for generations and produced authentic anarchists' (Prof. Josep TRUETA).

2. 'When intransigent, intolerant, intractable commissions or elements came to see me, I had no other recourse than to invite them to show me their trade union card, with the unvarying outcome; their cards were dated never earlier than the 1st, 10th or 15th of August [1936]' (J. P. Fàbregas, CNT economics councillor, *Buttletí trimestral de la conselleria d'economia*, no. 2, cited in A. Pérez-Baró, *Trenta mesos de col·lectivisme a Catalunya*, Barcelona, 1970, p. 47). A case in point was rent-collectors. Much hated, many were killed at the start of the revolution. The remainder joined the CNT for their own protection where they became 'ultra revolutionary', decided to collect all Barcelona rents and 'set about it as though they owned all accommodation. They frightened great numbers of the petty bourgeoisie whose interests – and even lives – were at stake . . .' (evidence of PEREZ-BARO).

dedicated much of its efforts to maintaining schools for the bourgeoisie's children while workers' children were deprived of secondary education, there could be little doubt. Two hundred and seventy-seven priests and 425 regular clergy were estimated to have been assassinated in Barcelona.[1] A great number of churches and convents were burnt, although some were saved thanks to the Generalitat's intervention. More than anything, it was the primitiveness of the anti-clerical persecution which most shocked the middle classes at the beginning.[2]

The thirteen-year-old daughter of a CNT tailor watched men dragging pews and religious objects from the church opposite her house in Gràcia, a Barcelona *barrio*, and setting fire to them. She and her mother were churchgoers, and her father didn't oppose them. The burning seemed unnecessary. When the men set about a near-by convent and María OCHOA saw, amongst the beds and furniture being thrown out and burnt, an embroidery frame which seemed too good to burn, she took it. Her father was angry; he said it was theft and ordered her to return the frame to be burnt.

—He was a very dogmatic man, a man who believed in his anarchist principles, a man who believed that everyone should think like him. I protested but it was no good. I had to take it back and put it on the fire.

They dug up the nuns' corpses, too, and displayed the skeletons and mummies. I found that quite amusing; so did all the kids. When we got bored looking at the same ones in my neighbourhood, we'd go to another *barrio* to see the ones they'd dug up there. In the Passeig de Sant Joan, they were exhibited in the street. Not for very long, but long enough for us to go and look. We kids would make comments about the different corpses – how this one was well-preserved, and that one decomposed, this one older; we got a lot of amusement out of it all . . .

There was a festive enthusiasm in the streets; the war, she thought, seemed a good thing. At home her father talked more about local politics than about the war; not that the latter was forgotten, but what happened in Barcelona seemed more important. He was particularly hostile to the masses of people flocking to join the UGT – 'opportunists without any political background', he called them. Soon, however, a black cloud appeared over the festival. A workers' patrol set up in a house on the corner of the street. It was guarded by two militiawomen. Each night a car drew up and sounded its horn.

—We soon discovered what it meant. People were being taken to be shot on the other side of Mount Tibidabo. It was horrifying, oppressive. The car would begin to grind up the hill and we knew the fate that awaited its occupants. My father didn't like it. He thought it quite normal that half a dozen big bourgeois exploiters should be liquidated. But not that all these others were being taken to their deaths . . .

The persecution of the clergy, the church burnings had made a deep impres-

1. A. Balcells, *Cataluña contemporánea, II (1900–1936)* (Madrid, 1974), p. 40.
2. In Catalonia the church was somewhat 'more open', republican anti-clerical sentiment less marked and the emergence of christian-democratic attitudes more developed than in central and southern Spain. See Points of Rupture, B.

sion on Maurici SERRAHIMA, a lawyer and leading member of Unió Democrática, the small Catalan Christian-democratic party, because of the long tradition in Spain of such events. He recalled an old street ballad which went: 'There were six bad bulls at the bullfight and so the people came out of the ring and burnt the churches.'

—I always maintained that, deep down, these burnings were an act of faith. That's to say, an act of protest because the church was not, in the people's eyes, what it should be. The disappointment of someone who believes and loves and is betrayed. It springs from the idea that the church should be on the side of the poor – and isn't; as, indeed, it hadn't been for a great number of years, excepting certain individual churchmen. A protest against the church's submission to the propertied classes. Not that this described the situation in Catalonia totally; with the growth of Catalanism, a movement within the church to open it to the world had started in the past twenty years . . .

SERRAHIMA gave shelter to eleven Capuchin monks from a near-by convent in the *barrio* of Sarrià. Fearing that his house would be searched, he managed to get them hidden elsewhere, and was then involved in getting Cardinal Vidal i Barraquer of Tarragona, who had been rescued *in extremis* by the Generalitat, out of the country. Returning from this mission – the British consulate regretted that as both the consul and vice-consul were on holiday it was unable to help – he found his home occupied by an 'FAI patrol'. His father had been accused of having hidden the Capuchins' money and had been taken off with one of his brothers who had volunteered to share his fate. SERRAHIMA saw that the armed workers had smashed a number of religious pictures and statues.

—'We are smashing this,' their leader had said to my father, picking up a San Francisco, copy of a famous statue, 'because we know it's a plaster reproduction. Were it the original in wood we would certainly not break it, for it is a work of art.' Meanwhile my mother, who had been blind for many years, was overcome by this sudden eruption in the house. The leader sent one of his men, armed with a pistol, to the local chemist to get rose water to calm her nerves. What a typical libertarian gesture, what a mixture they were! . . .

To the family's surprise, father and brother were released, but threatened with re-arrest if the friars' whereabouts were not revealed by noon the next day. After a long struggle with the Capuchin provincial, who was in hiding, SERRAHIMA managed to reach agreement that one friar would give himself up, and for the rest they would say they had lost track of them. The next day, realizing that they had taken action, the patrol pursued the matter no further; and the friar was soon released by the police – only to be shot by someone who recognized him later.

After his brush with the patrol, SERRAHIMA found the nervous tension too great to remain at home. All the Catalan ideals for which he stood were at stake. He went to the police to see if they could afford protection against the workers' patrols. 'Leave – that is all you can do,' he was advised. 'But – we can't *all* leave,' his father said; and so they agreed to remain.

To avoid being cooped up at home, he began walking round the city in the uniform of the times: shirt-sleeves and hemp sandals. The sight of the burnt churches depressed him; but there were other things that impressed him even more.

—In all my walks through the many different types of neighbourhood, I didn't see a single drunk. And that was a time which lent itself to excesses. Nor were there any sexual crimes; only once was one brought to my attention, and then without any real details. While there was total social disorder, you might say, there was no moral disorder. People were being assassinated – though in far fewer numbers than, propagandistically, has been claimed; in fact, relatively fewer than in other republican cities like Madrid, I believe – but at the same time the total decomposition that one could have expected did not occur . . .

Nevertheless, there could be no doubt that the struggle to win the Catalan middle classes was lost without thought by the libertarians. The consequences for them, for their revolution, and for the war were grave.

Let us repeat the phrase so often pronounced by our illustrious general, Queipo de Llano: the words 'pardon' and 'amnesty' must disappear from the Spanish dictionary.

***ABC* (Seville, 1 September 1936)**

We are fighting totally for Spain and for civilization. Nor are we fighting alone; 20 centuries of Western Christian Civilization lie behind us. We are fighting for God, for our land and our dead . . .

It has always been Spain's providential and historic mission to save the civilized world from all dangers: expelling moors, stopping turks, baptizing indians . . . Now new turks, red and cruel asiatics, are again threatening Europe. But Spain, today as yesterday, opposes them, saves and redeems civilization. Because this is a holy war, a crusade of civilization . . .

José Maria Pemán, monarchist poet
(Broadcast over Seville radio, 15 August 1936)

BLOOD AND GOLD FOR THE SALVATION OF SPAIN

Youth's generous blood must be prepared to be shed for the sacred cause of Spain. The gold of the wealthy is necessary for the same cause . . .

***Defensor de Córdoba* (15 September 1936)**

ANDALUSIA

In the first days of August, as the Catalan columns were being brought to a halt on the Aragon front, a motorized Army of Africa column, made up of legionaries and Moroccan *regulares*, headed north from Seville. Almost all the 8,000 men had been air-lifted from Morocco; amongst them was Lt BRAVO, of the *guardia civil*, who was impressed by the reception they were given. People came up to them in the streets and presented them with religious medallions, wine, water-melons, whatever they had to show their gratitude.

—There were still legionary NCOs who had doubts about the uprising – many had deserted at the beginning. But when we saw the welcome, I told them: 'Now you can't doubt that this is a popular movement.' For that is what it was. The Moroccan troops were scandalized when they heard that the reds were desecrating religious images. Girls were pinning scapularies on the Moors and I remember one old *regular* who said to them: 'No saint, no Jesus – but God, yes!' . . .

Travelling in commandeered lorries and advancing mainly by night, the force advanced 200 km to Mérida, in Estremadura, in a week. Three hundred and fifty kilometres ahead lay their final objective: Madrid.

Behind them they left a rearguard which was by no means secure: Granada and Córdoba were still outposts, the former isolated, the latter connected to Seville by only a narrow corridor along the Guadalquivir river. To the south, on the coast near Gibraltar, danger of attack from the Popular Front forces in Málaga (where the rising had failed) remained very real.

Episodes 1: Attack

The summer somnolence of school holidays continued for thirteen-year-old Carlos CASTILLA DEL PINO. After the Moroccan troops had taken his native San Roque,[1] near Gibraltar, life appeared to return to normal and shortly he was expecting to resume lessons with his tutor.

1. See p. 65.

On the night of 26 July 1936, the illusion was shattered: lorry-loads of Popular Front militiamen from Málaga arrived in the village vicinity. At seven o'clock the next morning, shooting was heard. The boy's uncles and others began to display signs of nervousness and placed mattresses against the windows of their house. Very soon a group of militiamen reached the door.

—Nine gunshots – I counted them – was the way they knocked. My uncle opened the door. Three men came in, two with shotguns and wearing white shirts with their sleeves rolled up, red neckerchiefs, red armbands. The other man wore a steel helmet, the first I'd ever seen, and sergeant's insignia; in his left hand a sabre and in his right a large pistol . . .

The men searched the house and the boy followed them. The two civilians – anarchists, for that was what he imagined them to be – appeared very nervous, more at finding themselves in a well-to-do house and in front of *señoras* than for any other reason, he thought. In one of the cupboards, under some clothes, one of them found something and gave a shout. It was a large crucifix, not the weapon he thought he had discovered, and he put it back. They stayed half an hour and then took his three uncles and a cousin away as hostages. His family were all monarchists; his father, now dead, had been mayor of the township under the Primo de Rivera dictatorship.

Outside shooting continued. Though he didn't know it, his uncles and cousin had been taken to the barracks where they were made to call on the army detachment and the *guardia civil* to surrender. Neither did. At noon there was another knock on the door. The boy opened it to see a Moroccan *regulares* lieutenant standing there; he informed him that his uncles and cousin had been shot.

—The women in the house, my mother and aunts, started to scream and wail. Under cover of their crying I slipped out. The lieutenant had said that my uncle Pepe, though badly wounded, was still alive in the hospital. I loved him very much . . .

Carlos ran through the streets. In the Calle de la Plata, he saw three bodies close by the pavement. Two men and a child. Later he learnt that one of the men had come out of his house to see what was happening and a Moroccan had shot him; his brother came out and he, too, was shot. Crying with grief, his son came out – and the Moroccan shot him.

There was still firing and, without being told to, he put his hands up. As he ran, he saw his uncle Juan's body, wrapped in a republican flag, being carried on an improvised stretcher. At the hospital, the doctor, whom he often accompanied on his rounds (for the boy already wanted to be a doctor), told him he could see his uncle Pepe. 'But he's badly wounded. Don't cry – ' He found him lying in a corridor. The small local hospital had only a few beds and they were taken by wounded *carabineros*. His uncle had been shot in the street and had managed to crawl to the doorway of a republican's house where he was shot again. His body showed twenty-one bullet wounds, one of them in the toes.

—When I saw him, the blood-stained bandages in which he was wrapped, I started to cry. I think he recognized me. Soon he died . . .

He came out. His other uncle and cousin were lying dead in the street. Uncle Miguel's face had crashed on the pavement with such force that the bloodmarks could not be removed and the paving stone had to be replaced. Then he saw a Moor across the street.

—'*Ala, paisa*, run, run,' the Moroccan shouted. He lifted his rifle and fired. I didn't see the man fall but later I learnt it was a well-known local anarchist. Moroccans were searching out militiamen and shooting them down like that. From a place called La Hasa on the outskirts, Moroccans and civil guards were firing down on the militiamen as they tried to turn their lorries round only 200 to 300 metres away to escape. It was a massacre.

I went home. I didn't feel what had happened as a great personal tragedy. Rather, as I related what I had seen, I felt something of a hero. No one at home dreamt of eating anything, but I was hungry and slipped away to the kitchen. All I could find was a tin of condensed milk which I gulped down . . .

The family spent the night in the infantry barracks in case the 'reds' returned. His uncles and cousin were the only right-wingers to have been shot; another twenty or so people had been taken to the cemetery, but the Moroccans had arrived in time. From the positions in which his relatives' bodies were found, it seemed that they had been shot as the militia retreated rather than executed in a planned way.

In the barracks someone said that half a dozen men had been executed against the wall at the rear. He and some others went to look. There were six bodies of republicans who had been shot. One of the corpses still had his pipe in his mouth.

The next day he and his cousins went to the cemetery to bury their dead. An infernal scene met their eyes. The cemetery was carpeted with bodies, at least 200 of them. They picked their way through, looking for their relatives. They wrapped them in the sheets they had brought and buried them themselves in the family vault, without coffins. Carlos didn't recognize any of the other corpses; they were almost certainly the militiamen who had been trying to escape.

The right-wingers continued their executions that night.

—An anarchist couple, whose son was a school-mate of mine, was taken to a village 25 km away and shot. From a falangist who was present, I later heard that the woman had been raped by the whole Moorish firing squad before being executed.

The five wounded *carabineros* were brought out of the hospital on stretchers and a Moor caught hold of each one by the feet and arms and tossed him into a lorry. The village medical assistant, who had to accompany them with a lantern, told me what happened. When they got out on the road, the wounded men couldn't stand up to be shot and the Moors bayoneted them to death . . .

His family decided to leave, to take refuge in Gibraltar. San Roque was virtually the front line. They set off the next day and made the short trip without difficulty.

Small insurgent columns from Seville and Córdoba were attempting to 'pacify' neighbouring townships and villages, with their large numbers of landless labourers. In *pueblo* after *pueblo*, the pattern repeated itself: attack; rudimentary defence; the slaughter of some or all right-wing local prisoners before the imminence of defeat; capture of the village and the summary execution (after summary mass court martial) of all who had 'aided the rebellion' (that is, defended their village, and thus the legal government). The declaration of martial law by the rebel military affirmed their claim to be the legal authorities. All those denounced by 'law-abiding citizens' as assassins, left-wingers, trouble-makers, non-churchgoers were certain to be court-martialled. Queipo de Llano's threats were not to be taken lightly.[1]

Rafael MEDINA, thirty-year-old falangist businessman, was a sometime leader of a flying column which operated in his home region west of Seville. It was essential, he believed, to take villages rapidly in order to prevent assassinations of right-wing locals which 'the reds, enraged at the thought of losing their villages, carried out at the last moment before our forces approached'. But who could deny that there was also violence on the insurgent side?

—I was opposed to the repression, did what I could to prevent it. However, martial law had been declared, military discipline was at stake, there was news of the atrocities being committed in the other zone. Our situation was precarious; had there been any weakness we might have found ourselves in a difficult situation. 'Fear preserves the vineyard,' as we say. But I would much have preferred that this harshness, this fear, had not existed on our side . . .

The Marquess de MARCHELINA, a retired artillery officer who had joined the Carlists in Seville five years earlier and was leading a *requeté tercio* in the re-conquest of Andalusia, was scandalized by the executions. Carlist ideals could not be reconciled with such actions, and he always protested about them. However, his attitude, he recognized, was not the normal one.

—The repression was a military tactic that, unhappily, has been repeated in all wars – a means by which authority is asserted, a sad law of war. The problem for the military was that their forces were small in number at the beginning, and they had to impose discipline. The outcome of the war didn't seem that certain at the start, the slightest vacillation might have been fatal; sabotage, bombings, even guerrillas might have started. Inevitably, injustice was done – as it is in every war . . .

1. 'I doubt if those village people hated us of the right as much as the Spanish Catholic clergy and we, its faithful servants, hated them.' The testimony of a *requeté* who executed left-wingers in Lora del Río, a township of 11,000, where some 300 – including at least one pregnant woman – were estimated to have been shot (see 'El comienzo: la "liberación" de Lora del Río (1936)', *Cuadernos de Ruedo Ibérico*, 46–8, Paris, 1975). According to the insurgents, 138 people were assassinated in Lora before it was taken (see *Preliminary Report on Atrocities by Communist forces in Southern Spain, 1936–37*, London, 1937). In El Arahal, a township of 12,000 with a long anarchist tradition near Seville, twenty-three right-wingers were burned alive in the jail shortly before the place was taken by the insurgents. In return, legionaries 'inflicted an exemplary punishment', the *Correo de Andalucia* of Seville reported on 25 July 1936, killing some 'seventy to eighty people between defenders, the executed and those who attempted to flee'.

The repression was not confined to townships and villages where assassinations had been committed. In a railway village between Seville and Córdoba, the church was burnt but no one was killed during the fortnight the workers held it. Then a punitive expedition arrived from Seville. As it advanced, it set fire to the shacks of the poor on the way to the railway station. Juana SANCHEZ's husband put on his railwayman's uniform and went to the station where he had been left in charge. He was arrested and brought back to his house where his wife and five children were awakened.

—As they took him away in the lorry I ran after it shouting '*¡Por Dios! ¡Por Dios!*' and one of them shouted, 'If you don't get back you'll die before he does' . . .

She tried to think what her husband might have done to be arrested. A member of the UGT but no militant, she recalled only one political action of his: participation in a pre-war May Day demonstration. He had come home and asked her if she had a bit of red cloth. Although her father was an old-style republican, she always kept a red hanging at home to drape over the balcony to celebrate a religious festival; and her husband said he would use it as a flag if she would sew the three letters UHP on it. She hadn't known what they meant and he had told her: '*¡Unîos, hermanos proletarios!*' ('Unite, brother proletarians'). She had worried about his going but it had all passed off quietly.

Two days after his arrest she went to the village, an hour's walk from the station, and discovered that he was being held with a great number of other men in the *casa del pueblo*. Shortly, he was removed to the gaol. Every day she walked to the village to take him his food until her ten-month-old baby fell ill; then a right-wing family in the village offered her shelter. She went to see the local priest who tried to calm her fears, but when pressed for assurances told her that he could do no more. ' "They've told me not to stick my nose into things. Don Jerónimo, I smell gunpowder about your head," was what one of them told him.'

A month later, her husband told her his name was on a list; he asked her to speak to the *guardia civil* and the Falange chief, both of whom told her they knew nothing.

—'They can say what they like,' my husband told me, 'we're all dead men in here. When you hear the cock crow that will be when they take us out.' He asked me to stay in the village and early next morning to bring him tobacco. 'But early, very early' . . .

She returned to the right-wing family's house where she intended staying awake in the doorway all night; but the wife persuaded her to lie down, saying that her husband could not be taken because he hadn't been tried. Some time during the night, in dream or reality, she heard the sound of a lorry and the singing of *Cara al Sol*, the falangist anthem. She ran to the gaol; the policeman on duty waved her to stop.

—'There's no point in your coming here. Your husband has been taken to Seville.' The feet went from under me, I sat down and cried. No one comforted me. Finally, I dragged myself to the landowners' club and waited for the

Falange chief, who was at mass. 'Recommend your soul to God,' was all he had to say.

That was it. I never heard or received any definite news of my husband again . . .

She was convinced that her husband had been shot against the cemetery wall in Seville. The father-in-law of another man shot with her husband tried to bribe the grave-digger to tell him who had been shot there and on what day. The grave-digger said it was impossible because people were simply brought there and executed without names being given. But he recalled a tall man wearing green shoes who had been shot that day; before dying he had cried, 'Criminals, I am the father of five children!' She was sure that was her husband.

—When I went to Seville by train I looked out of the window at the cemetery wall. It was riddled with bullet-holes. I would think, 'One of those killed my husband,' and a terrible feeling came over me. But I couldn't not look . . .

Let it be known to all the inhabitants of this admirable capital that I shall be the faithful and cold image of Justice; placing myself above all evil and cowardice, I shall work without rest to ensure that in our capital and its villages there remains not a single traitor who can in any way hinder the self-sacrificing tasks which the army and militias are undertaking to . . . place us amongst the most civilized of nations that, with blind Christian faith, are full of ambitionless hopes.

Everything for Spain! The homeland demands it, and those who do not feel the love that every good son must feel for the fatherland are not worthy of living in it and must leave or disappear for ever from Spanish soil . . .

Major Bruno Ibáñez, of the civil guard, on taking up his appointment as head of public order in Córdoba (23 September 1936)

CORDOBA

The large Andalusian towns, whether they offered resistance to the military or not, felt the full rigours of the repression. Córdoba, with a population of close on 100,000, had fallen to the military in a few hours and almost without resistance on 18 July. An artilleryman had been killed and a prominent CEDA member was reported to have been found assassinated in the streets. These were the only deaths.

Major Bruno Ibáñez's efforts did not belie the words of his address to the people of Córdoba when he took up his new post as head of public order. In his first six days in office 109 people were arrested, more than in any equivalent period since 18 July. The repression, however, had started with the uprising.

Luis MERIDA, a twenty-five-year-old Córdoban lawyer, joined the military as soon as he heard the cannon pounding the civil government building into submission, hoping for a *coup d'état* to 'restore order to the republic'. The Popular Front had brought nothing but disorder – the birth-pangs of the social revolution, in his view. What he wanted was a military coup which would suspend the constitution for a couple of months and re-establish authority.

There was no rapid coup; instead he found himself in an isolated city, 'an island in a sea of anarchism', without sufficient weapons to defend itself. He took part in a sortie to Seville to get arms. On the road, the party came across a dozen corpses, patently labourers from their clothes and sandals. They had been shot. He and a friend said the Lord's Prayer.

—The others with us in the lorry listened in hostile amazement. 'Those accursed dogs, they should all be killed,' they said. They couldn't believe that anyone would pray for 'reds' . . .

These were falangist comrades of his, for he had joined the Falange very soon after the uprising, feeling it impossible not to belong to an organization which united all those who were fighting, and feeling also a certain attraction for José Antonio Primo de Rivera, the Falange's founder.

On their return from Seville with a lorry-load of arms and ammunition, the men heard that their leader, a member of the prominent Cruz Conde family in Córdoba, had been questioned by General Queipo when he reported on the situation.

—'How many of them have you shot in Córdoba?' Queipo asked. 'None! Well, until you shoot a couple of hundred there'll be no more arms for you,' he said in that raucous voice of his. He needn't have worried because the city was soon living under a reign of terror . . .

Every morning, when they made a sortie from the town along the road to Málaga, they saw the corpses of men and women, face up, face down, in an olive grove – the result of that dawn's executions.

—The cellar in the Falange headquarters where they brought the people was like a balloon which filled in the evening and by the next morning was empty again. And that was only part of it. Executions were taking place daily in the cemetery and on the other roads out of the city. They could kill anyone they wanted . . .

Seeing a notorious local executioner coming down the street 'waiting for dawn' with a whore on each arm, he reflected that the man believed in nothing that he and his comrades were fighting for.

—There were two sorts of people here, as no doubt in the other zone: those who went to the front to fight, and the criminals who stayed in the rear. I hadn't joined the movement for this . . .

From the start of the war, Córdoba newspapers reported official police arrests daily; 'unofficial' arrests went unreported as did, with few exceptions, the executions. Sometimes the reasons for the police arrests were given: a man 'selling marxist novels'; a woman 'putting out a white flag during last Monday's air raid'; the inspector of a children's home, 'doing no good, teaching children to give the clenched-fist salute'; a 36-year-old woman, 'a known extremist going daily to the cemetery to see the corpses and on her return to her *barrio* making remarks against the movement'; a grave-digger 'protesting about military orders in the cemetery of Nuestra Señora de la Salud'. From 18 July to 31 December 1936, 1,049 such arrests, fifty-three of them women, were reported. A small proportion of the total, no doubt.

Two days after his appointment, Major Ibáñez – known locally always as 'don Bruno' – announced publicly that he was going to rid Córdoba and the province of 'every book pernicious to a healthy society'. Anyone who had 'pornographic, revolutionary or anti-patriotic' works must hand them in forthwith or run the risk of court martial. Two weeks later, he was able to announce that 5,450 books had been destroyed.

—My father, who was a maths teacher, lived in terror, recalled Roberto SOLIS, a Catholic law student. He was an educated man, a centrist republican, who spoke English and French and liked to read. I saw him destroy Engels's *The Holy Family*, a work by Bakunin, Molotov's *Fifth Plan* . . .

His father had an assistant, a pleasant and serious young man of twenty-two of whom he was very fond. One day the latter boasted to him that 'for fun' he was taking part in the nightly executions.

—'Last night we shot eight.' My father couldn't get over the shock. If that wasn't enough, he soon learnt that a university professor was taking his fourteen-year-old son to watch the executions. The son, Pedro, used to tell me about it.

In the early mornings I remember my mother, who was a Catholic of enormous piety, exclaiming '*¡Ay, por Dios!*' when she heard the firing squad's volleys . . .

If the town had been living under a reign of terror before don Bruno's arrival, it became a nightmare during his rule. Luis MERIDA saw him at a benefit bull-fight.

—As he came out of the ring people cringed. He had blue eyes, I'll always remember. To get out of his way the people would have incrusted themselves in the walls if they could. Everyone was electrified with terror and fear. Don Bruno could have shot all Córdoba, he was sent here with *carte blanche*. It was said that his whole family had been wiped out by the reds in some town in La Mancha. Whether it was true or not, he was a prejudiced, embittered man . . .

He was also exceedingly pious, attending mass regularly. He advised the people that by all the means at his disposal he intended to 'exile from this holy earth' the vicious and irrational vice of blasphemy. 'All great, prosperous and cultivated nations have always been profoundly religious; Spain, in the intimacy of its being, is nothing other than twenty centuries of struggle for Christianity.' Characteristically, his next target was the cinema. He banned all films of an 'immoral and anti-militaristic' nature; all Russian films – 'even those of ancient times or of the Czars' – and permitted only films of an elevated, patriotic and religious character. Soon the cinemas were showing *Military Manoeuvres in Nuremberg*, shot in Hitler's presence and constituting a 'formidable demonstration of the German state's war potential'.

But he never allowed such matters to distract him from the real purpose of his office: his reprisals were immediate and pitiless. When one night some Popular Front saboteurs blew up a stretch of the Seville–Córdoba railway line, he summarily executed the entire railwayman's brigade that was on patrol duty that night.

There were disadvantages to his methods; within a month of taking office, he had to admit to labour shortages in the building, stone-cutting and mining industries. It was still not impossible to flee the city.

What need was there in a place which had submitted from the start, where there had been no assassinations, to shoot so many people, wondered Alvaro MILLAN, a sales representative, who was arrested twice. Was it because Córdoba was close to the front?

—No. The same terror existed everywhere. They created a state on the basis of lies and terror. It wasn't only the working class which suffered. Before the war I was a member of a *tertulia* which had some forty middle-class members: schoolmasters, lawyers, politicians, sales representatives, etc. Only four or five, including myself, survived the repression . . .

A self-made man, who had started life selling bootlaces in the streets of Córdoba, MILLAN only escaped execution by the rapid intervention of two friends. The town's leading bookseller and a doctor who shared his cell were both shot. When he was released he went to see his friend. 'My life is no longer mine, it is yours. Please allow me to join the Falange – ' A lifelong moderate socialist, he saw no other means of finding personal protection, and it was a favour his friend could not refuse.

—I never believed it was possible to kill people the way they did here . . .

A right-wing agricultural machinery manufacturer, Pedro QUINTANAR had welcomed the uprising, but the repression which followed it was beyond all imaginable proportions. One day he was standing outside the bishop's palace when a friar came out.

—The priest of the cemetery of San Rafael went over to him and I heard him say: 'How many are there tonight?' The friar replied, 'Seventy-six.' The priest, who was a very religious man, put his head to his hand and said, 'Seventy-six! *¡Ay, por Dios!* It's atrocious.' The other replied: 'Seventy-six? Seven hundred it should be.' I overheard the whole thing. It was staggering . . .

*

The connection between repression and religion (if not the church as a whole) was clearly marked in some minds from the beginning. 15 August, feast day of the Virgin, turned into a day of blood in different parts of the insurgent zone. In Seville, the bodies of the executed appeared lying beside the wall of the swimming pool that was then located where the Plaza de Cuba is today. Relatives remember turning over the bodies trying to find their kin. 'Corpses were left in the streets to terrorize the population,' Anita MORENO, of the communist youth women's section, recalled.

—They took people and shot them without even checking their identity. It happened to a man in my street; they shot him before they found out he wasn't the man they were after. He had had no political or union activity at all . . .

Her husband, secretary of the Socorro Rojo (Red Aid) organization for Andalusia, was shot. Offered freedom if he took up a rifle and joined the Falange, he refused. 'I won't kill anyone, they can kill me first. Look at the hatred they have for us who never hated them.' The shock of his execution was so great that her milk dried up and she couldn't feed her baby. In fear of her life, she went into hiding where she remained eight years, her daughter growing up to believe that she was her aunt. A civil guard who came to look for her wrote in his notebook: 'She is not in her house. It is believed that General Queipo de Llano's edict has been applied to her.'

—While I was hidden my brother's *novia* was shot. She was a communist party member and was arrested early on. The guard at the gaol gave her mother the watch she had left. It had stopped at 4.30 a.m. Before being taken out, she had struck the watch against the wall so that her mother should know the hour of her death . . .

The news of the executions on the feast day of the Virgin in Pamplona quickly reached the Somosierra front where the Navarrese *requetés* and falangists who had taken the pass in the Guadarrama mountains were still stationed. Sensational accounts of the repression in the Popular Front zone were being published in the insurgent-controlled papers but little about the repression taking place in their own zone was allowed to appear. Least of all, the massacre committed by the Army of Africa after its capture of Badajoz, in Estremadura, 14 and 15 August in its advance on Madrid. Antonio IZU and his *requeté* companions were shaken by the news brought back from Pamplona by two of his company.

—'*¡Cabrones!*' some expostulated. 'Those who've stayed in the rear ought to be brought up to the front to fight. Send them here to face the fire!' I was particularly shocked because one of those shot was my favourite uncle – the black sheep of the family, my father's cousin in fact, who had become a socialist. And for that they had shot him, a man in his sixties . . .

—'This is barbarous,' said a Carlist lawyer friend of mine, recalled Rafael GARCIA SERRANO, falangist student, on the same front, when we heard that fifteen or so people had been shot on 15 August. 'If we permit atrocities we'll be on the same level and will lose the war.' What upset us particularly was that the executions had taken place on the patron saint's day of Navarre. They were shot as leading members of the Popular Front. It was the sort of thing that happens in all revolutions; the sort of thing that was happening at the front, too. No prisoners were taken by either side – and, happily, very few prisoners were being captured.

Very soon afterwards, we learnt of Lorca's death. How we got the news I don't know, for no newspapers published it in our zone. We took it badly, but believed that it was because of the poet's homosexuality. We couldn't imagine that it would be a political assassination. 'Yes, of course, they've shot him because he's a queer' . . .[1]

But, as Antonio IZU knew, the repression was not only in the rearguard. In a village in the Guadarrama mountains where he was stationed, the company commander, a falangist career officer from Pamplona, arrested all thirty-one people who had voted for the Popular Front; the village electoral returns had been found, the right had won by seven votes. After interrogating the Popular Front voters, thirteen were put in a lorry.

—Women gathered round crying; the falangists kicked them back, used their rifle butts on them. It was a terribly poor village, the peasants were half-starved wretches. The lorry set off for the rear, and I imagined they were being taken to Aranda de Duero . . .

Not long afterwards, by chance he discovered their fate. The *requetés*, after an attack, withdrew to a position nearby, where they were overwhelmed by a pestilential smell. By a small stream they discovered thirteen corpses so hurriedly buried that the toes of their sandals were sticking out of the earth. The *requetés* reburied them. As one was lifted out of the ground, some small change fell from his pocket.

—It was the village barber who had shaved us all, charging only 25 centimos; it was so little that we always gave him double. We made rough crucifixes, our chaplain said the responses. Later he confronted the falangist army officer and told him what he thought. The captain swore at him and threatened to shoot him if he didn't shut up . . .

1. Because of his world reputation as one of Spain's leading poets and playwrights, García Lorca's assassination in Granada has come to symbolize the barbarity of the insurgent repression. In his native city, with a population of about 125,000, 2,137 men and women are recorded as having been executed in the city cemetery – 'the flower of Granada's intellectuals, lawyers, doctors . . . along with huge numbers of ordinary left-wing supporters'. (I. Gibson, *The Death of Lorca*, London, 1973.) Many more, including Lorca himself, were executed beyond the confines of the city itself.

In these days in which military justice is pursuing its sad mission . . . an unusual number of people has been seen congregating in the place where the executions take place. Among them are children, young girls and even some ladies. These [executions] are public, it is true; but their enormous gravity . . . is more than sufficient reason for people, whose religious convictions are in many cases openly displayed, not to attend, even less take their wives and children . . .

Note from the civil governor's office
(Valladolid, 24 September 1936)

SEGOVIA

While the church hierarchy, with a few exceptions, maintained a prudent silence in the first six weeks, the same was not true of some priests who allowed their passions full rein. Dionisio RIDRUEJO, Falange chief in Segovia, listened with amazement to a sermon preached in the cathedral.

—'The Fatherland must be renewed, all the evil weed uprooted, all the bad seed extirpated. This is not the time for scruples – ' The sermon was evidently aimed at the three or four people who were trying to prevent the repression in Segovia, including myself . . .

For a fortnight they were successful; left-wingers were arrested but not shot. The roadside assassination of three or four people by Acción Popular militants and falangists caused a commotion. Two tendencies emerged, one legalistic, which believed that people should be arrested and tried, the other maintaining that a certain amount of terror had to be created by summary executions. The second tendency won the day when the Valladolid Falange took charge of the region and sent a delegate to Segovia to organize the repression.

—A special squad was formed, led by a very religious and sinister falangist from Valladolid. In place of the tassel on his cap he wore a Christ on the Cross. The squad's task, officially, was to arrest and take people to prison; but hardly any ever reached their destination. They were left dead on the roads. I and others attacked the squad leader, asserting that he could not be both judge and executioner. 'No, I take good care of these people,' he answered with complete confidence. 'They all have the chance to confess before they die, and therefore can go to heaven' . . .

The situation was aggravated by republican bombing of the town which did little damage but caused wounded (along with inevitable demands for reprisals on prisoners); and the closeness of the front, 35 km away.

—Looked at quite coldly, the terror could be justified. A guerrilla movement, an uprising in the rear, could have disintegrated the thinly held Alto del León front. Monstrous as it was, the military criterion of repression had its logic. Mola believed the purge should be rapid, Franco that it should be methodical and exhaustive; both had the same basic idea . . .

It was in Valladolid, where socialist workers from the railway repair shops had staged resistance, and where the Falange was strong, that the repression in Old Castile reached its maximum severity. 'The clean-up', as a falangist civil servant, Pedro JUAREZ, put it, 'was very thorough. The tram company garages were turned into a prison and were kept full a long time.'

JUAREZ had wanted to go to the front but, being a father of two young children, was assigned to guard duty in the rear. Valladolid was being bombed by a single plane almost every day, and there were rumours that the city's water reservoirs were going to be poisoned. He was put on guard duty at the reservoirs in the Campo de San Isidro.

—One morning we were ordered to form a cordon; the spectators were pressing too close to the firing squads carrying out public executions in the Campo. We had to keep them at least 200 metres away, and were given strict orders to prevent children joining the spectators.

The prisoners were brought from the tram garages. Among the dozen the first day I did duty, there were some I recognized from a village near mine. Imagine my feelings! All of them, including a woman, refused to be blindfolded. Like several others, the woman raised her hand in a clenched-fist salute and cried '*¡Viva la República!*' as the shots rang out.

For the rest of the week, while I continued on duty, a dozen people were shot every dawn. They included three more women. Two of them, as the firing squad took aim, lifted their skirts over their faces, revealing themselves completely. Gesture of defiance? Of despair? I don't know: it was for scenes like this that people went to watch. And then, when we returned to the city, the streets were completely deserted; all the spectators had disappeared into their homes, their beds. The city was silent . . .

—This was no illiterate mob which went to watch, reflected Jesús ALVAREZ, a liberal republican chemist. In the *casino*, people said to each other: 'Don't forget to be there tomorrow – ' These were people of social standing, sons of distinguished families, men who had received an education, people who professed to be religious. It was not a lumpen-proletariat, deprived of work, education, well-being like that on the other side; but it might just as well have been, for these bourgeois showed that all their education, culture, religion was nothing – skin-deep. So many went to watch the 'spectacle' – for that is what it was for them – that coffee and *churro* stalls were set up so that they could eat and drink as they watched . . .

The terror, he saw, was an important part of the counter-revolution; and the Falange did not shirk it. Though he was no admirer of the Falange, he had to admit, however, that the idealists in the main went to the front. It was the 'scum' left behind who did the assassinating, and the worst among them were the turncoats, the left-wingers who had joined to save their skins.

Because of the terror, people delated, denounced each other.

—The instinct of self-preservation. Imagine what it's like, day after day, to go out into the street, light a cigarette, walk to the café and act as though nothing is happening. For if you don't show your face you become an object of suspicion. Only by acting as though everything is perfectly normal can you show that you are above suspicion. You fear that if you hide your knowledge about someone else you will be executed; you hope that if you inform, your life will be spared. By becoming part of 'normality' the terror contributed to maintaining an appearance of normality. More than personal vendettas, of which there were enough, it was the terror which contributed most to its own perpetuation . . .

Some protests were made, the most famous being that of Unamuno, the most prestigious intellectual figure in the insurgent zone.[1] He was not alone. Eugenio VEGAS LATAPIE, editor of the monarchist *Acción Española*, felt sufficiently indignant to take the matter to the very highest level. Given the opportunity of accompanying the poet José María Pemán to see Franco, who not long before had reached the peninsula from Morocco, he raised the matter of assassinations.

—It was of absolute importance that these be brought to an end immediately. One heard rumours all the time of people being taken from gaol and shot without trial. Falangists even suggested to me that they would liquidate political enemies of mine. It was incredible, horrifying and a grave discredit to the cause. I stressed to Franco the necessity of ensuring that no one be shot without trial, however summary, and without the chance of defending himself.

Franco took no notice of me. As far as the repression was concerned, he knew very well what was happening and didn't give a damn. On information I gave him later, Pemán took up the case with Franco direct of the number of people who were being kept a year or more under sentence of death. Franco explained that this was necessary in order to be able to exchange them for prisoners in similar circumstances in the red zone. That was his explanation. But hardly any exchanges were authorized by the Franco regime during the war; and moreover, when the war was over and there was not even this excuse, the situation continued exactly as before, with people being kept under sentence of death for a year, if not longer. Franco displayed the simple, cold cruelty for which he was well known in the Foreign Legion . . .

At the local level, it was possible for one man to determine the outcome of the situation. In the village of Tamariz de Campos, Valladolid, Alberto PASTOR's

1. See below, pp. 205–9.

home village, no one was shot despite the pre-war violence in which he had participated.[1]

—I wouldn't tolerate it. From the start I said: 'You will answer with your lives for any killings that take place.' Tamariz must be the only village around here where no outrages were committed. Elsewhere local feuds resulted in assassinations. I was determined the same should not happen in my village. Some people were arrested, and one died in prison from illness, but none was shot . . .

In Pamplona, the Carlist regional chief issued an order a few days after the uprising that no Carlist was to carry out acts of violence and must do everything possible to prevent their being committed in his presence. 'For us, the only reprisals permitted are those ordered by the military authorities, who are always just and circumspect,' the order, signed by Joaquín Baleztena, stated.

—Bishop Olaechea of Pamplona, and Cardinal Gomá, primate of Spain who was on holiday in Navarre, congratulated my brother on his stance. But the note didn't go down well at Mola's HQ here. Officers told my sister, who had gone there to seek the release of a prisoner, that our brother's 'vaseline note' had made matters worse, Dolores BALEZTENA remembered. I don't believe there was complicity between the few falangist assassins who were carrying out their dirty work in the rearguard and the military; but there was certainly connivance. The military were the supreme authorities at that moment; had they wished to end the repression, they could obviously have done so . . .

Mola, whose original plans for the uprising included the arrest and 'exemplary punishment' of all political and trade union leaders opposed to the military, sent a telegram from Burgos on 20 August 1936 forbidding 'falangists and similar forces' to commit acts of violence in Pamplona. This followed a similar note from the local commandant two weeks earlier. On 15 September, the new civil governor reminded mayors that arbitrary arrests were forbidden. After a massacre of prisoners dragged from the gaol at Tafalla, Bishop Olaechea called for an end to the blood-letting. 'No more blood except that laid down by the Tribunals of Justice . . . We must not be like them . . . Not a drop of vengeance blood.' In November, the new military commandant had once again to repeat orders against violence committed by people claiming to belong to the militia.

—The repression was the great sorrow of the war. I was pleased when Bishop Olaechea protested; the clergy must speak out at wrong-doing. 'How can things like this go on? How can they allow it?' Carmen GARCIA-FALCES, a Carlist, asked her friends. The repression caused us grief because we believed we were fighting for Good. We knew many of the people who were being shot, and they

1. See Militancies 2, pp. 86–9. There was a belief, common to both sides, and not infrequently proven in practice, that personal courage could prevent an assassin from committing a crime. 'A courageous man can make a coward – for that is, essentially, what an assassin is – ashamed of himself and withdraw; for the courageous man says, "You will have to shoot me first if you want to carry out your dirty work." And that makes the other think of the consequences of his act, of his cowardice.' (Jesús ALVAREZ, chemist, Valladolid.) In Old Castile the inquirer will hear instances of village priests who, by a display of great personal courage, prevented their parishioners' execution. For an example, see Militancies 5, pp. 172–3.

seemed good people to us – why were they being executed? They had been tried, all right – but why shot? Our side was pursuing God's cause and God would never condone such atrocities. The assassinations of priests on the other side were terrible – but there the assassins weren't believers, it wasn't the same thing . . .

Despite the orders, prohibitions, admonitions, warnings, the killings continued. It was not surprising; nor was it a problem peculiar to Navarre. The short-term aims of pacifying a potentially hostile rearguard – a problem much more acute in other areas – coincided with the long-term aim of crushing the working class and its allies, leaders and militants, to exorcise the threat, once and for all, of proletarian disturbances, risings and revolution.[1] At the same time, moreover, the repression served to show the insurgents' supporters that the rising was not to be a simple change of political regime, but a profound change in the correlation of social forces: a counter-revolution, in short, in which they were implicated by the repression even if they did not participate directly in shedding blood.

1. The question of the number of victims caused by the repression on both sides still awaits a definitive historical answer. Oral history – except at the village level – does not provide accurate answers; in the large towns, because of their size, only documentary records (such as those provided by Ian Gibson in his *Death of Lorca* for the insurgent executions in Granada cemetery) will finally elucidate – if such is possible – what has been the subject of a series of unsatisfactory estimates from a variety of positions over the years. *Overall*, it can be safely supposed, the Franquista repression caused by far the greater number of victims, for the simple reason that it was more extensive in time, space and breadth. In space, it came to exercise its reign over the *whole* of Spain, capturing new territories and new, often largely hostile populations, throughout the war, while the republican territory receded. In time, because it continued fully operative for four years *after* the war ended. In breadth, because the class enemy – the industrial and rural proletariat (to name but that class) – was anything up to three times as numerous as the *whole* of the bourgeoisie. (If for no other reason than that they have a *larger* class to dominate, victorious bourgeois counter-revolutions have historically proven more bloody than revolutions.) The difference in attitudes was in itself indicative. The republican government (along with *all* parties and trade unions) condemned assassinations and, as its power increased, brought them under control. Although the insurgent nationalist authorities also ended random assassinations, no official condemnation was ever pronounced in the zone they controlled. The republic introduced Popular Tribunals which, despite defects, established trial by jury under the existing civilian legal code (see below, pp. 176, 177–8). The nationalist summary mass court-martials were little more than a device to 'legitimize' the repression. (As readers of the *Diario de Burgos*, which reported one such court-martial in Valladolid gaol which began in the morning of 2 September 1936, and was over by 3 p.m., may have reflected. In that time, the paper said, 448 prisoners accused of military rebellion – the usual charge against those who had resisted the military – were tried. Allowing for a misprint, it was a fairly average time for forty-four or forty-eight prisoners to be tried.) Some political parties in the republican zone operated parallel police forces and *checas* (interrogation/detention centres – named after the first Bolshevik security organization) which took justice into their own hands; after the initial moments this did not happen in the insurgent zone where the repression was rigorously, methodically organized and where a large part of the terror – perhaps the most cruel – was to keep prisoners under sentence of death for months, if not longer, never sure whether or not they would be shot tomorrow.

Militancies 5

JUAN CRESPO

Monarchist student

For him this was a paradoxical war. No sooner had he left the front at the Alto del León because he was 'fed up'[1] and returned to Salamanca, than he was setting off again to fight. This time under the command of Major Doval, the civil guard officer who had organized the repression in Asturias after the October 1934 uprising and who was now leading an expeditionary force to block an enemy offensive flanking the Guadarrama and threatening Avila. Only a few days earlier, Onésimo Redondo, the Valladolid falangist leader, had been killed in an ambush 40 km behind the lines; the insurgent rear was by no means secure.

—Again, we were going to have coffee in Madrid. When we reached Navalperal, on the road from Avila, we were ambushed. They were firing at us from all sides. We threw ourselves on the ground; thereafter, it was a question of each for himself. I threw my rifle away and began to run. Only the civil guards with a couple of machine-guns put up any resistance. I started running at 11 a.m. and I reached Avila, 40 kilometres away, still running, at 6 p.m. A marathon! . . .

He slipped back to Salamanca. There he received another piece of unpleasant family news. Before setting out the first time for the front, his uncle, the mayor of Salamanca and an eminent university professor, doctor and left republican deputy, had been arrested and assassinated. His body had been found beside that of the socialist deputy, Manso, 30 km away on the road to Valladolid. Now, during his second absence, another uncle had been arrested. Coming from the village of Morasverdes, where he was the town hall secretary, to buy his eldest daughter a pair of white gloves for her wedding, he had been arrested in Salamanca 'as a relative of my other uncle, Dr Casto Prieto'. Thrown in gaol and held without trial until May 1937, he was let out dying of a bladder complaint which received no treatment in prison.

—I decided to go to the village to visit my aunt who had brought me up for three years after my father died, and she asked me to stay on and take over my uncle's work until a new town hall secretary was appointed . . .

Nothing had happened in the village, a small but relatively prosperous place in the south of Salamanca province where the land was well-irrigated. The local doctor took charge. Under the dictatorship, he had been a member of the dictator's Unión Patriótica; in the opening period of the republic, a left republican thanks to his friendship with Crespo's Salamanca uncle; in the next period, jealous of Crespo's village uncle who occupied a more prominent post in the left republicans than he, he joined the CEDA. Now that times had changed, he became a falangist. But things on the village council, which he had appointed, were not turning out as he wished: the deputy mayor kept calling for votes and the doctor's proposals were being defeated.

1. See p. 116.

—So one day he went to Ciudad Rodrigo, the nearest big town, and returned with three or four falangists. They rang the town hall bell to summon the village to a meeting in the schoolhouse. The Falange chief sat in the teacher's chair. 'Strange things are happening in this village. Perhaps you don't realize that democracy no longer exists. The only democracy is this – ' and he pulled out his pistol. 'In view of this, be careful. The town council is hereby dissolved' . . .

A new council was appointed, the vexatious deputy mayor thrown out. On 15 August, feast day of the Virgin, falangists turned up on a sinister mission 'to get a few people'. As a couple of them were school-mates of Crespo they showed him the list of five people; one of them, the only woman, was his cousin, the daughter of his recently arrested uncle. From the names, he saw that it had been drawn up by someone from the village: 'the former deputy mayor's brother, in fact – another political turncoat, a man without an ounce of ideology. My aunt and uncle were his god-parents and here he was denouncing their daughter.'

Apart from arresting those on the list, the falangists intended to give a few others a 'good fright'. The mayor told them who was in need of such medicine. One of these was Juan, the son of the village poacher. Juan and his brother, both socialists, had volunteered for the insurgent army at the time of the rising; but Juan had the misfortune to be in the village on leave. 'I'm as patriotic as you – more than you,' Crespo heard him shouting as they beat him in the town hall. 'I'm in uniform – why are you beating me?'

—What irony there was in all this as the future would show! For the only two villagers killed in the war were Juan and his brother. Those two, who had poached everyone's game, who had been socialists, now became heroes of the Movement. Their names were inscribed on monuments, celebrated in a mass for the fallen which I attended in the village: there was the priest, who had always been denouncing them for stealing his chickens and eggs, saying mass for them; the corporal of the *guardia civil*, who was always arresting them, at the head of the guard of honour; the mayor, who had organized their beating by the falangists, giving the ritual cries. A moment of delicious local historic irony! . . .

Meanwhile the business of arresting those they had come for was getting underway. The mayor added some names to the list. Crespo didn't like the way things were going.

—In front of the town hall was the priest's house. No one liked him; he'd had an affair with the sacristan's wife and many approaches had been made to the bishop to get rid of him. I went in; he was having his siesta. I told his brother to wake him and I explained the situation. He heard me out and came with me to the town hall. As soon as he saw the falangists and the mayor, he said: 'No one is leaving this village. I am the priest and only I know the villagers' consciences. There may be some who don't go to church but there are none who are criminals.'

The Falange chief looked at him. 'Well, father, that's your view because you're the priest and it's your duty – '

The next move surprised us all. The priest threw himself on the floor in front of the doorway. 'Before any of my parishioners leave here, you'll have to pass over my body.'

The Falange chief was moved. 'Let's see if this can be arranged. Father, get up, please. I promise you that no one will be killed. I give you my word as a Catholic that I will take these people to the civil governor, no more. I will not put them in prison. If you wish, you may come with us.'

They arrested the cart-maker and the schoolmaster, the latter being the head of the local socialists. One of the others due to be arrested had already fled to the mountains, and the doctor wouldn't allow them to take my cousin because she had Malta fever. As they were taking the teacher to the car, his daughter, a very beautiful girl of twelve, threw herself at the Falange chief's feet and kissed them. So moved was he that he told her to get up and returned her father to her. So only the cart-maker was taken – and the next day he returned on the bus. They were saved by the priest and, in truth, by the Falange chief who was a decent man at heart. Only one of those who came had been a falangist before the war – one of the thirty-three in Salamanca. The rest had donned the blue shirt since the uprising . . .

CRESPO now heard that Renovación Española, the monarchist party, was organizing a volunteer battalion in Burgos, and for the third time in little over a month he set off as a volunteer for the front. He left behind an uncle in prison, an uncle assassinated, and yet another uncle in hiding. (The last of these, a CEDA member, was mayor of the municipality where the corpse of Dr Casto Prieto, the Salamanca uncle, was found. Soon he, too, was receiving threats to his life and, riding his horse halfway across the province to a small village near Morasverdes, he hid in a charcoal burner's hut. When he gave himself up he was clapped in gaol.)

—It was a civil war; the front was a sinuous line which divided friend from friend, brother from brother, which ran through many a particular home and even through bedrooms. In my family there were Carlists, liberals, republicans. My situation was by no means unique. I did what I could to alleviate the suffering of my relatives on the other side, did what I could to get my uncles out of gaol, but I went on fighting for my ideals. Not material interests, because I had none, but ideals: to end the chaos that the left and the CEDA had provoked; to restore law and order, authority and a national spirit. It had become a crime to cry *¡Viva España!* The Catalan and Basque autonomy statutes were the last straw. They were simply going to lead to independence and the end of Spanish unity. Every time there's a revolutionary situation in Spain, 'cantonalism' spreads like fungus. First Catalonia, then the Basque country, next Galicia – and in the end a village like Morasverdes – wants independence. Committees and juntas in every *pueblo*. There's no end to it. The moment a strong power disappears, Spain dissolves. The Spaniard only does what he wants. He is a king to himself who wants to be the king of everyone else. The Spaniard cannot be democratic – not because he lacks the education or culture, no – but because he is simply incapable of it. The republicans who believed the contrary were the most moronic of all. Without a world role, Spain had lost what Ortega y Gasset called 'the stimulation of a common programme'; without such a programme, rivalries and domestic problems could not be overcome. Spain was lost . . .

Although a monarchist, his sympathies lay with the Falange. Ever since he had read José Antonio Primo de Rivera's founding speech, he had been moved by his 'poetic prose' which, combined with the historic memory of Spain's past greatness and to a lesser extent with the Falange's social programme, influenced him strongly. Yet, for sentimental reasons, he remained a monarchist, believing that Franco was also one because, in the past, the king had favoured him; believing that the war would end in a dictatorship because 'that was what everyone wanted'. No one was concerned about what sort of dictatorship as long as it brought a return of authority and national spirit.

—The one thing I wasn't fighting for was the church. I fought on Franco's side without believing in God. At the age of thirteen, in the religious boarding school I was sent to in Salamanca, I had a religious crisis and stopped believing. We were saturated with religion there, there was nothing but saints – day in, day out. The first thing that struck me was the difference between what the priests preached and their personal conduct. Many of the younger friars who were studying to be priests had homosexual leanings and divided us pupils into the 'pretty' and the 'ugly'. The discipline was ferocious, it was just like a barracks. When I became an officer leading Moroccan troops – shock troops which, like the Foreign Legion, were full of adventurers and criminals – I was like a fish in water thanks to my training at school.

I became hostile to the church's social function. Spain has been dominated by religion – a religion imposed from above and used for instrumental social objectives. The Spaniard has never had deep religious beliefs as a result. Intransigently, many Spaniards have believed themselves the right arm of God; religion has been an emblem people have worn – like a football club badge. We've spent our lives building churches and burning them. And sometimes it has been the same people doing both.

I was fighting to create a better Spain. That would require sacrifices. The things going on in the rearguard were one of these sacrifices needed in order that justice might win. It was a necessary, if painful, part of the war. But I was also aware that it was necessary for us to prove ourselves *better* than the reds whose atrocities filled our papers. So, when my uncle was assassinated, I couldn't help wondering why a man who had done no one any harm, an eminent doctor and university professor, a man who had been elected to his position as deputy, should be killed for defending his ideals. How could we be making a better Spain if we were acting just like the other side?

But I went on fighting. The war went on. I didn't think too much about the rearguard, it was better not to. If you did, you might find yourself doing something foolish like throwing down your rifle. The thing to do was to aim to kill . . .

MADRID

Régulo MARTINEZ, president of the left republican party in Madrid, was busy trying to find rooms for the refugees fleeing to the city from Estremadura and Toledo, now that the Army of Africa had reached the Tagus valley, 180 km from Madrid. In three weeks it had advanced nearly double that distance from Seville, meeting little serious resistance. The militia columns were proving no match for the legionary and Moroccan units.

The capital's streets were jammed with peasant carts, herds of goats and sheep and peasant families. The week before, Badajoz had fallen. Rumours of the bloody massacre that had been wreaked on the defenders and civilian population of the Estremaduran capital immediately after the capture, were beginning to reach Madrid. Two days earlier, insurgent planes had bombed the capital.

At 9 p.m., MARTINEZ returned to party headquarters. The telephone rang; Marcelino Domingo, the party's national president, was on the line.

—'The people have stormed the Model prison and it is on fire,' I heard him say. 'The ambassadors of Britain and France have informed us that if the situation is not brought under control immediately, they will recognize Franco – ' 'I see – But – ' 'Yes,' he said. 'You're much better known in Madrid than I. The government has asked for representatives of all the Popular Front parties to go to the prison and meet General Pozas, the interior minister, to resolve the problem' . . .

He set off immediately. The air raid, which had hit the *barrio* of Argüelles, in which the prison was situated, had caused a lot of damage. It was the first air raid on Madrid.[1] There were civilian casualties, a young girl holding a doll was among the dead. The modern epoch of war had begun. The capital had no anti-aircraft defence (cinema projectors were later mounted on roofs as searchlights), there was no protection from raids. The people, thought MARTINEZ, wanted revenge. If they were being killed from the air, they were going to kill some of the right-wingers in the prison.

He had great difficulty getting through to the prison because control points had been set up everywhere. When he reached it, he found that more than twenty of the outstanding right-wing leaders being held there had been assassinated; but the fire was not burning so intensely.

As soon as General Pozas finished addressing the assembled Popular Front representatives, MARTINEZ asked for the floor.

—'The left republican party says that it is inadmissible that anything be done which harms the republic. And that is what has happened here today.' 'What do you mean?' people shouted. 'If you want to kill people,' I replied, 'let me tell you something. Long before you became a democrat or whatever, I was serving the republican cause – ' Again there were shouts. I realized I had to take a new tack. 'I demand the maximum punishment for the republic's enemies. In return I demand the maximum good sense from those who maintain they are the republic's friends. These sort of acts cannot be tolerated. You all know the threats that hang over the republic as a result of this assault and these murders – '

1. In the first weeks of the war, the republicans used their air superiority, such as an obsolete air force could provide, to bomb insurgent-held towns (Córdoba, Granada, Segovia, Valladolid, to name only these), causing civilian casualties on a scale reminiscent of First World War raids. The insurgent air raids on Madrid, using German bombers, would soon escalate to a level heralding the beginning of the Second World War.

'What are you proposing, then?' the people cried. 'The following. That none of us leave this room until we have agreed to set up tribunals on which, *de facto* and *de jure*, the people are represented through their political parties and organizations. This will ensure that the tribunals are not lenient in applying the law, the people will see to that. At the same time, the law will provide a counterweight to popular excesses. The Popular Front organizations must appoint their representatives and lawyers to this popular tribunal immediately.'

'Good,' said General Pozas. 'I'll inform the government that a popular tribunal is to be set up.' I heard the sound of a whistle; people began to put out the fire . . .

As he prepared to leave, a FAI militant came up. 'You're a man of good faith,' he said. 'Shall we go and look at the *fiambres* [lit. cold meats, corpses]'. MARTINEZ agreed. It was necessary, he thought, to put out the story that they had been shot while attempting to flee in order to justify, in some measure, a crime which should never have been committed.

The first corpse they came across was a former pupil of his. The FAI man looked at him. 'Do you feel sick?' He explained that he had taught the young man from the age of eight until he went to the university; he had been one of his very few students to become a falangist, had been involved in the attempted assassination of Jiménez de Asúa, a leading socialist deputy and professor, only a few months before.

—'I fully understand that he deserved his fate. But it affects me – ' We continued through the prison. We saw the corpse of Melquíades Alvarez. 'But this man was a democrat,' I expostulated. 'You're too honest,' an old socialist, who was standing near by, replied. He went on to recall a time before the republic, when Alvarez, founder of the reformist party and one of the king's councillors, had been met by a stony silence at a Bilbao political rally until he alluded to Pablo Iglesias, founder of the socialist party, who was on the same platform. Everyone cheered, the two men embraced. 'If you betray that embrace, the people will demand a reckoning,' the old socialist who was in the crowd had shouted. 'And he did betray it,[1] and there you see him now' . . .

The people, he thought, had the memory of an elephant. Every betrayal, every insult, every injury done to them – especially by their employers – was remembered. When they found themselves armed they took their revenge – not only on that person but on his father and grandfather, for it was an historic revenge.

—By 9 a.m. the next morning, the first Popular Tribunal was functioning. Its establishment put an end to the generalized wave of *paseos*; sporadic assassinations continued, but people could now see that their enemies were being tried. Before, they had felt that the republic was being too lenient . . .

The government instructed the population to lock their doors after 11 p.m. and call the police if unauthorized persons attempted to enter – further measures

1. By insisting on the execution of those sentenced to death after the October 1934 insurrection in Asturias and Catalonia and withdrawing his support – along with the CEDA – when the centre-right government refused to carry out the sentences.

which helped put an end to the indiscriminate killings. Amongst so many others, the latter nearly took the life of Pablo Neruda, then Chilean consul in Madrid. While dining one night at Carmencita's restaurant, 'militiamen' came to arrest him. He was saved by his friend, art professor Rafael SANCHEZ, who ran to the neighbouring security HQ, DGS (Dirección General de Seguridad), and called the police, who arrested the men, while offering profuse apologies to the Chilean poet.

Here, as in Barcelona, the revolutionary necessity of assuring the rearguard had been muddied by personal bloodletting, vendettas and arbitrary slayings.

—In those first weeks you heard people in queues saying – or even shouting in the streets – 'We've just come back from the Manzanares – there are seventeen today,' remembered Alvaro DELGADO, son of a shop manager who lived in the working-class district of Lavapies. Men, women and even children went to see the corpses; it was a spectacle. 'There was one today who was wearing silk stockings, I lifted up her petticoats and she had beautiful underwear on – ' That was one of the many remarks I overheard . . .

Among others, the communist party took action. Pedro SUAREZ, the communist clerk who had set out with his wife in a Madrid double-decker bus to fight at the Alto del León pass, was back in Madrid to see his wife who had been wounded after a couple of days at the front. Because of the assassinations he was ordered by his party to remain in Madrid. The rearguard was abandoned and all sorts of crimes were being committed, he was told. He and others were to serve in an auxiliary force at the orders of the DGS to try to stop them. They set up street controls. When a car was stopped, the occupants were asked for their identity papers.

—Then one of us would say, 'Anyone who does not wish to be in this car should say so now and get out.' This was in case someone was being taken for a *paseo*. It happened once, that I remember; when we disarmed and checked on the occupants, it turned out they were common criminals. Within three months we had put an end to the *paseos*. We couldn't stop the occasional assassination, it's true, but searches could now only be carried out by the police, who had to have a special Security HQ warrant – a white one by day, a red one at night – and a neighbour or the porter had to be present during the search and sign a statement of what had been found . . .

A non-political public prosecutor who was appointed to a Popular Tribunal and whose task it was not only to present the case against the accused but to act as 'defender of the law', found that there was rarely a miscarriage of justice if the jury had the law explained to them.

—It was when the law wasn't explained – which happened frequently because the judges were untrained or were right-wingers – that all sorts of outrage were committed . . .

There were, in fact, two sorts of tribunal. The first, in Fernando MORENO's view, was a perfectly constitutional creation set up to try people on charges of rebellion, sedition and other crimes against state security. The seven Popular Front parties and organizations each appointed two jurors and the tribunal was presided over by a professional judge assisted by two other judges. The jury's task was simply to find for or against the accused. The three judges were responsible for sentencing.

Created at the same time, and much less known, were the emergency tribunals (Tribunal de Urgencia). These, MORENO believed, were 'unconstitutional, illegal and flagrantly political': they could try people accused of 'disaffection to the republic'; could find people guilty retroactively – 'to have voted monarchist, or for the CEDA was sufficient cause to be sentenced'. The emergency courts could not hand down sentences of more than five years' imprisonment, while the Popular Tribunals could sentence to death. There was no appeal from either tribunal.

—The major problem was the lack of reliable judges and investigating magistrates. The judicial corps had been virtually dismantled after the uprising, judges had been arrested, assassinated, had fled. But not all the right-wingers had been removed. Because they were frightened for their lives, they acted either extremely harshly in order to prove their loyalty or else were so timid they refused to stick their necks out. On one occasion, I said to a fellow prosecutor: 'we must act impartially, see that justice is done.' 'No, we'll act as harshly as we can and may he who falls fall – ' That was the attitude of many right-wingers; it was a negation of justice . . .

Mario REY, falangist carpenter, who had been in the Montaña barracks and had managed to walk out through the crowds when they stormed it, was tried by an emergency tribunal (which in common parlance was also called a Popular Tribunal). After his escape from the Montaña, he had at first remained hidden in a friend's house. When he attempted to return home – his parents believed he had been assassinated – he was arrested in the street by the self-styled 'brigade of criminal investigation', led by García Atadell, a man of sad reputation, who was soon to defect with a considerable quantity of loot, be captured and executed in Seville by the insurgents. Released after a couple of days, REY was re-arrested for having no identification papers.

Worse than prison and awaiting trial, had been the hiding, he thought. School-mates, lifelong friends from his *barrio*, went to his home looking for him.

—Friends I'd played football with, got up to schoolboy escapades with, played truant with only a few years before, now wanted to kill me. How do you explain it? From one day to the next I had become a wild beast to be tracked down and killed. *¡Coño!* That was what was so brutal, so absurd, about a civil war . . .

By contrast, he was not maltreated under arrest or in prison.[1] At his trial, he was accused of being a falangist. He defended himself – the man who was

1. He was still there in November 1936 when the newly appointed anarchist head of Madrid prisons, Melchor Rodríguez, sent a delegate to Porlier gaol to inform the prisoners personally that nobody would be taken from the prison at night to be shot illegally. 'From that moment on, the arbitrary executions ended.'

On the other side of the lines, in Salamanca, General Millán Astray, founder of the Foreign Legion, visited the gaol on 1 January 1937 on behalf of Franco to give a similar assurance to the prisoners: no one would in future be taken from the gaol without trial and shot. (Evidence of a republican doctor who was imprisoned in Salamanca, then Franco's HQ.)

appointed to defend him not opening his mouth – maintaining that the Falange had been a perfectly legal organization before the war and that as a teenager he was too young to have any real political understanding.

—The trial lasted about twenty minutes. They acquitted me. As far as I know, I was the only falangist ever acquitted by a Popular Tribunal. They didn't know, of course, that I had been in the Montaña barracks . . .

In due course, he was released from Porlier prison. As he came out of the prison gates, a policeman stepped forward.

—'You – get up in there.' He pointed at the lorry and I climbed into it; there were others already there. I don't know whether they had been sentenced or not. We were taken off to a concentration camp where, with 500 or 600 others, we were kept for the next two years until the war ended . . .

All dictatorship is odious, all violence repugnant; yet, despite our pacifist sentiments, we revolutionaries have almost always had to resort to them to impose our ideas . . . A revolution carried out by the syndicalist organization's resolute intervention . . . can only have as its instrument of violence the dictatorship of the people in arms which refuses the establishment of any type of government.

Eleuterio Quintanilla, Asturian libertarian leader, speech to the national congress of the CNT during the debate on the Russian revolution (Madrid 1919)

BARCELONA

Over everything, still, there hung a pall of ambiguity. The Catalan anarcho-syndicalists had 'put off' libertarian revolution; and yet, daily, the revolution in Barcelona was taking root in CNT collectives and union-run industries. Hostile to 'power', the libertarian leaders had refused to take power, when in fact the CNT was the only power in Barcelona. They had opted to 'collaborate' in the anti-fascist militia committee which they proceeded to dominate while refusing to make the committee the real instrument of their power.[1]

1. An index of that power – which simple verbal threats sufficed to enforce – was the undoing of the already cited plan to bring *guardia civil* forces into Barcelona (see p. 142); and soon afterwards, obliging the communist PSUC to leave the government Companys had just formed (31 July 1936), and which at this moment was virtually powerless.

Power, like nature, abhors a vacuum. Even more so in the crucible of a civil war which is the politics of class struggle raised to the extreme of armed conflict. The means of production were largely in the hands of the Catalan working class, but political power was atomized in myriad committees; shared, though unequally, in Barcelona between the anti-fascist militia committee and the Generalitat; divided within the committee itself; divided again between it and other committees in Catalonia; divided between Catalonia and Madrid. Such dual (if not multiple) power, normal to an incomplete revolution, could not remain static.

—The CNT–FAI took power *de facto* without recognizing or taking responsibility for it. They should have taken power politically, as they had taken it in the streets, in the view of Sebastià CLARA, a CNT civil servant and one of the thirty signatories of the famous *treintista* manifesto which had split the CNT five years before. They should have taken over the Generalitat, changed its name to council or committee if they couldn't accept the word government, and ensured themselves the majority representation. If there were political crises *they* would have precipitated them, *they* would have proposed the solutions. The masses were looking for that sort of leadership, which only a government could provide . . .

In their revolutionary surge to take over the means of production – the objective of the anarcho-syndicalist revolution and the basis of libertarian communism[1] – the Catalan libertarians had overlooked one very 'material' element of power: finance. The Generalitat never lost control of Catalonia's banking and financial institutions, which were under the control of the UGT bank employees' union. From the start, the Generalitat appointed delegates in each bank, with the union's agreement, to control operations and prevent the flight of capital. The union carried out to the letter all the instructions issued by the Generalitat finance councillor and the central government, Joan GRIJALBO, a prominent union member, recollected.

—We had no plans to socialize or collectivize the banks: collectivization of individual banks is incompatible with running a banking system. There was some talk, at the start, of the UGT *nationalizing* the banks; but this was shelved when the Generalitat opposed it, and we realized it was impossible to haggle with the only authority capable of running the banking system . . .

Moreover, as he was well aware, the Catalan banking system was relatively weak at the time; the major banks in Catalonia were not Catalan but Spanish. To have nationalized them would have meant nationalizing banks throughout the Popular Front zone.

The Catalan libertarians' 'oversight' was perhaps less important than was often supposed. Pre-war Catalonia had never been able to 'cash in' its industrial weight for the political direction of the Spanish state; the bourgeoisie lacked one requisite for it: banking and finance capital. Now, for much the same reason, the Catalan revolution could not 'cash in' its specific weight; it did not control the

1. Points of Rupture, D, examines this problematic, as well as the *treintista* split.

country's financial resources; Madrid did.[1] Nevertheless the 'oversight' reveals something of the ambiguity of the libertarian revolution; for banking and gold are to capitalism what organized coercion – the police, judiciary, army – is to the state: the ultimate power. The republic had temporarily lost the use of the second, but retained the first. The libertarian revolution had gained neither.

From his position on the militia committee, Jaume MIRAVITLLES, the Esquerra politician, was growing pessimistic. Things, in his view, were chaotic. If they continued like this he – 'and the other representatives of the petty bourgeoisie, that's to say, of a class which could not take the helm of the revolution' – feared it meant losing the war. Dali wrote him from Paris: he wanted to set up a department in Barcelona, which he would head, to be called 'The Irrational Organization of Daily Life'. An historic project.

—'Salvador,' I wrote back, 'we don't need you, it's perfectly organized as it is.' There are historical moments when the slogan 'Freedom' is the correct one to mobilize people – as was the case to bring in the republic. But there are others when the slogan 'Order – Revolutionary Order' corresponds to the objective needs of the situation. And this slogan was being put out by the communist party; we could see the communists beginning to gain strength. The fact that power was slipping into their hands was perfectly understandable. But we couldn't get the CNT to understand it . . .

The dilemma was not the 'everything or nothing', 'CNT dictatorship or collaboration' which the libertarian leaders had formulated. It was a political problem of power. Collaboration was a pre-condition of working-class power. Only two months earlier, the CNT Saragossa congress had called for a revolutionary working-class alliance; now was the time to implement it. (In the changed circumstances, such an alliance would almost certainly have to include a *minority* representation of the petty bourgeoisie, but the CNT would have the dominant voice).[2] The decision was not taken until it was too late. The anarchists did not believe in *taking* but in *destroying* it. Their refusal to take it nearly led to their own destruction.

*

On 19 July, the unified socialist party of Catalonia, PSUC, did not exist; the

1. A Catalan commission which sought credits from Madrid was turned down by Caballero's new Popular Front government; so, too, was a request to transfer some of the Spanish gold reserves – the fourth highest in the world – to Catalonia. The refusals, said the CNT economics council delegate Joan Fàbregas, came because the government 'is not sympathetic to the practical works being realized in Catalonia' (J. Peirats, *La CNT en la revolución española*, Paris, 1971, vol. 1, p. 205). Certain libertarian elements then planned to 'expropriate' part of the gold held in Madrid, and mobilized 3,000 men for the task; the plan was turned down by the CNT national committee (see D. Abad de Santillán, *Por qué perdimos la guerra*, Buenos Aires, 1940; Madrid, 1975).

2. Patently, the revolution could not be taken to its ultimate, libertarian communist consequences – not if that revolution required the *unanimity* of the nation's masses freely and spontaneously declaring for it. But by ensuring itself the leadership of the proletarian revolution in progress in Catalonia, the libertarian movement would be in a strong position to determine future events, and not only in Catalonia. This required the forging of new instruments of power, of which the militia committee was an embryo. The libertarians' view that the CNT was itself such a power – the trade union having the task of organizing the revolutionary economy – militated against the creation of any new proletarian organs of power.

fusion of four small parties, including the socialist union of Catalonia and the communist party of Catalonia, was planned before the uprising, and precipitated by it. The PSUC began with some 6,000 members, about 2,500 in Barcelona.[1] The new party, which controlled the UGT, affiliated immediately to the Comintern: to all intents and purposes it was thus the Communist party of Catalonia.

Both PSUC and UGT grew tremendously. It was the same phenomenon as in the rest of the Popular Front zone: affiliations *en masse*, the determination – through weight of numbers, irrespective of 'quality' – to impose one organization's domination over the other. The phenomenon was made more acute in Catalonia by the obligation (imposed by the CNT) to join one or the other of the two main unions. Almost all the *treintista* unions rejoined the CNT; so too did a multitude of individuals in search of the protection of a trade union card. Fear of the CNT drove other unions, including the POUM's, into the UGT; fear of the revolution drove the mass of the petty bourgeoisie in the same direction. By November, the UGT's membership in Catalonia – which four months earlier had been barely one tenth that of the CNT's – actually slightly outnumbered the anarcho-syndicalists. This was an unbelievable situation compared to the past and was a reminder of the numerical importance of the petty bourgeoisie. The PSUC's strength, meanwhile, rose nearly tenfold to 50,000. This mass invasion of the socialist trade union by shop-keepers, office workers, employees who had lost faith in their traditional parties like the Esquerra – as well as the width of the PSUC's beckoning doors – aroused the libertarians' scandalized anger at what they conceived as a patently 'counter-revolutionary' move.[2]

Pere ARDIACA, a communist from before the fusion who became the editor of the PSUC's paper *Treball*, was in no doubt about what the situation required: a government which could govern.

—A revolutionary order had to be imposed on the rearguard. The militia committee was never, and never proposed becoming, the government. We wanted a Popular Front government in which all anti-fascist forces would be represented . . .

Keeping the anti-fascist sectors of the bourgeoisie on the side of the struggle was essential to victory, the PSUC asserted; such a strategy was not an obstacle to securing the proletariat's hegemony and furthering the revolution; on the contrary.

—We believed that all measures taken to win the war would strengthen, not

1. Though somewhat smaller than the dissident communist POUM at the outbreak of the war, the constituent parties of the PSUC had enjoyed a greater *political* bargaining power, securing the nomination (and subsequent election) of seven members of the victorious Popular Front lists throughout Catalonia in February 1936. The POUM had only one. For the PSUC's and UGT's subsequent rapid growth, see J. Bricall, *Política económica de la Generalitat* (Barcelona, 1970), pp. 120 and 315; Balcells, *Cataluña contemporánea, II (1900–1936)*, p. 43.

2. In other areas of the Popular Front zone, the induction of allcomers by the CNT caused similar deprecatory comment by socialists and communists. The socialist and republican parties alone did not open their doors to wholesale induction of new members.

weaken, this hegemony – especially as expressed in the union between the UGT and CNT – so that after victory the revolution would be consolidated.

For the revolution had not been made here. It's one thing to take over the means of production and another to ensure that the bases of the revolution are consolidated, that, ideologically, it has the people with it. Everything had been overturned; but that in itself guaranteed nothing, because the bourgeoisie could very well have returned to power. Everything depended on who won hegemony while the war was being pursued to a victorious conclusion. To do this required a certain order.

We were criticized by the CNT and POUM as being counter-revolutionary for organizing the petty bourgeoisie in a union, the GEPCI (Gremios y Entidades de Pequeños Comerciantes e Industriales), which we created to defend their interests. We believed that this social class, which could considerably help the country's economy until such time as the conditions for a socialist economy had been created and it would disappear as a class, had to be preserved. It was not a counter-revolutionary move, it brought forces into the ranks to help the revolution . . .

Not surprisingly, Juan ANDRADE, of the POUM executive committee, saw the situation somewhat differently. The PSUC looked for support to the petty bourgeoisie (which the POUM, like the CNT, failed to take account of) because it lacked any specific weight amongst the working class.

—But I don't believe this alone was the major cause of the PSUC's growth. The CNT was the reason. The latter terrorized so many people that, in reaction, they came to consider the communists as the party of order . . .

But the PSUC was not yet strong enough to confront the CNT head-on. Despite the former's growth, the libertarians were still the masters of Barcelona.

—The CNT had real power but it didn't know what to do with it; it had great revolutionary will, but lacked revolutionary consistency, thought ARDIACA. Even if it had taken power it lacked a programme which would have won the support of the majority of the Catalan people. Meanwhile, it continued to act much of the time as though it had taken power (without actually saying so) while at the same time apparently sharing that power with the petty bourgeois Catalan parties and us. It was a dual power situation without doubt – but dual power between one part of the proletariat and another, not between the proletariat and the bourgeoisie. That was why the situation became such an obstacle, why it had to be resolved . . .

Juan ANDRADE was dismayed on his arrival from Madrid to join the POUM's executive that the question of power was being posed neither by the CNT nor by his own party when, between them, they 'represented the real working-class strength in Catalonia'. He drew up a manifesto calling for a Constituent Assembly of Workers, Peasants, Policemen and Soldiers, which met considerable opposition from within his party executive, whose programme at that moment was one solely of increasing wages and improving working conditions. Finally, it was approved and the manifesto appeared on posters and leaflets throughout Barcelona.

—It was a call for the creation of a Soviet, of course. But you couldn't use that word, for the anarchists would immediately have labelled it authoritarian communism. In truth, the anarchists didn't know what they wanted. They had always called for revolution, said the revolution must be made, but never thought about what would happen when it had been. They went from concession to concession . . .

Viewing the Catalan situation from the distance of Asturias, where the CNT adopted an entirely different posture,[1] Ignacio IGLESIAS, also of the POUM, reflected that the Catalan CNT suffered from a 'superiority complex'.

—Having proven its strength in the streets, it believed it could do whatever it wanted, including humouring its political opponents. It didn't realize that the boot was on the other foot. Without political power it would not, in the last analysis, command either power in the factories or power in the streets. Because it didn't suffer from such a complex, the CNT in Madrid and Asturias acted with a much greater awareness of the political realities . . .

But the CNT militants, who had taken over factories and businesses in Barcelona, retained their trust in their organization, which, 'strong as a lion', incarnated their revolutionary aspirations and traditions: the libertarian transformation of society which would be realized by the proletariat's administration of the economy and the abolition of the state. The POUM leaflets and posters blew away, grew tattered in the wind. The CNT would determine its own decisions.[2] At the end of August, it did so. Again García Oliver cried: 'Either we collaborate or we impose our dictatorship. Choose!' Again the majority opted for 'collaboration' – but with a difference; this time it was to accept the invitation, repeatedly made by President Companys, to participate in the Generalitat government.

—The president hoped that if the CNT would join a government, the very stones of the Generalitat, the historic atmosphere, the seats, portraits, his presidency would contribute to structuring the amorphous explosion that had taken place, in the belief of MIRAVITLLES, who, like his party leader, Companys, thought that only a political solution of this nature could restore the situation . . .

No one, not even the CNT, doubted that some form of organization was necessary to fuse the disparate powers that existed. An Economics Council, semi-dependent on the Generalitat, and with CNT participation, had been set up in mid-August to structure and rationalize the revolutionary Catalan economy. But more was evidently needed. The choice was between working-class and Popular Front power; there were no alternatives.

The decision in favour of the latter was reached at a secret meeting and was taken – in accord with libertarian ideology – by the Catalan libertarians alone; only they could decide a matter which affected their region – though its impact

1. See below, pp. 239–41.

2. Workers' and soldiers' committees, organized by the CNT and UGT, functioned for a few months in the barracks, exercising surveillance over military commands, ensuring discipline and cooperation between the two unions; but neither proposed developing these into Soviets or new proletarian organs of power.

were national. The decision was kept secret. A few days later, in Madrid, Largo Caballero, the left-wing socialist leader, formed the first Popular Front government. This the CNT was not yet ready to join. Instead, it proposed for Madrid what it had failed to propose for Catalonia – a working-class government (called a National Defence Council to avoid the word 'government') with republican participation.[1] In what was to become a persistent pattern, the CNT reacted to – rather than acted on – political events. In the event its reaction came too late; a new Madrid government already existed.

Until then, for the previous six weeks, the petty bourgeois republicans had governed alone in Madrid. The government's sway had extended little beyond the capital, and even in the capital its power was tenuous, requiring the constant approval of the Popular Front committee.[2] It was becoming rapidly apparent that this 'dual power' situation, in which real power was scattered in fragmented local parcels, was detrimental both to the war and the revolution. The failure of the myriad committees to fuse into a revolutionary power that would overthrow the remains of the bourgeois state and mobilize the total energies of the population for the revolutionary task of winning the war had to – if the latter was not to be rapidly lost – lead to the restoration of an alternative power.[3] The latter, to be effective, had to include the working-class forces and 'bring under control' the fragmented and fragmentary revolution that had taken place, centralize and control the militias, organize and plan a coherent war effort. The real nature of this new power was immediately apparent to Juan ANDRADE in Barcelona, who greeted the formation of Largo Caballero's Popular Front government of socialists, communists (the first time a communist party had joined such a government in western Europe) and republicans, as 'the government of the counter-revolution'. (For this he was banned by the POUM executive from writing editorials in the party's paper, *La Batalla*.)

The establishment of this new government, whose creation respected established republican legal norms, represented the option – in the complicated initial moments of Non-Intervention – of trying to secure the aid of the bourgeois democracies in return for holding back the full development of the proletarian revolution. Very soon, Largo Caballero, who, as leader of the left socialists, had been insistently calling for revolution in the months preceding

1. To be formed of five members of the CNT, five of the UGT and four republicans. See C. Lorenzo, *Los anarquistas espanoles y el poder*, pp. 97–102 and 179–90 for details of these decisions.

2. 'If the committee did not approve the government's wishes, the latter remained wishes,' recalled Fulgencio DIEZ PASTOR, the committee's Unión Republicana secretary-general. 'Prime Minister Giral could never be sure that the Popular Front parties would obey the government's decisions, particularly the socialist wing led by Largo Caballero, who refused to join the government, because he was saving himself for the only task he saw fit: to take over the premiership and become the Saviour of Spain.'

3. See also p. 258. The lessons of nineteenth-century Spanish revolutions were illuminating in this respect, as Raymond Carr has shown: 'First came the primitive provincial revolution which spread "like a contagious disease" from town to town. In the second stage local Progressive politicians and notables captured the popular revolution, "restoring social peace" by setting up a Junta of respectable citizens . . . This may be called the committee stage of revolution . . . during which the central government abdicated control of the country to a network of local committees. The final stage, therefore, was the re-imposition, by a ministry that "represented" the revolution, of central government control.' (*Spain 1808–1939*, pp. 164–5.)

the war, was saying: 'First we must win the war and afterwards we can talk of revolution.'

The CNT initiative to form a working-class central government was hindered, in the eyes of Eduardo de GUZMAN, a CNT journalist in Madrid, by the libertarians' failure to take power in Barcelona. Important leverage, a revolutionary moment of great promise, was lost, in his view. Even if the total libertarian revolution were impossible at that moment, the revolution could have been pushed forward to the stage of a 'proletarian government, total working-class democracy in which all sectors of the proletariat – but of the proletariat alone – would be represented'.

—To make a revolution, power must be seized. If the CNT had done so in Catalonia, it would have helped, not hindered our minority position in Madrid. But they believed it was sufficient to have taken the streets, to have seized arms. They completely overlooked the importance of the state apparatus which, with or without arms, retains a very great weight. This error was due in part to the CNT's insufficient politicization; to be a-political does not mean that one lacks political sense; it means simply that one does not participate in the farce of elections. Politics exist; and revolutionary politics even more . . .

While heated discussions continued in Madrid, the Catalan CNT sprang its surprise: three CNT councillors (ministers) were joining the new Generalitat government. The militia committee was to be dissolved, and along with it all the local committees which were to be replaced by new town councils. The inevitable next step was decided three weeks later, in mid-October, and announced at the beginning of November: four CNT ministers were entering the central government. The Popular Front option had triumphed.[1]

The question of power had seemingly been resolved; in reality, the struggle was just beginning.

In the new Generalitat council – the name changed from government to satisfy the libertarians – formed on 27 September, Joan DOMENECH, CNT glassworker, became supplies councillor. Sitting with him were two other libertarians, five republicans, two PSUC representatives and one POUM member.

DOMENECH did not attend the libertarian meeting which decided on joining the Generalitat – he feared that his presence as head of the supplies committee could appear as a form of coercion, since he could expect to be appointed to the same post in the new government. But he believed the decision to join was the correct one. History was made when the opportunity arose, he thought, not by trying to force history. The war made the decision inevitable; the CNT couldn't allow itself to be trampled on by the political parties, it had to join the government. Not that the CNT militants were prepared for governmental tasks.

—How could we be? Our revolution had always been conceived of as abolishing all governments. Now all of us had to learn. We CNT ministers didn't have a 'line' like the communists. As long as we had no great problems, the CNT imagined that each of us was doing his job; the organization didn't

1. The significance of this option will be examined later (pp. 323–34); its content can be seen in Points of Rupture, E.

discuss our work. Only if there were a serious problem – and it hardly ever got to that – would there be a meeting of militants to discuss the organization's position . . .

Of course, the CNT would have been a lot stronger if it had had a defined line. But, he thought, it would not have been the CNT in that case. The CNT was like that – you loved it with all its defects or you left it. There could be no such thing as 'party discipline' because when you joined the CNT as a worker, no one asked what you believed or thought. A carpenter joined the wood-workers' union, a barber the barbers' union, and that was all there was to it.

—Certain FAI groups – not the FAI as a whole – tried to impose that sort of tyranny on the CNT; but each time they did, the base reacted: 'This far and no further,' they said. 'If you don't like it come and kill us – but in the streets, not here in the CNT itself.' . . .

DOMENECH's appointment was to be expected; but the manner of the other two CNT councillors' appointment reflected the organization's spontaneity. One, who had been a member of the CNT only briefly some twenty years ago and subsequently had been a member of the FAI (which refused, as such, to take part in the government), happened to be passing by when the names were being chosen and was offered the post. The other, Joan Fàbregas, had joined the CNT only after 19 July; in earlier times, he had been closely connected with the business world and the right-wing Lliga. But his financial and economic expertise were to play an important role in defining a legal status for the industrial collectives.

LAW

First Section

General Provisions

ARTICLE 1 In accordance with the constitution of the republic and the present Statute, Alava, Guipúzcoa and Vizcaya constitute an autonomous region within the Spanish State, taking the name of 'Basque country' . . .

(Madrid, 4 October 1936)

Autumn 1936

THE BASQUE COUNTRY

On 3 September 1936, a force of insurgent military and *requetés* from Navarre captured the frontier town of Irún, sealing the border between the Basque country and France. Henceforth, the only communication with the rest of the Popular Front zone outside the north was by sea or air. Before abandoning Irún, some of its defenders set fire to parts of the town. Ten days later, the Basque nationalists surrendered San Sebastián without a shot. A force of *gudaris* (Basque nationalist soldiers) remained behind to ensure that the city was not burned like Irún by the retreating forces; earlier, they had disarmed the anarchist militia which wanted to resist. The heavy street fighting which had put down the military insurrection in the city, the long siege of the Loyola barracks, which had not surrendered until 28 July 1936, had served to keep Guipúzcoa in the Popular Front zone for less than two months.

Despite the PNV's declaration of support for the republic on 19 July, and its participation in the defence junta set up in San Sebastián, it took nearly three weeks for the first of the Basque nationalist militia – Euzko Gudarostea – to be formed in Guipúzcoa.[1] Luis MICHELENA, then an office clerk in Rentería, near San Sebastián, and a PNV militant from the age of fifteen, immediately enlisted in the new militia, seeing action for the first time two days after Irún fell. He felt that his party's loyalty to the republican cause was absolutely natural, but that the PNV suffered from an excessively pacifist mentality.

—We kept thinking that we didn't really want to have anything to do with war, that war was a barbarous invention which should be abolished. It was the marxists and anarchists who were the first to organize, the first to understand what was really happening. They had had experience in the October revolution of 1934; they knew that this was for real . . .

While socialists, anarchists, communists and left republicans attempted to hold off the enemy at the front, the PNV, which had not been able to procure arms in any quantity, remained in the rear. Telesforo Monzón, a leading PNV member, had been sent to Barcelona for arms; the Generalitat and central government were able to provide no more than 1,000 rifles and six field pieces.[2] When Miguel GONZALEZ INESTAL, the CNT fishermen's union leader and delegate on the Guipúzcoa defence junta, heard what had happened, he told the PNV members that their party lacked credibility amongst his companions in Barcelona. 'A socialist, even a communist, would have been better.' The junta

1. Three separate juntas operated simultaneously in Guipúzcoa: the socialist-dominated junta of Eibar, the PNV militia command in Azpeitia and the Guipúzcoa defence junta under left-wing domination in San Sebastián. Relations between them were not always good, which did not contribute to military efficacy on this relatively small front (see Ortzi, *Historia de Euzkadi: el nacionalismo vasco y ETA*, Paris, 1975, p. 215).

2. M. de Irujo, *La guerra civil en Euzkadi antes del estatuto* (Bayonne, 1938, mimeographed), p. 60. The CNT made off with all the arms of the Loyola barracks, distrusting the PNV's commitment to the war effort.

delegated him to go to Barcelona where he saw García Oliver, Abad de Santillán and Companys.

—'The PNV has always shown great hostility to the CNT; but now that they have committed themselves to the struggle, things are different,' I told García Oliver. 'We must ensure that they continue to cooperate with us.' Everyone agreed, arms were collected, a train organized. It reached Hendaye, across the border from Irún in France, where it was held up by the French, who had sealed the border in anticipation of Non-Intervention. Irún meanwhile fell . . .

The PNV, with its base in the strongly Catholic, staunchly nationalist petty bourgeoisie, was incensed by the repression taking place in San Sebastián, and the subsequent burning of Irún. After a particularly brutal mass assassination of right-wing prisoners, Monzón, the PNV member in charge of interior affairs on the Guipúzcoa defence junta, resigned. The killings, in the PNV view, brought the republic into serious disrepute. Relations with the CNT were bad. The latter's view mirrored the former's; the PNV, in GONZALEZ INESTAL's opinion, was always reactionary.

—Irremediably hostile to anything that threatened a change in the political or social situation. Not that there was the time or opportunity to collectivize anything; we had the enemy on top of us from the start. But the Basque nationalists were much more concerned with protecting right-wingers and churches and fighting us than they were in defending the interests of the republic . . .

The surrender of San Sebastián pushed the front almost overnight some 60 km west to the borders of Vizcaya, the only Basque province still remaining in the Popular Front zone. Had the insurgents not been concentrating their attention totally on the advance on Madrid, they might have pursued their advantage to the gates of Bilbao. The seriousness of the situation seemed to some to be lost on the majority of the middle-class citizenry of that great industrial centre.

—A friend of mine who went there shortly before San Sebastián fell, came back astonished that people were still walking along the Gran Vía with their hats on as though nothing in the world had happened, while the atmosphere in San Sebastián was, to put it mildly, chaotic, recalled MICHELENA. But even in the most difficult times, towards the end, there was always a certain normality in Bilbao; the churches were open, priests walked the streets in their cassocks, and people continued to maintain their reputation of looking well-dressed in English-style clothes . . .

The failure to defend San Sebastián aroused some quite violent confrontations within the PNV, not to speak of the other parties, as MICHELENA remembered. The Biskai-Buru-Batzar (PNV of Vizcaya) believed that if it went to the defence of Guipúzcoa, where there were plenty of men but few weapons, the province would fall anyway and Vizcaya's defence would be prejudiced.

In Vizcaya itself, the PNV (unlike the other parties) sent no militia to the front until the last ten days of September when the enemy was almost on its borders. It was not till then that it was able to receive a consignment of arms. Despite its clear-cut declaration of adherence to the republic – which made the PNV the only non-Popular-Front political party to play a leading role in the republican zone during the war (ensuring thereby that the war would be fought not only between Spaniards but also between Basques) – there were members who, to say the least, were dubious. Juan Manuel EPALZA, an industrial engineer, believed that the PNV's adherence to the republican cause also meant above all that the party intended to maintain law and order in the rear and to prevent the left from considering it an enemy.

—Until the evening before, *our* real enemy had been the left. This was not because they were left-wing but because they were Spanish. And as Spanish, intransigent. We vacillated for two weeks or more, hesitating to ally ourselves with our former enemies. Had it been possible, we would have remained neutral . . .

The war, he thought, didn't really concern the Basques; it was a Spanish problem to be settled among Spaniards. But then, as the military invaded Guipúzcoa to the cry of 'Death to Euzkadi!' and assassinated Basque nationalists, there had been no alternative but to take up arms in self-defence.

Vice-president of the Bilbao Mendigoixales, the PNV's youth movement, EPALZA had earlier set out under Ramón Azkue, later head of the Basque nationalist militia, to form an embryonic militia force to control the rearguard.

—We were determined to prevent outrages, to ensure that the left-wingers didn't kill, steal, burn churches. We were between the devil and the deep blue sea. It was absurd, tragic – we had more in common with the Carlists who were attacking us than with the people we suddenly found ourselves in alliance with . . .

Pedro BASABILOTRA, who became secretary to the head of the PNV militia, also believed the Basques should have remained neutral. For if one side was bad, the other was worse. Only the news of the assassinations of Basque nationalists in Navarre and Guipúzcoa changed the situation.

—The right, for the moment, was even worse than the left. Assassinations committed by so-called religious believers, by people with so-called education, were even more unpardonable than those committed by the under-privileged and poor on the left . . .

If the PNV had not taken control of the rearguard from the start there would, he was convinced, have been the same assassinations as in the other parts of the Popular Front zone. Because of them, the republic would lose the war. Capitalism was cunning, it knew it had nothing to gain by intervening on the republican side; and even more so, when the Soviet Union intervened.

—But all the same, the left remained as dangerous to us as the fascists. We knew that if the war were won there'd be a second round to fight . . .

Juan Manuel EPALZA was already preparing for that 'second round'; the left would certainly turn on the Basque nationalists if they were victorious. He and others set up a second, parallel military staff with the aim of preparing to fight the left. Once the Basque country was granted its own government they were able to dispense with this, for then there was only one authority, and it was controlled by the PNV.

Without arms, the PNV found it impossible to train a militia.[1] After a meeting in early August of PNV youth, BASABILOTRA went round the villages calling for volunteers. Finally, on 20 September 1936, a consignment of arms the PNV had purchased in Czechoslovakia, and which travelled in part through Nazi Germany, reached Bilbao; some of the rifles were single-loaders.

The PNV militia reached the front just in time to help hold the line after the surrender of San Sebastián.

Two sectors of Basque nationalism did not share the doubts and hesitations of some of their PNV counterparts. The Basque nationalist trade union, STV (Solidaridad de Trabajadores Vascos), came out 'immediately on the side of the people', according to its president Manuel ROBLES. 'The working class had none of the hesitations which certain PNV elements betrayed.' As for Acción Nacional Vasca, which (unlike the PNV) had formed part of the Popular Front electoral alliance, it had – in the figure of one of its founders, Gonzalo NARDIZ – joined the Popular Front defence junta in Bilbao immediately, and ANV militants went straight to the front.

At the beginning of September, Manuel Irujo, PNV deputy to the Cortes, proposed, on behalf of the Guipúzcoa defence junta, the formation of a Basque government without waiting for Madrid's approval of the autonomy statute which was pending. The central government, about to be taken over by Largo Caballero, was not unaware of the party's intentions. It offered Irujo a seat in the cabinet in exchange for the statute. On 1 October 1936, the Cortes approved the statute, and on 7 October, at Guernica, José Antonio Aguirre, aged thirty-two, was elected leader of the new Basque government. The PNV held the key posts in the cabinet. The CNT, shortly to join the central government, was excluded from the Basque government on the pretext that the latter was composed of political parties, not unions. (Safe in the knowledge that it would refuse, Aguirre said he would accept the FAI in his government.)

Now that, after all these years, they had been granted the statute,[2] what did they need it for? That was what Juan Manuel EPALZA felt. 'We had guns in our hands now, we didn't need anyone granting us our autonomy. That was what I thought then, though today I can see I was wrong.'

Trifon ETARTE, of Jagi-Jagi (Arise Arise), the youth movement which had broken from the parent PNV before the war and come out clearly for an independent Basque state, had been to see Aguirre to suggest that Jagi-Jagi should

1. Unlike Catalonia, the Basque country had a pre-war arms industry, but no large stock of arms and ammunition to be seized from military dumps at the outbreak. Non-Intervention froze the supply of necessary raw materials to keep the existing arms factories producing fully. In August, the PNV seized the gold in the Bank of Spain in Bilbao and shipped some of it in fishing boats to France to purchase arms. In terms of heavy industry, however, Vizcaya, with all the resources of Bilbao's steel-making behind it, enjoyed a considerable advantage over Catalonia.

2. See Points of Rupture, C.

seize the first arms consignment before it could be unloaded to ensure nationalist superiority and the cause of Basque independence.

—Aguirre was horrified. 'That would be to betray the Popular Front.' I, who was only twenty-five, replied: 'The only betrayal I know is the betrayal of my country.' But Aguirre was much too honourable to take advantage of such an opportunity. We had always believed that the statute was a trap – a trap very similar to that in which Ireland had fallen after the First World War . . .

But in general there was cautious joy at the statute's approval. Jon MAURURI, a medical student and PNV member, summed up the feeling: people were happy but a bit suspicious. Would the republic have granted the statute if it had not been for the war?

—And was the republic going to regret it and abandon us? – as indeed it did. Would it think that it could leave us to be defeated and still win the war so as to use the victory to crush us once again? Who could know, who could say more than that everyone was our enemy then . . . ?

Concha ARRAZOLA, daughter of one of the first Basque nationalist town councillors in Bilbao and herself a leader of the nationalist women's organization, Emakume Abertzale Batza, had little doubt. The main enemy?

—The Spanish, of course. 'Red' or 'white' – they were brothers. We were 'cousins' – and by cousins we mean the person who pays the consequences. But we had such complete confidence in our leaders – such gentlemen they were – that our apprehension at finding ourselves allied with these left-wing Spaniards didn't last long . . .

Indeed, there was little enough cause for apprehension; Vizcaya was the least revolutionary area in the Popular Front zone. Industry remained in private ownership even if production was 'militarized' for the war effort; churches remained open.

—The working class made no demands. There were no wage claims. The working class was only too well aware of what was at stake in the struggle, believed Ramón RUBIAL, lathe operator and executive committee member of the UGT metalworkers' union. If they had to work overtime, they worked it at their ordinary hourly rate. Factory committees were set up to control and stimulate production, often taking the fastest worker as the norm and creating Stakhanovites . . .

After the PNV, the socialists were the strongest force in Vizcaya, recruiting mainly among the migrant mining labour force. But it was here, too, that the communist party had one of its major concentrations of strength, as the nationalist leadership of the party attested: three of the major party figures (Uribe, Hernández and Dolores Ibarruri–La Pasionaria) came from Vizcaya. Despite the communist party position that it was necessary to do everything to keep the anti-fascist petty bourgeoisie in the struggle – even to leave its leaders at the helm of the struggle – there were criticisms by party members (and later by the Spanish party itself) of the way the struggle was being waged in Euzkadi. A young communist miner. Saturnino CALVO, who had got a job for the first time now that his elders were at war, felt that pre-war conditions were being allowed to continue to the point where, in the initial months, it appeared almost as though there were no war. In the mines everything continued the same, the same bosses, the same foremen, the same hours; only the day wage was increased to equal the militiaman's ten pesetas. There was a lack of combative spirit, in his view.

—The Basque government didn't know how to make full use of the human and industrial potential available to it. And that was because the PNV wasn't a revolutionary party; it feared that if the war were won it would mean an advance for socialism – which it was hostile to. And yet a civil war is won or lost as much in the rearguard as at the front. Perhaps more . . .

Ricardo VALGAÑON, a communist foundryman, who had been in a column which set out from Bilbao on 19 July to help put down the uprising in San Sebastián, and was now manning the front at Orduña, felt that the revolution had been forgotten.

—Our only desire was to win the war; everything else was left for the future. The working class, the communist party of Euzkadi, made no claims on the Basque government. Even when our party paper, *Euzkadi Roja* (*Red Euzkadi*), attempted to point out that we were fighting not only for national freedom but to change the social structure, the PNV managed to get it censored . . .

The communist party, he thought, kept too silent. National liberation, of course, was the major social conquest for the people of Euzkadi at that moment; if the fascists won the Basques would lose their freedom and democracy. None the less, the failure to make any social conquests was inevitably to 'play into the hands of the Basque bourgeoisie'.

Only in those businesses where the management had sided with the insurgents or disappeared were new boards of directors and managers appointed. A government decree forbade anyone to hold more than one directorship; rents were reduced by 50 per cent as elsewhere in the Popular Front zone. For a factory owner like Juan MALZAGA, whose metal-window company had had a large contract before the war in the Madrid University city which was then under construction, work continued much the same as pre-war. Instead of metal windows he now made metal hospital beds. There was no attempt by the trade unions to take over or control the factory. About 60 per cent of his work force belonged to the STV, 30 per cent to the UGT and 10 per cent – 'a very aggressive 10 per cent' – to the CNT. But there was no trouble.

—The Basque nationalists were the reason, of course. They were middle class in the main, religious, conservative in the English sense of the word. The PNV's decision to ally with parties which stood for the destruction of the sort of society it believed in was the great drama of the Basque country; it created tremendous conflicts of conscience from which I believe this country has not totally recovered to this day . . .

Though his father had been a member of the PNV, and his family was totally Basque, MALZAGA's sympathies lay with the insurgents. They represented law and order and the means of living a 'normal life'. He, who had never had any faith in politics, who believed that the degree of a country's civilization could be measured by its capacity for compromise rather than the 'typical Spanish notion that one must defend one's ideals to the death', was convinced that a republican victory could lead only to a communist dictatorship. 'Quite irrespective of one's political ideology, people like myself felt the need to defend our fundamental interests.'

Episodes 2: Flight

MADRID

In the cubicle-sized actors' dressing-room, separated from his two friends who had been arrested with him hours before, he waited to be summarily tried and shot.

Disregarding the Union Jack and the strongly worded document the British embassy had authorized him to put up, three militiamen had hammered on the door. Assuming a slightly foreign accent, the 22-year-old Marquess PUEBLA DE PARGA had told them that this was a diplomatic flat. It gave a young falangist he was sheltering time to escape down the service stairs. Then he opened the door.

The militiamen, heavily armed and wearing red and black neckerchiefs, searched the flat. 'You're not foreigners, you're Spaniards, fascists,' they said when they found a Michelin map the marquess had spread out on a table with flags pinned on it to mark insurgent victories. Worse still, they found a shotgun in a cupboard. 'Arms as well! We've made a good haul.'

Under arrest, in the car, he thought: 'If they turn to the left, it means they're taking us for a ride. We'll be heading for the wasteland behind the bullring at Ventas. If we turn right, we'll be heading for the centre, a *checa*, we won't be shot immediately – '

The car turned right, stopped outside the Bellas Artes building in the Calle Marqués de Cubas. 'The FAI *checa*,' he thought. Men, women and children were milling about guarded by militiamen. On the first floor, in the ballroom, a scene that recalled the French revolution met his eyes: men of all ages, and a few terrified women, were sitting on the floor amidst piles of chalices, candelabra, religious objects, suitcases – some open, some shut. One of the militiamen pointed out a bedraggled man in a dirty shirt who appeared to have been mishandled because he was a priest. As soon as the marquess and two companions, to whom he had given refuge in his flat, were left unobserved, they went across to the man and, without ascertaining that he was a priest, confessed.

Waiting in the cubicle, the marquess remembered the sounds that had become familiar in the Madrid summer night: the car driven at great speed, the tyres screaming as it came to a halt, the engine revving fast. The noise of hammering on doors, the sound of the car a few moments later starting again. Sitting in the darkened dining-room of the flat, he and his friends had known that another victim was going to his fate.

The cubicle door opened. A militiaman took him into the theatre which was where the tribunal sat. Everything except the stage had been removed.

—In the middle now there was an enormous table covered by a black and red flag – or rather two pieces of black and red material crossed over each other, quite tastefully arranged. There were five people behind the table; one of them was a woman, who looked about thirty, dark and pretty. I was taken up to the table . . .

Two of the men questioned him. Why wasn't he at the front defending the republic? He had had time enough to think up answers to this sort of question. Because of his eyesight, he had been failed for military service. Moreover, he was a student who had been living in France and was in Madrid by chance. 'You're a fascist.' 'Of course not.' He was determined to brazen it out. The interrogation didn't last long. The questions had, all in all, been fairly non-committal. As he was being taken back to his cubicle, he saw his friend Enrique being brought out of his.

At dawn his cubicle door opened again; he, his two companions and some others were herded out of a side door and into a lorry. Again he was convinced that they were being taken out to be shot. But their destination was the interior ministry in the Puerta del Sol. Once they reached the cellars, he breathed a sigh of relief. They were out of 'the FAI's hands, out of the hands of the most ruthless and bloody force amongst the reds'. The next day, at dawn, to his despair, they were again put into a lorry, this time to be taken to a former religious school in the Calle General Porlier which had been turned into a prison. He had spent barely fifteen minutes in the classroom which was to be his communal cell when three militiamen appeared and grabbed him by the arm. 'Follow us.' Convinced that he was being taken to his death, fellow prisoners crowded round to protest. Swearing, the militiamen opened a passage, shoving him forward.

—We went down two or three floors, reaching a windowless basement, illuminated only by naked bulbs, from which I was taken through to a boiler room. I prepared myself to die; ever since our arrest I had been resigned to my fate. The enormous boilers in one corner, the great pile of coal opposite – it was an ideal place for an execution.

'*Canalla*, you're going to die now, you and all your class – ' One of them caught me by the shoulders and pushed me against the opposite wall. They stepped back and raised their weapons; took aim. Although I'd had a deeply religious upbringing, no religious thoughts crossed my mind. Rather, I felt a great wave of indignation. I don't know whether this was particularly Spanish, but my instinct of self-preservation expressed itself as anger. I took a few steps forward and began to insult them. '*Canalla*, you're going to kill an innocent person.' It was a banal thing to say, but at least not wholly undignified.

All this took much less time than it takes to tell. The men suddenly lowered their arms and one of them started to laugh. 'You're lucky this time, you're not going to fall. But you will die – ' They came towards me. My shirt was open at the neck and I had a gold chain on which two or three religious medallions hung, as was the custom then. One of them stretched out his hand and tore the chain from my neck. I didn't say anything. They pushed me towards the stairs . . .

When he reached the classroom, the other prisoners crowded round to comfort him, an act of solidarity that could have cost them dear.

In the following days there was no repetition of this senseless, brutal act. The marquess carved a chess set out of bits of chalk left in the classroom and played with a fellow prisoner. Two police alsatians with red and black collars patrolled the corridors with a militia warder who liked to expound anarchist theory to all who would listen. Every explanation ended with the example of the ants. 'You see,' was the triumphant conclusion, 'the ants have no commanders, but theirs is a perfect society.'

However, if the days were spent in relative safety, the nights were a different matter. After lights out, a militiaman or two might appear at the door, turn on the light and start to call out names from a list. Often they appeared not to know which prisoners were confined to which rooms and went through the whole list anew in each. The suspense was terrifying.

—A man answered '*presente*' when he heard his name; it was useless trying to hide. As he got up, the rest of us – thirty or forty crammed into the room – looked at him, trying with our eyes to give him solace and encouragement. Everyone I saw being taken out went with tremendous courage, serenity. It is one of the things Spaniards can be proud of, one of the things which heightened my awareness of life: the way they bore themselves as they went to their deaths. Then we heard the lorries driving away; the executions did not take place in the prison itself . . .

One morning in September, militiamen came into the room and called their three names. The marquess felt instinctively that things were all right, it wasn't a dangerous hour. Picking up their bedrolls as ordered, they were taken to the ground floor where they found a small, dark-suited man with a lively face who appeared to be in his fifties. His name was Juliá.

—'I am from the British embassy's economic section. I have come to take you to Atocha railway station; I think it is going to be possible for you to escape' . . .

Hardly able to believe their ears, they found themselves walking out of a side door of the prison and getting into a small black car with a Union Jack on the windscreen. Without further ado, Juliá set off for Atocha; when they reached the station, he took them to a room and told them to wait. 'Don't be frightened, no one will come in here.'

After several hours, he reappeared. 'Follow me. You can't leave. There has been a mistake – ' He drove them to an office of the British embassy's commercial section where they remained hidden for several days. A man of few words, Juliá explained little. Gleaning what they could, it appeared that the British embassy had taken some forceful steps when it learnt that they had been arrested in the flat which the marquess shared with a British diplomat friend who had left the capital before the start of the war. The government, concerned about its relations with Britain, considered the arrests a mistake; the Bellas Artes *checa* seemingly had come to share this view. 'Throughout the war, the flat was the only place under British protection to be broken into.'

From the moment their case became known, the likelihood of their being executed was dramatically diminished. But their escape was another matter. They got the impression that the acting British ambassador in Madrid knew of Juliá's initiatives and approved of them as long as they in no way involved the embassy which, officially, had shown itself reluctant to help individuals escape.

One day Juliá burst into the office: 'Come on, we're off.' In the Peruvian ambassador's house, where he took them – the marquess's friend Enrique was a relative of the ambassador who at that moment was in Lima – his face beaming, Juliá handed them forged identity cards.

—It was evident that this was an initiative he had taken on his own. During the days we had been in hiding in his office we had come to like him tremendously. A Catalan by birth, he was a republican and a mason. 'Your lives are in danger, it is a mason's duty to help anyone in danger.' Later we learnt that he had managed to save a considerable number of people. But when we looked at the identity papers – mine showed I was a FUE delegate on a mission to Alicante – we cried: 'But what are we going to do in Alicante? Do you expect us to swim to France?' 'You don't understand. There are German and Italian warships in Alicante. Relations between Germany, Italy and the republic haven't yet been broken. But they will be in a few days. If they can't help you, English ships also call there. I can see no other solution – ' It was evidently all Juliá could do. We decided to try . . .

Having drawn lots, it fell to the marquess to be the first to try to get to Atocha station. Dressed in a pair of overalls, he got past the control without difficulty and found a place in a coach directly behind the sleeping car, a stroke of luck that was shortly to save his life. With time to spare, he started to pace the platform when, to his horror, he saw a small figure bustling through the crowd of militiamen, soldiers, and war-wounded. He recognized her instantly.

—Nellie Cunningham, my old Irish nanny! From several yards away she cried out in English: 'My darling boy! – ' In her hands she had a bottle of whiskey and two cartons of cigarettes. 'Nellie,' I hissed, 'go away at once. You're endangering my life, don't you understand? Turn round and get lost in the crowd. Don't say a word – ' In silence, she turned away, obeying the order, and disappeared. Poor Nellie! She must have learnt on the grapevine that I was leaving. What an English scene! A man fleeing for his life and his nanny turns up! . . .

No one appeared to have noticed the incident. Shortly afterwards his friend Enrique turned up; but their third companion did not appear. Only later did they learn that his papers had been challenged at the control post and he had gone immediately to the Argentinian embassy to take refuge.

The train set off, the night passed uneventfully; in the morning, approaching Alicante, the marquess was looking out of the window at the landscape he had never seen before when, out of the corner of his eye, he saw a man in a tie and jacket coming down the corridor. He stopped in front of him, turned the lapel of his jacket over to reveal a badge: republican police.

—And then he said words I'll never forget. 'You are the son of the ex-duchess of Mandas, aren't you?' Out of weariness, or because I thought the game was up, I replied, 'Yes.' 'You are under arrest' . . .

In each carriage there was a militiaman; the policeman called him over to guard the marquess.

The policeman was young, rather plump. Racking his memory, the marquess managed later to place him: he had been an assistant in a bookshop where he bought all his university books and knew him quite well.

—Nothing is as true as Dr Johnson's saying that going to the gallows concentrates a man's mind. The mechanism of self-preservation leapt into action . . .

Sensing that the militiaman harboured no particular hostility towards him, he began trying to gain the man's confidence, saying that the policeman was a draft-dodger who was attempting to make trouble for him. The only hope of salvation lay in the sleeping car ahead where Juliá had told them the Argentinian minister was travelling. As the first houses of Alicante appeared, the marquess decided to try. 'I've got to go to the lavatory.' The militiaman made no objection. He went up the corridor and into the WC, rattled the bolt, re-opened the door and leapt across the communicating platform into the sleeping car. The conductor, still wearing the classic brown wagon-lit uniform, barred his way, but he pushed him hard to one side. By a stroke of luck, he saw the Argentinian minister in the corridor. He leapt towards him, saying who he was. 'I'm in great danger.' Without a moment's hesitation, the minister pushed him into his compartment and shut the door. Not for nothing was he known as Madrid's Scarlet Pimpernel. He told the marquess to stay there and went out. It was the last time he saw him. For at that moment the train was slowed down at the entrance to the station by an enormous demonstration come to welcome the war-wounded. A river of people swept past the window. The marquess realized that this was his chance. He opened the window and jumped out.

Lost in the crowd, he made his way out of the station and walked through the small city to the hotel Juliá had told them was the meeting-place of the Italian and German naval officers. Enrique, who had witnessed the scene in the train and believed he was now the sole survivor, arrived almost simultaneously outside the hotel. In low tones they discussed what they should do.

—It was a moment even more terrifying than being in the *checa* or prison. We had been so certain that we were going to die then that nothing much had mattered. But now that there was the chance of escape, life and death became a question of primary concern. Moreover, I had the police on my tail . . .

From the lobby they could see a large room whose parquet floor, potted palms, white wicker tables and white-jacketed waiters struck them, after Madrid, as incredibly clean and smart. Right at the back of the room five Italian naval officers were sitting; at a table slightly closer, a group of German officers.

—'What shall we do?' Enrique asked. I had no doubts. 'Go and tell the Italians your father is Franco's consul-general in Genoa. They'll help us, you'll see.' Enrique had a moment's indecision. 'But if they refuse, everything is lost. We'll have been seen – ' He was right, of course. But we had to risk it. I put all my powers of persuasion into propelling him those forty metres across the room. I saw him – can see him to this day – approaching the Italian officers, saw them stop talking, Enrique leaning across the table, murmuring something. Immediately one of them got up and accompanied Enrique across the room to where I was waiting. Without any explanation, he made a sign, saying: 'Follow us.' We went out of the door and past some militiamen in the street. A short distance away, I saw a place that looked like a mixture of toyshop and haberdasher's. *Casa Rossi* said the sign. We went in, the officer spoke to the owner. Without wasting a moment, the latter opened a door at the back of the shop and we went down some stairs into the basement. Soon Rossi returned to tell us not to move, the officer would be coming back to explain.

'From now on, you'll completely forget your true identities,' said the officer when he came back. 'You'll become two Italian naval deserters from the warships anchored in the bay. That is how we are going to get you out – ' The proposition seemed incredible. Our papers were already being made out, he said. I still remember my Italian name: Parodi . . .

The next day at dawn an Italian petty officer came to get them. He treated them brutally, as befitted deserters; they had been warned to expect it. They were taken to a republican police car which drove them to a jetty outside Alicante where a launch flying the Italian flag was tied up. The republican *carabineros* on duty appeared to be expecting them. Under close escort they climbed into the launch, which set off. The marquess looked back at the *carabineros* leaning over the jetty rail, looking bored, and a great yearning rose in him to shout *¡Arriba España!* 'But I rapidly thought better of it!'

Aboard an Italian destroyer, the two reached La Spezia; it was the end of their escape, but not the end of their war. The marquess returned to nationalist Spain in 1938 to join the Foreign Legion in which he served as a temporary second lieutenant until victory the following year.

Immortal hours of the national epic, of frenetic enthusiasm. Never has Spain throbbed, pulsated like this. The news of Toledo's conquest was announced over this very microphone: our listeners will have received it as such news must be received: on their knees . . .

Julio Gonzalo Soto, broadcast over Radio Castilla (Burgos, 28 September 1936)

CAPITALISTS

The National Movement, salvation of Spain, permits you in these moments to continue enjoying your dividends and rents

If you hesitate for a moment to lend your moral and material assistance, generously and disinterestedly, not only will you prove yourself unpatriotic, but ungrateful and unworthy of living in the strong Spain which is being re-born . . .

***Diario de Burgos* (21 September 1936)**

ATTENTION! ATTENTION!

Tonight, in a memorable broadcast from Radio Castilla you are going to hear the authentic voice of Spain in the plenitude of its power . . . The voice of the Caudillo, the chief, the guide, the maximum figure of the Spanish state. Spaniards and foreigners, General Franco is going to speak. ¡Viva Franco! ¡Viva Franco! ¡Viva España!

Broadcast over Radio Castilla (1 October 1936)

On 27 September 1936, Toledo was taken by Franco's forces which had turned from the direct advance on Madrid to relieve the Alcázar, the fortress-like infantry officers' school, set on a height commanding the city. Under Col. Moscardó, the Alcázar had resisted republican siege for seventy days. The half-shattered fortress had become a Popular Front obsession, and a great deal of time and effort had been invested in attempts to force its surrender while the enemy columns continued to close in. (The Popular Front militia – and later the army – never found it easy to leave an enemy redoubt in their rear.) Despite its diversion, the Army of Africa was now only 70 km from the gates of Madrid.

Two days later, an event of greater importance occurred: the national defence junta appointed General Franco head of the government of the Spanish state and *generalísimo* of the armed forces.

Until that date, insurgent Spain had been ruled by the defence junta which came into being at the outbreak of the war and was composed exclusively of military, under the leadership of the patriarchal-looking General Cabanellas. The junta's fundamental mission was to coordinate the military effort and to develop a state apparatus, more administrative than political, at first sight.

—The military had no clear political idea of what to do. They were opposed to public disorder, to the chaos that the revolution under the republic had produced; but nothing more . . .

Convinced that something had to be done, Eugenio VEGAS LATAPIE, editor of the monarchist *Acción Española*, set off to bring the heir to the Spanish throne, don Juan, from France to tour the front. He was certain that the military would expel the prince, which was indeed what happened – before he even reached the front. 'Mola, an upright man, supporter of law and order but no monarchist, was worried about the repercussions with the Carlists who didn't accept the Alfonsine dynasty.' VEGAS LATAPIE was himself nearly expelled from Spain as a result.

The military might have 'no clear political ideas' of what they wanted, but they had clear enough ideas of what they did not want. On 24 September 1936, the defence junta annulled all agrarian reform settlements made after the Popular Front elections and returned the land to its original owners;[1] and a day later outlawed all political and trade union activity in the zone under its jurisdiction. 'The marked national character of the movement, initiated by the army and supported, enthusiastically, by the people, demands the setting aside of party politics, since all Spaniards of goodwill – whatever their particular ideologies – are fervently united behind the army, the effective symbol of national unity,' stated the preamble to the decree. The repression was not limited to the liquidation of political opponents; it was to reach out to politics itself, even when practised by the military's supporters.

Many people in the insurgent zone, including the monarchist VEGAS LATAPIE, were critical of Franco's diversion to relieve Toledo, arguing that the latter was a 'sentimental' objective which would have fallen automatically if the main objective – Madrid – had been taken. The outcome, in this view, was that the republic was allowed to organize its defences; time was given for Soviet aid and the International Brigades to reach Madrid – 'and the war as a result lasted two and a half years longer'.

Col. Juan Yagüe, the Foreign Legion commander, had to relinquish command of the column advancing on Madrid shortly before because of illness and was stationed at Franco's HQ in Cáceres, where not long before VEGAS LATAPIE had protested to Franco about the indiscriminate assassinations in the rearguard. Col. Yagüe later related to the young monarchist how he intervened in the appointment of Franco as supreme commander.

—One day, Nicolás Franco, the General's brother, came up to Yagüe and for the first time addressed him by the familiar '*tu*'. 'Juanito, you're the only one who can persuade my brother. I've just returned from Lisbon and both the German and Italian ambassadors maintain that there must be a single, unified command. The present situation of two commands of the northern and southern

1. Having a month earlier already annulled the take-over of all estates which had not yet been actually settled.

armies cannot continue. It's particularly important for foreign relations, but also for everything else. Everyone thinks that the most suitable person is my brother. But he won't accept. You are the one who has the most influence with him, who can convince him – ' Yagüe, who was a man of incredible natural power, went over to Franco's door – there wasn't much formality at that time – knocked and said: '*Mi general*, may I come in? The ambassadors of Germany and Italy say we require a single command. It is necessary in order to achieve victory. We all think it must be you. If you won't accept, then we shall have to think of appointing someone else.' Yagüe then left Franco's office. A couple of minutes later, Nicolás came out overwhelmed with emotion. He caught hold of Yagüe, embraced, even kissed him. 'What did you say to him, what did you do? He has accepted – ' 'I simply told him that if he didn't accept we would have to appoint someone else.'

That evening, in celebration of the fall of Toledo, Yagüe made a brief speech after Franco had addressed the crowd from the balcony of his HQ. 'Today is a great day,' Yagüe began, 'but tomorrow will be an even greater day. Tomorrow, or very shortly, we shall have a general who will lead us to victory. And this general is – General Franco . . . '

Two days later, the generals met at an aerodrome outside Salamanca and the appointment went through, though not without resistance. Yagüe (who attended without a vote as he was not a general) pointed out forcefully that his legionaries and Moroccan troops wanted Franco as supreme commander. The military appointment caused less resistance than the political one. There was some confusion in the nationalist zone as to what Franco had been appointed to: 'Head of State' (as *ABC* of Seville named him) or 'Head of the Government of the Spanish State', as the *Diario de Burgos* correctly termed him. These confusions – compounded by the decree which gave him 'all powers of the new state' – were soon resolved: his first law, published on the day of his appointment, to establish a new state administration, referred twice to his post as head of state.

On the night of his formal assumption of power, General Franco made a broadcast setting out the aims of the new state. In social matters, work would be guaranteed and a day-wage assured; but workers would not be allowed to organize on class lines, and any 'combative activities' would be punished. Workers had obligations as well as rights; and these obligations were to 'collaborate in everything that constitutes the normal production of wealth'.

In religion, the new state, without being confessional, would 'concord with the Holy Catholic Church'. In agriculture, there would be 'constant and generous help' to the peasant to secure his economic independence. The national will would be expressed not by universal suffrage, which had been discredited, but through those technical organs and corporations which, 'in an authentic way, represent the ideals and needs of the new Spain . . .'

Of the three generals in the running, now that Sanjurjo was dead, Franco was indubitably the most likely choice. His military prestige combined with an apparent absence of defined political posture gave him an advantage over Generals Mola and Queipo, both of whom had republican leanings.

—'Moreover, if we had appointed Mola we would have lost the war,' General

Queipo de Llano told me later, VEGAS LATAPIE recalled. Mola was considered a magnificent administrator but a poor field commander. 'I couldn't be appointed because I was discredited; so there was only Franco,' he added. Queipo was discredited not only because of his past – attempting to overthrow the monarchy one day, the republic the next – but because of his current reputation. Franco won the day . . .

The new state administration – the 'Junta Técnica' – set up by Franco comprised seven commissions. The *generalísimo*, who had apparently taken no notice of the impetuous young monarchist when he addressed him on the dual need to stop assassinations, and to 'clean out' all revolutionary ideas in the rearguard, appointed him to the new culture and education commission, one of whose major tasks was to purge schoolteachers. The norms were made clear by the commission, which was headed by the monarchist poet José María Pemán: teachers who were 'professionally and morally irreproachable', but had sympathized with Basque, Catalan, or Galician nationalist parties without participating in the 'communist-separatist' subversion, should be moved to a different region; those who had belonged to, or sympathized with, Popular Front parties or secret societies (essentially, the masons) were to be sacked. Provincial commissions were set up to carry out the purges – a 'sacred mission', in the words of a circular.

—The purges were carried out with considerable severity; we were in the middle of a war. It was one thing that people were shot without rhyme or reason; another that education, which forms the future consciousness of a nation – and control of which is vital – should be purged . . .

None the less, many of the accusations made against teachers which fell on VEGAS LATAPIE's desk were 'absurd'. One was against a woman teacher who was said to have gone to mass only on Sundays and knelt only on one knee at the moment of the Host's elevation. 'Such a ridiculous accusation, of course, wasn't entertained.'

An Andalusian schoolmaster, who had been teaching in Burgos, was denounced for not having gone to mass once in the year he was there. He answered the charge by saying that it wasn't the custom in Andalusia for men to go to church, but had he known that it was the custom in Castile he would, of course, have attended. 'A witty response. There was such an inflation of religious belief during the war that those who hadn't believed in one God before now swore that they believed in seven.'

An Asturian teacher in a Castilian village was denounced for having taught the children a well-known song which begins: '*Asturias, patria querida, Asturias de mis amores* – ' ('Asturias, beloved homeland, Asturias of my loves'). The accusation said that as there had been a 'communist revolution' in Asturias in 1934, she must be a communist to have taught children the song.

—Incredible stupidities like this came to light. But some weren't so ridiculous. A *requeté* university professor came to see me one day. He said that his *requeté* sergeant – a marvellous fellow who had taken communion by his side that very morning – was accused of a terrible crime. A village schoolmaster under the republic, he had been ordered, as were all state teachers, to remove the crucifix from his classroom, and he had put the cross down the lavatory so that the children had to urinate and defecate over it.

While many people tried to protect themselves by joining the Falange, there were also some who did the same in the *requetés*. I appointed a special judge – a professor of medicine – to investigate the case. The evidence was incontrovertible; this '*requeté*' schoolmaster was thrown out of his job . . .

*

In Salamanca, the provincial commission's reports came to the rector of the university, Miguel de Unamuno, aged seventy-two. The reports often included a comment from the parish priest that the schoolmaster in question did not go to mass; considerable numbers of schoolmasters were socialists or left republicans. Unamuno, according to his son, Rafael, often drew a line down the side and wrote at the bottom: 'Nor do I'. The reports, which went to the civil governor, did little presumably to endear him to the new authorities. But, as he was one of the most prestigious intellectual figures of Spain, there was not much they could do. Moreover, he had welcomed the military uprising and been appointed to Salamanca's new town council. A republican deputy to the Constituent Cortes of 1931, he had soon become an outspoken critic of much the republic was doing. The first to articulate what was later to become almost a commonplace, he saw the uprising as necessary to save 'western civilization, the Christian civilization which is threatened'. Remaining a republican, he supported the military because he believed they had risen to defend 'an honourable republic'. The assassination of the mayor of Salamanca, Dr Casto Prieto,[1] a close friend of his; the assassination in Granada of Salvador Vila, professor of Arabic and Hebrew at the university, whose release from prison in Salamanca he had secured; García Lorca's murder – these killings angered and saddened him. Yet in a foreign newspaper interview he bitterly attacked the Madrid government; in response the latter sacked him from his post as lifelong rector of the university. On hearing the news Felisa UNAMUNO, his daughter, believed it would not be long before the military did the same.

—My father was enraged about what was going on in this zone; it was not what he had hoped for. He was convinced that the military and their supporters hated most what was best in Spain: Catalonia and the Basque country. 'Let's see if they don't become independent and then we'll go to Bilbao' – my father's birthplace – I said. 'That wouldn't be a bad idea,' he replied . . .

It was not long before the fate due to a perpetual critic in a situation where allegiance was demanded began to unfold. Salamanca was now Franco's headquarters; he had moved into the bishop's palace opposite the old cathedral almost immediately after his proclamation on 1 October. Eleven days later, the Day of the Race, in commemoration of Columbus's discovery of America, and the opening of the new academic year were to be celebrated at the university under the presidency of Unamuno, who was to represent Franco. At the last minute, doña Carmen Polo, Franco's wife, decided to attend also.

Juan CRESPO, the monarchist student, who had recently returned from the

1. Juan Crespo's uncle; see Militancies 5, pp. 171–4.

front to join his party's guard of honour at Franco's HQ, was on duty that morning; with the rest of the guard, he escorted doña Carmen to the university. When they reached there, he saw that they had arrived late, and room had to be made for the newcomer on the dais on Unamuno's right. As an admirer of José María Pemán, the civil poet of the nationalist cause, who was going to be one of the speakers, CRESPO remained at the door to listen. Eugenio VEGAS LATAPIE, who had accompanied Pemán, was on the platform. Felisa UNAMUNO was among the spectators in the hall.

—The first speaker, a professor of history, José María Ramos Loscertales, quoted a seventeenth-century Spanish writer, Gracián, who referred somewhat slightingly to the Basques and Catalans, recalled VEGAS LATAPIE. As soon as he said this, I saw Unamuno get out an envelope and start scribbling on the back. I wondered what he was doing since he was not due to speak . . .

Juan CRESPO: I imagined that he was going to draw something, or make a paper dart with the blue envelope. He was a good drawer. He went on doing something with his pencil, but I turned to listen to the speaker . . .

Few, if any, in the audience could know that the blue envelope in Unamuno's hands had contained a note from the wife of a protestant clergyman in Salamanca, who had been arrested, and whom Unamuno had tried to help. She said her husband, Atilano Coco, was accused of being a mason, which indeed he had become in England some fifteen years before. Unamuno advised her to go to see the Catholic bishop, and she had told him that the bishop refused to see her. When he pulled out the envelope, he knew there was virtually no hope of saving her husband.

Felisa UNAMUNO: When Pemán finished speaking, my father suddenly stood up and said that he must speak, since a Basque – himself – and a Catalan – the Bishop Plá y Deniel – were on the platform. Although it wasn't part of the programme, his action didn't surprise me; in fact, it would have surprised me if he hadn't spoken, since he took every opportunity of doing so; and even more so now, when it was necessary to protest . . .

Eugenio VEGAS LATAPIE: One of the speakers, he said, had referred disparagingly to the Basques and the Catalans. This was an outright discourtesy. The civil war was an uncivil war. Many cruel acts were being committed in Spain. It was one thing to conquer, another to convince ('*vencer no es convencer*') . . .

Felisa UNAMUNO: 'There is hatred but no compassion.' And hatred without compassion could not convince. To conquer was not to convert. Spain and the anti-Spain were as much on one side as on the other. On both it was the women who were providing a lamentable example: going to the front to enjoy the spectacle of death on the one side; on the other, with religious insignia sometimes worn, going to watch public executions.[1] There was hatred of intelligence . . .

1. These took place in Salamanca as in Valladolid (p. 167); but fewer people are believed to have been shot in the former than in the latter.

Juan CRESPO: 'You talk about the Basques and the Catalans,' he went on in allusion to the remarks about the Spain and anti-Spain, 'but here you have your bishop who is Catalan to teach you the Christian doctrine which you don't want to learn, and me, a Basque, who have spent my life teaching you to read and think in the Spanish language which you don't know . . . '

Felisa UNAMUNO: He had hardly spoken for more than a few minutes when General Millán Astray, also on the platform, shouted out: 'Let me talk, let me talk.' My father hadn't addressed himself to the general at all . . .

Juan CRESPO: From the door I saw the general, founder of the Foreign Legion, stand up and turn towards Unamuno. As always, Millán Astray's manner was exaggerated. Everybody fled from him in the street when they saw him coming – with his one arm, one leg, one eye – because he was such a bore with his patriotic harangues. He'd take one by the arm and talk on and on. But now he was plainly angry and stammering . . .

Felisa UNAMUNO: He started saying things it was impossible to follow. He was a madman. Anyone who heard him in the Plaza Mayor shouting, 'Everyone kiss, everyone embrace,' was aware of that. But then suddenly he shouted: 'Death to intellectuals! Long live death!' . . .[1]

Eugenio VEGAS LATAPIE: 'Death to the treacherous intelligentsia!' There was an outburst of cries so loud that although I was sitting close by, I couldn't hear what he said next. Army officers brought out pistols. Everyone obviously thought the shout was directed at Unamuno. Suddenly there seemed the possibility that the latter's life was in danger . . .

Juan CRESPO: Millán Astray's bodyguard, a short, pot-bellied Legion warrant officer, who had been half dozing behind the general, suddenly sprang up when he heard his general shout. Automatically, he aimed his sub-machine gun at Unamuno . . .

Eugenio VEGAS LATAPIE: Then Millán Astray shouted: 'Unamuno, take the arm of the head of state's wife!' . . .

Juan CRESPO: Franco's wife stood up with an aloofness, an elegance which I doubt she could repeat. With one hand she gestured to the legionary to deflect his machine-gun, and with the other she took don Miguel by the arm. Unamuno looked on the point of collapse. His head was sunk in his shoulders. With her other hand she made a gesture which we understood to mean she was summoning her guard. We formed up round the couple. Our lieutenant, perhaps on doña Carmen's instructions, took up a position on Unamuno's other side and placed an arm round his shoulder. We had to use our rifle butts to control the spectators who pressed forward. There were shouts and cries '*¡Rojo! ¡Cabrón!*' Franco's wife opened the door of her official car and told the lieutenant to take Unamuno home while she walked back to the palace . . .

1. The cry of the Foreign Legion. There is no written record of Unamuno's speech. The best reconstruction is in E. Salcedo, *Vida de don Miguel* (Salamanca, 1964). VEGAS LATAPIE alone remembers Unamuno making an attack on the army, accusing it of having shot Dr José Rizal, leader of the Philippine independence movement. The protestant clergyman, Atilano Coco, was shot.

Felisa UNAMUNO: I felt a great rage in me. To hear my father insulted, to hear, in the very university, someone shout, 'Death to the intelligentsia,' and only one person, professor Bermejo, protest, was intolerable. But I wasn't worried that the incident would have serious repercussions for my father. That much they wouldn't dare. They already had on their hands the stigma of Lorca's assassination . . .

At lunch, Unamuno was excited and nervous. The family already tried not to tell him too much of what they knew was going on because he didn't want to hear it. 'There's nothing I can do,' he said. He had been summoned to see Franco not long before and had protested about the assassinations and executions. Almost every day he visited the daughter of Filiberto Villalobos, education minister in the pre-war centre-right government, who had been imprisoned. 'The reds,' he told her one day, as she later related, 'are the colour of blood, they say; but these people here are the colour of pus – and I don't know which is worse.'

After lunch, as usual, Unamuno went to the *casino* for his *tertulia* – the customary chat with his regular circle of friends. His appearance provoked cries among the members: 'Red! Traitor! Throw him out! He's not Spanish!' His son, Rafael, heard the shouts and immediately went to accompany his father from the place; the old man insisted on leaving by the main door.

For the next two and a half months, until his death, Unamuno remained at home. A policeman was put on duty, allegedly to protect him. The *casino* cancelled his membership; the university senate met and 'withdrew its confidence', agreeing to ask General Franco to appoint a new rector. Two months after his dismissal by the republican government, he was dismissed by the nationalists.

Felisa UNAMUNO: Morally, if not materially, they killed him. When my brothers, who were in Madrid, heard the news they imagined the nationalists were responsible for his death, and both volunteered for the red army. One of them was wounded, losing an eye, almost as soon as he reached the front . . .

Falangists asked the family's permission to act as pall-bearers. As the coffin was placed in the niche, a falangist gave the fascist salute and shouted: 'Comrade Miguel de Unamuno!' '*¡Presente!*' cried the others, saluting.

Rafael UNAMUNO: I think they did it to show that the new regime, the Falange especially, was not responsible for my father's death. There were falangists who considered themselves on the left, and they were aware of my father's intellectual stature. In my opinion, they wanted to show solidarity with him and prevent his death being used against the regime . . .

It was a final irony, none the less. In the last months of his life he had made little or no attempt to hide his hatred of the Falange, which he held mainly responsible for the assassinations in the rearguard.

In two letters to a correspondent in the month before his death, he called the new state a 'stupid regime of terror', the war 'an imperialist-pagan African-type militarization', a 'campaign against liberalism, not bolshevism'. While retaining his faith in Franco, he now feared that the dictatorship would come to mean, as in Italy, 'the death to freedom of conscience, freedom of investigation, the dignity of Man'.[1]

COLLECTIVIZATION DECREE

The criminal military uprising of 19 July has produced an extraordinary upheaval in the country's economy . . . The accumulation of wealth in the hands of a continually smaller group of persons has gone hand in hand with the accumulation of ever greater poverty by the working class; since the former had no hesitation in unleashing a cruel war to protect its privileges, the victory of the people must mean the death of capitalism.

Barcelona, 24 October 1936. First Councillor, Josep Tarradellas. Economics Councillor, Joan P. Fàbregas.

Diari Oficial de la Generalitat de Catalunya
(28 October 1936)

The collectivism we are living in Spain is not anarchist collectivism, it is the creation of a new capitalism, more inorganic than the old capitalist system we have destroyed . . . Rich collectives refuse to recognize any responsibilities, duties or solidarity towards poor collectives . . . No one understands the complexities of the economy, the dependence of one industry on another.

Horacio Prieto, former CNT national committee secretary
(6 January 1938)

---

1. Unpublished letters from Unamuno to Quintín de Torre, dated 1 December and 13 December, quoted by courtesy of the Unamuno family.

It is not a question of proclaiming the failure of collectivization but of doing everything possible to ensure that the profound socializing significance of the Decree and its complementary dispositions are understood by the majority of workers, that they adapt themselves to it and become capable of directing their own destiny . . .

Albert Pérez-Baró, unpublished article (November 1937)

BARCELONA

The revolution – a word so often taken to have but one meaning – was being given a variety of definitions in its day-to-day organization in Catalonia. The militants, whose drive in taking over factories and enterprises had got Barcelona running 'normally' within a few days, interpreted the revolutionary moment in their own fashion. Collectivization, socialization, cooperativization – few people could give a precise definition of what was meant by the different terms being used. But one thing dominated the libertarian revolution: the practice of self-management – the workers' administration of their factories and industries. To have tried to take that right away, reflected Albert PEREZ-BARO, a politically independent civil servant with a long past in the working-class movement, would have been like standing defenceless in front of a flood.

—But, at the same time, it wasn't possible to leave each factory and enterprise to be run at the whim of the workers who had taken them over, or by their private owners: it could lead only to chaos. A structure had to be given to what had happened . . .

This structure was to be Catalonia's Collectivization and Workers' Control Decree, approved on 24 October 1936. The decree was unique in the Popular Front zone; nowhere, outside Catalonia, were industrial collectives given legal status.

Under the new law, industrial and commercial firms (the law did not apply to banks or the land) employing more than 100 workers, or whose owners had fled or been declared insurgent, were automatically collectivized. Firms with fewer workers could choose to collectivize if the majority of the workers and the owner(s) agreed – in firms of between 50 and 100 workers it required the decision of 75 per cent of the workforce. Works councils, elected by an assembly of the workers and representing all sectors of the enterprise, were to administer the collectivized factory, 'assuming the functions and responsibilities of the former boards of directors'. A Generalitat representative was chosen, in agreement with the workers, to sit on each council. Collectivized enterprises (and private firms under workers' control) in each sector of industry would be represented in an Economic Federation, in turn topped by a general industrial council which would closely control the whole industry. Fifty per cent of a collectivized firm's profit would go to an industrial and commercial credit fund which would have to finance all Catalan industry; 20 per cent was to be put to the collective's reserve and depreciation fund; 15 per cent to the collective's social needs, and the remaining 15 per cent to be allocated by the workers as they decided in a general assembly. Small businesses were not to be collectivized; a workers' control committee had the task of controlling production, working conditions and finance.

The decree, in PEREZ-BARO's view, did no more than legalize the existing situation, for the collectives already existed. It attempted to coordinate, codify and unite in a single practice what previously had been open to the interpretation of every trade union or workers' committee.

—And there were any number of interpretations. For many unskilled CNT workmen, the attitude was simply: '*¡Ja està bé!* (Everything's fine now!) The revolution has been made.' And they waited for manna to fall. Then there were the militant workers' committees which ran the enterprises as though they owned them, while others left the owner in virtual control, simply changing his title to manager. Then again, there were committees which – using a demagogic measure the Generalitat had decreed, by which it committed itself to pay workers wages for the time they had been on strike after 19 July – simply continued to present their weekly wage lists to the Generalitat, which went on paying them, instead of seeking to get their businesses going.[1]

By the time the decree was approved, three months after the start of the revolution, a great number of small businesses – artisanal enterprises in the main – had already been taken over by the CNT (and even UGT). These were not returned to their owners, and this later provided the pretext for the petty bourgeoisie's representatives on the Economics Council to launch heavy attacks and delay the decree's application . . .

PEREZ-BARO, who was appointed secretary of the commission overseeing the decree's application, believed that the new structure represented an attempt to seek points of concurrence between the anarchists, communists and petty bourgeoisie.

—Neither total collectivization, socialization nor nationalization. Ownership of industry lay not in the hands of the unions, the workers or the state. It belonged to society in general. Capitalism was not totally abolished, but its role was very much minimized. The basic premise of the decree was that the working class was to be supreme . . .

From the beginning, the CNT supported different solutions, both locally and nationally. At the latter level, Madrid had called for the 'classic' anarcho-syndicalist line of *socialization* of large industry, business and transport (by

1. This later became institutionalized as the 'pawn bank', through which the workers of deficitary enterprises received their wages in return for 'pawning' their company's capital equipment and inventory to the Generalitat – a measure which resulted in giving the latter virtual control of the enterprise.

which it meant that the unions should run, but not own, them), workers' control in other private enterprises and the planning of large industry. Barcelona, on the other hand, proposed *collectivization* of all enterprises without distinction, with profits to be handed over to a common fund administered by the Economics Council of Catalonia, which had been created in mid-August (under the auspices of the militia committee), to bring order to the Catalan economy.

It was doubtful that the CNT had seriously envisaged collectivization of industry (as opposed to agriculture) before this time. Joan FERRER, who as secretary of the CNT commercial employees' union was involved in the take-over and running of Barcelona's department stores, attended a plenum of the Catalan CNT regional committee in September, at which there was a heated discussion between the advocates of *socialization* and *cooperativization.* The bigger, more powerful unions, like the woodworkers, the transport workers, the public entertainments union, all of which had already socialized their industries, wanted to extend their solution to the rest of industry. The smaller, weaker unions wanted to form cooperatives, arguing that the latter would retain the identity of each firm.

—As the meeting was unable to come to a decision, an *ad hoc* committee was formed, of which I was a member, to thrash out the problem. We spent thirty hours without rest or sleep; finally the concept of collectivization was suggested, by Fàbregas, I think. Up to that moment, I had never heard of collectivization as a solution for industry – the department stores were being run by the union. What the new system meant was that each collectivized firm would retain its individual character, but with the ultimate objective of federating all enterprises within the same industry . . .

Fàbregas, who was one of the CNT's three representatives on the Economics Council and was soon to become the economics councillor in the Generalitat government, put forward the proposal as a sort of 'neutral ground', on which all could agree, FERRER believed. In this he was successful; but it didn't prevent those unions which had socialized – and this included the barbers and bakers who had closed down small shops and regrouped the industry under union management in big shops – from continuing their socialization rather than heeding the collectivization decree.

—To say that there was ever a general CNT policy about what to do in the new situation would be saying a great deal. It was ambiguous about the collectivization decree itself, in PEREZ-BARO's view. While it sent its representatives to the Economics Council – and there were those among them, like Andreu Capdevila, who did everything they could to see that the decree was implemented – the CNT at the same time pursued its own, unilateral objectives which were different.[1] Syndical collectivization or syndicalized collectives, I would call those

1. 'Indeed, I have a letter from Abad de Santillán, who was to become the CNT's economics councillor in the Generalitat after Fàbregas, in which he says: "I was an enemy of the [collectivization] decree because I considered it premature . . . It destroyed the autonomy and spontaneity of a work which (in its origins) was essentially popular . . . When I became councillor, I had no intention of taking into account or carrying out the decree; I intended to allow our great people to carry on the task as they best saw fit, according to their own inspiration" ' (PEREZ-BARO).

objectives; that's to say, collectives run by their respective unions, as though they belonged to them. The CNT's policy was thus not the same as that pursued by the decree – and this caused innumerable problems.[1] None the less, in giving a legal structure to collectivization, Catalonia embarked on a revolutionary social experience whose only antecedents were the Paris Commune and the Russian revolution of 1917 . . .

Militancies 6

ANDREU CAPDEVILA

CNT textile worker

A worker in the Fabra and Coats Spinning Company's factory in Barcelona, he had been called by the CNT's regional committee to take up a political post on the Economics Council of Catalonia which was drafting the collectivization decree. He, who had never had the slightest contact with any political party, who on election days always made a point of leaving the city at dawn for a hiking trip in the mountains 'to avoid the farce, the bribery and coercion, the trickery of the people who were being used by political parties', was now being called on to participate in an official organization.

He told the regional committee that he was doing a better job at his workplace than he could do on the council. Problems were beginning to arise in the factory where sales had fallen sharply as a result of the loss of a large part of the country – and market – to the insurgents. Full-time work was continuing, but the bulk of the production was being stock-piled. Although the workforce had joined the union in the past couple of years (where previously there had been no more than 125 CNT members in the dyeing section), the factory's 2,000 workers were known for their 'conservatism' and did not want to hear of collectivization. Conditions, he knew, were relatively better than in other textile plants; the British-owned company had made concessions: a 55- instead of a 60-hour week, crèches for women with young children, Christmas presents for all the workers' children. There was a long tradition of father-and-son workers which made the factory like a large family.

—I knew my fellow-workers' psychology, I could be useful there. Wishing to satisfy their aspirations, I didn't want the factory collectivized. We had set up a workers' control committee at the start, which had sorted out a number of problems, but the technical side of things remained in the old management's hands. However, with sales reduced by half, and the company's bank account almost depleted, we had to confront the imperative necessity of ensuring the workers' wages. The English owners gave no sign of life. We went to the local

1. The UGT, for its part, proposed at the time the cooperative organization of owner-abandoned industry, workers' control in the remainder of large industry, and the protection of the industrial and commercial petty bourgeoisie.

management and were informed that the British parent company expected us henceforth to work only three days a week . . .

The workers' committee called a general assembly which decided to send two of the local managers to Marseilles for discussions with authorized representatives of the parent company to put forward three alternatives: either the factory worked three days and the workers were paid for a full week; or worked a full week and output continued to be stock-piled; or surplus production from a full week could be sent to England for re-export. Whichever it chose, the company had to agree to pay full wages while the present abnormal situation continued.

—The two managers returned; the parent company was intransigent: they made only one concession – we could work three days and be paid for four . . .

Another general assembly was called. The workers' committee made it clear that it considered the company's attitude absurd. The assembled workers decided that they were not prepared to suffer hardships to benefit the company's shareholders, who had been making considerable profits for years; if someone was to make sacrifices, it would have to be the capitalists. By acclamation, the workers decided to collectivize the factory.

—It was while this was going on that the regional committee called me to take up the post. My knowledge of economics was very limited, I was a worker. I had never been in favour of the CNT entering any sort of official organization or government. Either we made our total revolution or remained in opposition. All social improvements come from the pressure of the masses in the streets and nowhere else. Politics corrupts, power corrupts . . .

Meanwhile, a works council had been set up and had taken over the factory's management, though leaving the former managers in their posts. One of the first steps taken was the abolition of piece-work, an objective which the CNT textile unions had long been fighting for. The first week, production fell by 40 per cent.

—We had calculated that if it fell by no more than 25 per cent it would be possible to fix a fair wage for all. But 40 per cent was impossible, it spelt the collective's collapse. We called a general assembly, called on the workers not to fail the collective attempts being made by the Spanish proletariat to achieve social justice. For several weeks production did not rise, we had to go round the shop floor, haranguing the women workers. In the end they managed to get production up to 70 per cent of its former level . . .

He noticed one big difference in the workforce after collectivization. Prior to the war, none of the workers 'knew how to talk'; if there was a claim to be made, he or one of his union companions had to meet the management. While the workers' control committee functioned, the mass of the workforce still didn't speak up. But the moment the factory was collectivized and there were general assemblies, everyone started to talk.

—It was amazing, everyone turned into a parrot, everyone wanted to say what he or she thought and felt. They obviously felt themselves in charge now and with the right to speak for themselves . . .

The CNT regional committee rang him again; there were very few cadres worthy of the CNT's complete trust, and he was needed.

—I spent several hours in a state of terrible nervousness. I knew I didn't have sufficient education to be in charge of the economy. I knew, too, in the revolutionary situation we were living through, when the workers had to take over the economy, that such problems as mine were bound to arise, especially when most of the working class was illiterate. I'd gone to work hardly knowing how to read or write, I'd rebelled when I saw the injustices done to the workers, especially the women. I'd joined the dyers' union, as it then was, and made friends with anarcho-syndicalists, vegetarians, nudists. I'd grown up in that sort of atmosphere. I never smoked, I never touched alcohol, I spent my life working and studying peacefully with my *compañera*; I had the opportunity of becoming a businessman, a foreman, but I always refused. I lived by my work, I never exploited others. I was an anarchist, but for all that I abhor violence. I was always opposed to the pre-war attempts by small groups to make the libertarian revolution by violent means. I was not a *treintista*, but I believed that the revolution had to spring from the proletariat as a whole, and that a great effort had to be made to raise the proletariat's level of understanding so that it would be prepared for the revolution.

From the age of thirteen, when I first joined the CNT, I held the belief that for man to live in conformity with the laws of nature, to live with mutual respect, the exploitation of man by man must end. To live healthily, to enjoy a tranquil conscience, a man must live soberly . . .

When he got to the Economics Council, Joan Fàbregas informed him that he was to be its Acting President. Within a month, he was presenting the draft collectivization decree for discussion. The debate lasted until 3 a.m. It was heated.

—The PSUC and Esquerra fought extremely hard to reduce the number of firms liable for collectivization, while the CNT–FAI held out for the most radical decree possible.[1] The reason the CNT had agreed to collectivization was that we could not *socialize*, as was our aim. The workers, as a matter of life and death, had taken over the factories – but the victory was not exclusively the CNT's. We couldn't, in consequence, take over and control the whole Spanish economy, couldn't socialize . . .

Collectivization brought order to the chaotic situation which had arisen as a result of individual unions taking over enterprises, in his view. All the parties and organizations solemnly agreed to respect the letter and spirit of the new law; 'but within three months the republican parties were systematically obstructing it; and soon afterwards, the communists were sabotaging it'.

Why had the CNT made any concessions?

—Because of our original concession; from the moment Companys offered the CNT power and it was turned down, the CNT's position became tragic.

1. The minimum figure of 100 workers for obligatory collectivization was a compromise between the different positions.

Companys was a much cleverer politician than any of us. Once we had compromised – knowing that we couldn't make our total revolution – every political party was able to manoeuvre and plot against us. They couldn't stand us because we were opposed to politics. As the war began to go badly, as the social aspects of the revolution frightened England and France, who imposed their Non-Intervention committee on us, so we slowly began to lose power.

International capitalism was determined to do everything in its power to force the failure of the collectivized Catalan economy. That is no idle statement. One day, talking with one of the Spanish former managers of my own company, I said I found it hard to understand why the British parent company had shown such intransigence – an intransigence which had led to the factory's collectivization.

'You're a man of good faith, Capdevila,' he said, 'but a bit naïve. What seems absurd to you seems entirely natural to me. The Coats board recognized the justice of the workers' proposals. But it isn't a matter of a dispute between the company and its workers; what's at stake is the life or death of international capital itself. All the capitalist monopolies have reached agreement to boycott the red zone and to give their unconditional support to Franco who represents the continuity of capitalism; the company has simply been carrying out this agreement . . . '

He wasn't wrong. I tried to reach agreement with two other international companies and they refused to discuss the matter or come to an agreement with their workers.[1]

As a member of the Economics Council, CAPDEVILA received a salary of 1,000 pesetas a month. The CNT regional committee took the decision that any CNT member who joined an official organization, and received a higher wage than in his previous job, should pay the balance to the committee. When he went to do so, after receiving his first month's salary, he was told not to bother: 'That was just an agreement, but it's not being put into effect.'

—That wasn't so important. The real problem was the possibilities of corruption that an official position afforded; the case of the man from Reus who offered me so much on every litre of olive oil if I would get him an export licence; the women who came in an attempt to save their husbands or brothers and would say, 'Well, if we can't settle the matter here, come to my house – ' And you knew very well what that proposition involved. I threw them out of my office. Once you compromised there was no end. All those dirty, sickening ways that politics bring with them and which result only in the people being swindled. I could have made millions – and I reached France without a *céntimo* in my pocket at the end of the war. I retained my morality to the very end . . .

With or without the collectivization decree's blessing, the libertarian revolution was collectivizing or socializing everything from the textile industry to greyhound racing in Barcelona.

1. For further discussion of the problem of foreign capital and collectivization, see Appendix A, p. 575.

Textile manufacturing, Catalonia's basic source of wealth, employing some 200,000 workers (nearly three times as many as in engineering, the second largest industry), was facing great problems. Dependent on importing the bulk of its raw material and on selling its finished products in the rest of Spain – one third of which approximately was now in insurgent hands – the industry had been in difficulties before the war started. When the workers took over España Industrial, one of Catalonia's largest textile plants, they found only enough money in the company's bank account to pay the 2,500 workers for a fortnight.[1] Luis SANTACANA, the CNT militant in the firm who had proposed to a general assembly of the workers that they take over the factory because the directors and managers had fled, knew that the worker-managed enterprise had been saved only because they had discovered a considerable amount of stock in the factory, which they sold little by little as they needed money to pay the workers' wages.

—That and war work saved us.[2] During the whole three years, there was never a week when the workers didn't receive their full wages, even if it had been possible to work only three days . . .

Although the factory had been taken over in the first flush of the revolution, it was not collectivized until the decree was published. There was little internal difference, in his view, between the two situations: the workers' committee now became the works council on which – in contrast to the past – a Generalitat supervisor sat and reported every three months on the state of finance, stocks, production, etc. The most important difference was that the workers' revolutionary conquest of their factories was now given legal status.

With one exception the workers' committee and later works council members continued to work at their normal jobs, holding their meetings after work on Saturdays. The exception was a member delegated permanently to remain in the office on duty.

—Those who have alleged that collectivization meant there were a dozen bosses where before they had been one are simply not telling the truth. I felt myself a servant of the collective; I didn't ask or expect any economic reward. At the technical level, I knew I wasn't sufficiently trained to be one of those running the factory; I'd only had six months' schooling in my life. But as far as social and economic – and to some degree even administrative – questions went, I felt capable enough. Any deficiencies I suffered from I believe I fully made up with will-power, enthusiasm and good faith . . . [3]

Twenty factory technicians who had remained at their posts dealt with

1. See pp. 139–40.
2. And also the deferment of payment on all company purchases made prior to 28 July, the date on which the workers got the mill running. See A. Souchy and P. Folgare, 'Raport sobre la actuación del comité central de la España Industrial', in *Colectivizaciones* (Barcelona, 1937).
3. 'I spent several hours in the España Industrial mill. A large number of the workers have spent the greater part of their working lives here and there is a sort of "mill-patriotism". When I questioned them on the improvements they wanted, I almost always got the same general, vague answers: freedom for all, socialism, fraternity . . . Very few made other demands, even for cultural facilities.' (H. E. Kaminski, *Ceux de Barcelona*, Paris, 1937.)

technical problems. ' "Each one to his place and to his work", had been the union's call to the factory. We knew very well that the technicians were necessary to us if the factory was to continue in production, and in consequence they were given two seats on the works council. They were able to improve some of the antiquated machinery in the plant and build showers for the workers.' The administrative staff also had two representatives on the council, while the manual workers had eight. Technicians and staff frequently found themselves out-voted 8–4.

Wage differentials were reduced, though not eliminated. Because of economic difficulties, it was impossible to raise the workers' wages; instead, the technicians and staff were asked to lower theirs. They replied by proposing a 20 per cent cut.

—That was magnificent. Achieved without any violence on our part. The money saved was used to pay pensions to workers who should have retired long ago, but couldn't because there was no social security or pension scheme. They received full wages in retirement . . .

SANTACANA was a believer in the 'single' wage as being the 'most perfect in terms of economic justice'. If needs were equal why should not wages be equal?

—We libertarians have a maxim which is binding: each shall produce according to his abilities, each shall consume according to his needs. Production is like a clock – each part is interdependent, if one part fails the clock will no longer show the hour. It's very difficult to determine which of the workers fulfilling so many different tasks is the most important. The miner digging out the coal, the worker transporting it to the factory, the stoker shovelling it into the factory furnace? Without any of them the process would stop. All should be paid the same wage; the only difference should depend on whether a man is single or married and has a family; in the latter case, he should get so much extra per dependant. Money, after all, has only a representational value; real value is what is produced . . .

But the 'single' wage could not be introduced in his plant because it was not made general throughout the industry. Women in the factory continued to receive wages between 15 per cent and 20 per cent lower than men, and manual workers less than technicians.

—Inevitably, collectivization could not resolve all problems; there were people who lacked self-discipline, a consciousness of what was demanded of them. There was a mechanic who stole a spanner. I told him he was no longer stealing from the capitalists, he was robbing himself and his fellow-workers. Under the old regime, he would have been sacked on the spot. 'Please, please, don't steal again' . . .

Within a fortnight the man was back and SANTACANA had to take disciplinary action. The collective, he said, would not sack him because he had children and needed his weekly wage. Instead, they were going to move him to a new section, the cleaning department. But that would require public notification.

—'You will write your full name on the blackboard, underneath it that you have stolen two spanners and that is the reason for your move to a section where you will have no chance of further theft.' 'No, no,' he cried, 'not the blackboard.' 'Yes,' I said, 'it can't hurt you to write the truth up there.' There were no more cases of indiscipline; the threat of the blackboard was sufficient...

The works council called bi-monthly or quarterly assemblies[1] of all the workers in a cinema or theatre to explain the current state of production, stocks, resources etc. After three or four months of the workers taking over, shortages of raw materials (the price of which had in some cases doubled owing to the fall of the republican peseta) had reduced the factory to a three-day week. Added to the shortage of cotton and dye-stuffs was the shortage of coal; the difficulties of receiving supplies from Asturias were almost insuperable, and the factory had on occasion to fire its boilers with wood. The CNT textile union looked after the sales as well as the import of raw materials for the factory, although smaller collectives were able to do their own deals with other collectives or even directly with individuals.

Under the decree, the works councils were considered to be 'assuming the functions of the former board of directors' and were answerable to the collective's workers. Each council appointed a managing director to run the plant on a day-to-day basis. The first director appointed by the España Industrial works council turned out to be unsatisfactory, and the technical section was asked to put forward a new candidate. They suggested a weaving technician, a man of liberal ideas, who was duly accepted.

Under the decree, the works council could be dismissed by the workers in a general assembly, or by the general industrial council in the case of 'manifest incompetence'. In fact, it rarely happened.

—Had such a vote of censure ever taken place in my mill, I would have been the first to have given up my post, and all the rest of us the same, I'm sure. The committee was not a dictatorship, it was elected by the base; and it was only right that those who had the right to elect should have the right to sack. Time was always put aside for 'any other business' at the end of general assemblies for any worker who wanted to criticize the way things were being run, or move a vote of censure. It never happened in my plant – and I don't know of any cases in any other factories. In any event, half the council was renewable by election every year under the decree . . .

The question of workers' trade union representation within the collective led, in SANTACANA's view, to some confusion. Before the war each factory had had a trade union committee; in many factories when they were taken over, it was this committee which was elected *en bloc* as the new workers' control committee or works council. Frequently, no new trade union committee was set up.

—Although it should have been, so that the workers still had their direct union representation to take up any grievance on the shop floor. It was a failure very common to the Barcelona area, a failure to understand the real situation created

1. Their periodicity was raised at the second assembly in October 1936, held two and a half months after the first. The factory committee said no decision had been reached on this question, but that no grave matters having arisen, it had not considered it necessary to call an assembly earlier (see A. Souchy and P. Folgare, op. cit.).

by a union moving from the stage of class struggle to that of self-management, a confusion between the two roles . . .

The workers of a particular mill section elected their own foremen; the latter were not permitted to earn more than they had before, but were relieved of direct work tasks. The foremen liaised on technical matters between the section and the works council.

Towards the end, when the factory was hardly able to work at all, the workers came in on Fridays to collect their pay. Few then turned out for the general assemblies – 'less from apathy than that they were out searching for food' – until the works council announced that all who didn't turn up would lose a day's pay.

But those sombre days were still in the future. Some of the problems facing workers in newly formed collectives were experienced in the department stores, which Joan FERRER, secretary of the CNT commercial employees' union, was able to observe closely.

—It came as a psychological shock to some workers to find themselves suddenly freed from capitalist tutelage. Exchanging one individualism for another, they frequently believed that, now that the owners had gone, they were the new owners. Though affecting white-collar workers in this instance, the problem was by no means confined to them . . .

As soon as the decree came into force, his union withdrew from the running of the stores since the concept of collectivization did not, in principle, admit union-management. This, FERRER felt, was an advantage, for the employees, who had to elect their own works council, now felt more directly involved in the running of the stores. Being at the orders of a union was, in his view, much the same as being at the orders of the state. Though the workers often felt themselves the owners, they also defended the enterprise as though it were their own.

—It was our idea in the CNT that everything should start from the worker, not – as with the communists – that everything should be run by the state. To this end we wanted to set up industrial federations – textiles, engineering, department stores, etc. – which would be represented on an overall Economics Council which would direct the economy. Everything, including economic planning, would thus remain in the hands of the workers.[1]

An attempt was made to federate the department stores; it failed. The works councils opposed it, considering the enterprises as their own and being unwilling to join a federation.

—It was understandable. Only a few months before, the traditional relationship between employer and worker had been overthrown. Now the workers were being asked to make a new leap – to the concept of collective ownership. It was asking a lot to expect the latter to happen overnight . . .

Other problems, directly related to the stores, were raised in the general

1. Industrial federations had been approved by the CNT in 1931 but their creation was combated by anarchist elements within the union and only a handful existed at the outbreak of the war. See Points of Rupture, D.

assemblies: they included sex discrimination – female assistants who complained of the Don Juan attitudes of their male counterparts. 'In the revolutionary fervour of the time, the latter was a subject the women took very seriously.'

Profits were not a problem – there were none, at least up to mid-1937 when FERRER joined the army. Any surplus there might have been was ploughed back into the stores; wages were raised, working conditions improved and other improvements made. This in itself was a success: the important thing, in his view, was that the stores continued to operate throughout the war.

In the smaller enterprises, those of between fifty and 100 employees, where collectivization was voluntary, one question that almost invariably arose was the role of the former owner. As a member of the trade union council attached to the Economics Council, FERRER attended many assemblies called by the workers to discuss collectivizing their enterprise which he, in a speech, would encourage them to do.

—Very often the owner would also address the assembly, practically bringing tears to everyone's eyes with the story of the sacrifices he had made to build up the firm – only now to see it threatened with collectivization. In these cases, I always suggested to the assembly that he be made the managing director, since the works council had to appoint one anyway. My idea was that the former owner was the most suitable person because, with his capitalist egoism, he would watch over the enterprise and make sure everything functioned as well as possible; he no doubt would one day be hoping to regain possession. My proposal was almost always accepted . . .

These former owners undoubtedly opposed any attempt to amalgamate their firms with others in order to rationalize their industry, since this went against their individual interests; but at the same time not all former owners were opposed to collectivization of their firms. Because of economic difficulties, many smaller companies could not continue to operate with the same number of employees on higher wages: collectivization was the only answer because the workers then 'had no other recourse but to keep their wages within the necessary limits'.[1]

Profit was not a matter in much evidence in most of the collectives, if for no other reason, in Eduardo PONS PRADES's experience of the woodworkers' union, than that 'no one would have thought it right if the union had acted simply like a capitalist enterprise'.

—The concept that prevailed was that the working class should have good furniture at cheap prices. Profit and loss was a secondary consideration, and I don't think that sales prices were studied very seriously in relation to unit costs. It was as though the revolution was all that mattered . . .

Unlike the Barcelona textile industry or the department stores, where each collective was an autonomous unit, the woodworkers' union had socialized its industry, taking over and managing everything from the felling of the lumber in the Vall d'Aran to the furniture retail shops. The union had nearly split over

1. Pérez-Baró, *Trenta mesos de col·lectivisme a Catalunya*, p. 87.

its policy, one section, dominated by the FAI, maintaining that anarchist self-management meant that the workers should set up and operate autonomous centres of production so as to avoid the threat of bureaucratization. A carpenter who wanted to join forces with another or a varnisher had the right to set up on his own, in this view. 'A concept of self-management that pre-dated capitalism, in effect.' Socialization won the day: the union ran everything.

It set up two big workshops, each employing up to 200 men, where those who had been working in small shops, which made up 75 per cent of all carpenters' shops in Barcelona, were found jobs. A union delegate would go round the small shops, point out to the workers that the conditions were unhealthy and dangerous, that the revolution was changing all this, and secure their agreement to close down and move to the union-built Double X and the 33 EU. The latter had existed before the war, but the union built two more floors for the finishing sections; it produced furniture, mainly tables and sideboards, and the union imported a great amount of French machinery for it. To get the foreign currency out of the Generalitat required considerable union intervention. PONS PRADES remembered the union leader, Hernández, storming out to the Economics Council, saying that if no currency were available there would be no more war work by the union. The latter now occupied about one third of the workforce, PONS PRADES estimated, and was employed making hangars for the air force, huts for the army, pontoon equipment, coachwork for lorries, etc.

In the retail furniture shops, usually also very small and as often as not run by the owner, his wife and an assistant, a union delegate was appointed. Very often the former owner was made sales delegate of another small shop, the same happening with the owners of the small workshops who became foremen in a larger shop when their places were closed.

—In fact one of my major surprises was to see how many of the newly appointed administrative heads of union sections were former owners or their sons, PONS PRADES observed. By then, the union had lost at least half of its best militants, between those killed in the streets of Barcelona and those – the greater number – who went to the Aragon front. Added to that, as soon as the call-up was made official, the industry lost all workers between the ages of twenty-one and thirty-two. The union's success not only in rationalizing and coordinating a whole industry, but in keeping it running throughout the war, in times of great economic difficulties, was in consequence all the more remarkable . . .

Inevitably, there were failures, most of which, in this view, could be ascribed to the militants' lack of preparation. It was 'the big dream – and each had his own idea of what should be done – but too many were not sufficiently capable of putting it into practice'.

The major failure, in his and other members' view (and which supported the original anarchist objection), was that the union became like a large firm. Its structure grew increasingly rigid. 'From outside it began to look like an American or German trust.' From within, while the workers had the possibility of expressing their criticisms and needs, it was difficult to secure any changes they wanted.

—They felt they weren't particularly involved in decision-making. If the 'general staff' decided that production in two workshops should be switched, the workers weren't informed of the reasons. Lack of information – which could easily have been remedied by producing a news-sheet, for example – bred discontent, especially as the CNT tradition was to discuss and examine everything. Fortnightly delegates' meetings became monthly and ended up, I think, being quarterly . . .

Despite these objections, the first Annual General Assembly renewed almost all the posts unanimously, as he recalled. For, at another level, those who now criticized the union's efforts had little moral ground for attempting to change everything since most of them had opted out of positions of responsibility from the start, saying that they were content to put in their eight hours a day, and 'left it to others to do the ungratifying work of creating the new structure. "No, I am not a person to give orders," was the frequent response. It was a common ideological position among CNT militants that to give orders to someone was self-degrading. But it meant also a loss for the union.'

On the other hand, the leadership always had the last word: it was wartime, socialization was working well, it was essential to maintain things as they were.

—The logic of the times – a logic not very close to the ideology which the majority of CNT members had imbibed. Nevertheless, the unease among union members never led to a strike or even an agreed platform of demands; but I think it would have been difficult to correct the union's increasingly rigid structure as time went on . . .

The union also assumed the role of looking after its members' physical and moral welfare; it organized an exchange system of its own with an agricultural collective in Valls to supply its cooperative foodshop; it built an Olympic swimming pool, a gymnasium and solarium at its Double X factory; and arranged a form of 'uniting a man and woman *freely and without coercion*' – a form of marriage ceremony to counter the trend of couples who, 'believing the revolution made everything possible', began living together and splitting up with too much ease.

The public entertainments union, like the woodworkers', socialized its industry, closing down some of the unprofitable neighbourhood 'flea-pits' – there were 112 cinemas in the city at the outbreak of the war – and transferred the staff to the *Cine Durruti*, the brand-new cinema the union built in the Gran Vía (today the Dorado) and the *Cine Ascaso* (today Vergara) which was already under construction.

Under an ambitious socialization programme, wages in the cinema industry were to be calculated according to an agreed differential rate depending on job. Sick pay and old-age pensions were established, six weeks' annual holiday granted, a clinic and a school were to be set up, cinema tickets were to be reduced in price and taxes to be abolished (an item, interestingly, left to the Generalitat to determine and carry out). In the theatre, however, there was to be a single wage rate. 'As a demonstration of the efforts being made, let it be realized that the greatest of opera singers, like Hipólito Lázaro, and the most humble of workers are going to get the same daily wage.'

A leading CNT militant, Marcos Alcón, called in his brother-in-law, Juan SAÑA, a fitter by trade who had been working in the famous glass cooperative at Mataró, to help reorganize the film production unit which had been making war documentaries and newsreels. Himself a CNT militant from the age of eighteen, who had seen the inside of thirty-eight gaols, SAÑA made it a condition of joining that feature films should be made. The unit began production of a cinematic version of the play *No quiero, No quiero*, by Jacinto Benavente, the Nobel prize-winning Spanish playwright. In SAÑA's eyes, the endeavour was designed to help the war effort; the republic needed foreign currency to buy arms and supplies abroad, and a feature film was a way of securing it.

—Everything that the republic could show abroad would be bought immediately and at a good price. Everything had to be done to win the war. While the collectives in Catalonia, on the whole, were a success, too many CNT militants put too much time and effort into organizing them when every effort was needed for the war. We should have concentrated all our efforts on winning the war – on the basis of the revolutionary conquests that had already been made – rather than making the revolution . . .

The fundamental error, he felt, lay in the failure to do what the enemy had done: overcome all political differences in order to create the type of unity which could win the war. Trying to avoid the 'scandalous divisions and disputes which wracked the republican zone', he devoted himself to the production of the only CNT-sponsored feature film of the collectivized entertainment industry. Halfway through, the male lead was arrested for high treason and espionage and was never seen again. On one occasion the entire company was thrown in gaol, while the 'PSUC, as they began to get the upper hand, made every sort of difficulty for location shooting'; but the film was finished in the end.

Almost the only problem SAÑA had not had to deal with was the 'single' wage introduced in the theatre. It came to a rapid end in dramatic circumstances one day when the famous tenor, Hipólito Lázaro, arrived at the Tivoli theatre where the union was organizing a cycle of operas at popular prices. He was to sing the lead. Before the audience arrived, he got up on stage and addressed the company.

—'We're all equal now,' he said, 'and to prove it, we all get the same wage. Fine, since we're equal, today I am going to collect the tickets at the door and one of you can come up here and sing the lead.' That did it, of course. There had been several previous protests. That night several of us union leaders met and decided at the very start that we couldn't leave until we had come up with a worthy solution . . .

It didn't take long. Top actors and singers, like Lázaro and Marcos Redondo, were to be paid 750 pesetas a performance – a 5,000 per cent increase over their previous 15 pesetas a day. Second- and third-category artists received large, but differential increases, while even ushers were given a rise.

—The single wage didn't work; the six weeks' holidays originally agreed on were, obviously, never given. But cinema tickets were reduced in price, tipping was abolished, the theatres were full to overflowing all the time – Azaña used frequently to go to the Liceo to the opera; we were able to clean up or shut down the music halls (where what went on on stage was less important than what was happening in the spectators' boxes), converting them into variety shows or vaudevilles, where the art lay in the spoken word, *doubles entendres*. Anyone coming on leave from the front would have thought Barcelona was a constant festival as far as public entertainment was concerned . . .

The collectivized entertainments industry was one of the very few to generate a surplus. Greyhound racing was one of the more profitable sides, along with the cinema. José ROBUSTE, a syndicalist party leader, who was president of the greyhound racing section of the entertainments union and a book-keeper at one of the tracks, helped collectivize the industry before leaving for the Aragon front. Everything worked perfectly, he thought. No one was thrown out of work, the old managers, trainers and staff were all kept on. Everyone got paid the same – 15 pesetas a day. Racing was popular, betting continued, the tracks made plenty of money: 100,000 pesetas were loaned to the cinema section which needed money to buy foreign films.

—Self-management by the workers meant making decisions on buying new dogs and that sort of thing. The dogs had always belonged to the companies which owned the tracks and we took them over. They were our means of production and reproduction: we bred from them. Otherwise things functioned the same. The only change collectivization made was that the product of our labour was now shared out differently from before; the work otherwise went on just the same. In a collectivized factory, the machines are operated by the workers in the same way, clerks carry out the same jobs, technicians do their usual work: there's no problem at all in passing from a capitalist to a socialist regime . . .

The workers' 'administration of the economy' implied, it seemed, taking over from capitalist owners and running enterprises without them. Between the one system and the other was there no rupture? Should the self-managed industries continue in the same mode to produce what the capitalist regime had found profitable to produce? These were questions that the anarcho-syndicalist movement was to be summoned rapidly to answer.[1]

In one field, armaments, the answer was ready-given: no such industry existing in Catalonia, everything had to be started from scratch. The machinery for recharging cartridges at the Sant Andreu arsenal had been put out of action when it was stormed by the populace; even the blueprints for the manufacture of shells had disappeared. Thanks to the initiative of a number of CNT metalworkers, in association with a military expert from the Oviedo arms factory, the beginnings of an armaments industry were improvised, and in early August the Generalitat set up a war industries commission. Within a couple of months, it controlled twenty-four major engineering and chemical factories turning out shells, explosives and armoured vehicles amongst other equipment. Pastry-kneading and beer-bottle corking machines were amongst the machinery pressed into service. Machinery for two complete cartridge-producing assemblies was purchased in Belgium; the Belgian government refused export licences and, after further delay, the machinery was bought in France. By October 1937,

1. For the view of the *continuous* passage from capitalism to socialism via self-management, as structural to anarcho-syndicalist ideology, see Points of Rupture, D.

more than 50,000 workers in 500 factories were directly involved on war production and a further 30,000 on auxiliary war work.[1]

La Maquinista, Spain's leading locomotive works, which the workers had taken over from the start, was declared a war industry by the commission. But it was being run – and had been from the beginning – as a collective. Joan ROIG, the only pre-war manager to remain, had been appointed assistant manager of the enterprise after his close escape at the workers' hands when he accompanied a company director to the bank to draw the workers' wages in the first week of the revolution. A liberal Catalan nationalist, he felt he understood the workers' need for equality, freedom and protection in their work. He was not opposed to collectivization and saw no reason why such an experiment should not succeed.

None the less, given the factory's potential, war production there was a disaster, he felt. The workers' indisputable initiative could not compensate for lack of technical expertise, added to lack of proper management and raw materials.

—The workers' committee and later the works council was never able to impose an efficient order of production; the original members, whose first president was a labourer – a great orator in the CNT style – weren't technically qualified to run the factory, let alone convert it to arms manufacture. Too much was left to luck, too much depended on the individual will of a few people rather than on the combined effort of the whole workforce. The majority of technicians weren't sympathetic to collectivization. I remember a Generalitat engineer saying that the reason was that none of the technicians had been shot. In a sense he was right. All in all, I don't think production ever reached 50 per cent of its potential . . .

The factory, moreover, never received orders for the sort of war material it was best suited to produce – large tanks, for example. No new machine tools were brought in; the factory's existing press forge, its milling machines and lathes were not suited for producing shells, grenades and anti-submarine depth charges. With adequate equipment, production might have reached 75 per cent of its potential, ROIG felt.

At the end of the first year, he helped draw up the collective's balance sheet, managing to strike a balance which showed neither profit nor loss.

—In fact, if the true position had been stated, it would have shown a financial disaster. The Generalitat was paying the wages against our invoiced deliveries; the only condition was that the latter should more or less cover the former. At the end of the war, when the owners took over again, they drew up new accounts which showed that the factory had made a loss of nine million pesetas in the three years. At the time that represented nearly 50 per cent of the company's subscribed capital . . .

Self-management, he came to think, could work only if the whole of collectivized industry, from the extractive to the transformation process, functioned properly; and this, patently, was not the case. It was only after the central government took over La Maquinista in November 1937, that things began to pick up, in his view. A young, intelligent engineer was appointed as manager,

1. See J. Bricall, *Política econòmica de la Generalitat*, p. 289.

more fitters and foundrymen were taken on, and some new installations opened. 'But I never trusted the military specialists who arrived with the government take-over. I was convinced they weren't putting all their technical expertise at our disposal – '[1]

In all truth, he felt, it was only when the old board of directors took over at the end of the war that the factory began to produce at pre-war levels again. The mass of the workers remained in the factory.

—There weren't more than one hundred who had been true revolutionaries and who fled. Once they were gone, the others did what no doubt they had wanted to do all along: work and earn their living. Within a few days of the end of the war the factory was working full blast . . .

*

In all, at least 2,000 industrial and commercial collectives were legalized and registered under the decree, according to the computations of Albert PEREZ-BARO. Despite the fact that the decree applied to all Catalonia, the idea that what was happening in Barcelona was necessarily happening elsewhere was erroneous. 'Those of us who didn't live in Barcelona at the time have always complained that historians have concentrated their attention on the capital and deduced that in places like Tarragona, Reus, Valls they were the same. They weren't,' commented Josep SOLE BARBERA, a lawyer and PSUC militant in Reus, a town of some 30,000 inhabitants in Tarragona province. An anti-fascist militia committee, on which he served, had been set up to replace the townhall; but there the comparison with Barcelona ended, for the CNT was not the dominant force or even the dominant trade union locally. An autonomous union organization, Federación Obrera Local, outnumbered both CNT and UGT and depended on neither. The Spanish socialist party, which almost immediately merged into the PSUC, followed by the POUM, which had 'gained considerable support by attacking the Popular Front as a reformist alliance', were the strongest political forces on the left at the start of the war.

—The relative equilibrium amongst the different forces, largely due to the local union federation, made Reus a very different place from Barcelona; a much more balanced place, with a much greater spirit of unity. The same was true

1. The Catalan war industries became one of the major points of friction between the Generalitat and the central government, which started taking over some isolated factories from the beginning of 1937. The conflict had been patent from the start of the war. In September 1936, the Generalitat asked that some of the munition-producing machinery from Toledo, threatened by the advancing Army of Africa, be transferred to Catalonia. Madrid's reply was categoric: 'Catalonia shall never make cartridges.' (See Bricall, op. cit., p. 291; also, *De Companys a Prieto, documentos sobre las indústrias de guerra de Cataluña*, Buenos Aires, 1939.) In August 1938, the central government, then in Barcelona, took over the whole Catalan war industry, provoking a cabinet crisis in which the Catalan minister, supported by his Basque colleague, resigned. Earlier, the Generalitat had refused to allow central government engineers and civil servants to set foot in its war factories. The take-over of La Maquinista led to considerable workers' unrest. In reply to a questionnaire issued by the Generalitat to the collective, the works council made no bones that there had been a decline in production which, six months later, was beginning to pick up (see *Contestaciones al questionari que ens ha estat adrecat per la Generalitat relacionat amb la requisa dels nostres talleres per la subscretaria d'armament del ministeri de defensa nacional*, mimeographed, Barcelona, May 1938).

wherever a certain equilibrium existed. Tensions certainly arose, the dominance of the CNT in Barcelona provoked a reaction which was reflected even in Reus – but it was not the determining political factor in the town . . .

There were important metal-working and textile factories in the town employing more than 100 workers which, under the collectivization decree, should have been collectivized.

—But none of them were. All industrial enterprises had workers' control committees – but the decree wasn't put into effect. The situation was so lax, so many decrees were issued that no one obeyed. In Catalonia generally, outside Barcelona, I'd say there were a great many industries which, though falling under the decree's scope, refused to collectivize and remained under workers' control[1] . . .

Neither Barcelona's revolutionary writ, nor that of the Generalitat, extended to all points of Catalonia. There was Popular Front local government in Reus; CNT–FAI domination in near-by Tarragona; trade-union government, without any petty bourgeois representation or link with the Generalitat, in Lérida under POUM inspiration; even in a CNT-dominated industrial town like Badalona, next door to Barcelona, the revolutionary process had its distinctive characteristics.

Within a few days of the military uprising, the town's thirty-seven textile mills were working again; the CNT textile union, of which Josep COSTA, a specialist foreman, was secretary, had ordered owners and managers to return to their posts which all but half a dozen had done.

—At that moment, we hadn't the slightest intention of taking over, expropriating or collectivizing any factory. We thought the uprising would be rapidly crushed and nothing much would change. What was the good of getting excited about collectivizing if, in the end, everything was going to revert to the former, capitalist, system? . . .

None the less, the union started to give orders – 'hardly in the anarcho-syndicalist tradition, it's true, but these were exceptional times' – to the union committee in each mill to set up a control committee of technicians, staff and workers to oversee and control production in agreement with management. A 'war tax' was imposed by the union on the profitable firms to support the 500 local men who had gone to the front and to help finance raw material purchases for the economically weaker firms which, it soon became clear, formed the majority; only half a dozen plants in the town, with its population of about 80,000, were profitable. Despite the fact that collectivization in Barcelona 8 km away was in full swing, the union didn't follow the capital's example.

—We didn't see the Barcelona textile collectives as models for our experience.

1. Another decree not put into effect in Reus was that issued by the POUM justice councillor, Andreu Nin, setting up Popular Tribunals. 'There was no need, I had the situation pretty well in hand,' explained SOLE BARBERA, who had been appointed judge of the main court. 'Within seventy-two hours of my taking over, the revolutionary tribunal which had been set up in the first days was dissolved, I had appointed a new prison director, and was shortly releasing many of those who had been arrested.'

Individual collectivized mills acted there from the beginning as though they were completely autonomous units, marketing their own products as they could and paying little heed to the general situation. It caused a horrific problem. It was a sort of popular capitalism . . .

The Badalona textile union leaders hesitated, unable to make up their minds to collectivize. The decree was still a long way from being made law. The news from the front was hardly encouraging; in the rearguard raw materials were already becoming short, inflation was setting in. Internationally, capitalism would not allow a repeat in Spain of the Russian revolution, COSTA was convinced. On top of everything, the divisions in the anti-fascist camp were apparent from the first days and – if not isolated and crushed by international intervention – the libertarian revolution would be jeopardized by political infighting. What was the point then of pushing the revolution forward?

—I'm sure there were thousands of CNT militants like me who saw that the whole thing made no sense; but the pressure came from the base, from the mass of workers who had been imbued for years with the CNT's revolutionary ideas. We militants couldn't now make a joke of the ideology and practice to emancipate the working class we had professed for so long. The revolution was like a dog shaking itself when it comes out of the water – the Spanish people shaking itself free of 400 years' injustice. There was nothing we militants could do but go ahead or shoot ourselves . . .

The final decision came when they heard news of the repression taking place in the insurgent zone. 'The assassinations, executions, showed us that capitalism was playing its last card – and we had to pre-empt it. We had to destroy that capitalism.' And so began an experiment that was perhaps the closest to a pure syndicalist revolution. The dangers of the big 'union trust' as of the atomized collective were avoided. Each collective was run by its elected management, sold its own production, received the proceeds and, as most of them were working for the war industry, got its own orders. But everything each mill did was reported to the union, which charted progress and kept statistics. If the union felt that a particular factory was not acting in the best interests of the collectivized industry as a whole, the enterprise was informed and asked to change course. 'The union operated more as a socialist control of collectivized industry than as a direct hierarchized executive.'

Piece-work was abolished, the working week reduced to forty hours (and soon to much less because of raw material shortages), the 'first social security system in Spain' created: full retirement pay, free medical care, free medicines, sick pay, maternity pay (two days' pay off work for the husband when his wife was giving birth), a clinic for specialist services and childbirth – the scheme being financed by a levy per worker in each collective that had the funds. An unemployment fund was created, and a proportion of those out of work were found jobs outside the textile industry.

—The one thing the union had to ensure was that workers were able to earn their weekly wage. We set up a compensation fund to permit the economically weaker collectives to pay their workers, the amount each collective contributed being in direct proportion to the number of workers employed . . .

There were about a dozen mills employing over 100 workers, the largest with nearly 1,000. Under the decree, the remaining two dozen firms already collectivized should have reverted to workers' control.[1] 'But, frankly, we didn't worry too much about the decree: the control committees carried out the union's instructions and the mills were as good as collectivized as far as we were concerned.'

Production dropped between 20 per cent and 30 per cent as a result of the reduction in work hours, but rose again 'after explanation that the success of self-management depended on each worker'. As supplies of raw materials decreased – before the war all but 2 per cent of the nearly 100 million kilos of cotton needed for the Catalan textile industry had to be imported – an attempt was made to rationalize the Badalona industry, closing down two or three of the small, uneconomic mills and distributing the workforce among the larger plants.

—We couldn't do more. Although such rationalizations were legal under the decree, we ran into the opposition of the UGT, which invariably invoked the Generalitat, especially after the PSUC's secretary-general Comorera became economics councillor. The latter could block rationalization very easily: at least half the collectives, within two years of the start of the war, had mortgaged themselves to the Generalitat in return for the payment of their wages. The Generalitat appointed an inspector and, to all intents and purposes, took over the factory. The collectives lost the economic freedom they had won at the beginning. We did everything we could to limit the numbers going to the 'pawn bank', but in those difficult circumstances we couldn't do enough . . .

From the start he had believed that collectivization efforts were doomed to fail. Like many other CNT militants, he felt, he would have been prepared to try to reverse the revolutionary current, but to do so required two prerequisites:

—The guarantee of a steady and continuous flow of arms from a capitalist country; and that we stopped being so touchy about our principles and showed ourselves willing to make compromises. The first was the most important. Aid from a capitalist country would have brought a change in our thinking because we would have had to assure that nation that we were acting in the defence of democracy – and nothing more. But no such aid was forthcoming; the only arms being received came from the Soviet Union, and this served to reinforce the communist party's position . . .

The dilemma which faced the anarcho-syndicalists, in consequence, was whether to press ahead with the libertarian revolution come what might, or renegue on it; the latter, as he saw it, meant tying the movement hand and foot to the communist party and the Soviet Union.

—The latter would have been like cutting out our guts, emptying our brains,

1. Only three mills had been originally left out, two because they were foreign-owned and one because the majority UGT opted to retain workers' control. 'I believe the Barcelona CNT told us not to expropriate the Swiss and French mills which had raised their national flags' (Josep COSTA).

denying everything we had been preaching to the masses. It would have meant handing back the factories to their owners and saying, 'Nothing has happened – ' This was precisely the communist party's *political*, if not social, objective in order to show the world that what was being fought for in Spain was a matter of a political regime, not a change of social order. When the communist party saw it was unable to dominate us, it set out to destroy us. What it didn't realize was that in destroying us, it was destroying itself. We were doing what the communists should have been doing; in destroying us it was destroying a strong, powerful, dynamic mass base . . .

*

The CNT soon became aware of the pitfalls and errors of collectivization, especially in the textile industry in Barcelona. In February 1937, four months after the decree's approval, a joint CNT–UGT textile union conference agreed that experience had already demonstrated that collectivization of individual plants had been mistaken, and that it was necessary to proceed rapidly towards a total socialization of the industry if ownership of the means of production was not once more to lead to man's exploitation of man. The works councils did not in practice know what to do with the means of production and lacked a plan for the whole industry; as far as the market was concerned, the decree had changed none of the basic capitalist defects 'except that whereas before it was the owners who competed amongst themselves it is now the workers'. Without the General Industrial Councils – the supreme body envisaged by the decree for each industry, which were not set up until nine months after the decree was approved – it was impossible to rationalize, cut out competition between collectives within the same industry and 'overcome the existing disorientation which exists in all branches of the industry'. Three months later, in May, a CNT commission castigated the 'exorbitant desire to collectivize everything, especially enterprises with monetary reserves, which has awoken among the masses a utilitarian and petty bourgeois spirit . . . Collectives have thought only of their debts, thus creating an unbalanced state of finance in other enterprises.'[1]

The woodworkers' union weighed in with its criticism of the state of affairs, alleging that, while small, insolvent workshops were left to struggle as best they could, the collectivization of profitable enterprises was leading to 'nothing other than the creation of two classes; the new rich and the eternal poor. We refuse the idea that there should be rich and poor collectives. And that is the real problem of collectivization.' In the non-collectivized sector, the union maintained, workers' control committees were responsible for a multitude of errors which included: raising wages and reducing working hours in the midst of a war; accepting 'vast sums' of money against imaginary capital assets from the Generalitat's 'pawn bank' – 'millions of pesetas spent on non-production which

1. A report of the February meeting in *Balances para la historia* (Barcelona, undated), mimeographed account of the Badalona experience; the May commission in J. Andrade, 'L'Intervention des syndicats dans la révolution espagnole', *Confrontation Internationale*, September–October 1949, cited in Broué and Temime, *La Révolution et la guerre d'Espagne*, p. 145.

has ruined the economy'; the creation of an enormous number of bureaucratic parasites, and committees which were often 'a thousand times more materialistic than the bourgeoisie' in their commercial dealings with the socialized woodworking industry.[1]

While thousands of workers contributed their wage increases to the support of the militias at the front, others of less ideological commitment came to consider that self-management or workers' control meant the guarantee solely of their weekly wages. In the large private sector under workers' control, this led to an unexpected result. Credit virtually dried up.

—The control committees, which had been given the right of joint signature with the enterprise's owner, or representative, to all money transactions, frequently refused to sign anything not strictly connected with wages. They refused credit. The result was that all dealings between enterprises were very soon reduced to cash transactions, recalled Albert PEREZ-BARO . . .

These difficulties might have been palliated if the industrial and commercial credit fund foreseen by the decree had been rapidly set up,[2] for one of its purposes was to channel funds from the wealthier to the poorer collectives. It was to be financed by a levy of 50 per cent of a collective's profits.

—This truly revolutionary measure – though rarely, if ever, applied – wasn't well received by large numbers of workers, proving, unfortunately, that their understanding of the scope of collectivization was very limited. Only a minority understood that collectivization meant the return to society of what, historically, had been appropriated by the capitalists . . .

Generalization about the collectives in their many and varied forms is impossible.[3] Some worked well, others badly. They were hampered by a great number of factors: no party or organization supported them (or at least the October decree) wholeheartedly, and some attempted to reverse the experiment. The decree itself – partly due to political in-fighting – failed to provide, either quickly enough or at all, the structure (General Industrial Councils, the credit fund) which would have articulated the collective enterprise into a coherent, planned totality; and added to all this was the unremitting official hostility of the central government to the experience which it saw as yet one more instance of Catalonia's determination to 'go it alone'.

The experiment lasted too short a time, in PEREZ-BARO's opinion, to be able

1. CNT–FAI bulletin, 25 December 1936, cited in Peirats, *La CNT en la revolución española*, vol. 1, p. 325.

2. The reason for the failure to create the Fund, connected with the problem of compensation for expropriated enterprises, is explored in Appendix, A.

3. At least five types of self-management can be distinguished: the 'individual' collective (or 'canton', in the expression of the time); 'socialization' (in which the union ran the whole industry); 'canton-socialization' (as practised in the Badalona textile industry, for example); 'canton-state control' (as operated in La Maquinista and in much of the armaments industry); and finally, collectivization, as laid down in the October decree (which can best be described as the project of economically federated cantons closely controlled by General Councils for each industry). The fact that only the latter two types were 'legal' added to the complexities. Alongside the collectivized sector, private industry functioned under workers' control.

to make a final judgement. As secretary of the decree's application commission, he was well-placed to have an overall view.

—But I believe that had it been allowed to continue, without being pulled either to left or right, and had further agreement been reached by common consent of the political parties and trade union organizations, the collectivized regime would have succeeded . . .

—The working class showed a splendid sense of initiative, agreed Sebastiá CLARA, old CNT militant and *treintista* leader. But that isn't to say there weren't stupid collectivizations. Take the barber shops. What in reality was being collectivized? A pair of scissors, a razor, a couple of barber's chairs. And what was the result? All those small owners who on their own would have supported the fight against fascism, now turned against us. Worse than having the enemy in front of you is the enemy in your midst. These people joined the fifth column, the GEPCI,[1] and it was the CNT which paid the bill . . .

Juan ANDRADE, of the POUM executive, was highly critical of the whole experiment. The anarcho-syndicalist workers had made themselves the owners of everything they collectivized; the collectives were treated as private, not social, property. Socialization, as practised by CNT unions, was no more than trade union capitalism.

—Although it wasn't immediately apparent, the economy as run by the CNT was a disaster. Had it gone on like that, there would have been enormous problems later, with great disparities of wages and new social classes being formed. We also wanted to collectivize, but quite differently, so that the country's resources were administered socially, not as individual property. The sort of mentality which believes that the revolution is for the immediate benefit of a particular sector of the working class, and not for the proletariat as a whole, always surfaces in a revolution, as I realized in the first days of the war in Madrid . . .

One of the first men killed on the Madrid front had been a POUM militant, and his funeral provided the occasion for an enormous demonstration. Before it, the CNT undertakers' union presented the POUM with its bill. The younger POUM militants took the bill to ANDRADE in amazement. He called in the undertakers' representatives.

—'What's this? You want to collect for your services while men are dying at the front, eh?' I looked at the bill. 'Moreover, you've raised your prices, this is very expensive.' 'Yes,' the man agreed, 'we want to make improvements – ' I refused to pay and when, later, two members of the union's committee turned up to press their case, we threw them out. But the example made me reflect on a particular working-class attitude to the revolution . . .

Joan GRIJALBO, bank clerk and UGT representative on the Economics Council, was more sanguine. Had the collectives functioned as badly, had there been as much disorder as was sometimes claimed, the war would not have

1. The PSUC-organized trade union for the petty bourgeois entrepreneurs and artisans.

lasted thirty-two months. The Catalan UGT was not opposed to collectivization as such; but it was resolutely opposed, like the PSUC, to trade union (or autonomous working-class) power.

The Council's youngest member at twenty-five, GRIJALBO was less impressed by the libertarians' casual approach to administrative matters. On one occasion, when the Generalitat lacked sufficient ready funds to pay wages and was preparing to send someone to the Bank of Spain in Cartagena, Abad de Santillán, the CNT economics councillor, told him to make out an IOU and go to the CNT to draw the 500,000 pesetas needed.

—There was the CNT lending the Generalitat money! An illustration of the anarchists' way of doing things, their mistaken concept of administration. Moreover, if the CNT had half a million pesetas in its coffers to lend, it meant they had a lot more – and the money must have come from confiscations . . .

But apart from the CNT's attitude to such matters, an attempt was constantly made to make people aware of their responsibilities in managing the collectivized economy. At least 5,000 company directors and managers were present, he estimated, at a huge meeting to celebrate approval of the collectivization decree. Given the very grave economic problems brought on by the war, he felt that the collective experience was fairly successful.

Though the collectives' achievements cannot be meaningfully quantified, some of the economic problems they – and their workers – were living through can be given statistical expression. As the indices opposite show, overall Catalan production fell in the first year of the war by 30 per cent, and in the cotton-working sector of the textile industry by twice as much. Overall unemployment (complete and partial) rose by nearly a quarter in the first year, and this despite the military mobilization decreed in September 1936.[1] The cost of living quadrupled in just over two years; wages (as far as can be ascertained) only doubled. Inevitably, the working class bore the brunt of the civil war. The relatively frequent insistence on – and pride in – the fact that the collectives managed to pay their workers wages even when there was no work must be seen in this context. Industrial prices rose less sharply than the cost of living and at a slower pace than the wholesale raw material index, suggesting that collectives heeded the Economics Council and later a special price commission. It also meant they generated little or no apparent surplus, and even less so if they were paying 'unproductive' wages. This in turn meant that the money due to go to the credit fund to finance, and eliminate disparities between, collectives was impaired.

Despite the errors in practice, the collectivization decree (widely believed in Catalonia to have influenced the later, post-war Yugoslav experience) stands as a revolutionary monument in industrial self-management. Through every difficulty, including bitter internecine political struggle, the Catalan working class kept collectivized production going for thirty months of war.

1. Complete unemployment dropped by some 10 per cent while partial unemployment doubled, owing mainly to the short-time working in the textile industry. It is worth recalling that the same phenomenon occurred (in a non-revolutionary context) in Britain during the first year of the Second World War, and that it took two more years before unemployment ceased to exist.

CATALAN INDICES

1936–9[1]

	Cost of living, Barcelona (July 1936=100)	Industrial production, Catalonia (January–June 1936=100)	Industrial prices, wholesale, Catalonia (January–June 1936=100)	Raw material prices, wholesale, Catalonia (January–June 1936=100)	Overall unemployment (complete and partial) (January–June 1936=100)
December 1936	147·1	71·1	119·8	120·3	135·7
(February 1937)[2]	(164·2)	—	—	—	—
(April 1937)[2]	(185·4)	—	—	—	—
June 1937	196·4	70·1	160·6	166·9	123·6
December 1937	357·8	59·8	196·8	207·3	(Nov.) 120·1
June 1938	367·1	32·9	—	—	—
November 1938	453·3	(Sept.) 34·0	—	—	—

	Industrial production: cotton products (January–June 1936=100)	Industrial production: engineering–machinery (January–June 1936=100)
December 1936	59·0	160·9
June 1937	36·6	122·9
December 1937	13·7	41·7
	(no further data)	(no further data)

1. Source: Bricall, op. cit. Industrial production, prices and unemployment have been recomputed to give the January–June average as base.
2. Included to show inflation increase immediately prior to May events (see pp. 374–83).

The question that must be asked of the experiment is not, however, the usual one of whether the collectives were a revolutionary success, but whether they were the adequate revolutionary response to the needs of the moment: winning the war. Was it necessary to take over more than large industrial and commercial enterprises, transport, the banks in order to consolidate the revolution and win the war? Was the Catalan revolution serving itself and the war effort by allowing, within a collectivized system, the continued existence of a market economy, lack of controls, a variety of types of self-management, and large numbers of deficitary collectives? By failing to ensure the revolutionary redistribution of labour, the rapid rationalization of the textile industry (where, after a year, partial unemployment had risen from 6,000 to 36,000)? So staunch a defender of the collectivization decree as Albert PEREZ-BARO addressed himself to the essence of these questions seven months after the start of the revolution. Laying the blame on all sectors for the difficulties encountered, he did not spare the workers themselves:

'. . . the immense majority of workers have sinned by their indiscipline; production has fallen in an alarming manner and in many instances has plummeted; the distance from the front has meant that the workers have not experienced the war with the necessary intensity. The former discipline, born of managerial coercion, is missing, and has not been replaced, owing to the lack of class-consciousness, by a self-imposed discipline in benefit of the collectivity. In an infantile manner the workers have come to believe that everything was already won . . . when in reality the real social revolution begins precisely in the period of constructing the Economy' . . . [1]

A harsh answer; but then these questions were not often asked by those who maintained that the war and revolution were inseparable, and only too often answered – with a blank negative – by those who believed that the revolution must wait on the successful outcome of the war. The polarization of that polemic obscured many real problems.[2]

1. Prologue to a pamphlet, *Col·lectivitzacions i control obrer* (February 1937), cited in Pérez-Baró, *Trenta mesos de col·lectivisme a Catalunya*, Appendix 1, p. 191.

2. See pp. 323–7 below for this and the communist reaction to the libertarian revolution as a whole. In January 1938, eighteen months after the start of the revolution, the CNT at its Enlarged Economic Plenum in Valencia revised many of its previous postures. It agreed to differential salaries, a corps of factory inspectors who could sanction workers' and works councils; the administrative centralization of all industries and agrarian collectives controlled by the CNT, and effective general planning by a CNT Economics Council; the creation of a syndical bank; the development of consumer cooperatives. The following month, in a pact with the UGT, it called for the *nationalization* of mines, railways, heavy industry, the banks, telecommunications and airlines. (CNT interpretation of nationalization meant that the state took over an industry and handed it to its workers to manage; the socialists interpreted it as meaning that the state ran the industry.) However, as was only too often the case, the CNT reaction came too late, and the resolutions, though representing an important ideological shift, remained consigned to paper (see Lorenzo, *Los anarquistas españoles y el poder*, p. 233).

Fuego, fuego,
Entrar a Oviedo
Coger a Aranda
Y echarlo al agua

Fire, fire,
Enter Oviedo
Catch Aranda
And throw him in the water

Children's song in Gijón sung to the tune
of a chocolate advertising jingle

COMRADES: The Spanish working class, at war and at work, is forging a Spain which must be fundamentally different from that which we had to live under before the fascist uprising . . . We know, however, that this is not the moment to try to introduce a total social revolution . . . either of a libertarian communist or state-run nature. This statement in no way means that proletarian pressure to achieve the COMPLETE SOCIAL REVOLUTION must be postponed . . . for the process has already entered its final stage and is guaranteed by the Alliance of our two Trade Unions.

In accordance with the above, we recognize as part of the present historic reality the following forms of property:

A. Nationalized
B. State-controlled or State-run
C. Cooperative
D. Private

Asturian UGT-CNT pact (14 June 1937)

Asturianos: A fellow-Asturian, a lover of the Fatherland and the Republic, I, Colonel Aranda, send you my warm greetings. I beg all of you to cooperate in this labour of saving the Fatherland; let every man pick up a rifle, let every man do his duty . . . We must put an end, once and for all, to this era of innumerable crimes perpetrated under cover of a love for Democracy and the Republic which their authors do not feel . . .

Colonel Aranda (First radio speech, Oviedo, 19 July 1936)

ASTURIAS

Some of the questions that the Catalan revolution posed were being answered under different conditions in Asturias. Less than two years after the October insurrection, the industrial and mining region was again in the throes of revolution. In many aspects it was, initially, a repeat of the October commune. In the mining villages the workers took control of the mines, sent men to the front only a few kilometres away, organized the distribution of food and set up their own workers' patrols. As everywhere in the Popular Front zone, power was dispersed in dozens of local committees, but here a particular proletarian tradition was at work. Not for nothing had socialists, anarchists, dissident communists of the BOC, trotskyists and communists of the PCE (Partido Comunista de España) risen and fought together in October to the cry, UHP.

Oviedo, the capital, had fallen to the military without fighting on 19 July, thanks to the stratagem of Col. Aranda, the military commander. An attempt to duplicate his success in Gijón, the Atlantic port and CNT stronghold, had failed. The combination of armed workers and police forces beat back a poorly executed sortie from the Simancas barracks to which the troops retreated; besieged in the convent turned barracks, 200 defenders held out for over a month. But the rest of this mini-Barcelona of the Atlantic, with its 60,000 population, was in the hands of the workers under a war committee dominated by the anarcho-syndicalists.

To the south, in the mining valleys, a Popular Front committee under socialist domination held sway in Sama de Langreo. For a couple of months, these two different proletarian-led organizations – on which the same parties and trade unions were represented – ran their respective zones barely 40 km apart. The working class had taken power. The absence (in contradistinction to Catalonia) of a politically influential petty bourgeoisie outside beleaguered Oviedo and rural western Asturias, made the question of power more easily answerable. Between the two proletarian zones, in the midst of the densest working-class concentration of all Spain, Col. Aranda was landlocked in Oviedo at the head of the insurgents.

Militancies 7

RAFAEL HERNANDEZ

Socialist railwayman

As soon as the CNT set up its war committee in Gijón, he had been appointed its secretary and Labour representative. The anarcho-syndicalists had not doubted for a moment that all political forces who stood against the military rising had to be represented. The war committee took over everything. His first act was to call a meeting of all trade union representatives. Each industry should appoint a delegate, he told them, and the delegates should form a sort of Economics Council to look after all production which was to be entirely in the trade unions' hands.

The syndicalist response, unorthodox in socialist thinking, was none the less not exceptional among socialist trade unionists. And perhaps even less so in a strongly anarcho-syndicalist town of small workshops and artisans' enterprises like Gijón. Hernández had gone to a school run by Eleuterio Quintanilla, the great anarchist leader, and there had become friendly with many who later became outstanding CNT militants. Although his father, a railwayman, was a member of the UGT, this made little difference in his relations with anarcho-syndicalists.

—Although there were fights between the two unions, there was a personal level at which we all got on; because of the constant battles with the employers, we in Asturias were always aware of the class struggle and the common enemy in front of us. It was that which bred a tradition of unity . . .

He had become well known in Gijón for his combativeness in organizing the workers on the Gijón–Langreo colliery railway. In his early twenties, he had joined the company after military service in the air force. He had been involved in the abortive republican rising against the monarchy in December 1930, at Cuatro Vientos airfield outside Madrid, been court-martialled and sentenced to twelve years in a disciplinary battalion. Released only four months later, on the republic's proclamation, by none other than Ramón Franco, General Franco's aviator brother who had taken part in the rising, he returned to Gijón. The impossibility of getting work there made him think of returning to Argentina where he had spent five years from the age of fifteen. On the point of emigrating, a job on the colliery line turned up. Of the 2,000 workers in the strongly anti-union company, a dozen, he found, belonged to the UGT, eight to the CNT and thirty to the company union. He had fought that, and with others had managed to unionize the line and affiliate the union to the UGT. It was this struggle which, at the age of twenty-seven, made him well known to the anarcho-syndicalists, and led to his post on the war committee.

—The revolution was fabulous. In the first days, committees sprang up in every *barrio* quite spontaneously, setting up communal eating places, re-quisitioning food, issuing vouchers and so on. They demonstrated the in-stinctive sense of initiative derived from so many years of proletarian struggle – but they were a bit chaotic. It got nearly to the point of there being a committee in each house . . .

Although fundamentally in favour of the committees, he had to go round to tell them that the war committee would handle the town's affairs and that their existence only added to the confusion. At the same time, the war committee re-established the police force, dismissing those chiefs and men whom it dis-trusted, but otherwise leaving the force intact. It took over the 17 million to 18 million pesetas in the Bank of Spain in Gijón in order to prevent the money being stolen.

—Pillaging was a problem we had to confront immediately. I remember the money being counted and checked before it was handed over to the Popular Front committee in Sama de Langreo. The other banks were put under our control and we appointed delegates in each . . .

His revolutionary initiatives included some urban renewal. Bathing huts, belonging to a local property owner, which blocked traffic on the front, were ordered to be knocked down and burnt; all the town's old wooden newspaper kiosks met the same fate. Then it was the turn of a block of houses belonging to the bathing-hut owner which stood in the way of traffic, followed by the old hospital, and finally the church of San José.

—All my life, I'd heard how the municipal authorities had wanted that church built to one side so that it wouldn't block the street. But the all-powerful ecclesiastical authorities had resisted such moves and built it in the middle of the street. So I had it knocked down . . .

The ruling classes of Spain had always seen only their own immediate interests, he thought. In historical perspective they were dwarfs, pygmies who had failed their mission: to care for the future of the nation. They had failed to see what was needed – an agrarian reform, above all, to give the starving peasantry land to work; they should have taken the nobility's land for the hungry labourers, should have modernized agriculture to bring it up to the level of that of France and England. But the ruling classes always refused. 'October 1934 was the awakening of the two great forces that were to fight out the civil war – '

Along with thousands of other militants, he had spent from October 1934 to February 1936 in prison as a result of his participation in the insurrection. The revolution then had been transitory; now there was time to prove what the working class was capable of.

As a railwayman, the most inventive of his revolutionary innovations con-cerned, appropriately, the railways. Three track sizes existed in Spain: the inter-national gauge, used on only two railways, one out of Barcelona, the other the colliery line on which he had worked; the mainline Spanish wide gauge, the same as the Russian; and a narrow gauge used on coastal and inter-provincial lines, such as the one between Oviedo and Bilbao. The latter was an important rail link at that moment, as Asturian coal had to be freighted to Bilbao to fuel the steel mills.

—It meant loading the coal on to the international gauge colliery line out of the coalfields, and then unloading it, wagon by wagon, on to the narrow gauge rolling-stock to continue, via Santander, to Bilbao on the only direct rail link. This manual unloading and reloading was costly, slow and inefficient. The head of the railway works department, whom I had appointed, came to see me and said there was a possible solution – the laying of a third rail within the international gauge track to convert it to a narrow track . . .

He saw the possibilities immediately and set out to implement them. It required manufacturing special points and switching gear. The third track was laid and the narrow gauge wagons were able to reach the pit-head at Langreo directly. It worked well, and later in Barcelona, he thought of introducing a similar solution.

Meanwhile, despite constant attacks, the Simancas and engineers' barracks of El Coto continued to offer resistance in Gijón. The war committee's major efforts were aimed as much if not more at reducing these strongholds than at organizing the revolution. Finally, artillery was brought in. Positioned behind sandbag parapets on an open field that served as a football pitch within machine-gun range of Simancas, they opened fire at point-blank range. On the roof of the Hotel Asturias, where he had gone to watch, Dr Carlos MARTINEZ, former parliamentary deputy, saw several rounds fired without effect. Then a shell hit the roof and very soon flames began to leap up. 'It was a lucky hit which set light to the wooden rafters.'

Earlier, in a daring sortie, Rafael HERNANDEZ had crawled to a transformer in full view of the barracks and cut off the electricity supply. Then he and the anarchist militants Carrocera and Onofre García and others raced from the last houses facing the barracks; knocked out a machine-gun nest protecting it with dynamite, and blasted holes in the ex-convent walls.

—Under fire from ground level and with a fire in the roof above their heads, the defenders retreated inside. We started to attack through the holes in the walls . . .

In a last heroic gesture, the defenders called on the insurgent cruiser *Almirante Cervera* to open fire on the barracks itself. 'Defence is impossible, the building is burning and the enemy is coming in. Fire on us,' said the last radio message. Within a short time, amidst scenes of slaughter, the barracks had fallen. It was 21 August. For over a month, a couple of hundred defenders had tied down the Gijón militiamen and kept them from joining the siege of Oviedo or from combating the insurgent columns coming from Galicia to Oviedo's relief. Precious time had been won and lost.

*

The revolution in the predominantly socialist mining valleys did not follow the same trajectory as in Gijón. The powerful socialist Mineworkers' Union did not lay claim to the mines.[1] Instead, miners' committees controlled work in the pits under the same foremen and technicians as before.

—The control committees' functions were what their name suggests – it was not their task to operate the mines. We didn't dispute the technicians' and foremen's right to direct the work, most of which, in any case, consisted in maintenance, recalled Paulino RODRIGUEZ, a socialist miner in Sotrondio in the Nalón valley. There were large stocks of coal at the pit-heads; English dumping before the war meant that Asturian coal couldn't compete in its home market . . .

Eventually the mines came to be run by mixed committees of technicians, administrators and miners; decisions taken by the manager responsible for running the colliery had to be approved by the workers' delegates appointed by the mineworkers' union.[2]

In the neighbouring steel town of La Felguera, a traditional CNT stronghold, the anarcho-syndicalists made no attempt to collectivize the Duro-Felguera iron and steel works, which employed nearly 4,000 workers. As in October 1934, a workers' control committee was set up, composed entirely of CNT militants, who soon discovered that production was impeded by the loss of engineers who had fled or gone into hiding. Two politically uncompromised engineers from the works were found in Bilbao and returned when asked to by the workers' committee, which did not technically manage the works but exercised considerable weight on those who did.

—We made no attempt to introduce libertarian communism, we didn't want to collectivize everything, recalled a leading FAI militant and steelworker, Eladio FANJUL. We were fighting the war and making our revolution at the same time. But we did nothing that we felt might prejudice final victory in the war . . .

But while striving for victory it was necessary to create the bases of the revolution which, after victory, would remain to be completed, he thought. There could be no doubt that it was necessary for the workers to feel that they were fighting to shape their own destinies, for them to feel that they were making the revolution at the same time as the war, if they were to contribute every effort to final victory.

Mario GUZMAN, a blast furnaceman at the works and president of the CNT metalworkers' union in La Felguera, while at the same time a POUM militant – a combination no longer acceptable to the CNT in Barcelona – concurred. The working class would not mobilize to defend petty bourgeois leaders like Azaña and Companys; the proletariat needed assurance that after the war the revolution would be consolidated in ways which were not possible during the war.

—But that didn't mean trying to achieve the total revolution; it meant laying

1. Although it would have been well able to do so. Before the republic it bought out the bankrupt San Vicente mine and ran it profitably, and later took over three or four other mines in the mountains. It financed the great Oviedo socialist newspaper *Avance*, created *casas del pueblo* in all the major mining villages, a theatre in Sama, a miners' orphanage, etc.

2. See F. Jellinek, *The Civil War in Spain* (London, 1938), p. 413.

the bases. The Catalan CNT made a big mistake – and so too did my own party – in wanting to make the revolution immediately in Barcelona. The CNT here wasn't like that . . .

While collectivization of industry, mines and the land was not the order of the day – the Asturian CNT standing in any case for socialization of all the means of production – domestic consumption tended to be collectivized. In Sama de Langreo, where the socialist-led Popular Front committee had originally established itself, daily life was being organized on much the same lines as during the October commune. It was, thought Ignacio IGLESIAS, a student and POUM militant, who had been called from the siege of Oviedo to take up the post on the revolutionary supplies committee he had held in October 1934, a kind of war communism. All the shops were taken over and combined into one store.

—Everyone received ration vouchers for free food, household supplies, and clothing. Money wasn't officially abolished, but soon there was nothing to buy – since the food and clothes shops had been taken over (and at that time there wasn't much else in the way of consumer goods); then money lost its use. Bars closed down. To be seen drinking in one would have been considered counter-revolutionary – it wouldn't have occurred to anyone, it would have been a moral betrayal of the revolution. And since no one went to them, they closed . . .

This war communism did not extend to the producers of food, the peasantry of Asturias. No attempt was made to collectivize them.

—It would have been totally counter-productive to have tried to do so in the middle of a war, stressed FANJUL of the FAI. Smallholders are jealous of their property, they want to work their own land, be their own masters. The land here was well divided, there were no great problems on that score. All efforts had to be bent to winning the war . . . [1]

The centralization of power in the hands of the provincial Popular Front committee, which in September moved from Sama to Gijón, and two months later took the title of council, was achieved with relatively little friction. Though the Gijón war committee resisted dissolving itself for a couple of months, other local committees were replaced by new town councils. Unlike their Catalan, Aragonese or Madrid counterparts, the FAI in Asturias had no hesitation in joining what was in effect a government under a president who was appointed by the central government as its delegate.

Differences over revolutionary positions caused tensions within the council but these were less sharp than in Catalonia. The problem, as in Barcelona, of the expropriation of small traders and shopkeepers arose, particularly in Gijón,

1. Later, when power was concentrated in the Council of Asturias (see below), the communist agriculture councillor expropriated some large insurgent landowners, whose lands were let out in small plots (as tended to be the custom), and the renters were given the usufruct of the land. Sharecropping was abolished and some former communal grazing lands restored. 'Our long-held claim that the land should be for him who worked it was now met,' recalled a socialist youth peasant's son who no longer had to pay rent to a local landowner who lived in Madrid. 'A lot of the farmers no doubt continued to pay the rent secretly to insure themselves against the future; but we didn't.'

which was a city of small commerce and industry. The socialist party here came to the defence of the petty bourgeoisie, and tried to have such businesses as the bakeries which the CNT had taken over returned to their owners.[1] Though the polemic was sharp, the CNT attempted to resolve the conflict by persuasion rather than force.

—We didn't want to have tests of strength with the socialists although we disagreed with them. Our policy was to stay on good terms with them until the war was won; then we would see, commented Ramón ALVAREZ, the former CNT regional committee secretary who had become fisheries councillor . . .

In effect, the socialist-led Council of Asturias on which, after December, the libertarian youth joined the CNT and FAI, supervised union control of any industries socialized on anarcho-syndicalist lines. The fishing industry, after livestock-rearing the most important source of wealth in Asturias, with coal in third place, was a case in point. As fisheries councillor, ALVAREZ oversaw the industry which the trade unions had taken over and were running as a socialized enterprise.

—Not collectivized, as has often been said. Although the CNT was by far and away the majority union, we set up a commission of three CNT and three UGT delegates to direct and administer the industry. Each of these had a different responsibility. My job was to supervise the administration of an industry which, basically, was being run by the trade unions . . .

He managed to persuade the Council that the canning industry should be incorporated into the socialized fishing so that the profits – 'canning was the most profitable side' – were returned to their rightful source, the fishing industry in its totality.

Despite friction, despite differences between the anarcho-syndicalist and socialist positions, the CNT and UGT were able to reach agreement on the fundamentals: the nature of workers' control, the extent and aims of the revolution at that moment (neither libertarian communist nor orthodox state-run socialist), the types of property they would recognize ('nationalized; state-controlled; cooperative; private'), and the overriding need for proletarian pressure to achieve the 'complete social revolution' which must not be postponed. The problem of power had been resolved: the proletarian organizations controlled the Council of Asturias, on which the petty bourgeoisie was represented by only two out of fifteen councillors. Thanks to the revolutionary

1. 'The trade unions can and must control production to ensure that this runs as efficiently and economically as possible. But when it comes to the distributive trades, the trade union cannot play this role,' thundered Amador Fernández, socialist trade councillor. 'We are determined that interference (in this sector) must end. As long as the concept of private property has not been abolished, we have to respect the rights of all . . . Let it be clear: the trade unions are trade unions, control is control, the government is the government, and the owner of a business is the owner, subject only to the limitations and controls that the legitimate organs of government dispose.' (Cited in J. A. Cabezas, *Asturias: catorce meses de guerra civil*, Madrid, 1975, pp. 53–4.) However, the boot was sometimes on the other foot. The UGT chemists' assistants took over the Gijón chemist shops because their owners were 'fascists'; the libertarian youth councillor of health, Ramón Fernández, ordered them returned to their owners. (I am indebted to A. Masip for this information.)

positions of the socialist and communist[1] masses, and the revolutionary realism of the Asturian libertarians, both the need of revolution in order to win the war, and the practicable extent of the revolution within the limits of the war, were defined.

But on two crucial issues, the organization of warfare and the means of overcoming localism, the Asturian revolution was no more immediately successful than elsewhere. On both these matters, the communist party took issue with the libertarians and socialists.

By mid-September 1936, two relatively small insurgent columns had captured nearly half Asturias and advanced to within 25 km of Oviedo, which was still under siege. In the mountainous terrain of the interior, where the only roads wound through deep ravines and over high passes, the revolutionary miners had been unable to stay the advance of the two columns from Galicia and León. In October 1934, they had pinned down government troops for a fortnight in the Vega del Ciego; Alberto FERNANDEZ, a socialist youth member, had been wounded there; but the feat was not to be repeated. Suffering from pleurisy, he had left his sick-bed to fight the advancing Galician column. In an action on the heights opposite Candamo, when their ammunition ran out, he and the militiamen fought with stones. But nothing, not even the Narcea and Nalón rivers, could keep the enemy from advancing on Oviedo. The militiamen fought bravely, but tended to retreat when there was any threat of being cut off. Another October veteran, José MATA, a socialist miner, was wounded as the enemy advanced.

—We were all volunteers; there was no military discipline. We got demoralized at the enemy's constant advance. We kept saying, 'Let them advance, we'll get into boats and disembark behind them.' But we didn't; it would have taken a real army to do that . . .

The Asturian Popular Front was handicapped by an even greater lack of trained armed forces than elsewhere: not a single army or civil guard unit had remained loyal, and the majority of the assault guards were with the insurgents in Oviedo. There was a great ammunition shortage, a lesser but also serious shortage of arms. The resistance of Simancas barracks in Gijón had tied down militiamen who should have been combating the advancing enemy. When at last, on 21 August, the barracks fell, Rafael HERNANDEZ, the socialist railwayman and member of the Gijón war committee, believed that an all-out attack

1. Despite the communist party's rapid growth and influence, especially in the army, it did not come to exercise the same political weight in Asturias as in other regions. On the two occasions of major crisis in the Council, socialists, libertarians and republicans joined in taking issue against the communists. In April 1937, the communist party failed to get its slate elected to the UGT leadership and lost the shared leadership it had held with the socialists since the previous September. The JSU, which almost everywhere else followed the PCE line, in Asturias did not do so to the same extent, and showed a tendency to unite with the libertarian youth (see A. Masip, 'Apunte para un estudio sobre la guerra civil en Asturias', in *Sociedad, política y cultura en la España de los siglos XIX–XX*, Madrid, 1973). A solid 'centrist' socialist leadership, a UGT unwilling to threaten its alliance with the CNT, isolation from the main area of the Popular Front zone, and the absence of Soviet aid and advisers on anything like the scale of the central zone were some of the contributing factors to the PCE's failure to assert its control to the same extent as elsewhere.

on Oviedo should have been launched immediately. Even without military organization, if they had attacked *en masse*, wave upon wave, they could have taken the city, he thought.

—But it was argued that it would cost too many casualties; the besieged were organized, and we would have to organize also. Capt. José Gállego, an army officer who was on holiday in Gijón, and reported to me on the war committee, stressed the need for military organization. At one level, that was correct. But an army officer is as good as the material he has to work with; he's trained to command a militarily structured unit. If he hasn't got that he's like a chauffeur who's been given a cart to drive . . .

The problem had another aspect, as Dr Carlos MARTINEZ, former parliamentary deputy who was now acting as an 'unofficial liaison man' between the war committee and Capt. Gállego, soon saw. While the committee trusted Gállego, amongst the militiamen there was a certain lack of confidence in all army officers. Nothing discouraged an officer more than to know that he was not trusted by the men he was trying to lead. 'He needed support, wanted me, as a republican, to bear witness to his conduct, his loyalty and courage which were all quite remarkable.'

In the absence of a nucleus of trained military units, the revolutionaries would have to invent new tactics, new forms of fighting. It was a problem common to all fronts, and it was one which the *ad hoc* militia units, formed in the first days, were nowhere able to resolve. Not even in Asturias where some prior experience existed and where, even more importantly, the terrain was admirably suited for defence.

—All we had was guerrillas. By which I mean groups of men who went where they wanted. Someone would shout, 'Heh, a woman says the Galicians are down there and we're surrounded.' They'd pick up their stuff and get out, remembered Ramón ALVAREZ, representing the FAI on the Gijón war committee. That was why the insurgent columns could advance.[1] It was only when we gave up guerrilla fighting and formed an army – however bad it was, however late in being created – that we had some victories . . .

The communists had been pressing hard for militarization; the concept of guerrilla warfare was discredited. The majority of the CNT – though not the majority of La Felguera militants – agreed on the need to form a regular army. But before it could be achieved it was decided – against communist advice, which believed that all forces must be directed against the Galician columns – to stage an all-out assault on Oviedo.

1. These had their own share of 'amateurism', according to an Asturian falangist youth who was able to escape from his home town and join the Galician column after walking four or five days across the mountains: 'It was pretty much of a walk-over until we reached Grado, about 25 km from Oviedo.' Given a rifle, a pair of army trousers and a beret he tagged along in the column which was composed mainly of soldiers, under the command of a bearded, retired Lt Colonel wearing a Moroccan campaign uniform and nicknamed the 'Lion of the Rif' by his men. 'For us volunteers there wasn't much discipline. After we took my home town, I used to leave the column and go home for the night when I felt like it.' (Faustino SANCHEZ.) No doubt, the military elements were not allowed similar liberties; and the Galician peasantry was to become renowned in the course of the war for its fighting ability on the nationalist side.

Ten thousand militiamen, perhaps more, were laying siege to the city which, with its arms factory, had been the natural objective of the October revolution. Never fully captured then, taken by Col. Aranda's guile now, the city was becoming something of an obsession. This time it must fall. But the logic of one situation was not necessarily that of the next. Oviedo's capture was of little strategic importance, apart from the arms it might yield. A blockade that neutralized Aranda's small force in the city and released thousands of men to attack the advancing columns, or to strike into the enemy's rear, would have been a more appropriate revolutionary revanche for October 1934. (What fear there had been in Old Castile of the Asturian miners in the first days of the war! Their frustrated attempt to reach Madrid then was not to be repeated; Oviedo absorbed their attention for seven of the fifteen months of the war in the north, and they launched no other major *offensives* except for those on the city.)[1] Localism was again to be proven the leitmotif of the Spanish revolution.

*

Ever since he had been appointed military commandant of Asturias after the October insurrection, Col. Aranda had believed that he would be called upon to defend Oviedo once more against the revolutionaries storming in from their mining villages. Surrounded on almost all sides by heights, Oviedo was no easy city to defend. Moreover, Aranda had been disappointed (as had others in cities where the insurgents had won easy victories) by the relatively low number of volunteers in the first moments. The centre of the city was bourgeois and predominantly right-wing;[2] memories of October 1934 had not been erased; the colonel had expected more than the 856 volunteers who reported to the Pelayo, Rubín and Santa Clara barracks.

In all, he had some 3,000 men to defend a city of 60,000 inhabitants. Of these, nearly 900 were civil guards ordered into the city from their posts in the province. But Aranda's carefully studied plan of defence depended less on men than on fire-power: just under 100 Hotchkiss machine-guns which he sited in five strategic nuclei around the 15-kilometre perimeter to lay down 'curtains of fire'. There was no initial shortage of machine-gun or rifle ammunition: 2 million rounds were in store. (As a result of the October insurrection, the government had reinforced the Oviedo and Gijón garrisons.) 'Aranda's tactics were something absolutely new for the time,' one of his officers recalled. 'A city as vulnerable as Oviedo could be defended against a numerically far superior force by fire- rather than man-power.' The shortage of defenders meant, however, that he could not hold the whole of Mount Naranco, which rises to a height of 600 metres above the city, leaving the besiegers a privileged position.

Throughout August, while life continued normally in the city, Aranda improved his positions with offensive thrusts which kept the besiegers in doubt

1. The extraordinary difficulties of the war in the north, cut off from the rest of the Popular Front zone, without control of the sea or – later – air, and with shortages of every sort must be remembered. So, too, must the subsequent Asturian contribution to the *defence* of the Basque country and Santander, and the Asturians' own resistance, especially in the battle of El Mazuco, in the autumn of 1937.

2. See J. Girón, 'Un estudio de sociología electoral: la ciudad de Oviedo y su contorno en las elecciones generales de 1933', in *Sociedad, política y cultura en la España de los siglos XIX–XX*.

as to his intentions, though no one believed a break-out was possible. Even so, as José ALVAREZ, a grocer's lad, discovered, the perimeter was by no means impenetrable. Having from one day to the next found himself in an insurgent city, separated from his girlfriend 5 km away in a village in the Popular Front zone, he determined not to let the geographical vagaries of the civil war deter his courting. For over two months, he crossed the lines frequently. It wasn't difficult.

—The first time I even walked past a *guardia civil* machine-gun post on the main road in full daylight, with my UGT membership card in my pocket, moreover, and no one said a word. I came back from Colloto a different way, through the Mercadín *barrio*, where I crossed from then on . . .

It was, he had to admit, a sentimental rather than a political act. He never took out political messages or engaged in spying. Once in a while the republican besiegers would ask him questions, but they seemed well enough informed by the many people crossing the lines.

On Mount Naranco, the positions were little more than 200 metres apart. As dark began to fall the opponents shouted across at one another.

—'This is radio Panchito,' we'd call through the megaphones we'd made. 'Calling Arturín of La Felguera – ' 'What do you want?' 'Arturín, would you like some cake?' 'What cake? You lot are dying of hunger – ' '*Coño*, Arturín, you're a good man, come over to our side.' 'Shit on the mother who bore you.' 'Don't use that sort of language, you sons of whores.' 'And you – you call yourselves Catholics and you swear worse than us.' 'Well, give us a song then,' we'd shout. And they'd start to sing Asturian ballads . . .

One day, as Ricardo VAZQUEZ-PRADA, a falangist journalist, recalled, his side suggested swapping newspapers in no-man's-land. For half an hour the next day, while they exchanged papers, they talked; there were people they knew amongst the attackers. Aranda put an end to the practice.

From the first days, the besiegers had cut off the city's water supplies, leaving only the contents of the reservoir, which formed one of the strong points of the perimeter; water was strictly rationed and there was none for sanitation. Old wells had to be re-opened, all water had to be boiled; but even this precaution was to prove insufficient. This, however, was the only serious hardship until the beginning of September; there was little fighting, the cafés remained open, people were able to stroll in the evening *paseo* along the Calle Uría. The warehouses of Oviedo, which traditionally supplied a large part of the province, were full; there was no immediate shortage of food.

From early September, however, air raids and artillery bombardment became intensive. On 4 September, the defenders estimated that 1,500 bombs were dropped on the city; the gas, light and telephone systems were cut and the city blacked out. Four days later, supported by an armour-plated steamroller, the besiegers launched their first heavy attack at San Esteban de las Cruces, the most distant outpost, on the road leading to the Nalón and Caudal mining valleys. In an attempt to drive off the Popular Front planes, the defenders set up an artillery field piece on sandbags to fire as an anti-aircraft gun. After twelve hours of fighting the attack was beaten off.

Jesús-Evaristo CASARIEGO, student, journalist and *requeté*, had left his house in his reserve officer's uniform to report to the barracks as soon as Aranda had risen. As he left home, his mother embraced him.

—'I am sorry to have to say farewell to you and to know where you are going; but I would be sorrier to see you stay.' Then my wife, who had recently borne us a daughter, said: 'I would prefer my daughter to become an orphan rather than that her father should prove himself a coward' . . .

In saying that, he thought, she had fulfilled the words of the Bible, the words of Ruth: 'Your God shall be our God and your people shall be our people,' for her father was a socialist, albeit a moderate one. On opposite sides, both loyal to their respective ideals, just one more of the many politically divided families.

Despite Aranda's alleged republicanism, his friendship with Prieto, the rumours that he was a mason, CASARIEGO had confidence in him. As long as he had been in Asturias he had acted as an officer loyal to the honour of the army. There had never been any real doubt that he would rise. But if he hadn't, the *requetés* and falangists would have taken to arms. 'We knew we would be killed in any case if the reds took the city. We would die fighting' . . . [1]

As it was, the air raids and artillery shelling were hitting not those manning the perimeter but the civilian population in the town. The mortality rate among children and the aged, caused by living in unhealthy cellars without proper sanitation because of the water shortage, rose very considerably. However, the outcome of the bombing and shelling was not the one the attackers expected. 'Instead of lowering the defenders' morale, it stiffened their will to resist, inspired a hatred of those who bombed targets of no military value.' VAZQUEZ-PRADA, the falangist journalist, saw people he knew to be Popular Front supporters pick up a rifle and join the defenders after an air raid. In particular, a socialist whose family was wiped out.

—'Those aren't revolutionaries, they're criminals,' he said as he joined us. He fought very bravely. It was more dangerous to be in the city than at the front. The bombing and shelling were counter-productive for the reds; we never had to fear a rising among the civilian population' . . .

A large mass of the inhabitants was neutral, CASARIEGO thought. A very rough idea could be got by estimating that some 2,000 out of perhaps 10,000 men between the ages of sixteen and forty volunteered in the course of the siege. The more militant left-wingers had fled or been imprisoned. 'Those who still lived in hope of the left's triumph were too small in number to give cause for fear of a rising; the time was hardly ripe for anything like that.'

José ALVAREZ, the grocer's lad, believed that the lack of any such threat

1. Some months earlier, when planning of the uprising was still in its preliminary stages, José María MOUTAS, CEDA parliamentary deputy for Oviedo, had sounded Aranda out. 'I can still hear his words. "Look, Moutas, I am always ready to take part in anything serious, but not in childish ventures." He knew that I had been implicated in the 1932 Sanjurjo rising. He was an extremely cool, objective man, who had been careful not to express any opinions openly on his arrival, other than a personal disapproval of the Falange.'

stemmed rather from lack of organization. Taking advantage of a Popular Front offensive, a rising in the city could have been staged with decisive results.

—Half the population wanted the town bombed to force the defenders to surrender and put an end to the whole thing. Once you'd got used to the air raids there was little to fear; it was the artillery shelling which was much more accurate and deadly. But there was no organization, I don't even believe that spying was systematically organized . . .

By the end of September he was finding it more difficult to get out of the city to see his girlfriend. He continued to work in the grocer's shop, no attempt being made to oblige him to volunteer for the city's defence (although the military obliged all able non-volunteers to spend two or three days a month working as labourers on fortifications). Supplies were becoming restricted: meat, potatoes, eggs, milk, cider – Asturian staples – were now unobtainable. Professors began making petrol from coal in university laboratories to supply military vehicles. Typhoid grew to epidemic proportions and José ALVAREZ fell victim. For those in good health, the epidemic was not particularly dangerous, but the old and feeble were unable to resist. Sickness, during the ninety-day siege, took an estimated 1,000 civilian lives, the same number as were killed in air and artillery raids. But one form of death Oviedo was almost unique in being spared, despite the bombardment, despite the memories of October 1934: no political prisoners were executed, no *paseos* took place, no vendetta assassinations were committed while the siege lasted. Given what was happening everywhere else – and what would happen later in Oviedo itself – this was perhaps the most remarkable achievement of the defence in a city where the loyalty of a part of the population could not be automatically assumed.

—It wasn't the moment to be executing people, thought Salvador GARCIA, an advertising agent and one of the few non-party men to volunteer from the first day. Our aim was to defend the city, not to shoot prisoners. Even a case of sabotage in my artillery barracks, when a soldier was accused of causing an ammunition store to blow up, was not punished by death . . .

GARCIA had lived through the October revolution in Oviedo. He was a man who 'liked law and order', who thought politics was divisive and that the dictatorship of Primo de Rivera had been a 'perfect time'. Under the republic there had been nothing but disorder, which had got even worse after the Popular Front electoral victory. There was going to be another revolution, he had seen the plans. Though he had never joined a party in his life, he had had no hesitation when the moment came. 'I knew what I had to do.'

*

At dawn on Sunday, 4 October, the Popular Front offensive on Oviedo began. The next day would be the second anniversary of the October rising. The Galician columns, which had been reinforced with legionary and Moroccan units, and were now commanded by Col. Martín Alonso, were only 25 km away; but they had been held there for the past fortnight by a resistance which at last was beginning to coalesce. The Popular Front aim was to take Oviedo before the columns could advance. Commanding a group – there were no formal military commands – José MATA, the socialist miner who had already been wounded fighting the Galician column, believed it important to take the city to capture the large store of rifles and machine-guns and to give a boost to the militiamen's morale.

The offensive had been hastily organized, thought Manuel SANCHEZ, an Oviedo cabinet-maker. A communist party member, he had been among those who had set off for Madrid on 19 July at Aranda's suggestion. That had been a mistake, as comrade Lafuente, a party militant had warned. Was this offensive also an error?

—We had had virtually no training, we were all still volunteers, still wearing overalls. We went into the attack with ancient single-loading Czech rifles which we had just received . . .

From the south-east at San Esteban de las Cruces to the north-west on Mount Naranco, the offensive unfurled. Aranda's front line strength in men and ammunition had already been halved by the rigours of the past month's fighting. The advance position on Mount Naranco, the Loma del Canto, fell after four days' bitter fighting and heavy artillery barrage from the Popular Front field pieces barely 1,000 metres higher up the slopes by the sanatorium. Between the two lay the beautiful ninth-century church of Santa Maria del Naranco.

As VAZQUEZ-PRADA, the falangist journalist, retreated from the Loma del Canto to new positions around the church of San Pedro de los Arcos, he saw an assault guard lying beside the church with a head wound. 'Get me out of this hell,' he begged. 'I carried him just a few steps to a first aid post in the main street. We were fighting in the city now, yet I never for a moment thought the reds would take it.'

—'They're here, they're here!' the two assault guards cried as they ran into my house. They were in rags, without rifles, almost dead with exhaustion. Very shortly, the streets running parallel to the North Station, a couple of hundred metres from my house were being raked by republican fire, recalled José ALVAREZ, the grocer's lad. . .

After a week's heavy fighting, the defenders had been forced to withdraw from all the positions on the perimeter that had served them so well: the water reservoir, the hermitage of Christ Enchained, the cemetery, the lunatic asylum of La Cadallada. There was no second line of defence, no machine-gun ammunition left, only one tenth of the rifle ammunition of a week earlier remaining. From the south-east, through the working-class *barrio* of San Lázaro, and from the west through La Argañosa, the miners advanced.

—We cut through the walls of houses to get up the Calle Magdalena. The defenders were so close we had to set up mirrors to be able to stand guard without being in the line of fire. Most of the fighting was done with hand-grenades, but their mortar fire was punishing. We suffered heavy casualties . . .
Anselmo PAÑEDA, a socialist youth miner, considered himself lucky to be only slightly wounded. The miners waited under cover of dark listening to the artillery fire before attacking, recalled his companion, Misael MARTINEZ.

'When thirty shells had exploded, we charged. It needed no training – only knowing how to count' . . .

In La Argañosa and in the Calle Marqués de Gastañaga, the defenders set light to blocks of houses to prevent the miners' advance.[1] Jesús-Evaristo CASARIEGO, who was in command of one of the defenders' assault groups, knew they were fighting for their lives.

—We were like wild animals at bay. We were prepared to burn the city, to create barricades of fire between us and the enemy. We were fighting street by street, house by house, storey by storey, room by room. We weren't prepared to surrender under any conditions. Win or die, there was no other choice . . .

His home, in the Calle de la Independencia, fell into enemy hands; his wife and six-month-old daughter fled to the cellar of a house in the centre. The daughter of a socialist, the wife of a nationalist, she said she wanted to die with her husband. His eighty-year-old grandmother, his mother, sisters and two young brothers remained in the hands of the attackers. 'The reds didn't maltreat anyone; indeed, one of their officers even gave the children some condensed milk from his kit.' Hardly any ammunition remained.

—Fifteen rifle rounds each was all we had left. 'Well, we've still got bayonets and balls,' we said . . .

Nationalist aviation dropped 30,000 rounds of rifle ammunition. Only 500 men remained, including the lightly wounded and sick, able to bear arms. The attackers were almost in the city centre; preparations were being made to withdraw to previously selected strongholds where resistance would be carried on to the end.

Three days after being wounded in the throat, Salvador GARCIA, the advertising agent who had volunteered as soon as the uprising began, insisted that he be allowed to return to duty. So many wounded were lying in the hospital that no doctor had had time to examine him. A medical assistant, a good friend of his, offered to bring him civilian clothes and to make out a certificate saying he had been wounded by firing in the street. He had lived through the October revolution, was convinced that the miners were going to take the city.

—'You know what that means – ' His words convinced me that my place was beside my companions who were fighting to the death. The first doctor refused, but the next understood and discharged me. My throat was bandaged, I could hardly speak. But I could handle a rifle, you don't need to talk to shoot . . .

His artillery unit ran out of ammunition and became infantrymen. The Fresno electricity generating plant was captured and the city blacked out. Only the fires of burning buildings lit the night sky, and oil lamps the cellars which the civilian population had been unable to leave for nearly a fortnight. Aranda moved his HQ from the arms factory into the Pelayo barracks. Over the radio, powered by a car battery, he sent a message to the defenders exhorting them

1. The measure, natural in defence of this sort, caused an uproar only two months earlier when Popular Front forces used it in their last-ditch defence of Irún in the Basque country. Not the least of the critics were the Basque nationalists.

to fight like Spaniards to the end. A radio message to the Galician column said ammunition was exhausted, but Oviedo would resist to the last man.[1]

The Popular Front offensive had dragged on, had been costly in men and ammunition too. In the south-eastern sector, in the Calle Campomanes, José MATA was pinned down. Advance into the city was difficult, bloody. He cursed the day they had left for Madrid three months before. If they had been like the CNT in Gijón and remained, things would have been different. Every house had to be destroyed before the defenders were put out of action.

—The *guardia civil* defenders wouldn't surrender – they had to be killed. A single machine-gun in a house pinned us down; it took artillery to reduce the house to rubble before we could advance. The numbers of casualties were enormous – 5,000 wounded we had on both fronts . . .

On the western side, the advance had penetrated deeper; there was fighting in the Plaza de América, and almost at the walls of the hospital. Manuel SANCHEZ's unit had advanced through the houses, outflanking the Casa del Jabonero, one of the defenders' strongholds. He was trying to snatch some sleep when he was woken and told that a squad leader and some men had got drunk and had set off for the centre. He went after them. Singing at the top of their voices, they were not far from the Calle Uría, Oviedo's main street, when he caught up with them. It was evident to him that the Popular Front forces could have virtually walked into the city that night.

The next morning, summoned to a meeting with their communist column leader, Damián Fernández, SANCHEZ and other leaders were told that Oviedo could be taken now but that the Galician column was advancing rapidly to the relief. It was vitally important to protect the artillery factory at Trubia near by which was threatened. 'To lose it would be a serious defeat, whereas Oviedo could be taken later. Moreover, ammunition was running short – '

In the city, VAZQUEZ-PRADA was posted in the cupola of the Banco Asturiano building with a machine-gun. 17 October had dawned sunny; the offensive was entering its fourteenth day. The front – it was impossible to speak of a line – was almost in the centre. Like every other defender's, his nerves were worn thin. Only the memory of October 1934 sustained his determination: a sports reporter on the local right-wing paper *Región*, he had been caught by the revolutionaries, his rib-cage buckled in by their rifle butts, had almost been shot. The rapid intervention of a communist leader who had stopped the men beating him, and of a doctor cousin who had him removed to another ward in the hospital where he had been taken unconscious, saved his life. Seeing that he had disappeared, his persecutors believed he had been shot, and his death was entered on the hospital records. When he recovered, he joined the Falange, rejecting both marxism and capitalism, for he had suffered both, having begun his working life at twelve in a machine shop after his lawyer father had died.

In the cupola beside the machine-gun he could at least enjoy the sun. These were the last moments. There was only one thing to do: die fighting.

1. The best day-to-day account of the fighting from the defenders' side is Gen. Aranda's own *Informe Técnico*, of which a résumé is contained in A. Cores Fernández de Cañete, *El sitio de Oviedo* (Madrid, 1975), pp. 103–12. See also O. Pérez Solis, *Sitio y defensa de Oviedo* (Valladolid, 1938).

—If the reds took the city we would all be assassinated. I drank in the sunshine. On the social security building there was an aircraft observation post. Our planes appeared and began attacking the enemy positions. Suddenly I saw don José Rubio in the observation post gesticulating. His voluminous cape spread open, his head was bare. I heard him shout: '*¡Moros en la cuesta!*' [Moors on the hill]. It sounded almost like that old warning shout, '*¡Moros en la costa!*' [Moors on the coast]. I grabbed binoculars, looked up at Mount Naranco; there were Moors on the crest. 'We're liberated, freed!' I shouted. Shortly, there was a tremendous explosion on the mountain-side; the reds were blowing up their ammunition dumps. Then we knew for sure they were retreating . . .

In the evening, fog closed in. The relief column was not due to enter the city until the following day. Fighting was still continuing. Jesús-Evaristo CASARIEGO was in a position close to the Plaza de América when he heard shouts: 'We are the Galician column. *¡Viva España!*' Next to him a soldier shouted: 'It's a lie,' believing it to be an enemy trick. CASARIEGO went forward with a captain. Aranda, who had been informed, ordered every precaution to be taken. Thanks to the fact that one of the defenders' officers recognized the commander of the column's advance party, Capt. Jacobo López, the newcomers' identity was established.

—The Galicians, mainly volunteers, came in with their bayonets dripping with blood. They had had a bitter fight in the railway depot before breaking through. Aranda received Capt. López by the light of a car's headlamps in the doorway of the Santa Clara barracks. The captain saluted. 'At your orders, *mi general.*[1] The advance guard of the relief column of Galicia has arrived. *Sin novedad* . . . '

On the other side of the city, in the Calle Magdalena, the socialist miners saw flares and bengal lights being fired from the centre. They suspected the worst. The next day they heard the news and received orders to withdraw to their original positions.

—I was only an ordinary militiaman, I couldn't tell the reason for these orders, recalled Anselmo PAÑEDA, socialist youth miner. I thought that if we had continued we could have taken the city. Instead, we withdrew, abandoning all the positions we had captured – a couple of which, a few days later, we were ordered to take again . . .

Despite great bloodshed and heroism, no revolutionary revanche could be wrested from history for October 1934. The attempt foundered on the lessons learnt by the defenders from two years earlier. The ninety-day siege had been withstood, and the nationalists had won a narrow corridor to the city which remained beleaguered until the war ended in the north a year later.[2]

1. Aranda had been promoted in the course of the siege, his general's insignia being dropped by parachute.

2. Only four months after the October offensive, the Popular Front launched a second all-out attack on the city. With the militia now militarized and greater weaponry available, the February offensive was even more costly in men and arms. It failed in its three objectives: to cut the narrow nationalist corridor, to seize Oviedo and to take pressure off Madrid, then in the closing stages of the Jarama battle.

The Galician relief column in October brought the rigours of the nationalist repression to

MADRID WILL BE THE TOMB OF FASCISM

¡No pasarán!

Every house a fortress, every street a trench, every neighbourhood a wall of iron and combatants . . .

Emulate Petrograd! 7 November on the Manzanares must be as glorious as on the Neva!

WIVES –
TOMORROW PREPARE TO TAKE YOUR HUSBANDS' LUNCH TO THE TRENCHES, NOT TO THE FACTORY

VIVA MADRID
WITHOUT A GOVERNMENT

Militancies 8

TIMOTEO RUIZ
Communist peasant

Lying wounded in the open lorry – there were no ambulances – he saw men, women and children at work everywhere in the Madrid streets, filling sandbags, building barricades. Loudspeakers were blaring out insistent calls to the people to resist. In hospital that night he fell asleep happy, convinced that the capital would resist.

Seventeen years old, a corporal in the communist-organized 5th Regiment,

Oviedo. The day before the second Popular Front offensive, Leopoldo Alas, rector of Oviedo university, the republican son of the famous novelist 'Clarín', was executed. The grocer's lad, José ALVAREZ, witnessed the execution, lifted on the shoulders of fellow prisoners. Arrested shortly before, beaten up so badly that he was unable to get up from his prison mattress for a week, ALVAREZ was soon condemned to death on charges of not having joined the army (although his age group had not been called up), of being a socialist youth member (which was untrue), and of having crossed the lines (which was true, although no evidence was produced). He owed his life to an elderly *guardia civil* lieutenant who defended him at the trial and secured commutation of the death sentence. Of the twenty-five prisoners who had been court-martialled with him, all but three were shot.

he had been fighting in retreat from the Army of Africa for the past two months. In the last stretch, between Toledo and Madrid, he was wounded. Under-age, he should not have been at the front.

—When I came from my village in Toledo province with a few other local youths who like me wanted to fight, we met a lad in Madrid from the village who had joined the communist youth. He told us that the best unit was the 5th Regiment which the communists were forming. I needed my parents' permission because I was too young. One day we were training when I heard my name on the loudspeakers ordering me to report to the commandant's office where my father was waiting. I ignored the order – I knew they'd never find me . . .

Almost immediately, he was made an NCO. Each recruit was asked if he had had any military training. In his village of Los Navalmorales de Pusa, an ex-legionary had given the socialist youth some training – without arms – before the war. So he said, 'Yes.' 'Right, you're a corporal.'

—I had very little idea of what was involved; all I knew was that I wanted to do what I could. In the village I had been one of those who three years before had organized the socialist youth. I didn't know much about socialism – I was only fourteen – but when I heard what had happened during the Russian revolution and that the large landowners had disappeared and the land was given to the peasants, my imagination was fired. Shortly afterwards, I and some others were arrested for writing 'Long Live Russia' on the village walls. We were too young to be taken to court; the mayor and the local *guardia civil* commander agreed to punish us by shutting us up in the townhall cell every Sunday – the only day of rest and enjoyment – until the day's festivities were over. The punishment lasted more than four months. That was the sort of feudalism we lived under.

Five large landowners practically owned the village. Apart from some 500 smallholders like my father, the rest of the 4,000 inhabitants were landless day-labourers who every morning waited in the village square to be chosen to work by the foremen of the big estates. There was work for all only at harvest and olive-picking times. The only way the landless labourers could keep themselves and their families alive was by cutting firewood on the communal land in the mountains. But this was forbidden, and the *guardia civil* confiscated the wood if they caught the men . . .

His father made ends meet only by going out to work for the large owners; under the agrarian reform he received some land but the soil was so poor that he left it untilled.[1] There were four children in the family, and they lived on *gazpacho* and chick-peas. A chicken at Christmas was a 'big event' and meat was an unknown treat.

On 18 July, he was out irrigating his father's smallholding when, at 2 a.m., his brothers came from the village to tell him the military had risen. He ran back to the socialist youth headquarters.

—'What are we going to do? We've got no arms; we've got to defend ourselves and the republic.' The only thing anyone could think of was to go to the seignorial house in the village belonging to Joaquín Costa's brother, don

1. See Points of Rupture, A.

Tomás. He had a collection of old armour there. I remember with what pride I received the lance with which I set out to defend the republic. Others went with old swords, bucklers, breastplates. We set off in a small lorry for the neighbouring village to see what was happening. We found they had cut down trees to block the road; the barrels of a couple of old shotguns poked through the branches. It was a scene from another age, a war of long ago . . .

After a month's training, his No. 10 Steel company left the 5th Regiment's barracks in a former convent in Madrid for the Talavera front not far – but on the other side of the Tagus river – from his home village. Meanwhile, he joined the JSU and later would become a member of the communist party. The company was issued with old military uniforms and Mexican rifles; the men had received rifle and hand-grenade training. The company had no machine-guns, but included stretcher-bearers and casualty equipment, which was rare amongst the militia.[1]

—As we got close to the front, I was surprised to see cars and lorries, many of them bearing the letters CNT–FAI, coming back from the lines. The men said they were returning to Talavera to sleep. Was this possible in wartime? When I got to the front, I saw that the only units which had a certain discipline – self-imposed, by and large – were those of the 5th Regiment . . .

At the beginning, he found himself facing Moroccan troops and the Foreign Legion. It was enough, in his experience, for someone to shout that the Moroccans were attacking for panic to spread. His unit stood up to them in hand-to-hand fighting in trenches outside Talavera for a couple of days; but after a heavy artillery barrage, the break came. 'The ease with which they shelled our positions was what made the biggest impact on us. It demonstrated their strength and our weakness, for we seemed to have no cannon to reply. It was demoralizing.'

Remaining bunched on the roads, the militia units were easily cut off or, fearing encirclement, retreated. For two months, the withdrawal continued to the gates of Madrid. The last 70 km from Toledo, however, took a month.

Each time his unit retreated there was great disorder and it was easy to lose contact with the company. This created a serious problem. His company was armed with Mexican rifles; the next Steel company had Russian rifles; the

1. The 5th Regiment, which stemmed from one of the five volunteer battalions created in Madrid after the uprising, became a regimental training depot for twenty-eight steel companies, which were created to set an example of discipline, and other units sent to the front. The Regiment grew from 600 to 6,000 men in under ten days; the four other volunteer battalions originally created remained on paper. 'I don't think the communist party at the beginning knew its initiative would be so successful; it was something that was simply improvised,' explained Fernando TAFALLA, architectural student and communist sympathizer who joined the Regiment in its first days and helped organize its infrastructure. 'All those who joined were not communists, but the latter were in the majority.' The Regiment's inspiration derived largely from Vittorio Vidali ('Carlos Contreras'), the Comintern's delegate in Spain, who became its political commissar – an appointment the Regiment was the first to initiate on a general scale. Compared to the ordinary militia columns, the 5th Regiment units displayed a higher degree of organization and military discipline, but did not reach the level of the International Brigades. On its incorporation into the newly formed Popular Army in December 1936, the Regiment claimed a membership of 60,000.

ammunition was different for each. A man who lost his company ran the risk of having no ammunition if he had to join another unit. But the worst was always feeling alone, exposed.

—You could never be sure whether the column to your right or left was still there, or whether you were in danger of being encircled. It couldn't continue like this. We had to have a single command. I was filled with joy when I heard that the militias were to be militarized. Not because I knew anything about military problems, but because for too long I had known what it meant not to be able to count on the units on either side . . .

A friend of his, a brave lad, made off on his own each time the company took up a new position. Asked where he was going, he replied: 'To see where we're going to retreat to.'

—He was right. Each time we took up a new position we could be sure we'd be retreating again the next day. But when we got to Madrid, I said to him: 'You won't have to look behind you any longer. There's nowhere to retreat to now' . . .

The Madrid militia had had to face two tests unknown to the Catalan militia in Aragon: a professional fighting force in the Army of Africa; and the bitter experience of constant defeat. None of the militia units, including the 5th Regiment, was able to withstand the onslaught of the first. The second was driving home – however slowly – the need for a different concept of war. The revolution was failing on two related scores: no proletarian power had been created, no revolutionary Valmy had been capable of routing, if only temporarily, the main enemy force. The militias were the manifestation of the 'dual power' vacuum: each party and organization had its own military headquarters, its own supply services, its own transport which attended to the requirements of its columns with scant regard for the rest. Such central staff as there was was in no way able to formulate a common plan of action and allocate available supplies of men and munitions according to an effective plan. There was rivalry, if not open hostility, between different columns. The failure to create a proletarian power capable of mobilizing the population's total energies in the revolutionary task of winning the war must lead to the establishment of a different power capable of organizing the war effort. The creation of such a power was the aim pursued by the communist party, for which the socialist revolution, even if underway, was not on the historical agenda.[1] With its acute understanding that the Popular Front was facing a large-scale civil war rather than the sequel to a military coup, the party was the only one able to offer a coherent alternative to the power vacuum which seemed inevitably to be leading to defeat. 'Discipline, Hierarchy and Organization,' *Mundo Obrero*, the party organ, thundered only two days after the uprising had been crushed in Madrid. But it would take time. Before the change could be completed, the revolution's failures were suddenly reversed, its unrealized potential dramatically revealed, in the defence of Madrid.

1. For the communist party's analysis, see pp. 323–7 and, for its pre-war origins, Points of Rupture, E.

The sound of war had been plainly heard for some time in Madrid; every day saw the enemy getting closer. The first Russian tanks thrown into a counter-offensive failed to stop the advance;[1] by 6 November 1936, the Army of Africa had reached the suburbs of the capital – a relatively small force of some 20,000 men which, in three months, had fought its way some 400 km from Seville and now stood poised to take a city of over 1 million inhabitants. A population which had struck a leading CNT–FAI militant returned from San Sebastián in September with its apparent insouciance. Miguel GONZALEZ INESTAL thought Madrid was mad after his experience in the Basque country,[2] where 'everybody was virtually living in the front line, everything was devoted to the war effort'. In Madrid, at the beginning of September, the front still seemed very distant, he thought, the war a long way off. The people hadn't realized what was about to hit them.

—With a few exceptions – to speak of my own organization (and the others were the same) – people weren't taking the war seriously. The few thousand militants who were at the front knew what was at stake; but the majority simply remained in Madrid, quite content with what had been done, content to remain complacent spectators . . .

By 6 November, eve of the nationalist offensive on the capital, things had changed. In a dramatic, last-minute move, the government of Largo Caballero, which the anarcho-syndicalists had just joined, left Madrid for Valencia that day. With it went the leaderships of the political parties and organizations. A silence fell: people retreated to their homes, confused by what initially seemed an open confession that the capital could not be defended.

José VERGARA, agricultural ministry official, walked that night from the ministry in the Plaza de Atocha through the centre to the Calle Sagasta. Not a soul was about; he saw houses with doors open, everything looked abandoned. Artillery fire was plainly audible. There was nothing, he felt, to prevent Franco's troops walking into Madrid.

—The war was lost – had seemed lost to me for some time. The military leadership was patently absurd, the internal political fighting savage. It was impossible to win with such confusion, such lack of decisive action. It was all over . . .

Others did not share this view. On the roof of the left republican party's new headquarters in the Círculo Mercantil in the Gran Vía, Régulo MARTINEZ, the Madrid party president, was calling over a loudspeaker on the population to rally to the capital's defence. The Madrid left republican committee had

1. A member of the Non-Intervention Committee, the Soviet Union denounced Italian violations of non-intervention and, in October, began to send war matériel to Spain. This included about 100 tanks and the same number of fighter planes; both tanks and planes were superior to their German and Italian equivalents. As this aid arrived, the Popular Front government opened a base at Albacete for the many thousands of foreign volunteers being recruited, under Comintern auspices, to fight in Spain, and who were now formed into International Brigades. Simultaneously, a start was made in the creation of the Popular Army. At the end of October, the Popular Front government sent a large proportion of its gold reserves to the Soviet Union to finance arms purchases.

2. See p. 189.

refused to leave with the government, whose hurried departure seemed to MARTINEZ a disaster. But there was talk of a defence junta being set up; and while there was life there was hope. With each passing hour, thought Lorenzo IÑIGO, secretary of the Madrid CNT metalworkers' union, the population was getting over its initial shock. A general feeling of indignation arose. People prepared themselves to fight.

—We libertarian youth were outraged that a government should flee in the face of the enemy. Some of Cipriano Mera's militiamen stopped members of the government in their flight and wanted to force them to return to Madrid . . .

Victoria ROMAN, a university student, saw young children beginning to drag cobblestones to where men and women were raising barricades. She was due to leave the city, but suddenly she felt she couldn't go.

—I felt myself completely identified with the people of Madrid. 'I'm staying,' I told the evacuation people, who wanted me to accompany the children I had been looking after to the Levant. I didn't belong to any political party; I was a typically undisciplined Spaniard, prepared now to do anything to prevent fascism triumphing. 'No one can leave Madrid at a time like this,' I told them . . .

Almost alone, the communists defended the government's action, arguing that it could not remain besieged in the capital and govern effectively. Narciso JULIAN, communist railwayman who had returned to Madrid from Aragon and was now commander of the armoured train brigade, was critical of the scores of people who had left or attempted to do so in the government's wake.

—Without any excuse these people fled while the masses began to prepare to defend themselves amidst a desperate shortage of arms. We organized a railwaymen's battalion and went to the war ministry to arm it; but there were no arms, and the battalion had to set out for the Casa de Campo and arm itself from the dead and deserters . . .

The Franco army, which was in position to launch its initial offensive on the day of the government's departure, delayed its attack by twenty-four hours. The population began to rally to the calls going out from all quarters for trade unionists to report for mobilization.

—'*¡No pasarán! ¡No pasarán!*' That's what you heard and saw everywhere all of a sudden, recalled Pedro GOMEZ, a UGT turner. It was like an ad which says 'Use instant shaving cream' and you do. Everyone believed it . . .

A few hours earlier, as the government left, enemy shells began to whistle over the factory where GOMEZ worked. It was the plant where the famous English double-decker buses had been assembled before the war and which had been converted to ammunition production. The workers' committee put out the word to evacuate all the machines and tools.

—'They won't capture any of this,' we said. We were in charge there. I hadn't seen any of the former bosses because by the time I joined the plant three or four days after the uprising the factory committee had been elected. My older brother worked there as a turner and he taught me the job; I had been working in a small workshop making tortoise-shell combs before. So we piled all the machinery and equipment into lorries and moved to the north of the city out of artillery range. Then my brother and I went home. My mother looked at my brother. '*Anda, hijo,*' she said, 'there's fighting to be done.' 'Wait a minute. Let's see if it passes.' But when he saw it wasn't going to go away, he set off; he hadn't far to go to the front . . .

For the past month, Julián VAZQUEZ, communist garment workers' union leader, had been organizing a tailors' battalion. He and another union leader bought some books, amongst them an excellent French infantry manual, and set about training the men. Most unions organized battalions on the same lines. On 7 November 1936, the communist party issued orders that only women were to remain in the rear.

—The communist party had been calling for the capital's defence to be organized when Franco's army was still in Estremadura. A socialist said to me: 'You're scaremongers, you're trying to attract new members.' 'If the party has said it, *me cago en la leche*, it must be true,' I replied. I had blind faith in the party. And now it had come true. But our tailors' battalion had no arms. So we communist union leaders set off to wait in a trench in Carabanchel until there was a spare rifle, leaving the battalion behind . . .

—At union headquarters the men stood silent, hands in pockets, waiting to go, recalled Pablo MOYA, a UGT turner. There were more men than rifles. An elderly couple turned up. The president of the socialist party's East Circle came to ask what they were doing. 'We've answered the call, we've come to do what everyone else is doing – ' He asked them to go home; they refused. They had to be taken off almost by force. When some rifles came, the men went off, not singing, but silently, fully aware of what was at stake. They knew what might happen, and they preferred to die rather than let it happen . . .

—My mother got a bit of firewood and a few litres of oil; she was prepared to boil it and pour it on the enemy soldiers' heads if they came in. It was like 2 May,[1] thought Josefa MORALES, a secretary. But different, too. On the one hand the fear of what would happen if they got in – we remembered Asturias after the October rising; on the other, complete faith that the city would resist . . .

In the garment workers' union secretariat, the women members remained all night at their posts. They could hear gunfire from the lower *barrios* of Usera and Carabanchel, see the flashes in the sky. At the North Station, María DIAZ accompanied her engine-driver father when the railwaymen's battalion was ordered out to the Casa de Campo as the Franco forces began their attack. The men were without arms, the battalion had just been formed.

1. 2 May 1808, when the Madrid populace rose against Napoleon's forces – an episode commemorated in Goya's famous painting.

—There was chaos, confusion. We didn't know where the enemy was, didn't know whether they had cut us off. We were sent out as reinforcements in case the line broke; we had to get our arms from the dead . . .

Within a few hours the railwaymen were ordered to return to the North Station. María DIAZ looked out of a window and saw aeroplanes overhead. 'Those must be bombs, what else can they be?' she said to herself as she watched the objects falling. The explosions threw people to the ground. No one was prepared for what was happening, she thought. Her father, a lifelong republican, had torn up his left republican party card when the government refused to arm the workers at the start of the uprising. Like him, she considered herself a republican. But now, in the station, she saw that while all the railwaymen were prepared to defend the republic, there were some who were different, who stood out by their discipline, their seriousness, their respect for others.

—I learnt they were communists. I asked to join the party. 'No,' they said, 'you're only sixteen, you'll have to join the youth movement.' But I didn't want that; I insisted until they let me join the party . . .

The sky was grey, it was cold. The city seemed to reflect the sky's colour, thought Alvaro DELGADO, the fourteen-year-old son of a shop manager who used to watch the men leaving for the sierra in the mornings of the early days of the war. Now he was watching men filing out of a communist party locale in Atocha and others from a socialist party branch in the Calle Valencia. They were in their ordinary clothes, rifles in their hands. Some of them carried canned fruit tins filled with dynamite.

Overhead, he heard the distinctive sound of the 'Three Marías' – the popular name for the three-engined German Junkers – which flew over nearly every day on bombing missions. Adults and children gathered in the streets, oblivious to the risks, to watch the bombers. But that day, the boy saw some small planes with snub noses he had never seen before which began attacking the 'Three Marías'. What were they? They bore the republican emblem. In the dogfight, enemy planes crashed to the ground; people cheered. Until then the republican air force had rarely attempted to fight off the enemy. These were Russian fighters, the *chatos* (snub-nose) as they were rapidly baptized. The situation suddenly seemed transformed.

—When the government left, we felt betrayed. People talked openly in the streets about the enemy being in Carabanchel suburb already. Everyone expected the enemy to take the city. But they didn't. The climate began to change. There were calls everywhere to defend the city. 'Better to die than to live on your knees,' as La Pasionaria said . . .

—This was the moment when we liked the Russians, recalled Pablo MOYA, the UGT turner. It was marvellous to see those Russian fighters knocking the German planes out of the sky. The streets were full of people cheering and clapping. The Russians had come to our defence, we felt great sympathy for the USSR. Later, things changed . . .

On the ground, the nationalist command was surprised by the stubborn resistance; fearful of attacks on their extended flanks, they had thrown only 3,000 troops into the main assault through the Casa de Campo on the first day, 7 November, with a further 2,000 engaged in diversionary attacks. That night, the hard-pressed republican command, which Caballero had put in the hands of General Miaja, enjoyed a stroke of luck: the nationalist plan of operation was discovered on a dead enemy tank officer. This gave the hurriedly organized republican staff the opportunity to reorganize the defence. Meanwhile, a defence junta, under General Miaja, had been set up. Composed of members of the Popular Front organizations – with the exception of the POUM which was vetoed by the communists, and the FAI, but with the inclusion of the two other branches of the libertarian movement – this was to become the revolutionary organ of power in Madrid. The bulk of its members were little-known militants, many of them under thirty years old. The communists and the JSU – most of whose leaders, including Santiago Carrillo, the secretary-general, now joined the communist party – were the dominant force.

During this crucial period, the largest single massacre of right-wing prisoners in the republican zone took place. About 1,000 prisoners evacuated from the Model Prison were slaughtered by their guards in Paracuellos de Jarama and Torrejón de Ardoz, two villages north-east of Madrid, while officially being transferred to new prisons.

Like many others, José MERA, a schoolteacher and UGT member, spent the night of 7–8 November waiting for the summons to go to the front. Along with university professors, teachers and porters who had answered their union's call, he spent the night in a building in the Castellana. Nobody had come to tell them what to do; they had no arms.

—Before dawn on 8 November I heard a sound that seemed like a miracle. *Tring-tring-tring* – the Number 8 tram on its normal route. I could hardly believe my ears. 'They haven't got in then,' I said to myself . . .

In the Plaza de Antón Martín, not long afterwards, Alvaro DELGADO heard a song he didn't recognize, saw a group of well-uniformed soldiers wearing large blue berets and pulling machine-guns on rubber wheels behind them. They didn't look at all like the militiamen in overalls the boy was used to seeing. These wore boots, had steel helmets attached to their belts, rifles slung over their shoulders, and some were carrying sub-machine-guns with cartridge drums on top, he observed. They were singing the *International* – but in a foreign language. They gave him the impression of great strength.

—The arrival of the International Brigades impressed us all, remembered Eduardo de GUZMAN, a CNT journalist. And that first one, the 11th, was the best of the lot. Revolutionaries who fought magnificently, with a military organization and discipline the militias by and large lacked. In some ways they taught the militias how to fight. They dug foxholes which no one had thought of doing before . . .

No one in Madrid, he believed, could ever say a word against the brigaders, even if most of them were communists and they were under communist command. At that moment everyone was united in the face of common danger.

There were no party rivalries. A revolutionary spirit existed, everyone fought side by side, irrespective of organization or political creed. He would never forget the CNT building workers' union which ordered its members to report with their lunch baskets because the union was not responsible for their food.

—The civilian population was the most impressive of all. Everywhere I went I saw people building barricades. A lot of them, militarily speaking, were useless, but they raised the population's morale. It reached tremendous, euphoric heights. Mikháil Koltsov, the *Pravda* correspondent, said to me one day that he didn't understand the Spanish. 'As soon as they see Moroccan cavalry they start to run. And then one says to the other: "You're a coward," and the other replies, "I've got more balls than you," and he stays there and allows himself to be killed. How do you explain that?' Koltsov was right: how do you explain it? . . .

In the Calle de los Embajadores, several women were shouting at two or three militiamen who were coming up from the river Manzanares and Usera beyond. 'Cowards, chickens, where are you going?' Lorenzo IÑIGO, of the CNT metal-workers' union, heard them cry. 'If you aren't brave enough to be in the front line, then give us your rifles because we haven't got any. We'll go down to take your place.'

Victoria ROMAN, the university student who had refused to be evacuated, was working in the motorized brigade HQ when a dispatch rider came in.

—'They're in the Calle Ferraz,' he said. He was carrying a piglet he'd found somewhere. The Calle Ferraz! I didn't know what to do. If they'd given me a machine-gun, I'd have gone out and used it. Everything was obliterated except the passionate desire to defend the city against the enemy. The enemy that had refused to accept the people's freedom to elect the government they wanted. That was what angered me so profoundly, made any sacrifice worthwhile to prevent their victory . . .

In raincoat, collar and tie, with a blanket under one arm, José MERA set off for the front. After hearing the welcome sound of the tram bell, a doctor he knew had come in and told him he needed a draughtsman for his artillery battery. The doctor had been in the army only a couple of days and, being a mathematician as well as a doctor, had been put in charge of a battery. MERA set off with him to El Pardo, where he found another teacher and an industrial engineer as part of the battery which was attached to the International Brigade *Commune de Paris* battalion under the Frenchman, Col. Dumont. The brigaders impressed MERA deeply. The idea that men had come from all over the world to fight for the republic raised the population's morale. Their discipline was something to marvel at, he thought.

—I saw them lying in pouring rain day and night, completely silent, just waiting for the enemy. All of us who had suffered from the lack of discipline on our side, from the very disagreeable assassinations, who had become convinced that a war could not be won like that, saw in the brigaders what a real army would have to be like . . .

Kitted out in his father's leather jacket, hunting boots, gaiters and cap – 'one of those soft, classic German caps like Dimitrov was pictured wearing after the Reichstag fire' – Arturo del HOYO, a university student, went down to the Plaza de Cibeles and caught a No. 37 tram, which took him and the newly formed Youth Front battalion to the front. A few days before they had received arms: rifles that looked like those the Abyssinians had used to fight the Italians. 'Each had a barrel about two metres long.' When they reached Usera suburb, they found they had to relieve a CNT battalion.

—They had good rifles and didn't want to hand them over. There was a bit of a struggle. Orders were that units had to hand over their arms on leaving the front. We won the day, however, and took up our positions properly armed. The same can hardly be said of our dress. My father, a railwayman, had lent me his shooting clothes; but one of my companions was wearing shirt, tie, raincoat and shoes – and that's how he remained dressed for the months we stayed at the front . . .

But it was his mother's reaction which surprised him the most; she had not said a word against his going to fight. Normally, she would be running after him in the street to make sure he was wearing a raincoat and didn't catch cold. 'Now she thought it natural, it was as though I was going to the office to work. What a change there was in mothers' attitudes in those days!'

—'To the front – five *céntimos*,' the tram conductors began calling out. José BARDASANO, a painter and poster designer, saw a tram leaving from close to the Plaza Mayor to go to the Puerta de Toledo which was now nearly the front. It was full of barbers who hadn't even had time to take off their white smocks and were still carrying their combs . . .

He had never believed the enemy could take Madrid, had designed a poster called *7 November*. It showed a young lad shouting 'To Arms!' By then the workshop he had set up had enormous hoardings ready to put up on houses damaged by air raids or shelling. 'Fascism struck here', 'Terror hit here', they proclaimed. At the start of the war, he had won a poster competition organized in the Plaza Mayor. In front of each entry there was a ballot box and the people voted for the poster they liked best. His poster, called *1936* and showing a militiaman breaking the Falange's Yoke and Arrows emblem over his knee, had been awarded the only prize. Thereafter, he received so many commissions that he set up La Gallofa workshop, run as a collective, to handle them . . .

There was no doubt in Régulo MARTINEZ's mind that the communists and the JSU were playing an important role in raising morale, in exhorting the population to defend the city. At the communist party's celebrations on the anniversary of the Bolshevik revolution, his left republican party headquarters received a telephone call saying that the Soviet ambassador regretted the absence of a left republican representative. MARTINEZ, as president of the Madrid party, was chosen to go, and when he reached the Monumental theatre he found Dolores Ibarruri (La Pasionaria) addressing the crowd. The speeches were being broadcast to the world.

—She was praising the communists, maintaining that they alone were defending the city. I rose to speak. It was not the communists but the *people* who were fighting, I said. The communists didn't take that too well, but the people stood and cheered as I spoke of the times when *madrileños* had risen to defend their liberty . . .

Day after day the nationalist offensive continued; day after day, the militias, backed by 3,500 International Brigaders and soon by a somewhat smaller number of men from the Durruti column in Aragon under its leader, resisted desperately. This was no longer combat in open countryside but battle in working-class streets and suburbs the defenders knew well. Most important was the fact that several of the first new mixed brigades of the Popular Army were thrown into the fray. Though only half-formed, barely trained and equipped, they were a more effective force than the old militia columns. Added to which was Soviet aid: fighters, tanks, artillery and advisers, not to speak of food and clothing. In Lister's mixed brigade, the first to be formed, the troops ate Russian ham and wore Russian jerseys and trousers. But even the militia were no longer the autonomous units of the past. Manuel CARABAÑO, the fifteen-year-old libertarian youth, veteran of the storming of the Montaña barracks and the retreat to Madrid, was fighting in the anarchist del Rosal column. Instinctively and without discussion, the column began to accept orders from the military staff, he observed. The orders came – no one asked where from – and were obeyed. But the defence in his view was a people's defence. From a military standpoint, the people's contribution was perhaps not very important; but when it came to morale and supplies it was vital. For the first two weeks he and his companions lived on whatever civilians brought them.

—Wine, sandwiches, bread, chocolate, *paellas*, stews – they brought us everything they had. Many of them died; they were fearless. My *centuria* took up position in houses on the other side of the river. Four or five men and a boy of fourteen brought us a tin of tunny and some bread. We asked them to bring ammunition. The next day another lot arrived with food and cardboard boxes containing fifty rounds of rifle ammunition. They kept us going like that for a week . . .

Civilians not only brought supplies but picked up fallen men's rifles and fought. CARABAÑO recalled a forty-five-year-old bricklayer, 'the classic Madrid mason, who played his game of cards and got drunk every Saturday, paid his union dues but nothing much more', who joined his unit to fight, and remained for the rest of the war.

José SANDOVAL, a draughtsman who was soon to become the communist party secretary of the first mixed brigade commanded by Lister, was convinced that the civilian population's role in maintaining the combatants' morale was crucial. Men, women and children were prepared to do anything to support the troops.

—I think the communist party played a vital role in rallying the people, for the party decided without a moment's hesitation to call for all-out defence of the capital. There was a real understanding between the party and people of Madrid . . .

After eight days of bitter fighting, the break came; legionaries and Moors stormed the river and reached the University City beyond. It was 15 November. Furious counter-attacks by the International Brigade recaptured the Hall of Philosophy, but they could not throw the enemy back across the river. Two days later, the nationalists attacked again and occupied the Clinical Hospital, which was on the very edge of Madrid; it was to be their farthest point of penetration.

—'We need men in the West Park,' the voice on the other end of the phone said. 'All right,' I replied, 'you can count on us.' Salvador LOPEZ, a civil servant and UGT member, set off with some companions. When we got to the West Park, adjoining the University City, we found a section of men and they said: 'Here's the trench, get in it, we've got to defend this.' I was handed an Italian rifle; it was full of dirt. I set about cleaning it with the only thing I had – a tin of Nivea cream which I had kept from an outing in the sierra before the war . . .

The trench was rudimentary, little more than a ditch with a few sandbags, and its defenders were all civilians. They remained there for five days without moving. Each trade union organization sent up cold rations. Later, thinking about it, LOPEZ wondered if he and the others like him hadn't been mad to jump into a trench without any training.

—But at the time the enthusiasm, political conviction and determination to defend Madrid were overwhelming. The defence was a popular effort. If that example had been set from the beginning matters would have turned out very differently . . .

In the church of San Francisco, where she and another woman were cataloguing the paintings for the government commission which had undertaken the protection of the nation's art, Carmen CAAMAÑO heard the shouts echoing in the street outside: 'The Moors! The Moors!' She ran outside. Women in the street were crying: 'Get upstairs with the oil, get the knives – ' She looked round but could see no troops, although the church was quite close to the Casa de Campo.

—Then the shouting died down and the word went round that it was not '*los moros*' but rather '*los toros*' [bulls] which had escaped from the slaughter house and were running wild in the streets . . .

But some nationalist armoured vehicles with Moorish troops managed to reach the city streets before being repelled. A US journalist came to see Régulo MARTINEZ to confirm a rumour that the militia had discovered a new way of combating tanks. The president of the Madrid left republicans offered to take the journalist to the scene. When they reached the Cuesta de San Vicente, MARTINEZ found a militiaman who had witnessed an armoured car being blown up.

—'Will you tell this journalist how it was done?' 'Oh, it wasn't anything much.' I knew that the militia had repelled the vehicles with tins filled with dynamite. 'But how could you beat off armoured vehicles without proper weapons?' the journalist insisted. 'Oh well,' said the militiaman, '*echando cojones al asunto*' [with guts]. The journalist asked me what he had said and wrote it down carefully. A week later, I was shown a copy of an American paper in which I read that Madrid militiamen had invented a new anti-tank device called '*echando cojones al asunto*' . . .

The description was not inaccurate; without anti-tank weapons, only personal bravery could stop what the militiamen feared above all – 'as the Romans must have feared Hannibal's elephants' – the enemy's tanks. Julián VAZQUEZ, the communist garment workers' leader, was reminded of the Soviet film *The Sailors of Kronstadt* which he had seen shortly before when a detachment of naval orderlies leapt out of the narrow trenches in Usera suburb and charged. But then he saw an even more amazing sight. One of these sailors, a man he later learnt was called Antonio Coll, threw himself on to the ground in the path of three enemy tanks, let them nearly reach him and then threw his bombs. Two were blown up, the third turned tail and fled.

—Coll was killed; but tanks were no longer seen as invincible juggernauts . . .

A peasant emulated the sailor. At a mass rally, La Pasionaria called on him to explain how he had blown up the tanks. Narciso JULIAN, the communist commander of the armoured train brigade, heard his reply.

—'Well, look, it's – it's very easy. You lie on the ground with a bomb in your hand and you let the tank get to within three metres and you throw the bomb at the tracks. If it explodes, the tank blows up on the spot. And if it doesn't – if it doesn't explode – ' He stopped, not knowing how to continue. 'If it doesn't,' he added finally, 'the tank crushes you . . . '

Everything, thought JULIAN, depended on popular initiative. When they received their first Soviet tanks, crews had had to be rapidly trained; a specialized business which in the Soviet Union could take a year. Madrid taxi-drivers were pressed into service. 'This is exactly the same as driving a taxi except that instead of a wheel you've got two levers.' People who knew trigonometry were needed to operate the range-finders; the latter were removed. So too were the radio receivers, which were replaced by signalling flags. Where the radio had been there was room for three more shells. The Soviet advisers found it difficult to believe that tank crews were being trained in forty days. They came to see. JULIAN watched the taxi-drivers manoeuvre their tanks in perfect formation; but not content with this display, the Soviets wanted to see a gunnery test and selected a tank at random, ordering it to fire from standstill at targets set up at different ranges.

—First round – a bull's-eye. Amazement. The Soviet officer ran to congratulate the tank commander. 'How did you do it?' 'Oh well, you know – ' All this was being translated. 'Let me see,' cried the Soviet. He got inside the tank, the gunner opened the catch, looked down the barrel at the target, put in his shell and fired. Another bull's-eye. Imagine what the Soviet had to say to that! Well, they just had to learn that we hadn't time to lose. Popular initiative had to make good many deficiencies . . .

Hand-to-hand fighting in the buildings of the still uncompleted University City continued for days with complete disregard for life. But again, *in extremis*, people and soldiers combined to hold the enemy. Though neither side gained terrain, it had to be counted a republican victory. For forty-eight hours Madrid suffered constant, heavy air raids by Nazi bombers of the Condor Legion. The Spanish capital was the first to experience the future fate of London, Dresden, Coventry, Hamburg. But the population could not be bombed into submission.

—Knowing you could be killed at any moment from the air you thought you might as well die fighting, asserted Josefa MORALES, the secretary. The bombing didn't do the enemy any good. It made people angry, more determined to resist. House committees were set up to control the movements of residents, to prevent looting during raids; it was a form of civilian control but it didn't go further than that. After a time you became fatalistic; I refused to go to the shelter when the siren sounded . . .

On 19 November, while inspecting the lines round the Clinical Hospital where, it appeared, a unit of his was withdrawing against orders, Durruti was fatally wounded. Rumours immediately circulated as to the origin of the bullet.

—The first was that he had been killed by the communists, according to Eduardo de GUZMAN, the CNT journalist. We denied that categorically. Then it was said he had been killed by one of his own men; this was equally false. Recently, it has been said that his sub-machine-gun went off accidentally and that he shot himself. This is also untrue. The truth was really very simple. Foolishly, he got out of his car at a position barely 500 metres from the Clinical Hospital where some of his men had taken up positions behind a night-watchman's shack. A burst was fired by the enemy from the Hospital. As soon as I received the news I went to the hotel where he had been taken and talked to the people who had been with him . . .

Manuel CARABAÑO, the fifteen-year-old libertarian youth member, had heard Durruti address a joint meeting of the Madrid defence junta and the general staff shortly before. The CNT's contribution to the war would be total and absolute, CARABAÑO recalled him as saying. The libertarian representatives on the defence junta had voiced their agreement.

—When he was killed many of us thought that his statement – a repetition of his famous phrase that the CNT renounced everything but victory in the war – was the cause of his death. We didn't talk about it openly, for that would have been too risky, but we attributed his death to a FAI group . . .

Durruti died early the following morning, 20 November; at much the same hour, José Antonio Primo de Rivera, founder of the Falange, who had been tried in Alicante prison, was taken from his cell and executed in the prison courtyard.[1]

1. Plans to exchange him, as attempts to rescue him from Alicante prison, where he was being held at the outbreak of war, had failed. At his trial, he defended himself by reading out editorials from the Falange organ *Arriba* to show that his views were different to those of the insurgent military. He was sentenced to death on 17 November. For the effects of his execution in the nationalist zone, see p. 316.

Left *in extremis* by the Caballero government to organize the capital's defence, General Miaja rapidly became the symbol of popular resistance.

—'I was like someone standing on the sea-shore who sees a man drowning,' Régulo MARTINEZ heard him say during the defence. 'Suddenly the spectator is given a push, falls into the water and in order to save himself starts to swim. The drowning man grabs him and is saved. "You're my saviour," shouts the man. But what I want to know is' – Miaja liked talking in allegories – 'who pushed me in?' . . .

MARTINEZ was attending a dinner given for his left republican colleague and former prime minister José Giral who, he observed, found it impossible to understand how the Madrid population had rallied to defend the city. Evidently in Valencia, where Giral was still a member of the government, there had been complete surprise at Madrid's resistance. Meanwhile, Miaja was continuing:

—'I'm the man who was pushed in, but here are the real tacticians: Rojo and Casado. These are the officers who have achieved the miracle, if that's what it is, who have carried out the staff planning so effectively in the face of the complete lack of confidence in the military' . . .

Miaja was turned into an idol, and an idol, reflected MARTINEZ, was needed in those desperate moments. Moreover, on several occasions, pistol in hand, he rallied troops who were faltering in the front line when the enemy was pressing towards the heart of the city, displaying considerable personal courage in the process. But then courage had been common currency in those November days, and not only among the capital's inhabitants but also among the peasant refugees who had flooded in from Estremadura and Toledo. People who had suffered all their lives, who knew what the republic's defeat would mean to them, he thought, they had turned out to be magnificent defenders of Madrid.

*

By the last week of November there was a stalemate in the fighting. Hitler and Mussolini had meanwhile recognized the nationalist regime; Soviet aid had come to the Popular Front just in time. The defence of Madrid had confirmed the evidence of the very first days of the war: the fusion of disciplined fighting forces and a determined civilian population prepared for every sacrifice could hold the enemy. It remained to be seen what conclusions were drawn from it – not least by the communist party which had contributed so decisively to the defence of Madrid. 'For people to fight, to fight with an exalted frenzy, it is essential that they believe in something, that they know the struggle has a meaning,' noted the *Pravda* correspondent, Mikháil Koltsov, in Madrid on 7 November.[1] The lessons to be learnt could condition the future course of the war.

In the nationalist zone, which had prepared altars, courts martial, food supplies and celebrations for the capture of Madrid, there was the inevitable disappointment. 'Madrid remains a general obsession,' wrote the *Defensor de*

1. See M. Koltsov, *Diario de la guerra de España* (Paris, 1963), p. 193.

Córdoba, on 23 November. 'There are those who think that taking a large city is like taking a cup of chocolate,' said General Queipo de Llano in one of his nightly broadcasts from Seville, adding that he had never believed the task would be easy.

Bitter battles – the Jarama, Guadalajara, Brunete – remained to be fought around Madrid as the nationalists sought to encircle the capital, and the republicans to cut off the besieging army; but for the next twenty-eight months the front line would remain almost exactly where it had been drawn in the November fighting.

Episodes 3

Repression

As though the assault on the capital heralded the enemy's total extinction, November witnessed an intensification of the repression in some areas of the nationalist zone. It was 7 November, the first day of the nationalist offensive, that Francisca de LEON arrived outside the Jesuit convent of Jesús del Gran Poder in Seville to be turned away by the guards.

—'Go away, daughter, go away, your mother doesn't need coffee and food now,' they said. I knew what that meant . . .

Her mother, sister of José Díaz, secretary-general of the Spanish communist party, had been shot. She turned and left, still carrying the food basket. 'I don't know how I managed to reach home.'

As soon as the uprising occurred in Seville they had tried to flee. She, her four brothers and sisters, her mother, an aunt and the latter's two children. With so many young, they had not been able to get far, hardly beyond the gates of the city, where they were given shelter by a woman. The police came looking for them, threatening to shoot a youth on the spot unless their whereabouts were revealed. When her mother saw what was happening, she cried out, 'There's no need to kill anyone, I am Pepe Díaz's sister.'

Arrested, she, her mother and aunt were taken to the Jáuregui cinema which had been turned into a prison. It was packed; more than 2,000 people, she believed, were crammed into the place from which all the seats had been removed but where there was still no room to lie down to sleep. Throughout one night, eighteen-year-old Francisca was interrogated in an attempt to get her to give the names and whereabouts of party members. She saw many of her companions being taken out, tied together, to be shot. One group she remembered was of girls who worked in an olive factory.

—When the man came in at night with the list and started calling out names, panic spread like wildfire. But the women always answered when their names were called. Hope remained until the last moment . . .

The day after her interrogation, she was released and went to look for her brothers and sisters who had remained in the stranger's house beyond the city walls. When she returned with them and her two cousins, she found her house had been turned upside down and much of it smashed.

—In the first days they shaved women's heads, forced castor oil down them and led them in their underclothes through the streets to sow terror in the working-class districts. In the mornings you could see mothers crying for sons or husbands who had been shot. Bodies were left lying in the streets without burial. The working class was completely terrorized by the repression . . .

She returned to work in the glass factory, where she was employed at 2·50 pesetas a day painting designs on glass which others had drawn, to support her brothers, sisters and cousins while her mother and aunt continued in gaol. Her mother, who was forty-three, had never been a member of the communist party. With five children to bring up after her husband died in an accident, she had had to work very hard.

—She earned her living selling bread house-to-house. She was a very good woman, but she had no political beliefs. All she used to say was that communists must be good because her brother was good and he was a communist . . .

Every day Francisca took the two women their food. Until 7 November.

The next day she returned to see what had happened to her aunt; she had been moved to another gaol. Francisca was able to get in and talk to her for a minute. She explained the tragedy. The guards had come to take them both, but her aunt's nine-month-old baby, whom she was still breast-feeding, woke up and started to cry.

—'We'll leave that one and take only the other,' the guards said. Then a discussion started between my mother and aunt, her sister. My aunt wanted to be the one to be taken. 'Let them shoot me because you have got more children than me.' My mother replied: 'No, I will be the one because your children are still so young – ' And she stepped forward and they took her. They wanted to blindfold her before she was shot, but she refused: she would die with her head held high because her brother, José Díaz, merited that of her. 'Shoot me, but shoot me quickly,' she said . . .

Her aunt was kept in prison for another eighteen months; her young brothers were thrown out of school and her aunt's two children, who hadn't been christened, were forcibly baptized. A godmother and godfather were chosen and the children were given new Christian names.

Early in 1938, she, her siblings and her aunt and her children were exchanged for two of General Queipo de Llano's sisters who had been in the Popular Front zone – one of the few exchanges to take place during the war. Francisca joined her uncle in Valencia.

Social equality is nonsense. Look at nature, at the work of God, and you will see that no two things are equal. Equality among men is impossible.

Queipo de Llano (Speech on inaugurating a cheap workers' housing site, March 1937)

The land is the permanent seedbed of Spain. Many have lived on its wealth without ever having a drop of sweat on their brows. Others have been constantly stooped over the land to find themselves forced to sell their products at low prices . . .

Azul, falangist (Córdoba, August 1937)

WORKERS

It is you who are triumphant now . . . All that is asked of you is that you give a day's work for a day's wage. In return you are being given real independence and an implacable defence against your eternal enemy: the political bosses of left and right. You don't believe it yet, but time will convince you.

Guión (Córdoba, January 1937)

Winter 1936

Episodes 4

Return

Public prosecutor of the High Court of Madrid, Francisco PARTALOA crossed from Gibraltar to La Linea and the nationalist zone, his arrival motivated by a sense of patriotism. At the frontier there had been no problems; the nationalist officer in charge of the local security forces had come to welcome him. Now, only a day later, the same officer was telling him he was under arrest. 'You are a very dangerous person, I understand – '

This was not what he had been led to believe by General Franco, who had replied to his letter from Paris by saying that he was the very sort of person the nationalists needed. The latter had even published a propaganda pamphlet which used his case to illustrate the illegalities being committed in the 'red' zone: his dismissal from office, his forced flight to France from Madrid where, on his return from his Almeria holiday at the outbreak of the war, he had been shocked to find that people were being assassinated at will, *checas* functioning, an 'uncontrolled rampage' taking place. Very shortly he had come into conflict with a communist trade union leader who was attempting to expropriate a *marquesa*'s jewellery which was deposited in a Madrid bank.

—'Do you realize what your attitude can mean?' the communist said to me. 'Yes, it can cost me my life; but it is my duty as public prosecutor in this case to oppose you.' I didn't believe there was any justification for depriving the *marquesa* of her rights; but that night I didn't go home to sleep which was just as well because they came to get me . . .

From that moment he knew he had to escape. Informed of his case, the republican minister of justice regretted that he was unable to guarantee his safety. None other than the director general of the security forces took him into his office and hid him until he managed to get a plane ticket out of Madrid – on a German plane bound for Paris. 'Not only did he get me the ticket but he gave me three pounds of gold which I put in my shoes.' His last night in Madrid he spent in the Model prison – a voluntary prisoner because he thought it was the safest place to be. The next day the assault of the prison took place;[1] several of those slaughtered were friends of his.

After four months in Paris he decided to leave for the nationalist zone. He wrote to Franco and to Queipo de Llano, a good friend of his. He belonged to no political party. Although a friend of President Azaña in the past, he had broken off relations with him when the latter became actively involved in politics. In a judicial career, he believed, one should not be politically involved.

1. See pp. 175–6.

He came to his decision to return from a sense of patriotism and the conviction that 'a fire cannot be put out by running away from it'.

—It was up to Spaniards to solve the problems of Spain. My wife advised me not to return. 'The nationalists are just as brutal as the reds,' she maintained; but she came with me when, on New Year's day 1937, we left Marseilles by ship for Gibraltar . . .

The morning after their arrival in La Linea, across the border from Gibraltar, his wife wanted to return briefly to the latter to buy some silk stockings. He went to the security forces' commandant to get a pass; after the latter had read a sheet of paper lying on his desk, he looked up and said: '*¡Ay señor!* this is very disagreeable. This piece of paper informs me that I must arrest you.' . . .

—'In that case you had better carry out your duty,' I replied. I was taken to a military barracks where a captain called Manuel Jiménez said to me: 'Prepare yourself, for tonight you are going to be executed.' He spoke in a matter-of-fact manner, sitting in his office: there was no question of a trial. I didn't lose my composure. 'Why are you going to shoot me?' 'You know the reason as well as I.' 'I don't know at all, but I do know one thing: if you shoot me tonight you'll regret it tomorrow. Don't you know where I've come from? If I had anything to hide I wouldn't have come.' . . .

Unfortunately for him, he did not have on him the letters from Franco and Queipo de Llano. The captain refused to allow him to use the telephone to ring Seville. But his wife, on her own initiative, had done so and spoken to Queipo de Llano, who was about to leave for the Marbella front where the offensive along the coast towards Málaga was under way. Before leaving, he was able to send orders that PARTALOA was to be transferred to Seville prison until he returned. It was a stroke of luck.

Only later did PARTALOA discover that the cause of his arrest was the allegation that he had stood as a communist candidate in parliamentary elections. The *denuncia* had been made by a man from Almería, now in Algeciras in the nationalist zone, whom PARTALOA had helped on several occasions in the past and who had heard of his arrival . . .

Transferred to Seville, PARTALOA reached the prison at 2 a.m. Queipo's wife had telephoned to say he was coming and was to be treated with every courtesy. He was told he could spend the night in a room where a fire was burning. He pulled up a chair, but soon some Moorish troops came in. He had never liked Moors and he asked to be taken to a cell. As the warder opened the cell door he saw that there were some twenty men crammed into a tiny space trying to sleep on the floor. The prisoners began to protest.

—I said I understood but that I didn't want to spend the night in the same room with Moors. As soon as they heard the word Moors they leapt up, exclaiming. They were right. Ten minutes later the cell door opened again.

'All those whose names I call get up and step forward. It's no good trying to hide.' The warder called three names. The prisoners stepped forward. I'll never forget the last one, he couldn't have been more than sixteen or seventeen, and he was rolling a cigarette. He went on rolling it until it was finished, got up and turned to us: 'I wish you all better luck,' he said, and went out. That scene is engraved on my memory. The men were taken out, their jackets removed, their hands bound behind their backs with rope or wire, and they were led away to be shot.

They hadn't been tried; by Spanish law, no one under eighteen could be sentenced to death. It was enough, as I was soon to see in Córdoba, for the head of public order simply to put a cross beside a name on a list . . .

Released from Seville prison, where he personally had been treated well, he went to see Queipo; it had been his intention to take over the running of social affairs in the general's zone – an intention which included taking over all the large estates and dividing them up amongst the peasantry. Queipo, he was sure, would have agreed; but after his reception in the nationalist zone he felt unable to take on the task.

—'Look, don Gonzalo,' I said to Queipo, 'a dog is the only animal you can beat and which will come and give you its paw. I haven't had a happy reception here; I'm sorry, but you can't count on my help.' 'What you have said is well said, and your decision is very just,' he replied. And so I went to Córdoba where, in the past, I had served as a public prosecutor . . .

Not, however, to practise. For his dismissal from his post by the republican authorities for being a 'fascist' was now followed by his dismissal by the nationalists for not having supported the military uprising. The two dismissals were published officially in both zones within a few days of each other. They satisfied him equally, for they showed that he supported neither 'fascism' nor 'communism', both of which he hated as totalitarian.

—But let me say this quite clearly. I had occasion to witness the repression that was being carried on in both zones. In the nationalist zone it was planned, methodical, cold. The authorities didn't trust the people and imposed their will through terror. To do so they committed atrocities. In the Popular Front zone atrocities were also committed. That was the similarity between the two; but the difference was that in the republican zone the crimes were committed by an impassioned people, not by the authorities. The latter always tried to prevent crimes; my own case of being helped to escape is only one of many. It wasn't so in the nationalist zone. There more people were shot, it was scientifically organized . . .

Day after day he attended courts martial in Córdoba, observing nationalist justice at work. The courts martial were no more than a 'mask of legality', in his view, trying and sentencing, in a single day's mass session, thirty or forty people without for a moment attempting to ascertain whether the accusations against them were true. 'Death sentence, death sentence, death sentence.'

—The officers on the courts were honourable men, but they knew very little about law and saw sedition in everything. They often asked my advice. I'm happy to recall that I managed to save eighteen people from execution. It meant sitting in silence day after day, witnessing the atrocities that were being committed – I couldn't intervene unless asked, my reputation as a 'red' would have meant that I would have lost what little moral authority I had over them if I had tried – in order, occasionally, to be able to do something . . .

But when Major Ibañez – don Bruno – the civil guard officer who had been appointed head of public order in Córdoba,[1] sat proudly informing him of the purge he was carrying out, PARTALOA felt too frightened to tell him straight to his face what he thought. 'It was the most humiliating experience of my life.' Don Bruno justified the repression by maintaining that Spain had to be 'rid of these bad people'. Bad people?

—He got hold of the list of the workers' representatives on the joint employers–workers' committee in Córdoba under the dictatorship before the republic and had every single one of them shot. I know that for a fact, because I was the president in 1930 of seven such committees, and I was able to do something that I believe was unique in labour relations there: to get all seven to agree unanimously to new wage rates. The workers' representatives, some 100 in all, were fine men; in those committees they overcame the class struggle to reach agreement with the employers. And he shot them all!

Tremendous atrocities. One other example, no more. A certain count, a good friend of don Bruno's, told me this himself. One day the count discovered that a friend of his was to be shot that very night. He jumped into a car and caught up with the lorry taking the men to their execution. As his friendship with don Bruno was well known, he was able to stop the lorry, and he ordered his friend to be taken off. The head of the squad refused, maintaining that he was under orders to deliver eighteen corpses – corpses, not prisoners – to the cemetery. The count then grabbed a passer-by, ordered him on to the lorry, and took his friend off. The hapless man was executed with the rest . . .

SEVILLE

General Queipo de Llano ran the nationalist zone of Andalusia and Estremadura like a viceroyalty. With the working class – such as remained – cowed, with trade unions abolished and wages restored to their pre-Popular Front levels, he set out to introduce a regime which assured the 'harmonious co-existence of capital and labour'.

'I ask you, workers, does disorder, anarchy and gangsterism suit you better than a government which imposes freedom from above? The real freedom, which ends where that of your neighbour begins?' he asked in a speech at the opening of a building site for cheap workers' housing. Capital and labour were dependent one on the other; but while there was an apparent equality between them, no such equality existed among men, for such was not 'natural'. However, he promised that no great fortunes would be made in future while people were dying of hunger. As a gesture of intent, he forbade employers to sack workers without 'prior authorization from the regional labour office'; and abolished employers' associations, for 'it is not fair that workers' organizations should disappear while employers have associations to defend their interests, interests which must be abolished'.

Convinced that the major part of the ills which afflicted Spain originated in

1. See pp. 161–3.

its 'abandoned state of agriculture', he set in motion a number of projects. One of these was to drain and put into cultivation 100,000 hectares of the marshlands along the Guadalquivir from Seville to the sea to provide work and homes for several thousand families. As the state could not spend large sums of money, he told the landowners involved, at a meeting, they would have to contribute in proportion to the size of their holdings. When asked for their opinion, none answered. The engineer in charge of the project informed the owners that the scheme's cost of 4 million pesetas could be reduced to only one third of that total by 'the use of personnel whom the general will put at the scheme's disposal'.[1] Thus reassured, they gave their consent.

—With the result that an area where hardly any rice was grown before has become the most important rice-growing area of Spain, exceeding even that of Valencia, explained Prudencio PUMAR, a lawyer, who was to become involved in an even more ambitious project under the general's auspices.

One day in October 1936, he and some friends agreed, in casual conversation, that Seville – 'birthplace and heart of the nationalist movement' – needed industry. One of the men commented that cotton was grown successfully in Andalusia but that there was no processing industry. They formed a committee and took their idea to Queipo. He backed it wholeheartedly.

—Any worthwhile initiative suggested in good faith always found his support. We got in touch with the technical junta of the newly formed Burgos administration, and met considerable resistance: the Catalans on the junta didn't want to see a textile plant in Seville. At that time, apart from a very old cloth factory, the only industry in the city was engaged in the transformation of agricultural products, mainly olives . . .

Less than a year later HYTASA was launched with a capitalization of 100 million pesetas. Difficulties in getting foreign exchange out of the Burgos administration to buy machinery in Switzerland – 'we wanted only the best' – were overcome with Queipo's help. For an initial outlay of 700,000 pesetas the company was able to buy machinery worth 10 millions. At the beginning the company's originators had difficulties in subscribing shares. 'The people of Seville weren't used to the idea of industrial ventures; it took quite an effort to sell small numbers of 1,000-peseta shares at par to raise the capital; but we managed that, too.'

HYTASA was the only integrated textile factory in Andalusia.[2] Raw cotton prices were fixed for the farmer – calculated on equivalent guaranteed prices for maize and chick-peas – and the prices of finished textile products were also regulated. Given the shortage of textiles in the nationalist zone – the bulk of the industry being in Catalonia – HYTASA's initial success was virtually guaranteed; production in the first years averaged some 50 million to 60 million pesetas annually. But, in PUMAR's view, the reasons for success were more profound; the secret of the nationalist economy resided in the fact that there was law and order in the zone.

—Security, safety and confidence. I wasn't a political person; yet I supported

1. *ABC* (Seville, 23 June 1937).
2. The company employed 2,500 workers and was capitalized at 3,500 million pesetas in 1973.

the uprising because life had become impossible. You couldn't walk the streets in safety. One of Queipo's major successes was to rid this zone of strikes. People knew that authority existed and that something unpleasant might happen if they tried to strike; Queipo wouldn't have tolerated any such thing for a moment . . .

With this tranquillity, he felt, it was only natural that business confidence existed and that the new authorities were able to secure help from abroad, especially from Germany, Italy and Portugal. 'Help that was given to those who respected law and order, who inspired confidence, to an army that was always advancing.'

The confidence inspired by the nationalist zone was by no means limited to the European fascist regimes: convinced of where its real interests lay, international capital subscribed to the nationalist war effort in no uncertain manner.

The insurrection having succeeded only in agricultural provinces which, in 1935, contributed less than one third of the state's taxes, the nationalists started the war at a considerable economic disadvantage. Measures such as postponing payments on the national debt and on 60 per cent of all war supplies, as well as new taxes, still left more than two thirds of the necessary finance unprovided. Without Italian and German aid, estimated in total at over £116 million ($570 million), they could not have carried on the war. On top of this they were able to buy £15 million ($76 million) of war-related supplies from the dollar and sterling countries.[1] The Texas Oil Company delivered nearly 2 million tons of oil on long-term credit and without guarantees between 1936 and 1939; British mining companies lodged no protest when the Burgos regime exported half their ore to Nazi Germany at an artificially low peseta exchange rate. Exports flourished – sherry sales, mainly to Britain, reached nearly £2 million in 1937, their highest level for many years, and the US contracted to buy $4 million worth of the 1938 olive crop.[2] Surplus wheat from the two previous years' crops which was still in storage was shipped to Germany. In 1937, the nationalists were able to export to the sterling area products worth £12 million and to Germany approximately half that amount again; the total exports of undivided Spain two years earlier had been only 20 per cent higher.[3]

Queipo concerned himself not only with his area's economy but with welfare problems. He was determined to provide Seville's needy inhabitants with cheap housing. There could be little doubt of the necessity of such a project: of the city's 267,000 inhabitants, 90,000 were estimated to be living in rooming houses, packed on average five to a room, while another 20,000 lived in shanty towns around the city.[4] 'The home is the seat of the family, and the Christian family is the fundamental base of a vigorous and strong nation,' declared the preamble to Queipo's housing decree of December 1936. Fourteen months later, 360 houses were said to have been built or to be under construction, a figure which was given as 1,000 by December 1938.

The land, however, was Queipo's chief concern. Within six weeks of the

1. See R. Whealey, 'How Franco Financed His War – Reconsidered', *Journal of Contemporary History* (January 1977). Also G. Jackson, pp. 414–17, and R. Tamames, *La república, la era de Franco* (Madrid, 1973), pp. 345–8.
2. See J. de Ramón-Laca, *Cómo fué gobernado Andalucía* (Seville, 1939).
3. For a view of international capital's reaction to the Popular Front zone, see Appendix, A.
4. According to de Ramón-Laca, op. cit.

rising, he had set up a marketing board to fix minimum prices for wheat, flour and bread; in the autumn he decreed that no farmer could sow less wheat than his previous five-year average and took measures to make seed available; in March 1937, he founded a provincial savings bank to 'redeem the small farmer from usury, making possible loans at a modest interest of 5 per cent p.a. in place of the 5 per cent per month which some people demand'. The matter of quashing the agrarian reform settlements he did not have to handle; the national defence junta in Burgos took care of that.[1]

Near the hamlet of Santa Cruz, some 25 km from Córdoba, José AVILA's family became tenant farmers on one of the duke of Medinaceli's estates which had been expropriated and distributed to peasant settlers under the agrarian reform law.[2] The settlers had fled, the wheat was still standing; the uprising had started as the crop was ready to harvest, and livestock had been let in to graze it. AVILA's family was offered the tenancy because the original tenant had been assassinated in neighbouring Espejo – one of some sixty people to suffer that fate in the township. 'Tenant farmers for the most part – our sort was the backbone of a place like that.' AVILA and his family fled the township and got to Córdoba, to return when Espejo was captured. His oldest brother ran the estate, their father having died, while he and two younger brothers acted as foremen. None of them received a wage; on Sundays, their mother, who was the legal tenant, gave them a tip. 'That was how we lived then. I was twenty-nine at the time.'

But in other respects, he found, there had been a dramatic change. There were no labour disputes, no trouble of any sort, everything went smoothly, tranquilly.

—What a contrast to pre-war! Strikes disappeared, it wasn't even necessary to outlaw them. For who was going to organize a strike now that there were no political parties? This fact convinced me that previously the strikes had been politically motivated, that the labourers struck on orders from others without really knowing why. It was a labyrinth from which we had at last managed to escape . . .

It was a large estate for the times. To farm its 1,000 *fanegas* (650 hectares) without mechanization was the equivalent of farming 2,000 hectares with tractors and combine harvesters, he estimated. At harvest time, the estate required up to 120 men, at other times between forty and fifty, with twenty-four yokes of mules. Even so, it was extensive farming, in space and time: each year in rotation one third of the estate was left for grazing, one third grew a fallow crop of legumes or maize and the remaining third grew wheat. To bring in the harvest took two months, compared to two weeks with mechanization, and the same was true of ploughing.

Along with labour peace, prices and profits remained fairly stable during the war, in AVILA's memory. Anyone who rented land from the duke of Medinaceli, Spain's largest noble landowner with 79,000 hectares, was considered fortunate in Espejo.

1. See p. 202.
2. For a description of the settlement, see Points of Rupture, A.

—We used to say that it was better to rent from him than to own the land; other owners charged twice as much. We paid 30 pesetas a *fanega* per year, the same rent, I remember, as in my youth. The duke of Fernán-Núñez also rented his land cheap, and both allowed their tenants to pass on their leases to their sons. They could do this, I suppose, because they had so much land, so much rent coming in . . .

Although income fluctuated depending on the year, he calculated that after all costs, including wages, rent and taxes had been deducted, profits averaged about 20 pesetas a *fanega* of land on the estate. 'Rents were a fair barometer of profits at the time.'

*

The small and medium-sized peasantry in the nationalist zone, particularly the wheat-growers of Old Castile, could not count on such profits. Well aware of needing their support for its cause, the Burgos regime took an important step towards remedying one of the great rural ills: the lack of a guaranteed outlet at a guaranteed price for the peasantry's wheat crop. The creation of a national wheat service to achieve these aims was welcomed by the peasantry. Not for nothing did a nationalist newspaper write that 'Wheat has been one of the principal arms of combat in our struggle.'

—Before the national wheat service, a farmer who lacked the financial means to store his wheat crop was forced to sell it immediately. That meant low prices, commented Antonio GINER, the son of a farmer with 120 hectares of wheat land in the Old Castilian village of Castrogeriz, not far from Burgos. At the outbreak of war my father had two crops stored; he was lucky to have the resources. By announcing guaranteed prices in advance each year – prices a little higher than those before – and purchasing the wheat as soon as it was harvested, the wheat service did away with all this . . . [1]

The national wheat service was an integral aspect of the new regime's overall control of the economy, and its determination to guarantee production and distribution (the 1937 wheat crop was decreed of 'national utility' by Franco, and anyone impeding the harvest would be found guilty of rebellion under martial law). Other measures, especially in the matter of securing loans, were also taken to help the peasantry. What had the pre-war republic offered? Precious little. The new lease laws and an agrarian bank, which would have helped this peasantry, had either been emasculated or not approved. Labour costs had risen, wheat prices had fallen. Only the Catholic agrarian syndicate, modelled on the Belgian example, played any significant role in helping the Old Castilian peasant, providing cheaper artificial fertilizer, seed corn and other supplies than he was able to procure from private dealers. It also established granaries in each village where the peasant members could store their wheat if the price was low; and in Castrogeriz, when the situation became especially

1. 'It served also to even out the supply of wheat. Previously, prices would be forced up after a time by the non-sale of the crop by those who could afford to store their wheat, thus ensuring the better-off a bigger profit in the end. The trap of borrowing money at high interest rates to finance storage in the hope of getting a better price in the end – a price that often didn't cover the interest – was eliminated by the new wheat service . . .' (José AVILA).

bad under the republic, it paid the farmers between 60 per cent and 70 per cent of the market value of their crop in ready cash to keep them going. Given the low level of mechanization, medium-sized peasants were also employers of labour, if only at harvest time. They felt the effects of wage claims and strikes as much as, if not more so than the large owners. Labour peace, law and order, were important issues.

—Within two days of the start of the war I was happy, recalled a day-labourer in Castrogeriz. Life was quiet and peaceful again. What a stroke of luck that this man Franco came along! . . .

José ALFARO was one of the village's 150 day-labourers, the majority of whom lived in caves under the castle.[1] The leaders of the labourers' union had been arrested in Burgos on the first day of the uprising, court-martialled and shot. Other union members fled to the surrounding hills, but these provided no hiding places and they were forced to return to the village. Summary courts martial did the rest: some twenty villagers were executed. Not all of them deserved their fate, reflected ALFARO; 'they were workers like the rest of us who had been taken in by the leaders.' The latter had coerced labourers to join their union; like many others, he hadn't wanted to join because they attacked religion, attacked everyone who went to church.

—I was brought up to believe in God by my mother. She was illiterate, but she taught me religion when, as a child, I went with her to the fields where she worked. I went to mass. The union leaders called me a blackleg, the landlords' scum. They wanted the revolution, wanted to get paid without having to work. I didn't want that. My mission in life is to work – not to get paid for doing nothing . . .

He was not alone in feeling that the war brought peace and tranquillity; Fernando SANCHEZ, a ploughman in the village, shared the opinion that the war was a good thing.

—Once the left had gone we could all work for a day's wage peacefully again. There was plenty of work, we all worked as hard as we could. With the youth away at war, we older men had to work even harder – but we were happy . . .

—It was before the war that we knew war, explained Antonio GINER; once the war started everything was peaceful. We could get on with farming again. We suffered very little, the fronts were a long way off. Everyone helped each other out; even the *señoritos*, who had never worked on the land, lent a helping hand. Some land went out of production because farmers lost sons at the front, there was some drop in production, but it wasn't much . . .

—There was a tremendous spirit in the village, everyone put his back into it, recalled a local grocer's son, Joaquín SUÑER. We all knew that the only alternative to winning was to lose the war; and people were determined to win . . .

1. See also p. 84. The village, with a population of some 2,500, had ten large-holding landowners, fifteen medium-holding peasants and about 130 small-holding peasants owning between 25 and 30 hectares – the amount of land one pair of mules could till. Most small peasant owners were also renters or sharecroppers, adding to their smallholdings by leasing land. The relatively high proportion of day-labourers for a Castilian village added to social unrest.

Aged eighteen, SUÑER was quick to volunteer for the Falange militia. Before the war, to the best of his knowledge, there had been no more than half a dozen falangists in Castrogeriz. But now one had to join something or remain under a cloud. One couldn't remain neutral. His father was a CEDA member.

—But like most of the youth of my age I joined the Falange. For a simple reason: the Falange came round the villages telling the people they had to volunteer for the war. It wasn't a matter of choosing really, the essential thing was to defend the cause . . .

And the cause was being defended essentially by the peasantry of Old Castile, León, Galicia and Navarre; it was they (and in particular the latter two regions) which provided the shock forces of the nationalist army.[1]

The contradictions inherent in this situation did not escape some on the nationalist side.

—The peasantry was fighting in fact to defend the rights of the large landowners, the big wheat farmers, the owners of the sugar beet factories who exploited them. How could this impoverished peasantry defend interests that were totally opposed to theirs? Only through the mechanism of religious ideology which made them identify the nationalist cause with their own, thought Dionisio RIDRUEJO, the Falange chief. Ideology, spiritual and mental structures, were more important than material interests in this case. These smallholders were anti-socialist, anti-communist, and the idea of the marxist revolution taking place in the other zone was repugnant to them . . .

Called up to serve in the nationalist army early in 1937, Paulino AGUIRRE, the philosophy student caught in the limbo of a hotel on the Ebro at the start of the war, found himself serving with poor peasants from the Rioja region. After a month in barracks, his infantry company was sent to the Basque front. As the troops entrained there was a call for all students to step forward; the two or three to do so were made corporals on the spot. When they reached the front, a further selection was made and AGUIRRE found himself a sergeant. Throughout the brief training, and now in action, he wondered about the soldiers under his orders. Did they have any clear idea of what the war was about?

—It didn't seem like it. Perhaps deep down they had, although I fear not even there. Their only awareness seemed to be that of obedience – obeying the orders given, not thinking. And the same was true of a great number of officers, especially those who had risen from the ranks and who had never thought they would have to fight a war . . .

But if, as he felt, there was no real awareness of the issues at stake, there was always a strong feeling on the nationalist side that victory was assured. It stemmed from the conviction that military coups in Spain were usually successful, and from the fact that victory seemed normal to the right, since the latter was accustomed to being in power. By the end of the war, two years later, it

1. It was not until 1938 that Franco, dubious of their political reliability, used ordinary conscripts in major battle; even then, the Galician and Navarrese divisions, with the Foreign Legion and Moorish *regulares*, remained the army's vanguard force (see S. Payne, *Politics and the Military in Modern Spain*, p. 389).

was no longer the case that soldiers didn't know what the aims of the struggle were. 'They had had to hear and read enough propaganda by then to make up their minds.'

Obedience to orders was no light matter: the nationalist zone was under martial law. And no one could forget the repression that was taking place.

A republican sympathizer answered his call-up by the nationalist forces knowing he was going to have to fight for the 'wrong' side, but fearing further reprisals on his father, a republican doctor in Salamanca who had already been arrested, tried and fined. César LOZAS, an engineering student, had a valid pretext for refusing to serve: dual French–Spanish nationality, but he decided against using it; the new regime might not consider it sufficient. There was no way out but to serve. And that, he believed, was what the majority of the peasant recruits in his infantry company – he was the only student – felt. They were not politically motivated to fight.

—They were swept along by events, they lacked the ideological awareness that would have motivated a serious attempt to desert. Moreover, any such attempt could cost you your life – and even if you succeeded, reprisals could be taken on your family. There was considerable terror in the rearguard . . .

Another republican from Salamanca who served in the nationalist army as a doctor found the peasants making good soldiers, tough, used to a harsh life.

—Cannon fodder, sheep to be led. They were no one and knew nothing. Those who were politically active had been imprisoned or liquidated. Everything in the rearguard was 'cleaned up'. The proof can be seen in the fact that there were no acts of violence or sabotage in the nationalist rear – that was how effective the purge was . . .

But, despite republican propaganda to the contrary, no amount of terror could weld together a successful army. Military discipline was rigorous; but the nationalist peasant soldier did not, in the last resort, go to the front under any greater coercion than did the republican conscript. Rafael GONZALEZ, a student who served on the Andalusian front, found that the majority of the peasants in his battalion were pleased to be in the army. Most of them had lived a very hard life on the land; in the army they found they were being fed for nothing and for doing nothing. This was particularly true of soldiers on fronts where there was little action.

—They would remember that they would be a lot worse off at home. The only ideological indoctrination – if one can call it that – they received was the military one which asserted that Spain was in danger, the *patria* had to be saved. Since resistance was impossible, they joined up with resignation – the sort of attitude that the great mass of people always shows in these situations . . .

One thing, in his view, alleviated the resignation. The peasants thought of themselves as part of a victorious army. As a result, their objective became the personal one of taking part in the capture of a capital city, Madrid, Barcelona, Valencia. 'For many of them, who had never left their hamlets before, this offered a bright hope for the future.'

Religion, resignation, fear of reprisal. But there were certainly other reasons which determined that a peasantry, whose standard of living was often little higher than the landless day-labourers', should fight for the counter-revolution. 'Patently, their own class interests,' observed a student who volunteered for the nationalist forces at the age of seventeen with the ambition of making a career of the army. Ignacio HERNANDEZ, an *alférez provisional*, led peasant troops in the north, at Teruel, on the Ebro, was wounded seven times and decorated as many. The peasantry, he recalled, knew only too well that in the republican zone smallholders were being 'driven at gun-point' into collectives, despite the communist party's efforts to prevent it.

—The 'nationalist' peasantry was fighting for the defence of its property, its land. If this meant identifying itself in the first instance with the cause of the landed obligarchy, big finance, the military – well, that was better than the alternative of being deprived of its smallholding, its plot . . .

As long as any woman is kept as an object and is prevented from developing her personality, prostitution, in fact, continues to exist.

Mercedes Comaposada, editor, *Mujeres Libres* (December 1936)

Prostitution presents a problem of moral, economic and social character which cannot be resolved juridically. Prostitution will be abolished when sexual relations are liberalized; when Christian and bourgeois morality is transformed; when women have professions and social opportunities to secure their livelihood and that of their children; when society is established in such a way that no one remains excluded; when society can be organized to secure life and rights for all human beings.

Federica Montseny,
former CNT minister of health and social welfare (1937)

In Catalonia, the woman has always been the centre of the family . . . The man, here, at the end of the week, gives his whole wage to his wife . . . Women have won not only equality in public life and in work but have possessed it for a long time within the family.

Federica Montseny (Interview with H. E. Kaminski, 1937)

MADRID and BARCELONA

Women were playing a large and important part in the Popular Front war effort, working in factories, farms, hospitals, in industrial and rural collectives. The depths of the revolution were, at one level, nowhere better revealed than in the change of attitude towards women in a traditionally male chauvinist society. Rosa VEGA, a schoolmistress who remained in Madrid, found the change remarkable. In the blackout, during the siege, she walked home after spending long hours preparing medical supplies.

—It was so dark that I often bumped into people in the streets. But never once was I molested or in any way made aware that I was a woman. Before the war there would have been remarks of one sort or another – now that was entirely gone. Women were no longer objects, they were human beings, persons on the same level as men. There were many bad things, without doubt, in the Popular Front zone, but the fact that both sexes were humanly equal was one of the most remarkable social advances of the time . . .

—The war bred a new spirit in people, it was amazing, remembered María SOLANA, a unified socialist youth member. I was often sent round villages on propaganda missions with other party youth and there wouldn't be enough beds. I, the only woman, would sleep in the same bed with two or three youths and nothing would happen – absolutely nothing. There was a new sense of human relationships . . .

At the start of the war many women donned overalls and pistols and went to the front. 'They included a large number of prostitutes who caused more casualties due to venereal disease than did enemy bullets,' recalled a nurse, Justina PALMA, another JSU member. After the battle of Guadalajara in March 1937, a call was put out for women to leave the front.

—Dolores Ibarruri, La Pasionaria, came to the front to tell the women that their place was in the rearguard where they would be of more use to the war effort. Lorries were drawn up to take the women back. But a childhood friend of mine, and a number of others, didn't leave. I never found out what happened to my friend, but I believe she was killed fighting . . .

In Barcelona, similar new freedoms were being experienced by women. Margarita BALAGUER, an eighteen-year-old seamstress in a *haute couture* fashion house which she had attempted unsuccessfully to collectivize, found the liberation of women the most rewarding of all the revolutionary conquests. For as long as she could remember, she had fought the accepted notion that 'men and women could never be friends'. Now she found she had better friends among men than among women. A new comradeship had arisen.

—It was like being brothers and sisters. It had always annoyed me that men in this country didn't consider women as beings with full human rights. But now there was this big change. I believe it arose spontaneously out of the revolutionary movement . . .

The daughter of a cabinet-maker and former CNT member, she used to go to an anarchist centre after work in the invoice department of the plumbers' and electricians' collective.[1] At the centre plays were staged for the benefit of war widows, women knitted soldiers' sweaters and wrote letters to soldier pen-friends; there, too, sex education classes were given. An anarchist in his mid-twenties explained the male and female reproductive functions, 'talked about physical contact between men and women'. Nothing like this had existed before the war.

—I found it excellent. The classes were mixed and I think they helped us, men and women, to develop a new way of understanding, just as much as in gaining information. It was a way of getting rid of all the old taboos. A real liberation . . .

Abortion was legalized under controlled conditions, centres opened for women, including prostitutes and unmarried mothers, birth control information disseminated and 'marriage by usage' instituted whereby cohabitation for ten months, or less if pregnancy occurred, was considered marriage.[2] Despite these considerable gains, the revolution did not fundamentally alter the traditional roles or – but rarely – the customary inequalities of pay. Women continued to launder clothes, cook, keep house and look after children; they continued to get paid less than men.

1. 'A job I'd had to take when our attempt to collectivize the fashion house failed.' On the pretext that the situation was 'precarious', the owner sacked forty dress-makers, seamstresses and apprentices after the uprising. Margarita BALAGUER suggested getting the garment workers' union to collectivize it and to make clothes for the militia. 'At the CNT union they gave us a bit of paper. None of the other girls wanted to confront the *señorita*, the owner, so I went. She turned red with anger and said it was an impudence that one of her seamstresses should do such a thing to her. She refused to have anything to do with it and simply closed down her business. There was nothing we could do.'

2. Instituted in April 1937, this measure was later reversed due to the prevalence of bigamy. The first two measures were due to Federica Montseny as CNT health minister. The libertarian-influenced *Mujeres Libres* (Free Women), which grew to 30,000 members during the war, organized a women's trade union in Madrid and Barcelona in public transport and food services. While its members saw themselves engaged in the struggle to liberate themselves from the traditional roles and oppression by men and capitalist society, the federation appeared rarely to challenge these roles in practice during the war (see T. E. Kaplan, 'Spanish Anarchism and Women's Liberation', *Journal of Contemporary History*, vol. 6, 1971; also L. Willis, 'Women in the Spanish Revolution', *Solidarity Pamphlet* 48, London, 1975). The communist party organized a number of women's organizations, including the Anti-Fascist Women's Organization, the Union of Young Mothers, the Girls' Union, etc.

—We went on washing clothes for the men; it seemed normal enough, especially when we had to do everything we could to help those at the front, remembered María SOLANA. I used to go to a socialist militia barracks. It got me into trouble with my fellow-communists; not because I went to wash clothes but because I was working for the socialists. They wanted to know why. 'Because they haven't got enough people, whereas our forces have. I'll go where I'm most needed.' The answer didn't satisfy them at all . . .

In an anarcho-syndicalist collective in a small lower Aragon village, the sixteen-year-old daughter of a CNT smallholder experienced both the liberation of revolution and the frustration of the seemingly impermeable male–female roles.

BECEITE

—What joy, what enthusiasm we felt! The revolution had happened. One has to live through it to know what it's like. Now we were all free, no one had to work for anyone else, when you went out to till the land you weren't thinking of the *cacique* or boss . . .

It was marvellous, thought Pilar VIVANCOS, to live in a collective, a free society where one could say what one thought, where if the village committee seemed unsatisfactory one could say so. The committee took no big decisions without calling the whole village together in a general assembly. All this was wonderful. But the role of women – that hadn't changed. There was much talk but little action.

—The men were sincerely dedicated to furthering the revolution, but they didn't understand that the revolution had to be made in depth, at all levels. The revolution has to begin at home. In truth, the question of women's liberation wasn't posed as part of the revolutionary process, at least not in my experience. Perhaps things were different in Catalonia, but in Aragon the woman's place was in the kitchen or working the land . . .

There were no women on the village committee. When the latter needed more hands in the fields, the delegate told a group of women to report the next day. Otherwise Pilar stayed at home. Sometimes the women would lend a hand on neighbouring collectives. In that way, a group of young girls from her village became friendly with the socialist youth girls in near-by Valderrobres. 'How we were criticized and attacked in our village for that. The FAI was especially intransigent, sectarian, it didn't want us to have anything to do with any organization that wasn't anarchist.'

But, she felt, the women themselves were partly to blame for not pressing women's liberation further.

—We women, who had to make the women's revolution, in truth understood very little of what women's emancipation entailed. We lacked the necessary education and culture . . .

Puritanism increased as a result of the anarcho-syndicalist revolution. A cousin of hers started to live with a woman in the village and came in for considerable criticism by the villagers. Not to get married was 'living like animals', they said. (The village committee performed marriages and burials, interring people in the cemetery without religious ceremony.) 'They couldn't see that my cousin and the woman had chosen freely to live together. And *free union* was what anarchists preached!'

—What criticism an anarchist's wife or companion who wore lipstick had to face – *ouf!* And the husband – they would say he wasn't a man to let his wife paint herself. Until the age of twenty I never wore lipstick. I remember going to the front once. An anarchist militant – a beautiful woman – who was there said to me: 'Don't take any notice of what *they* say about make-up. The men here only go after women who wear lipstick' . . .

Soon Pilar had to confront this puritanism herself. One of Durruti's companions of the *Nosotros* group, Miguel García Vivancos, was the commander of the 25th division, formed from anarcho-syndicalist militias, including the Carod-Ferrer column.[1] Pilar's brother-in-law, who was serving with the forty-two-year-old Major Vivancos, invited him to their house for a meal. Pilar served at table.

—I was just a village girl. All evening Vivancos kept looking at me. I went red as a beetroot. 'Don't blush,' he said, and that made matters even worse, I blushed all the more. He was very good-looking, tall, thin, dark-skinned with striking blue eyes. He had a great, human vitality. After the meal he left. One day, some time later, my brother-in-law returned and said that Vivancos wanted to come for a meal.

'He's not coming because of me or you,' he told my sister. 'He's coming for Pilar.' The word went round the village and stirred up gossip. He arrived; he said that he wanted to talk to me.[2] I agreed. I was in love with him. My parents were scandalized – but who could say no to Vivancos?

The CNT national committee had words with him, asking what he was doing with such a young girl. 'At least be discreet about it,' they said. 'Discreet! You're a bunch of reactionaries,' he replied. 'You're worse than the Bolsheviks.' 'You must be mad,' they said. 'Mad – of course I'm mad. Haven't you ever been in love? I'm mad about her and I've no reason to hide it.' He knew they all had their mistresses. Here was this streak of puritanism again, and Vivancos attacked it for what it was – hypocrisy.

Whenever he had a few hours free, he would let me know and we would meet. I liberated, emancipated myself. We slept together, we became the couple we were to remain all our lives, for we never married. I believe that people respect each other more without marriage. Not being married is a freedom – not a freedom to do as one pleases but the freedom to be oneself in a human relationship . . .

1. See pp. 132–5. Carod's column liberated Beceite on its march towards Saragossa in the first weeks of the war. Carod became a commissar and later the division's political commissar.
2. The traditional formal male request to be accepted by the woman as her suitor.

MADRID

Many thousands of women and children were evacuated from Madrid; but many thousands also remained. Among the latter were great numbers of domestic servants who had been left behind when their masters set off, somewhat earlier than usual, for their summer holidays. To provide employment for them, and to assist the war effort, the communist-led Anti-Fascist Women's Organization set up new workshops where they made uniforms and clothing for the militias and army. At the same time all out-workers were 'concentrated' in these new shops, the largest of which had between 2,000 and 3,000 women workers; they were run as collectives, with the full agreement of the communist leadership of the garment workers' union, under workers' self-management.

—We always insisted that the workers should run their own workshops, unlike the CNT which tried to impose union control, explained Petra CASAS, communist secretary of the UGT garment workers' union. Self-management was our principle for the collectives. It was not the union which gave the orders. Each shop elected its own management council, and each council was represented on a union coordination committee where joint problems were thrashed out. But each workshop was autonomous. The communist party was in complete agreement with this; it believed that each collective should be free to manage its own affairs . . .

As soon as the garment collectives were operating successfully, they were told to open their own bank accounts and to negotiate their own contracts with the army's purchasing department. All money left over after wages and payments for raw materials was to be placed in the banks so that it could be used for the war effort. The collectives were profitable enough to set up their own canteens and libraries, and to pay sick pay. Each canteen had its own van which went round the villages looking for food to supplement the rations.

Petra CASAS was called one day to the biggest of these collectives in the Calle Abascal: a strike had broken out. A great number of teenage girls worked in the collective, and they had gone on strike, claiming that the food was bad and that a woman sent by the union had been seen wearing a religious medallion. When the collective had opened, CASAS had told the workers that they were the owners, there were no other bosses.

—Now they were turning up for work late, taking time off when they wanted, because they felt they were the bosses. I told them they were striking while men at the front died to save the country from fascism; if they had been working for a capitalist boss they wouldn't have been able to take time off . . .

This was their factory, she continued; how could they know who had earned her wage if some took time off whenever they felt like it? They should start a record of hours worked. As to the woman with the religious medallion, she was a member of the union's secretariat, a Catholic and an excellent worker who enjoyed the union's full confidence. Finally, the workers had to realize that each factory was responsible for organizing its own food supplies and that, in wartime, these were bound to be irregular. 'They accepted what I said and returned to work.'

At the start the union took over all factories and workplaces whose owners had disappeared until a workers' committee and a manager had been elected by the shop-floor. Thereafter these factories, usually the bigger ones, operated with much the same autonomy, according to union leaders, as the collectives, although they were not given that name. Where owners had not fled, workshops were placed under workers' control – which the communist party interpreted strictly as *control*, not management, which remained in the owners' hands.

—The communist party gave us strict instructions from the beginning, remembered Julián VAZQUEZ, a communist member of the union's leadership. The union was not to carry out any arrests – that was a matter for the police; it was not to take over the whole industry – that was a matter for the state; it was not to take over small owners – for that was to expropriate the petty bourgeoisie. These instructions we faithfully carried out . . . [1]

Militancies 9

MIGUEL NUÑEZ

FUE-JSU education militiaman

The change in awareness revealed in the new attitudes towards women was reflected in another area also. Overnight, as though the revolution had unleashed the pent-up hopes of generations, education became a matter of pressing urgency, even in the front lines.

—It was quite remarkable to see peasants and workers devoting time and energy, even under fire, to learning to read and write; to see with what attention they listened to poetry and literature which we read to them. Most remarkable of all was the questions they asked . . .

Not yet sixteen when the war started, he had volunteered immediately. He belonged to no political organization, only the FUE, but it was not long before he became a member of the JSU (and later the communist party). Too young to fight, he was sent to an auxiliary service which, within a short time, became the culture or education militia where he became not just a teacher but also a combat militiaman. Teacher and student were both fighters.

—The fusion between culture and the army of the people was complete. Learning was not something exterior to the men or the struggle they were engaged in. At the beginning I used to ask myself what these workers and

1. The instructions never forbade the creation of collectives, whether industrial or rural; but the communist party inveighed against 'forced' collectivization, anarcho-syndicalist 'socialization' (union management), the single or family wage and other tenets of the libertarian revolution. The basis of much of the communist attack on collectivization concerned less the actual question of collective work (Stalin's rural collectivization was at its height) than the more vital question of *who* controlled it. See below, p. 372.

peasants were really fighting for at the risk of their lives. The only answer I could find was: all those things which the enemy, the reactionary forces of this country, have for so long deprived them of. And access to culture was one of these . . .

It was not a revolution that sought only justice, a settling of accounts with the exploiters, but a revolution which sought to conquer all that the people had been deprived of. Here, at last, was a people standing on its own feet. The movement of the masses was something magnificent.

When all the men in his unit had learnt to read and write – 'which cost a number of them serious effort' – it moved him to see with what excitement they picked up a newspaper and, almost spelling the words out, read it. It was as though they had crossed a tremendous barrier. Then they almost invariably sat down to write two letters. The first to their wives, telling them that they had learnt to write. The second to La Pasionaria, to infórm her of the good news. 'We are not only fighting the enemy, we are learning too, you can count on us – '

Classes were given when and where possible, usually in the mornings and in the rough shelters put up by the men. If he was lucky, he'd find a large piece of blackboard and some chalk, but if not, he would use large sheets of paper and draw or paint on them. Each time the unit moved, the equipment, however rudimentary, had to be left behind. Time and again, the men's initiative – one of the revolution's major revelations for him – was displayed as one found a couple of chairs, another a bit of chalk, another a piece of wood that would serve as a bench, or a bit of blackboard to set up the school again.

—It wasn't a question of waiting for a superior to give an order, for instructions to come from an officer or political leader. No, everything came from the people. It was fabulous. All the qualities and capabilities which capitalism prevents from developing were suddenly revealed by the revolution. Peasants who had never heard music listened to concerts in an impressive silence, or to the great poets like Alberti and Miguel Hernández reading their poetry. The immense strength of the people, their courage, fraternity, comradeship, appeared with overwhelming force . . .

An international delegation of writers and journalists visited his unit and wanted to attend the classes. They appeared impressed by what they saw, and suggested that, after the war, it would be necessary to continue the experiment with education militias going out into the countryside until not a single illiterate remained.

When one of his companions was killed, the other cultural militiamen gathered their units together to give a joint lesson – the fallen man's last lecture, delivered from notes he had left, on the 'golden era' of Spanish history, the epoch of Philip II.

—It was an analysis of the period which, in school, had always been presented to us as 'golden' but which the dead man's lecture showed had been based on the exploitation and misery of other peoples, something that had never been said before. But we said that the best lesson the fallen man had given was his personal example: in his death in combat the fusion of culture with the people in arms had been given true expression . . .

One of the education militiamen in his unit was something of a mystery. He taught grammar and geography, but refused to touch history, which the others found passionately interesting. One day it was revealed that the man was a priest who had fled his parish at the start of the war and had managed to hide out in the unit. It caused a certain commotion amongst the men. The education militiamen decided to take his case as the subject of a lesson, underlining two themes: the ecclesiastical hierarchy's responsibility in siding with the fascist reaction against the people; and that they, personally, held no hatred for this priest. The themes were not received without argument. Not everyone was convinced by a long shot.

—However, the priest's own attitude helped him considerably. As soon as he knew he was discovered, he displayed a willingness to discuss the matter openly and frankly, and his fearlessness won him a certain sympathy. Moreover, like the rest of us, he had been fighting rifle in hand against the enemy. And he went on to say that he believed history was on the side of the poor, not the rich. He came out of it pretty well, indeed freed of the fear with which he had been living. But he would never teach history, claiming that he knew nothing about it . . .

What impressed Núñez most was the profound democracy of the masses which the revolution had initiated. When he thought today of a society without exploiters and exploited, without the mistakes that had been committed in the name of socialism, it was of that democracy he thought.

—The masses in movement, when everything is put at the service of the revolution. As a petty bourgeois, I learnt everything from my contact with the masses during the war. If I am where I am today, in the front line of the struggle,[1] it is because my experience during the war was decisive. Life isn't worth living for anything else. You can only live for the people . . .

Not that the revolution should be idealized. There were mistakes, pettiness, egoism, cowardice, even in the revolution's finest hour at the start when everything had to be improvised, when a worker suddenly found himself the commander of a militia force, when the people were mastering their own destiny. A revolution was not just light but shade too.

—Mud, cowardice, misery, they all exist as well. But it was none of these things that most struck one. A revolution is a process. It is difficult to be a coward when your companions are being brave. Or at least to be one for long. For us marxists, the lesson is never to forget the people and what that people bear within them. That is the source of everything . . .

---

1. A member of the PSUC leadership, he was living in clandestinity in Barcelona at the time of the interview in 1973.

MADRID

In the rear, as at the front, educational expansion and reform – the field in which the republic had achieved most – was being given a new impetus by the revolution. The transformation of traditional attitudes, patterns of awareness laid down long before and which lagged behind the rapid socio-economic change, would come only as a result of new forms of experience opened up by the revolution. Education was a vital area; in the rear, many of the old pedagogical attitudes were being radically altered.[1]

Marisa SOLER was among a group of Madrid teachers who, at her union's call at the start of the war, took over a school of some 300 working-class pupils which a religious order had abandoned. The changes they proposed were not effected without considerable resistance from the children.

—We changed all the textbooks. Under the old system, the girls were taught needlework and prayer; the boys manual trades and prayer. All the textbooks were religious ones – the main one being the catechism . . .

The teachers' major problem as far as teaching was concerned – religion was no longer part of the curriculum – stemmed not from the children but from the fact that not enough new textbooks were being published. Where the real problems began was when they tried to change other practices. For example, under the former regime, the girls had to wear shirts when they took a shower.

—'No one needs anything but soap to wash themselves with,' I said. 'But *señorita*,' they protested. I pointed out that each shower was completely enclosed and that the boys' and girls' showers were separate; they had immediately imagined that the boys would use theirs. Still they were unhappy, the older ones especially. 'You're making us get water all over our bodies which are exposed – and that is a sin.' 'You've been inculcated with the idea of sin and you are unable to tell what is and what is not sinful,' I replied . . .

Another change which aroused the girls' protest was the school's sexual desegregation, the fact that boys and girls were allowed to play together at recreation time. The teachers believed in encouraging a healthy relationship between the sexes, telling the girls that boys weren't their enemies, and the boys that they must not mistreat the girls, for they were all companions.

The showers, desegregation, the absence of religion – all these 'sins' led to increasing trouble from the older girls.

—'You're not believers,' they said to us. Their former teachers had been good, we were not. They used their perfectly understandable affection and admiration for their old teachers to fight the changes we were making. In the end I decided

1. In Catalonia, the CENU (Consell de l'Escola Nova Unificada) carried out a remarkable scholastic programme and displayed an unparalleled political unity in doing so. 'In setting up CENU, agreement was reached that only educational matters – not politics – should be discussed. The PSUC must be given full credit for their loyal cooperation throughout in the organization's work,' in the words of a CNT schoolteacher and CENU president in Sabadell, Ramón CALOPA. Even after the May events (see pp. 374–83), which led to the outlawing of the dissident communist POUM, the POUM vice-president of CENU remained at his post, defended by the communists of the PSUC.

to take a step I would have preferred to avoid. I asked three or four of the oldest girls to come with me to the former directress's office . . .

There she laid out a series of photographs on the table; they were of a woman naked except for black stockings in different poses in front of a mirror. Today the photographs, she thought, might seem laughable but at the time they were distinctly pornographic.

—'Do you recognize this woman?' One of the girls began to cry. 'Yes, it is our directress.' I hadn't wanted to go this far. Another of the girls asked forgiveness, she hadn't known. 'No one knew,' I answered. 'But remember, someone took these photographs. You see, this is the sort of false virtue we have to struggle against in order to reach real virtue' . . .

Most important of all, she felt, was to try by every possible means to prevent the children being traumatized by the war: the boys, in particular, many of whose fathers had gone to the front. She and the other teachers told them that the war was being fought to ensure that in future their fathers always had jobs, that their families would never again go in want. Little by little, both the boys and girls settled down, until – because of the siege – all schools were closed down as the children were evacuated. Later, some schools reopened for children whose parents did not want them to leave.

*

More muted than in Barcelona, a revolution was changing the face of Madrid a few hundred metres behind the front lines. The capital, essentially an administrative centre pre-war, was hardly industrialized: 25,000 metalworkers, engaged almost totally in small workshops, and some 40,000 building workers made up the bulk of the labour force (compared to Catalonia's 200,000 textile workers, 70,000 metalworkers and an equal number of building workers). None the less, an important munitions industry was being built up.

In a reshuffle of the Madrid defence junta some three weeks after its creation on the very eve of the nationalist offensive on the capital, the CNT gave up the department of Information and Propaganda in exchange for War Industry; twenty-four-year-old Lorenzo IÑIGO, secretary of the CNT metalworkers' union, and a member of all three branches of the libertarian movement, set about organizing the engineering industry for the war effort.

From the beginning, he saw, engineering could not continue in small, scattered workshops; it must be concentrated in one place to become efficient, and to be safe from the constant air raids and shelling which were disrupting production.

—We couldn't afford the sort of collectivization they were carrying out in Barcelona, their autonomy in production and administration. Nor could we afford the luxury of carrying on in their sort of commercial spirit. We were living on the front line . . .

He came up with a simple idea: the city's entire metalworking industry would be put into an underground railway tunnel some 7 km long which, at the start of the war, was being built between the Atocha station and the new ministries. He went to see General Miaja who agreed, but said he would have to ask the government in Valencia. The next day Prieto, the socialist leader who as public works minister before the war had planned the tunnel, sent a message asking what madman had come up with the idea.

—'Well, madmen sometimes come up with good ideas,' I said to Miaja. 'If you've no objection, we'll go ahead without waiting for further government permission.' And that's what we did . . .

Technicians managed to make the tunnel waterproof, and arranged an internal layout which gave access for lorries along one side of its length while work bays were laid out on the other. Then came the business of getting the owners to agree to move their shops into the tunnel.

—As a good libertarian, I couldn't simply send armed men to all the workshops and order the machinery to be sent to the tunnel. I called all the owners to a meeting. '*Señores,* we are at war. I need all your machinery for war production. I need you too' . . .

The owners, he told them, would be in charge of their own equipment, as foremen or skilled workers at the head of a team. An inventory of all machinery would be made and their property guaranteed; when the war was over they would be free to remove their equipment. All agreed. Within two months, the capital's entire engineering production was working sixteen hours a day underground, undisrupted by air raids.

Technically and administratively, the 'tunnel' was controlled by IÑIGO's department, which also paid the workers. 'A sort of self-management from above.' For Pedro GOMEZ, a UGT turner, working in the 'tunnel' was like working in a state factory. Production norms came from above, from the workshop committee and the technicians. Work conditions were excellent. Wage differentials existed but they were not large. There were no strikes. Once things were organized, work continued round the clock in three shifts.

—The norms needed no enforcing. If the night shift had produced 300 shells, the day shift would do its utmost to beat it. We never had to stop work for shortage of materials, only for electricity cuts as the war went on. Above us we had six metres of earth: there was no fear of bombing or shelling. There was only one problem – not enough unity at the top. We were united enough on the shop floor, there were no great problems between UGT and CNT workers. But it needed someone to prevent all that bickering and dissent at the top if we were to win the war . . .

One day General Miaja, the defence junta president, refused to sign the weekly wage cheque, alleging that the government in Valencia had ordered him to fund no more war production. IÑIGO set off for Valencia to see Prieto. 'Miaja at that time was a tool of the communists who knew they couldn't get rid of us libertarians without evicting us from war industry.' Prieto assured him the government had given no such order and dictated a message to be sent to Miaja. At the same time he read the report on arms production IÑIGO had taken with him. How was it possible, he asked, for Madrid to produce shells at a unit cost lower than Barcelona or Valencia?

—'For a very simple reason, *señor ministro*. Madrid metalworkers are putting in all the hours needed without overtime.' Prieto asked if we could produce shells for other fronts. I explained that we couldn't produce enough for our own needs yet . . .

Instead, IÑIGO asked Prieto's permission to buy the necessary equipment to produce rifle ammunition, explaining that special groups of militiamen each morning collected spent cartridge cases from the front lines for reconditioning. Madrid could produce only the lead bullets, but insufficient cases were being recovered, and the capital was totally dependent on the government for supplies. He showed the minister a Belgian catalogue and told him that the Catalans were buying such equipment.

—The Catalans were more advanced in arms production than we in Madrid. I had already exchanged 7,000 shells produced in Barcelona for several tons of copper. 'You Catalans are very commercially minded,' I had said to my CNT counterpart. 'I won't sell you this copper, I'll exchange it.' Prieto said the government had no intention of spending a *céntimo* on any machinery for Madrid; if it were purchased, it would be installed in Valencia or Catalonia . . .

The government in Valencia was finding that the defence junta it had left behind in Madrid as a last-ditch measure had become the government of Madrid. There were those in Valencia who thought that Miaja, a popular hero if no politician, was acting as though he were the head of the government of Spain. From his post as sub-secretary of the interior ministry in Valencia, Sócrates GOMEZ, of the JSU, expressed the concern of a sector of the government.

—A certain duality of power arose. Miaja, who was easily manipulated by the communists, interpreted the instructions he received from Valencia with some wilfulness. He had to be severely reprimanded and told to obey instructions . . .

The growing power of the communist party lay behind the concern. The defence of Madrid, the weight of Soviet aid and the Comintern-organized International Brigades which had arrived in the nick of time, allied to the party's determination to organize everything for the war effort and its opposition to pushing forward the socialist (not to speak of the libertarian) revolution, was winning the PCE considerable prestige among those who found the other parties and organizations wanting in clear policies or threatening to their interests. The Madrid defence junta was the only government organ in the Popular Front zone on which the communists had a dominant position. Eventually it was they who provided the government with the pretext for dissolving it.

The junta was riven with internal conflicts mainly between the communists and libertarians. Foreshadowing what would shortly lead to a dramatic confrontation in Barcelona, a communist junta councillor was shot and wounded at a libertarian road block on the outskirts of Madrid. Subsequently, assault guards on the orders of the communist public order councillor disarmed some fifty CNT militants for failing to have arms licences. Finally, in April 1937, Melchor Rodríguez, the anarchist prison director in Madrid, published precise details of torture carried on in unauthorized communist prisons in the capital, and blamed José Cazorla, who had taken over from Santiago Carrillo as public order councillor. Largo Caballero, the prime minister, used the ensuing scandal to reassert the government's authority and dissolve the junta.

IÑIGO recalled the last meeting. Miaja informed the junta councillors of Caballero's decision.

—Carreño España, the left republican representative, looked across the table at Cazorla and said: 'You' – and he used the plural to indicate he meant the communists, not just Cazorla – 'are the Juan Simón of the defence junta.' Juan Simón is a grave-digger who buries his own daughter in a popular Spanish ballad. He was right. Even though the fronts around Madrid were stabilized by then, the junta could have continued to play an important political and moral role in the capital . . .

A role that might have stayed the creeping demoralization that was to set in months later as the rigours of the war's second winter were felt, that might have prevented the tragic events which two years after the junta's dissolution brought the war to an end.

Episodes 5

In hiding

Ever since the uprising in Madrid he had stayed at home, fearing that he might be arrested or sent to the front. Militiamen from the Bellas Artes *checa* had come to the flat with an order to search and arrest. He had denied nothing, having long since made the decision always to tell the truth. Yes, he was a member of the Catholic Youth organization, had been for several years; yes, he had many religious books, but the republic guaranteed freedom of religion. One of the militiamen wanted to arrest him, but another opposed the idea so resolutely that in the end they left to report back to the *checa*. The militiaman who had argued against his arrest was a mechanic who often went to his father's shop for spare parts. While not a member of any party, his father was a businessman sympathetic to the right, while he, Enrique MIRET MAGDALENA, was a university student of chemistry, a 'clerical Catholic' much influenced by the type of christian democracy best represented by Giménez Fernández, the former CEDA agriculture minister. Before the war, he had intended to go abroad to study to become a Jesuit.

One day he was told that a list with his name on it had been found during a militia search of the Jesuit Provincial's house, and he was advised to hide. Angered at the Provincial's folly in keeping such a list, his father agreed he should go into hiding and they set about looking for a place. He fast learnt his first lesson.

—None of the people whom I expected to help was willing to do so, while, out of the blue, the person I least expected gave me shelter: our landlord who lived in the same house. After a month things became too difficult for him and I had to find another place. Once again, a woman I didn't know, a friend of a friend, helped. She took me to the Cuban embassy where she knew the porter, going to the extreme of accompanying me in person, which was risky since I had no papers if we were stopped in the street . . .

After three weeks in the Cuban embassy, all those who had not been given formal permission to seek refuge there were thrown out. Given shelter by another acquaintance, he was finally able to get himself accepted at a building which the Paraguayan embassy had taken over. It was March 1937, and he was to remain there for two years until the war's end.

The conditions in the building were primitive. Six refugees slept on mattresses on the floor of his bug-infested room which was about 15 foot square; in the daytime, they rolled up the mattresses to make a bit more room and lived in the corridors. They never saw daylight since the blinds were perpetually drawn so that no one could see in from the street and discover how many were sheltering there. They had always to talk in whispers so that the militiamen on duty outside couldn't hear. There was no heating and, because food was so scarce, they suffered from the cold. At Christmas 1937, their meals consisted of sugarless barley coffee for breakfast; a bowl of hot water spiced with red pepper and a few grains of rice, with a piece of bread about one centimetre thick at noon, and the same in the evening.

—We calculated that our total daily intake was under 600 calories. There were fifty or sixty of us, but the embassy applied for only twenty-five ration-cards. Of the rations received, the *chargé d'affaires*' mother-in-law sold half on the black market and kept the proceeds. Some managed well enough on the diet, but others preferred to leave the embassy and run the risks outside rather than continue on so little food . . .

The majority of the refugees were conservative Catholics and monarchists, with a handful of falangists and Carlists. As a clerical Catholic, he had believed the counsels the clergy had been giving and had sympathized with the military uprising. The problem began when he started to live in the embassy with people who said they thought as he did. The first thing he noticed was that the most religious among them were also the most conservative, in everything from religion to politics.

—On the other hand, the majority didn't give a hang about the church or Catholicism. They were Catholics, but their Catholicism was a sort of social security for the other life. I began to feel like a fish out of water. I had never been able to understand why so many Catholics equated the monarchy with their faith. I felt myself a republican. But at the same time, the republic was anti-clerical, I felt. Now, in the embassy, I came to see that the clergy had practised a great deception on us by asserting that to be Catholic meant to be conservative, and anti-Catholic to be on the left. Even the republic's anti-clericalism came to seem healthy when I viewed the people around me . . .

They were concerned, he saw, with only one thing: revenge. Their fantasies, articulated day after day – 'for talking was an endemic disease' – revolved about what they would do when they got out of this situation: 'kill, kill, kill – all the workers, all the republicans, all the reds.' Everything that smacked of social progress was automatically condemned; yet they had no religious grounds, as far as he observed, on which they could base such attitudes.

Among the refugees was a priest in his forties, an exemplary man who at 5 a.m. daily celebrated mass in secret with only MIRET MAGDALENA present. It made him think of the catacombs, of the authentic simple mass, an experience he would never forget. But the other refugees didn't like the priest.

—It was curious, those clerical Spaniards seemed at heart to harbour a certain anti-clerical resentment. They showed it plainly in the embassy by their treatment of the priest. When they saw that sexual jokes and stories upset him they made a point of telling them in front of him; they reserved their vulgar remarks for him and in general treated him with disrespect.

Since I had to remain in the embassy with these people, I decided that I would hold staunchly to my Catholic principles but without arguing with anyone. That, too, had a curious result: I was respected by the others because they saw that my conviction was absolute, and this in turn had tangible advantages. My suitcase was the only one from which nothing was ever stolen. There was no solidarity whatsoever, even amongst people whose lives were in danger. The most ferocious egoism was unleashed in that place; frequently I asked myself what could religion mean to them when each thought only of saving himself and displayed not the slightest concern for his neighbour . . .

Some of the refugees maintained they had contacts with the fifth column, but MIRET MAGDALENA suspected it was all talk. The republicans, however, infiltrated *agents provocateurs* into the embassy. A man who had 'taken refuge' put it about, little by little, that some militiamen were in his confidence and that it was possible to escape by paying a certain sum.

—Without attempting to check up on what the man said, people put their names down on a list, so great was the desire to escape to the other side. The first five to leave agreed that once they reached the nationalist zone they would arrange for the radio to give a certain password. It never came. Later we learnt that they had gone through the famous 'tunnel of death'; this was supposed to be a secret tunnel in Carabanchel which led from the republican to the nationalist lines. In fact it was a trap. Such was the fear in the embassy that no one dared confront the man whom we were all convinced was a republican agent; the decision was taken simply to expel him . . .

As many as 20,000 people were estimated to have taken refuge in Madrid embassies at one time or another, especially in the first months of the war. Only some 10 per cent to 15 per cent of these remained by the end of the war. Many, although by no means all who wished to, were evacuated. Some, like David JATO, falangist student union leader, left for safer refuges when the nationalist failure to capture Madrid made it evident that the war was going to continue for months, if not years. Looking back on it, he thought, the idea of frontally attacking a city of 1 million inhabitants with a shock force of only a few thousand troops was a complete folly. Unless there was a deeper reason.

—From what Franco said after the war, it may well be that he had come to the conclusion that a rapid end to the war would leave half the country, half the population with its political ideals intact. A civil war, he said, was quite different from an international war. The latter ends with the conquest of enemy territory; but in a civil war military occupation of enemy territory is not the final goal . . .

One of the several buildings taken over by the Finnish embassy in which JATO had taken refuge was forced to open to republican police and the refugees were arrested. This hastened JATO's determination to leave; he got out thanks to his family's friendship with a Frenchman with whom he went to live. Embassies issued their nationals with a document to post on their doors.

—Once the terrible days of November and December 1936 were over, these documents proved effective. The two worst periods of assassinations were from July to September and November to December. After that, though never totally ended, their numbers were very considerably reduced . . .

He got hold of false documents showing he was sixteen instead of nineteen; he had always looked younger than his age. As time went on it became increasingly easy to get hold of false papers.

—As the repression eased up, a sort of breach opened in the republican administration, and all sorts of things became possible. There was another reason. Within six months of the start of the war the majority of the best militants in the red zone were dead. They had been the first to go to the fronts, the first to be killed. Those who remained in the rearguard were not, ideologically speaking, the same men . . .

Episodes 6

Liberation

María Carmen QUERO, aged nine, peered through a crack in the window of the Málaga clinic, where, for nearly six months, she had been hiding. It was the morning of 8 February 1937. In the street she saw two Moors crouching, ready to shoot at the top-floor windows. Then a red and gold flag appeared on the balcony opposite. 'Ay, mama, there it is!' she shouted. They flung open the shutters and breathed in the fresh air. In the street below they saw people embracing. Tanks began to roll by, bearing soldiers in plumed hats who carried olive branches. They were singing a beautiful song.

—'Who are these people, mama?' 'I don't know,' she replied, but then suddenly she said: 'Italians!' The streets were full of blue shirts and people giving the fascist salute. Where had so many falangists come from all of a sudden? . . .

The night before they had heard people shouting in the streets, children crying, the sound of mules, oxen, carts. Entire villages from the surrounding countryside appeared to be pouring through the city along the only escape road to Almería. 'It was like the exodus of the Jews from Egypt.' Why were they fleeing, her mother, doña Pepa, asked sadly.

Pepa LOPEZ came from one of those villages herself. Her husband, a lawyer and former CEDA parliamentary deputy, had gone into hiding as soon as they heard the mob advancing towards their house on the day the war started. A couple of minutes later, with an instinct born of long years lived close to the peasants, she was throwing off her *señora*'s dress and slipping on an old smock. She replaced her shoes with a pair of hemp sandals, grabbed three bracelets which she had inherited from her mother and put them in a basket under a pile of tomatoes, pimentos and other vegetables. Holding on to her children, she hurried from the house looking like a street-seller.

—Once I got out into the street I ran to a cousin's house. From there I saw the furniture being dragged out of our house and burnt in the street. My cousin was frightened. Within twenty-four hours we had to look for another place . . .

—One after another of our relatives began to fail us, recalled María Carmen. Their faces turned white when we asked them for shelter. There came a moment when no one would take us in. That was the saddest experience of my life . . .

After wandering the streets in shirt-sleeves and a beret, her father had been given shelter by a medical assistant. He was on the point of turning himself in, hoping friends on the left would come to his help. The assistant's daughter wouldn't let him carry out his plan and arranged for her fiancé's family to shelter him. 'Rejected by relatives, he was saved by people he didn't know . . . '

Doña Pepa moved to a poor civil guard's house near the women's prison. The chauffeur and maid accompanied her. One day the porter at their house managed to smuggle out some of her clothes, amongst them a new tricorne hat resembling a civil guard's. As soon as she saw it she went to the window and threw it out.

—'But mama, your hat!' I cried. 'Bah, a hat,' she replied sternly. I watched it spinning through the air. With it, for me, vanished a whole epoch. A hat had gone; it summoned up everything . . .

A few days later their chauffeur warned them that a neighbour had recognized María Carmen. They had to move again. Their last resort, an aunt on the outskirts of the city, refused them. She suggested that doña Pepa try to get into a clinic run by an outstanding gynaecologist, Dr José Gálvez. 'A devout, right-wing Catholic, a saint revered by all social classes in Málaga', he took her in on condition that she contact none of her family.[1] María Carmen was allowed to join her. She slept on a sofa in her mother's room. The clinic was full of re-

1. Dr Gálvez's two daughters were married to men who had become famous as nationalist aviators: Joaquín García Morato and Carlos de Haya. The latter's wife was being held prisoner in the city. She was later exchanged for Arthur Koestler who was captured when Málaga fell to the nationalists.

fugees: the ancient prioress of a Carmelite convent who had arrived in her full nun's habit after the convent was burned; an archbishop's sister, a number of politicians' wives, priests whom no one saw.

María Carmen got up praying and went to bed praying; she had never prayed so much in her life. She prayed for her aunt and her niece whom she read in the paper had been arrested. The niece had belonged to the JAP. Every time there was an air raid the reds took out prisoners and shot them. One day – she later learnt – her aunt was being tied up ready to be taken out when someone shouted from the door: 'That's enough for today.'

María Carmen grew pale; her mother complained she wasn't getting enough exercise. Dr Gálvez pulled a piece of string out of his pocket: 'Skip with this twenty times a day and you'll get exercise,' he said in his kindly voice. The windows were permanently shuttered to prevent anyone seeing in.

One day they heard shouts in the street. The nursing nuns told everyone to go down to the basement. Outside the shouts grew closer, louder. 'Let's go in and get them!' María Carmen was old enough to know what that meant.

—I felt at that moment as though I had been born only to die. We all knelt and prayed. Even Dr Gálvez thought the reds were going to break in. 'As long as it doesn't hurt too much,' I said to myself . . .

The shrieks were the same as those of the mob which burnt houses on the first day of war, doña Pepa recalled. 'Have you ever heard that sound? No? Well, it's better not – ' The women were worse than the men. This war was terrible, a war between lower and upper classes was much worse than a war between nations. She supported the army's desire to restore order. But at the same time she had to admit that for the lower classes it was an army of occupation.

—And when you provoke the masses – sssh – that's when things become dangerous. Passions overrun, they can't be stemmed. Frightening things happen. The lower classes hated those who had power; don't they always when there is such inequality? . . .

The shrieking – could it be? – was growing fainter, the mob was moving away. Finding it hard to believe they rose from their knees.

Only later did they learn what had happened. A mother and son had been dragged through the streets. The mother, an old woman, wore a metal truss for her hernia; someone had taken it for a secret radio. A crowd gathered. As a result of the manhandling the old woman had died.

The clinic faced the cathedral. Doña Pepa saw men bringing out religious statues and dumping them into a lorry. The heads appeared to have been split by an axe. She was reminded of the church burnings of May 1931, a month after the proclamation of the republic. Within a short while, the people who had taken part in the burnings were bringing holy images out in procession or standing by and applauding as they passed. 'How do you explain that? *¡Dios mío!* The people who destroy holy images kiss them – '

Refugees from the villages began to live in the cathedral. In each corner María

Carmen could see a family cooking over a fire, sleeping on mattresses, defecating in the Patio de los Naranjos.

—At night all the lights were on and there was a thick fog inside. I saw people sitting in the pulpit smoking and talking as though they were in a club. People died in there and were brought out in coffins . . .

One day the maid who made the bed and cleaned the room arrived in a terrible state. 'They're coming, and they're killing as they come . . . ' 'Don't be stupid,' doña Pepa replied, 'they don't kill anyone who hasn't committed a crime.' Later, during the day they heard cannon fire. The front was crumbling fast. They were frightened, they didn't know how things would end. 'Yes, I know,' Dr Gálvez said to doña Pepa, 'it's our land, the land we love – '

None of the feared last-minute resistance by stubborn or anguished defenders occurred. Instead, the latter escaped as best they could. Spearheaded by Italian tanks, the direct offensive on the city lasted barely three days: its capture at very little cost gave the nationalists their first Mediterranean port and wiped out an important Popular Front territory in the south. The repercussions of the loss were felt at the highest levels. Not yet strong enough to attack the prime minister, Largo Caballero, directly, the communist party attacked General Asensio, his secretary of war. The general was dismissed.

María Carmen stepped on to the pavement. Her feet felt as if they had gone dead, the pavement seemed like cork. She felt herself sinking into it. Doña Pepa pulled her by the hand. 'Come on, child, we're going to see your father.'

A few minutes earlier a tall and beautiful lady had arrived at the clinic with her son. She told doña Pepa that her husband was safe in her house. They set off. In the reception room, at the top of a marble staircase, stood a man with a beard, wearing a beret and a leather jacket. He looked like a militiaman, María Carmen thought.

—Soon our problems began. My father said he felt depressed at being left alive. Almost all his political acquaintances had been assassinated. Then people came to ask him to make accusations against left-wingers. The purge was under way. He refused. We began to hear of the courts martial, the executions. Every day there were hundreds of cases. 'Twenty death sentences,' my father would exclaim. 'What is happening?' He was a criminal lawyer. Before the war when he had a death sentence on his hands he wouldn't be able to eat or sleep. 'Don't tell me about the courts martial, they make my blood freeze,' he said.

Like everyone of my age, my youth seems to have been nothing but disaster and violence, tragedy and horror: sometimes on account of the reds, other times because of the whites . . .

The proscription in Málaga was ferocious. The Italian government ordered its ambassador to take up the matter directly with its Spanish nationalist ally as 'a moral question affecting the reputation of both Spain and Italy'. In a radio broadcast a month after the city's capture, General Queipo de Llano made no bones about it. 'We are unfortunate enough to be forced to shoot plenty of people in Málaga, but all after trial by court martial . . . It must be borne in mind that those who are condemned to death are inexorably executed because we do not intend to imitate those weak governments of 1934!'[1]

Episodes 7

Escape

Two friars sat in the train taking them through the Andalusian countryside. One of them, the superior of the missionary community for the Holy Land and Morocco, had made the trip to Granada especially. Being an important churchman, he had had no difficulty in securing the necessary passes and safe conducts, including one from General Queipo de Llano personally, to make the trip. It might have surprised the nationalist authorities if they had seen the spare friar's habit the superior was carrying in his bags and which, on his arrival in Granada, he delivered to a house in the centre of the city. Their surprise would have been greater still had they known that, sitting beside him in the train, disguised in the habit, was the twenty-eight-year-old socialist schoolteacher and lawyer he had travelled through half Andalusia to rescue from the city which had already witnessed the assassination of its most distinguished son, García Lorca.

It was the second time that a churchman had saved Dionisio VENEGAS since the military uprising in Granada. A moderate socialist, member of the UGT schoolteachers' union, he had very rapidly learnt of the repression being carried out against his colleagues. One day his mother-in-law crossed the street to the cathedral where she spoke to a priest.

—A saint of a man, that don Francisco. At dawn the following day I went across the Gran Vía to the cathedral where he hid me in one of the towers. Every day my wife brought food in a basket which she left at the bottom of the stairs. I remained hidden there five weeks . . .

Desperate to have someone to talk to, he sent the priest a message; the latter replied that he was unable to visit him because it was too dangerous: another priest was one of the major instigators of the executions that were taking place in Granada and which were aimed in particular at intellectuals.

One day his sister arrived and told him that the superior of the Franciscan order from his home town of Chipiona, near Cádiz, had come to take him away. In the basket she brought was the friar's habit, and he put it on with only a pair of pyjamas underneath. Then he went out into the cathedral precincts where a street photographer was brought to take a picture of him. This was attached to a paper which the superior had with him and which he now took to the military authorities to demand a pass for this lay-brother he had come to fetch.

None of this might have happened had it not been for the convent burnings

1. Broadcast on Seville radio (7 March 1937).

of May 1931, which had made such a disastrous impact on Catholic opinion.[1] A liberal republican, VENEGAS's father, who was head lighthouse keeper in Chipiona, had gone to the convent to offer refuge to the friars in his official residence. Although the offer had not been needed, the superior, Fray Agustín Zuluaga, had never forgotten the gesture. When VENEGAS's father had vainly attempted to discover his son's fate after the uprising – the new civil governor of Granada, Valdés, had replied to an inquiry from his opposite number in Cádiz: 'whereabouts unknown, probably with the enemy' – the superior had immediately offered to set out to find him.

—The first night we spent in a convent en route. The superior of the order there asked Fray Agustín who I was. 'Oh, he's a red lay-brother I'm taking back with me,' I heard him reply to my horror. Both of them laughed. When I remonstrated with him he replied I had nothing to fear, I was in his territory now and everything was peaceful. I wasn't so sure: on the train I had seen a falangist guard, a man I had known since childhood, and he looked at me hard and I think recognized me, although he didn't say anything . . .

Despite his fear, they reached the small seaside resort of Chipiona safely. VENEGAS was given a cell in the convent while he thought out his next move. He and a couple of friars who had managed to escape from Málaga, still in the Popular Front zone, consoled each other. Victims of circumstances, they had – on both sides – been fortunate enough to escape. It was thought unwise that he should suddenly reappear in the town – even to see his father – until precautions had been taken. He persuaded the superior to speak to the new civil governor of Cádiz, Eduardo Valera Valverde. A retired cavalry officer, the latter had been civil governor of Seville at the time of Sanjurjo's abortive rising in 1932 and had been tried for his alleged failure to put down the rising. Acquitted, he retired to Chipiona where he had come to know VENEGAS whom he treated like a son.

The superior returned with a message from Valera saying everything was all right and handed him a package containing a falange uniform and blue shirt. He put it on and asked the superior to send for his father. The latter was overwhelmed with joy. He spent a couple of days at home and then appeared in the streets as a fully fledged falangist, evading as best he could the constant questions, for people were astonished at his sudden return in the guise of a falangist. The situation did not seem entirely safe, and Valera Valverde suggested he go to Cádiz where he would be a member of the civil governor's family. He gave the young man a vague job as his private secretary, but he had no real work. For five months, until the end of February 1937, he amused himself in Cádiz.

A month earlier, Córdoba newspapers announced in rapid succession that Major Ibáñez – don Bruno – the public order chief in Córdoba, had been promoted to civil governor of the city. Only a short time elapsed before another announcement said he was being replaced by Eduardo Valera Valverde.

—Queipo de Llano came to Cádiz and told Valera Valverde that don Bruno had been such a disaster that Valverde had to take over. He didn't want to go, but

1. See Points of Rupture, B.

he had no choice. I went with him. In Córdoba everything continued without problem until the summer of 1937 when suddenly the tranquillity was shattered. I could see things were going on in the civil government building that I didn't understand . . .

For some time, without his knowledge, the authorities in Granada had been summoning Valera Valverde to hand him over; the latter had repeatedly refused, had even sent his private secretary, chief of the Cádiz Falange, to Granada to find out what was happening. The latter returned without a satisfactory answer. Finally, the civil governor received a formal order to hand him over. 'Everything will be all right,' he told him, 'I shall do everything necessary to protect you.' Unable personally to accompany VENEGAS to Granada, he sent his private secretary with him. For two or three days in Granada, lodged in a comfortable hotel next to the Alhambra, he waited while the secretary had talks with Pelayo, don Bruno's equivalent, who assured him that VENEGAS would probably have to be expelled from Granada for a year but nothing worse.

—That suited me; I was happy to go to Seville where I could practise law. We went to the military commandant's office to confirm the arrangement. I waited several hours while the secretary talked to the commandant. When he came out he told me he was sorry, the commandant refused to accept the arrangement. I was to be arrested immediately and court-martialled . . .

He was clapped in gaol. In October 1937, he was court-martialled with twenty others, accused of aiding the rebellion (i.e., defending the legally constituted republican government), of defending lay education, of having exercised influence on the republican civil governor of Granada and of being a mason. He was sentenced to life imprisonment.

—Not one of the accusations was true. I was not a mason – as the special tribunal for the repression of masonry and communism which they set up later recognized; I had never been inside the civil government building, let alone influenced the governor; the latter had refused to distribute arms to the people on 18 July and I had certainly not taken part in any resistance to the military uprising. No, I was the victim of some private grudge by someone I have never been able to identify . . .

At the end of the war his sentence was reduced to twelve years; and he was released in 1941, having served four.

CORDOBA

Sacked as public order chief after four months in office; sacked as civil governor barely a month after his appointment, Major Bruno Ibáñez was given command of the 18th *tercio* of the *guardia civil* in Córdoba. Barely a week passed before he was relieved of his command.

—People in bars openly celebrated the fact that he had gone, even in front of the police. They believed he had been shot, which wasn't true, recalled a local baker, Juan POSADAS. The people said that if he had been allowed to stay he would have had all Córdoba shot. So great was the fear that people fled the city every night – there wouldn't have been anyone left to work if it had gone on much longer . . .

—Once the dirty work had been done, they got rid of him, thought Roberto SOLIS, a Catholic law student. The executioner is only useful for a certain length of time . . .

Francisco PARTALOA, the Madrid public prosecutor whose arrival in the nationalist zone from France had nearly cost him his life, was told by Queipo de Llano that he had been responsible for sacking the infamous major.

—He told me personally that when he found out what don Bruno had been doing he wanted not just to sack him but to give Cordobans the satisfaction of having him shot publicly in Las Tendillas – the city's main square. But General Mola demanded his services in the north. Córdoba was lucky to be rid of him; Eduardo Valera Valverde, his successor as civil governor, was a humane man . . .

. . . The good National-Syndicalist state rests on the family. It will be strong if the woman at home is healthy, fecund, hard-working and happy, with the windows of her home and soul open to the sweet imperial dawn that the sun of the Falange is bringing us.

Azul (Editorial on the 2nd national council of the women's section of the Falange, February 1938)

May no home be without light nor any worker without bread

Francisco Franco

What we shall never do is put women in competition with men because women will never succeed in equalling men; if they try, women will lose the elegance and grace necessary for a life together with men . . .

Pilar Primo de Rivera (Opening speech to national council of the women's section of the Falange, February 1938)

ONE FATHERLAND, ONE STATE, ONE CAUDILLO

The Margaritas of Tafalla

Solemnly promise on the Sacred Heart of Jesus

1. To observe modesty in dress: long sleeves, high necks, skirts to the ankle, blouses full at the chest.
2. To read no novels, newspapers or magazines, to go to no cinema or theatre, without ecclesiastical licence.
3. Neither publicly nor in private to dance dances of this century but to study and learn the old dances of Navarre and Spain.
4. Not to wear makeup as long as the war lasts.

Long live Christ the King! Long live Spain!

Spring 1937

While in the ideological perspectives of the nationalist zone women were 'complementary' to men, seeking 'neither votes nor equality of rights but rather equality of sacrifices and duties', they were participating fully in the war effort. The latter had 'shaken Spanish woman from her apparent civic lethargy in the home and thrown her to work in hospitals, clothing workshops and, above all, in the marvellous *Auxilio Social*,' commented a falangist newspaper.[1]

Auxilio Social (Social Aid) began in Valladolid and was arguably the most important practical social work undertaken by the Falange during the war. In the view of Dionisio RIDRUEJO, poet and orator who had been promoted from Segovia to chief of the Falange in Valladolid, *Auxilio Social* illustrated the idealism and politicization that was taking place in the nationalist zone.

—Political involvement reached its highest level in recent Spanish history in both zones during the war. People were willing to volunteer for self-sacrificing work. Those who started *Auxilio Social*, which was first called Winter Aid and was an exact copy, down to the emblem, of the Nazi organization of the same name, demonstrated great idealism. The immediate cause of its creation in Valladolid by Onésimo Redondo's widow was the enormous number of fatherless children due to the repression . . .

The first thing the new organization did was to open public dining halls for needy children where they received not only food but clothing and medicine. The example soon spread from Valladolid to other provinces. Financing followed the German model: weekly collections, money boxes, flags. Gradually, the organization created family-style orphanages where young girls were put in charge of a group of young children, usually not exceeding fifteen, who lived as a family in a house.

—The basic concept underlying the organization was to substitute public solidarity for public charity; and while the organization remained fairly small and there was this intense sense of public-spiritedness, it worked well. Later things changed . . .

The organization cared for the old as well as children. Within a year of its foundation, it was feeding more than 4,000 young and old in Córdoba province daily.

The Carlist Margaritas ran a hospital and front lines' organization. Indicative of the tension within the nationalist zone as to the aims and political outcome of the war, some of its leaders felt that not enough attention was given to their organization.

—The women's section of the Falange was given every sort of help to develop and expand, observed Dolores BALEZTENA, head of the Pamplona Margaritas. We wanted to play a positive role in the post-war. Our suspicion that we were

1. *Azul* (Córdoba, 9 January 1938).

deliberately held down proved justified in the end. We were tolerated only while the war lasted . . .

But as long as it lasted there was important work to be done. Carmen GARCIA-FALCES, a Margarita and Pamplona bakery worker, now found herself doing unpaid overtime every day. Not only was there more bread to be baked for the front, but after work she went to make bandages because, like so many other things needed for the war, these were in short supply.

—I don't know how we won the war with all the shortages we suffered from. Girls went to make hand-grenades in a small family foundry which, before the war, produced agricultural implements. The manufacture of the grenades was simply improvised by a few people, and the girls worked there in their spare time without pay. Everyone did everything necessary for the war effort without thinking of rewards . . .

The evidence of war was soon visible in the streets of Pamplona, as of every other city, which filled with war-wounded: men without legs, arms, blind. They were youths of her own age, so many of them people she knew. It was horrible; and yet mothers didn't often cry at the death of their sons.

—The war was a Crusade; their sons had gone to Heaven and that was their consolation. '*Chica*, how fortunate you are, you already have a son in heaven,' was a remark one often heard . . .

In the hospital where Dolores BALEZTENA worked a nurse told her she had never seen anyone die with the faith and resignation of the *requetés*.

—'One day as I was passing by the bed of a gravely wounded man,' she told me, 'he called and, groaning with pain, asked me to stretch out his arms in the shape of a cross. I did so, thinking that it relieved his pain. "No, sister, it's not for that," he replied. "It's because I want to die like Christ on the Cross" ' . . .

Dolores BALEZTENA used to accompany the war-wounded home sometimes when they were released from hospital. So many of them who had volunteered, she saw, were poor, owned nothing but 'the air they breathed and the sun that shone on them'. She remembered one in particular. He had lost an arm. When they reached his house, a very poor place, his mother could hardly contain her tears; his father looked at him sadly, thinking that he could no longer help with the farm work.

—'Well, haven't I got another arm to help you with?' the wounded man asked. And he went out to feed the chickens. The poorer the home, the greater the sacrifice, it seemed to me. If communism had triumphed, these anonymous heroes would have lost nothing; indeed, materially, they would have gained. The fatherland, for which this *requeté* had given his arm and so many had given their lives, owed him no more than a tiny plot of land from which, by hard work, he was able to earn his daily living. But spiritually, he would have lost everything, and it was for this – to defend his religious beliefs, his ideals – that he had gone to war.

How well I remember another war-wounded, a man whose leg had been amputated, and who said to me in the hospital where I was nursing him: 'If it hadn't been for God, we wouldn't have gone' . . .

*

A new state was being consciously formed in the nationalist zone. Designed to carry the class war to its ultimate consequences, this new state was to be a better instrument than the old for waging a civil war. Its very creation gave a revolutionary impulse to the counter-revolution. A 'new life' was under way.

—All the normal routines had been overturned by the war; but a sense of impermanence, provisionality, arose also because everyone was aware – an awareness encouraged by the regime – that a new life, a new country, a total change was being made, recalled Paulino AGUIRRE, the liberal philosophy student. To a certain extent, this newness corresponded to reality: the right had broken with the legitimate regime and was inventing a new order which, for being new, was that much more fragile. The newness didn't give one freedom – that would be too noble a word; but it gave one the feeling of living within a process of creation, and the consequent sensation of social elasticity which people could take advantage of. Of course, there was a harshness; the political colouring was falangist. But even this harshness was somehow exterior: the ornamental and show aspects of fascism which the regime adopted . . .

The sense of participating in, experiencing the creation of a new social structure which was to resolve the class conflicts of the past five years brought satisfaction to the middle class. Life in the rearguard was peaceful and, most important, there was no notable shortage of food. An exalted patriotism, a religious fervour, an ardent conviction that the war would be won, maintained middle-class morale. The failure to take Madrid was recorded but shrugged off, the Italian defeat at Guadalajara – last of the series of attempts to encircle Madrid in March 1937 – laughed off. Málaga had been captured meanwhile; the campaign was starting to take the north.

—Everyone had an absolutely blind faith in Franco's leadership; there were hard battles for sure, but people never lost faith in the final victory. The other side seemed to have all the advantages, the big cities, industry, the main ports, the gold reserves. But they lacked our victory morale; we were always sure we would win, reflected Tomás BULNES, Onésimo Redondo's collaborator in the sugar-beet growers' union in Valladolid . . .

Even the 'defeated' sometimes felt relief. A Málaga chemist, Isidro ANTUÑA, a lifelong republican, member of the radical socialist party and a mason, felt that after the nationalist conquest life returned to normal again.

—What do I mean by normal? That anyone could do what he wanted as long as he didn't say anything which gave offence to the authorities. That was the thing: *silence*. Thoughts were best kept to oneself. Apart from that, no trouble at all. You could do what you wanted. After the chaos before the war, after the fearful domination of the reds for seven months during the war, it was a relief. I had always been more frightened of a proletarian revolution than of a military uprising which I had known for years was bound to happen . . .

The *silence* covered many things, especially in Málaga where the nationalist repression reached new levels of ferocity. But for those participating in the creation of the new state, the apparent 'elasticity' of the social structures offered revolutionary opportunities.

Militancies 10

DIONISIO RIDRUEJO

Falangist leader

Having found in the falangist variant of fascism a solution to his personal situation, he was determined to help lay the bases of the falangist revolution. Young, dynamic, a powerful orator and poet – he had written a stanza of the Falange anthem *Cara al Sol* – his rapid promotion to the leadership of the Valladolid Falange put him in a position to make the attempt. The key, he believed, was the falangist syndicalist principles. These meant organizing the business firm or enterprise *syndically*: the managerial, technical and labour sides must form a single community which would be hierarchically structured according to the functions of each, not on the principle of ownership or non-ownership. His interpretation of the Falange's corporative syndicalism, he knew, was not widely accepted; corporative, or vertical, syndicalism, could mean the subjection of the workers to the bosses, or the subjection of managers, technicians and workers to the superior economic interests of the nation as a whole.

—In truth, I had to invent a large measure of these ideas, since they were more implicit than explicit in Falange ideology. It was only in the second phase of José Antonio Primo de Rivera's thinking that syndicalism had been mentioned as a form of self-management of the economy, and it had been worked out fully only in regard to the land. In this phase, José Antonio was striving to go beyond Mussolini-type fascism of a corporative state modelled on Catholic thinking, to discover a form in which traditional Spanish utopian syndicalism could be used to collectivize the economy. I understood his thinking to mean that the economy must be run by a vast federation of trade unions representing the different branches of production which would lead to self-managing industries within a planned economy . . .

Primo de Rivera, son of the former dictator, believed that the Italian and German models could not transcend their countries' personal dictatorships. Fascism would have to be made anew in each country.

—José Antonio was never completely at ease in his role as a fascist leader; he lacked the high degree of resentment which marked petty bourgeois fascist leaders. He was a rather shy man at heart who entered politics to defend his father's memory, for he felt that the dictator had been betrayed by his own class, the upper class. While very critical of the latter, José Antonio knew only too well that, in as far as his own class wanted a domesticated fascism, he was in some respects its instrument. This made him all the more hostile to it. At the same time, he was attracted by the parliamentary system and believed that the British Empire was magnificent. He always had a copy of Kipling's *If* on his table. But as Spain could not be a parliamentary imperialist nation, he found himself advocating a new solution . . .

Though critical of Italian fascism and Nazism, Primo de Rivera was clearly a fascist.[1] Indeed though few would admit it today, all falangists had felt themselves fascists, had been attracted to politics by fascist models.

—We spoke like fascists, saluted like fascists, wore fascist uniforms and aspired to fascist ideals. At the same time, we believed that fascism as it existed was an excessively limited type of nationalist reaction to the situation which had arisen from the end of the First World War, and was not a sufficiently substantive doctrine to become the third force between an outworn liberalism and an unacceptable marxism . . .

It was as this third force that Falangism had attracted him, solved his personal contradiction. Born in a small Castilian town, he had received a 'traditional Catholic, patriotic upbringing'. He was the only male in his family, his father having died. His mother lived on income and he grew up without a firm idea of the relationship between money and work. At home, they received few newspapers and he was not well-informed. 'In short, I came from what I call the "traditional class".'[2]

Aged eighteen when the republic was proclaimed, his personal crisis started when he went to the university at the Escorial run by Augustinians. A small but lively socialist group, composed mainly of building workers, existed amidst a generally conservative and Catholic community, and he began to feel himself attracted to socialism. At the same time, he had religious reservations about being unambiguously committed to the left. The fact that large sectors of the left were violently hostile to the church, engaging in polemics which he found unnecessarily crude, influenced him and, he believed, great numbers of the petty bourgeoisie. Though not uncritical he remained convinced of the validity of traditional Catholicism.

Ill at ease in this contradictory situation, caught between a nonconformist social posture and traditionalism, his crisis was ended, his problem solved, when the Falange came on the scene.

—You could be a revolutionary and still be a conservative, a nonconformist and a conformist. There was no need to reject your traditional upbringing, especially nationalism. Indeed, the latter formed part of the new equation: the diminished state of Spanish society, the poverty of large sectors of its inhabitants went hand in hand with the loss of Spain's power as a nation. The fact that Spain

1. It is now known that from early 1934, Primo de Rivera was financed to the tune of 50,000 lire (the equivalent of $2,600 or £530) a month by Mussolini. See M. Gallo, *Spain under Franco* (London, 1973), pp. 48–9; Angel Viñas, *La Alemania nazi y el 18 de julio*, pp. 168, 500–501.

2. For his description of the provincial petty bourgeoisie, see Points of Rupture, B.

was a poor, semi-industrialized country, dominated by foreign – especially British and French – capital was in large part the cause . . .

He found himself accepting the critical categories of fascism. The latter he understood as the riposte of those countries defeated in the First World War or dissatisfied with the colonial carve-up which that war had consolidated. British national imperialism had shown these countries that there was an equivalence between internal prosperity and colonial expansion. In other words, the metropolitan proletariat could be satisfied at the expense of a colonial proletariat. The other reasons were obvious: the bourgeoisie's reaction to the Soviet revolution and the international capitalist crisis of 1929; and also, in his view, a sort of 'dogmatic contagion of a Bolshevik thesis, namely that revolutions were the work of a minority substituting for the masses'.

—I accepted all these uncritically. Only an enlightened minority can transform the country; a proletarian revolution destroys the traditional elements of a society, cuts the latter off from its own history. Only territorial expansion can provide the conditions which will produce general prosperity in the metropolitan country, thus reducing class differences and finally eliminating the class struggle . . . [1]

Once in the Falange, he felt himself on the extreme left of the movement. This motivated his concern for implementing the falangist revolution during the war. The countryside concerned him most – it was also where Primo de Rivera had most systematically worked out his ideas in terms of creating large cooperatives of smallholders. The Falange defended small owners, whether industrial, agricultural or artisanal, believing that this form of ownership provided incentives which were otherwise unobtainable. However, his revolutionary attempt was not helped by the Falange's rapid growth from some 75,000 members at the outbreak to several hundred thousand within a few months and close on 1 million by the end of the war. The newcomers who joined en masse were right-wingers.

—Falangists like myself with more ideological commitment began to favour the entry of left-wingers into the movement. Within the nationalist camp, the Falange after all represented the most left-wing posture possible. For sectors of the previously non-unionized proletariat – large numbers of the Castilian day-labourers, for example – the Falange was an acceptable solution. For the hostile there was a powerful initial argument for joining: the repression. In the Falange a man had a chance: he was either accepted or shot.

Cases of left-wingers joining became so notorious that the right called the Falange the FAIlange. Firstly because our flag was the same red and black;

1. 'We didn't believe that Spain could in fact expand territorially since the colonial carve-up had already been made, and what Spain might now get was hardly likely to be economically profitable. Spain had lost money for long enough in Morocco. In consequence, the demands for territorial expansion – in North Africa and the return of Gibraltar – were largely rhetorical, although great emotional rallying cries. In this, the Falange differentiated itself from Italian fascism with its clearly defined policy of territorial expansion; it differentiated itself from Nazism by having no racist policies which would, in a country as racially mixed and as Catholic as Spain, have been nonsense.' (Dionisio RIDRUEJO.)

secondly because of our pseudo-revolutionary demagogy, and lastly because we accepted everyone . . .

Despite its mass membership, the Falange never became a mass party, in his view. It lacked the leaders and the internal dynamic. It was a hierarchical party, much more similar to an army than a mass party – 'and there's nothing less like a mass party than an army'. Sovereignty of the party never lay with the base, it resided in the 'leadership'; and since there was no real leadership, sovereignty was nowhere. Had it been a mass party, the base would have produced its own leaders.

José Antonio Primo de Rivera's imprisonment and subsequent execution by the republic had left the Falange leaderless. There was no one of his stature to replace him; potential leaders, like Onésimo Redondo or Ruiz de Alda, had also been killed. The myth was propagated that José Antonio was still alive, while a collegiate junta, over which Manuel Hedilla, a Santander worker, presided, took over on a provisional basis. The myth, he believed, was both decisive and disruptive.

—Decisive in maintaining morale and in postponing the leadership struggle amongst the mediocre contenders. Disruptive in making it easier for the leadership to be taken over from outside. Without an obvious leader, the Falange was left headless, and it was all the easier to put a noose around it and strangle it.[1]

To translate falangist–syndicalist principles into practice, he started to organize the trade union. He met passive resistance from the workers.

—They found that the *sindicato* could serve them as a place of refuge – and that was about the measure of it. In any case, it didn't last long, for after Franco took over, there was an outright capitulation and we had to accept two unions, one for management, the other for workers, within the national-syndicalist structure. This duality, with the important role allotted to union bureaucrats, portended little more than what in fact happened: the Franquista vertical trade unions.

What I didn't see then was that the military – which, politically speaking, I would have called a neutral force – would be influenced by the old conservative forces so that the war would end with all our efforts negated and the wealthy classes dominating again. The counter-revolution to our revolution went on throughout the war but, believing we could win, I went on fighting for our revolutionary principles . . .

1. 'To begin with we believed the news of José Antonio's execution; then a conflicting report saying that he was alive and being held hostage gained unconditional credence. It made political sense, after all. Even Franco believed it. Serrano Suñer [Franco's brother-in-law who was about to become the dominant political personality in the nationalist zone] told me on one occasion that Franco was convinced José Antonio had not been executed. Franco was jealous of him; he could see that the Falange masses had no other ideology, no other myth than that of José Antonio. Franco felt this as an insult. He maintained to Serrano Suñer that José Antonio had been handed over to Russia and that the Soviets had castrated him. Franco patently believed what he wanted to believe. José Antonio could no longer overshadow him as a man or a myth. The former had been destroyed by his castration, the latter by his being alive, not a dead martyr . . .' (Dionisio RIDRUEJO.)

The 'strangling' of the Falange, in RIDRUEJO's words, was shortly to be carried out in public. Talks between falangist and Carlist representatives on the fusion of the two movements had taken place two months earlier, without concrete results. Franco now decided to bring about the unification – and with it the final suppression of the other remaining political parties – by decree.[1] Head of the new movement would be none other than the head of state. The old parties, argued his brother-in-law Serrano Suñer, a former CEDA deputy who had recently escaped from the Popular Front zone, did not answer the needs of the moment. The military uprising had been a movement *against* republican disorder and the threat to the nation's unity. The situation now was similar to that faced by the Catholic Kings at the beginning of their reign in the fifteenth century; here was the possibility of founding a new state . . .

The manoeuvre to unify all political organizations in one body under his command – a logical continuation at one level of the decree banning political and trade union activity issued before Franco's appointment as head of government – had another important dimension. Keeping the noose round its neck, it would strangle not so much the Falange but the falangist populist anti-capitalist elements; 'revolutions' such as RIDRUEJO was proposing were to be dealt a death blow.

Taking advantage of a confused situation arising out of a leadership struggle within the Falange, Franco imposed his decree on 19 April 1937. Manuel Hedilla, who the day before had been congratulated by the Caudillo for having won the leadership battle, was arrested a week later, court-martialled and sentenced to death. Although the sentence was commuted, Franco had crushed the main populist element in the Falange.[2] Within nine months of the start of the war, Franco was head of state, *generalísimo* of the armed forces and head of the only political movement[3] authorized in the nationalist zone.

On guard duty at Franco's HQ in Salamanca when the unification decree was announced, Juan CRESPO, the monarchist youth, heard the Caudillo speak. When the guard was relieved, he went home, took off his tailor-made uniform

1. A Carlist politician, Count Rodezno, said later that Franco had told him before the event that unification was necessary to prevent the resurgence of right- and left-wing dissension and the class struggle. The left, he said, was joining the Falange; the right the Carlists. Unification would permit the more extremist falangist elements to be counter-balanced by the Carlists (see J. del Burgo, *Conspiración y guerra civil*, pp. 777–8). Potential civilian contenders for power were being removed without difficulty. Fal Conde, the Carlist secretary-general, had been exiled by Franco the previous December for attempting to set up Carlist military academies without his approval; don Juan, Alfonsine heir to the throne, had been escorted from the country earlier (see p. 202); Gil Robles was in exile in Portugal; don Xavier, the Carlist pretender, would be asked to leave Spain six months later.

2. Hedilla was kept in solitary confinement for four years. 'I heard Franco say more than once later, when some problem arose, that he regretted not having Hedilla shot. Hedilla had struggled within the limits of his possibilities to contain the repression, without going so far as to condemn it. He protested about falangist participation in it; and also about the "orgiastic" aspects of the war – the proliferation of bodyguards, arms, cars. But he was a man who lacked any talent for leadership; discreet, prudent and, in the last analysis, weak, he made it easier for Franco to take over.' (Dionisio RIDRUEJO.)

3. Given the portmanteau title of: Falange Española Tradicionalista y de las JONS, usually abbreviated to FET. Its political secretariat was made up of second-rank figures under Serrano Suñer, who became secretary-general.

and cape, packed them up and went to the barracks where he handed them in.

—'I am not in agreement with the statement made by His Excellency, the Generalissimo,' I told our chief, Miralles. 'I hereby resign from the militias.' I didn't return home, expecting to be arrested, but went to the infantry barracks as the place where they would be least likely to look for me. I was disgusted. I couldn't see why, because a man banged his fist on the table, we should suddenly now all have to believe the same thing . . .

How could parties of such different ideologies be amalgamated? he wanted to know. It was one thing to defend common interests; another to be forced into a single party. While he disagreed fundamentally with the latter, the former remained important enough to keep him believing in the need to fight the war. Within a couple of weeks, he was at the front again, his age-group having been called up.

When RIDRUEJO heard the news he wondered whether it was not his duty to take Salamanca militarily. Had he found three or four others in positions of command willing to support him, he would have captured the city and taken Franco prisoner.

—Naturally, the Foreign Legion would have moved in the next day and captured us. But, much more important, such a move on our part would have brought the war to a halt. I didn't dare take the step – who would have? In other circumstances, if there hadn't been a war, the Falange would have killed Franco. None of us could accept our forced capitulation, our unification in which we had not had a word to say . . .

He was with Hedilla drafting a memorandum demanding that Franco's measure be reconsidered, when the police came to arrest the Falange leader. Accompanying Pilar Primo de Rivera, sister of the Falange's founder, RIDRUEJO went to see Franco. Aged twenty-three, and looking even younger, he was taken for a bodyguard and not allowed in, until finally Serrano Suñer redressed the situation. Once in Franco's presence, RIDRUEJO let flow a cataract of grievances.

—I told him that a political party was not a regiment and could not be treated like one; if he proposed becoming a political leader he would have to interpret the wishes of the party's base. The worst way of inspiring confidence in party members was to imprison their leaders. He listened to all this quite calmly, betraying nervousness only by a slight movement of his lips. Pilar was patently scared, thinking that no one should talk to Franco like that. After we left, he apparently said to Serrano Suñer that I seemed quite a sharp lad. An hour later, when I got home, I received a tip-off that I was about to be arrested. It seemed that after his relatively friendly reception of me, Franco rang the bell for the police . . .

He took refuge in the Falange militia HQ under General Monasterio and waited to see what would happen, emerging unscathed soon afterwards.

Other pre-war falangists, like Rafael GARCIA SERRANO, who was working on the Falange paper *Arriba España* in his native Pamplona, were equally opposed to unification. In their view it meant that the Falange had lost a commanding position. Unification could be justified on military grounds, but never politically. GARCIA SERRANO carried his opposition to the point of never officially joining the new organization.

—There were many like me. We could no longer be assured that our ideals would inspire the future. Though I admired Franco greatly as a general, I knew he was not imbued with falangist ideals. The threat José Antonio had so clearly seen and warned against – the danger of being overwhelmed by right-wingers after a successful rising – was coming true. Serrano Suñer had been a CEDA deputy, and that was enough to disqualify him totally in my eyes. The Carlists were reactionaries. 'A pride of lions led by lambs', a Carlist canon once correctly remarked. Their leaders displayed only the very right-wing aspects of Carlism, a movement which had, after all, in its deep Spanish roots, certain affinities with anarcho-syndicalism . . .

While some Carlist politicians were found to serve in Franco's unified organization, the bulk of the Carlist movement was opposed. Marquess de MARCHELINA, commanding a *tercio* of *requetés* in the south, saw it as a totalitarian coup d'état.

—We expelled from our ranks all those who collaborated with it. It was evident from the moment Franco took over political and military power that the state was becoming falangist. The latter we saw as an extension of German and Italian fascism. Nothing could be further from our ideals than totalitarianism . . .

But what could they do? Had they risen to oppose unification they would have been shot – worse, the war might have been lost. Troubled, worried, they continued to collaborate. Under cover of the new organization he saw that instead of the social justice he was fighting for, the old ruling capitalist order was being given a tremendous boost.

On the Guadarrama front, Antonio IZU, the peasant *requeté*, told his captain that if he was ordered to wear the falangist blue shirt (which, with the *requetés'* red beret, became the uniform of the new movement), he would burn it. In his brother's company of the America regiment on the Guadalajara front, the men had burnt the blue shirts; and when a *requeté* subaltern was arrested for leading the opposition to unification, his troops refused to go into the attack.

—They mutinied. An attempt was made to disarm them but they made it clear that they would resist. Only when the *alférez* was released did they end their action. The Falange never inspired any confidence in me. It was a totalitarian, centralist movement, without respect for the *fueros*. And the way they carried out the repression during the war – well, they had a different mentality to us . . .

While unification pleased neither Carlists, falangists nor monarchists, the three movements shared a profound anti-liberal, anti-marxist posture, a concept of 'organic democracy'[1] and a loyalty to the uprising which they had helped

1. Basic to organic democracy (as opposed to 'inorganic' bourgeois democracy) is the concept that the class struggle can be overcome by the harmonious cooperation of different social groups within a single corporation. Class trade unions, political parties and universal suffrage

precipitate. The major enemy lay on the other side of the lines; and in the trenches, despite occasional friction, unity was an imperative of war.

—We were there to fight a common enemy. When the war was won there would be time enough to settle our differences, thought Alberto PASTOR, farmer and falangist from Valladolid. Unification was a logical continuation of what I had considered necessary when I commanded the Falange militias at the Alto del León in September 1936. Although the Falange command in Valladolid opposed me, I imposed collaboration with *requeté* units. It was the only way to win the war . . .

Not that he was blind to what was going on. Remembering that the 1931 republic had declared itself in its constitution a 'republic of all the workers', he coined a phrase to describe the nationalist zone. 'Ours is a national-syndicalist state of all the *alféreces provisionales*[1] under the command of the military and the clergy.'

But for the 'utopian' falangists like RIDRUEJO every day brought another disappointment; they hoped that they might still influence the political situation, but not much else.

—I was coming to realize that the revolution we had hoped to make was impossible. Eighty per cent of those being executed in the rearguard were workers. The repression was aimed at decimating the working class, destroying its power. In eliminating those whom our revolution was to benefit, the purpose of the revolution was itself eliminated. The reasoning behind the necessity for the purge was the sophism (shared moreover by both sides) that the enemy was a *minority* which was forcing the great mass of those on the other side to fight. Destroy that minority and order would be restored. The repression in the nationalist zone was carried out in cold blood, purposefully and methodically, to destroy that 'minority'. It was a class war. Not everyone, certainly not the petty bourgeoisie on the nationalist side, recognized it as such, or they would have been on the other side. But the ruling class certainly knew it. Franco was its most lucid exponent; his crusade was but another way of expressing it . . . [2]

---

are abolished. 'Our regime will make radically impossible the class struggle because all those who cooperate in production will constitute an organic totality,' in the words of José Antonio Primo de Rivera. An individual's three 'functions' – as worker, as member of a community, as member of a family – are represented within an organization of corresponding interests. In the fascist/falangist variant, the state is all important and the corporations form an integral part of it; in the Catholic version, these corporations exist *prior* to the state and thus the latter occupies a lesser, subordinate role. This was the Carlist position (explaining their hostility to the Falange's totalitarianism) as well as the long-term perspective of the CEDA pre-war. Where the latter two differed was on the means to achieve the desired goal. The monarchists also favoured a 'strong, corporative state' as a means of ending the 'ruinous era of the class war', in Calvo Sotelo's words. Organic democracy was the common political denominator which Franco espoused, converting it into one of the means of dominating civil society for forty years.

1. The volunteer temporary second lieutenants who were trained, partly by German military instructors, in rapid courses to officer the nationalist combat units. Their death rate was so high that a temporary lieutenant became known as a permanent corpse.

2. Not usually credited with this formulation, Franco used the word 'crusade' in the first week of the war while still in Morocco when he called on the army to have 'faith in the outcome of the crusade', according to *El Defensor de Córdoba* (25 July 1936).

We are motivated exclusively by the desire to defend the democratic republic established on 14 April 1931, and revived last 16 February.

Jesús Hernández, PCE politbureau member
(Madrid, 8 August 1936)

Has the working class in arms now to defend the democratic republic? Is the working class of Catalonia and Spain sacrificing itself and shedding its blood to return to the republic of Sr. Azaña? (*'No!' shouted the audience*) . . . Comrades, all the concrete problems of the democratic revolution, which the bourgeoisie failed to carry out in five years, have been resolved by the proletariat in arms in as many days. (*Applause.*)

Andreu Nin, POUM leader (Barcelona, 6 September 1936)

First we must win the war and afterwards we can talk of revolution.

Largo Caballero, prime minister (30 October 1936)

It is necessary, above all, to ensure the collaboration of Azaña and his group to help them overcome their hesitation. This is necessary to prevent the enemies of Spain considering her a communist republic and thus to avert their open intervention which is the greatest danger for republican Spain . . .

Letter from Stalin, Molotov and Voroshilov
to prime minister Largo Caballero (21 December 1936)

There are some who say that at this stage we should fight for the socialist revolution, and there are others who say that we are practising a deception, that we are manoeuvering to conceal our real policy when we declare that we are defending the democratic republic. Nevertheless, comrades, we are fighting for a democratic republic, and furthermore, for a democratic and parliamentary republic.

Santiago Carrillo, JSU secretary-general
(Speech at first JSU national conference, January 1937)

It should be clearly understood that we are not fighting for the democratic republic. We are fighting for the triumph of the proletarian revolution. The revolution and the war are inseparable. Everything that is said to the contrary is *reformist counter-revolution.*

CNT-FAI Boletín de Información (January 1937)

What do the comrades of the *CNT* accuse us of? According to them we have diverged from the path of revolutionary marxism. Why? Because we defend the democratic republic . . . Well, this republic is of a special type. A parliamentary democratic republic with a profound social content such as has never before existed . . .

Mundo Obrero, PCE organ (Madrid, March 1937)

Civil war being the continuation of class politics by other means, politics inevitably conditioned the means and ends on both sides. In the Popular Front zone, the failure of the proletarian revolution to consolidate itself politically and militarily in the very difficult conditions of the first three months, meant the emergence of a new political option. It was expressed in a slogan: Victory in the war first as the guarantee of making the revolution.

If the war were not won, maintained the communists (with the agreement of the republicans and right-wing socialists), the revolution could not triumph. Losing the war meant losing the revolution. Who could dispute this elementary proposition? Except by standing it on its head: if the revolution did not triumph, the war could not be won. Losing the revolution meant losing the war. Either way there was polarization. War-and-revolution, revolution-and-war.

And then – what revolution? Democratic? Socialist? Libertarian? Centralized, de-centralized, self-managed, state-run? The answer would determine the course of the war. In the life-and-death struggle being waged against the common enemy, many lives were to be lost – assassinated – in the bitter polemic between working-class organizations aroused by the question.

—It was *the* great theoretical and concrete problem of the war, recognized Josep SOLE BARBERA, Catalan communist lawyer. Could revolution co-exist with the anti-fascist struggle, or must the latter dominate and political problems remain subordinate until the end of the war? Were the people fighting to defend the republic of February 1936, a democratic, liberal, open republic, or were they fighting to transform that republic into a socialist, syndicalist or some other type of republic? We communists maintained the former . . .

In accord with the communist party's pre-war political line,[1] the revolutionary upsurge sweeping the Popular Front zone was carrying through the bourgeois democratic revolution. This had to be completed before the socialist revolution could appear on the historical agenda. The transformation of society which was indisputably taking place, thought Francisco ABAD, a communist soldier, would eliminate feudalism on the land and in the economy. The stages in the political and economic development of a society could not be by-passed; the bourgeois democratic revolution had to precede the passage to socialism. Meanwhile, it was impermissible that the revolutionary situation should be used to take measures opposed to that revolution – like the workers seizing factories and running them.

—That wasn't a revolutionary measure; moreover, it was carried out not by the government but by political organizations. We were opposed to it. We were engaged in a civil war in which the republic's total potential had to be mobilized. If we began by taking away from certain capitalists their factories and workshops, production would be disorganized, paralysed. Such so-called revolutionary measures went far beyond what the people were ready for, what they wanted. Our party could not go against the will of the people . . .

Even as it lost strength to the Caballero Popular Front government, this

1. Points of Rupture, E.

inchoate, multiform revolution continued to defy the Procrustean efforts to fit it into its correct historical stage. The communist party, in consequence, had to reformulate its definition of the revolutionary stage. Early in March 1937, an amplified plenum of the party's central committee in Valencia heard that the struggle had gone beyond the republic of February 1936, to a 'democratic, parliamentary republic of a new type and with a profound social content'. It would not be a democratic republic like that of France or any other capitalist country, said José Díaz, the party's secretary-general. 'We are fighting to destroy the material foundations on which reaction and fascism rest; for without their destruction no true political democracy can exist . . . ' The large landowners, the financial and industrial oligarchy, the politico-economic power of the church and the army were the bases which had to be destroyed.

'And now I ask: To what extent have [they] been destroyed? In every province we control, big landowners no longer exist. The church, as a dominant power, has likewise ceased to exist. Militarism has also disappeared never to return. Nor are there any big bankers and industrialists.' The guarantee that these conquests would never be lost lay in the fact that the 'genuine anti-fascist people' – the workers, peasants, intellectuals and petty bourgeoisie – were armed. 'And precisely for that reason, because we have a guarantee that our conquests will not be lost, we should not lose our heads . . . by trying to introduce experiments in libertarian communism and socialization . . .'[1]

The destruction of the old ruling order, as José Díaz observed, had already been achieved; the revolution had not limited itself to 'defending the republic established on 14 April and revived last 16 February' as the communist party had maintained at the start of the war. Communist militants in the front lines around Madrid, like Miguel NUÑEZ, an education militiaman, were well aware of the depth of the popular explosion.

—It was a thorough-going revolution. The people were fighting for all those things which the reactionary forces of this country had so long denied them. Land and liberty, an end to exploitation, the overthrow of capitalism. The people were not fighting for a bourgeois democracy, let's be quite clear about that . . .

—True, the socialist revolution was not on the agenda for us, recalled Narciso JULIAN, communist armoured train commander. But what was quite clear was that the struggle for democracy and socialism was linked. There was, in Lenin's words, no Chinese wall between the two. Democratic conquests which the republic had been unable to make were now being achieved with incredible speed. Not all of them were orientated towards the war effort; many were made with a wider view of future perspectives. We continued to struggle for socialism, but we didn't believe, like the anarchists, that everything could be achieved in one fell swoop . . .

A profound revolutionary rupture had occurred, thought NUÑEZ. The first

1. J. Díaz, *Tres años de lucha* (Toulouse, 1947), pp. 295–7.

real land reform, over 5 million hectares of land distributed, the major industries and the banks under workers' control – 'a control which admittedly sometimes went too far' – the old oligarchy swept aside. 'This was a national revolutionary war, like South Vietnam. National because it was essential to incorporate the anti-fascist petty bourgeoisie who had to be offered certain guarantees, a democratic perspective.'

Would it not have been appropriate to have created revolutionary structures to lead this democratic revolution? Soviets?

—No, had we done so we would have been changing the historic phase. It would have assumed that we were making the socialist revolution. Instead, certain 'forms of being' I would call them were being created, not to organize power but to win victory in the war. The Popular Army, whose creation absorbed our energies even to the detriment of other things, was the prime example. Moreover, if we had come out in favour of socialism, fascism would have found allies the more easily. The democratic countries imposed Non-Intervention on the republic as it was. What would they have done if we had come out immediately for socialism? They would have left fascism's hands even freer . . .

He was convinced that the road to socialism was the one the communist party was following. But rather than spend time discussing what this revolutionary transformation of society should consist of, it was more important to sacrifice everything in order to win the war. It was sufficiently revolutionary to throw back fascism, save democracy. 'If we saved democracy, the people would give the final answer – '

The dichotomy of war first, revolution later, represented, in this view, a false dilemma.

—A play on words, observed José SANDOVAL, communist party organizer of the 11th division. On the one hand because a profound revolution was being made; on the other, because it was common sense that to devote all one's energy to making the revolution with the enemy at your gate was like tending your garden and ignoring the elephant about to trample all over it . . .

The real problem, he believed, did not lie in the fact that one sector was bent on making the revolution and the other in devoting all its energies to the war. The real problem was – how to make the revolution, what sort of revolution and how could this revolution, given that the former ruling class's power had been destroyed, contribute to winning the war. 'Had there been no revolution, it would have been impossible to sustain the war for three months, let alone three years.'

The revolution that the communist party was pursuing, in his view, was being made in the course of the war against fascism. It had to be made with all those forces prepared to defend democratic liberties at home and abroad. No communist ever believed that France or England would intervene directly; but to protect her rear, France might allow arms purchased in the Soviet Union and Mexico to be shipped to the republic through her territory, for example. The French and British failure was lamentable. But the communist party's strategy of seeking alliances with all democratic forces in the fight against fascism remained correct all the same.

—It corresponded to the needs of the international communist movement[1] and to the internal needs of republican Spain. It countered the myth that we Spanish communists were Bolsheviks bent on making the communist revolution. A revolution was being made – but a new sort of revolution, one that opened up perspectives of a socialist revolution later. This was not the revolution of a single party. Our revolution was seeking new, pluralistic paths to socialism . . .

In the first eight months of the war, the communist party more than doubled in size to 250,000 members. Their social composition revealed the source of the new recruitment. Alongside 87,000 industrial workers, artisans and shopkeepers and 62,000 landworkers, there were 76,000 peasant owners, 15,500 middle class and 7,000 intellectual and liberal professionals. The petty bourgeoisie made up 40 per cent of the party;[2] 55 per cent was rural-based, consisting of either peasant owners or landworkers.

The strength of the communist party was to have a coherent policy where others had none; to be monolithically united where others were split.[3] 'The party knows what it wants and where it is going,' in José Díaz's words. Its determination to shape the revolution to the correct historic stage which, at the same time, opened 'democratic perspectives' for a petty bourgeoisie terrified by the libertarian revolution in order to keep that class in the anti-fascist struggle, had brought it success in membership and influence. Along with Soviet aid and the party's indisputable dedication to the military effort, defence of small property, especially rural, was a decisive factor. The communist party proposed the peasantry's complete freedom. Even the petty bourgeois Esquerra's measure requiring all Catalan peasants to join a single union to sell their crops and control prices was viewed with displeasure because it 'suppressed the peasants' total freedom to sell their produce and killed all stimulus to produce more'.[4] It proposed to give the peasantry as their property the estates confiscated from landowners who had sided with the military rebels.[5] War and revolution was to be prosecuted with free enterprise in the rural rearguard.

1. In the same way as the creation of the Popular Front had corresponded to the 'complementary, not contradictory' needs of the Soviet Union and the Spanish democratic revolution. See Points of Rupture, E.

2. Not including the shopkeepers and artisans included by the party amongst the industrial workers. Guy Hermet (*Les Communistes en Espagne*, Paris, 1971) estimates that the industrial proletariat comprised no more than 25 per cent of the PCE's membership between 1937 and 1939. This would mean that shopkeepers and artisans formed 10 per cent of the party, raising the petty bourgeoisie's share to 50 per cent of the membership.

3. Any who did not follow the line, like Juan Astigarrabía, secretary of the Basque communist party, were in difficulty. See p. 397, n. 1.

4. See *Guerra y revolución en España, 1936–1939* – the official party history of the war – (Moscow, 1967), vol. 2, p. 31. In August 1937, the communist agricultural minister, Vicente Uribe, published a decree regularizing agricultural cooperatives.

5. This was blocked by the socialist ministers who sought nationalization of expropriated estates which the communist minister was forced to accept. However, the PCE's criterion that only those owners who had intervened directly or indirectly in the uprising should be subject to expropriation was upheld. For further consideration of the land question see pp. 372–3.

Defence of the democratic republic stood to make larger gains for the communist party than if it had decided in the first months of the war that this stage was completed and a new historic phase had opened, for the libertarians and left socialists already occupied the latter terrain. The proletarian revolution, on the other hand, lost a great deal. However, as the Spanish section of the Third International (under a relatively new and young leadership – José Díaz, the secretary general, had been a party member only seven years) the PCE would have found it difficult to pursue options unapproved by the Comintern. And the latter, which had dispatched some of its leading figures to Spain, was categoric. In Stalin's words, it was 'necessary to prevent the enemies of Spain considering her a communist republic . . . '[1] Irrespective of how far the masses had advanced, external (the Soviet Union's desire for an alliance with the bourgeois democracies of Britain and France against Hitler) and internal reasons (the communist party's desire to keep bourgeois democrats in a wide anti-fascist alliance and ensure the benevolence of Britain and France) coincided in the inappropriateness of advancing the historical stage.

The politics represented by this Popular Front option were translated into concrete and specific policies which determined how the war was fought. Theory, historical stages, here became life-and-death realities, as the combatants knew. Among them Timoteo RUIZ, the young peasant who started the war with a lance in his native village and later joined the 5th Regiment and the communist party, felt that not everything was right.

—A great mistake was being made in thinking that the war could be waged with classic strategies. This wasn't a traditional war – it was a civil war, a political war. A war between democracy and fascism, certainly – but a *popular* war. Yet all the creative possibilities and instincts of a people in revolution were not allowed to develop . . .

This, he believed, was firstly because some government leaders lacked faith in ultimate victory, and secondly because some socialist leaders were more frightened of a revolutionary triumph, which would have meant a major communist advance, than they were concerned about winning the war. The government was made up essentially of bourgeois elements representing capitalist interests who were always hoping that England and France would intervene to secure victory and hand them back the bourgeois republic on a plate. Indeed, as long as help was expected from England and France the fact that a revolution was being made could not be admitted.

—It was as though we had to be ashamed of the revolution, as though we were frightened they would get wind of it abroad. The pre-war republic was still supposed to exist. That was a shamefaced way of making a revolution. It tried to turn us into 'good boys' who didn't want to go any further than the re-establishment of the bourgeois democratic state. The principal factor that conditioned everything, I believe, was expecting help from England and France. It meant the limitations on legalizing revolutionary conquests, respect for certain types of property – some of which, of course, had to be respected –

1. Stalin's letter to Largo Caballero (21 December 1936).

the use of traditional military strategy, the creation of a new army on regular army lines . . .

Until the end of the war, when he crossed the Catalan frontier into France and saw train-loads of arms held up by the Non-Intervention committee, he firmly believed that, out of self-interest if for no other reason, England and France would help the republic. But when he saw the trains he began to think that the republic should have relied solely on its own efforts.

—Found other ways of fighting the war – and of fighting to win. For if we hadn't been convinced that the democratic countries would come to our aid, different forms of struggle would have developed. If we had realized from the start that we were alone – even opposed to the bourgeois democracies which were boycotting us – it would have become a popular, revolutionary war . . .

One of the forms of popular war would have been guerrillas. How was it possible, in a country which had invented the word, not to have sustained a proper, coordinated and coherent guerrilla in the enemy rearguard? It was a question he had often asked himself during the war. It was a major revolutionary failure. The only explanation he could find was that the war was being fought in a traditional military manner rather than as a political, civil war. Irregular warfare, supported by a popular revolution, instead of pitched battles, would have considerably reduced the effectiveness of German and Italian aid to Franco, which was designed for regular warfare, he thought.

There was no doubt in his mind also that the revolutionary energy and spirit needed to maintain such a war was eroded by the fact that, apart from agrarian reform, no laws institutionalizing the revolution were approved.

—Fighting and dying, we sometimes thought: 'All this – and for what?' Was it to return to what we had known before? If that was the case then it was hardly worth fighting for. The shamefaced way of making the revolution demoralized people; they didn't understand. I think the communist party demonstrated the most correct understanding of what the war was about . . .

It could not have done much more; it did not have the strength, he believed. To have got rid of the bourgeois elements in government and developed the revolution's full potential would have required an alliance with the revolutionary sectors of the socialist party, 'would have meant taking over the government and displacing all the other forces'. But the party's growth was largely due to its position on how the war should be waged – as a continuation of the Popular Front policy. And he believed this was correct because it was essential to retain the petty bourgeoisie in the anti-fascist alliance.

—In the last analysis, a revolutionary leader was needed who could understand how the people felt, who would not take the war as a military exercise. Someone who didn't believe the war could be won by creating the same sort of army as the enemy army, by fighting the same sort of traditional war . . .

The failure to fight a different revolutionary war was in itself part of a larger problematic, thought Paulino GARCIA, a communist student who had been one of the first political commissars in the 5th Regiment and supported his party's call for the creation of an army in place of the militias: the need to put politics in command.

—It was easy to say that the war was being lost because Germany and Italy were helping Franco, and England and France were not helping the republic. Who could deny the importance of this? But it was not the sole answer. We had to be asking what lay in *our* power to do, what possibilities were there which we hadn't seized, what tasks hadn't we carried out . . .

First, the evident need to mobilize popular energy in a united effort to win the war made it essential that working people should be able to see that their sacrifices were going to lead to what they wanted to achieve. This, in his view, meant making the revolution in order to win the war.

—'But a more revolutionary course will only frighten the democracies,' people said. What nonsense! The capitalist democracies were frightened enough already by what was happening in Spain. 'Stalin won't agree,' said others. But was that the case? Would Stalin not have had to do what he did anyway – and a lot more, perhaps – if we had pursued a more revolutionary course? Could he afford to be seen betraying a proletarian revolution? . . .

Here, he thought, the communist party had failed its role, had failed to see how to overcome the historic tragedy of the Spanish working class – its ideological and organizational divisions. By leaning towards the reformist sectors of the socialist party and UGT, the communist party poisoned its relationship with the CNT and lessened the possibility of unity. And the most combative, revolutionary sectors of the Spanish working class were in the CNT; to overlook them, to ignore the greatest human potential a revolutionary party could hope to enlist, was an error of incalculable consequence.

This error, in his view, was conditioned by the communist party's excessive dependence on the Soviet Union. The latter (correctly or incorrectly was not of concern in this context) was pursuing a policy of alliance with the bourgeois democracies to confront fascism. It was correct that communist parties everywhere should *link* their policies to this Soviet policy; but it was not correct that they should subordinate their national policies to the USSR's supposed international interests. The Chinese, who defended the Soviet Union's and their own national and revolutionary interests, showed the way.

—Could we not have done something similar? The Spanish problem was so enormous that Stalin would still have been obliged to send arms. But we didn't do it, I believe, because we lacked a leadership with a profound theoretical understanding of the situation. This lack of theoreticians, common to the whole Spanish working-class movement, led to the communist party's blind obedience to the Soviet Union. This in turn reinforced its hostility to the CNT . . .

There was a large sector of the libertarian movement with which it would have been possible, he thought, to have reached understanding. It was necessary to explain to its more politicized sectors (as well as to the revolutionary sectors of the UGT) that neither libertarian communism nor socialism was possible at that moment.[1] A powerful enemy stood before them and there were many democratic forces prepared to fight it.

—We had to explain that these limitations must be taken into account, but that *at the same time* we had to set ourselves firmly on a revolutionary course – a long-term one. We had to conquer positions that could not later be taken from us. Had this been done we would have avoided the situation in which the communist party put the war before everything else and the libertarians made the revolution their prime concern. Such a policy would have neutralized both the extremist elements and the reformists. Instead, the communist party chose a way of posing the problem which ensured that a solution was impossible; when it didn't choose yet another course, that of drowning its opponents – in blood, as often as not . . .

*

The Popular Army was being built in the mould of the anti-fascist Popular Front regime which, under socialist leadership and with the participation of the other working-class forces (less the POUM), was bringing the revolution 'under control'. In reaction to the uncoordinated militias under their different political commands, the new army was to be a regular, disciplined, hierarchized force under professional command. As such it fought with great bravery, winning some important battles but no decisive victories. It represented the people in arms, but it did not develop a strategy of people's war.[2] The failure was political. The implementation of the Popular Front's complementary policies of aligning the petty bourgeoisie nationally, *and* the bourgeois democracies internationally, in the anti-fascist struggle, precluded such a revolutionary development.[3]

In the absence of the former ruling classes, the regime which was emerging was patently not the pre-war bourgeois republic, although the republican constitution remained in force. With the exception of the first six weeks, every cabinet throughout the war was dominated by working-class organizations led by the socialists. As the communist party's options and influence gained ground

1. As, in effect, was done in Asturias where the initiative was taken by the UGT and the CNT and the outcome was applauded by the communist and republican parties. See UGT–CNT pact, p. 244.

2. There can be no historical guarantee that a people's war would have triumphed. International isolation, absence of bases outside the national borders, continuing lack of working-class unity might have proved too heavy a burden. But many factors favoured it: among them, the terrain, the great length of sparsely manned fronts, the vulnerability of the enemy rearguard (which, in fact, never felt its victory morale seriously threatened), Franco's traditional military thinking, the lack of anti-insurgent weaponry, and, above all, historic memories and recent experience: the guerrilla warfare of the Napoleonic era, the victories of 18–20 July and of Madrid in November through the fusion of armed forces and civilians. In his letter to Caballero, Stalin advised him not to overlook the creation of peasant partisans in the enemy's rear. The Popular Army included a guerrilla corps which raided but did not form a *maquis*; the latter existed, in isolation, in some parts of Andalusia and later Asturias. (For the experience of a guerrilla in Asturias, see pp. 426–30.) Guerrillas, partisans, etc. would, of course, have formed but part of a protracted people's war strategy.

3. As it did others, such as declaring Spanish Morocco's independence to undermine the enemy's rearguard and disrupt one of Franco's major sources of recruitment, the legalization of revolutionary conquests on the mainland, etc.

(and especially after Largo Caballero was ousted as premier), the regime could with some justification be called a 'democratic republic' – a labile regime in which, despite working-class governmental domination, no class was yet totally dominant. The decisive moment of filling in the contours of the democratic revolution remained, in the communist view, still to come.

First, victory in the war. The communist concentration on building the instrument to achieve victory – the Popular Army – was not divorced from its position on the revolution. In order to consolidate the latter once victory had been won, it was necessary for the proletariat to become the hegemonic power in the course of the war.

—An important element of power is the military. Having an army of proletarians formed in the war, with proletarian officers in command, a proletarian police force, this hegemony would be assured as long as there was no foreign intervention, explained Pere ARDIACA, editor of the PSUC's paper *Treball*. The people's total identification with this process would, in itself, be an obstacle to such intervention, we believed. With the military and police in proletarian hands, the government would be able to start on the road to socialism . . .

Very rapidly, the Popular Army's crack forces were communist-led, the political commissariat was communist-dominated,[1] Soviet aid and influence were political facts.[2] When the moment came to embark on the next revolutionary stage – the march towards socialism, which, in the Comintern's book, could only be led by one of its national sections – communist domination of these forces would be a critical factor. Were it not for this, hegemony of the proletariat could have been consolidated in the first weeks of the revolution.[3]

The near exclusive emphasis on the war at the front, on military victory, gave rise to a failure which, in a civil war, no people's army could afford. It neglected the rear.

—The communist party sent its best militants to the front; its dedication to the war effort was admirable. But as a result – and I think this was its major error –

1. Jesús Hernández, communist minister and later head of the political commissariat, said after leaving the party that hundreds of communist and JSU 'organizers' invaded military units. 'Our officers were given categoric instructions to promote the maximum number of communists to higher ranks, thus reducing the proportion of promotions open to members of other organizations. But it is my duty to state that while this reckless policy was being carried out, the communists did not cease fighting the enemy and their resolution and discipline at the fronts showed them to be better than the best, a fact that facilitated the proselytizing work we had undertaken.' (Bolloten, *The Grand Camouflage*, p. 231.)

2. The fact that the Soviet Union was the only large supplier of arms and that the government had sent the bulk of Spain's gold reserves to Moscow meant that the influence was more than equal to the aid.

3. By supporting the formation of a workers' government based on a UGT–CNT alliance to the exclusion of the republicans. Such a government, or junta, was mooted at the end of August 1936. Participation, on the basis of making the revolution necessary to win the war, would not have excluded fighting to keep the petty bourgeoisie in the struggle. The new Soviet ambassador is said to have opposed the move and suggested the eventual outcome: a Popular Front government under Caballero. See F. Claudín, *The Communist Movement: From Comintern to Cominform* (London, 1975), pp. 703–4; also, Broué and Témime, *La Révolution et la guerre d'Espagne*, p. 180.

the party at certain periods lost its very important ties with the masses in the rear, recalled José SANDOVAL, communist party organizer of Lister's 11th Division. This was particularly noticeable at the end of the war in Madrid; the links which the party had forged with the capital's population during the glorious days of November 1936, had been undone. A large part of the rear-guard was undermined by defeatism. The communist party was so dedicated to the war effort that it did not sufficiently consider the possibility of defeat . . .

Morale at the front remained high; defeat seemed impossible. But failure to understand the threat from the rear was, ultimately, failure to understand the conditions of victory at the front. It meant relying on the technical strength of an army (which was almost always inferior to the enemy in technical means), not on the strength of the masses, the revolutionary fusion of civilians and armed forces. It overlooked the lessons of the defence of Madrid, in which the communist party had played such a notable role, consecrating the dichotomy which set 'the war' above everything. In the midst of the terrible privations in the rear, it reflected the way the revolution had been forced back. Reaction to the excesses of the ultra-left revolution, which had done its share of demoralizing sectors of the rearguard, now led to a different form of demoralization: depoliticized defeatism.

—There was virtually no politics in the rearguard at all, remembered Antonio PEREZ, socialist youth militant of the JSU who in the last days of the war joined the communist party. We were all so absorbed in our tasks at the front that it was left to a few political leaders to express their parties' views in the rear. There was almost no mass political involvement. That made us very vulnerable. The decomposition in our ranks occurred in the rear, not at the front . . .

The real evidence of this was yet to come. There were other reasons involved, as some communist militants recognized.

—Whatever the communist party proposed should be done was taken by the other organizations as a threat; they always feared that we intended to seize power, that Soviet aid was designed to strengthen us, when in fact it was for the republic's defence, explained Francisco ABAD, communist soldier. This fear remained alive throughout the war. It resulted in a ferocious anti-communism reflecting an accumulation of hatred towards the Soviet Union. For this state of affairs, which undermined the possibilities of resistance and defence, we were all responsible. At such a critical moment in history, we were unable to lay aside our political and personal interests for the common interest of the people . . .

They hadn't been able to do what the enemy, with less material and human resources at his command, had done: put everything at the service of the war effort. Instead, he lamented, they had engaged in a constant internecine political struggle. But even when the communist party made concessions, they were seen as some obscure plot directed by the USSR to take power. 'And due to the Soviet Union's direct presence in Spain this distrust increased day by day.'

Sócrates GOMEZ, Antonio Pérez's comrade in the Madrid socialist youth, came to the conclusion that it was, paradoxically, the communist party's failure to subordinate everything to the overriding needs of the war that caused the demoralization in the rear.

—The communist party tried to absorb, monopolize everything, acting with the wildest sectarianism. Instead of unity, there was the opposite. The war was being fought for the freedom of Spain, not to win a victory which would hand the country over to the communists who, in turn, served the interests of another nation. But from the propaganda, the large posters of Stalin, etc., the impression was gained that Spain was in the Soviets' hands. That only alienated large sectors of the population on our side and helped the enemy . . .

He was no anti-communist, couldn't call himself a marxist if he were. He believed that, as marxists, it was necessary to find points of convergence with the communist party to begin the march towards socialism. But when he thought that such collaboration was both possible and necessary during the war he found the opposite.

—To be a socialist where the communist party or JSU was dominant was virtually equivalent to being a criminal. Instead of unity, anyone who protested – as I did at the communist party's domination of the JSU – was slandered, blackened and sometimes physically eliminated. The communist party never attempted to take account, calmly and coolly, of differences of political opinion; they launched instead into insults, slanders, defamations . . .

The communist party gathered strength, he observed, because it opened its doors to virtually anyone. The socialist party, on the other hand, excluded new members for a considerable time, believing that the war was not a time for 'party building'. The formation of the Popular Army meant there were posts and jobs to be handed out.

—Accept a communist party membership card – and promotion. I don't say this lightly, I know what I'm talking about. The communist party grew strong on this procedure. A membership card, a post. It made a big impact on people who had no particular political loyalty. Had the communists acted with sense and loyalty there would have been no problems, I believe. Even some of the party's leaders – and I don't mean the renegades – subsequently came to recognize that the party's sectarianism had been outrageous. The 'morale' front, which is as important, if not more important, than the actual fighting front, was demoralized by the communist party . . .

A communist youth member of the JSU national committee and an FUE leader, Ricardo SALER, corroborated some of the charges. While he firmly believed in the revolutionary transformation of society during the war, he came to believe later that the communist party's constant calls for unity in the republican camp were made for tactical rather than any other reasons.

—I don't believe that we sincerely ever thought that a socialist or a republican could think like us. Let alone an anarchist or, even worse, a trotskyist. Our real purpose was to absorb the other parties. So much so, that in the youth organizations we had members who, while officially representing republican parties, were in fact communist party members or very close to our positions . . .

A moderate socialist, the art historian José LOPEZ REY, who had been seconded to the foreign ministry in Valencia, believed that there was a general desire to be rid of the Russians and even the communists. The latter fought bravely, were dedicated to the war effort. But a large majority of republicans, he believed, would not have accepted an unqualifiedly communist regime.

—If the republic had won, I'm sincerely convinced that Juan Negrín, Caballero's socialist successor as prime minister, would have got rid of the communists immediately. None of this could be said, of course, for the simple reason that we couldn't afford to alienate the only country that was helping us. There were many opinions about Soviet aid, but one thing must not be forgotten: the show trials were being held in Moscow. Most of us found these trials repugnant . . .

Irritation, if not anger, at communist political 'monopolization' affected liberal republican militants also. Andrés MARQUEZ, left republican youth leader and political commissar, found that the continuous and insistent propaganda about leading communist figures, the 'ostentatious symbols', the big portraits of Stalin and Lenin created an atmosphere in which only the communist party appeared to exist. The communist policy of respect for petty bourgeois property he saw as a tactic to attract this class to the party which, at the same time, in its meetings and newspapers, 'always spoke of the triumph of the revolution and communism'.

—I had no doubt that if we won the war the communists would come out, above everything and everyone, for a 'second Russia' of a Stalinist type . . .

We renounce everything except victory.

Durruti (August 1936)

We want the revolution here, in Spain, now and not perhaps tomorrow after the next European war.

Durruti (September 1936)

We are carrying on the war and the revolution at the same time.

Durruti (Madrid, September 1936)

The reformists, the republicans also say they want to make the revolution. But they tell you that they want an orderly, well-made revolution; Lenin also came up against people who wanted a revolution in Russia made by well-educated, clean workers. These people think the revolution is like a train which arrives on time at the station, and then the station-master says: 'gentlemen, we have reached the social revolution.'

Revolution is not, cannot be, like that . . .

Andreu Nin (Barcelona, April 1937)

The only dilemma is this: either victory over Franco through a revolutionary war, or defeat.

Camillo Berneri, Italian anarchist (Barcelona, November 1936)

The libertarians lacked the rigorous certainties of the communist party on the crucial issues of war and revolution. Durruti's statement, 'We renounce everything except victory', was often adduced to mean that the revolution must be sacrificed to win the war. Given his other statements of the time, it was dubious that he meant to go so far. Rather – as the first anarchist leader to realize that the working class was facing a civil war – he was aware that sacrifices in traditional libertarian aspirations would have to be made if the war were to be won.

A range of opinion, from those like Eduardo de GUZMAN, CNT journalist in Madrid, who believed that only by making the revolution was it possible to win the war, to others who took Durruti's 'everything' to include any further revolutionary advance, co-existed within the libertarian movement. GUZMAN was convinced that only the people's revolutionary *élan* had crushed the military in Barcelona and Madrid, and saved the capital in November. 'It was the grave mistake of all working-class organizations, including the CNT, to sacrifice the revolution in order to win the war.' The libertarians in Barcelona had made a serious error in not taking power from the start, in overlooking the fact that the state apparatus had considerable weight, even when disarmed.

—The petty bourgeoisie was inevitably opposed to the proletariat. The communists were recruiting in this class, and in alliance with the petty bourgeois republicans were bound to gain strength if the Generalitat and the central government were reconstituted . . .

The CNT had failed to push home the idea of setting up a trade union government in the first couple of months when there was no effective government at all; a revolutionary moment of great promise had been lost, he thought. This was due perhaps to the CNT's insufficient politicization; to be a-political, anti-political, did not mean to have no political sense. It meant simply not to participate in the farce of elections. 'Like it or not, politics existed – and revolutionary politics doubly so!'

In his view, none of the working-class organizations had matched the historic demands made of them. There was, in the working class, a great desire for unity, a desire 'to carry through the total revolution'. At the very least, total working-class democracy, in which all working-class parties and organizations would have participated on an equal footing.

From the moment the Catalan anarchists had accepted collaboration with the Popular Front forces in Barcelona, Lorenzo IÑIGO, libertarian youth councillor for war industries on the Madrid defence junta, had not believed it would be possible to make the libertarian revolution. But what he did believe was that it would be possible to make partial revolutionary conquests of a libertarian nature which would ensure, when the war was over, that the pre-war petty bourgeois republican regime could not return to power. Meanwhile, the communist party's stand for a 'democratic republic' appeared to him as no more than a political 'slogan'.

—Designed to attract to the party and to keep within its ranks the petty bourgeoisie; to attract the bourgeois democratic powers; and to combat the experiment in self-management on which we libertarians were engaged . . .

In Barcelona, libertarian views were as divided as elsewhere. Andreu CAPDEVILA, CNT acting president of the Economics Council, expressed the view that 'having made half a revolution, we of the CNT wanted to finish making the revolution and win the war, while the communists said: "Just win the war – " ' In the opinion of Joan MANENT, ex-*treintista* and CNT mayor of Badalona, not even the most extremist FAI militant in Catalonia believed that the total social revolution could be made while the war was being fought. Once the war had started, the people's will was geared to winning the war, not to making a revolution.

—The first aim had to be to win the war; the revolution could come later. The collectives which had been created stood as the libertarians' revolutionary stake in the future when the republic would emerge victorious from the war . . .

Durruti's companion and successor as leader of his column, Ricardo SANZ was convinced that the war had to be waged and won as rapidly as possible before the social revolution could be carried to fruition.

—I can't count the times I rebelled against those in the rearguard who wanted to enjoy the fruits of the revolution without thought of those at the front. Almost from the start, the people who triumphed in the rearguard didn't give a damn about the future of a people, a nation. And with them triumphed not disorganization but discouragement, demoralization of all those who could contribute to the triumph of the social revolution. The rearguard! Combatants who went on leave returned – if they returned at all – disgusted with the life they had seen. The low life people were living, it was much worse than had existed under the capitalist regime . . .

The contradictory currents in the libertarian movement were summed up by an Aragonese libertarian leader, Macario ROYO, who had experienced the collectivization in his native region and was about to serve on the CNT national committee.

—We knew – it was so obvious, we all said it – that if the war were lost everything would be lost. Durruti's statement is but one example, and it has no more significance than that. On the other hand, if we of the CNT came out and said that making the revolution was not our concern, the enthusiasm of libertarians in fighting the war would have been entirely dissipated. Why? Because, ideologically, all libertarians were convinced anti-militarists. To have to serve in an army was the biggest contradiction they could face. Their only hope, therefore, was that if the war were won thanks to their sacrifice, society would be transformed. Everyone of us held these two images simultaneously in his mind . . .

It was in the military field that the gap between these two simultaneously held but unsynthesized concepts was most rapidly revealed. Should the militias, which had been incapable of holding back the Army of Africa on the Madrid front, or of advancing further on the Aragon front, be 'militarized', converted into the Popular Army the communist party was demanding? For Miguel GONZALEZ INESTAL, the CNT fishermen's union leader who had returned to Madrid from San Sebastián soon after the start of the war, there could be no doubt: militarization was an inevitable necessity.[1] In the Basque country, with the enemy on top of them almost from the first day and the sound of artillery fire clearly heard, there was not even time to discuss it. The libertarian militias might be well supplied with food, medical supplies and light arms thanks to their powerful trade unions, but they would receive no heavy arms, which were coming from the Soviet Union and were controlled by other political forces, including the communists, unless they were part of an organized army. The CNT national committee accepted militarization, and GONZALEZ INESTAL was appointed to visit all the fronts to convince the CNT columns of the need. Everywhere he put forward the same argument.

—'You can't expect to be equipped with heavy machine-guns, artillery, etc. when your column is not trained to use them and you lack the personnel with the skills to serve them. You cannot plan offensives without overall planning, and without such offensives how do you expect us to carry on a war?' When I spoke to them man to man, comrade to comrade, they understood. I had difficulties convincing the Durruti column in Aragon and the del Rosal column on the Madrid front; with the Iron Column before Teruel I failed . . .

1. As personal experience had convinced other CNT militia leaders, like Saturnino CAROD on the Aragon front (see pp. 132–4).

The del Rosal column, which had tried to turn back some of the government ministers when they left Madrid the day before Franco's forces launched their offensive on the capital, accepted militarization only under great pressure. Manuel CARABAÑO, the fifteen-year-old libertarian youth member who had participated in the assault of the Montaña barracks and fought in the defence of Madrid, was amongst the opponents. Even though the column had accepted orders from the military command during the fighting in the capital, it was a completely different matter to become a military unit. CARABAÑO fought with all his energy against it: anti-militarism was an essential aspect of libertarian ideology, something revered and respected in the organization.

—A professional army, moreover, would lead to the creation of a state and any state was an oppressor. Militarization went hand-in-hand with the hierarchical type of communist organization. We weren't defending the democratic republic, which was essentially a bourgeois republic, we were fighting it. The war for us was a revolutionary war against fascism *and* the bourgeois republic . . .

Discussions on the matter continued in the column until February 1937. Then one day military forces arrived, cleared them out of their positions on the Teruel front, and took them in lorries to Cuenca. The CNT national committee threatened to expel them if they continued to refuse militarization. Cipriano Mera, the leading anarchist on the column's war committee, had accepted militarization after initial opposition. (Although his bitter sarcasm at the CNT Saragossa congress just before the war had contributed to the defeat of García Oliver's proposal to create a libertarian militia force that could crush a military uprising, he went on to become one of the leading anarchist military commanders and disciplinarians of the war.) The men were given leave passes which stated that, on their return, they would be 'totally militarized'. They accepted because the majority had already done so. CARABAÑO, moreover, had begun to think that their fight was misdirected: it should have been concentrated on the call for a disciplined *political* Popular Army.

—We weren't waging a simple military war, we couldn't form a purely military army; within the revolutionary context in which we were fighting, it had to be a political army. But it had to be disciplined. The libertarian movement took a long time to realize this. We didn't think it necessary to have a central military staff to give us orders; we thought that strategy and tactics could be decided by our own organizations . . .

He added three years to his age to make him eighteen and was appointed a lieutenant, surely one of the youngest officers in the Popular Army. When he and his companions went to a Madrid hotel on their return from leave to hear their appointments, the first name to be read out was that of a man who had been a waiter; he was appointed a major. 'Major of the mother who bore you,' he shouted, 'I'm a good anarchist!' There was uproar. He refused his appointment (only to be promoted lieutenant on the field of battle later). Many others also refused to become officers. However, there were few desertions, unlike in the Durruti column where a large proportion of men abandoned the front, many with their arms, rather than be militarized.

—We were enthusiastic enough in the end, although we never accepted formal army discipline. I refused to wear uniform; I sewed my officer's insignia on to a black leather hunting jacket and wore corduroy trousers. We never saluted. We said hallo and good-bye; officers and soldiers continued to be friends, went on calling each other '*tu*'. An officer had always to remember that his actions would be judged by the organization. We had a highly developed sense of justice . . .

As CARABAÑO had sensed, the fight against militarization was a blind alley if no concrete and effective revolutionary alternative could be proposed. Here, as in other spheres, the libertarians reacted to events which the communists were already beginning to shape. Refusing militarization (and posts) meant that the CNT lost almost any chance of seriously influencing the shape of the Popular Army which, in the end, they had to accept. Macario ROYO, Aragonese representative on the CNT national committee, believed that this was the libertarians' major error. Where they refused posts, others accepted them, not only in the army but in all the new organizations.

—The libertarians were making the revolution, carrying on the war, but refusing to take on positions of responsibility. They failed to understand that theory was one thing, practice in wartime another. When the first exams for political commissars were held, not a single CNT member passed. Illiterates had been sent, the CNT lacked men with education . . .

Illiterates could make fine revolutionaries, he reflected, but they were no good at the front reading a map. Some maintained that the CNT had been discriminated against, but this wasn't the case. As a result, the organization started a 'Durruti training school' with CNT teachers and was soon turning out militants who passed the exam.

*

For the dissident communist POUM in Barcelona, the war and the revolution were 'inseparable'; the party was opposed to the creation of the Popular Army. Ignacio IGLESIAS, political editor of the POUM paper *La Batalla* from early 1937 and veteran of the October 1934 rising in Asturias, expressed the party's position. There could be no triumphant revolution unless the war was won; but the war would not be won unless the revolution triumphed. 'No one in the POUM – or the CNT for that matter – ever claimed that the revolution had to take precedence over the war.' The POUM's opposition to the Popular Army was based on revolutionary postulates: it was wrong to create a regular army since to do so was to pose the war in the same terms as the enemy. This was what the communist party was doing. But it was not a classic war, the situation did not require a regular army with hierarchized commands which inevitably destroyed the revolutionary spirit of the working class, but a popular revolutionary army. If the premise were accepted that the war could be fought only in the traditional manner – which was why the question of guerrilla warfare was never properly considered – the simplistic but true conclusion had to be reached that the enemy was bound to win. He had an army, trained soldiers, superior arms. Moreover, the premise ignored the important question of self-reliance. Those who stood for making the war and revolution simultaneously could not expect aid from Britain and France.

—How could we? Logically, international capital stood closer to Franco than to us; and within the republican zone, closer to the republicans and communists than to the anarchists and POUM. But the anarchists, with their utopianism and their complaisant attitude towards petty bourgeois republican parties and politicians, whom they had always favoured over working-class political parties, failed to understand this . . .

Hostility to the creation of the Popular Army[1] stemmed also from the fear that the communist party would dominate it. At the same time, the POUM was aware that the militia system had failed to create the revolutionary force under a single command which was so vitally needed to win the war. The party proposed a 'red army' on the Bolshevik model, with soldiers' committees to 'control the officers and prepare the army politically', in Juan ANDRADE's words. Unlike the communist party, which dissolved its 5th Regiment into the nascent Popular Army, of which it then formed the political nucleus, the POUM continued to maintain its separate militia. Its call for the creation of a 'red army' in the first months of the war met the Catalan CNT's opposition since for the latter the militia was a prolongation of the anarchists' defence groups which had proved themselves so effective in urban settings (but less so in the open countryside). Moreover, the CNT had no need of revolutionary lessons from an 'authoritarian marxist' party which had been its main rival for the allegiance of the Catalan working masses before the war.

Failing to attract a large sector of the anarcho-syndicalist movement to its general positions on the prior need for the working class to take power to consolidate the revolution and win the war, the POUM and the revolution were bound to be isolated. To win over the libertarians, with their visceral aversion to 'authoritarian marxism' and their hostility to 'power', was no light task. POUM–CNT relations were cool; any CNT union threatened with falling under dissident communist domination had, in the recent past, been expelled; the POUM had set up its own trade union federation, FOUS (Federación Obrera de Unidad Sindical), in reply. But the CNT was where the mass of the workers remained.

Although the largest working-class party, with the second largest trade union organization (after the CNT), in Catalonia at the start of the war, the POUM was accorded only one seat by the CNT on the Anti-Fascist Militia Committee, the same as the nascent communist PSUC.[2] In a few weeks, the POUM had grown ten-fold to nearly 40,000 members; yet it was not a question of numbers alone – the PSUC soon had the same number – but of *political* weight. At the

1. The Valencia section of the POUM, to the right of the party in Barcelona (as the CNT there was to the right of the Catalan CNT), supported the creation of the Popular Army and believed that 'we could win the war without making the revolution, but we couldn't make the revolution without winning the war. In Barcelona they were certainly fixated on the revolution' (Luis PORTELA, POUM).

2. See p. 142.

national level, the party, which had been in existence for only ten months at the start of the war, had not had time to develop. Lacking a real base except in Catalonia, its political influence on a national scale was considerably less than that of other parties. And within Catalonia, it had to prove to the CNT militants that its positions were the only ones which could defend the revolution they had made against their own organization's original decision.

In the eyes of some of its leading militants, the POUM made a number of political mistakes. The first, underlined by IGLESIAS, was to have dissolved its own trade union into the UGT rather than the CNT when the latter ordained that only two trade union organizations – itself and the UGT – should exist in Catalonia, and decreed obligatory membership of one or the other.[1] The party lost its union base without the corresponding advantage of establishing a channel to the CNT workers and militants in their unions.

The POUM followed the CNT into the Generalitat government, having lost the long battle against liquidation of the Anti-Fascist Militia Committee. This was an even greater error, in the view of Wilebaldo SOLANO, secretary of the party's youth movement. To allow the Generalitat to take over the Anti-Fascist Militia Committee when the committee should have become a workers' government and taken over the Generalitat – what a tremendous mistake!

—The CNT must bear the responsibility. We didn't carry enough weight on our own to prevent it happening . . .

Juan ANDRADE, the 'only party executive member' to voice opposition to the POUM's collaboration with a bourgeois government, knew that he would be expelled from the party if he voted against it. An editorial he had just written in *La Batalla* calling the formation of the Largo Caballero Popular Front government 'counter-revolutionary' had raised a storm of protest in the party, and a central committee plenum had decided he should no longer be permitted to write editorials. None the less, the real problem that faced the party in its decision whether or not to join the Generalitat government concerned the POUM's legality.

—If we refused to join, the Stalinists would have used it as a pretext to outlaw us, and we wouldn't have been able to maintain our militia forces. This would have been an additional reason for refusing us recognition as an anti-fascist party. We had no intention of outlawing ourselves in a revolutionary situation, cutting ourselves off, in this way, from influencing the masses. We knew the fate that awaited us as Russian influence grew, but we wanted to continue making our positions known to the workers for as long as possible . . .

—The POUM was already under attack for various reasons, recalled SOLANO. Many militants feared our isolation, particularly from the CNT, if we didn't

1. The general attitude in the printworkers' union, one of the three main FOUS unions, was summed up by Adolfo BUESO, POUM printworker who had joined the CNT as long ago as the First World War, and was opposed to joining the UGT now. 'If we return to the CNT we won't be allowed to play any role, the FAI will continue to manipulate everything as before.' Affiliation to the UGT was as individual members, not as a union. 'Once the FOUS was in the UGT the communists, with their usual techniques, managed rapidly to gain control.'

join. Once in the Generalitat, it escaped the CNT completely that it could use it as an instrument to develop the mass struggle in order to create a real workers' government. Without a political line, the CNT was lost. The notion of forming a bloc with the POUM, which we put to them, went unanswered. But I don't believe events would necessarily have changed if we hadn't joined. I'm not sure we could have convinced the CNT to change course. It had the mass of the workers, it was a tremendous popular force, a mixture of primitivism and idealism. It hadn't evolved towards revolution; it was an organization that had sprung from the country's guts with a fighting revolutionary spirit. A colossus – with a head of clay . . .[1]

When, after less than two months, the POUM was evicted from the Generalitat under communist pressure, ANDRADE observed, the CNT referred to the matter as a 'quarrel between two marxist parties' and said it wanted nothing to do with such disputes.

—Little did they realize that our fate would be theirs in due course. It was them the Stalinists wanted to liquidate. But with its love of rhetoric, the CNT simply answered: 'No one can attack the lion of the CNT' . . .

If the CNT leadership remained intractable, what of the CNT membership? Could a sizeable section be brought over to the POUM's positions? One phenomenon was apparent to ANDRADE: the CNT workers saw no need to join a revolutionary marxist party because, when they contrasted the (superficially) revolutionary positions of their own organization with the simply democratic ones of the socialists and orthodox communists, they believed their organization's tactics still held the guarantee for the continued development of the revolution. In other words, the anarcho-syndicalists believed that their organization, like their revolution, was sufficient unto itself. Was enough done, however, to criticize openly these *superficial* revolutionary positions to the CNT membership? Or did the POUM ride on the CNT leadership's coat-tails?

—Sometimes, frightened of breaking with the CNT, I believe we did, explained SOLANO. We should have pursued a tougher policy. Before the war, when we had to fight the anarchists in order to be able to hold meetings in certain Barcelona *barrios* they dominated, our toughness paid off. They respected that. If Maurín had been with us, perhaps things would have been different; he was a lot more abrasive than Nin. The CNT was more critical of Maurín, liked Nin better, but the former carried more weight with them . . .

To impose the POUM's policies, thought Ignacio IGLESIAS, required more than 'the correct political line'; it required strength. The former did not guarantee the latter. And it was the CNT which had the strength. To appeal to its base we would have had to speak in an idiom that was acceptable to those who had been formed, or at least influenced, by another, anarcho-syndicalist language.

—We didn't succeed. We were too demagogic, like most minority parties. We

1. Joaquím Maurín, POUM secretary-general, who was caught by the uprising in the insurgent zone and held prisoner, had called it a 'colossus with feet of clay'.

sloganized, instead of tackling real problems in the way the anarcho-syndicalists could understand . . .

But the question of *what* was explained was even more crucial. Calling for the working class to take power – 'get the bourgeois ministers out' – Nin told the libertarians six weeks after the uprising that if they were prepared to take over, bourgeois power would be destroyed. The question of the dictatorship of the proletariat admittedly separated marxists and anarchists; but this dictatorship must be understood, said the POUM leader, as including 'the whole working class, the dictatorship of the popular classes. No organization, whether political or trade union, has the right to exercise its dictatorship over the other organizations in the name of the revolution'. Working-class monopoly of power abolished the class enemy's political rights and freedoms.

Calling on the anarchists to draw the practical conclusions from the fact that, at that moment, the bourgeoisie exercised no freedom or political rights, and to accept his definition of the dictatorship of the proletariat, he went on: '*compañeros*, I can assure you then that today the dictatorship of the proletariat exists in Catalonia.'

This was patently untrue; hardly a kilometre away an exclusively petty bourgeois Catalan government was sitting at that moment, however powerless it might seem. (Less than three weeks later, the POUM would, moreover, join it, together with the other working-class organizations.) The bourgeoisie's power had been gravely damaged but it had not been destroyed. However, as Wilebaldo SOLANO understood it, Nin was trying to explain, didactically, to the libertarians that their view of the dictatorship of the proletariat, of what had happened in Russia, was wrong. He was trying to get them to understand the need to create a workers' government, to get them over their hostility to dictatorship, which they had recently repeated, so that they would establish the political power to articulate and consolidate the economic and armed power they had already won.

—He was misunderstood then, as he was misunderstood when, in April 1937, calling again for a workers' and peasants' government, he maintained that the working class could still take power without recourse to armed insurrection. What he meant was that the weight of the working class remained so great that, with sufficient political will, bourgeois power could still be overthrown. The strength of the CNT and POUM in the factories and army was such that insurrection was unnecessary, *given that the workers were armed*. It would be sufficient for them to announce to the Generalitat that they had taken power. The government would probably have given way without bloodshed. But it required a determined political will. All this was a far cry from the charge levelled at Nin that he was in favour of the peaceful road to revolutionary power. How could anyone think that when, in fact, the working class was armed? . . .

Ignacio IGLESIAS also felt that Nin was correct – but only inasfar as he was referring to Catalonia. 'The fact of the matter was that at that moment Catalonia's importance with respect to the rest of Spain had considerably diminished. By then the republican state had been recreated.' If Nin's perspective had been pursued, it would have meant Catalonia's secession or independence from the rest of Spain, he felt. In every revolutionary movement there tended to be a loss of perspective as the focus narrowed on to the immediate; Nin had suffered from this, as he had also from the 'very Spanish fault of making categorical statements and seeing issues in local rather than national terms'. Real possibilities of making a revolution and winning the war had existed for the first three months of the war, but these had died with the formation of Caballero's government and the Soviet Union's intervention.

To what extent these political errors affected the course of the CNT's development remained an open question. Few CNT militants, even among the growing numbers who feared for their revolution, conceived of allying with a political party, but believed rather in returning to pure anarchist principles or consolidating trade union power.[1] Even the more 'politicized' CNT militants could not conceive of an alliance with the POUM. 'The POUM was a political party, the CNT was not,' said Joan MANENT, a former *treintista*, by way of explanation. Moreover, the POUM, like the communist party, was critical of anarchist collectives – 'trade union capitalism' – and opposed to 'forced' land collectivization.[2] Many libertarians might agree with the POUM on these points; but they were not attracted to marxism by hearing it from the minority POUM.

At the one level where the POUM might have expected CNT comprehension and solidarity – its unremitting anti-Stalinism and denunciation of the Moscow show trials then taking place – the party found that the anarcho-syndicalist movement's reaction was 'to keep quiet'.

—'What's going on in *La Batalla*?' the editor of the CNT's *Solidaridad Obrera* asked me when we met in the street one day, recalled SOLANO. 'You're shooting trotskyists every day.' I exploded. 'You receive the same Havas newsagency reports as we do. We publish them and you throw them in the wastepaper basket, that's the difference.' 'Ah,' he said, 'don't worry about Russia. We've got our own problems here.' 'What! All these years you've reproached us about Kronstadt and the terror in Russia,' I said, 'and now that it is really happening and they're shooting revolutionary leaders you're all keeping quiet. In fact it's *you* who are helping to shoot them by not publishing the news' . . .

The CNT leaders were willing to make many sacrifices not to alienate the main supplier of arms. Even their traditional 'anti-communism' was not a cause for *rapprochement* with the POUM. And in the last resort, and however unwillingly, the CNT 'base' followed its leadership, as events in Barcelona would shortly prove.

Like the CNT leadership, the POUM had been overwhelmed by the revolution at the start. The question of working-class power had not been on its agenda, and when it was placed there by the force of events, the party concentrated on it to the exclusion of many other problems.

1. A further description of this, and the relationship with the POUM, will be found on pp. 374–83, concerning the May events in Barcelona.

2. 'Jordi Arquer, the POUM leader, once asked me why his party wasn't admitted to the CNT's Council of Aragon. I answered that this was a revolutionary experiment of our own which had nothing in common with his or any other party – the POUM did nothing to foster rural collectives.' (Juan ZAFON, CNT propaganda delegate on the Council of Aragon.)

Perhaps the most important of these, as Ignacio IGLESIAS found to his surprise on his arrival in Barcelona early in 1937, was the question of the petty bourgeoisie. In a series of articles in *La Batalla*, he attempted to formulate the party's position.

'Up to the present the workers' organizations have not practised the correct revolutionary strategy with respect to the petty bourgeoisie . . . In the name of an intransigent and infantile revolutionaryism, the petty bourgeoisie has been rejected, or else the working-class organizations have fallen under that class's domination, hegemony and leadership. That is the meaning of the Popular Front policy at the present, a policy which binds the working class unconditionally to the organizations and parties of the petty bourgeoisie and, through them, to the big bourgeoisie. The correct policy does not lie in this route, but in attracting the petty bourgeoisie to the revolutionary movement.'

To achieve this, he wrote, it was necessary to 'demonstrate that the working class is not opposed to the petty bourgeoisie or to its particular interests. Neither the small carpenter's tools nor the tailor's sewing machine are socializable objects to be taken from their owners. We must destroy the legend that the revolutionary proletariat is opposed to the small industrialist.'

The expropriation of the petty bourgeoisie undertaken in the first moments and which was justified by the need to impose a sort of 'war communism' was the antithesis of socialism. 'The passage to socialism cannot be made in a brusque and sudden manner, leaping intermediary stages . . . At the moment, only large industry, transport, large commercial enterprises and the banks should be socialized. That is more than sufficient (for the working class) to keep power. Socialization of small industries and workshops is of no interest . . . '

But a point of importance remained to be stressed. 'We, the revolutionary proletariat, want to win the petty bourgeoisie for the revolution, which will resolve our common problems. But we are opposed to the petty bourgeoisie exercising political hegemony. We support its economic demands and work for the solution of its problems, which can only be satisfied within the framework of the revolution and socialism; but we deny it (political) leadership, for when it enjoys that it inevitably falls under the dominion of the bourgeoisie.'[1]

—By the time I wrote the articles it was already too late. It should have been done at the beginning. For if we weren't able to attract the petty bourgeoisie to the revolution by solving its problems (instead of criticizing or neglecting it as was done at the start), it would swing behind whoever did – and in this case it was the communist party . . .

*

War and revolution; revolution and war. How often, recited backwards or forwards, these three words were used. The triumph of the revolution to ensure victory in the war, the victory in the war to ensure the triumph of the revolution. Words can be a terrible trap. The terms of each slogan were as much separated as joined by the simple word 'and'. How rarely the conjunction was removed to form an adjectival phrase: *revolutionary war* – to furnish an answer to the

1. I. Iglesias, *El proletariado y las clases medias* (Barcelona, 1937), cited in V. Alba, *Historia del POUM* (Barcelona, 1974), pp. 146–7.

twin questions: Which type of revolution? What sort of war? The two were more than 'inseparable'; they had to be fused into a new whole.

—But no one tried to make the synthesis; or if they did, they didn't come up with an effective answer, observed Albert PEREZ-BARO, of the Catalan collectivization commission. Instead, the political struggle polarized around the two slogans, around the question of Soviet aid, which the communist party used to strengthen its positions continually throughout the Popular Front zone . . .

It was not totally idle to speculate whether such a fusion could have been achieved, as Paulino GARCIA earlier suggested. It would have required a shift of the communist party to ally with a sector of the libertarians and revolutionary socialists. Was such a solution totally impossible, particularly in Catalonia where it would have served as an example to the rest of the zone? Josep SOLE BARBERA, lawyer and PSUC militant, believed that failure to work in that direction was one of the two major errors committed by his party during the war. The PSUC's policies were far too influenced by the Comintern.

—The latter's political perspectives, conditioned by situations and problems totally foreign to the problems and interests of the republic, deformed many of the PSUC's positions. This was most evident in the party's line on the POUM and the CNT. Durruti was no Ukrainian anarchist who had raised the smallholding peasantry against the revolution – and yet we frequently used the same denunciations that Lenin had used against Makhno in the 1920s. The POUM was not a trotskyist organization as anyone with a concern for politics was fully aware. Trotsky was hostile to the policies Nin and the POUM were pursuing. But the PSUC acted as though it were . . .

The PSUC should have made the maximum effort, he felt, to attract the sector of the CNT which had understood Durruti's famous phrase about sacrificing everything except victory to positions closer to its own. He believed it could have been done.

—Instead of which, the PSUC committed the cardinal sin of doing the opposite. It made charges that weren't true, accused militants of the CNT and POUM of being virtual traitors, enemy collaborators. The party's views on the adventurism and infantilism of the more extreme CNT sectors should have been made as *political* charges, with proven examples as they arose, rather than anything else. But that wasn't how things were done: the party applied an entirely too mechanistic policy in its relations with the CNT and POUM . . .

The result was to lead to two civil wars within the civil war; to communist victory in the first and defeat in the second. And with it, finally, defeat in the war.

AGRARIAN REFORM DECREE

Article 1. It is agreed: that the state expropriate without compensation all rural property, of whatever size and use, belonging to persons, their spouses and legal entities on July 18, 1936, who intervened directly or indirectly in the insurrectional movement against the republic . . .

Vicente Uribe, agricultural minister, PCE
(Madrid, 7 October 1936)

The Council of Aragon will respect the peasants' right to work the land individually or collectively, in order to avoid any discontent which the rapid social transformations of the first moments may have caused. Although the Council will defend smallholders, it will – as agreed between the UGT and CNT – strive to prevent the return of the despicable system which existed prior to 19 July . . .

Joaquín Ascaso, president (CNT) of the Council of Aragon
(Radio broadcast, 19 July 1937)

As far as the collectives are concerned, there is not a single Aragonese peasant who was not forced to join. Any who resisted suffered terroristic attacks on their persons and property. Their land was taken from them, they were forced to work from sunrise to sunset on sweated day labour, receiving a wage of 95 centimos. Any who refused were deprived of bread, soap and their most basic needs. All privately held stocks of food were taken over. Well-known fascists were put in positions of authority in municipal councils . . .

Frente Rojo, PCE organ (Valencia, 14 August 1937)

ARAGON

It was over the land question that the sharpest differences arose and Aragon became the centre of the storm.

In the first days of the war, the militia columns – CNT-led in the main – sweeping towards Saragossa and Huesca had taken about three quarters of Aragon's land mass. It included some fertile zones but, overall, it was the poorer agricultural areas that had been captured.[1] In such relatively difficult conditions, rural libertarian collectivization began to take root and spread: 275 collectives totalling 80,000 members by February 1937; 450 collectives with 180,000 members three months later . . .[2]

Was collectivization being forced on an unwilling peasantry, as the communists maintained, or was it spontaneous, as the libertarians often argued? Was it undermining the war effort, turning small and medium peasants against the Popular Front, or consistent with revolutionary aspirations and the needs of the war? These were the questions that had to be answered. With two thirds of the country's wheat lands in enemy hands, adequate food production was essential to meet the needs of the growing Popular Army and the nation's three largest cities.

Aragon was a region of small and medium-sized peasant holdings. Large estates of 100 hectares or more covered about one fifth of the total land,[3] less than the overall Spanish average. The proportion of smallholdings was above average.

Although the CNT had considerable strength in Saragossa city, it was much weaker in many of the rural areas, as Saturnino CAROD, former propaganda secretary of the CNT regional committee, knew from his work in the villages. In some there was a flourishing CNT, in others the UGT was strongest, and in only too many there was no unionization at all.

The son of a poor landworker from a small Aragonese village, CAROD was well-placed to understand the peasant's situation, and he had no hesitation, as a column leader, in arguing that it was not the moment to introduce total collectivization which, he felt, could harm the war effort. It was essential to keep the peasantry's allegiance in the struggle.

—I knew only too well how the peasant clings to his plot of land. He should not be forced to join a collective if he wanted to keep his own land. Only the

1. The three Aragonese provinces produced 7·6 per cent by value of Spain's total cereal crops pre-war. Of this Saragossa province produced over half, Huesca just over a quarter and Teruel slightly more than one fifth. The best wheat-growing lands of Saragossa were in nationalist hands. Yields in Huesca province, especially in the Monegros steppe lands, were notorious for their tremendous fluctuations depending on rainfall; while Teruel, one of the most sparsely populated provinces of Spain, which sowed one third of Aragon's pre-war cereal lands, harvested only 21 per cent of the total crop (by value), an indication of the quality of the land. See E. Malefakis, *Agrarian Reform and Peasant Revolution in Spain*, p. 45, and *Bases documentales*, vol. 7, p. 344; also F. Mintz, *L'Autogestion dans l'Espagne révolutionnaire* (Paris, 1970), p. 99.

2. Mintz, op. cit., p. 102. Less than half of Aragon's 1 million population lived in the three quarters of the region under republican control.

3. Medium holdings (10 to 100 hectares) covered about one quarter, and smallholdings just over one half of the land, representing about 1 per cent and 98 per cent of the total holdings respectively. See Malefakis, op. cit., pp. 16–17 (although it should be noted that his figures include Logroño).

lands of those who had fled and communal village lands should be collectivized, I maintained, and the collectives be given legal recognition . . .

The advice was not heeded. Very rapidly collectives, in which not only the means of production but also of consumption were socialized, began to spring up. It did not happen on instructions from the CNT leadership – no more than had the collectives in Barcelona. Here, as there, the initiative came from CNT militants; here, as there, the 'climate' for social revolution in the rearguard was created by CNT armed strength: the anarcho-syndicalists' domination of the streets of Barcelona was re-enacted in Aragon as the CNT militia columns, manned mainly by Catalan anarcho-syndicalist workers, poured in. Where a nucleus of anarcho-syndicalists existed in a village, it seized the moment to carry out the long-awaited revolution and collectivized spontaneously. Where there was none, villagers could find themselves under considerable pressure from the militias to collectivize – even if for different reasons. There was no need to dragoon them at pistol point: the coercive climate, in which 'fascists' were being shot, was sufficient. 'Spontaneous' and 'forced' collectives co-existed, as did willing and unwilling collectivists within them.

Forced collectivization ran counter to libertarian ideals. Anything that was forced could not be libertarian. Obligatory collectivization was justified, in some libertarians' eyes, by a reasoning closer to war communism than to libertarian communism: the need to feed the columns at the front. Macario ROYO, an Aragonese CNT leader, believed that collectives were the most appropriate organization for controlling production and consumption, and ensuring that a surplus was made available for the front.

—Everything was disorganized. The columns depended on the villages, they had no other source of supply. If there had been no collectives, if each peasant had kept what he produced and disposed of it as he wished, it would have made the matter of supplies much more difficult . . .

By abolishing a free market and in effect rationing consumer goods, mainly food, the collectives controlled the local economy. Feeding the columns without payment became a source of pride or resentment, depending on the villager's ideological commitment. But for ROYO, as for most Aragonese libertarians, the matter did not end there. The fundamental purpose of founding the collectives was social equality.

—That each should produce according to his ability, each consume according to his need. Equality in production, equality in consumption. To supply everyone equally in the collective as well as the columns at the front – this was the principle and usefulness of the collectives . . .

Nevertheless, even where the initiative had arisen spontaneously, collectivization did not lack its coercive moment. Inevitably, in ROYO's view, for this was revolution. And revolution always meant imposing the will of an armed minority – 'in this case, an anarcho-syndicalist minority made up essentially of the younger, idealistic militants, the ones who get things done'.[1]

1. The contradiction between the use of force and libertarian ideals was, ROYO believed, one that had always existed in anarchism. 'To establish libertarian communism means making the

The opportunity missed in Catalonia was seized by the libertarians in Aragon: the power vacuum they found there (the three provincial capitals and the corresponding state apparatus being in nationalist hands) was filled by a CNT council. ROYO was called to attend a plenary session in Bujaraloz, Durruti's headquarters, in September 1936 to consider the matter and draw up a report on the projected council's constitution. He was convinced of the need for such a body because, in his view, Aragon was being treated like a colony by the Catalans and Valencians. A representative of the Catalan Generalitat had toured Aragon making propaganda when the first age-groups were called up, as though Aragon belonged to Catalonia. 'If we were going to have to belong to a government, we didn't want the Generalitat, we preferred to belong to the central government.'[1]

The CNT column leaders, most of them Catalans, opposed the council's creation.

—They spoke threateningly of the rearguard, were hostile. They acted more like thugs than idealists. Arms brutalize men, I thought. The union representatives from the villages weren't going to have any say, it seemed. Then Durruti arrived. 'I have waited all these years for the revolution. Now it has happened. The 14,000 men in my column are with me, I believe, because they agree with me. My men and I are at the disposal of the villages and their unions . . . ' I wasn't a Durruti supporter, I'm nobody's man, but at that moment he was perfect. He shut up all the other column leaders . . .

The CNT Council of Aragon became the only libertarian-dominated governing body in the Popular Front zone.[2] Its propaganda delegate, Juan ZAFON, the sole Catalan serving on a body whose councillors were appointed – 'counter to CNT tradition in which all posts were elected by the base; but we were at war and had to improvise' – saw it as the regulatory body of the collectives rather than as a government. Its aim was to foster further collectivization 'as part of the war effort'; at the same time, the collectives were an attempt to create a model, an example for the future of what, once the war was won, a new libertarian society would be like.[3] But first the war had to be won: he and his companions agreed with Durruti's famous statement.

---

revolution; revolutions are made only by force. Everything that is imposed by force has to be maintained by force. The outcome may be communism but it isn't libertarian. If it were, it wouldn't be communist, for the simple reason that the mass of the people aren't communist. Libertarian communism could be established only if the majority of the people already supported communism and then started to organize that communism *freely* – '

1. Juan ZAFON (see below) maintained that the Generalitat's propaganda machine under Jaume Miravitlles rejected his approach to coordinate their propaganda to which the central government had readily agreed, and stated that it would continue to send its propaganda and cinema lorries to Aragon. ZAFON threatened to expropriate them if they were sent. There were also protests when the militia columns requisitioned foodstuffs, livestock, etc. which threatened to 'ruin the whole region' (Lorenzo, *Los anarquistas españoles y el poder*, p. 120).

2. In exchange for government recognition, it admitted Popular Front parties (with the exception of the POUM) in November 1936, though the CNT retained majority representation.

3. Perhaps because rural collectivization was being pursued more rapidly and extensively in Aragon than in the heartland of anarcho-syndicalism itself, Catalan militants tended to stress the war communism aspect of collectivization, while Aragonese militants emphasized the social revolutionary aims.

—While engaged in our revolutionary experiment, all our propaganda concentrated on the defence of the legally constituted republican government. That might seem contradictory. We didn't think so. The people had expressed their will in the 1936 elections and we had to defend that will, while collectivization served both the war effort and our vision of the future. We were attempting to put into practice a libertarian communism about which, it's sad to say, none of us really knew anything . . .

The free, independent municipality, the collective which abolished the exploitation of man by man, the federal structure which linked each village at district and regional level and, after supplying the needs of the villages and fronts, channelled what surplus was produced to the council, which in turn could sell or exchange it with other regions or abroad; 'all this had been talked and written about, but it had been no more than a slogan until then.'

MAS DE LAS MATAS (Teruel)

With a population of 2,300, Mas de las Matas was a relatively prosperous village of small- and medium-holding peasants. Whereas other lower Aragonese villages lived off wheat and olive crops, Mas de las Matas enjoyed extensive irrigated lands along the river Guadalope which grew large vegetable and fruit crops. More important: the dry land was good and retained moisture; even in a dry year the wheat crop did not fail as it did once every five years or so in other villages. Yet more important, the land was well divided, everyone having some irrigated as well as dry land. 'Equality had real meaning here,' in the words of a self-defined right-winger. 'There was no one who could live without working, no one who had to spend his life seeking a day's wage.' Surprisingly, perhaps, the village was an anarcho-syndicalist stronghold which, in the third of the pre-war libertarian uprisings (December 1933), declared for libertarian communism, forced the *guardia civil* to surrender, burnt local archives and the land registry. The rising was quickly subdued and about 130 villagers arrested and gaoled.

At the start of the military uprising, many libertarians, on instructions from the CNT regional committee, left the village for the fortified town of Morella and from there they joined the Carod column as it advanced into their region. Among them was a twenty-six-year-old cabinet-maker who had joined the CNT in Barcelona, participated in the December rising and was to become one of the protagonists of collectivization. Before reaching their native village, which offered no resistance, Ernesto MARGELI and his companions had taken an important decision: no one was to be imprisoned, let alone shot. MARGELI had never conceived of revolution as meaning that 'half the world has to be killed so that the other half can live. Just because they imprisoned us was no reason for imprisoning them.' For every person killed the revolution would make half a dozen irreconcilable enemies out of their family and friends, he told his companions.

In the village they formed an Anti-Fascist committee, composed half of CNT militants (all elected and including a communist party member) and half of republicans who had a long history in the village. But as more militia forces continued to arrive, as the problem of supplying them became more acute, and as the disorganization of the initial period did not give way to anything better, several CNT members, including MARGELI, realized that something had to be done.

—We were living through a revolutionary moment; it had fallen into our hands. Even if the people weren't prepared, we had to make the revolution now . . .

They called an assembly at which they proposed that a collective be formed. It was something they had always talked about. They explained that if the land were collectivized, if all the different plots were combined, production could be rationalized and increased with less effort through the use of machinery. They spoke of their revolutionary ideals to transform society; they wanted 'the purest form of anarchism'. The assembly agreed.

It was in September, about six weeks after the start of the war. By then collectives had been formed in other villages, predominantly north of the Ebro river; the example was catching on. The nearly 200 CNT members in Mas de las Matas were morally obliged to join the collective. It meant handing over their lands and tools, livestock (with the exception of the one or two pigs each family fattened yearly), stocks of wheat and other produce. The collectivized land was divided into some twenty sectors and each sector was assigned to one work group of about a dozen men, neighbours from the same street, who elected their own delegate or leader. Money was immediately abolished. All produce from collectivized land was to go to 'the pile' for communal consumption; each would produce according to his ability, each would consume according to his need.

—I was so enthusiastic, so fanatic that I took everything in my parents' house – all the grain stocks, the dozen head of sheep, even the silver coins – and handed them into the collective, recalled Sevilla PASTOR, of the libertarian youth, who came from a prosperous peasant family which owned two houses and more land than they could work with family labour alone. So you can see I wasn't in the CNT to defend my daily wage; I was in it for idealistic reasons. My parents weren't as convinced as I, that's for sure . . .

MARGELI put his cabinet-maker's workshop with all the tools and machinery into the collective, for what had been set up was not just an agricultural collective.

—No, no! It was a general village collective. We set up a collective carpenters' shop in a garage on the outskirts of the village where the seven or eight local carpenters made furniture for the collective, carried out repairs – all done free on a collectivist's house – and worked on building projects with the masons who were also collectivized. We built a barber's shop where all the village barbers worked, a collectivized butcher's and so on . . .

Elected secretary of the collective, MARGELI argued from the start against obliging republican party members to join the collective. Something of the sort had been done in neighbouring Alcorisa and it had turned out badly and had to be reversed. None the less, there remained a problem: because landholdings were so numerous and the plots so scattered, rationalization of landwork was made difficult if many peasants refused to join. Machinery could not be introduced unless there was extensive cultivation.

—Our next move was a mistake – the biggest of all, I believe now. We obliged all right-wingers to join. Coerced them morally, not physically, but coerced them all the same . . .

An ugly incident had occurred shortly before. A band of armed men had arrived from Alcañiz, the nearest large town, to 'clean up the village in the name of the CNT'. Its first action was to arrest the local Anti-Fascist committee and take its members, including MARGELI, to the townhall were they were locked up. The committee was accused of 'cowardice' for having refused a purge. Within a couple of hours, six men had been shot on the road leading from the village. There was absolutely no justification for this action, in MARGELI's opinion; the assassinated men had not risen against them, had submitted with more or less good grace to the committee's orders. 'Their assassination was an utterly un-anarchist mode of behaviour which, unfortunately, not all the companions were sufficiently educated to understand.' The following day the Anti-Fascist committee called a village assembly and offered its resignation *en bloc* for having been unable to prevent the assassinations which it unanimously condemned. Several villagers spoke, expressing confidence in the committee, which finally received a unanimous vote of confidence.

The incident, following on the burning of the church by 'uncontrollables' on the day the village was taken by the returning libertarians, posed a considerable threat. Who could tell if it might not be repeated (as it nearly was, though few were to know, by some villagers serving in the Carod column; alerted, the committee was able to take preventive action); violence was everywhere. Within a short time, 2,000 of the village's 2,300 inhabitants had joined the collective.

Lázaro MARTIN's father and older brother were among the six assassinated men. One of the better-off village families, they owned 2 hectares of irrigated and 12 of dry land; his father had belonged to an agrarian syndicate – 'the syndicate of order' as it was locally known – before the war. But it wasn't politics that caused the assassinations, thought MARTIN; it was personal hatreds, vendettas. 'It was enough for one family to be better off than the next for there to be envy.' When collectivization occurred, MARTIN had to join. At first he worked in the collective store, later on the land.

—At first we all thought, 'Well, all right, we'll obey the new order. If things change later, so much the better.' In time of war you've got to expect this sort of thing. It's bad luck if your land is expropriated, there's not much good worrying about it. If that was all that had been at stake we would have put up with it and worked in the collective without any problem, as though nothing had really changed. But taking lives was another matter. It was their big mistake. If it hadn't been for the assassinations, one wouldn't have known there was a war . . .

Even if the conservative peasantry was willing to accept collectivization as a 'war measure', MARGELI remained convinced that the collectives should have been voluntary. The question of the division of the land could have been solved by agreements on exchanging peasant holdings so that the collectivists' lands formed a continuous whole. People who were forced to join did not work with pleasure, worked as little as possible, he observed. The peasant was very individualistic; he had to be persuaded by example.

Another of the collectivist experiments, the most advanced, was also proving unviable. If it was possible for a person to produce according to his ability, it was not possible for people to be left to consume according to their needs. The leap from a capitalist society of scarcity to a communist society of abundance, where neither communism not abundance existed, was doomed.

—People were throwing away bread because it was free, remembered Macario ROYO, the CNT leader, who was a native of Mas de las Matas but spent most of the war on tasks outside the village. It was tragic for us who had aspired to a libertarian society, but we had to face it. Wastage couldn't be permitted. We had to put a wage on people's work and a price on the products. We had in fact to introduce rationing . . .

While some collectives introduced their own paper money (having abolished national currency) and paid a family wage to the collectivists, others worked a form of rationing without money. Both were designed to control consumption. The elimination of money, or its substitution by currency valueless outside the collective, was aimed at preventing the accumulation of capital in private hands. While assuming that money above a certain quantity was synonymous with capital, and while overlooking the elasticity of choice money provided, these collectives did not ignore the actual money value of their products: pre-war prices were used to fix the value of produce exchanged between them; and also the value of some products supplied by the collectives to their members.

—We thought that by abolishing money we would cure most ills, observed MARGELI. From an early age, we had read in anarchist thinkers that money was the root of all evil. But we had no idea of the difficulties it would cause – it turned out to be one of the biggest mistakes. And having different money in each village only added to the muddle . . .

Mas de las Matas did not introduce money but a rationing system. Each family had its ration card: 100 grams of meat, 500 grams of bread, so much sugar, rice, wine per head per day free. Each adult male was allocated a clothing quota of 200 pesetas per head per annum, which could not all be spent at once. In MARGELI's recollection, the system was unwieldy but worked; a family wage would have been preferable.[1] According to MARTIN, the right-wing youth who worked for some time in the collective store, the rations were set too high at the start and, as the stocks which had been taken over were depleted, the rations had to be reduced. None the less, the villagers did not go hungry.

All the taverns were closed. 'We libertarians were always hostile to bars because they were the source of vice, arguments and fights,' recalled Sevilla PASTOR, who had handed over his parents' possessions. Only the large room in the CNT centre was left open and there people could drink coffee or non-

1. Adopted in many rural collectives, the family wage consisted of a basic day-wage for all working family heads, plus a wage for each dependant which varied according to whether he or she had reached working age or not. The wages were paid in the collective's currency. (See also p. 367 n.)

alcoholic beverages. Wine was distributed as part of the ration for private consumption at home. Gambling was suppressed.

PASTOR was happier working in the collective than he had ever been. A large part of the happiness stemmed from knowing that he and his companions were working for the good of the village as a whole. There were others, he realized, who didn't share his enthusiasm because they felt that instead of working for themselves they were working for others. But the committed libertarian youth worked harder in the collective than before the war, believing that the war demanded it of them.

—We knew we weren't prepared to achieve our real goal – libertarian communism. The collective's purpose was to increase production for the war effort and to prevent speculation and private profit. Remember, all trade was in private hands at the start of the war. Now the collective controlled it. When the war was won, we thought, we would continue on our collectivist path, but everyone would be free to decide whether they wanted to remain in it or not . . .

Although he bore hatred for those who had killed his father and brother, Lázaro MARTIN found that to live and work in the collective was 'no hardship at all'. He found himself working a good deal less hard than before when he had been used to going out to the fields at day-break, and returning at sunset.

—But now we didn't go out until the sun was shining overhead, and we stopped a lot earlier too. Each work group looked after its own interests up to a point. If we were weeding a melon patch, each of us would have a melon or two, with our delegate's knowledge. It was like everything: ideals are one thing and personal interests another[1] . . .

But it was the republicans and socialists who did not join the collective whom he pitied most. As long as they worked their land on their own they had no problems, but if they as much as got their brother or a neighbour to lend them a hand, then the trouble started. The 'individualists' were supposed to have only as much land as they could work on their own, and any infringement by calling on outside labour was leapt on.

Another medium-holding peasant's son, Jaime AVILA, who found himself in the collective, had no objection to the work – 'it's an obligation to work anyway' – and was pleased to have got a new jacket and a pair of trousers from the collective store, something he had not been able to afford before. Nor did he find it unduly strange to work without pay. In a great many farmers' homes sons did not get a wage.

—Nor did their parents, of course. Until the crop was sold they didn't get any money for their work. That was country life; work wasn't valued in terms of a daily wage. When there's a job to do, country people go out and do it. And that's what we did. It wasn't a regime of terror, you couldn't call it that. All the same, we saw things we had never seen before. What sort of things? People being shot, some after trial and some without. And so everybody had to do what *they* said . . .

1. Some fifteen months later, MARTIN managed to cross to the nationalist lines; after three nights in the mountains, a guide led a party of eighteen across.

If the experiment had continued longer, he felt, they would have seen if it really worked. What would happen when the stocks ran out? Could they be replenished? As it happened, the wheat harvest in Aragon that year had been very good, and the olive crop to come was similarly excellent. As long as there was food and clothing people were more or less content. But in a bad year? He felt that in the work groups there was always a shirker, and as soon as another saw him taking things easy the example spread. Why should one work harder than another?

—Not that it was better to work on your own, I don't mean that, but it was necessary to have a stimulus, a drive – and that was what was missing. We people here weren't of the quality needed to make the experiment work; more than mutual respect was necessary for that. And meanwhile what was happening in the rest of the nation? In one place one lot was in charge, and across the lines another lot. The strongest would force the weakest to give up their system and impose their own. It was a mix-up and a mess I never understood . . .

Florentín CEBRIAN's father had resisted joining the collective. A right-winger, he owned only half a hectare of land, which was insufficient to support a family of five children. Florentín, at the age of twenty-one, went out to work as a labourer; when his father at last joined the collective 'from force of circumstances or fear, I've never known', he too had to join. He did not mind the work, but he resented receiving no pay. 'Everybody at work likes to know why they're working and for whom.' When he went out to work it was to earn a day's wage. Now he got his food instead.

—But there was a war on, you had to bear that in mind. I used to say to myself, 'This isn't going to last for ever. Nothing is eternal.' I had heard people talk about the war in Cuba. That had come to an end, and I imagined one day this war would end too . . .

The collective attempted to reconcile the peasantry to the new system by allowing each collectivist a small, irrigated plot to grow vegetables for his own home. The men worked there on Sundays. Similarly, everyone was allowed to keep chickens and to rear rabbits at home. The two or three village motorbikes which had belonged to small businessmen were expropriated and given to the shepherds of the large herds formed from the previous privately owned head of stock. 'It was time to improve the shepherds' lot, we thought; they had always had the hardest, most oppressed lives, and so now we spared them having to walk long distances,' Sevilla PASTOR, of the libertarian youth, remembered.

In almost every collective there was one general wish which, when fulfilled, brought immense satisfaction: the introduction of agricultural machinery where there had been none. In many collectives, as in Mas de las Matas, this was a threshing machine which ended the laborious task of threshing by mule and winnowing by hand. The collective procured a Czech machine powered by an electric motor in time for the 1937 harvest. It was 'paid for' by the collective's produce of beans, fruit, and cattle stock with which the collective had run up a credit with the Council of Aragon. The latter had found the foreign currency.

As the chief village in a rural district comprising eighteen other villages, Mas de las Matas was responsible for the district's exchange of produce. An account – expressed in pesetas and at pre-war prices – was kept for each village in the district warehouse, and exchanges carried out through the Council of Aragon.

—There was no inflation, prices were fixed. Without realizing it we had created an economic dictatorship! It went against our principles, we would have had to change it with time, explained MARGELI. But I came to the conclusion that someone has to be responsible for giving orders; things couldn't work simply with people doing as they wanted . . .

He began to see that assemblies, in which many anarchists put all their trust, were not always the best vehicles for selecting the people to be in charge because those attending the meeting often did not take sufficient account of a person's psychological suitability for the post. And choice of the correct person was what mattered most.

—We held village assemblies only to discuss special matters, like fixing the bread ration, or schools. The women attended, of course. They, for example, wanted to continue to bake their own bread. The collective provided freshly baked bread daily whereas the women, traditionally, baked only once every ten days or so, and the bread went stale. But the women liked their old ways, didn't want to change. The assembly decided against them. There was a lot of talk at these assemblies – too much. We should have talked less and worked more! . . .

A characteristic concern with education occupied the collectivists. From the start of the war the village schools were re-opened to keep the children off the streets, and students called in to replace teachers absent on holiday. MARGELI made a special trip to Barcelona to fill a lorry with rationalist school books. He also managed to procure a duplicator, a ciné projector and some children's films. A new school was built in a farmhouse for children from outlying areas who had never been able to attend school; education was made co-educational, a school magazine started, a theatre group set up. Once a week the collective's committee met to discuss matters with the teachers, insisting that the schools must want for nothing.

—A young woman teacher said she had never known anything like it. Previously it had been impossible to get funds for education. We were always prepared to adapt our ideas in every area of collective life if things didn't work. That was the advantage of our collectives over state-created ones like those in Russia. We were free. Each village could do as it pleased. There was local stimulus, local initiative. True, the problem of inequality of resources existed; there were rich and poor collectives, and this was something that had to be tackled, as it was at the 1938 special CNT economic conference in Valencia which proposed the creation of an Iberian syndical bank. Meanwhile, we suggested that villagers from the poorer villages, where there was a surplus of labour, should go to work in more prosperous collectives. But the people were stubborn, they didn't like the idea of moving . . .

*

The Mas de las Matas collective was undoubtedly among the more successful.

In Macario ROYO's view this was because of the existence of a relatively prosperous, independent peasantry. 'As a result, many of the young people had a good education, a good grounding in libertarian thought. It wasn't a poor day-labourers' village – ' A socialist from a neighbouring village in the province of Castellón, Emilio SEGOVIA, who travelled extensively through Aragon on business and was opposed to the total collectivization that was being carried out, admired the Mas de las Matas collective. He remembered going to see one of the richest men in the village who had joined.

—'How come you're a communist now?' I said. He had more than enough land, wine, olive oil to live comfortably. 'Why? Because this is the most human system there is.' In Mas de las Matas it worked really well. I remember them sending a man who suffered from an ulcer to Barcelona to be cured. It cost them 7,000 pesetas, a considerable amount of money at the time. More than the man would have been able to raise for himself . . .[1]

ALLOZA (Teruel)

Some 30 km from Mas de las Matas, on a small prominence in the centre of a large bowl of arable land, stands the village of Alloza. In the 1930s, Alloza was both smaller (population 1,800) and less prosperous than Mas de las Matas. Its economy was based on the traditional wheat, olives and wine; a year without rain meant no wheat harvest. Though a few villagers had joined the CNT in Barcelona, there was no union in the village. Politics functioned in a manner common enough in rural Spain: the monarchy's liberals and conservatives became the republic's left republicans and CEDA members. Power remained in the same hands; the change of regime at the national level meant only a change of shirt at the local. In the Justice of the Peace's words, the village was like a vat of olive oil – 'so calm that it seemed the republic had not been proclaimed here'.

At the outbreak of war, with rumours that the insurgents were advancing from Saragossa some 100 km to the north-west, and anarcho-syndicalist columns setting out from Barcelona to the east, the villagers chose an ingenious course: they set up a committee composed of left- and right-wingers to protect each other whatever side arrived first. 'A form of mutual aid to prevent a blood-bath; it was fear of what might happen which made it possible, of course,' explained Mariano FRANCO, CNT member and smallholder's son, who was responsible for the initiative.

Within a few days an armed group claiming to belong to the CNT reached the village, sacked the church and set fire to religious images, including some locally famous copper reliefs from the Calvary above the village. Mariano FRANCO finally managed to get them to leave.

—It was an unequal struggle; they were armed and I wasn't. But I had joined the CNT at the age of sixteen, had been fighting for my ideals – which evidently

1. Contemporary anarchist accounts of the Mas de las Matas collective are contained in G. Leval, *Collectives in the Spanish Revolution* (London, 1975); and A. Souchy and Bauer, *Entre los campesinos de Aragón* (Valencia, 1937). No such accounts exist for the following collective in Alloza.

they didn't share – for nearly half my life. With the moral strength that gave me, I was able to confront them . . .

A few days later, the Carod column reached the village and continued on to Muniesa. FRANCO, who had known Carod in the Barcelona CNT, had already set off to join the column. Alloza was now, and remained for the next eighteen months, only a few kilometres behind the front line. Barely a week later, militiamen from two neighbouring villages came to make four arrests in the village; the prisoners, who included a priest and a civil guard lieutenant, were taken to Carod's headquarters where a militia committee condemned them to death. Mariano ALQUEZAR, a large-holding peasant and right-wing deputy mayor of the village, was one of the four. He was accused of being the village's leading fascist. 'In fact, I wasn't a falangist – although I would have been if I could. My family was traditionally right-wing, my father had been the local leader of the Conservatives, and we were called *caciques* in the village.' Convinced from the moment of his arrest that he was going to die, he did not deny the charge. He remained calmly waiting in the cell for his hour to come.

—Suddenly Mariano Franco appeared. I could see he was deeply upset. He was an idealist, completely opposed to people being shot. This wasn't what he was fighting for. He didn't mention the priest and the civil guard lieutenant, who were both from Alloza originally and had returned there to hide. Franco couldn't save them, but he got me and the other man released. I returned to the village with my companion who almost immediately fell ill and soon afterwards died . . .

Angel NAVARRO, a smallholder, had seen the men being driven away. 'Now it's going to start,' he thought and began to shiver. A former CNT member in Barcelona where he had gone as a building labourer because his father's land was too poor to support the family, he was shortly appointed president of the village committee on Carod's and Franco's recommendation. His sole concern became to avoid bloodshed in Alloza where, as he knew, opinion generally favoured the insurgent rather than the Popular Front cause.

One day a car drew up and half a dozen militiamen got out with a list of people they had come to arrest.

—'Yes,' I said. 'Have you eaten supper, companions? No. Well, let's go and eat and we'll talk about it then.' We went to the inn which was run by a relative. I sent out the town crier to find the man who held the keys of the collective store to fetch a good ham, a carafe of wine. When the militiamen had eaten one of them said: 'Come on, we're in a hurry.' I feared the worst. Instead, one of them put his arm round my shoulder. 'Comrade, everyone should be like you, act as you have.' They left. That night in Alcorisa they shot a lot of people . . .

There had been other incidents of this sort earlier. It was in this climate that, in the autumn of 1936, collectivization took place. Until the CNT representatives of the district committee came to tell them to collectivize, nothing had changed on the land.

—We agreed to collectivize – simply to ensure that lives were spared. If we did what we were told there would be no cause for reprisals. Otherwise I feared for what might happen – and to us on the committee in particular . . .

A village assembly was called. NAVARRO explained that the initiative came from outside. 'They've come and told us other villages have collectivized and they want everyone to be equal.' The CNT representatives had stressed that no one was to be maltreated, had suggested how to organize the collective. NAVARRO proposed to the assembly that work groups be made up of family and friends and that each group work its former lands, although all produce would have to go on 'the pile', i.e. to a collective warehouse.

—The collective wouldn't have been formed if it hadn't been for the terror. In fact, given the choice, I wouldn't have joined myself. If everyone were good and just – not egotistical and two-faced – a collective would be fine to work and live in because union brings strength. But I knew what we were really like . . .

Once the decision was taken, it was formally left to the peasants to volunteer to join. Mariano Franco came from the front to hold a meeting, saying that militiamen were threatening to take the livestock of all those who remained outside the collective. As in Mas de las Matas, all privately owned stocks of food had to be turned in.

Juan MARTINEZ, a twenty-eight-year-old medium-holding farmer, who belonged to the left republicans but considered himself a-political, had considerable quantities of olive oil, wine and wheat which, with other stocks in his wife's small shop, had to be handed over. He was left without anything, 'cleaned out, in fact'.

—But I realized there was a war on and everyone had to make sacrifices. 'Look, *chico*, material interests aren't the most important thing at the moment. What we've got to ensure is that no one is assassinated.' Everyone felt the same . . .

Once the work groups were established on a friendly basis and worked their own lands, everyone got on well enough together, he recalled. There was no need for coercion, no need of discipline and punishment. People worked just as hard as before. The owners of the land knew what crops needed sowing in their fields, everyone knew how to work the land. A collective wasn't a bad idea at all.

—To work in common is by no means stupid. It meant large concentrations of land instead of small, scattered plots, which saved time and effort. We didn't live worse under collectivization than before – or only to the extent made inevitable by the war. Those who had had less – and there were quite a few of them before – now ate more and better. But no one went short . . .

He shared, however, the generalized dislike for having to hand over all the produce to 'the pile' and to get nothing except his rations in return. Another bad thing was the way the militia columns requisitioned livestock from the collective, issuing vouchers in return. Having been appointed livestock delegate, he went on a couple of occasions to Caspe to try to 'cash in' the vouchers unsuccessfully.

As elsewhere, the abolition of money soon led to the 'coining' of local money – a task the blacksmith carried out by punching holes in tin disks until paper notes could be printed. The 'money' – 1·50 pesetas a day – was distributed, as the local schoolmaster recalled, to collectivists to spend on their 'vices' – 'the latter being anything superfluous to the basic requirements of keeping alive'. With the money he could go to the café – there were only two kept open: one for the collectivists and one for the 'individualists' – and have a cup of coffee (no spirits were served; the bottles had been taken away), or his wife could buy a quarter litre of milk or extras like peaches when they were in season.

In the schoolmaster's view, the reaction of many of the independent local peasantry was not as equanimous as Juan MARTINEZ's. Along with the doctor, chemist, barber, shoemaker, etc., Alfredo CANCER, the schoolmaster, was collectivized.

—The peasantry disliked having to give up their crops. 'A thousand *dobles* of my olives have gone to "the pile". *Virgen del Pilar*, when will the fascists come?' one of them said to me. He wasn't worried about the Virgin, he was concerned about his olives . . .

Well over half the small- and medium-holders felt like him, thought CANCER, who now received only food and a tin disk for 1·50 pesetas a day in place of his previous 250 pesetas a month salary. He was living on potatoes, bread, lentils and a bit of rice. He had no pig to rear.

—I went to the committee and they said: 'Go to Tío Enselmo' – that's the way they say the name Anselmo – 'and he'll give you half a pig, for he's got two.'

'Tío Enselmo,' I said, 'I've come for half a pig – '

'And this pig,' he said, looking at me, 'who has reared it?' 'You.' 'And if I have reared it, whose is it?' 'Yours.' 'And if it's mine, why have you come for it?' 'I've been told to by the committee. But if you don't want to give it to me, I won't take it. It's harder for me to have to come to ask than for you to have to give it to me. My sister gets headaches living only on fried potatoes – I think she's anaemic, and a little meat would do her good.'

'Take it then,' he said . . .

He had the same story when he went to get a sack of potatoes on the committee's instructions. The peasants did not want to give up what they considered was theirs; 'that was the only reason they favoured the fascists.' On the other hand, he observed, the poor who had lived on little more than bread, potatoes and water were certainly much better off than before, for now they got olive oil, rice, sausages, meat.

—Had I been one of them I might well have thought like them and wanted the new system to continue. It wasn't that the anarchists' ideals were bad – they were simply utopian. I was no property owner and had no reason to be hostile to them out of fear of losing my wealth. Nor was I political. It seems fine that I should teach the shoemaker's son free and the shoemaker should make me a pair of shoes for nothing. But what really happened was a loss of incentive. That is, unless you were a don Quixote or a saint. We Aragonese are independent-minded, freedom-lovers, healthily proud. Without freedom, what is there? . . .

As far as his school went, the collective obtained everything the children needed free of charge, made parents respect the legal school-leaving age of fourteen – 'before they took their children out of school at twelve to look after the livestock' – and generally showed a great concern about education.

Freedom could be subject to many definitions; but there was no doubt that for many peasants it meant continuing in the way they were accustomed to.

—The immense majority in the villages round here didn't want to be collectivized, admitted Angel NAVARRO, the CNT village committee president. They didn't believe the collectives could work with everything going on 'the pile'; they felt they had to ask for what was theirs by right – it was like having to beg . . .

The opponents of collectivization included CNT members and those close to them. One of the talking points in Alloza was the refusal of Mariano FRANCO's father to join.

—There was I, the leading village collectivist, and I couldn't even persuade my father. He said the collectivists didn't work properly, the leaders didn't know how to do things. He preferred to stay outside working his own land like a slave. People said it did the collective's reputation a lot of harm. I'd tell him the collective had produced more wheat that year than the village had ever harvested before. He'd reply that the year had been a specially good one. I couldn't oblige him to join; we weren't living under a dictatorship . . .

As it was, considering that it was a war economy, the collectives were very successful, he thought. Still the majority of the collectives were imposed, not spontaneous, for the revolution was not being made.

—We had no option. Our sole objective was to combat fascism and win the war, nothing else. Of course, obligatory collectivization caused many problems with smallholders. With time, years of propaganda perhaps, we could have shown them that with less expenditure of energy they could produce more. Co-operatives wouldn't have served the same purpose: the land would still have been scattered in plots, time would have been wasted going from one to the other – they weren't the correct economic solution . . .

The collective matched Mas de las Matas in acquiring a threshing machine by an exchange of olive oil. Moreover, the village administered the local lignite mines, which the miners had taken over, and sold coal to Barcelona, thereby securing a useful source of revenue to procure food supplies the collective itself did not produce. But one problem which afflicted the collectivization experiment almost everywhere was vividly demonstrated in Alloza: the shortage of administrators. Most of the people appointed to the collective's committees were right-wingers, Angel NAVARRO recalled.

—The man who ran the accounts and did all the paper work, who bought and sold on the collective's behalf, was a *falangista*. When the nationalists took the village they made him mayor. What else could you expect? We, the poor, had only one concern before the war: to go out and work the land, while the others, with education, ran the village . . .

Militancies II

SATURNINO CAROD
CNT column leader

The problem preoccupied him: so many of the villagers in the collectivization experiment were illiterate that, when he went to see how a collective was working, they often did not understand what he meant when he asked if they were keeping accounts. They replied that if they needed something for the village they got hold of a lorry – often one lent them by the Carod column – and made an exchange with another village.

—It seemed almost impossible to get them to understand the need for accounts; such bureaucratic necessities were opposed to the romantic, idealistic ways they were pursuing in all good faith . . .

He had argued against the abolition of money which was based on a confusion between money and capital; the error was rapidly illustrated when the villages had to print their own. And he was insistent on the need for accounting.

—'Yes, yes, we're keeping accounts now as you suggested,' they'd tell me, producing a bit of wire bent in the shape of a hook on which there were stuck cigarette packets, wrappings from other products or the margins of newspapers, which bore the marks of several lines or strokes. In some cases, where there was someone who knew how to sign his name, you'd perhaps find the word Alcañiz as well. But never the article or products to which these scratches corresponded. Even more typical was a bamboo cane split down the middle. Both sides were notched in such a manner as to indicate what had been bought and sold, and the buyer's and seller's half fitted together exactly. Despite their lack of formal education, and thanks to their natural intelligence, these people achieved very considerable successes. In organizing work no one could better them, for they knew, from their long experience of cultivating the land, what had to be done and how . . .

He himself, the son of a landless day-labourer in the small village of Moneva (close to his column headquarters now at Muniesa), had been illiterate until his early twenties. At six, he had begun earning his keep; at times, to help keep his eleven brothers and sisters alive, he had been driven to begging or to looking for snails, edible fungi, herbs or whatever else he could find. At the age of twelve he was a ploughman, working for a peasant with a medium-sized holding; later, he followed the wheat harvest across the Castilian plain, reaping with a sickle. By the age of eighteen he had left the village, as so many Aragonese were forced to do. It was the end of the First World War. He crossed France; at the German border the sight of the enormous quantities of marks being exchanged for a few pesetas frightened him, and he turned back. Reaching Barcelona finally, he became a building labourer; and there, again like so many Aragonese migrants, he joined the CNT. He attended union meetings, spoke but vanished when there was any question of being elected to a union post. Maurín, then of the CNT, later secretary-general of the POUM, discovered the reason and suggested to his workmates that they cut out the headlines of newspapers to teach him to form syllables and pronounce them. It was during the worst era of governmental and employers' repression of the CNT in Barcelona,[1] and soon he had to flee to France. His group had been on its way to shoot an employer when they met a priest who was bearing the viaticum and was accompanied by police.

—We refused to kneel, as was the custom, or to obey police orders. The employer we were after was a very bad man who refused to recognize the union or any of the workers' demands. Our refusal to obey police orders resulted in a shoot-out and we all scattered . . .

When an amnesty was declared on the republic's proclamation, he returned from exile to live and work in Saragossa. Soon elected to the CNT regional committee, he made it a condition of his acceptance that the committee undertake peasant organization. He had always felt himself a peasant; but he knew that within the CNT, despite its massive rural strength in Andalusia, there was hostility, not only – and understandably – towards the landowner but towards the small peasant as a property owner. As propaganda delegate, he began a series of public meetings in the villages of Aragon to organize amongst the smallholders.

His opposition to total collectivization at the start of the war stemmed from his awareness that many of the people fighting in his column were smallholders, and that a great number of different tendencies were represented: republicans, socialists, liberals, Catholics, libertarians. To collectivize, he argued at a CNT regional plenum, might provoke dissension amongst the non-libertarian peasantry and the combatants at the front. He knew only too well how the smallholder clung to his plot of land.

—It's a part of his being, he's a slave to it. To deprive him of it is like tearing his heart from his body. He must not be forced to give it up to join a collective . . .

Collectives, formed from land belonging to owners who had fled and from communal land, should act as an example for the future; they should help, rather than hinder, individualist smallholders so that they would be encouraged by their example;[2] meanwhile, the small peasantry should form cooperatives.

But once collectives had formed, it was his duty to support them in every way possible. He found himself saddled with the responsibility of conducting the war in his sector and of helping the collectives in the rear. He used his influence with his companions in the rear to ensure that the peasants' needs were attended to rapidly and unbureaucratically; loaned the collectives lorries and technicians; and made a special trip to talk to the CNT's national committee secretary, Mariano Vázquez, to suggest that book-keepers or people capable of keeping accounts should be sent to the collectives.

1. See Points of Rupture, D.

2. In which he was following Kropotkin's teachings in *The Conquest of Bread*: the revolution would not dispossess the smallholders but would 'send its young people to help them reap the corn and bring home the harvest'. (See Leval, *Collectives in the Spanish Revolution*, p. 86.)

Convinced that capitalism spawned the all-enveloping megalopolis at the expense of the stagnant, isolated rural village, and that neither represented the post-capitalist future, he set out to realize a revolutionary vision of his own: the creation of an agro-town. The aim was both economic and social. By creating a viable rural economy it would be possible to prevent migration from villages whose existence no longer corresponded to historical necessity but where people continued to eke out a miserable existence, deprived of the most elementary means of satisfying their human needs.

He chose the village of Muniesa, where he had his headquarters, because it had good road communications, and started with the building of farm installations to rear chickens and rabbits, and later pigs and cattle. Bricklayers and carpenters serving in his column worked at their respective trades while ordinary militiamen and a handful of peasants worked as labourers.

—Next to the farm was a flour mill on which I spent the equivalent of nearly 200,000 pesetas converting and re-equipping it to mill the grains grown in the region. My aim was that all the mill's waste product should be used as foodstuff for the farm's livestock. Soon we had two large blocks completed for rabbit-breeding, and an incubator with a capacity of hatching 24,000 chicks every twenty-one days . . .

Here the peasantry from the outlying areas would find work. But it was necessary to create jobs for women, since their migration often led to that of the men. He planned to develop the region's bee-keeping and the use of honey in the manufacture of sweets and *turrones*, which would provide female employment, as would a small meat-canning factory.

—Despite everything that is said about the liberation of women, one must take into account woman's social role, particularly as mother, and protect her from the sort of work that requires great strength. It was not right that a single woman who needed to earn her living had to work the land like a man . . .

The social purpose of the agro-town was to provide the educational and recreational facilities so sorely missing in the small villages: not only schools, but theatres, cinemas, libraries. At the same time he bore in mind that the larger the city or town, the less intimate were the relations between its inhabitants and the greater the inhumanity.

—Solidarity should come first in all human societies. In a town of 15,000 to 30,000 inhabitants, everybody more or less knows each other, and each respects his neighbour and is willing to lend a hand when the latter needs it . . .

The CNT national committee sent foreign technicians to see what he was doing. They valued the project at 9 million pesetas, he recalled.

—We had spent hardly anything. Then they asked me for the plans. I said I was sorry. They assured me they wouldn't use them for any other purpose than to study what was being done. Finally, after some to-ing and fro-ing, I said: 'No one can see the plans because they're here – in my head.' And that was the truth. Whenever I went to the farm I would say to the bricklayers:

'Lay me out a section here of such and such a size; we're going to use it for chicken-rearing.' The general ideas were mine but they were carried out by skilled workmen, militiamen and peasants.

Perhaps we were dreamers. Utopians. Yes, all of us; but remember that even liberalism was a utopia until it was realized, and then socialism appeared the utopia. We were (and remain) convinced that one day the utopia of ours – the most utopian of all perhaps – will be realized; for if it isn't, man will not be content . . .

Others were as concerned as Carod at the lack of trained administrators. Félix CARRASQUER, the FAI schoolteacher who, on the day of the military uprising, had been expounding his plan for a CNT people's school in Barcelona, put his idea into practice in his native Aragon. The boarding school he started on his own initiative in Monzón for some sixty students between the ages of fourteen and eighteen, all peasants' children who had been elected by their respective collectives for the six-month courses, was to prepare them practically and theoretically for administering collectives.

Every Sunday, the school travelled to different villages. CARRASQUER noticed the difference between those which had spontaneously collectivized and the others. In the former, where the CNT had existed before and the small peasantry was used to running its own holdings, things went well. But where the collectives were formed by CNT militiamen or where CNT militants had forced people to collectivize, things were often very different. He was called on more than one occasion to settle disputes.

—'You have got to leave people free to decide what they want to do,' I reminded the fanatical anarcho-syndicalists who insisted on forcing smallholders into the collective. But it wasn't a widespread problem, because there weren't more than twenty or so villages where collectivization was total and no one was allowed to remain outside . . .

In February 1937, rather tardily in comparison with Catalonia or the Levant, the CNT held an extraordinary congress in Caspe to discuss the creation of an Aragonese regional federation of collectives. CARRASQUER attended as a delegate; he was convinced of the need for a federation. Each collective had by now got into the habit of sending its own produce in its own lorry to Barcelona or somewhere to exchange it for other products. Without a federation, there could be no solidarity, no communitarian sense of self-management. But it was a long hard battle before the congress could be persuaded.

—Knowing our militants, knowing that each would want to make his speech, I let them all talk first. Then I got up. The 'cantonalism' of the collectives spelt the ruin of the movement, I said. A rich collective could live well, a poor collective would have difficulty feeding its members. 'Is that communism? No, it's the very opposite. Whose fault is it if one village has good land and the next has poor?' The congress was persuaded of the need for a regional federation. Then I outlined the need for a national federation. 'But you've just persuaded us to create a regional federation and now you want to destroy it,' was the reaction I got. It illustrated one of the problems the movement confronted . . . [1]

*

Self-managed autonomy could, in a collective, turn into the autonomy of 'managers' over the 'managed'. This, at least, was the experience of Fernando ARAGON and his wife Francisca, both staunch CNT supporters, in the important collective and district centre of Angüés, close behind the lines on the Huesca front in northern Aragon. A smallholder and day-labourer, ARAGON had joined the CNT nearly twenty years earlier in Barcelona, and would have given his life to defend it, because for as long as he could remember he had hated the bourgeoisie. 'A stone on the road isn't worth much, is it? Well, I'll tell you: I wouldn't even give a stone to a bourgeois – '

The collective set up in Angüés was total; no one was allowed to remain outside. He welcomed the collective's creation. Wasn't this the moment they had been waiting for for so long? When at last they were rid of the bourgeoisie, especially the half-dozen landowners with as much as 200 hectares each of the best land, who had been grinding him and his fellow workers into the dust.

—When we brought in the wheat crop – an excellent harvest because we had worked hard and it had rained at the right time – we knew we were right: all that grain which had been sown, reaped and threshed with our labour had previously gone to benefit the landowners who did nothing. How sad to think of what those landlords had been making out of us before; how happy we were now to see the fruit of our labour providing food for the collective, the whole village . . .

Three or four of the peasants with larger holdings tried to leave the collective, but the committee controlled all the sources of seed and fertilizer and there was nowhere, now that money had been abolished, where they could buy what they needed. They had to remain in. But they worked unwillingly, he observed: they hadn't their hearts in it, the hopes he and his companions had for the future. But soon he saw that it was not only the reluctant peasants who had no desire to work: it was the twenty-odd members – 'where three or four would have been enough' – of the village committee. The younger men went round with pistols stuck in their waistbands, looking – 'but not working' – like revolutionaries. The older men labouring in the fields commented that amongst their number were several who could no longer work hard on the land but could do a committee job. (ARAGON excluded himself for he was illiterate, and he knew that on the committee it was necessary to have some learning.) But what was even worse was that the committee members were lining their pockets: all the best food ended up in their houses. The collective produced considerable quantities, all the village's needs were met, except when the committee refused to distribute stocks. ARAGON's wife, Francisca, had twins; they were expecting only one baby and lacked clothing. He went to the committee and explained his need.

1. Among the major agreements reached at the congress were those to abolish *all* money, including local currency, and substitute a standard ration book; to permit smallholders to remain non-collectivized as long as they did not 'interfere with the interests of the collective' from which they could expect no benefits; to organize the collectives at district rather than local level; and to refuse the Council of Aragon the monopoly of foreign trade. (See Leval, op. cit., pp. 83–90, 197, 203; also Mintz, *L'Autogestion dans l'Espagne Révolutionnaire*, pp. 100–102.)

—They turned me down. 'If we give you anything, all the pregnant women will come begging.' 'Is this what the revolution is about?' I said to them. I knew they could provide something, even if only a few bits and pieces of cloth. 'Is this why we're fighting the fascists? Is this why I'm working in the collective? To be refused a small request – a need for a newborn? Until I get clothes for the child, I won't do another day's work.' They didn't like it; they knew I had been in the CNT a long time. They gave in . . .

But that wasn't the end. One of the twins fell ill with a kidney complaint. Having no faith in the local doctor, Francisca wanted to take the baby to a doctor in Barbastro, the nearest large town 30 km away. She went to the committee.

—There were always half a dozen of them there – men. There wasn't a single woman member. They refused me transport, it was all needed for the front. They told me to walk. They had three or four cars they had expropriated from the bourgeoisie which they were always riding about in. I got angry and asked for money so that I could make my own way to Barbastro. They refused. 'It was your idea to abolish money so that we should all be equal. What sort of equality is this? You ride round in cars when I need to take my child to the doctor.' They still refused . . .

Her father had been a CNT militant, her first husband had been killed during a strike in Barcelona, she had helped her brother-in-law, a CNT member, to escape from a ship that was taking him and others to deportation after the great 1933 tram strike in Barcelona. But she wouldn't have a single good word to say of the revolution as she lived it in Angüés. She lost both her twins – they caught measles and died.

—There was great discontent. The women talked about it. We went out to work in the fields – and it was right that we should. But why didn't the wives of the committee members have to go? If things went on like this, we would have to get rid of the committee. I wanted to leave, but I couldn't. We had no money, no means. Moreover, the committee had guards posted on the roads. It was terror, dictatorship . . .[1]

—There was no way of getting rid of those committee members. They had the arms, recalled ARAGON. We couldn't vote them out, they only called a general assembly when one of them got fed up and wanted to leave. Or else if there was something very important to decide. Of one thing I'm convinced. Had we won

1. The problem of collectivists' freedom to leave villages – permanently or on trips – exercised the imagination of observers from the start. With the abolition of money, the collective held the upper hand since anyone wishing to travel had to get 'republican' money from the committee. This meant justifying the trip. In those times, it must be remembered, travel was not likely to be undertaken unless there was considerable need. In Mas de las Matas, the collective prided itself on sending people to Barcelona for specialist medical attention; and the collective paid the bus fares of families to visit their sons at the front. But for a person without a union card to leave the village, even on a short trip, it was necessary to get a pass, according to a right-winger. Ill-health in Alloza was seen as a valid justification and the schoolmaster's father-in-law left to have a hernia operation, taking the opportunity not to return. As lorries went frequently to Barcelona with produce it was not difficult to get a lift. Conditions obviously varied from collective to collective and, as in many other aspects, generalization is impossible.

the war, we workers would have had to fight another to get rid of those sort of people who were only out for themselves. Another revolution, there was no other way. Until that was possible, I went on working, nothing could shake my faith in the collective itself. I would have fought and died to defend it, as we thought was going to be necessary when the communists came. For, despite everything, those were the best years of my life . . .

*

For detractors of the Aragon collectives, Fernando ARAGON's experience was more or less typical; for supporters, exceptional if undeniable. As one of the few collectives where everyone was forced to join, it was certainly exceptional; total, it became, in this experience, totalitarian.[1] At stake was an inner democracy which directly expressed the collective's will. Arbitrary conduct by those elected could only be prevented by ensuring their immediate recall if they failed to carry out the majority will. Such recall was not built into the collective structure here or elsewhere; too much, in consequence, depended on the 'good' (or 'bad') faith of those in positions of responsibility.

—In trying to create their free society, the anarchists were obliged to use force. I've had peasants come up to me almost crying with rage, saying they weren't against the collectives – 'but they've taken everything from me and forced me into it and that's dictatorship.' At some of the assemblies I attended, men walked round armed, hands on pistols . . .

Antonio ROSEL, a communist foundryman who, thanks to the CNT, had managed to escape from Saragossa three months after the start of the war, visited villages in lower Aragon as a UGT delegate in the company of a CNT militant to sort out problems. (The two unions in Aragon had signed a 'unity in action' pact which included agreement to 'help and stimulate' freely constituted collectives while respecting the freedom of the smallholding peasantry.) The communist party, he stressed, was *not* opposed to collectives as such. Where a landowner had disappeared and his estate had been taken over by day-labourers who wanted to work it collectively, the party had no objection.

—If a whole village freely decided to form a collective, that was fine. The trouble was that anyone who knew lower Aragon knew only too well that no such thing would happen. The peasantry *en masse* would not freely opt for such a solution, they preferred cooperatives to collectives. It was different for the landless labourers. People had to be given a choice. But the anarchists wanted to impose their maximalist revolution right from the start – and among a peasantry that lacked the understanding and consciousness for such a revolution. It was an anarchist dictatorship . . .

ROSEL, who had started life as an anarchist, did not feel that he was a syste-

1. Whereas in Mas de las Matas and Alloza it was possible to talk to supporters and detractors of the collectives, I was unable (for extraneous reasons) to do the same for the Angüés collective. No contemporary descriptions exist in Leval, Souchy, Mintz or Peirats. A village of 1,500 inhabitants, Angüés was an important centre with thirty-six collectives within its district in February 1937, a number which grew to seventy within the next few months (Leval, op. cit., p. 70). The testimony of Fernando ARAGON and his wife – a view of the inherent undemocratic dangers contained within the collectivization experiment – must stand on its own.

matic detractor of anarchism. One day, when communism had been in existence a long time, the scientific basis for the advance to libertarian communism might appear. But not like this. Revolutionaries with real revolutionary awareness would have understood, he thought, that the revolution being imposed in Aragon was contrary not only to the peasants' interests but to the interests of the war. It was obvious to him, as it was to the communist party, that the war had to be won first; then the revolution could be made. Not only were the anarchists trying to make the revolution first, detracting effort from the war, but the Council of Aragon, as an autonomous government, was prejudicial to the conduct of the war which required in his opinion a strong central government. 'As a result, our differences with the anarchists were absolute.'

Absolute differences that were finally to be decided in blood. The core of the problem was to find an agrarian structure which ensured the peasantry's allegiance to the anti-nationalist cause *and* the highest possible agricultural production. Was it collectivization – of often unwilling peasants whose allegiance might be lost but whose output could, theoretically, be rationalized and controlled? Or private enterprise, which assured the peasants' allegiance (in as far as they felt any loyalty to a republic which had done precious little for them), but allowed them to hoard or abstract a portion of their crops which reached the cities only through the black market?

Anarchist domination in Aragon, overthrown within thirteen months of the start of the war, did not last long enough to provide a conclusive answer. Production measured by only one year's grain crops in a region of known yield fluctuations like Aragon could not be definitive evidence. (None the less, it should be noted that the sole wheat crop harvested in Aragon under collectivization – 1937 – showed an increase of 20 per cent over the previous year, which had been a good crop, while in Catalonia, where agrarian collectivization was less widespread, it fell by the same percentage.[1] More significantly, land sown to wheat in Catalonia dropped by as much as 30 per cent in Lerida province and 25 per cent in Tarragona province in 1937 compared to the previous year.)[2]

*

The collectivization, carried out under the general cover, if not necessarily the direct agency, of CNT militia columns, represented a revolutionary minority's attempt to control not only production but consumption for egalitarian purposes and the needs of the war. In this, agrarian collectives differed radically from industrial collectives which regulated production only. Long before rationing was imposed in Barcelona, Aragonese collectives – although benefiting from

1. Republican agricultural ministry figures, cited by Thomas, *The Spanish Civil War*, p. 559. The figures showed a small drop in the Levant – at the time less collectivized relatively than Aragon with 340 collectives; and a 16 per cent increase in Castile where there were 230 collectives comprising about 100,000 members. (Leval, op. cit., pp. 150 and 182.) At the height of the movement in July 1937, some 400,000 agrarian collectivists worked in about 800 collectives in the Popular Front zone, by no means all of which were libertarian-organized. (Mintz, op. cit., p. 148). Aragon thus represented just over half the total collectives and just under half the total collectivists at that time.

2. See Bricall, *Política económica de la Generalitat*, p. 44. Other Catalan cereal crops showed either little improvement or actual drops; potatoes and vegetable production, on the other hand, increased.

stocks of the recently gathered wheat harvest which served as their founding capital – had imposed it on themselves: a rationing which had a redistributive effect – overall, people ate better. Control limited inflation, private speculation and hoarding, and released surplus production. Despite the fact that the youth which formed the bulk of the revolutionary minority went to the front, productivity was maintained, if not increased. Schooling improved and cultural achievements dear to libertarian hearts were introduced. For the revolutionary minority a new world might well be dawning – a world of revolutionary conquests which mobilized them against the common enemy. But the other side of the balance sheet showed the costs.

The absence of a libertarian strategy in relation to the petty bourgeoisie was again evident. Coercing peasants into collectives not only ran counter to libertarian ideology, but was no way to ensure their loyalty; there were other ways of enforcing control on production and consumption.[1] As many Aragonese libertarians came to recognize, the collectives functioned better when they became voluntary. The egalitarian control which resulted from collectivization was vitiated in part by its localism. While the latter provided a source of communal identity, localism ran counter to egalitarianism – 'rich' and 'poor' collectives co-existed – and prevented the emergence of an effective revolutionary power. (The attempt by the Council of Aragon to provide a coherent structure was not successful and, apart from other defects, represented a 'localism' writ large.) The utopian elements of the experiment, mainly the abolition of money, complicated matters. The arbitrariness of some committees indicated the limits of libertarian democracy which could only be overcome by elected and revocable delegates answerable to a general assembly. Thus even as a form of war communism, collectivization suffered from serious defects.

In the libertarians' eyes, Aragon was to be the anarcho-syndicalist example to the world. This it might have become if the revolution in the rear had been capable of initiating and sustaining a revolutionary war at the front. Revolution and war would then have found their exemplary synthesis. This did not happen.[2]

1. Many libertarians outside Aragon felt that collectivization there had been pushed unnecessarily far. Antonio ROSADO, an Andalusian CNT militant who was appointed coordinator of all CNT collectives in unoccupied Andalusia, advocated a much more moderate approach. 'People weren't ready for such extreme measures. We expropriated no land, setting up collectives exclusively on estates that had been abandoned, and with any land that smallholders wished to bring in. Otherwise, the latter were left free to continue working their own land as before and to sell their produce freely.' (By the end of the war, 300 collectives with 60,000 members existed in unoccupied Andalusia, according to ROSADO, many of them worked by labourers who had fled the nationalists.)

Collectivization did not necessarily guarantee control of production and consumption in every circumstance either. Jacinto BORRAS, editor of the CNT's Catalan peasant paper *Campo* and a long-time advocate of rural collectivization, observed that the Catalan collectives looked very different in the last year of the war (by which time Aragon had fallen to the nationalists). 'The privations awoke the peasantry's egoism. The youth had gone to the front, leaving the collectives in the hands of older men whose mentality had not necessarily changed. In the dire circumstances, it was only natural that people thought first of themselves and their families . . .' Collectives, like individuals, could hoard food when shortages arose.

2. Or rather, it happened only embryonically. Militiamen helped the collectivists at harvest and ploughing time. 'And I've had collectivists come up to the front line with shotguns and farm implements to help out when we were hard pressed on the Belchite front,' recalled CAROD, the column leader. 'It was a sign of the tremendous solidarity that existed.'

The libertarian revolution did not prove itself in the only manner that could have guaranteed its success: by defeating the enemy, by sweeping him back.

*

The major struggle within the republican camp being what it was – the struggle for political dominance over the popular revolutionary movement – the anarcho-syndicalists could expect to come under attack in Aragon as elsewhere. The peasant question was one of the major areas of the communist party's anti-libertarian offensive. From the beginning the party had adopted a totally distinct land policy. This was seen in the communist agricultural minister's Agrarian Reform decree of October 1936, which expropriated for the state without compensation all land belonging to those involved in the military uprising. Small tenants on expropriated land were given the perpetual usufruct of their holdings within certain size limits. Where there were no small tenants, the usufruct was given to peasant and agricultural labourers' organizations to work collectively or individually as the majority decided.[1]

The pre-war republic had failed to implement agrarian reform; within a month of joining the government, the communists had legislated it. Land for the peasantry fitted squarely into the historic phase of the bourgeois democratic revolution.

The party's newspaper *Frente Rojo*, of Valencia, hailed the decree as 'the most revolutionary measure taken since the military uprising'. What the paper overlooked was that this 'most revolutionary measure' had already in good part been taken by the day-labourers and militant peasants without waiting for any decree. Its real importance lay rather in the fact that it gave the peasants *legal* right to the land they had themselves seized, and was the only legislation giving *de jure* recognition throughout the Popular Front zone to a revolutionary conquest.

Application of the decree within the limits prescribed required, in the communist party's view, a 'firm and tenacious struggle against uncontrollable elements who, in the name of "revolution" and "libertarian communism", were trying to submit the peasantry to a new oppression'.[2] In deeming expropriable only those owners who had intervened in the military uprising, the decree did nothing about village *caciques* and labour-employing peasant owners who had intervened actively in the exploitation and repression of labourers and peasants pre-war but not in the uprising. Anarcho-syndicalists and the left-wing socialist Landworkers' Federation bitterly criticized this lack, the latter in particular demanding that it be made good. The communist party was adamant in its refusal. The need to form a 'rearguard of steel', in *Frente Rojo*'s words, came down in reality to the defence of the right-wing as well as republican peasantry, despite the fact that communist protection of the former could only exacerbate friction at village level where memories were long. To the control, however defective, proposed by the libertarians of agrarian production and consumption,

1. As we have seen (p. 326 above) the communist party originally proposed giving the expropriated land to the peasantry as its property, and consistently argued for the peasantry's complete freedom in the production and sale of its crops.

2. *Guerra y revolución en España, 1936–1939*, vol. 2, p. 274.

the communist party opposed peasant free enterprise within the limits of size of holding laid down by the decree.

Peasant realism – the acceptance (as evinced by smallholding peasants hostile to collectivization in Mas de las Matas and Alloza) that war inevitably brought controls and restrictions – suggested that communist polarization in defence of the peasantry was unnecessarily sharp; when it came to free enterprise, the peasantry would most adequately place its trust in the true capitalists on the other side of the lines.

From early 1937, there were clashes over collectivization, and deaths in Castile, the Levant, Catalonia. A particularly bloody incident occurred in January in La Fatarella, close by the Ebro river in Catalonia, in which some thirty peasants who had resisted collectivization were killed. In June, however, Vicente Uribe, communist agricultural minister, issued a decree declaring all rural collectives legal 'during the current agricultural year'. This was necessary to ensure that agricultural work for the time of the year should be undertaken 'as satisfactorily and speedily as possible' and to avoid 'economic failures which might chill the faith of the landworkers in the collective form of cultivation they chose freely when they confiscated the rebel exploiters' lands'. The threat of undermining the collectives as the wheat harvest approached had evidently gone too far.[1]

Who are the enemies of the people? The enemies of the people are the fascists, the trotskyists and the uncontrollables.

José Díaz, secretary-general PCE (March 1937)

In short: what really concerns Stalin is not the fate of the Spanish or international proletariat, but the defence of his government by seeking alliances with some states against others.

***La Batalla*, POUM organ (Barcelona, November 1936)**

---

1. Within little more than a year, under the Agrarian Reform decree, over four million hectares of land in the Popular Front zone – excluding Catalonia or the Basque country – were officially taken over. This represented the equivalent of one fifth of the total arable land of *all* Spain pre-war, suggesting that decisions on who had intervened directly or indirectly in the military uprising, which were initiated at local level, received a fairly wide definition. (For an instance of local power exercised in a contrary sense, see R. Fraser, *In Hiding* (London, New York, 1972), p. 147.) Evidence that the communist party was not opposed to collectives *per se* is demonstrated by the fact that the Institute of Agrarian Reform, under communist control, had given 50 million pesetas worth of credits, implements, seeds etc. to collective farms by June 1937. But to qualify, the collectives had to legalize their situation with the Institute; this, on principle, many libertarian collectives refused to do.

One of the manoeuvres of the press which has sold out to international fascism consists in the slander that the Soviet Union's representatives are in fact conducting the republic's foreign policy . . . *La Batalla* in its 24 November issue provides material for such fascist insinuations.

Press statement issued by the Soviet Consul General (Barcelona, November 1936)

We anarchists have reached the limit of concessions. If we continue giving up ground, we shall within a short time be completely overwhelmed, and the revolution will be no more than a memory.

***La Noche*, libertarian (Barcelona, March 1937)**

It is a very serious moment. The destiny of the proletariat is at stake. The POUM has repeatedly voiced the alarm. Will it be heard by the other revolutionary organizations?

Andreu Nin, *La Batalla* (March 1937)

BARCELONA

The definitive clash between these opposing views came not in the countryside, but in Barcelona. The city had experienced neither the unity of purpose effected by enemy fire nor the bitter but glorious days of Madrid's defence. In addition, Barcelona was farther from the front than any other major republican city. The libertarian revolution was running into resistance. The political tensions which arose throughout the spring of 1937 were increased by the first tastes of hardship. Food was in short supply and there were long bread queues. In April, women demonstrated in the streets against the cost of living, which had just risen a further 13 per cent on top of the increases that had already added nearly two thirds to the index since the start of the war. Never self-sufficient in food,

Catalonia had a population density pre-war nearly double that of the whole of Spain; a massive influx of refugees, especially after the fall of Málaga in February 1937, had added to the pressure. With the nation's largest city to feed, the question of food became critical. The CNT supply organization, which depended on an exchange system, had been suppressed by 'a stroke of the pen' when Joan Comorera, the PSUC leader, took over the portfolio in the Generalitat government in December 1936. 'You fools,' Joan DOMENECH, his CNT predecessor, told his companions, 'don't you realize that whoever fills men's stomachs influences their minds? By this petty manoeuvre you've destroyed everything that we've created in the past months.'[1]

Comorera publicly accused his predecessor of incompetence; DOMENECH responded by reproving the PSUC leader for abolishing the controls he had set up and establishing a free market in food.

—I knew that if supplies weren't controlled a black market would spring up. I practised a sort of dictatorship over supplies and prices. I had already organized seven ship-loads of food and other essentials from the Soviet Union. By saying there were shortages, Comorera created them because people rushed to buy whatever they could. Two months later, he had to introduce rationing, which I had wanted to avoid, although I had had ration cards printed in case the need arose. And when the Russian ships arrived, as all but one did under his tenure, he received them as though he had organized their dispatch . . .

Comorera insisted that his predecessor had run up debts of 36 million pesetas, half of which he had now paid off; there was a month's supply of wheat, and delays in distribution were due to slow unloading. Pere RIBA, a close associate of Comorera, was called to the Barcelona docks; a phone message said an anarchist group had captured a load of flour. He confronted the men, arguing that the flour belonged to the Generalitat. 'We don't recognize the Generalitat or anything to do with it.' An argument started, a shot rang out, and the lorry driver's mate standing next to RIBA dropped dead to the ground.

—How could you organize, consolidate the revolution with people like that? Comorera sent me to London and Marseilles to close down the libertarian trading offices.[2] The anarchist idea of export was to seize a load of champagne, a load of black stockings, a load of this or that, put it all on a freighter and send it to London to be sold. The owner of the champagne, who had fled to England, slapped an injunction on the cargo which an English court ordered embargoed. But what struck me most was the naïvety of sending black stockings to England where surely only waitresses would ordinarily wear them . . .

To the man in the street, the argument about food supplies appeared 'entirely

1. See pp. 144–5 for Domènech's food organization. A Generalitat crisis in December 1936, which ousted the POUM, resulted in Domènech being shifted to the public services portfolio. 'It was a manoeuvre by García Oliver, Durruti and other libertarians who decided that the CNT must control the war councillorship. They tried to keep their plan quiet, using the crisis to exchange the portfolio of supply for that of war' (Joan DOMENECH). García Oliver, who had been acting as virtual Generalitat war minister, had shortly before been appointed a CNT minister in the central government; the *Nosotros* group was doubtless concerned that his absence might threaten libertarian control of the Aragon front.

2. Set up outside Domènech's ministry, according to the latter.

byzantine'. Living in Tarragona, a small town surrounded by countryside, Edmón VALLES, an unaffiliated left-winger sympathetic to the CNT, remembered going hungry under both systems. There was chaos in Tarragona from the start. When the CNT collectivized food distribution, the system worked, in his view, only because the wheat harvest was just being brought in and there were stocks. By the winter of 1936–7, people were going hungry.

—But the communists were no better at organizing food supplies. To live on one's rations was to go hungry; inefficient distribution, moreover, meant that you would eat nothing but broad beans for a fortnight, lentils for the next couple of weeks, chick-peas for the next and so on. Lack of food was one of the major factors in the war-weariness that overtook Catalonia. The republic was unable to solve it . . .[1]

Under this issue, as under every issue, lay the question of power: the CNT's failure to consolidate its revolution *politically* in the first weeks and months of the war. Having refused to take power, the libertarians had joined the Generalitat government, believing this the best way to protect their revolution. Firm in the conviction that power in the factories and streets was the determining factor, they accepted three posts in a cabinet of six liberal republicans, two members of the PSUC and one of the POUM. Within a fortnight, the government decreed the dissolution of all the committees that had held power locally in Catalonia, and their replacement by administrative bodies with the same political composition as the Generalitat. Within two months, the dissident communist POUM had been evicted (its anti-Stalinism having made it the target of the Soviet Union, the Comintern and the Spanish communists) without protest from the CNT. Within six months, the Esquerra republicans and PSUC felt strong enough to order the dissolution of the armed workers' patrols which had been set up in the first days of the revolution. In future, police forces were to belong to no political party or organization; along with factory collectives – many of them already 'in pawn' to the Generalitat[2] – the workers' patrols were seen as the last vestige of proletarian power.

'No more concessions; we can retreat no further,' the CNT proclaimed, withdrawing from the Generalitat. The POUM called yet again for a workers' and peasants' government. The crisis lasted three weeks before a new cabinet was announced. It differed little from the previous one, and not surprisingly, it lasted barely a fortnight. A POUM member of the armed workers' patrols, Miquel COLL, saw the ambiguities of the proposal to 'disarm the rear'.

—The patrols, in fact, were no longer revolutionary, were no longer serving the purpose they had been set up for. The members lacked discipline, weren't carrying out their duties, had become lax. On revolutionary grounds, the Generalitat would have been right to abolish them. But the Generalitat – or rather the PSUC which was behind it all, a communist party without an ounce

1. A year after the PSUC took over supply, its trade union, the UGT, was complaining of the 'disorganization in the supplies of food and its enormous expense'. Whereas inflation in the first six CNT months pushed the cost of living up by 47 per cent, the next six PSUC-dominant months saw it rise by 49 per cent.

2. See p. 211n.

of communism – had very different ideas. They wanted to control the entire police force in order to be able to take over strategic strongholds, like the Telephone Exchange, which were still controlled by the CNT . . .

A week after the new cabinet's formation, a leading PSUC–UGT leader (and former *treintista*), Roldán Cortada, was assassinated. The CNT denounced the murder which the UGT attributed to FAI 'uncontrollables'. The funeral was turned into a massive demonstration of communist strength. A central government force took over Catalan frontier posts from the CNT, and at Puigcerdá three anarchists were killed. Andreu CAPDEVILA, who had been taken from the factory floor to become the CNT's acting president of the Economics Council, and who was now the Generalitat economics councillor, was aghast that workers were killing each other. During a cabinet meeting, he turned to Comorera.

—'This is something that shouldn't be allowed to happen. Workers being murdered by fellow workers.' Comorera, barely raising his voice, replied: 'Oh, it's of no particular importance.' He wasn't a man who really felt anything about the working class; a bourgeois, cold and ambitious, he had given himself over body and soul to the communists . . .

The May day parade – the first since the revolution – was banned by the Generalitat; while massive UGT–CNT rallies were jointly organized in Valencia and elsewhere, people in Barcelona went to work as usual. All the organizations were on the alert. In the CNT woodworkers' union, Eduardo PONS PRADES heard that the libertarian defence committee of Poble Sec had ordered some boxes to be removed from the basement: hand-grenades and short arms. The spark that set off the explosion came on Monday, 3 May. During the siesta hour, police forces led by the communist police commissioner moved into the Telephone Exchange in the Plaça de Catalunya, which a CNT-dominated workers' control committee (as such, legally recognized by the collectivization decree) had held since the start of the revolution. There was shooting, the CNT telephone workers resisted, and the news spread like wildfire through an already tense city. Pere RIBA, Comorera's close associate, recalled that he had known of the decision since a party executive committee meeting several days before.

—'Pedro' [Ernö Gerö,[1] the Comintern adviser to the PSUC] always attended these meetings. Perhaps it was he who brought up the matter, though I can't be sure because I didn't attend the meetings. It was high time such a step was taken. The CNT listened in to all the conversations between the central government, the Generalitat and abroad. That couldn't be allowed to continue. We had tried unsuccessfully to get a member on to the control committee to stop the listening in. So it was decided to take more energetic measures.[2] Of

1. Later to become Hungarian deputy premier, famous for his role in support of the Russians during the 1956 Hungarian uprising.

2. Central government ministers, as well as President Azaña, were reported to have had 'incidents' when talking on the phone. The latter was said to have been in the middle of a conversation with President Companys a couple of days before when he was cut off by a voice which told him he had been talking long enough.

course, had the PSUC been in a position to listen in to telephone conversations it would have done so also. The party always wanted to be well-informed . . .[1]

For several months, RIBA remembered, it had been openly said in inner party circles that the situation with the CNT–FAI could not continue. 'These people are going to have to be eliminated,' Comorera told him on one occasion.[2]

It was unlikely, however, that this was considered the opportune moment for anything as drastic; more probably, the PSUC and its Esquerra ally expected the CNT, as usual, to protest at the Telephone Exchange take-over and then, unwillingly, accept it. Instead, this turned into a trial of strength. Fighting broke out which lasted, intermittently, for five days. On the one side, the PSUC, Esquerra, Estat Català and police forces; on the other, the libertarians and POUM.

The dissident communists of the POUM were unhappy at the turn of events: they had not wanted this to happen. But, recalled Juan ANDRADE of the executive committee, once the workers were in the streets, 'we had to support them.' Moreover, the party saw that the repression was aimed at it.

—The Generalitat's step in taking over the Telefónica was counter-revolutionary; but it was also just. The CNT acted as *owner* of the exchange, controlling calls, listening in, censoring even. This state of affairs couldn't continue . . .

For the PSUC the fighting was a *putsch* by a group of 'uncontrollables' which included anarchists and POUMists.

—The POUMists provided the political platform for the *putsch*, explained Pere ARDIACA, editor of the PSUC newspaper *Treball*. As I saw it, there were two aspects to this platform: the revolution had to be made at all costs, even at the expense of sacrificing the left-wing petty bourgeois forces which could help in the anti-fascist struggle. Secondly, the Soviet Union's aid was designed to arm the communists in order to liquidate anarchists and the POUM, and to install a Soviet-style communism in Spain. The POUM's paper, *La Batalla*, is there to prove it! Today I believe it is necessary to correct some – but only some – of the ideas we of the PSUC held at the time . . .

By dawn on Tuesday, the barricades had gone up. With the exception of the area around the Generalitat, CNT and POUM workers held almost the whole city. Behind the barricades, CNT companions explained to Eduardo PONS PRADES, the young libertarian of the woodworkers' union, who had just arrived on his bicycle, what was happening.

—'The Chinese [the libertarians' name for the communists] are trying to sabotage the revolution. They're going to take over the collectives, the workers will simply have to work and keep quiet under their heel.' It seemed true.

1. 'Later, Comorera had me appointed secretary to General Pozas, a supposed PSUC member, who took over as commander of the Catalan army. He made it clear enough that I was to act as a party informer' (Pere RIBA).

2. In March 1937 José Díaz, PCE secretary-general, called for the elimination of those 'agents of fascism – trotskyists disguised as POUMists' – a reflection of the accusations being made at the Moscow show trials.

When I produced my CNT membership card to a group of civilians who stopped me, they shouted that it was shit. 'You'll see what's going to happen. You think you're revolutionaries, but all you are is a tribe of defeatists, as Comorera called you' . . .

The historical memory of Kronstadt and the Ukraine and the Bolsheviks' liquidation of the anarchists, he thought, remained very alive. Inside the woodworkers' union headquarters, the atmosphere was like that of the first days of the war.

—'Only this time we're going to make the revolution properly, so it puts down roots deep and strong.' As for the 'politicians', their fate was already decided: labour battalions where they could redeem their counter-revolutionary 'political' sins . . .

Leading anarchists, communists, socialists and President Companys broadcast appeals to end the factional fighting. García Oliver, CNT minister in the central government, who long ago had called for the CNT to take power in Barcelona, rushed from Valencia. In a bathetic radio speech, he proclaimed all those who had been killed his brothers. 'I kneel before them and kiss them.' Instantly, behind the barricades, his speech was baptized *The Legend of the Kiss* – the title of a light opera.

—'Another Judas!' Hernández, the woodworkers' leader, exploded. 'What's the good of reminding us that we're at war. He should have thought of that a long time ago – and let us get on with making the revolution which is our job. As though the war had any meaning if we can't make the revolution at the same time!' . . .

On the other side of the barricades there were moments of demoralization. Manuel CRUELLS, Catalan nationalist, felt the same fear he had known on 19 July when he fought the military: 'We're going to lose, we're caught in a trap.' From behind a cobble barricade, he could see the PSUC holding out in the Hotel Colón in the Plaça de Catalunya; it gave him hope that perhaps the trap would not be sprung. In any case, he wasn't fighting to crush the CNT.

—At that moment in fact I was a CNT member. To be a syndicalist was quite distinct from supporting anarchism, the FAI. I was fighting to put an end to the CNT's irresponsibility. I was disillusioned by the anarchist revolution and knew that, as a Catalan nationalist, I had to fight on the Generalitat's side. But I had no illusions about the communists. I could see that Companys had no alternative but to play their card since he couldn't rely on the CNT, although it was the latter which geared into the mentality of the Catalan working class – something that certainly couldn't be said of the PSUC . . .

Companys announced a new four-man government. On his way to take up his new post as Generalitat minister, Antoni Sesé, the UGT secretary-general, was killed. The fighting intensified; assassinations increased. The Italian anarchist, Camillo Berneri, one of the most original of libertarian thinkers, was arrested with his collaborator Barbieri and murdered. The central government in Valencia began to intervene, sending two destroyers to the port, and taking over police and defence from the Generalitat. In Valencia, the CNT viewed the situation with gravity. Joan MANENT, Badalona CNT leader and private secretary to Peiró, the CNT minister of industry in the central government, thought it catastrophic. 'It was as bad as though we were going to lose the war the next day. The communists staged a provocation and the CNT, always ready to take the bait, fell for it . . .'

—But what did all these manoeuvres and traps matter, reflected his companion, Josep COSTA, Badalona CNT textile leader, if little by little we were being reduced to mere spectators of our own slaughter? Our blood boiled. We had Barcelona surrounded; it only needed the word and we would have cleaned out the communist plotters and their dispossessed, intriguing petty-bourgeois lackeys who were sabotaging the revolution. The war would have ended sooner – with Franco's victory – no doubt, but it would have spared us having to go on to the same result two years later; would have saved us being the scapegoats for so many things we never did and which were later held against us. But the CNT wasn't prepared to order troops to leave the front, for that would have let the enemy through. There was only one man who could have put an end to the provocation: Durruti. He wouldn't have hesitated a moment . . .

Unknown to most, the CNT had in Barcelona 500 well-armed and equipped men (all that remained of the 3,000 who had gone to Madrid) of Durruti's former column, now under the command of Ricardo SANZ, Durruti's companion and successor. They were returning to the Aragon front where other units of the division were prepared to move on Barcelona; they had telephoned SANZ to ascertain his intentions. He replied that he was at the orders of the CNT, the organization would have to decide. He went to see García Oliver.

—'Listen,' I said to him. 'What haggling, what bargaining is going on? What's to be done? The division – ' 'Ah no, there's to be none of that,' he replied. So I knew. None of my troops moved to decapitate the reactionary movement which was the cause of it all. Our representatives in the central government called instead for a cease-fire. My personal feelings didn't matter; I was a disciplined man, a military commander . . .

The CNT leaders continued to call for an end to the fighting. Wilebaldo SOLANO, secretary of the POUM's youth movement, JCI (Juventud Comunista Ibérica), accompanied Nin to see the CNT regional committee leaders. The POUM leader explained that this was a moment of rupture: the working class had risen, held arms. The movement, which had started spontaneously, must either go forwards or back.

—We believed we had to take the offensive, demand the Generalitat's resignation, confront the problem of creating a government of the working-class organizations – to seize power . . .

The means, SOLANO thought, were at hand. There had been no difficulty in forming a CNT–POUM column in the north of the city, the Gràcia *barrio*, which was ready to advance on the PSUC headquarters and the Generalitat.

—'Yes, that's all very interesting,' the CNT leaders said. 'But things mustn't be allowed to get too complicated.' Their members had 'shown their teeth', as one of them put it. 'Companys will now reflect on the matter, the situation will probably change, become more radical – and then we'll confront the PSUC and all that lot.' Nin explained again. The revolution had reached a critical juncture. It wasn't a matter of simple government changes. We were at war with Franco, the situation in Catalonia might not be understood in the rest of republican Spain. The revolution had to pass on to a more advanced stage; this had to be explained on the radio, in the press. It was urgent. In effect, he proposed forming a liaison committee to lead the struggle, formulate programmes, take up the problems connected with power. But he didn't hammer home the point, he was waiting to see their reaction.

No, they said, we were going too far. Nin always said interesting things, they appreciated him – but this was dramatizing events! They refused to reach agreement. As we got up to leave, one of them patted us on the shoulder and said, 'It's been a pleasant evening together.' I'll never forget it as long as I live. I'd crossed the city from barricade to barricade twice in a few hours simply to be told what a pleasant evening we'd had . . .

A small anarchist organization, the Friends of Durruti, came out openly against the CNT leaders, calling for a revolutionary junta, with the POUM's participation because the party had come out on the workers' side. Until then, its relations with the POUM had been notably cool. The call found little echo.[1] What carried real weight in the CNT was the neighbourhood defence committees, the middle-level militants who had made the revolution by taking over factories and workplaces in the first days, and who felt that their revolution was being betrayed. Frustrated by the rise of an official communist party where none had seriously challenged them before, angered by its large intake of petty bourgeois whom they saw as their enemy, these militants were fighting not for political power but to crush the PSUC and its allies.

—It was they who had mobilized the people when the *Telefónica* was attacked, it was they who had arms, who were the first to man the barricades, stressed SOLANO. The Friends of Durruti have subsequently been portrayed as the perfect group of anarchists who had evolved to marxism. A seductive myth, but a myth nonetheless . . .

The POUM leadership had no confidence in them, SOLANO knew. In his neighbourhood, the CNT–POUM committee was about to give the order for

1. The group was formed of anarchist militants from the Durruti column who had refused militarization and abandoned the front to return to Barcelona 'with their arms and equipment', according to Jaime Baliús, one of the group's prime movers. The proposed revolutionary junta was to be composed of combatants from the barricades. 'We did not support the formation of Soviets; there were no grounds in Spain for calling for such. We stood for "all power to the trade unions". In no way were we politically oriented. The junta was simply a way out, a revolutionary formula to save the revolutionary conquests of July 1936. We were unable to exercise great influence because the Stalinists, helped by the CNT and FAI reformists, undertook their counter-revolutionary aggression so rapidly. Ours was solely an attempt to save the revolution; at the historical level it can be compared to Kronstadt because if there the sailors and workers called for "all power to the Soviets", we were calling for all power to the unions.' (Jaime Baliús, letter to the author, April 1976.)

its column, which included officer cadets from the training school, to march on the centre when the POUM youth leader was called to the phone.

—It was Nin. He told me not to give the order. As long as the CNT was opposed, we could take power militarily but not politically. Nin feared – and he was right – that the events would be totally misunderstood in the rest of Spain. There were such enormous disparities beween Madrid, Valencia and Barcelona. A revolutionary government backed by an army and controlling the radio could have explained the situation to the combatants at the fronts; even then, even had the CNT unanimously agreed with us, it would have been a risky affair. Alone with the CNT neighbourhood defence committees – which carried little weight outside their own *barrios* – things were quite different . . .

The POUM lacked the political credibility, he thought, to swing over the mass of CNT workers from their own organization and leadership. To have broken with their organization at a moment like that ('it wasn't, after all, a trade union congress from which they could walk out, set up a new organization and later propose reunification') was a big step to take. The difference between being in opposition within an organization and openly breaking with it was often forgotten, he thought. 'I didn't give the order, we didn't move from the barricades.'

It was nearly over. Juan ANDRADE, of the POUM executive, managed to reach the seminary where the CNT regional committee had its headquarters. It was a question of terminating the fighting as advantageously as possible.

—'It's not a question of taking power, if that's what worries you,' I explained. Power could have been taken, I was convinced, but not held, for the central government would send forces. But if the Generalitat were taken in a rapid offensive, it could be used as a lever in negotiations to ensure immunity for all those who had risen.[1] The CNT leaders refused, assuring me that nothing would happen. But we were already convinced that when the fighting ended the repression would be unleashed on us . . .

While he was there, Federica Montseny, the anarchist minister in the central government, broadcast yet another appeal to end the fighting.

—The CNT militants were so furious that they pulled out their pistols and shot the radio. It sounds incredible but it happened in front of my eyes. They were absolutely furious – and yet they obeyed. They might be anarchists, but when it came to their own organization they had tremendous discipline. As soon as they were told to, they started to dismantle the barricades, including ours. 'Wait, you're not taking these down yet,' we said . . .

By Friday, the city was almost back to normal: 5,000 assault guards arrived from Valencia and took over 'like a conquering army'. The five days of fighting, which had on the whole been defensive, took an inordinately high toll: 500

1. Throughout the fighting, President Azaña had been besieged in the Catalan parliament building where he lived. Jaume MIRAVITLLES, the Esquerra politician, managed to get out of the Generalitat to visit him. 'What would have happened if someone had captured him and used him as a hostage to negotiate conditions? Happily, no one thought of it except Azaña himself who was tormented day and night by the possibility.'

dead and 1,000 wounded. The assassinations, particularly of anarchist militants, after the fighting ended added to the toll.

*

There were two victors: the central government and the communist party. Using Largo Caballero's refusal to suppress the POUM for having 'organized the May *putsch*', the communist party, in alliance with the right wing of the socialist party, succeeded in its earlier-conceived aim of ousting the left socialist prime minister; he had not proven himself the leader required by the times. Having conformed to the overall communist strategy of containing the revolution in order to prosecute the war with (hoped-for) British and French aid, he had not conformed to the communist demands on the actual conduct of the war. The fall of Málaga three months before had shaken the Popular Front. By containing the revolution he had lost the revolutionary base which was a potential alternative source of power; by refusing to repress that base he gained no new source of power. Symbolically, only the vanquished, the anarchist ministers, stood behind him in his last crisis.

Juan Negrín, the new, moderate socialist premier, had none of Caballero's hesitations. He would prosecute the war resolutely enough to satisfy the communists, clamp down on any revolutionary or autonomist stirrings, and at the same time prosecute his own, secret peace feelers to negotiate an end to the war. A distinguished physiologist of the *haute bourgeoisie*, his tremendous personal vitality fitted him for the task of leading a bourgeois democratic struggle while shrouding the ambiguities of his aims.

It was not only those on the wrong side of the barricades who suffered defeat. The Esquerra was deprived of control of its police forces and army by the central government[1] and soon lost its *raison d'être*: Catalan autonomy.

The CNT withdrew from the central government, and was soon to be provoked into withdrawing from the Generalitat. But it was the POUM which took the full initial force of the communist attack.

On the Sunday after the fighting ended, José Díaz, PCE secretary-general, addressed a large audience in Valencia. 'Who, if not the trotskyists, inspired the criminal *putsch* in Catalonia?' he asked. The fascists went under many names; one of them was trotskyists. 'That is the name many secret fascists use who talk of revolution in order to create confusion. Everyone knows it, the government knows it. What is the government doing in not treating them like fascists and exterminating them without consideration?'

The POUM was not trotskyist, as many PSUC militants who had been prewar members of one of the POUM's two constituents, the Bloc Obrer i Camperol (BOC), knew.[2] It was anti-Stalinist.

1. Shortly Catalan police and even firemen were being transferred out of Catalonia, more Catalan war industries were taken over, the central government moved to Barcelona to impose tighter control and, finally, the entire war industry came under government control.

2. And as the POUM had officially declared in December 1936 when it rejected the Second (socialist), the Third (communist) and the Fourth (trotskyist) internationals as incapable of being the 'instrument of the world revolution'. It condemned the last of these for its 'sectarian character' and for 'lacking roots in the masses'. *Izquierda Comunista*, the other POUM component, whose leaders included Nin and Andrade, had belonged to the Fourth International until 1934.

—The revolution in Spain began just as Stalin's crimes were beginning to be known. The show trials were taking place, recalled ANDRADE. There was a feeling of terror and indignation amongst the revolutionary left internationally. The POUM represented the new revolutionary current that could stem the Stalinist tide, it challenged the Comintern and the Soviet Union. This was why Stalin had to liquidate the party . . .

—There were party militants who said it would be better to drop our criticism of the Soviet Union. They were frightened. But we continued. It is one of the POUM's historical merits to have condemned Stalin's policies, the Moscow trials, affirmed SOLANO . . .

But the communist party would have got rid of the POUM under any circumstances, believed Ignacio IGLESIAS, *La Batalla*'s political editor, because it 'could not permit another, independent communist movement to exist'.

—It had nothing to do with trotskyism. Even if we had been reformists to the right of the PCE they would have liquidated us. We thought the communist party was bourgeois and conservative; we were mistaken. It wasn't 'right' or 'left', it simply followed the line laid down by the Soviet Union's state interests at the time . . .

In other parts of the Popular Front zone there was incomprehension about what had happened.[1] In Madrid, however, Eduardo de GUZMAN, CNT journalist, felt that a great opportunity had been lost in not making good the CNT's initial error in July of failing to take power, an essential of revolution.

—They could have smashed the communists and republicans in Barcelona, driven the revolution forward everywhere. The CNT might then have taken power in Valencia and Andalusia, if not in Madrid. The aim, of course, would have been to reach an agreement with the other parties that would have been much more favourable to us and to the revolutionary cause than handing power over to Negrín . . .

The 'ifs' of history are unending. It did not happen. Who would take responsibility for unleashing a full-scale civil war within the civil war while there was still hope of defeating Franco? GUZMAN's opinion was not widely held;[2]

1. Even the POUM was split. The Madrid section, which had been refused representation on the defence junta by the Soviet ambassador's intervention, and subsequently had its radio and press closed, published a statement disassociating itself from the POUM's position in Barcelona. (The small Madrid section, which had undergone considerable trotskyist influence in the preceding months, was 'the victim of a public opinion hostile to Catalonia', according to ANDRADE.) The Valencia section published a note 'regretting' the events, although not specifically condemning them (Luis PORTELA).

2. Significantly, Cipriano Mera, the outstanding CNT military commander on the Madrid front, makes only a passing reference to the May events in a footnote in his memoirs. 'When I asked him the reason, he said they received the news late on the front and didn't understand its significance' (Ignacio IGLESIAS).

hostility and doubt were the more usual reactions. Nin was right. The long-standing and generalized suspiciousness of Catalonia in the rest of the Spanish state made it only too easy to misinterpret the revolt – which took place as the enemy was closing in on Bilbao in the north – as a stab in the back, possibly to separate Catalonia from the republic. 'If the anarchists are trying to break up the republic, the sooner troops go up there and settle the matter the better,' thought the socialist youth militant, Antonio PEREZ, on the central front. The correlation of forces had already moved against the proletarian revolution, against Catalonia.

*

The denial six months earlier by the Soviet consul general in Barcelona (the old Bolshevik Antonov-Ovsëenko, who led the storming of the Winter Palace, and was soon to be recalled and shot by Stalin) that the Russians intervened in the republic's affairs, as the POUM had alleged, was now to be shown in its true light. On 16 June, after a semi-clandestine meeting of the POUM's executive committee (the party's paper, *La Batalla*, had been suppressed a fortnight earlier) Andreu Nin walked across the Ramblas to the POUM offices above the Café Moka. One of the bodyguards, Miquel COLL, formerly of the armed workers' patrols, was about to accompany him.

—'No, no,' Nin said, 'I'm only just going across the street.' I insisted. Since the May events, our orders were that no executive member was to leave the Virreina Palace on the Ramblas where they lived and met without being accompanied by one of us guards. 'No, *coño*, it's not worth it,' he repeated. He didn't want to put me to any trouble. He went out. That was the last we ever saw of him . . .

The police had come from Madrid. Six days after his arrest on trumped-up espionage charges, Nin was assassinated in Alcalá de Henares, near Madrid, where – alone of all the POUM leaders – he had been taken. Officially, not even the new prime minister, Juan Negrín, could find out where Nin was. Luis PORTELA, founder member of the PCE and now on the Valencia POUM provincial committee, went to see the new socialist interior minister.

—'If you know where Nin is,' the minister said, 'I'll put a police force and cars at your disposal and you can free him.' It would have been comic if it weren't so tragic. It was he – the minister in charge of police and security forces, not we – who should have known where Nin was . . .[1]

Jaume MIRAVITLLES, the Esquerra politician and former secretary of the Catalan Anti-Fascist Militia committee, travelled to Valencia on Companys's behalf with a verbal message that the president of the Generalitat was 'enormously surprised' that Nin had been arrested on charges of spying for Franco.

1. It was not an isolated case, as PORTELA later discovered. On his fifth visit concerning two POUM militants the minister had ordered released from prison and who were still being held, PORTELA confronted him with his powerlessness: 'Comrade Zugazagoitia, I think you should leave your desk, take that guard's rifle and his place on duty outside the door, and let the guard sit at your desk. Because your orders are evidently totally ineffectual – '

He wanted it known that any trial must be conducted with absolute impartiality and all evidence thoroughly proven. MIRAVITLLES saw Manuel Irujo, the newly appointed Basque minister of justice who was 'very concerned and plainly knew nothing about the case'. Then he went to see Col. Ortega, a Negrín appointee as director general of the security forces (DGS) and a wartime communist party member.

—'A document bearing the initials A.N. and revealing a great number of war secrets has been found on the body of a known spy,' he said to me. 'The initials are those of Andreu Nin. In due course, the government will be informed of all the details. But at the moment, as it is a very serious espionage case – ' 'This is the first time in the history of spying that a spy signs – if only with his initials – a compromising document,' I replied. 'Supposing A.N. were Amadeo Núñez or Andrés Nova – what then?' Ortega got up bad-temperedly, saying that he considered my remarks insulting and would take it as expressing my personal opinion and not that of President Companys. 'That's right,' I said . . .

The communist outrage, the direct work of the GPU (the Soviet secret police), demonstrated the Soviet Union's clear determination to use Spain at any cost for its purposes, even if it meant reducing the republican government to powerlessness in its own territory. Until Trotsky's assassination four years later, it was Stalin's most heinous *foreign* crime, and did considerable damage to the moderate image of the new Negrín government which communist policy had so long called for.[1]

The POUM was outlawed, its 29th division on the Aragon front forcibly disbanded by the communists and its commander, Rovira, arrested – contrary to military law which forbade the arrest of divisional commanders without the defence minister's express authority. The communists took the law into their own hands – the law they had made so much of defending in the first months of the war against the 'uncontrollables', whose assassinations they now repeated. POUM militants, officers of the division, fled. Many of the communists who disbanded the division were known to the POUM officers as old, pre-war militants.

—'We're anti-fascists, you know that, we've been in the struggle together a long time,' Ramón FERNANDEZ, a POUM carpenter pre-war and now a captain, remembered telling them. But it made no difference. I had to flee to Barcelona where I was able to enlist in a mainly Basque brigade as a sergeant . . .

Adolfo BUESO, veteran militant printworker, was sheltered by some friends in a village near the French frontier. 'When the enemy hunts me down, I can understand it; but when those who claim they are on the side of the working class do so – no!'

1. As a cover-up, *Mundo Obrero*, the Madrid PCE organ, published a sensationalist story that Nin had been sprung from prison by Falange agents and was in Burgos.

Militancies 12

JUAN ANDRADE
POUM leader

The police who arrested Nin rounded up forty more ranking POUM militants. He escaped because, on Nin's insistence, he had gone to the doctor's.

—'A revolutionary's health is vital,' Nin insisted, reproaching me for not taking it seriously. We were on our way back to the executive committee offices from our clandestine meeting place whose existence everyone knew. I went to the doctor. The police arrived asking for Nin and me. The communists hated us equally; we had both been in the communist party and had become trotskyists. I might well have followed the same road to death as he . . .

As soon as she heard of Nin's arrest, Andrade's wife ran out to warn him. Only a couple of hours earlier, in the Moka café, two republican officers of the International Brigades, he later was told, had apparently warned a POUM militiaman that Nin was about to be arrested. The militiaman had informed Nin but he took no notice. 'None of us believed the situation was serious enough to risk our arrest.'

On his arrival at his new hiding place, Andrade found the police waiting. A Swiss woman POUM member who lived there was a GPU[1] agent – 'one of only two agents to infiltrate the party'. He and others were taken to the main Barcelona police station, and at midnight, he, Gorkin and Bonet, fellow executive committee members, were bundled into separate cars. Three convoys set out.

—In mine there was a car in front full of foreigners only – Poles, I think – and another behind also with foreigners. In my car there were four Madrid policemen – former socialist youth members. Whenever we stopped on the road, it was the car in front that gave the signal. The Madrid policemen would take us into a bar to have coffee while the foreigners remained outside . . .

When they reached Valencia they were kept in solitary confinement in police cells. The socialist and CNT warders gave them news when their communist chiefs weren't about.

—'Do you know what's happened? Nin has disappeared. We of the CNT have begun a great campaign about it – ' That impressed me, but I must admit that even then we didn't really think we were in danger of our lives . . .

An international campaign started, especially in England and France. The Independent Labour party sent a delegation to Valencia to investigate; the CNT continued its campaign. Finally, Manuel Irujo, the justice minister, was able to order their release. They came out of gaol, officially free, to be met at the gates by police who bundled them into a car and took them to Madrid, first to a communist *checa* in the basement of a hotel, later to one in a church in the

1. The Soviet secret police organization.

Paseo de Atocha. There he was interrogated by three former socialist youth students now turned communist agents.

—What did I think of Trotsky? Of Stalin? Questions like that. An idiotic interrogation, but quite obviously their intentions weren't of the best. I gave them as good as I got. There were tremendous shouts. My comrades feared I was being beaten up. 'No, no,' I assured them on my return, 'they were such fools, those interrogators, I let them have it' . . .

He remained convinced, however, that the POUM's repression had taken place without the agreement of the PCE leadership.

—The GPU carried it out on its own. Once it had happened, the communist party had to agree to it; but they hadn't given their prior consent. In fact, La Pasionaria is said to have exclaimed: 'No, it is still too early – ' a phrase that can readily be explained. The Spanish communist leadership knew the situation in Spain and feared the CNT and socialist reaction; they were wrong as it turned out – there was none . . .

A founder-member of the Spanish communist party, a Treasury official and journalist, he had become one of the leaders of Left Communism, the Spanish section of the (trotskyist) International Communist League until 1934, and continued to think of himself as a trotskyist; but he did not carry on fractional work inside the POUM, which had his complete loyalty. He was not, however, in agreement with the trotskyists in Barcelona, nor with much that Trotsky wrote about the events there. In particular, the accusation that the POUM had capitulated during the May events and that it would have been easy for the working class to take power. Such power as might have been taken would have been rapidly isolated and overcome by the central government, in his view. During the fighting, when he had gone out from the virtually permanent sessions of the party's executive, trotskyists had come up to him and said: 'It can't go on like this, there's no rhyme or reason to it – '

—They were terrified, they thought the situation was turning out badly. In that they were only displaying their sound sense: anyone could see there was no real way out, that the movement lacked head and feet. Those trotskyists weren't posing the question of power. When the central government announced its intervention in the Generalitat, Jean Rous, the Fourth International's delegate, came up to me. 'I can't see any solution to this situation,' I said; and he replied: 'No, nor can I. There isn't any.' It was only after the events that they came to a different conclusion, writing to Trotsky that the situation was ripe for working-class power. The trouble was that Trotsky believed everything the trotskyists in Barcelona – a great number of whom were foreigners, petty intellectuals of mediocre calibre – wrote him . . .[1]

1. During the fighting, the diminutive Bolshevik–Leninist section of the Fourth International put out a call for the disarming of the police forces, a general strike in all but war-related industries 'until the resignation of the reactionary government', the complete arming of the working class and for committees of revolutionary defence in shops, factories etc. 'Only proletarian power can assure military victory.' (See F. Morrow, *Revolution and Counter-revolution in Spain*, New York, 1974, p. 144.)

After several weeks, Andrade and his comrades were transferred from the *checa* in Madrid to the state prison in Valencia. An FAI police chief in Madrid, whom he knew, came to see him and to offer his services to ensure that the transfer was made safely. The next day he returned saying there was nothing he could do, the communists would not allow him to accompany them to Valencia. Then the justice minister, Irujo, sent an assault guard captain, a Basque like himself, to escort the prisoners.

—A rough and ready sort, a peasant, but a fine man. 'Minister Irujo has sent me to guarantee your safe transfer. Have no fear for your lives, my men will guard you.' We were taken out and put in a prison wagon. In front, went a car full of plain-clothes communist police; behind the same. It was really quite funny. We had to stop three or four times to urinate. The communist police surrounded us and the assault guards surrounded the police. We got to Valencia safely . . .

Sixteen months after his arrest, he and five other ranking POUM militants were tried by the republic's newly created special espionage tribunal on charges of spying and collaboration with the enemy. All six were acquitted of the charges, the evidence having shown, in the court's words, that 'all of them were proven long-time anti-fascists'. None the less, they were found guilty of having rebelled against the constituted government during the May events in Barcelona. He and three other members of the executive were sentenced to fifteen years;[1] one, Jordi Arquer, to eleven years, and the remaining two acquitted. The POUM and its youth movement were formally outlawed.

—It was my first real shock. I simply couldn't believe that Nin was a fascist agent, recalled a PSUC militant, a pre-war socialist youth.

When the PSUC had formed, Alejandro VITORIA had suggested that the POUM be asked to join, for it had within its ranks, in his opinion, the most militant marxists in Catalonia. But no attention was paid to his suggestion; even worse, the PSUC had affiliated immediately to the Comintern which had isolated the party from the POUM, the CNT and the socialists in the rest of Spain, thus reducing the possibility of an understanding with these organizations.

—And now this. I obeyed the party line about the POUM, but without conviction. To have protested would have been to start an internal party struggle when unity and winning the war was the main priority. But it caused me remorse, personally and politically . . .

1. Imprisoned in Barcelona, they were moved the day before the city fell in 1939 to a village near the French frontier. Hoping to use their safe release in France for his own protection, the prison director had got the justice minister's permission for the move. By chance, the communist army commander, Enrique Lister, set up his HQ in the same village. ANDRADE: ' "If they find us here they'll liquidate us tonight," we said to one another. It was only because the GPU agents were so frightened at Barcelona's collapse that they had forgotten about us. Many militants were executed during the flight into France. We insisted that the prison director move us immediately; he managed to find Catalan guides to lead us across the mountains into France that very night.'

He was not alone; but he was in a minority. The PSUC played no part in Nin's assassination, Pere ARDIACA, editor of the party paper *Treball*, asserted categorically. The executive committee never discussed the question of liquidating the POUM.

—That was a matter for the PCE central committee and the representatives newly arrived from abroad. We certainly considered the POUM as traitors, as spies and enemy agents whose sole task was to disrupt republican unity in order to prevent victory in the war. This belief, which today we must correct, obviously determined a particular attitude on our part, quite independently of the fact that there may have been one or two enemy agents in the POUM's ranks. The same could be said of the PSUC – indeed, we had to expel people, and people high up in the party's ranks, the leadership even. I had been in the BOC before joining the communist party, so I knew that its militants were honest and sincere in their revolutionary beliefs, even if those were different to ours . . .

If his party had pursued the same policy with the POUM as with the CNT, meeting jointly from time to time, the POUM's policy, he was convinced, could have been influenced and the May events prevented. Instead, the PSUC had held to its positions, contributing thereby to the POUM membership maintaining its positions because they saw themselves under attack from the PSUC.

—My party had no hand in Nin's assassination; that I can state categorically. The assassination took place in Madrid. Everyone knows who was responsible, but I'm not in a position to name names because officially I don't know. None the less, there can be no doubt whatever that any charges against Nin should have been heard, at the very least, in a court. His assassination is a heavy legacy indeed.

Though we had nothing to do with the POUM's persecution, we regarded it with favour. Later, at the POUM trial, we were stupefied by the evidence given, but at the same time it never occurred to us to protest because we shared the prosecution's opinion . . .

*

Two months after the POUM's repression, Negrín, the prime minister, issued a decree dissolving the Council of Aragon: 'moral and material needs of the war imperiously demand the concentration of authority in the hands of the state.' Aragon was the CNT's last bulwark; to strike a blow against it was to strike another blow in the battle for central government control over Catalonia, for Aragon was Catalonia's battle front and also to some extent its agricultural hinterland. The harvest was just about in, the first full crop under collectivization.

The communist agricultural minister's decree legalizing the collectives for a further year was now revealed as a hollow promise to ensure the harvest was reaped. Lister's 11th division was sent to Aragon; the communist commander was ordered by Prieto, the socialist defence minister, to carry out the government's dissolution decree. His forces swept through Aragon, arresting CNT leaders, including the Council of Aragon's president and other councillors, as well as village collectivists. Before leaving for Aragon, the division's political delegates told the men that the CNT had set up the council in order to establish a libertarian communist regime, recalled Timoteo RUIZ, the peasant lad who had started the war with a lance and was now a junior staff officer in the division.

—We were told that the peasantry was hostile to the council and frequently crossed to the enemy lines. When we got there we went round the villages disarming the people. We told them there was a war on, that it was being fought to defend the republic and ensure the triumph of democracy, and that the peasantry must be respected. What they were doing didn't correspond to the needs of the war. The peasants welcomed us as though we were their liberators, delighted to have their lands, tools and livestock back and to be able to work their land as they wanted . . .

Overwhelmed by the way the peasantry appeared to have suffered, the collectivization seemed to him 'the most counter-revolutionary experience of the war'. One peasant came up to him and said that when 'those men with red and black neckerchiefs and bristling with arms came through here they seemed to me like the *guardia civil* – only worse. The *guardia* used to lay down the law here – but they didn't tell us how to work our land.'

—What we were determined to put an end to was the dragooning of the peasantry into collectives, not the collectives themselves. We weren't opposed to the latter – how could we be when we were encouraging their creation everywhere? No, it was forced collectivization, the abolition of money, which demoralized the peasantry and stopped them from working as hard, which we were opposed to . . .[1]

Antonio ROSEL, the Aragonese communist foundryman who had listened to so many peasants' complaints about the collectives when he served on a joint UGT–CNT commission, was arrested by a communist military patrol in the streets of Caspe. He produced his party card, informed the troops that he was a member of the communist party's regional committee.

—'We don't give a damn about anyone or anything here. We're in charge and that's that.' They couldn't have cared less. Lister was proclaimed a liberator by the people. But he overstepped his orders. It required a great deal of care to ensure that in liquidating a bad experiment we didn't go to the other extreme. But that was what happened. We went from an anarchist dictatorship to a communist one. People who had been, and always would be, enemies of the working class because their interests were fundamentally opposed, were now given encouragement and support simply because of their hostility to the CNT. Later, these same people turned their hostility on the communist party and the republican government . . .

His experience was a clear indictment of the dangers inherent in out-and-out support of the anti-libertarian peasantry. At the same time, few libertarians were prepared to defend their own creation, the Council of Aragon. In the opinion of Ernesto MARGELI, secretary of the Mas de las Matas collective, all

1. For RUIZ's and another communist's favourable experience of rural collectivization – and the differences between communist and anarchist modes of collectivization – see Appendix, B.

but one of its members, the economics councillor, had proven themselves useless. Macario ROYO, the CNT national committeeman who had been on the commission which set up the council, had lost confidence in its president, Joaquín Ascaso, and Ortiz, the commander of the 25th division. 'Their headquarters was more like a house of pleasure than anything else,' he observed after a visit to complain that they were preventing collectivists from fetching fertilizer from a warehouse which they had declared in a war zone. 'If it had been the communists or republicans sabotaging the collectives, I might have understood. But no! It was CNT militants.' There hung over some of the Council's leading members a cloud of immorality which was offensive to libertarians.

Ernesto MARGELI was amongst those arrested. Taken to Lister's command post in an olive grove near Caspe, he was interrogated by an officer.

—'You're not defending this flag,' he said, pointing at the republican flag in the room. 'And what about you?' I replied. 'It's the Russian flag you defend!' The officer shouted at me angrily. Then he started questioning me again. They were obsessed with the idea that the CNT had stocks of arms, an ammunition dump in Aragon somewhere . . .

One night he and the other prisoners were lined up against a wall under car headlights; the attempt to frighten them into talking was clear enough. MARGELI always gave the same answer. He knew nothing – but even if he had known he wouldn't tell them. 'None of you ever belonged to a working-class party or organization before the war. You're all new.'

Released after five days, thanks to the CNT national committee's intervention, he returned to Mas de las Matas the day before Lister's troops reached it. Having been originally arrested while on a trip from the village, he was now arrested again. With the exception of one companion, who had already shared his fate, all the others on the village committee fled to the safety of a CNT division in the neighbouring township of Hijar.

Lister's men ordered a new village council appointed, composed of republicans – 'a bit soft, but not right-wingers' – examined the accounts of the municipality and the collective, and questioned the men about jewellery collected on behalf of the Council of Aragon. On none of these scores could they find anything illegal; MARGELI and his companion were allowed to go free. They were told to call an assembly of the collectivists. Assault guards attended.

—Everyone was told that he was free to leave the collective if he wanted. We asked each member individually. The right-wingers, those who had been obliged to join, took the opportunity of leaving. There may have been villages where Lister's men dissolved the collectives, but not in Mas de las Matas . . .

Nor in Alloza where the same procedure was carried out by a group of assault guards. Juan MARTINEZ, the medium-holding peasant there who had thought the collectives were not a bad idea, remembered the moment when a captain told the villagers they were free to choose.

—Most of the people left, and were happy to do so. Those who remained – about a quarter of the original number – were under no pressure to do so; nobody bothered them, nobody tried to break up their collective. In fact, one or two of the peasants with bigger holdings left their land in because they were frightened the situation might change again . . .

Several hundred CNT militants on local and regional committees were arrested and some killed. The aim of the sweep appeared to be not to smash the collectives, but to smash CNT domination in Aragon.

Estimates as to how many people remained in the collectives after the communist action are difficult to make. Ernesto Margeli, who shortly afterwards enlisted in the 26th (ex-Durruti) division, estimated that in Mas de las Matas it was as high as 60 per cent. In Alloza, where pre-war there had been no CNT, it was significant that perhaps one quarter of the collectivists refused to leave.[1]

—The people now showed more determination to keep their collectives going, more solidarity. Older peasants, men of forty-five or fifty, many of whom had never belonged to the CNT before, expressed their determination to continue the experiment and asked for advice and guidance, recalled Félix CARRASQUER at his school of collectivist administrators. In fact, things were much easier now that the younger militants were out of the way, there were none of those byzantine discussions of the past . . .

At the front, there was a considerable movement among CNT troops to retaliate. Sevilla PASTOR, libertarian youth member from Mas de las Matas serving in the 26th division, was prepared to leave the front and fight it out. He, and others like him, were restrained by their commanders who told them that other, diplomatic means had to be found to solve the problem.

—Many different thoughts went through my mind. But in the end it always came back to the same thing: the most important objective was to fight the main enemy, the one in the trenches opposite. Most of us felt like that . . .

Saturnino CAROD had great difficulty persuading his troops not to abandon their positions to fight the communists in the rear. Had they done so then, or three months before during the May events in Barcelona, the way would have been left open for the enemy to walk into Aragon and Catalonia, he thought. That catastrophe was avoided only because he and others in similar positions were able to contain the troops. But seeing the equipment Lister's division deployed in tanks, machine-guns and machine-rifles caused him further despair. 'We hadn't realized the difference between our divisions and theirs until then. Now, with rage in our hearts, we realized how under-equipped we were' . . .

Once the sweep was finished there were fraternization gatherings. CAROD began to wonder whether Lister (whose division was used as a shock force, not for manning the lines) had not come to regret his action, for he began to offer

1. Compared to mid-1937, the number of agrarian collectives increased by 25 per cent throughout the Popular Front zone to the end of 1938, while the number of collectivists dropped by nearly half (see F. Mintz, *L'Autogestion dans l'Espagne révolutionnaire*, p. 148). The relative increase of rural collectives was actually larger, for by early 1938 Aragon had fallen to the nationalists and was not included in these figures. A somewhat similar sweep had been made by Lister through certain areas of the Levant prior to Aragon; there, too, peasants were given the option of leaving collectives.

his services to various villages and collectives in the region. Relations between communist and anarchist units improved somewhat, although never to the point CAROD believed necessary. Throughout the war, he reflected, the anarcho-syndicalists lived with their eyes fixed on the front line *and* turned towards the rear.

—Always expecting to be stabbed in the back, always knowing that if we created problems, only the enemy across the lines would stand to gain. It was a tragedy for the anarcho-syndicalist movement; but it was a tragedy for something much greater – the Spanish people. For it can never be forgotten that it was the working class and peasantry which, by demonstrating their ability to run industry and agriculture collectively, allowed the republic to continue the struggle for thirty-two months. It was they who created a war industry, who kept agricultural production increasing, who formed the militias and later the army. Without their creative endeavour, the republic could not have fought the war . . .

*

The last word on the collectives can safely be left with the nationalists. An official report on the Levant, issued a year after the end of the war by the nationalist ministry of industry and commerce, wrote: 'The number of collectivized industries and businesses has been truly extraordinary; it can be said that almost the totality of industry and commerce operated in this form. At the present time there remain groups which have not been totally de-collectivized; this is because of the passivity shown by those concerned who, seeing that their attitude does not endanger them, are doing everything possible to delay de-collectivization.'[1]

Not even enemy victory had yet crushed the movement.

1. *Comisión de incorporación industrial y mercantil, No. 3*, 'Estudio sobre la riqueza del Levante Español' (Valencia, 1940). I am indebted to Regina Taya for bringing this document to my attention.

I have decided to end the war rapidly in the north. The lives and property of those who surrender with their arms and who are not guilty of murder will be respected. But if the surrender is not immediate, I shall raze Vizcaya to its very foundations, beginning with the war industry. I have the means to do so.

General Mola, Proclamation to the people of Euzkadi
(March 1937)

Summer to Autumn 1937

EUZKADI

While the issues of war and revolution were being fought out in the republican rearguard, the Basque country and Santander were falling to the Franco forces.

Having failed to take Madrid, the nationalists turned their attention totally on Vizcaya, beginning their campaign at the end of March. It was immediately marked by air raids on open towns behind the front, which was no more than 40 km from Bilbao at its farthest. Mola's boast was no idle threat. In Durango, a town of 10,000 inhabitants, 250 were killed in two air raids on the first day of the offensive. A volunteer army chaplain, Father José Maria BASABILOTRA, rushed to the town where some troops of his unit had been caught on their return from leave. Bombs had fallen on two churches as communion services were being held, and several nuns had been killed in a near-by convent. Father BASABILOTRA saw the planes of the Nazi Condor Legion – 'grey, rather beautiful and sinister' – on their second raid. He went to the cemetery. People started to emerge from the coffin niches in the walls where they had taken refuge. Rows of corpses were laid out, men, women and children. He was stunned. 'They've done this to demoralize us at the front.' It was to become an important element of enemy strategy, he later saw.

The Basque government, in which the PNV was the dominant force, had organized its own army. Here, the issue of war and revolution did not arise: there was no revolution. More than any other republican region, Euzkadi exemplified a nationalist bourgeois approach to the conflict. For most Basque nationalists, the war was being waged in Euzkadi's defence against an external aggressor – 'the Spanish, white or red' – to retain their country's autonomy, not to make revolutionary changes in the Spanish state and society.[1] When the central government decreed the formation of an army of the north (Asturias, Santander and Euzkadi), the Basque government maintained it had been 'wrongfully' created and refused to accept it.[2]

—Of course, militarily, there should have been a single command. But there was no understanding between us and the others – the Asturians and the people from Santander. We found it very hard to feel Spanish. Whether one likes it or

1. See pp. 189–95. Certainly, Euzkadi's President Aguirre affirmed (December 1936) that the war was being fought between the old capitalist order, which the privileged classes had risen to defend, and 'the profound sense of social justice which many workers felt'. This must be read in the context of his government's declared programme proposing that the worker be given access to capital, to profits and the co-management of enterprises (see Ortzi, *Historia de Euskadi*, pp. 222 and 224); Aguirre, moreover, saw the war in its widest implications.

2. A few weeks later, Caballero, the Spanish premier, assured President Aguirre that no such thing as an army of the north existed. The general whom Caballero had appointed to command it was, not surprisingly, dismayed and moved his HQ to Santander. Neither the Basque nor Catalan autonomy statutes gave the right to maintain an army; in the circumstances it was almost inevitable that both should do so. But whereas the Catalan forces, the bulk of them under CNT dominance, covered a continuous line in Aragon, the same was not true in the north where three distinct but adjoining regions were fighting more or less separately.

not, that's the truth, asserted Juan Manuel EPALZA, a leading PNV militant...

There was a different concept of liberty and democracy; the religious question aggravated everything, he thought. How could one mix units where some gloried in their Catholicism, like the Basque nationalists, and others in their anti-clericalism? Moreover, he and others feared that when the central government appointed Capt. Ciutat, a communist party member, as chief-of-staff of the army of the north, it heralded 'a complete infiltration by the communists'.

The government's non-revolutionary conduct of the war was criticized shortly before the enemy offensive began by the Popular Front parties (which included the small Basque nationalist party ANV (Acción Nacionalista Vasca), but not the dominant PNV) in Euzkadi. They called for the fusion of the existing militias into a popular army under the single command of the army of the north (the ANV alone opposed this, maintaining that the command should be 'conditional'); the appointment of political commissars; the 'energetic elimination' of the enemy in the rear; the nationalization of all industry needed for the war effort, and the banking system; and workers' control and participation in the direction and administration of all enterprises. Although the socialist party was the major working-class force in Euzkadi, the programme corresponded fairly closely to making good the criticisms the Spanish communist party had been levelling against the Basques – and in particular against the Basque communist party leadership – for allowing the PNV to dictate the terms of the war.[1] But the Popular Front parties continued to participate in the government. Gonzalo NARDIZ, the ANV agriculture minister, remembered no great political differences until the defence of Bilbao.[2]

Basque nationalist battalions, manned in the main by the peasantry, formed the largest single element of the army. Even its junior officers were aware that the chief-of-staff, Col. Montaud, a career officer, who enjoyed the confidence of President Aguirre, was a defeatist. Lt Luis MICHELENA, ex-bookkeeper from Rentería in Guipúzcoa and PNV militant, believed he should have been shot. It wasn't a question of disloyalty as much as the way the colonel conceived the war effort.

—He always had the idea that any operation he planned would turn out badly. But then few of the professional officers in the Basque army were much good. The majority had a civil servant mentality, lacking initiative and understanding of the popular forces they were commanding. In short – they were suspicious of the people . . .

With the exception of one offensive the previous November at Villareal, which had failed in its attempt to draw forces from the Franco offensive on Madrid, the

1. The communist party of Euzkadi was an 'autonomous' branch of the PCE. It defended the right of self-determination and independence for Euzkadi, and its leaders were Basque-speakers. After the fall of Bilbao, the PCE's charges were taken to their conclusion: Juan Astigarrabía, the Euzkadi party's secretary-general, and a minister in the Basque government, was expelled from the party.

2. With the exception of the central government's proposal to send non-Basque political commissars. 'Only the communists were prepared to accept; Astigarrabía even threatened to resign, but when he saw that the rest of us were united, he remained in the government.' (Gonzalo NARDIZ.)

Basque army had launched no major attacks since its creation.[1] In Basque nationalist eyes, and not without reason, too much effort in the north had been concentrated on Oviedo.

On 20 April, after a fortnight's lull due to bad weather, the Franco offensive resumed. At the same time, the nationalists hoped to starve Bilbao into submission by imposing a blockade which the British Admiralty readily accepted as effective until disproved by a British merchant ship, the *Seven Seas Spray*, which sailed in with 3,500 tons of food. By 24 April, the enemy had made an important breakthrough in the hills of Inxorta; and in the ensuing panic it seemed as though little would stop the Franco forces advancing to Bilbao. Two days later Guernica was blitzed by the Condor Legion.

*

'*Amatxu*, the church bells are ringing,' Ignacia OZAMIZ's three-year-old son kept saying as, from early morning, the bells tolled out warnings of enemy planes in the vicinity. The front was barely 20 km to the east at Marquina as the crow flies. Four months pregnant, she had put her child – the youngest of four – to bed after lunch when her husband, a local blacksmith, sent her a message to go down to the shelter. People had seen a big plane – the *abuelo* – over the mountains.

Until the past week, she thought, with the exception of food shortages and the dead being brought from the front for burial, the war had hardly affected Guernica. Six months before, José Antonio Aguirre, newly elected head of Euzkadi's autonomous government, had knelt under its famous oak tree, where in the past Spanish monarchs or their representatives had sworn to respect the Basque *fueros*. Guernica, a town of 6,000 inhabitants lying between hills 30 km to the north-east of Bilbao, was a symbol of liberty and tradition for the Basques. In a few hours it became the universal symbol of fascist terror.

Monday, 26 April was market day. The livestock market had been suspended for the duration of the war, but the ordinary market, Ignacia OZAMIZ recalled, continued as usual. Father Dionisio AJANGUIZ was on his way to his home town from his parish of Aulestia, halfway to Marquina, to spend the afternoon chatting and playing cards with fellow priests. One of them, whose mother that very morning had offered them a glass of cognac each not to go to Guernica, was accompanying him. They had drunk the cognac and set out. He had taken no heed even of his own brother's admonitions; Father José AXUNGUIZ had been warning his parishioners at Marquina not to continue the traditional practice of going to Guernica on market day.

—It was an outing for the youth; buses brought people from as far away as Lequeitio on the coast. The people lacked war training. I blame the Basque authorities. They shouldn't have allowed the practice to continue, they were responsible for a great number of deaths. Those of us who lived virtually on the front, as in Marquina, had learnt the importance of building good shelters. But in Guernica they hadn't taken adequate precautions; the shelters were

1. Seven battalions – volunteers as far as the Basque nationalists were concerned, for the party leadership would oblige no one to fight outside the borders of Euzkadi – had participated in the February offensive on Oviedo, See p. 254, n. 2).

rudimentary. I kept telling my mother: 'Build a good one.' 'Poor child, poor child,' was all she could say . . .

As Father Dionisio AJANGUIZ walked into Guernica, a solitary Heinkel III flew over and dropped half a dozen bombs. 'It was the people's salvation; they ran from their houses to the shelters.' He was still half a kilometre from the centre when he saw nine planes appear, flying low, from the direction of the sea. He threw himself on the ground as the first bombs fell.

Hearing the explosions, Ignacia OZAMIZ, who had taken her husband's advice and gone to the shelter next to her house, thought the end had come. So did others.

—'Ignacia, where have we come to die?' the church organist from my home village said. 'Here – ' I replied. The shelter was packed: 150 people at least between neighbours and people who had come for the market. The bombs crashed on the near-by hospital, killing twenty-five children and two nuns. Debris fell on the shelter, and we thought it had been hit. It was little more than a roof of sandbags, narrow and short, in the patio next to our house. Soon it filled with smoke and dust. '*Amatxu,* take me out,' my son began to cry in Basque. 'I can't breathe . . . '

Her eldest daughter, Manolita AGUIRRE, had gone with girlfriends to the plain that began at the edge of the town. There had been no school that day. As they were playing, they saw the planes coming. Workers shouted at them to get into the shelter close by the small-arms factory. As they ran in they heard the *tat-tat-tat* of the fighters' machine-guns. An old man pulled out a religious medallion and gave it to her to kiss. 'Pray, child, pray, the planes are bombing us – '

—The fighters dived down and machine-gunned people trying to flee across the plain. The bombers were flying so low you could see the crewmen, recalled Father Dionisio AJANGUIZ. It was a magnificent clear April evening after a showery morning . . .

Between the waves of bombers, the priest scrambled to look for a safer place than the side of the road. Amidst the crash of bombs, Juana SANGRONIZ hoped she could die without seeing the cause of death. When she ran into the shelter people had shouted, 'Don't let her in – '. She was a Carlist, had been arrested with a number of others and kept in gaol for three weeks in Bilbao. She hadn't been out of her home, not even to go to mass, since her release, unable to face the indignity of being seen under guard like the other women. But her *novio* had dragged her into a house near the church of Santa María where people were sheltering. She was sure she was going to die. She heard the bombs whistle, the frightening explosions. People cried that it was dangerous to keep the mouth shut.

—One had to put a stick or something between one's teeth. My *novio* tried, but I kept telling him, 'Leave me in peace.' He was a strong man, but he was trembling with fear . . .

The house on one side of the shelter, and then Ignacia OZAMIZ's house on the other, began to burn. The smoke poured into the shelter. Someone drove a cow in. It started to shriek.

—All the smoke came in with it. We had to keep our mouths shut, we could hardly see each other, and the smell was awful, remembered her seven-year-old daughter, KONI. I didn't think of dying, I was too young perhaps. But I thought we were going to suffocate . . .

—People started to panic, recalled Ignacia OZAMIZ. 'The house is on fire, we're going to be burnt alive,' they screamed. *Gudaris* guarding the shelter let no one leave. One man tried to force his way out with his young child. 'I don't care if they kill me, I can't stand it here.' He was pushed back. 'Keep calm,' the soldiers shouted . . .

The town was beginning to burn, the wooden rafters catching alight. After the high explosive bombs, successive waves of planes dropped incendiaries.

From the shelter of an iron-ore bore hole about a kilometre from the town, Father Dionisio AJANGUIZ saw the roofs catching alight. Even at that distance he found breathing difficult because of the smoke. He feared that at least half the town's population must have been killed. 'And that's what would have happened if they had dropped the incendiaries earlier instead of towards the end' . . .

A pall of smoke rose into the sky. Between waves of bombers, Juan Manuel EPALZA, now serving in the war industries' chemical section, who by chance was lunching at a factory on the outskirts of the town, came out of an air raid shelter to look. Thoughts of Nero crossed his mind. The bombing was of a different intensity to any that he had suffered.

After some three hours it ended. As Ignacia OZAMIZ and her two children emerged from the shelter, she saw the town was alight. 'Don't cry,' her husband consoled her. 'We've got our hands, we're unharmed, alive.' But she could think only of her eldest daughter and her mother, neither of whom had been in the shelter with her. Her house in Asilo Calzado was burning from the roof. Her husband rushed in to rescue papers and money.

—'Oh, if only you'd managed to save my sewing machine,' I said. He went back in. As he came down with the machine, he found the staircase alight. He threw the machine out of the window, only just managing to jump out himself. 'Woman, I got your machine but it nearly cost me my life.' 'Why did you go up?' 'To do you a pleasure.' The machine broke in its fall on the air raid shelter we'd just left, but I picked up the head, and I've got it still . . .

As her eldest daughter, Manolita, came out of the shelter on the edge of the town – where none of the industrial plants, including the small-arms factory, had been hit – a wave of heat struck her face. She told a man that she had to join her parents who were in the blazing ruins she could see beyond the railway station. Together, they skirted the town along the railway track to reach the main road. A *gudari* carried her on his shoulders to reach her burning house, one of the first on the street into the centre.

Everywhere people were fleeing. The water main had been broken in the raid, and there was little to be done to put out the fire. Juana SANGRONIZ was led out of the blaze by her *novio*. Crying uncontrolledly, she refused to look back at the burning town. Ignacia OZAMIZ's husband ran to rescue his crippled mother; he arrived too late. She and three other old women had been burnt alive. Leaving their house burning, the family made their way out of the town by a path known as El Agua Corriente; the main street through the centre was impassable. As they reached the higher part, they saw that the area around the oak tree had not been hit. That night, given shelter outside town at the home of the Count of Arana, one of whose sons her husband had managed earlier to get released from gaol, she had a miscarriage. Her husband took her to a relative's farm. She left her four children with her mother. Little did she think it would be three years before she saw them again.

—'And to think that we shall be blamed for this,' I said to Dr Junod, the Swiss Red Cross representative, as we walked through the still burning ruins a few hours later. Juan Manuel EPALZA had just returned to Guernica from Bilbao. 'No,' replied Dr Junod, 'that's impossible.' 'You don't know the enemy we have in front of us,' I replied . . . [1]

Demoralization of the rearguard was an important element of war, thought Father José Maria BASABILOTRA, chaplain in a Basque nationalist unit, who had been in Durango after the air raid nearly a month before. It became more important as married men were called up: concerned about their families in the rear, they were more easily demoralized and in turn demoralized the youth who were the best combatants.

—The effect of Guernica on the soldiers of my JSU battalion was much worse than if they had been in combat and suffered casualties, reflected a seventeen-year-old communist miner, Saturnino CALVO, who was stationed barely 10 km away. To know that women and children were being killed in the rearguard – we saw the ambulances on the road below our positions – demoralized them. I won't say it lowered their combat-spirit – the battalion was almost entirely Basque-speaking – but it affected them deeply . . .

*

For seven more weeks, the Basque army – its previously politically affiliated battalions formed at last into five regular divisions – defended every metre of the 30 km of hilly terrain before Bilbao. Col. Montaud was replaced as chief-of-

1. The international protest and the slow but steady erosion over the following decades of the Franquista propaganda story that Guernica had been set fire to by the Basque militia can be followed in H. Southworth's *La Destruction de Guernica* (Paris, 1975). It was a story which some right-wing local people subscribed to, if only by their silence. Juana SANGRONIZ (Carlist): 'Our consciences were uneasy about it. After living through the raid, we knew only too well that the destruction had come from the air. The reds had hardly any planes, we knew that too. Amongst our own we'd admit the truth: our side had bombed the town and it was a bad thing. "But what can we do about it now?" we'd say; it was better simply to keep quiet. The propaganda was so patently untrue.' The exact number of dead has never been satisfactorily established (see Southworth for an examination of the conflicting evidence). The Basque government at the time put the figure at 1,654 dead and 889 wounded – but the government could not establish an accurate count since three days after the raid, the front having broken at Marquina, Guernica fell to the Franco forces.

staff and President Aguirre became commander-in-chief. It was the communists, particularly the Soviet advisers, stressed Gonzalo NARDIZ, ANV minister in the government, who suggested the latter appointment. 'They understood the great importance of nationalism in the Basque army; without it, I doubt if there would have been such resistance.'

In Bilbao, which in the Carlist wars of the previous century had three times withstood siege, and was now defended by a 'ring of iron', fear that the Guernica blitz might be repeated was widespread. Every time the frequent sirens sounded, industry, business and offices came to a complete halt.[1] People saw the few remaining Basque fighters take off.

—'They're only five,' the right-wingers said, rubbing their hands. Then one day there were no longer five but four; then three. Ana María ADARRAGA, fifteen-year-old daughter of a merchant navy purser, was one of hundreds who spent all day by the railway tunnel close to her home in Luchana on the estuary's right bank. I remember the enemy planes bombing frequently – but never the Altos Hornos steel works and the shipbuilding yards right across from us on the opposite bank. They must have thought they were going to be using them pretty soon . . .

Her four brothers and sisters had been evacuated to England. Since Guernica, over 13,000 children had been sent to France, Belgium, Switzerland, England and Russia. Food had been a problem since the winter. 'Chick-peas, rice, black rye bread, fish. We were going hungry. The blockade was ferocious.'

Rations in January were down to 50 grams of rice, chick-peas and vegetables, and 250 grams of oil per person per day. The difficulty of feeding the population – Vizcaya, like Catalonia, was not self-sufficient in food – was increased by the 100,000 refugees from Guipúzcoa. The fortuitous arrival of a large consignment of chick-peas from Mexico just before the start of the war had to some extent saved the situation.

Ignacia OZAMIZ's four children from Guernica had arrived in Bilbao, unknown to their mother who was expecting them at the relative's farm where her husband had taken her after her miscarriage on the night of the blitz. A friend of her husband's had picked up the children in his lorry. Three days later, when the nationalists occupied Guernica, the family was stranded on different sides of the lines, neither knowing if the other were alive.

After the blitz of their home town, the children now experienced the bombing of Bilbao. Living with an aunt in a house in the city's centre, they went from the third to the first floor, where mattresses had been piled against the windows, when they heard the sirens; it was the only shelter they had.

Confused and sad, they heard children saying wherever they went: 'Have you seen my parents?' and parents asking after their children. They went hungry, eating orange peel, if they were lucky to find some lying in the street, and raw carob beans. At last, with the enemy at the gate of the city, their uncle managed to get them on the last ship to leave Bilbao. They drove through a heavy air raid to the port. Their uncle went aboard, gave the captain a package containing pistols from the small-arms factory he owned; the ship was already

1. J. Zugazagoitia, *Guerra y vicisitudes de los españoles* (Paris, 1968), vol. 1, p. 276.

full. The children went up the gangplank. Shouts rose from the people thronging the quay and who were still trying to get their children aboard. 'It shouldn't be allowed, they're rich people's children.' Alone again, not knowing where they were making for, they set sail; after three days at sea they heard that Bilbao had fallen.

*

The 'ring of iron' had been pierced a week before, after a heavy pounding by artillery and bombers at a point near Larrebezúa where it had not been finished. The Franco forces knew where to attack;[1] at the start of the campaign, the engineer Goicoechea, who had been working on the fortifications, defected to the enemy.

—We had trusted him, considered him one of ours at heart because he came from a PNV family, Juan AJURIAGUERRA, president of the Vizcaya PNV, recalled. It may seem as though I'm trying to excuse him; on the contrary, I consider it an additional charge against him . . .

In fact, it was the second betrayal; the first engineer who initiated and planned the defensive line had been executed for trying to pass information to the enemy. Goicoechea, his assistant, continued to work on the line. His defection was common knowledge among the troops – so much so that an enemy reconnaissance plane was nicknamed after him. But in Ramón RUBIAL's opinion, the iron ring was virtually useless anyway. The socialist turner, who was now in command of the 5th socialist battalion, found that the concrete pill-boxes were not camouflaged, and the trenches were wide and straight. 'We had no confidence in it. Bilbao had to be defended in positions outside it . . . '

—If it could be, reflected Pedro BASABILOTRA, secretary to the head of the PNV forces. The enemy bombed and bombed. We were without air cover. Every day the central government promised us war material – and every day it failed to arrive . . .

Air superiority was decisive. The Condor Legion did not repeat the Guernica blitz; it experimented, instead, with incendiaries on the pine-clad slopes of the hills, setting fire to them. After abortive attempts, the central government managed to get seven fighters to Bilbao in a direct flight from Madrid. There was a generalized resentment among Basque nationalists at its failure to send more effective aid. There was talk again that all Spaniards were the same, that the central government was as hostile to the Basques as was the insurgent military.[2]

1. Gen. Mola, who had been in command of the offensive, was killed in an air accident at the beginning of June, a week before the final attack on Bilbao.

2. The central government believed that the Basque government was suing for a separate peace. In May, an uncoded cable from the Vatican setting out terms agreed by Franco and Mola for Euzkadi's surrender had – in error – been sent via Barcelona rather than London for onward transmission to Bilbao. The central government did not pass the message on, but sent a bitter denunciatory cable to the Basque government which was unaware of the cause. Preoccupation about Vizcaya's resistance was a factor in Largo Caballero's downfall after the May events in Barcelona.

But, as Ramón RUBIAL perceived, Vizcaya lacked a sufficient hinterland to be able to keep war matériel, even planes, safe from enemy air attack. As it was, even the little Basque artillery could hardly be used in daylight because it was spotted and bombed.

—All our fighting had to be done at night; under cover of darkness we recaptured positions lost by day . . .

In Saturnino CALVO's JSU battalion, enemy artillery, especially the German ·88 cannon, was more feared than the bombing to which, after initial panic, they had grown used. The seventeen-year-old communist miner believed that by fighting in the mountains with a proper network of defensive positions they could have held the enemy off.

—But it required a war policy of the sort that the Basque government was unwilling to carry out. A scorched earth policy, a revolutionary type of war like in Madrid. We enjoyed a great advantage – the rugged terrain – which the defenders of Madrid lacked . . .

With the 'ring of iron' pierced, the centre of Bilbao lay only 10 km away within heavy artillery range. In the city, observed Dr Carlos MARTINEZ, the former parliamentary deputy just arrived from Paris on his way home to Asturias, there was calm. Artillery fire was plainly audible. The city's fall was patently imminent. He walked along the Gran Vía. Under President Aguirre, order had reigned in Vizcaya throughout the war: priests and property had been respected, he saw. He went into a shop and bought two jackets of English material without any formalities – no ration cards, no vouchers. He wouldn't have been able to do the same in Asturias. Perhaps many were waiting for the Franquista victory, he thought.

The communists called for all-out resistance, maintained that spades, properly used, were as effective as fighters against enemy raids. The disadvantages of a war of position, a last line of defence, became clear: once pierced, what other positions were there to fall back on?[1]

The Basque government decided to defend the city and at the same time to evacuate the population. A city without its population would not be another Madrid, however heroic its soldier-defenders might be.

By the morning of 19 June, a week after the initial breakthrough, the enemy was in command of the heights on both sides of the city. The order was given to abandon Bilbao; the road to Santander was left open by the enemy for the retreat. From the staff headquarters in the Basurto civil hospital, Ramón RUBIAL set out on foot to escape. As he made his way along the road, the sight of the streams of civilians in flight with all their possessions depressed him. Why had Bilbao not been another Madrid? No international brigaders to raise the population's morale? Lack of the war matériel which had reached Madrid in the nick of time? It was difficult to know. Veteran commanders had come from

1. Given the type of war that was being fought, however, fixed defensive lines could prove their worth, as the XYZ line demonstrated the following year. Built into the mountains, the fortifications – with trenches capable of withstanding 1,000-lb bombs – prevented the nationalists taking Valencia (see Thomas, *The Spanish Civil War*, p. 834). By comparison, the iron ring was poorly constructed, unfinished and betrayed.

the central front, a shipment of Czech arms had arrived, more men had been called up, a new commander of the army, General Gámir Ulíbarri, a Basque, appointed. It had all come very late. The enemy superiority in the air had been overwhelming. Still, it had taken the enemy seventy days to cover the 42 km to Bilbao.

Along the same road as the socialist battalion commander, Pedro BASABILOTRA was escaping in a car protected with mattresses. When he reached Castro Urdiales, the first town in Santander, a Russian major confronted him. —'Are you Basque?' he said, forming the words very slowly in Spanish. 'Yes.' 'The Basques are cowards.' 'Come out in the street and repeat that. What sort of soldier do you think you are?' The Russian had the mentality of a shoemender, thought the secretary to the head of the Basque nationalist forces. 'Destroy Bilbao? It was impossible to defend. It was stupid to die there when we could get our forces out so as to continue the fight'. . .

The night before, in a characteristic gesture, the Basque nationalists had released all their right-wing prisoners and passed them through their lines to the enemy zone.

Militancies 13

JUAN MANUEL EPALZA
PNV engineer

It had fallen on him to transfer the prisoners. If he couldn't, he was to remain in the Larrínaga prison and defend them from any and everyone until the enemy arrived. Then he was to escape. How? 'Swimming', the official replied. The mission was unofficial; the Basque government, which had left for Trucios to the west, knew of the plan but would not officially give the order. If things turned out badly, he would be held responsible, would have to take the blame.

He set off. It was another of the many tasks the war had saddled him with. A war, he thought, that had been lost from the moment the Army of Africa had been able to cross to the mainland, from the moment it became clear that Germany and Italy were going to support the insurgents. Well-led, the Spanish army always gave of its best. The little hope for the republic had been knocked on the head by Non-Intervention. Train-loads of arms waited in France while Irún fell on the other side of the river separating the two countries. The blame for all that lay with the government of his glorious majesty – and Blum wept. What a scene!

And the republic? Anarchy. Instead of assassinating, burning, expropriating, an army should have been organized immediately to counter-attack. The enemy had always held the initiative. Look at Catalonia. Despite its great economic potential, it had been incapable of waging a proper offensive on the Aragon front. Instead – endless committee meetings, talk, debates. *POUM-pim-pam* – even killing each other. Just a week after Guernica, they were fighting in the streets of Barcelona. How could you win a war like that?

Aged twenty-five, with degrees in law, industrial engineering and business administration, he came from one of the very few upper-class Bilbao families to have espoused Basque nationalism. His father, a director of the Banco de Bilbao – one of the leading Spanish banks which his great-grandfather had helped found – had been a PNV deputy. His family spoke only Basque at home. His second language was French, his third German, his fourth Spanish.

—Love of our language was one of the essential elements of nationalism. Kept alive by the peasantry and the church, it was a bulwark of religion, for the language knows no blasphemous words. (In the confessional one says to the priest that one has used 'Spanish words'.) Language, religion, Basque patriotism, liberty and democracy, those were the constituents of nationalism. The upper class in Bilbao looked down on nationalism as 'rustic', provincial; they were centralist and liberal in the English sense of the word . . .

The Basques were Basques; and Euzkadi their homeland. It was as simple and as complicated as that, he maintained. They were not Spanish, even if they carried Spanish passports. Once that was recognized, the task of formalizing the relationship between Basques and Spaniards could be tackled; but not until then. The PNV was like a resistance movement whose aim was to get rid of the oppressor and win Euzkadi's freedom. Its members came from all classes; possibly, when liberty was attained, it would split into its constituent class elements. The Basque spirit, he thought, was individualistic, closer to anarchism than socialism. The latter, openly centralist, drew its support in Vizcaya almost entirely from the workers who had migrated there from other regions. The socialist party had been the main enemy before the war.

Vice-president of the Bilbao Mendigoixales, the PNV's youth movement, he had believed at the start that the war was a Spanish problem and the PNV should remain neutral: how could the Basque nationalists ally themselves with those who were their major enemies – the left?[1] They had been forced to only because they'd been attacked; all the same, he had spent as much time during the war looking over his shoulder, fearing the stab in the back from his allies, as looking forward at the enemy in front.

—Even if we won the war, what was the point of allowing the country to fall into the hands of the communists and anarchists? . . .

He wasn't a communist witch-hunter; but he didn't like communism, nor did he want to have to choose between one form of dictatorship and another. Had he been forced to, he would probably not have chosen communism for 'their dictatorship lasts longer than others'.

Ahead lay the prison. What an absurdity, he thought, to be rescuing potential enemies, ensuring their safety! The Basques valued human life above everything.

1. See p. 191.

—Not to stain our hands in blood was always as big a problem for us as winning the war. Perhaps even bigger . . .

Five months before, at the beginning of January, after a German air raid, an infuriated mob had assaulted the prison. Soldiers of a UGT battalion who had been sent to repel the mob joined in the massacre, killing some 200 prisoners before the Ertzaina (the newly formed Basque police) arrived. Basque nationalist opinion was horrified;[1] Radio Bilbao broadcast the names of those murdered, a special tribunal was set up to judge the guilty, six of whom were sentenced to death. Coming after two assaults on prison ships anchored in the estuary the previous autumn, it had been a tragedy. The Basques, he was convinced, were not prepared to be thought of as Spaniards, whether 'red' or 'white', who assassinated people; the Basques were different. Another prison assault and a great number of Basque nationalist units would have abandoned the front. Even now, at the last hour, the 900 prisoners in Larrínaga and in the adjoining Carmelo and Angeles Custodios convents, which had been turned into prisons, could not be left to their fate.

He found the prisoners lined up, awaiting orders. They had been given picks, shovels and blankets to make it look as though they were a work force going out to dig trenches. He and three previously selected military men set out up the road to Santo Domingo; two Basque nationalist battalions had retaken the heights the day before at enormous cost. At the last corner he sent the three men on their way. He couldn't let the prisoners cross the lines without knowing first that it was safe.

—The three men would make the trial run. It was a moonlit night and the civil guard's bald head shone in the light. I gave him my beret. I was determined that the prisoners should only cross at a place held by Basque nationalist troops. I could imagine the massacre if some unit we couldn't trust spotted the prisoners and opened fire . . .

As he waited, giving time for the emissaries to cross, a lieutenant of the Basque nationalist Itxasalde battalion arrived, very frightened, with orders for him to return to the prison a kilometre down the road. A group of soldiers from a left-wing battalion had seen the prisoners drawn up and seemed about to take action. The *gudaris* guarding the prison had given orders for the prisoners to set out immediately. Going down, he found the prisoners in a long column behind the Basilica of Begoña. Some of them were armed, the *gudaris* had seen to that.

—I'd have done the same. We had only enough *gudaris* from our decimated battalions to protect the column's rear. I gave the order for the prisoners to drop their spades and pickaxes. I'll never forget the noise they made. Then the order for the column to move, the armed men to remain at the crossroads. It

1. 'Some of us believed that the government, despite all the difficulties it faced – among them the fact that the police force had had to be created from scratch – could have acted more effectively and rapidly to prevent the massacre, and at a party meeting we resigned. But we accused no one of responsibility, accepting our own in what was a terrible blot on our reputations' (Juan AJURIAGUERRA, president, Vizcaya PNV).

was one of the few times in my life that I swore: they weren't walking fast enough . . .

The column included sick men on stretchers; it was 3 km from the prison to Santo Domingo. In the full moon, the column of 900 men winding up the road was plainly visible to those in the rear, who included Ernesto CASTAÑO, ex-CEDA deputy from Salamanca. Down from his normal 70 kilos to 30, he clutched a sub-machine-gun given him by a *gudari*. Little did the prisoners know that on the road behind them, EPALZA was preventing a shoot-out between Basque nationalist and socialist-led troops who had been alerted to the movement but were not sure what was happening. Finally, at his insistence, the commanders of both parties began negotiations.

—I was trying to gain time so that the column could get as far forward as possible. In the middle of all this we discovered that the armed prisoners and *gudaris* I had ordered to remain guarding the cross-roads had passed over to the enemy lines. I had no desire to join them. The war might have seemed lost from the first day, but that was no reason not to continue fighting. A friend of mine, whom I had been hiding in my house, suggested I remain in Bilbao. 'What – so that your friends can cut off my head?' '*Hombre,*' he replied, 'what do you expect them to do to someone with ideas like yours?' That was the mentality the right-wing displayed . . .

Twenty minutes after EPALZA had successfully concluded his mission and withdrawn across the river to the centre of Bilbao, the bridges were blown up. The central government had ordered all industrial plant to be destroyed if the city could not be defended. The left bank of the estuary, from Bilbao to the sea, contained the bulk of the republic's heavy industry. Three plants were totally evacuated, and some machinery taken from other large plants;[1] but cartridge, mortar and high explosive plants were left intact, not to mention shipbuilding yards, heavy engineering works and steel-making plants. Among the latter, Altos Hornos at Baracaldo was the most important steel works in Spain. The left-wing units withdrawing from Bilbao expected it to be destroyed.

– What was the point of blowing up the bridges if Altos Hornos was to be left intact? asked Ramón RUBIAL, socialist battalion commander. All it needed was to blow up the main power plant in the works, and steel-making would have come to a stop for a couple of years . . .

Few knew why it did not happen; but Gonzalo NARDIZ, ANV agriculture minister in the Basque government, did, for he was instrumental in seeing that the works remained undamaged. Two or three days before Bilbao fell, President Aguirre invited him and General Gámir, commander of the army, to go with him to Baracaldo.

—A member of my party, Luis Urcullo, was the commander of the local

1. *Guerra y revolución en España, 1936–1939*, vol. 3, p. 140, n. 4, cites a list of the plants and equipment, drawn up for the army of the north's chief-of-staff.

battalion. There had never been any discussion in the government about blowing up Altos Hornos; the question was never posed. We talked to Urcullo, insisting that his mission was to defend Altos Hornos and, as far as possible, to prevent it being blown up. We didn't give him written orders, we didn't even have to say out loud what was on our minds; it was something understood between us, *sotto voce*, by hints . . .

It would, moreover, NARDIZ felt, have been difficult to have given orders to the contrary since most of the battalion members came from Baracaldo and depended on the steel plant for their livelihood. President Aguirre's objective was to avoid any destruction which would leave people unemployed and open to enemy reprisal. EPALZA, for example, believed that no other policy was possible.

—If the first and only Basque government set about implementing a scorched earth policy, destroying the country's productive capacity, our people would never have understood. We knew that it was betraying our allies to leave our factories intact, but it would have been an even greater betrayal of our people to have destroyed everything and left them without work . . .

And in any case, the defeat might be shortlived. Juan AJURIAGUERRA, president of the Vizcaya PNV, was convinced, as were other members of the party's leadership, that a European war was going to break out and the Franco regime would be overthrown.

—We didn't want to blow up the people's wealth which we would soon take over again. Even though things didn't turn out like that, I wouldn't like to say categorically that it was a mistake not to blow up Altos Hornos . . .

Other PNV militants believed, however, that militarily speaking it was a serious error.

—The fact of the matter was that we never really succeeded in acquiring a military mentality, maintained Luis MICHELENA, the PNV militant from Guipúzcoa. We were always civilians who had been forced to fight a war . . . [1]

*

Four days after Bilbao's occupation, the victors placed all industry in Vizcaya under military control.[2] For the first time the Franco regime had an industrial and mining base. Production was ensured. Within six months, iron-ore output, which under the Euzkadi regime had dropped from its pre-war level, was exceeding that level by nearly 6 per cent per month. Not having to suffer a blockade, the Franco regime was, by the following year, able to export 60 per cent of this output – Britain (by agreement with Nazi Germany) taking its

1. Before passing judgement on the lack of sabotage of war industries in Vizcaya, it is necessary to recall that neither in socialist-dominated Asturias, as we shall see, nor in CNT Catalonia was there any large-scale sabotage before defeat.

2. At the same time, the *concierto económico*, the right of self-taxation, was abolished for Vizcaya and Guipúzcoa. In the words of José Maria de Areilza, Count of Motrico, newly appointed mayor of Bilbao: 'The horrible, sinister nightmare called Euzkadi has been conquered . . . Vizcaya is once again a piece of Spain by pure and simple military conquest . . .'

pre-war share – which provided an extra £1,700,000 revenue per annum. In addition to Vizcaya's war production, which could supply all his fronts – not just the north – Franco won a valuable source of foreign currency to import further war supplies.[1]

After the battle of Brunete on the Madrid front, planned by the republicans to relieve pressure on the north, and fought to a bloody stalemate throughout most of July, Franco was free to resume the northern campaign. In less than a fortnight in August, Santander, the second of the three northern republican provinces, was captured – a largely Italian victory, conceded by Franco in compensation for their recent defeat at Guadalajara.

In a previously negotiated arrangement, 25,000 men and 3,000 Basque nationalist officers capitulated to the Italians at Santoña in eastern Santander. It was the denouement of the Basque nationalist participation in the war.

The Basque units, which had done as much as any others to try to stem the rout as the Italian offensive gathered momentum, fell back on Santoña instead of Santander. Supported by a Basque nationalist battalion and on PNV orders, Juan Manuel EPALZA deposed the Santoña military commandant and took over the town.

—Then, half in jest, half seriously, we proclaimed the only independent Basque republic to have existed. A government was formed with all the normal portfolios except finance. I became vice-premier and justice minister.

For many of us Basque nationalists the war had ended with the fall of Bilbao. It is inadmissible to admit it, but that was the truth. We had asked the central government to send warships to transport our army to Catalonia; we had been refused. We weren't in our country any longer; where was the liberty and democracy for which we had fought in Euzkadi? Nowhere – in neither republican nor Franquista zones . . .

This feeling was widespread; it had led to a meeting a fortnight after the fall of Bilbao between PNV leaders and their military commanders, who agreed that surrender was out of the question but that the politicians should seek a solution. Earlier Italian feelers to negotiate Vizcaya's surrender had been rebuffed; now contacts were re-opened. Juan AJURIAGUERRA, who was convinced that the Basque army was neither materially nor morally in a condition to continue fighting, travelled behind enemy lines to negotiate a pact with General Roatta, commander of the Italian forces.[2] Two PNV members came away from discussions in Rome with Ciano, the Italian foreign minister, convinced that Mussolini was prepared to honour the pact. The Basque government was not involved; the initiative was an exclusively PNV matter, the

1. See Whealey, 'How Franco Financed His War – Reconsidered', *Journal of Contemporary History*, nn. 27 and 28, p. 151.

2. Under the pact, all Basque officers were to be allowed to leave – 'our aim was that they should be transferred to Barcelona to take up new commands'; no Basque soldiers were to serve in the nationalist army; there would be no reprisals against civilians. The Basques, in return, would surrender their arms, maintain public order and guarantee the lives of right-wing prisoners in the zone around Santoña. 'The negotiations weren't very tough. The Italians didn't try to impose more conditions. All they wanted really was their little victory' (Juan AJURIAGUERRA).

Basque nationalists hoping to secure more humane treatment from the Italians than from the Spanish.

Determined to comply with the pact, Basque nationalist commanders tried to disarm Basque communist units, like Eugenio CALVO's in Santoña, which wanted to continue fighting, and refused to allow a communist captain on a mission from the army of the north's general staff to address their men.

AJURIAGUERRA returned – in Haile Selassie's plane which the Basque government had purchased – from a second negotiating mission in France, to surrender with the Basque forces. As the Italians entered Laredo, he was taken to General Roatta's headquarters, where the Italian army commander confirmed that the pact would be honoured.

—Everything was in order. Nothing was said at that moment about the fact that we had not fulfilled the time limits which had been set.[1] There were no last-minute hitches . . .

Many Basque officers embarked on the *Bobie* and the *Seven Seas Spray*, two English ships which had arrived in Santoña at the request of the Basques. Among them were Pedro BASABILOTRA and his brother, Father José María. The former spoke to the captain who assured him they would be sailing with the tide. The two men went down to the holds, where black crewmen gave them some chocolate, to get some sleep. They woke at dawn to find the ship still there.

—The next thing we knew was that some small vessels flying the Spanish colours entered the port and Italian troops came aboard and ordered us all to disembark. They said they had to check that no one's hands were stained with blood . . .

There was nothing in the pact that permitted such a measure, recalled AJURIAGUERRA, although it might have been tacitly understood between them ('though I don't now remember that it was') that no one who had committed a blood crime would be allowed to leave.

—Once the officers had disembarked, the problem arose of what to do with them. As the Dueso prison was empty – we had released the right-wing prisoners – it was decided they should go there – but not as prisoners; it was to be their living quarters, and for several days the gates weren't even closed . . .

In the prison, EPALZA heard General Roatta say that if Franco continued to oppose the implementation of the pact, the Italians would send a cruiser to take off the Basque officers.

—They tried to carry out the agreement, but they didn't have the guts. One day someone shouted, 'Look out, they're lowering the flag.' Until that moment only the Italian flag had flown over the prison. A company of Spanish soldiers

1. 'The surrender plan I had negotiated included a series of stages, with different sectors surrendering in successive steps. We weren't military experts and we miscalculated; later – after who knows what pressures from Franco – our failure was used to justify the Italian pretext that we had broken the pact, although their officers on the ground maintained that it was valid. Indeed, when the Italians entered Laredo, they kept saying: "there are no Spaniards, only Italians and Basques here . . ."' (Juan AJURIAGUERRA).

marched in, with prison officials, to take over. Ajuriaguerra gave the Italian commandant such a dressing down, told him so many home truths about his country, his regiment and himself that all he could do was salute and leave . . .

The prison gates closed; the pretence was at an end. Mass courts martial began. Sentenced to death, expecting to be executed, Juan AJURIAGUERRA wrote a letter of protest about the Italian betrayal to be delivered after his death to General Roatta. (Unknown to him, the letter was smuggled out of the prison and delivered to the Italian consul in San Sebastián, who protested to Burgos at the executions taking place, thereby possibly saving some lives.)[1]

Meanwhile, in the rest of the republican zone, the Basque nationalists were accused of betrayal. AJURIAGUERRA disagreed. The Basque army had not surrendered until after the fall of Santander where the enemy offensive had turned into a military walk-over.

—The central government had told us it could send no aircraft; and after the loss of Bilbao, morale was low. Our people felt very deeply that they should not have to fight outside Euzkadi – as before the war they had not been called on to do military service outside their own territory, which was one of Vizcaya's *foral* rights. Morale in the Santander army was low; it was higher in Asturias, but the latter fell not long afterwards. The Asturian propaganda that anyone who looked towards the sea was a coward, served for little: the Council of Asturias and the army's general staff escaped in the end by ship. We in Santoña remained: the secretary of war in the Basque government, the head of the Basque militias and five other party leaders, including myself . . .

No one could doubt their personal integrity and bravery. But other aspects of Basque nationalism, no doubt, helped determine the situation, as Pedro BASABILOTRA saw.

—If Franco had been clever, he would have told our troops that they had fought bravely, cleanly and surrendered honourably. Having said that, he would then have called for volunteers to join his army to take Madrid. I'm convinced that 80 per cent of our troops would have responded to such a call on the spot. I judged that from conversations I had. They felt betrayed by the republic which had constantly promised and failed to deliver weapons. While in Madrid we heard they had arms and planes . . . [2]

1. On 15 October the first carefully selected prisoners were shot on the beach: two PNV political leaders, two PNV army leaders, two STV (Basque nationalist trade union) leaders, two socialists, two communists, two anarcho-syndicalists, two republicans. While the repression in Vizcaya was less ferocious than elsewhere (320 prisoners were executed in the Dueso and Larrínaga prisons between October and the following July, according to R. de Garate's *Diario de un condenado a muerte*, Bayonne, 1974), it was a common experience to spend two years or more, as did AJURIAGUERRA and Luis MICHELENA, amongst many others, under sentence of death, uncertain from one day to the next whether the sentence would be carried out.

2. Twenty years after the war, President Aguirre told the American historian Stanley Payne that one third of the Basque country supported the anti-fascist coalition, one third was opposed and one third neutral (see Payne, *El nacionalismo vasco*, Barcelona, 1974, p. 238).

The war is an armed plebiscite . . . between a people divided: on the one side, the spiritual is revealed by the insurgents who rose to defend law and order, social peace, traditional civilization, the fatherland and, very ostensibly in a large sector of the population, religion. On the other side there is materialism – call it marxist, communist or anarchist – which wants to replace the old civilization of Spain by the new 'civilization' of the Russian soviets.

Spanish bishops' collective letter (1 July 1937)

My dear Iñaki:

In a few hours I am to be executed. I die happy because I feel Jesus close to me and I love as never before the only homeland of the Basques . . . When you think of me, who has loved you like a father, love Christ, be pure and chaste, love Euzkadi as your parents have done. Visit my poor mother and kiss her forehead. Farewell until heaven. I bless you a thousand times.

Esteban

Letter from the Basque poet, Esteban de Urquiaga,
to his friend Iñaki Garmendia,
shortly before being shot on 25 June 1937

Militancies 14

ERNESTO CASTAÑO

CEDA lawyer

The column of prisoners from Bilbao's Larrínaga gaol walked through the night to reach the nationalist lines, unaware of the threat which Juan Manuel Epalza was dealing with in their rear. In the moonlight, Ernesto CASTAÑO tried to make out his side's lines. He felt like a man who had spent his last night on earth and was prepared no longer for this world. Arrested in the Basque country where he had been helping to prepare the uprising, the ex-CEDA deputy had not allowed his morale to drop during his confinement or because of the harrowing experience of the mob's assault on the prison. His suffering, he felt, was more than rewarded by the renovatory idealism being shown in Franco's Spain. The Belgian consul, on his visits to the prison, had told them that the same crimes and assassinations were being committed in both zones; the prisoners refused to believe him, hated him for trying to turn them against Franco. 'We were totally convinced that a better Spain was going to be created out of sacrifices like ours.'

Ever since the prison massacre of the previous January, the Basque nationalists had protected them with almost paternalistic attention. They had thanked the prison director and chief warder, told them they would be considered members of their families when they were released, would do whatever was necessary for them. The two were among the prisoners now, having chosen to escape with them. Their fears that the Franco regime would punish them had been laid to rest by the prisoners themselves.

—'Rest assured, we are creating a new Spain,' we told them. 'The authorities – civil and military – will thank you for your conduct and all you have done' . . .

The uprising had been the only way forward, he thought. The republicans' refusal to tolerate the right's access to power, the regime's need for class war, especially in the countryside, had doomed it to failure. He had fought the republican–socialist coalition, becoming one of the main organizers of the Salamanca Agrarian Bloc which, while affirming its allegiance to the republic, had expressed landowning and farming reaction to the coalition's legislation and agrarian reform.[1] He had gone to gaol for urging farmers not to sow wheat where yields were not high enough to make the crop profitable, and had been sentenced to exile. In the bitter struggle against the new regime, he reflected, the defence of material and religious interests became imbricated. Every possible force had had to be recruited against the republic's class war, its agrarian policies, its sectarian, anti-religious legislation. Everything had combined, each of them had been in the front line.

Bringing up the rear, he saw the head of the column stop. They had arrived. Safety! A *requeté* colonel received them, their political affiliations were noted, food was handed out.

1. See Points of Rupture, A.

—But we could hardly eat, hungry as we were, we were so happy to breathe this new air, be where we had longed to be for so long. We informed the authorities that the two prison officers were under our protection. Then Falange leaders from Bilbao arrived and struck the two men in the face. We were horrified, we attacked the falangists, tore their clothes. But the two prison officers were taken off and thrown into gaol. This was our first sign of what was going on. We were deeply disillusioned. One of my prison comrades said he would rather go back to prison. We thought, to begin with, that it was a matter of personal falangist brutality; soon we realized that it was a general state of affairs – something that had been planned and prepared from before the uprising . . .

The prisoners, he among them, testified to the prison officers' conduct, and eventually they were freed and allowed to return to Bilbao. But not before they had been given a rough time. Meanwhile, longing only to be in the bosom of his family, he returned to his native Salamanca. Little by little, as he heard what had been happening, he could see that there was little shared sentiment between those like himself who had been imprisoned in the red zone and those who had been free from the first day in the nationalist zone. The latter, living in the throes of euphoria, had taken advantage of the triumph to wreak vengeance on their personal enemies, on those against whom they held a grievance. Vendettas were being pursued at every level of the social scale, including the church. His dismay was increased when, less than a fortnight after his release from prison and the end of Basque resistance, with its vexatious demonstration that defence of Catholicism was not synonymous with the nationalist *Cruzada*, the bishops of Spain published a collective letter addressed to the bishops of the world. In it the Spanish hierarchy justified its support of the military uprising; the church had been the victim of attacks under the republic; but it had always sought to respect the established authorities. It had not desired the war, and now thousands of monks, nuns and priests were being martyred in the republican zone.

'Because God provides the most profound bonds holding together a well-ordered society – as was the Spanish nation – the communist revolution had to be, above all, anti-God.' The 'civic-military' uprising had attracted the healthiest elements of society in defence of the 'fundamental principles of every civilized society'. The war was an 'armed plebiscite' between the spiritual and materialism. The bishops pointed to a political future which bore the ideological hallmark of a corporative nationalist state: 'The fatherland implies fatherhood; it is a moral ambience, like that of a vast family, in which the citizen fulfils his total development; the national movement has created a current of love which has concentrated on the name and historic substance of Spain, averse to those foreign elements which have brought us to ruin . . . '

The letter enhanced the new state by officially identifying its cause with that of the church. Order – the order of the property-owning class – and religion were one. The Vatican (which had been careful not to condemn or admonish the Basques publicly) shortly recognized the Burgos regime.

The church's support of the right, CASTAÑO felt, was deplorable; it stirred his religious consciousness in a way that even the heavy attacks on the church under the republic had not done. His view of the ecclesiastical hierarchy, which throughout the republic he had defended, changed.

—And I believe that was true of the majority of real Catholics. Half out of fear, half out of ambition, the church failed its duty to speak out against the crimes being committed. Its passivity tacitly countenanced the repression, while at the same time accepting generous benefits from the state. Even if it meant going to the wall, the church should have spoken out . . .

The church, he now saw, had not played a Christian, educative role in Spain. It had laid more importance on outward show. As a result, Catholics had drunk not at the well of Christ but of the water of a church that revealed an unworthy egoism. 'We were brought up not in the love of God but in the misery and chains of Purgatory. We had to discover God for ourselves.'

It had been impossible to understand this before; he, too, had been brought up in the outward show, the 'tricks and swindles'. Now, in his daily dealings with the church hierarchy, he saw that the bishops had betrayed him. There was an emptiness which he alone would have to fill with God.

Still no voice rose to say clearly what the majority of real Catholics like himself felt; they kept quiet for fear that they might be wrong, might harm the public good. It had been a grave error, he thought, one of incalculable consequence for the future.

But if it was impossible to speak out, it was possible to withdraw all active support from the new regime, even while continuing to hope for its military victory so as to avoid a return to the anguished pre-war situation. He turned down an offer by Serrano Suñer, the Caudillo's brother-in-law and a major political figure in the new regime, to run its vertical trade union organization. To have accepted would have been to admit that those – the majority now – in the nationalist regime who blamed the CEDA for all the pre-war failures were right; he was not prepared to make any such admission, was proud to have belonged to the party. Nor, he told Serrano Suñer, could he accept the principle of vertical trade unions. The nationalist movement, which he had travelled the country to help bring about, for which he had spent nine months in gaol, was not the one he had hoped for; his active participation was at an end.

The bishops' collective letter was not the church's first intervention in the war. Less than three weeks after the uprising, Bishops Múgica and Olaechea of Vitoria and Pamplona respectively – both of which cities were in insurgent hands – addressed a joint pastoral to the Basques of their dioceses stating that it was 'absolutely illicit' for them to join forces with the enemy – 'this modern monstrosity, marxism or communism, seven-headed Hydra, synthesis of every heresy.'

A long Basque Catholic tradition of wariness of the Spanish ecclesiastical hierarchy did not lend to ready acceptance of the pastoral which theologians and politicians in the Basque country agreed lacked validity because their bishops were in insurgent hands.[1] News was not long in reaching Vizcaya that the insur-

1. 'We argued that, as a result, the bishops – both Basques – were unable to ascertain what was going on. The theologians agreed. Ordinary people would ask us after mass if we had heard of the pastoral and reached a decision. When we told them we had, they went on their

gents had shot fourteen Basque priests in neighbouring Guipúzcoa after its conquest. At much the same time Bishop Plá y Deniel of Salamanca put forward the concept of the 'religious crusade' in a pastoral. The relationship of the two events did not escape the majority of Basque priests. Chaplain in a *gudari* company, Father José María BASABILOTRA's conviction of the meaninglessness of the slogan 'For God and For Spain' was reinforced. A crusade?

—Ludicrous. Who could believe that generals, whom we knew were not believers when the war started, were now fighting a religious crusade? We tried to raise ourselves above this sort of thing. Our only thought was the hurt being done to the faithful by a war we had neither started nor provoked . . .

Another priest, Father Luis ECHEBARRIA, religious director of the federation of Basque schools, was emphatic.

—From the start the capitalists were on Franco's side. Religion doesn't reject capitalists; but when it is they who rush to the defence of religion, then all I can say is that Jesus Christ knew what to make of it. The Basque people, who are probably more Catholic than any other in the peninsula, were totally opposed to the concept of a crusade. To maintain that defence of religion was the cause of the war is an untruth . . . [1]

Outside the Basque country, clerical support for the uprising, while virtually inevitable, was not always a linear process, even in Old Castile. Father José FERNANDEZ, a parish priest in Valladolid, believed he was typical of most of the clergy in his initial support of the uprising which he hoped would restore law and order and respect for religion which had been so severely persecuted under the republic, in his view. In the first days of the rising he did what he could to help the military.

—But very soon the majority of us clergy withdrew. The reason was the assassinations. They were totally unjustifiable. Even worse, they were being ordered and condoned, if not actually carried out, by people who declared the uprising a crusade, who came out wearing religious insignia, scapularies and *detentes*. On the other side it may have been worse, but there the assassinations weren't being carried out in the name of religion . . .

---

way without asking more; they had absolute confidence in our judgement' (Juan AJURIAGUERRA, president Vizcaya PNV). The tribulations of Bishop Múgica, an extreme right-wing Integrist who supported the military at the start and was exiled by them within two months of the rising, reflected some of the drama of the Spanish hierarchy's relations with Basque nationalism. In Rome he protested to the Vatican at the insurgents' execution of Basque priests, refused to sign the bishops' collective letter but equally refused representations from the Basque clergy to rectify his joint pastoral. His public and private postures remained very different; he had, he said, been told 'to keep silent'. In 1945, however, he broke his silence in *Imperativos de mi conciencia* (Paris, 1945), in which he expressed his previously held private views and excused himself for his public stance. (See A. Onaindía, *Hombre de paz en la guerra*, Buenos Aires, 1973; also J. de Iturralde, *El catolicismo y la cruzada de Franco*, Toulouse, 1965, vol. 3.)

1. Both Fathers BASABILOTRA and ECHEBARRIA were court-martialled by the Franco forces along with nearly fifty other Basque priests and sentenced respectively to twelve years and life imprisonment; both spent three years in confinement before being exiled to parishes in New Castile.

With the exception of four or five bishops, he believed, the majority of the clergy now reserved its positions; but it did not speak out in protest about the killings.

—We couldn't. For a start, who was there to accuse? The assassinations were carried out anonymously – you couldn't point a finger at the killers. And to have protested openly – this was another reason – would in those impassioned times have been to declare oneself on the enemy's side . . .

There was silence instead. But as the new regime repealed all controversial republican religious legislation, particularly in respect of education, and gave the church new privileges – in effect uniting church and state in a national Catholicism – so the clergy came to demonstrate its open support for the regime. 'Things were settling down, the assassinations were less frequent, the church became used to its new, privileged situation.'

This did not necessarily mean that the bishops' collective action was seen as much more than war propaganda – 'simplistic as propaganda must be, non-sensical in fact', in Father FERNANDEZ's view. On the one side all was white, everyone was good, religious.

—On the other, only black anti-religion. Equally simplistic was to speak, as the bishops did, of the new religious fervour everywhere apparent in the nationalist zone. An effervescence, nothing more, an exterior show which served the nationalists' cause. There was no real change; the indifferents remained indifferent, the religious what they had always been . . .

GIJON (*Asturias*)

Such reflections were unsustainable in the hold of the collier turned prison ship where Father Alejandro MARTINEZ was being held in the Asturian port of El Musel, near Gijón. The 'purity of feeling', which Ernesto Castaño had known throughout his confinement in Bilbao, the sense that the sacrifice was necessary to create a better Spain, was almost the sole consolation available to prisoners. But Father MARTINEZ had long been convinced that to save themselves it would be necessary to rise.[1] Most Catholics, he was convinced, saw the civil war as a crusade of liberation; almost all approved the bishops' collective letter.

—The republic had shown its hatred of the church from the start; in consequence, we supported Franco's rising as soon as it took place . . .

1. See Points of Rupture, B.

Militancies 15

FATHER ALEJANDRO MARTINEZ

Madrid priest

Had not the Spanish people always followed their clergy with either a candle or a club in their hands? His students at the Madrid seminary where he had taught since his ordination in 1923 asked: 'Father, why has the church always been on the side of the right?' And he answered: 'Because the left has always kicked and beaten the church to the right.' Popular hatred dated from the middle of the previous century when the church, deprived of its landed wealth, had to seek support from the rich in order to be able to continue its work, he explained, 'to found the many colleges, sanatoria, hospitals and other institutions it had created'. Socialism had deliberately fostered an anti-religious feeling in the working classes and amongst the intelligentsia. The ignorance and passion of the masses had proven fertile ground. (If anything, the women were the most extreme. More religious than men, but more passionate when they lost control. Schopenhauer was right, he thought: the longer the hair, the smaller the intelligence.)

A hundred years earlier, during the slaughter of priests, a mayor of an Aragonese township had reported to the government: 'The massacre of priests is continuing here in the midst of the greatest order.' It had started because the people had believed a rumour that priests had poisoned the wells. If they could believe that, they could believe anything, not least that the church was not concerned about the poor. In killing priests they believed they were doing a very necessary, even God-ordained task in finishing off vermin. They had forgotten Napoleon's words: 'He who eats priests dies of the eating.'

He had caught the last train out of Madrid on the eve of the uprising to spend his summer holidays with friends in the seaside town of Luanco, not far from Gijón. His friends had been arrested and imprisoned; he had been confined to house-arrest for seven months, then held in the local church with other prisoners. There he experienced a moment of great danger. Militiamen arrived from Gijón with a list of people to be taken; one of the men was the cousin of a local committee member. The latter protested that his cousin was not to go. 'Give us another, then, it's all the same to me. I've got orders to take fourteen,' said the militiaman in charge.

—So they woke up the first man they happened to come across – a *practicante* who had done absolutely nothing, and that night he and the other thirteen were shot...

Cut off from news of Madrid, he did not know that his brother, a priest at El Pardo, just outside the capital, had been assassinated in August. Only later did he learn from the local grave-digger how he had met his fate.

—He was a mystic, a man completely withdrawn from the world. The reds (to use the terminology of the time) called him an enemy of the people. He had many rich and aristocratic penitents whom I sent him, for I was rector of a small church on the Paseo de Recoletos, an aristocratic quarter of Madrid. That was his death warrant. They came for him one night and took him to the cemetery at the top of the hill where, facing the sierra Guadarrama, he had so often read St John of the Cross.

'Will you give me five minutes to recommend myself to God?' They agreed. Then he turned to them. 'In the dark you are not going to be able to aim properly, are you? But if I stand against the whitewashed wall of the convent you will be able to see me.' The first shots didn't kill him. Lying on the ground, he called to them: '*Chicos*, you will have to administer the *coup de grâce*, you haven't killed me' . . .

In June 1937, the Council of Asturias decided to abolish make-shift prisons and he was transferred to El Coto gaol in Gijón. Neither he nor any of the priests incarcerated with him were physically maltreated, nor were any executed. After the fall of Santander, he and some 200 other prisoners were transferred to the prison ship in the port of El Musel. The move coincided with the start of the nationalist offensive on Asturias: the prisoners aboard the collier were exposed as hostages to the air raids of the important port. (When the offensive gained momentum, the Council of Asturias protested about the air raids to the League of Nations and threatened to kill prisoners in reprisal.)

—Every time they suffered a set-back it was we who suffered. One night, by the light of an acetylene lamp, we were ordered on deck. I realized immediately what was afoot – a *saca*. I was sure my last hour had come, they knew only too well that I was a priest. They selected thirty prisoners, many of them good friends of mine, and shot them. I still can't understand why I was not among them . . .

He had already been denounced by a fellow-prisoner for hearing women prisoners' whispered confessions through a rivet hole in the bulk-head separating the two holds. ('One or two love letters also passed through, but they didn't reach their destination, I made sure of that. It was a good thing our gaolers didn't mix the men and women, I'll grant them that. War demoralized people and a civil war doubly so.') Woken in the middle of the night to explain how he could confess the women, he showed the militiamen the hole. 'Bah!' they expostulated when they saw how small it was, and ordered him to desist. 'But it was I who had to carry the burden of fear.' Might he not have suffered the fate of the three or four prisoners who had been taken out to sea in a rowing boat not long before and shot?

But if it was not the fate of priests to die, it was their misfortune to be humiliated. When he first saw himself covered in fleas he believed it was the end of the world; but this was nothing compared to his gaolers' evident delight in tormenting priests. He was made to clean out the bilges with his bare hands when the pumps broke down. The venerable parish priest of Luanco, who had been president of the fishermen's brotherhoods on the Cantabrian coast, was treated even worse.

—'They accuse me of being the persecutor of the working class – ' he would say. 'That's quite normal,' I replied, 'that's what they accuse me of, too.' 'But in these newspapers' – he indicated an enormous bundle – 'there are articles of mine written over the past twenty-five years defending the fishermen's interests.

I am sure that they will serve as evidence in my favour before a Popular Tribunal.'

In one of the searches, a guard asked don Faustino about the newspapers. He explained. The guard said that was interesting. He sat down on a coil of rope and with a pair of scissors carefully cut out, newspaper by newspaper, each article. When he had finished, he crumpled the articles into a ball and threw them overboard. 'And with what's left you can wipe your arse . . . '

Like don Faustino, the priest, almost all new prisoners maintained their innocence as soon as they were brought aboard. 'I have done nothing,' was the endless refrain. He had a standard answer: 'Ask the others here what they have done.'

—And then I would add: 'Examine your conscience and ask yourself if that is not why we're all here: *for not having done anything*. If we had done what we ought to have done many years ago, perhaps we wouldn't be where we are now' . . .

Surprising as it might seem, he reflected, the republic had come in with ecclesiastical support, particularly in the Basque country and Catalonia. Barely a month had passed when the convents were fired.[1] People started to shout, 'They're coming, they're carrying petrol cans', and he left the seminary and went to a near-by friend's home from where he rang up and ascertained that his church was not under attack. He was about to have lunch with his friends, when the nephew of the lady of the house arrived and had words with her. What this apparently fervent, devout man said to her he didn't know.

—But she turned to me and said: 'Don Alejandro, you will have to leave immediately; my nephew tells me your presence compromises me very gravely.' Recommending myself to God, I left the house and walked home through the crowded streets without trouble. But I now knew what to expect of the republic – as did all believers. The republic committed suicide that day . . .

Indisputably, in his view, the church burnings (which he maintained the new regime had tolerated if not actually instigated) had divided the country. Thereafter the republic had continued its absurd, impetuous religious persecution, incarnated in anti-clerical laws, the dissolution once more of the Jesuits, the offensive against religious education. Nothing could be achieved by legal means. The Popular Front electoral victory, following on Gil Robles's terrible mistake of believing he could collaborate with the republic, had done no more than confirm this.

—Not that I took part in anything. If someone asked me whether I was on the left or the right, I answered simply: 'I am a priest.' But most of us believers saw the civil war as a liberation from that absurd persecution of the church. We Spanish clergy loved Spain and didn't want to see the country dismembered by separatism. Those were the reasons which justified our supporting the uprising. And if, once in a while, things didn't turn out as we might have wished, if Franco's army was not the band of archangels we imagined while in prison, that was not exactly our fault . . .

1. Points of Rupture, B.

ARMY IS IN SITUATION MORAL DEFEAT, WE LACKING MEANS MAKE IT FIGHT. STRENUOUS EFFORTS RAISE MORALE... STRICT RATIONING EFFECTED DUE FORCED SHORTAGES. WE SEEN NO SUPPLIES YOU SAY SENT . . . LACK RIFLE ROUNDS, RAW MATERIALS. URGENTLY NEED CHICK-PEAS, RICE, BEANS, OIL, POTATOES, FLOUR AND HAM SUFFICIENT FOR 1,200,000 INHABITANTS . . .

**Telegram from Belarmino Tomás,
president of the Sovereign Council of Asturias,
to the central government (September 1937)**

ASTURIAS

Father MARTINEZ's sufferings were not to last long. After six weeks of bitter resistance in the mountainous terrain,[1] the Asturian forces began to crumble before the nationalist offensive. Isolated in the last Popular Front territory in the north, the Council of Asturias had declared itself a sovereign government and dismissed General Gámir Ulíbarri, supreme commander of the army of the north. The communist party opposed the declaration of independence, but the socialists, backed by the libertarians and republicans, stood firm. Asturias prepared to emulate Madrid; no one was to 'look towards the sea' – the only means of escape.

In one week in mid-October the tables turned. The front started to collapse, panic swept the rearguard whose morale had been severely tested by shortage of food and air raids. The military command advised the council that resistance was impossible. The communist councillors called for all-out resistance, in accord with instructions cabled by Prime Minister Negrín. The majority decided otherwise.

The night before – travel by road was possible only at night because of the air raids – Paulino RODRIGUEZ, miner and socialist mayor of Sotrondio in the

1. The defence of El Mazuco pass in eastern Asturias, where for thirty-three days forces commanded by Carrocera, a libertarian steelworker from La Felguera, held out in hand-to-hand combat as positions were taken, lost and retaken, was the most outstanding of these actions.

Nalón mining valley, had his last talk with Belarmino Tomás. The president of the council assured him that the evacuation of all those with political responsibilities was about to begin. RODRIGUEZ returned to his village on 17 October to find that a battalion had arrived with orders signed by the commander-in-chief of the army of the north to destroy all industries and strategic sites: mines, electricity generating plants, bridges, etc.

—'I agree that everything must be blown up,' I told the battalion commander. 'But first the population's evacuation must be assured. We cannot blow up the mines on which the population depends for its livelihood; if we do, the people will only heap curses on the few who have been able to leave' . . .

RODRIGUEZ secured the officer's agreement to wait three days before carrying out his orders. He spent the time gathering evidence to present to the general staff to support his plea to evacuate the population or leave the mines intact. On the night of 20 October, he travelled to Gijón with two comrades, one of them a CNT member. When he got there he found people running wildly through the streets. He forced his way into Belarmino Tomás's office only to find him gone; people were desperately packing papers in boxes and sacks. He saw that people were hurrying towards the port. He thought he should join them. 'But the battalion commander was waiting for me in Sotrondio. What would happen in the village? I decided to return – '

Throughout the night the fishing boats set sail from El Musel. The day before a bomb had fallen beside the collier prison ship in the port where Father MARTINEZ was confined, killing eleven of the prisoners and wounding a further fifty. No reprisals were taken for the raid; instead, the prisoners were taken off the ship and returned to their original prisons under orders of Col. Franco, commander of the Trubia arms factory, who remained to surrender Gijón to the nationalists.

—Divine providence saved us. Had the reds found us aboard the ship as they started to flee that evening, they would surely have slaughtered us, thought Father MARTINEZ, aware, moreover, that the collier's steering gear had been immobilized a few days earlier to forestall the unlikely threat that the prisoners might seize the ship and sail it out of the port. Now it would not serve those hastening to flee . . .

*

Aboard the fishing smack *Toñin*, making at most eight knots, Dr Carlos MARTINEZ, former parliamentary deputy, was trying to get some sleep. He had returned four months earlier from Paris where he had been serving on an arms purchasing commission; after the fall of Bilbao he had been in little doubt that Asturias would be conquered, but while people were fighting and dying to defend his country he could not remain abroad.

He had been one of the first of the sixty passengers to board the now crammed smack. The captain had failed to appear. Happily, a young Basque with some experience of the sea had turned up and they had set off.

Suddenly he was wakened by a beam of light; the *Toñin*'s engine slowed, then stopped. He knew what had happened; they had been caught by the nationalist cruiser *Almirante Cervera*.

Passengers began tearing up party membership cards; revolvers and other arms were thrown overboard. On the deck all the passengers were lined up and searched; wallets, papers, arms there had not been time to dispose of, passed behind backs down the line and splashed into the sea. In fear, a passenger leapt overboard, but the cruiser's crew took it to be an accident and fished him out. Their major concern appeared to be that the smack was proceeding without navigation lights.

—To our surprise, we heard one of the passengers demanding to be allowed aboard the cruiser. At first he was refused, but in the face of his insistence they finally agreed. When he returned, he told us what had happened . . .

The man had managed to see the ship's captain, explaining that the passengers aboard the smack were people of modest means fleeing the air raids on Gijón. To prove his point that the escapees were not Popular Front supporters, he pulled a piece of paper out of his pocket showing that a consignment of cocoa worth a considerable sum of money had been expropriated from him. In the course of the conversation, it became apparent to the man that the cruiser's captain was unaware of the mass exodus from Gijón that night, or else he would not have spent so much time with the smack. The Basque youth had also been ordered on board the cruiser where he was given instructions to set a certain course which would take the *Toñin* to a 'bou' – an armed nationalist fishing ship.

—As we set off some of the passengers panicked, believing the cruiser was going to fire on us. It was an impressive moment for sure, that huge warship towering above us, the immensity of the sea and sky. But when it became apparent that we weren't going to be sunk, an argument broke out among the passengers about whether to try to escape. The Basque seaman paid no attention. I decided to go back to sleep. I was woken by a cry. 'We're saved!' The Basque had set a course which, far from taking us to the 'bou', was heading so far north we might have reached Greenland had we not eventually turned east once out of danger . . .

Many who set sail later were not so lucky; caught by nationalist warships they were forced to sail to Galicia where the passengers were confined to concentration camps.

On 21 October – four days after the first anniversary of the relief of Oviedo – the nationalist army entered Gijón. Father MARTINEZ saw the prison ship he had so recently left filling with his warders, and felt that a certain justice was being done. But he was surprised when Col. Franco, the republican army officer who had stayed to surrender the town, was arrested, court-martialled and shot within the week.[1] The repression that started seemed to him of an 'inopportune rigour', it was as though a 'certain species' of human being had to be liquidated. Things were being done that should not have been done. The military prosecutor demanded so many death sentences and with such speed that he was nicknamed 'machine-gun'. Many of those being executed had carried out others' orders; the real criminals were getting off. Not all were even being tried, for there were *paseos*. Among those to die without trial was the prisoner who

1. Col. Franco had previously been court-martialled by the Popular Front forces in Asturias and acquitted.

had denounced him aboard the prison ship for hearing the women's confessions. The police, who had arrested him on some other matter, asked Father MARTINEZ if he wished to see him 'before they took him a bit further'.

—'I know what you're going to do with him,' I replied. 'No, I don't want to see him.' They laughed. I knew they would take him for a ride, and that was a bad thing, of course. But at a court martial, he would certainly have been meat for the gallows, given the circumstances of the time . . .

The church, correctly, he thought, did not protest officially and openly about the repression. Had it done so it could only have helped the enemy.

—Obvious atrocities are one thing – they must be protested about. But this was another matter – it could only provide the enemy with propaganda and deprive the uprising of its authority; that would have been risky for everyone. On the other hand, individual priests, and the church privately, did a great deal, I'm convinced, to mitigate the repression. The 'machine-gun' prosecutor in Gijón was soon replaced by another who was so lenient that he became known as 'catapult'. Justice is a serious matter and must be carried out seriously, without going to extremes like this . . .

No, Franco's army was not the crusading band of archangels he had imagined in prison. The troops sacked and looted Gijón as though it were a foreign city. These were things that should not have happened. On the other hand, a 'half-mad' priest who had given the clenched-fist salute when the 'red' Dean of Canterbury visited Asturias, maintaining before the English cleric that he was the 'only free priest in Asturias', was given the choice of prison or lunatic asylum by his bishop. In prison, the bishop said, 'Something might happen to him'; the lunatic asylum would be safer. The priest chose the latter, and in due course died there.

*

Whilst the nationalist troops were still entering Gijón, Paulino RODRIGUEZ tried to locate the battalion commander in Sotrondio who had the orders to blow up the coal mines. Unable to find him, he gave instructions to the sentries at the mine where the dynamite had been stored to allow none of it to be removed; then he returned to the townhall to destroy papers, especially charges laid against people which would be dangerous for those who had signed them. Tortured in the repression after the October 1934 rising, RODRIGUEZ had no illusions about what was in store. The battalion commander did not reappear.

Around Oviedo, still besieged by the Popular Front forces, the front was calm. José MATA, a socialist miner and veteran of October 1934, was in command of a battalion; he had refused to accompany his brigade commander to Gijón to find out whether resistance was to continue. At 8.30 that evening he received a message from him saying he should be in Avilés at that hour to be evacuated. He gave orders for the brigade's documents and papers to be burnt. Then he made for Sama de Langreo in the Nalón mining valley. He couldn't leave his men; he would have died of shame to abandon companions who had joined him on the first day in the struggle against the military. 'They were captains and lieutenants who would be considered by the Franquistas as politically responsible as I.'

In Sama de Langreo he and other commanders met. Some believed they should stage a last-ditch resistance.

—They were going to shoot us anyway, there was no hope. They hadn't forgotten October 1934 – and then we'd been mere soldiers. Prudence won out. It would have been stupid. We couldn't have resisted more than twenty-four hours. They had only to shell us from the heights to raze the town. We decided instead to make for the mountains . . .

Episodes 8

Fugitives

Paulino RODRIGUEZ and two fellow-councillors left the Sotrondio townhall, having declared the town council dissolved. All the funds were carefully accounted for and left behind; they had run up a white flag on the building. The three men made for the RODRIGUEZ farmstead where there was a *chamizo* – a very narrow gallery which he had cut to dig his own coal. While his two companions gathered dry grass for bedding, he went to tell his mother they were there, and to fetch blankets.

José MATA and fifteen companions made for the mountains of the Puertos del Aramo south of Oviedo where they hid for a fortnight. But they were in countryside they didn't know well; the first betrayals took place. They decided to return to the Nalón valley where they were known. A few days after their return new falangist recruits began denouncing villagers. Beatings, assassinations began. 'We'll have to go to the sierra,' they said and they set off. Little did MATA think that eleven years of guerrilla life were opening before him.

*

Hearing the firing squads' volleys from their hiding place in the gallery, RODRIGUEZ and his companions realized that things were going to be worse than even they had imagined. It was 27 October 1937; fifteen people had been shot, their bodies left unburied, in the near-by village of Blimeo. The three men set about making their hiding place more secure, moving out only by night. One day they heard the stones and earth at the entrance being moved: local lads looking for a place to hide who, when they realized that people were already there, covered up the entrance again and left. But the fugitives feared they had been discovered and decided to leave. His two companions set off for the townships of Barredos and Laviana. RODRIGUEZ believed his only hope lay in taking to the sierra. He made for home first to ask his mother's advice. There he found his sister had made a hiding place under the hay in the shed next to the cowstall for his brother and his unit commander who were both wounded.

—She said I should join them. She had dug out a sort of tunnel in the floor under the hay and widened it a bit at one end. That's where we hid . . .

He set out to make the hiding place safer, laying planks over the tunnel so that if there was a search bayonets prodded through the hay would not reach them. But it was not long before they heard that police forces were burning hay-sheds to force fugitives out. RODRIGUEZ started to dig a tunnel from the shed to the kitchen of the house.

*

No preparations had been made for guerrilla warfare in the sierra while the war lasted; no training, no supplies, no arms caches, no radios. The men who took to the mountains were the remnants of a defeated army. They formed small groups, each independent of the other, of between half a dozen and twenty men each. There was no organization, no overall command.

—It was very difficult to form a real guerrilla from a conquered army. A lot of men were there by force of circumstance, not all were political by any means. Adventurers, people without political ideals, who had fought in the war, been implicated in something or other and now couldn't return. For a real guerrilla, the men must be trained, not only militarily but politically; must be convinced of what they are fighting for; must volunteer for it. Men of steel, undaunted by despair, prepared to go days without food and sleep, ready to sow terror. There has to be a purpose to make such an existence viable. In the circumstances, we lacked many of these things . . .

They were on the defensive, in fact. Had they launched a real guerrilla war, sabotaging the enemy rear, it would have all been over quickly, he thought. The enemy would have responded with a yet more ferocious repression against their families and comrades. The people would not have continued to support them. That was what happened after the enemy's final victory in the war: they sowed fear. For every person the guerrillas killed, they responded by killing twenty or fifty. Happily for MATA, his immediate family had been able to get out, but even then they assassinated his third cousins. 'If my mother had had to remain behind, I'd have committed suicide rather than let them kill her because of me.'

At the start, living in mountain huts in Peñamayor, a roadless sierra to the north-east of the Nalón valley, and in the mining villages, the guerrillas moved about with relative impunity. In the villages, the miners, who were very often also peasants, could be relied on. The guerrilla groups limited their actions to avenging assassinations to frighten the enemy from committing others. It was more a question of survival than of taking the offensive. Sabotaging the mines, MATA believed, would not have served the republican cause, however useful the coal output now was to the enemy.

—It would only have hurt the people, discredited us in their eyes; and within a year they would have got them working again. Meanwhile, Franco would have been able to buy all the coal he needed, as he was able to buy oil . . .

Throughout the first winter, with the enemy rearguard manned by new conscripts called up by the Franquista army, civil guards and falangists, there was little attempt to hunt down the guerrillas. But the following spring an entire division was sent in to liquidate them. Cowherds kept the guerrillas informed. While the troops beat the mountains, most of the guerrillas were in the villages and townships; as soon as the troops left, they moved back to the sierra. 'Until the end of the war we didn't have any important engagements.'

Later, they had to live by hold-ups. MATA's first was on the San Vicente coal mine, which the Asturian miners' union had owned and operated for years and the enemy had expropriated. The guerrillas requisitioned the wages. After such actions, which took time to plan and execute, the groups split up, each man going his own way.

—I'd disappear, no one knew where I went. I needed to rest, recuperate mentally. There was a time when you had to be on constant guard; you never knew whether one of the men with you had gone to see his girlfriend or to talk to the *guardia civil*. Once a friend of mine, a socialist youth member, tried to assassinate me; he had killed two others already. We got him first.

We became as quick on the draw as cowboys in westerns. A doctor in Mieres whom I went to consult in broad daylight about my rheumatism gave me a piece of advice. On the table in front of him I had placed four hand-grenades and two pistols. 'There's nothing wrong with you. Eat a lot of meat, it makes one's reactions faster. Look at lions and tigers compared to non-carnivorous elephants.' He was right. We ate plenty of the fascists' livestock. One night, on a path, I found myself face to face with a police corporal. He wasn't looking for us, he was going to see his wife. 'Good evening, where are you going?' he asked. Before I could reply, my companion had shot him dead. 'What did you do that for? I knew him, it was so-and-so,' I said. 'I didn't know who he was. All I saw was a policeman with a gun,' my companion replied . . .

*

Once the tunnel reached beneath the kitchen, Paulino RODRIGUEZ felt safe. His sister had been taking the earth out to the fields to bury under manure so as not to arouse suspicion. On either side of the kitchen stove there was a recess or closet. RODRIGUEZ began digging out a room beneath the kitchen in such a way that the closet would make an entrance to it. He made a trapdoor of iron and concrete, which resembled the tiles, to place in the floor of the closet. Then there was the problem of light. The initial solution, a flex from the kitchen, was dangerous: it might be seen. He drilled underground until he reached the mains entry into the farmhouse, and wired up a new light, bypassing the meter. Then the three fugitives spent the day sleeping and the night reading or listening to the radio his sister brought and which they wrapped in blankets. They spent twenty-eight months like that.

His sister cut off all communication with his wife and children. The latter were being harshly persecuted to give away his whereabouts.

—My nineteen-year-old daughter died of the treatment she received at the hands of the police. My sister told me of her death, but not the cause. I didn't know the punishment they were having to suffer . . .

*

RODRIGUEZ was still in hiding when, in January 1939, a few days before the fall of Barcelona, José MATA and 800 guerrillas set off in different columns for the coast and possible escape. The guerrillas communicated with France, using rice water to write between the lines of letters which contained eulogies on Franco. Indalecio Prieto, no longer a minister in the central government, had made arrangements for a boat to be waiting in the small port of Tazones on the Villaviciosa estuary.

Some of the older, sick men who were to be got out – men who had been in hiding in houses and other refuges – were sent in advance to the rendezvous. For MATA and the men in Peñamayor it was a matter of a night's march across the mountains to reach the concentration point in a pine wood two hours from the port. Guerrillas from Mieres, Langreo and all the surrounding areas assembled there at dawn. Twenty-five of the men were wearing Franquista army uniforms. The plan was that they should report to the small garrison in the port as a relief section and take over. The uniforms came from men who had fought in the republican army and had subsequently been called up by the nationalists. When MATA arrived at the pine wood he found the advance party was not there.

—An enemy patrol, which was searching for some deserters, came across them quite by chance; our men opened fire – and the plan was given away. The enemy brought in reinforcements and began to attack. We managed to keep them at bay all that day and, under cover of dark, we began to withdraw in a fighting column. The next day the *guerrilleros* from Langreo and Mieres fought another battle. Fifty-seven men were killed, most of them because they left the column. In a well-disciplined guerrilla column there's no danger unless you're betrayed or the enemy is very strong. We split up again into small groups and returned to the sierra . . .

*

One of the two companions with whom Paulino RODRIGUEZ had first hidden in the gallery was caught and 'sang' before being shot. A search party went to the RODRIGUEZ farmhouse, but so well-constructed was the underground hiding place that they were not discovered. The fugitives had been warned by their contacts of the coming search. When the police and falangists found nothing, they set off for the gallery, taking his sister with them. His mother insisted on accompanying her. It was snowing heavily. When they reached the mouth of the gallery, the falangists' leader ordered his sister to go in. 'If they shoot, the bullets will be for you – and mine will be for your mother.'

—Knowing we weren't in there, my sister wasn't afraid. She had taken the precaution of putting some tins and bottles in the shaft to show that we had been there recently. She even 'found' a bit of the lining of my beret. She was able to convince the falangists that we had left the gallery not long before but without saying where we were going. They searched the mountains until dawn and then gave up . . .

*

Eighty per cent of the guerrillas in the mountains were UGT and socialist youth members, MATA estimated. There were communists, anarcho-syndicalists and non-party men also. In those first years there were few political differences.

—We ate from the same dish, took part in the same actions; we were all in the same situation – when men's lives are at stake there can't be very deep differences. I often went on actions with communists. Fundamentally, I think the base is always united – it's at the top that disagreements occur. My divisional commander during the war was a communist and we got on very well. He was the sort of man who would have disobeyed his party had it ordered him to take measures against me. We socialists in any case are different – if the party ordered me to do something I was opposed to I'd tell them to go to hell . . .

When the Asturian socialist party reorganized in clandestinity, it formed a mountain resistance committee made up of Antonio Llaneza, son of the former mineworkers' union leader, Antonio Florez and MATA. The latter went under the *nom de guerre* of 'Tamayo', an anagram of Yo Mata (I Mata). While the war lasted, the guerrillas had no contact with the republican government; their only contact – via intermediaries – was Prieto.[1]

1. At the end of the civil war, in April 1939, things began to change for the guerrillas. The regime now attempted to wipe them out in direct attacks against their mountain strongholds and indirectly by reprisals on their civilian support. The latter were more successful than the former. 'Guerrillas began to get demoralized as a result of the defeat in the war and many gave themselves up. Others, too young to have fought in the war, later joined us.' In 1940 MATA and others tried to break out and reach France, but were forced to fight a battle in the Picos de Europa, the highest range in the north, where MATA was wounded. He returned to the Peñamayor area where he commanded a guerrilla division of some forty men. Their actions included many more shoot-outs in the villages in search of food and supplies. Arms and ammunition were captured or bought – indirectly – from the *guardia civil*: 'They were so poor in the hunger years after the war that they'd sell ammunition at one peseta a round.' Leading falangists fell to the guerrillas' guns in reprisal for the repression which included the slaughter of twenty-two people in Pozo Funeres in 1948. With the end of the Second World War and evidence that the Allies were not going to intervene in Spain, the socialist *guerrilleros* called on their party either to support the struggle and assign it an objective or to abandon it after eleven years. The latter course was chosen and Prieto took charge of getting the men out. At 10 p.m. on Saturday, 21 October, 1948, after a summer spent in preparation, a French tunny fishing boat arrived off the small Asturian port of Luanco. Only MATA and one other knew the details of the plan. Under the noses of the *guardia civil* in their barracks by the port, thirty-one people, including a woman, leapt aboard. 'The whole operation was over in three minutes, the boat didn't even tie up. There were others we wanted to take off but we couldn't get in touch with them. At 4 a.m. on Monday, 23 October, we were in San Juan de Luz in France.'

Ten months after the end of the civil war (and twenty-eight months after it had finished in Asturias) Paulino RODRIGUEZ emerged from hiding. He had written to the civil governor that he was willing to give himself up and stand trial on condition that he did not have to surrender to falangists or give information as to who had hidden him. His terms were accepted; on his emergence he was reasonably treated, given safe-conduct papers and not charged. His wife reproached him for having come out of hiding. 'The only thing they will let you do is attend my funeral. After that they'll kill you. In the short time left, someone must be found to look after the children. It is they who are going to suffer for all this – ' She told him of the beatings she and their daughter had received in the *guardia civil* barracks, how the latter had lost consciousness and died soon afterwards. His wife had told her torturers that she knew where her husband was hiding but wouldn't tell them. She wouldn't be the cause of his death.

'A fortnight after I came out of hiding, she died. My daughter was dead too. All from the maltreatment they received protecting me. And I lived.'

Episodes 9
Silences

When the boy saw the corpses of the fugitives they had hunted being brought down in garbage carts, his sympathy for the nationalist cause began to change.

Juan NARCEA was twelve. His father was a mining engineer in Pola de Lena, Asturias, and a supporter of Melquíades Alvarez's reformist party. At the start of the war a socialist miner warned the engineer that his life might be in danger. He pooh-poohed the idea. In October 1934, the miners had guarded his home and life. Things were different now, the miner insisted: the engineer's three brothers had been imprisoned and so had two of his sons, Juan's older brothers. Finally, his father agreed to leave for a village near Teverga where the family had a country house; the rest of the war in Asturias he spent pursuing his favourite sport, fishing

Juan accompanied him. Life in the country house was pleasant enough – more pleasant than in his native Pola de Lena where, in the first weeks of the war, two older boys had descended on him as he was making a birdcage and beaten him with a compressor pump hose. As they beat him they called him the son of a bourgeois.

—They did a fairly good job on me. Children were then clearly divided between right and left. Before the war there were two kids' football teams in the town, one for the right- and the other for the left-wing. As long as it remained at the level of sport there wasn't much trouble, but now the differences were becoming much sharper . . .

The divisions existed within his own family; the war was being fought among his own brothers. The eldest, José, was a doctor, a man of liberal beliefs who never took an active part in politics and probably voted left republican. The next brother, Francisco, a lawyer by training and clerk of the townhall, was an 'extreme conservative'. The third, Timoteo, was a dentist and a member of the communist party. The fourth, Leopoldo, was a chemist and a member of the Falange. A sister and two more brothers, of whom Juan was the youngest, and who were too small to have clearly formed political views, completed the family.

—At home, before the war, we all got on very well as brothers, but there were violent political discussions in which my father acted as moderator, for he was a very moderate man . . .

At the beginning of the war, militiamen came to the house and arrested Francisco and Leopoldo. Nine people, including a former mayor, were shot in the township; but the family did not fear for the lives of its two members.

Soon the brothers were suffering different fates.

—The eldest, José, the liberal, was persuaded that it was his duty to join a militia column as a doctor, and he served in a CNT battalion – which was where, it seemed, most right-wingers served. Francisco, the conservative, was released from prison and forced to join a battalion (but not one belonging to the CNT) as a sort of punishment. As he was a lot better educated than anyone else, he soon found himself in an important administrative job in his unit, and seemed to me to be one of its commanders. Leopoldo, the falangist, was taken to Gijón prison and then sent to a disciplinary battalion to build fortifications; he had a pretty bad time of it.

Timoteo, the communist, had left Asturias before the war, partly for political reasons, because life was difficult for him since my mother was an ardent Catholic and president of Acción Católica until her death. He went to Algeciras, opposite Gibraltar, where he was active in local politics and – as we later learnt – attempted to organize resistance to the military uprising. He was executed there on 3 August 1936.[1] My older brothers knew of his death via the International Red Cross, but they didn't tell my father . . .

As the war progressed, Juan felt himself on the nationalist side and waited for Asturias to be 'liberated'. Militiamen came to search the house one day. His relatives, thinking that a sick-bed was a useful hiding place, stuffed religious objects under the sheets beside him. The militiamen's leader, a schoolmaster, asked what was wrong. A cold. He looked at Juan's throat, gave him some pills and sat down on the bed. Immediately he leapt up. 'What have you got there?' Thinking no doubt that he had discovered weapons, he put his hand under the sheet and pulled out a crucifix. Looking surprised, he put it back. 'Keep quiet about all that,' he warned the boy, and went to tell his relatives how to treat his cold.

At last the fronts crumbled, the nationalists advanced.

—The first nationalist soldier I saw was a very young man – so young that he seemed only a lad even to me – riding a fine horse and wearing a helmet. It was that day or the next that my father heard the news that his son Timoteo had been executed in Algeciras. From that time until his own death seven years later, he never raised his head again. He was completely overwhelmed with grief . . .

Juan, too, was shocked. He had been very fond of his brother. All the children in the township had liked Timoteo who told them stories which many of them could remember forty years later – stories which always contained a social message.

—But perhaps because of the impassioned atmosphere after the nationalist victory in Asturias, or because my brother's death seemed something of a blot on the family's reputation and I tried to repress it – or again perhaps because my relatives tried not to talk about it – for some or all of these reasons, I continued to sympathize with the nationalists. In some way or another I was able to dis-associate the nationalists – whose campaigns outside Asturias I plotted on maps

1. 'One of my brothers recently went to Algeciras to locate his grave. The cemetery keeper remembered Timoteo and his execution. He showed my brother the cemetery records for his burial. It said simply: "Charity – for the common grave." A similar entry stood beside a long list of people who were executed there.'

– from my brother's assassination. It was only later, when I saw other things, that suddenly reality was borne in on me . . .

One of these things was the sight of the fugitives being brought in dead. Manhunts were organized by the military and villagers to shoot them.

—When they killed some of them – people who had fled, who were living in the mountains as guerrillas to a certain extent – they celebrated their success with a sort of fiesta, with plenty of food and drink. One of the dead, I remember, was a neighbour of mine, the son of a bourgeois, who had become a socialist. His father was assassinated when the nationalists took Pola de Lena; and his son, who had married in the trenches – that's to say, without a religious ceremony – fled with his wife and baby to the mountains. They were hunted down and shot in a mountain shack: father, mother and baby. Then the corpses were brought down. Several hundred people were killed like this. I was only a kid but I can remember the names of at least thirty of them . . .

During the war, as after it, there was a silence among the brothers about Timoteo's execution. No one talked about it.

—No one wanted to talk about it. After the war it was a question of keeping alive; there was considerable fear. My falangist brother was wounded fighting for the nationalists on the Aragon front and died in 1944. Francisco, the second oldest, also served in the nationalist army as an officer. The family was divided by the war. It is only recently – nearly forty years later – that I and the brother immediately older than I have tried to find out the actual circumstances of Timoteo's death . . . [1]

Episodes 10

Evacuees

About a month before the fall of Gijón, the Council of Asturias, which had previously prohibited all evacuation, permitted a great number of children to be sent abroad. Some 1,200 youngsters, between the ages of two and twelve, embarked on a French freighter in the last week of September for St Nazaire; there, they boarded a Soviet passenger ship for the voyage to Leningrad. It would be more than twenty years before many of these evacuees were to see their native land again.

Twelve-year-old Nicolás FERNANDEZ, from Oviedo, had been in a summer camp when the war started. At the end of the three-week holiday, the children

1. A silence that descended, not untypically, on the second generation also. As Juan's nephew, Francisco's son, explained: 'The civil war was never discussed in my family. My father's brother was shot by the Franquistas; my mother's father, who lived in Valdepeñas, was shot by the reds. My father had a lot of medals which, on his death, we found; but he never told me on what fronts he had fought or any of his experiences. All I knew about his war is what I learnt for myself. At home there was complete silence.'

were told they could not return home because there was a general strike. After waiting fourteen months, his whole camp was evacuated to the Soviet Union. Juan RODRIGUEZ ANIA, the eleven-year-old son of an Oviedo policeman, who had managed to get his six children out of the city in the early days of the siege before meeting his death fighting with the Popular Front forces, was also aboard, with his brother and two sisters. At their orphanage they had been given the choice of going to England, France or the USSR. Their uncle, a communist, had chosen the latter.

The arrival in Leningrad Juan remembered as 'like reaching paradise after being in hell'. As soon as they had had a medical examination and a bath, the children were shown into an enormous room where a profusion of suits were hanging from hooks. Each child could choose what he wanted.

—We ran round taking a pair of trousers here, a jacket there. The suits were split up, but the Russians didn't seem to mind. Then we were taken to the Astoria Hotel, one of the best in Leningrad. We had never seen a hotel like it. They ended up by having to remove the room telephones because we spent all day 'ringing up', talking to no one, of course. They gave us enormous meals in the hotel restaurant, and the orchestra played for us – *La Cucaracha*, it always was! . . .

While Juan and his brother and two sisters remained in the hotel for several months – moving later to children's houses in the city – Nicolás and others were sent to House No. 1, a former workers' rest home, some 45 km from Moscow. To begin with it was the food that made the biggest impression on him: a large plate of caviar, followed by porridge, eggs, bread and butter, cocoa, for breakfast; half a chicken per child for lunch – 'It was amazing!' But in a short while he began to realize that this was but a small part of what they were being given. The Russians were determined that they should lack nothing; not merely the essentials, but the best.

—Our football team was trained by a first division player from Moscow; our dance group by a Bolshoi ballerina; our orchestra by a master of the great theatre orchestra. We had our own football stadium, ice rink, motorboats on the reservoir, cinema. Once our group said it wanted to go up in an aeroplane. We were taken 200 km to a flying school where, I remember, my pilot was a young woman. Later, they gave us a complete aeroplane – a trainer in perfect flying condition – so that we could study it . . .

—It was unforgettable, recalled Juan. The Russians looked after us with the greatest devotion, spoiled us endlessly. The fact that they had been through a civil war themselves made them even kinder to us, although the Russians have a great love of children at all times. We, who were little more than savages really, lived the life of *grandes señores* . . .

One day, his house was taken round the Mikoyan chocolate factory where each worker told them about his job and gave them sweets. Their pockets bulging, they wondered what the manager would say when they were taken to see him. But instead of reproof, he told them how he had taken part in the revolution, had been a worker in the factory himself before becoming manager;

finally he produced two boxes of chocolates for each child. Laden down, they climbed aboard a tram and began to throw sweets out of the window.

—To our great surprise, children in the streets began to pick them up. 'What are they doing that for?' the boy next to me said. We were so spoiled, we believed that everyone else was like us. It was a terrestrial paradise and we couldn't imagine we were an exception. Later, when we had to confront reality, it caused some of us quite a shock . . .

There was no comparison, thought Nicolás, between Spanish and Russian education. In the Soviet Union nothing was left to chance, everything was programmed and planned. All the teaching was in Spanish for the first years, but followed the Russian syllabus with Russian textbooks rapidly translated into Spanish. 'The teachers were real slaves of the pupils.' Not the smallest detail was overlooked. A man stood at the door every morning in winter as they left for their classrooms to make sure that each child was wearing galoshes. Each group had an instructor who was with them from the moment they got up until they went to bed to see that they washed and dressed, got to meals and to class. It was her task to see that the children's clothes and shoes were in good shape, to ensure that they did their homework. At the beginning of the school year, each group met with its instructor and planned exactly what it wanted to do on each Sunday and free day throughout the year. The question of not knowing what to do on a Sunday never arose: the zoo, ballet, the theatre – nothing was left to chance.

—The patience they showed us was incredible. If we had been in Spaniards' hands we would have been beaten more often than I'd like to imagine. But the Russians, never! I don't recall a single case of punishment amongst the 500 of us in House No. 1. And we were barely civilized! Compared to Russian children, we were more spirited, did things more hurriedly, without giving a damn; our temperament was different, we were pure anarchists, everything centred round the individual. Moreover, there were the problems of getting used to the food, the language, the climate, not to speak of feeling homesick at the beginning. Yet we made the change without trauma. It was entirely thanks to the Russians' kindness and persuasion. No Spanish potentate's son ever lived the life we lived in those first years . . .

—I have such happy memories that, were it possible, I would put my name down to live it all over again, exclaimed Juan.

*

For two years, many of the children had no news of their parents. The Russians were always concerned lest they lose touch with their native culture, and Spanish teachers were brought from Spain to help those who had accompanied the children when they were evacuated. Amongst the new volunteers was Rosa VEGA, the Madrid schoolteacher for whom the revolution had brought such remarkable changes as a woman.[1] She had meanwhile joined the communist party, 'mainly out of enthusiasm for the Soviet Union', and was keen to go there for she believed that the USSR was educationally very advanced. In Valencia,

1. See p. 286.

where she had been evacuated, she had had the opportunity of putting new teaching techniques, especially the 'centres of interest' method,[1] into practice. She found the Soviet Union's concern for the children's indigenous culture very praiseworthy, and she set off for Moscow in early 1938 full of hopes. Once there, she was assigned to a Russian school where the Spanish children were taught in a special section using Russian methods.

Her first shock was to find even the youngest children being taught by subject – fifty minutes of arithmetic, fifty minutes of Spanish, etc. The content of each teaching period was, moreover, rigorously laid down. 'If we went beyond it we were considered undisciplined.' The lessons, she reflected, had evidently been designed for children with a slower learning rate; Spanish children tended to be more lively than the Russians of the same age, while the latter were more conscientious, more stable, but also more placid and docile. After a time, the Spanish teachers were able to persuade their Russian counterparts to allow the Spanish children to be taught faster, and several were able to complete two years in one. Other problems, however, rapidly confronted her.

—It was evident that there was considerable fear of individual initiative. In each of the older children's classes, one of the pupils was appointed as invigilator to walk up and down to ensure that the children were studying – a sort of policeman. In Valencia I had been able to leave the pupils, even those who were supposed to be difficult, to get on with their work alone because they were interested in what they were doing . . .

A Spanish-speaking Russian woman was assigned to the teachers as supervisor and attended the classes, taking notes. At weekend self-criticism sessions, she would ask why such and such a child in such and such a class had been scratching the table while the teacher was writing on the blackboard.

—'I couldn't see what the child was doing behind my back,' I'd reply. 'But the child is committing an outrage against Soviet property,' she retorted, and she didn't mean it as a joke. 'More discipline is needed.' Her peculiar ideas of discipline took up the best part of those meetings. Rather than self-criticism, she tried to turn them into criticism of others to keep us feeling frightened and insecure. But then, her task was not to be constructive; it was to be a policewoman to ensure that none of us made remarks hostile to communist orthodoxy. There was a lot of terror, a lot of fear; it was the height of Stalin's show trials . . .

An Italian who translated the Russian textbooks into Spanish used to ask Rosa VEGA to look over his translations. But any suggestion of a stylistic change brought the immediate response: 'It doesn't matter if it doesn't sound quite right, the important thing is that the original Russian meaning should not be distorted.' Worse was to come; one day, the Italian disappeared. 'Thinking he was ill, we asked where we could find him and were told, very bluntly, not to bother.'

She fell ill and had to go to hospital. The doctors believed that she was suffering from a nervous complaint. Secretly, she felt it was true. The reality of

1. The choice of a theme which would be studied in all its inter-related (linguistic, mathematical, geographical, etc.) aspects by children in work groups.

the Soviet Union had come as a great shock after the propaganda in Spain. She was surprised to find that the USSR was poorer than her own country, that life for Soviet citizens was very hard, that clothes were still rationed and that food seemed expensive in relation to wages. As to the political conditions – they were patently harsh.

—But in complete contrast to all this was the quite extraordinary love and affection the people had for children, invalids, the old. Never in my life have I been treated with such affection as when I was in hospital in Moscow. I saw that everyone was getting the same attention and care as I. It confirmed everything I had seen in terms of the ordinary Russian's concern for others; at the human level it was admirable. At the educational level – *¡nada!* . . .

Using her illness as a pretext, she returned to Spain after six months. Before she left, women wanted to buy her clothes, her silk stockings. 'How can you Spaniards who are only just beginning to make the revolution, dress so much better than we who have made the revolution?' the other teachers constantly asked.

Once in Spain, she wanted no more to do with politics. She felt disillusioned by what she had seen. In Spain, thanks to the aid the Soviet Union was providing the republic, it had seemed normal to join the communist party. But in the Soviet Union, she had felt as though she were in prison, had come to value freedom and independence as never before.

—The party asked me to give talks about my experience. I limited myself to describing how well the Spanish children were being looked after, because that was a positive experience. For the rest – and I wasn't an educational expert – I kept silent for I didn't want to offend anyone . . .

*

The Basque country, where nearly 14,000 children had been evacuated, provided the single largest contingent of evacuees; but only a relatively small proportion were in the Soviet Union, the majority having been given refuge in France, Belgium and England.

In a convent in south-west France, the four AGUIRRE children, who had been separated from their parents after the tragic air raid on Guernica and put aboard the last ship to leave Bilbao, awaited their final destination. The children wanted to get out of the convent where the conditions were bad; but when they heard an announcement – 'All those wanting to go to Russia, form up and put their names down' – 'all those wanting to go to Belgium' – Manolita, aged nine and in charge of her siblings, didn't know which queue to join. 'Russia, Belgium, Isle d'Oleron – it was all the same to us, one or the other might be wonderful.' In the end there were thirty children left. The French communist CGT took them over, lodging them in a castle which had once belonged to Napoleon some 80 km from Paris. Koni AGUIRRE, aged seven, remembered the cups of milky coffee, the French butter . . .

—What excellent care and attention we received! They gave us classes in every subject except religion. At first I longed for the prayers my grandmother had taught me in Basque; I longed for my parents. Sometimes I would go off on my own and cry, just thinking about my mother and father, my country. I could never forget the day of the air raid. Life seemed to have begun for me on that day. I could hardly remember anything of my life before it, even my first communion only a fortnight earlier. Everything had been wiped from my memory except the knowledge that we had no home to go back to. My last memory of Guernica was seeing our house in flames . . .

Eight months passed before they had news that their parents were alive. Their mother, living now in the village of Ibarranguelua, some 10 km north of Guernica, was offered help by a Frenchman married to a woman from Guernica, to get her children back. A Franco-sympathizer, he offered to accompany her and to pay the costs. She went to the *guardia civil* in Guernica to try to get papers. They refused her. She was dangerous, they said. 'I? A woman who has lost her four children, who has lost everything, who has done no one any harm? Dangerous?' As a result of all this her husband was briefly arrested.

In Guernica itself a band was brought to play in the ruins one Sunday. Many of the original inhabitants had not returned; some streets remained impassable, the charred shells of houses were still standing. The band was to attract people back. 'Do you know what I have just seen?' said a priest who was not from the town. 'I have seen people dancing in a cemetery.' 'A cemetery?' 'Yes. People are still buried under the rubble – '

Hearing that efforts were being made to secure the children's return, the CGT evacuee director called Manolita in to ask if her parents were Franquistas. No. Communists? No. 'They're Basque nationalists,' she said. The director asserted that no child would be allowed to return as long as Franco controlled any part of the peninsula.

—So our idea became one of hoping and waiting for that gentleman, Franco, to leave Spain so that we could join our parents again . . .

Meanwhile, they were so well looked after that Manolita believed that another three years and they would have ended up communists.

—Yes, agreed Koni. It was as though in place of religion they took special care of children. And as a religious person, I believe that if I had to choose between the two, the care was more important than the religion . . . [1]

1. In the end it was the Second World War and Hitler's advance into France which got them back to the Basque country. 'In 1940, nearly a year after the civil war ended, I received a telegram saying they were being sent to Bilbao. I went there to wait for them. My delight at seeing them getting off the ship was marred by the way the Spanish nuns pushed them about as though they were lepers, almost a sub-human species . . .' (Ignacia OZAMIZ, their mother).

Juventud del Siglo XX
Que preparas con ardor
Un mundo libre de trabas
Mundo del trabajador . . .

Juventud del Siglo XX
Madrid está llenito
De fascistas 'camuflaos'
Cobardes y 'enchufaos' . . .

Pero cuando la victoria
Lleguemos a conseguir
A todos los emboscados
Les haremos que trabajen
Para que puedan vivir . . .

Youth of the twentieth century
Who are eagerly preparing
A new world freed of fetters
A world of the working man . . .

Youth of the twentieth century
Madrid is full
Of undercover fascists
Of cowards and string-pullers . . .

But when the victory comes
Which we are going to ensure
We'll make these draft-dodgers
Work to earn their living . . .

Words put to the tango tune, *Siglo XX* (Madrid)

Somos los hijos de Lenín
Y nuestro padre es un cabrón
Porque nos manda resistir
Con las lentejas y el arroz

We are the sons of Lenin
And our father is a bastard
Because he's ordered us to hold out
On lentils and rice alone

Words covertly sung by right-wingers when
La Joven Guardia, the communist youth song,
was played

Winter 1937 to Summer 1938

The winter of 1937–8 was bitterly cold and it snowed heavily on the central and Aragon fronts. Spirits in the republican zone were momentarily raised by the capture of Teruel, the only town of size to be occupied by the Popular Army. From Barcelona, Jaume MIRAVITLLES, Catalonia's propaganda chief, hastened to see Prieto, the socialist defence minister, to propose a massive propaganda campaign to mark the largest republican victory to date. Prieto refused; the republican army could not hold the town for more than three weeks.

—I saw then that the war was lost. The offensive had been carried out simply as an attempt to bring about a negotiated settlement to end the conflict . . .

A bitter nationalist counter-offensive threw the Popular Army back. The anarchist-led 25th division, which had been badly mauled in the initial offensive, was ordered back into the line. Saturnino CAROD, the division's political commissar, refused to counter-sign the order. It was inhuman to send men into battle without proper equipment and arms. Thumping the table, the divisional commander, García Vivancos, exploded.

—'If there are no arms we'll fight with sticks and stones, with our nails. This order has got to be carried out.' We were still discussing it when a fresh signal arrived ordering the 118th brigade of the division to report to Galan's army corps. We set off . . .

It was snowing hard. On arrival, García Vivancos remained with the men in the uncovered lorries while CAROD went in to report. Around a stove he found a group of men who offered him coffee. They began to talk. 'It wasn't long before the eternal theme of unity between the communist party and the CNT was brought up.' He said this was a matter to be dealt with directly between the leadership of the two organizations. As a disciplined member of the CNT he would obey whatever decision the national committee reached. But one of the men present insisted, saying that as a well-known militant he could put pressure on the CNT to agree.

—In their attempt to persuade me, they argued that the future of Spain lay in the unity of the communist party and the CNT, that the war would be won by the two organizations. They proposed that the communist party should form the political organization of the CNT, and the CNT the trade union organization of the party . . .

He replied again that this was not the moment to discuss the matter. His men were freezing outside, he needed orders and especially the arms which the brigade had been instructed were waiting for them. The tone of his voice was rising in anger when one of the men put his hand in his pocket and brought out a communist party membership card.

—'Take this, or none of the arms you see there will be given to the 25th division. I looked: in a shed at the back there were arms enough to re-equip the men.

They included Maxim machine-guns which we had never had. 'I'll get the men off the lorries and we'll pick up the arms.' 'You'll do that only when you accept the membership card.' I presume it must already have been filled out, for I don't suppose they expected me to sit down and do so myself at that moment. I gave them a piece of my mind. One of them put his arm round my shoulder and said, 'Calm down, Carod, there's no need to get upset. The comrades have not posed this matter correctly. You Spaniards are all the same. Don't worry, everything will be sorted out.' I recognized the man: Ercoli. It was only later that I learnt his real name: Togliatti, the Italian communist leader . . .

Unplacated, CAROD stormed out. He ordered his men to make for another army corps HQ on the same front. From there he spoke by telephone with the general commanding the army of the Levante. The latter sounded angry and ordered the brigade to remain where it was. But this did not solve the problem of arms. The lieutenant-colonel in command of the army corps assured him that there was a dump near by sufficient to re-equip the entire division. He had not even finished speaking when a signal arrived from the front. Pounding the table, the colonel exclaimed: 'The entire dump has just been captured by the enemy.'

*

Using the recapture of Teruel as a springboard, the nationalist army rolled forward and by April 1938 had reached the Mediterranean at Vinaroz. Taking all of republican Aragon and a part of Lerida province, it stood poised to advance into the heart of Catalonia. Prieto's self-fulfilling forecast had been proven more than true. After the loss of the north the previous autumn, the remainder of the republican zone was now cut in two. Hitler, meanwhile, marched into Austria.

BARCELONA

In their advance the nationalists captured the hydro-electric plants at Tremp, in Lerida province, which supplied Barcelona. Old steam-generating plants in the Catalan capital had to be pressed into service. Production dropped again. Air raids aggravated the disruption, although some factories – like the new Maquinista Terrestre y Maritima workshops – were noticeably being spared, no doubt on their owners' pleas. But more than 750 houses had already been destroyed in the city when the worst of the raids began. Every two to three hours, day and night, Italian Savoias bombed the city for forty-eight hours, beginning on the evening of 16 March. People fled the capital.

Hearing the crash of bombs in the Carrer Carmen just off the Ramblas, and the Red Cross man's shouts for help, Eduardo PONS PRADES, the young libertarian of the CNT woodworkers' union, jumped into a car. He was on leave from a machine-gunners' training camp, and it was the first time in his life that he had driven. Outside a baker's, a dozen women's bodies were lying; three wounded women were put in the car and he set off for the Clinical hospital. From there he was sent to fetch two surgeons from their homes. 'I could see from the fright on their faces that they realized I hadn't driven before, that they might die in the car as easily as in the raid.' The novice driver, who at the front was convinced he would not be harmed, was now himself certain that he was going to be killed by a bomb.

The weather was cold and rainy, and many of the people fleeing the city had to sleep in the hills. Soon the centre was almost deserted, the streets deep in broken glass.

Filling the car with petrol at one of the few garages still open close by the Plaça de la Universidat, PONS PRADES heard the bombs falling closer and closer. He and the attendant looked at one another; the next moment he felt himself lifted up in a whirlwind of hot air and dust and tossed across the street. He fell stunned. The blast from the bomb, which had fallen on the Coliseum cinema, struck the neighbouring buildings with such force that they collapsed like a pack of cards. Rushed to a first-aid centre, PONS PRADES heard – as did many others – that the bomb had fallen on a lorry carrying high explosives which happened to be driving down the Gran Vía at that moment.

Almost all the casualties from the big explosion passed through Professor Josep TRUETA's hands. Head surgeon of Barcelona's largest hospital, his method of treating war wounds had already made history – one of the great innovatory processes to result from the war.[1] For some time he had been observing the evidently experimental types of air raids the Italians had been carrying out on the city and its solid stone houses: the combination of explosive, high-explosive and penetrating explosive bombs, followed by incendiaries. Anti-personnel bombs had also been used. But the March air raids were different in scale. The only comparison, in his view, was Guernica.

—The raids were meant to test the population's capacity of resistance. By the time they ended, there were 2,200 casualties in my hospital . . .

On seeing the casualties from the 'big explosion', Professor TRUETA immediately denied the story that the bomb had fallen on a lorry carrying high-explosives. Casualties reaching the hospital in the following forty-eight hours confirmed to him that another two explosions of similar magnitude had occurred in the city, although they were less noticed because they caused fewer victims. They were, he was convinced, some sort of super-bomb which the Italians were trying out.

The raids took their toll in casualties and demoralization. But people reacted in protest, even right-wing acquaintances of Professor TRUETA who complained at the barbarity of the air raids. 'How can the Caudillo allow this sort of thing – '[2]

1. The most striking part of the treatment, which he had slowly developed from his pre-war experience of road and industrial accidents, was the immobilizing of the wound in a plaster-of-Paris cast; but this was only one – and indeed the last – of the five stages in the treatment. The others were: early surgical intervention made possible by efficient ambulance services; cleansing the skin and wound with non-toxic materials such as soap and water; the meticulous removal of all foreign matter and the excision of all devitalized tissues; open drainage with dry gauze and no skin suture; and finally, immobilization in a plaster cast. Of the 1,073 war fractures he treated with this method in the course of the war, only six died. (See *Reflections on the Past and Present Treatment of War Wounds and Fractures*, mimeographed, undated, speech by Prof. Trueta to US Army medical conference.)

2. Mussolini declared his delight that the Italians were horrifying the world. In Britain, France and the US the raids raised a storm of protest. Thirty years later, Franco declared – contrary to Ciano's statement that Italian air raids on Barcelona two months earlier, in January 1938, had been carried out without consultation with any Spanish commander – that 'all the air

A liberal, who had not espoused Catalan nationalism, who admired England – 'I always thought Catalonia could have been like England, despite its different history' – Professor TRUETA remained at his post though he had long been convinced that the war was lost. Lack of organization, failure to create an army rapidly, the anarchist mentality alien to the Catalan middle classes, had ensured defeat. Never neutral, he felt hostile to everything.

It was a widely shared feeling. A joke went the rounds of the Catalan nationalist petty bourgeoisie. 'Which is the best day of the week? Answer: The day this lot leave and the others haven't arrived yet.'

—It expressed our situation as Catalans exactly, reflected Eulalia de MASRIBERA, whose father, a liberal Esquerra businessman, had had to go into hiding after a threat on his life. A staunch Catalan nationalist, she found herself torn between values that had not previously been contradictory: between defending a legally constituted republic and a republic of disorder, chaos, assassinations; between being a Catalan and a Spaniard; between religion and church-burnings; even between members of the same family taking opposite sides. Liberal Catalanists like us were caught in the middle. We couldn't identify with one side or the other. There was I, with my father's life threatened by this side, and yet knowing that the other side, the Franquistas, were determined to put an end to Catalan autonomy. It was all this that made the war so sickening for us . . .

Militancies 16

TOMAS ROIG LLOP

Lliga Catalana lawyer

—We middle classes simply withdrew to our homes and hoped the whole thing would be over as soon as possible, and the situation prior to 18 July restored . . .

To begin with, he had hoped that the republic would restore order and win the war. Although his party, the Lliga Catalana, had lined up with the counter-revolutionary bloc in the 1936 general elections, nothing justified the military uprising. It could only threaten what had cost so much to win – Catalan autonomy. By the same token, what could justify the wave of violence that swept the city after the uprising was crushed? The violence of the popular reaction shocked him. Churches and convents were burned, people assassinated before anyone even realized that the uprising had become a civil war.

Had it not been for this violence against the church, Catalonia would have

---

raids were always carried out by special decision of the Spanish command'. (Lt Gen. Francisco Franco Salgado-Araujo, *Mis conversaciones privadas con Franco*, Barcelona, 1976, p. 494.) Whether this statement could be applied to Guernica, where the Franquista version continues to maintain that the Condor Legion acted without knowledge of the Spanish high command, is a moot point.

been a solid bloc against the Franco forces, he thought. Admittedly, the church had not been all that it should, had been insufficiently concerned with ordinary people; but if anywhere, it was here and in the Basque country where this had been least true. The attack on the church had been what most angered the profoundly religious Catalan middle classes.[1]

It was these classes which formed the base of Catalan nationalism; in the towns, the liberal professions, the shopkeepers and artisans; on the land, the peasantry. The people who lived their Catalan culture, their language and traditions, in a deep and meaningful way. This middle class abhorred violence, which clashed with the Catalan tradition of conciliation, of seeking means of dialogue rather than confrontation – the English model, the 'political ideal'. The nationalist middle class was not separatist; separatism, he observed, had been supported by only a small minority which had never played a dominant role in Catalonia's political destinies. For all that, as soon as Catalans of different tendencies got together in support of their historic personality, the people of Spain began to view the matter with considerable hostility. There had been very few exceptions to that rule. It was explicable by the fear that Catalonia would separate from Spain – 'something that in fact was inconceivable: geographically, economically – even mentally – it was an impossibility.'

The middle classes had an important role to play in the war effort. Their hopes for the restoration of law and order had been disappointed. Only one way existed, he believed – and that was used too late. Against the disorder, violence and indiscipline of the FAI which, in the last – if not the first – analysis had been responsible for the republic's collapse, the communists' disciplined violence had to be used. Only a well-organized party could control an extreme situation which otherwise led automatically either to worse chaos or to a right-wing backlash. But it had not been until Negrín came to power and sent SIM[2] agents to the city that an end had finally been put to the indiscipline and violence. By then it was too late; the middle classes had withdrawn.

—When we saw that the attacks – not only on religion but on middle-class businesses and workshops through collectivization – were not going to be ended, we pulled out of the struggle. Became neutral, you could say. Didn't give ourselves up to the war effort. This, I believe, was decisive to the outcome of the war. We withdrew, we could see no purpose to a war we had been dragged into and which we had never wanted . . .

As a Catalan nationalist, there were dangers, however, in an attitude of neutrality which could, in the last resort, only favour an enemy resolutely opposed to the Catalan cause. Contrary to the proverb, the devil known appeared worse than the devil unknown.

—We never believed that Franco would impose a regime which increased the divisions between Spaniards. We thought that after a short period following his

1. His opposition to the republic's anti-clerical legislation, in particular the suppression of religious orders, had led him, indirectly, to join the Lliga Catalana, representing the conservative big bourgeois Catalan nationalist interests (see also Points of Rupture, C).

2. Servicio de Investigación Militar, the counter-espionage and political police organization created by the republican government after the May events in Barcelona.

victory, he would allow former political parties to re-establish a political order, since he had the army behind him. We imagined he would allow exiles to return. We never thought that his forces would crush Catalonia . . .

One of the very few Lliga members to remain in Barcelona, he was deprived of his living as a lawyer. His life threatened more than once, he turned down the chance of escape abroad which Cambó, his party leader, offered, because it meant leaving his wife and three children behind. He found a job in the town-hall which did not pay enough to keep them alive, and eked out a living by going round the countryside filling out official forms for illiterate peasants. When they asked what they owed, he looked around: 'that rabbit,' 'that chicken,' and returned home full of triumph.

A post office worker he knew told him he had packets of Canary tobacco stored away which he didn't dare sell. 'You're frightened? Well, I'm not,' and he bundled the tobacco into a large suitcase and set off for the butcher's, the baker's, the grocer's.

—People were crazy for tobacco – and this post office worker was being sent regular supplies which, by some fantastic stroke of luck, were never intercepted . . .

His work sometimes took him to an FAI office. At first he went without tie or cap.

—'What have you taken your cap off for?' the FAI man would say. 'You're a rotten bourgeois, rotten through and through, what's the point of trying to hide it?' So I'd put my cap back on. Then I'd go to the Esquerra party office to try to get some condensed milk for my children. 'Why don't you stop wearing a cap?' the man would say, looking at me. 'It's very impolite these days to wear a hat or cap. Especially when you're not in your own home.' A cap or beret – no one in the first months dared wear a hat – became a symbol of the contradictions of life in Barcelona.

If only all the republican forces had lined up solidly against Franco and bent all their energies towards winning the war, none of this need have happened. Franco could not have won, however much aid he received. All the large cities were on the republican side! But now it was too late . . .

The shadow of things to come had not yet lengthened over the Catalan bourgeoisie. The visible, hostile presence of the revolution, threatening their socio-political interests, their vision of Catalan autonomy, outweighed the enemy spectre on their borders which threatened autonomy but not – it still seemed – their fundamental class interests.

A confirmed Catalan nationalist, Juana ALIER none the less supported the Franco forces throughout the war, well aware that they were irreconcilably opposed to Catalan autonomy. The wife of one of the city's largest millers, she wanted the military's victory to 'put an end to the sort of life we were being forced to live, to bring in a new life'. She felt everything was disintegrating around her; it couldn't continue like this.

Not that, in some ways, she had been unfortunate. Although she had voted for the Lliga in 1936, she had always been able to count on the protection of the FAI militants in her husband's mill. In the past, her husband had looked after the families of FAI workers in the mill when they were in prison. On one occasion, when she had been denounced for removing papers and valuables from the family *torre* which the unified socialist youth had taken over, these FAI workers prevented the socialists from arresting her, and sent a couple of armed men to guard their flat. During the May events, she and her husband stayed in the mill, knowing that under FAI protection they would be safer there than at home. Her husband, who had voted for the Esquerra in 1936, had joined the CNT and had been appointed to the city's flour-milling committee. He and his brother – who, to all intents and purposes, as a member of the mill committee, continued to run the family enterprise – received wages which were higher than the ordinary workers, and quite sufficient to live on. The mill committee always saw to it that the former 'bosses' received not only their fair share but a little more of the food obtained by the committee's 'sale' to farmers of mill residues for cattle fodder. Until the very end, she could not complain about food.

Her husband wasn't frightened. Not a single mill-owner who had remained in the city had been killed. As long as there was work one would always be able to live, her husband said.

—If 'all this' lasted a short time, he would get his mill back; and if it lasted a long time – then what did it matter? He was more philosophical about things than I. I was more bourgeois, I needed security. I'd always been frightened of not having enough to live on. If one had some capital, one had security. That's what I missed . . .

Her 100-hectare estate in Tarragona province had been taken over by the workers once the wheat harvest was brought in. Until then, they had sent the foreman and an armed worker each week to Barcelona to collect their wages. Her brother's paper factory in Lerida was also taken over. But thats he had managed to handle, setting up a committee in the head office in Barcelona to run the business side. Everything had to be run by committee these days! Hers consisted of an office boy and a clerk, who both unreservedly supported her, and herself. The important thing was to prevent anyone else taking over.

—And to ensure that the factory workers got their wages each week. As long as they were paid there was no friction. The committee was just running out of money when Lerida fell to the advancing nationalist forces, putting an end to the matter . . .

Despite her energy, her will to resist, she felt herself falling apart, as though without bearings in a life that was totally impermanent, transient. One of the most important bearings of her former life had gone: religion. She desperately missed not being able to go to church. She managed to have her first child baptized clandestinely in 1937 by a priest who came to the house – but only with water. By the following year, when things were slightly easier, the priest returned with the sacramental objects, they took communion and the child was baptized again.

—Were we to go on for ever like this? Was worship to be abolished for the duration of the war or for ever? I didn't know. It was part of a world that had been lost. I prayed for the 'whites' to win, so that we could start a new life. Not the way they won in the end – but who was to know that then? . . .

Though 'law and order' appeared to have triumphed in Barcelona after the May events, this did not reconcile large numbers of the Catalan middle class to the new course of events. Juana ALIER's husband felt threatened by the growing strength of the communists; he returned from talks with Joan Comorera, the PSUC leader and Generalitat economics councillor, dispirited.

—'I don't know what will happen to the FAI,' he said. He didn't feel entirely safe any more . . .

But this was an exceptional view. More common was the opinion that the anarcho-syndicalist revolution was 'like being in a plane which you know is going to crash', in the expression of Marcel CANET, the son of a small textile manufacturer in Badalona who had been taken over.

From the moment that he had answered the government's call to reservists two days after the start of the war, but was ordered out of the Barcelona barracks by FAI militants on the pretext that no army was going to be formed, he had felt (as an Esquerra member) that the libertarians' response to the needs of the war was tragically chaotic.

Returning to his father's mill, where, in the manner typical of much of the Catalan bourgeoisie of the time, he had begun work at fifteen sweeping the floor, he found that on trade union orders the workers had taken over. The man appointed president of the factory committee was a stoker.

—He decided that my father was going to have to do his job instead. Become a stoker. My father was a republican, a lifelong Catalan nationalist. After working hard and saving all his life, he had managed to start the mill ten years before. What folly to make an enemy of someone like him! The great majority of middle-class Catalans were hostile to the military rising – but an even greater majority came to hate the revolution the CNT was trying to make . . .

His father refused to comply and left for Barcelona where, for a time, he went into hiding. But he was never troubled, no one went after him, and he soon returned to Badalona to live.[1]

Receiving 10 pesetas a day – half his previous salary – like all the other workers, his son continued in the mill as a manager, supervising production, taking up complaints from clients, trying to find customers. Relations between him and the mill committee, which was in charge, were mutually respectful.

—Meanwhile, the workers went on working just the same. There were about sixty women and eight men. To them it made no difference, in the last analysis, who was putting the pressure on, whether owner or committee. It was they who knew how to do the job. What made a difference was how things worked higher up. The relationship between different economic sectors, the overall economic situation – and it was there that chaos really existed . . .

1. Where the CNT textile union continued to pay him the same wage as other workers though he did not return to his mill, according to the union's secretary, Josep COSTA.

CANET observed with amazement that when the mill committee went to Barcelona on business they hired a taxi. He and his father before the war had always gone by train. They didn't own a car.

There was no doubt in his mind that the enterprise was going to flounder. The workers, in his view, were totally naïve when it came to running a business.

—It's something you don't learn overnight, it comes to you from experience, or perhaps it's innate. I felt as though I were someone who could read, read the writing on the wall, while those on the committee were illiterate . . .

He had suggested earlier to his father that they flee. 'I have done nothing, I have no reason to leave,' his father replied; and so they had stayed.

As the factory went onto short-time as a result of shortages of raw materials, CANET volunteered for the Pyrenean regiment formed mainly of Catalan nationalists. The local anarchist committees which (until the May events) controlled the borders, attacked the regiment when it was sent to the frontier area to train, taking some of its commanders as hostages. The Generalitat informed the regiment that it was powerless to intervene.

—If there was nothing the government could do, what could we do? I decided the only thing was to get out. One only fights if one has got something to fight for. I wasn't an anarchist, I wasn't a communist, the republic of 1931 in which I believed was no longer the republic that existed after July 1936. I could see no reason to continue fighting for it. I wouldn't have left simply because of what was happening in the factory. If that had been the case, I should have escaped to the other side and fought to restore our property rights. I couldn't do that. Money wasn't the most important thing; ideals mattered more. And my political ideals were simply no longer represented by Catalonia as it was . . .

He and a cousin, both skilled mountaineers, packed haversacks, took their skis and set off. In a blinding snowstorm, they crossed a mountain pass into France far from any military post. From there CANET made his way to America and to a new life – a neutral in the struggle.

As the war progressed, there were other causes of disaffection. One outcome of the May events had been the central government's progressive takeover of the Generalitat's functions, especially in matters connected with the war effort. Josep ANDREU ABELLO, Esquerra deputy and president of the Barcelona High Court, believed that this was a major error which sapped Catalan resistance.

—The Generalitat's powers were being steadily eroded until, in the end, they were virtually reduced to nil. As a result, large numbers of Catalans came to believe that this was no longer *their* war. The great spirit which had moved the masses at times of crisis suddenly began to disappear. A sense of defeat permeated the hearts of most Catalans; added to which were the air raids, the hunger, the overall war-weariness . . .

ANDREU ABELLO noted that the working class had a great deal more optimism that the war could be won than did people like himself in positions of authority.

—That was the problem. While we were probably better informed and could hardly be optimistic, the masses – with their greater simplicity – were preparing for the revolution after the conflict; in this confusion we were losing the war . . .

Not that it was being lost because of the revolution; it would have been lost anyway, he thought. The parliamentary democracies' failure to rally to the republican cause had assured defeat from the very first day. The failure was hardly surprising. The war, the last ideological war, coincided with the nadir of democratic ideology. Daladier, Reynaud hadn't an ounce of ideology, in his view. As for Chamberlain, he displayed an English tranquillity-seeking egoism which betrayed his lack of understanding of what was at stake – even for Britain's own prosperity.

—The majority of French and English lived through our war with an indifference and lack of generosity that left us entirely unsupported. It was a terrible thing . . .

Food was by now a constant preoccupation; nobody starved, but people were going hungry. Some curious advantages accrued from this unhappy situation, as Joan GRIJALBO, the UGT bankworker who was serving on the economics council, recalled. He occasionally returned to his former bank to look at its state of affairs. He could remember the time in 1935 when, to celebrate its twenty-fifth anniversary, the bank had given a banquet and he had spoken on behalf of the employees. They were devoted to the bank's future, he said, but they had many concerns which the union was taking up: wage rises never happened spontaneously or miraculously. 'I recommended to the bank's directors that they bear in mind the concept of social justice. At that, as one man, they walked out of the hall.' The Spanish bourgeoisie, he reflected, was the most reactionary in Europe. 'It wanted to continue to live well by refusing to allow the proletariat's standard of living to rise to European levels.'

As he went over the bank's accounts, he was amazed to see the way people continued to save. Catalans had one of the highest per-capita savings rates in Europe during the war, he calculated. But there was one firm which was on the verge of bankruptcy: a bicarbonate of soda company.

—Nobody was buying its product any longer because no one was suffering from indigestion . . .

Episodes 11

Imbroglios

Food supplies were Joan MANENT's major concern as CNT mayor of Badalona, the industrial town of some 80,000 inhabitants 8 km up the coast from Barcelona. Agricultural production within the city limits had virtually collapsed. The CNT agrarian collective had failed. The half dozen day-labourers who were in the CNT – members of the foodworkers' union, for there was no anarcho-syndicalist agricultural union – had expropriated most of the twenty-odd large owners' lands and had tried to do the same to the some 400 smallholders. CNT union leaders in the town had prevented them taking over the latter who, in the main, belonged to the Esquerra's *rabassaires* (smallholding peasants') union.

—Not only that, the day-labourers ran the collective so badly that some of the *rabassaires* who wanted to join the CNT were put off and joined the UGT instead. We sent a couple of well-prepared militants to administer the collective, but they refused to stay, seeing that it was going to lead to a shoot-out. Even the FAI opposed the way the labourers were running things. In the end we managed to get them thrown out and sent to the front, but by then the damage was done . . .

On the other hand, a UGT agricultural collective, formed in part from large holdings and in part from the plots of smallholders who wanted to join, and run by a couple of former CNT members who had left because they had come to blows with those who had been running the CNT collective, functioned very successfully, in MANENT's opinion. 'It was paradoxical, perhaps; but then all revolutions are like that – '

The food problem, none the less, remained acute. And it was made more so by some of the industrial collectives; amongst them, the important Cros chemical factory, now a collective working flat out for the war effort. Operating an exchange system, the factory's 2,000 workers received food supplies for every so many tons of fertilizers they produced.

—Over and above their ordinary rations, each worker might get about 15 kilos of food a fortnight from their exchanges. The same was true of the other chemical- and metalworkers in the town. There was great discontent among the rest of the population at this inequality . . .

MANENT organized a meeting of collectives and consumer cooperatives and insisted that all food supplies should be handed over to the CNT supplies committee to be equitably distributed among the whole population.

—The CNT unions were agreed; but the workers refused. It wasn't the first time I encountered the egoism of individual collectives . . .

Appointed mayor in July 1937, after the anarcho-syndicalists had refused to participate in the new Negrín government – he had been private secretary to Joan Peiró, the CNT industry minister until then – he had found the town hall in a serious financial plight. It had insufficient funds to pay even its own staff, and had to appeal to the Generalitat for funds.

—The reason was that there was no income. The collectives refused to pay any taxes – not a soul would pay a *céntimo*. There we were trying to live libertarian communism while people forgot their duty to the collectivity. It was a proof of the irresponsibility which many people displayed. Each collective, as I soon saw, only too frequently thought first of its own interests . . . [1]

1. The impossibility of collecting taxes from industrial and agrarian collectives was an important factor in the central government's hostility to them, particularly under Negrín who had been finance minister before becoming prime minister.

MANENT threatened to resign unless the food situation were put on an equitable footing. The CNT national committee secretary, Mariano Vázquez, had to come to ask him to continue at his post. Nothing was achieved to change the food situation.

The arrival of the central government in Barcelona brought a new problem. An attempt by the Generalitat to take over a TB sanatorium being run by the CNT-led municipality in a former monastery had been staved off without too much difficulty. But when the central government decided to take it over – Negrín's niece was a patient there – the matter became more complicated.

The sanatorium was set up in the monastery during the revolution as the result of a long-standing anarcho-syndicalist claim. During the republic the Carthusian monks had suggested to the municipality that they would look after the town's TB patients – a disease with a relatively high incidence in Badalona – if the municipality would meet the medical expenses. A disused building above the monastery could be used for the purpose. A week after the October 1934 insurrection, all the patients had been returned to the Badalona hospital without warning. The CNT demonstrated, demanding that the monastery itself be taken over as a sanatorium.

In July 1936, as soon as the military uprising was crushed, some 2,000 people attacked the monastery, burning its pharmaceutical laboratory and nearly burning its library, reputedly the third most important in Catalonia for its *incunabula*. The CNT dispatched men to prevent it.

—But we were unable to prevent the crowd bringing thirty-eight monks, including the prior, down to Badalona to kill them. Two were killed and two wounded en route. Seeing men armed with pikes bringing the monks in I thought I could see the guillotine waiting in the square, so much did the scene remind me of the French revolution . . .

He and other CNT leaders had taken precautions, assembling 200 of their militants in the square where the mob was threatening to kill the monks. Pistol in hand, the militants arrested the crowd's ring-leaders, and took the monks back to the monastery.

—'You call yourselves the Anti-Fascist committee, you've taken over the town-hall and now you're saving monks. How can you act like this?' The crowd couldn't understand what was happening . . .

Within a few days, the committee realized it could not adequately protect the monks, among whom there were many foreigners – French, English, Japanese, etc. Committee representatives went to see President Companys and asked him to repatriate the monks in order to avoid an international incident.

As soon as this was done, the local CNT set about realizing its aim of converting the monastery into a sanatorium, knocking four cells into one to make wards, bringing in new beds and equipment, including an X-ray machine, and appointing CNT guards to protect the place. The latter also worked in the vegetable gardens which kept the sanatorium self-sufficient in food and provided a surplus for the aged and orphans in Badalona.

One day, some of the guards were cleaning old straw from an upper storey when they found a trapdoor. Beneath it were stairs. Fearing that someone might be hidden there, for two or three monks had escaped, they went down. In an underground room they found a stockpile of arms – about 100 Mauser and Winchester rifles with 100,000 rounds of ammunition. The rifles were packed in grease and labelled.

—We went to see the prior who was wounded in hospital. He denied all knowledge of the arms. But a monk who was also wounded told us the story. The rifles had been delivered by four men in donkey-drawn carts shortly before October 1934. The weapons were for the monastery's defence and for use by right-wingers; but they had not been used. We found the men who had delivered them, and they confirmed the story. They had picked up the cargo of rifles from a ship which had unloaded them up the coast from Badalona . . .

The Generalitat's attempt to take over the sanatorium was staved off by a proposal to accept patients from the whole district if the Generalitat would subsidize the cost. But the central government's attempt, backed by a company of assault guards who arrived at the sanatorium, arrested all the CNT guards and took over, was another matter. MANENT immediately summoned the heads of all the police forces at his command. CNT militants, in conjunction with their forces, were going to retake it, he informed them.

—There was some hesitation on the police chiefs' part. They had only some fifty men with which to face the assault guards. But I assured them that with our men we would be sufficiently strong. The police commander suggested he telephone the assault guard commander, but the latter replied that he had his orders and would defend the sanatorium to the death . . .

Seeing the impasse, a CNT member telephoned the Generalitat. Faced with the possibility of armed confrontation, President Companys suggested a compromise.

—The assault guards would be withdrawn, but the position of the sanatorium must be 'legalized'. A public meeting, attended not only by Companys and other Generalitat officials but by prime minister Negrín himself, could celebrate it. 'You'll have to lay on a lunch for everyone, of course,' he said. When the town councillors heard of the scheme, they all wanted to attend the banquet. 'Yes, you shall attend,' I said, 'but Manent won't – ' When the day came, I shut myself in my bedroom, told my wife to tell everyone I had gone to Sabadell, and remained there until the affair was over . . .

It was just as well. That evening the libertarian youth of Badalona organized an enormous women's demonstration. They marched on the townhall to protest that a banquet had been laid on for government ministers when there was hunger and suffering among the civilian population.

—It takes great diplomacy to deal with a mass of enraged women. I asked them to send in a delegation. They recited their protests. I told them I hadn't attended the banquet. 'We know that. All the same there are stocks of food in the municipal warehouse which aren't being distributed – ' I knew the real purpose of all this: it was an attempt to get rid of the councillor in charge of supplies, a member of the PSUC, who was a friend of mine for all that. I had a sudden brilliant idea.

'We shall all march to the warehouse now, I and the town councillors with you, and inspect it. If there is a single gram more food there than there should be, you can hang me from the nearest tree – ' 'Manent, what have you promised them?' one of the town councillors said. In truth, I was only half sure myself that everything was in order . . .

With the demonstration of women following, they set off. When they got there – 'luckily for me' – there wasn't even a *bacalao* in the warehouse. Convinced, the women disbanded.

As a result of all this MANENT again tried to get agreement on the equitable distribution of food supplies.

—And again I failed. The parties and organizations all agreed in principle; but did nothing in fact. They were frightened of abolishing their members' privileges. So I resigned as mayor . . .

New arrivals to Barcelona from battle zones often found the atmosphere of a rearguard city frivolous; despite the food shortages and even the air raids, the war – at least on the surface – seemed a long way off. The new arrivals' impressionistic view was sometimes reinforced by a critical insight into the way things were being run.

Appointed commandant of the Barcelona transport commission, Rafael HERNANDEZ, socialist railwayman from Gijón[1] who had managed to escape by ship from Asturias, found the railways running very badly. 'The reason was that no one was in charge.' There were no schedules, each train was a 'special' which meant that it had to go from station to station waiting for a clear line. He decided that this had to end.

—But there was no way of doing it. The station-masters were no longer in charge of their stations. Instead, there was a station committee, made up of guards and representatives of other railway personnel, and an engine drivers' committee. If the latter decided against the former's decision to run a train to the frontier, for example, it didn't run . . .

A single person had to be in charge, HERNANDEZ believed. He found people who were willing to assume responsibility if they were backed by higher authority. Would he provide it? That was what he was there for, he told them. He summoned station-masters and sub-masters and told them it was their task to run a scheduled train service under his command. Anyone who opposed them would be thrown in gaol. If they failed in their duty it would be on their heads.

He found the railway workshops in a similar state of disarray. In one, the boilermaker who had been put in charge was laughed at by the engineers and technicians since he lacked all idea of what had to be done.

—I ordered him back to the boiler-making section, re-appointed the former workshop head and told him he was now responsible for seeing that repairs were properly carried out . . .

1. See Militancies 7, pp. 239–41.

Small things surprised him: the great number of carriage seats which had been ripped out by people to make themselves leather jackets; nothing like that had happened in Asturias. Andalusian refugees billeted in fine country villas tore out doors for firewood in winter. They couldn't be blamed, the fault lay with those who organized their housing and who had not taken the trouble to tell the refugees where they should go for firewood in the mountains. Of course, the fundamental cause of all this disorder lay with the military who had started the war. 'None the less, the lack of any sense of property, the lack of culture, astonished me.'

Among CNT militants the outcome of the May events, the growing strength of the PSUC, and the economic difficulties encountered by the collectives all made for demoralization. Josep COSTA, CNT textile union secretary in Badalona, and Joan MANENT's companion there, believed that the general mass of workers was less affected.

—But we came to the conclusion that we didn't know what we were fighting for any longer. We'd reached a situation in which nothing seemed worthwhile. So most of us went to the front, to fight and be killed . . .

At the front, morale was high, especially among the youth, even those who had been called up, in PONS PRADES's experience. Though not yet seventeen, he had volunteered for the army, falsifying his age, not long after the May events. The effect of the latter on the CNT woodworkers' union had been 'catastrophic'. Although work continued, there was a sense of material and moral defeat which permeated everything. Nobody talked about it; 'It was just like an impending death. We were all waiting for the union to die of a heart attack.' But at the front things were very different.

—As long as the war wasn't lost, everything hadn't been lost; that was what we all felt. And once the war was won, all the problems could be reconsidered. Even defeats like that of May could perhaps be overcome . . .

Hopes to be shattered; but whose tortured shadows were to rise again, a year later, in a second civil war within the civil war which without settling the former, finished the latter, opening the gates of Madrid to the enemy . . .

MADRID

The winter had been very hard; when blizzards struck during the Teruel republican offensive, it had snowed heavily in Madrid. The people, he thought, were beginning to lose heart. Or rather, those people who wanted only to 'eat and live', who wanted the war to end, however it ended. Régulo MARTINEZ, president of the Madrid left republican party, still had faith in victory; yet he could not help but see that large sectors of the population no longer shared his faith.

—They were like sand, these masses, absorbing whatever came their way. Their morale was falling very rapidly. The soldiers at the front never went without food, but they knew that their families in the city were going hungry, and that was bad for morale too . . .

There was the problem of the refugees; in the panic evacuation of the countryside as the enemy advanced on the capital in that already distant autumn of 1936, many had come who had been supporters of village *caciques*, he reflected. At the beginning, when he had found them places to live, they had given of themselves in the defence of the city; but now they were among the first to become demoralized.

The front line remained where it had been traced in blood during the November offensive. Nationalist artillery continued sporadically to shell the city from Mount Garabitas, in the Casa de Campo, although there were no more direct assaults. In the *barrio* of Argüelles, facing the University city, few houses remained intact. An area so close to the front was also an area in which it was relatively safe to hide. Standing in the doorway of a house, a man watched three children playing behind a cobble barricade in the sand of the street. Only two families lived in the three still habitable houses; one was a chemist whose children he taught, to earn money because, as a leader of the clandestine Falange, private work was safest. As he watched, spent bullets from the University city splattered against the barricade and the walls of the houses. Three mortar shells suddenly exploded over the roofs. The children's mother looked up. 'You had better come in now, it's getting a bit thick.' It was as though it had just started to rain. 'That was the way the people of Madrid lived.'

Women hung out their washing on the barbed wire entanglements; children went to school in air-raid shelters, and to the Gran Vía to pick up red hot shrapnel. It was a favourite sport of Alvaro DELGADO, the fifteen-year-old son of a clothing store manager. The shelling did not usually start until 6 p.m. The lads would wait in the side streets on the south side of the Gran Vía until they heard the cannon open fire, the whine of a shell in the air, and the boom as it exploded against the Telefónica. Then they rushed into the street for the hot metal.

—It seemed a very precious thing for us kids to collect. One evening, when things got a bit hotter than usual, I took shelter in a shoemaker's shop; when the smoke cleared, I saw a man in the street whose head had been blown off . . .

The Gran Vía was known as Shell Avenue. A current joke was to ask whether the 17 tram had arrived. 'No, the only thing that comes by here is the 15½' was the stock answer. The latter referred to the calibre of the enemy shells.

It was the only city where you could go to the front by tram. Girlfriends and *novias*, knowing that their boyfriends had an hour or two off duty at the front, would take the tram to see them.

—And there, behind barricades and parapets, you could see them making love with firing going on all round them. Now and again a couple would be killed and their bodies found still clasping each other in a last embrace, Régulo MARTINEZ remembered . . .

People got used to anything, he thought. He was taking a short cut through the Plaza de Bilbao behind the Telefónica building – the highest edifice in the city, the enemy's main target – when he saw two kids of about eight and six playing marbles. An old woman was sitting in the entrance to a cinema taking the winter sun. Suddenly, a couple of shells, missing their target, fell in the square. One exploded, the other buried itself in the ground. One of the kids looked up. '*Abuela*, they're firing. Go home, *coño*, only men can be outside now.' Turning to his companion, he said: 'OK, it's your go – '

—I could hardly believe my ears. I went up and said: 'And you too, get home quickly, it's dangerous here.' They looked up at me and said: 'Go home? What for?' . . .

People 'vaccinated' themselves with shrapnel fragments, and went to the cinema to forget. The Marx brothers; Soviet films. Enemy shelling seemed to many Madrileños to coincide with the time when the cinemas came out. 'Soldiers who had gone through the worst of the fighting at the front were killed leaving a cinema in the Gran Vía at night.' For youths like Alvaro DELGADO, half the excitement was the fear of whether they could get to safety when the shelling started. 'If you could reach the Plaza del Callao and the corner of the Calle Preciados, you knew you were OK.' One evening he was watching an American film, something to do with Mexico, when the noise of the shooting on the screen seemed somehow to get a lot closer and, all of a sudden, the lights went out: a shell had hit the cinema.

The centre of the city was always full of people; but the closer you got to the Plaza de España, the fewer people you saw. From there on, the cobble barricades began and sentries stopped people from approaching the front.

Pushing his father's handcart through the streets on delivery errands, he liked to stop at all the political party offices and read their wall newspapers. Often they included poetry by Miguel Hernández, Lorca, Alberti, Machado, and he wanted to read them all. In the main squares, enormous posters portrayed the faces of communist heroes – of Stalin, Lenin, La Pasionaria, Lister – as well as anarchists like Durruti. 'But never a poster of the prime minister, Negrín, and hardly ever one of Azaña.'

Most children, by now, had been evacuated; some, like Jesús de POLANCO and his family, had even succeeded in reaching the nationalist zone. His father, manager of a Santander dairy company in Madrid, had been caught by the uprising in Santander; his mother, right-wing and religious, had been left to look after the six children without any means since her husband's bank account was frozen. The children began to go hungry. Relief came from the waiters of La Granja el Henar, the famous café which her husband's company owned in Madrid, who brought them food and even gave her money.

—Our one remaining maid had a militiaman *novio*, a very nice man who, when he came on leave, would draw his rations and bring them to us. In the midst of everything, there was a tremendous sense of humanity . . .

In fact, he reflected, the left helped the right a great deal during the war. Not a single charge was laid against anyone in his house by the left republicans living there. 'In that sense, the civil war only began after the war, when the right-wingers began denouncing people as reds – ' Not that they had escaped without trouble by any means. Police and militiamen had come seeking his father. One of the policemen had been so moved by his mother's shattered nerves and the sight of the six children that he had calmed her down and given her a piece of paper which stated that the flat had been searched and nothing found. If anyone tried to search the flat again, they were to be shown the paper; if they persisted, she was to call the police.

—Which, on one later occasion, she did when militiamen appeared. As soon as they heard what she was doing, they gave up their search. My poor mother, what she went through! I gave her no peace. I was only six; I wore a pair of overalls on which I had had UHP embroidered. 'You're all fascists and I shall denounce you,' I used to say to them. They didn't think it was much of a joke at the time . . .

Through the offices of the British embassy – his father was a friend of the British consul – the family was evacuated a year after the start of the war. Five hundred women and children set off in a convoy of buses by night for Valencia where they were taken aboard a British hospital ship which disembarked them at Marseilles. From there they went by train to Hendaye to cross into nationalist Spain. Never in his life would he forget the scene as they walked across the international bridge.

—The whole expedition burst out singing *El corazón santo tu reinarás*. People threw themselves on the ground to kiss Spanish soil. Others started singing *Cara al Sol*, the Falange anthem, and I remembered that a few days before the start of the war my aunt had given me the first five *duros* [25 pesetas] I'd ever had for singing it for her on her saint's day . . .

The change was tremendous, overwhelming, he remembered. From hunger to abundance, from poverty to relative affluence. There were no air raids, no cause to worry. Public enthusiasm for the nationalist cause in Burgos where he stayed with an aunt and uncle was tremendous. On the Espolón, he met a neighbour who had lived in the flat above his in Madrid who gave him a kiss: a naval captain called Luis Carrero Blanco who had escaped via an embassy.

Shortly, Santander would fall. One day, a man came to the door and asked if it was his uncle's house. Suddenly the stranger threw his arms round the boy and embraced him. ' "*¡Hijo mío!*," he cried. 'I hadn't the faintest idea who it was . . . ' His father had driven to Burgos immediately on his release from the sanatorium in Santander where he had been confined after the prison director and doctor had shown him how to fake the symptoms of TB.

*

Despite the defeats, despite all the difficulties, the militiamen who came to Alvaro DELGADO's father's shop in Madrid always seemed in great spirits, were never in doubt that the war would be won in the end.

—Next door to the shop in the Plaza Antón Martín was the Bar Zaragoza which was locally known as the syphilis bar; the army men who went there for the whores often brought them next door to buy something. There was no shortage of clothes and suits for a long time, and the soldiers had plenty of money. While they were serving them, the shop assistants always asked for news of the front. It didn't matter what setback had just occurred, the men were always optimistic; and their faith was shared right to the end by the Madrid working class . . .

The lack of food was debilitating. Queues for bread and milk had started early on in the war. One had to join the queue by 7 a.m. in order to make sure of getting something later in the day; family members took turns spending a couple of hours each in the queue. It was where people talked, it was where he had experienced a new type of revolutionary fraternity. Everyone was addressed as '*tu*', there were no ties, no hats to be seen, everyone appeared to be wearing sandals.

But those days were over; the food shortages had only got worse. Everyone was suffering from vitamin deficiencies, great boils came out on his neck and under his arms. His hands were broken with chilblains. A bowl of lentils, a bit of rice occasionally, livened up with some *chirlas*, a mush of flour – that was all he ate. He never saw meat, never tasted coffee.

—I've often thought that from 1936 I didn't eat properly again for another ten years. People went home early because of the hunger and cold; and on those dark nights the only light would be the sky lit up with the reflections of shooting . . .

Vitamin deficiency was sending Pablo MOYA's sister-in-law to her grave. The UGT turner made a special trip to his native village to collect a ham his sister had managed to get. He left it to his sister-in-law and his children to eat. There was a generalized spirit of self-sacrifice, even though they were all nearly dying of hunger. Not that a whole day ever went by without something to eat.

—A tiny bit of bread, lentils – the famous Dr Negrín pills, as we called them – rice, that was about it. And the cold – I've never seen rain and snow like that second winter of the war. There was nothing to heat ourselves with. People tore out doors and windows for firewood. And yet I never lost faith in our victory. I had a workmate whose brother-in-law was a political commissar in El Campesino's division. Every morning I used to call him across and say, 'Tell me the latest, even if it's a bunch of lies.' It sounds ridiculous, but I wanted to hear him say that so many new tanks, so many planes, so much more ammunition had arrived – even if it was untrue. I had a blind, mad faith in our winning the war . . .

It seemed impossible to be neutral and remain on any part of Spanish territory. However much there was to criticize about one side, a choice seemed inevitable when faced with the prospect of the other winning. But it was not out of the question. José VERGARA, former agrarian reform chief in Toledo,[1] felt that the impossibility resided not in siding but in choosing: both seemed equally repugnant to him. He sent his Mexican-born wife and children, via the British embassy, to the nationalist zone where he knew they would be safe and fed, while he remained with his parents in Madrid. He wanted to have nothing to do with the nationalists – 'in any case they'd have shot me for having worked on agrarian reform' – or the republicans. The former seemed bent simply on restoring the old Spain; the latter were a disaster, had proven it in their conduct of the war which patently they were going to lose. For a liberal, neither represented a viable future. He turned down the offer of a high-ranking post in

1. Points of Rupture, A.

the commerce ministry which was made to him on Negrín's suggestion. He explained that he was disillusioned with the republic.

—'And what will you do when the war is over, then?' asked the politician on the other end of the line from Valencia. 'What will *you* do?' I replied . . .

He found work in the scientific investigation institute in which, among others, Julián Besteiro, the moderate socialist leader, played a leading role. Called up, he procured a piece of paper from someone he knew to say that he was unfit for military service. He dressed in a suit, tie and hat and was never stopped in the street for an identity check.

—They must have thought I was someone important to dress like that. One day I was in the tube when I became aware that two men were saying something critical about the war. 'Shut up, we're being overheard,' one said. The other looked at me and turned back to his companion. 'It's all right, he can't understand, he's a Russian' . . .

VERGARA lost 30 kilos. One of Encarnación PLAZA's friends wore four skirts simply to look a little fatter – the fashion then not tending to the skinny. Her father was a medical colonel in the republican army; they lived in the upper-class Salamanca *barrio* which the nationalist artillery spared. When she went out into the street, the other children made underhand, malicious comments about her father, a staunch republican.

—Though we all came from the same class, those children were hostile to us for 'being on the other side'. It was the first time I heard anti-republican remarks . . .

Such an experience was no novelty to Alvaro DELGADO, whose family, as so many, was divided; his mother's side was 'exceedingly right wing', while his father's brother was 'practically a founding member of the communist party.' At the start of the war, his mother's family had had a hard time and she had tried to get his communist uncle to help. Whether he had or not, young Alvaro did not know; what was certain was that very soon his mother's side became a lot better off than the rest of the family. They moved to a large flat out of danger of the shelling which they shared with two other families; the husband of one of them held an important post in the townhall and seemed able to procure all the meat he wanted.

—One of my cousins was a draft-dodger who got himself a job as a clerk in the SIM, the counter-espionage service; he belonged to the clandestine Falange. We, who were on the left, had virtually to beg food from my right-wing family who always seemed to have enough bread, soap, milk. In fact, I used to go to the SIM headquarters where my cousin would give me green soap for washing clothes, and condensed milk . . .

The right, he reflected, as he pushed his father's handcart through the streets, might not be very intelligent – 'in Spain it has always been characterized by its cultural philistinism' – but when it came down to the practical realities of life right-wingers organized themselves better than the left. Which was not surprising really, when one considered that they had much more experience of administering property and wealth, since they owned almost all of it.

*

Without military victories to offset hunger, cold and air raids, the mobilization of the rearguard became increasingly difficult. While morale at the front remained high and defeat seemed impossible, the rear was beginning slowly to crumble. 'There was virtually no mass political involvement any longer.' The communist party was losing the close ties it had forged with the people of Madrid in the November days.[1] The fervour of the revolution was gone; the linked policy of aligning the bourgeois democracies abroad and the democratic petty bourgeoisie at home in the anti-fascist struggle meant pursuing the alliance with right-wing socialist and liberal republicans. (Amongst the latter, there were many who, like Régulo MARTINEZ, the Madrid left republican leader, felt that communist propaganda was constantly trying to prove that the 'communists alone existed', and feared that if the war were won, they would proclaim another 'Stalin-type soviet regime'.)

It was surely no accident that *Mundo Obrero*, the communist party's main Madrid organ, staged a revolt at this moment. The Spanish people, it wrote, would not make the revolution according to the wishes of capitalism. 'The people will triumph despite capitalism's opposition. Without pacts or intermediaries. And they will set the popular revolution on the course that the popular will considers opportune.' More importantly, the paper said it did not believe that the 'only solution to our war is that Spain should be neither fascist nor communist because France wants it like that'.

From Barcelona, where the government and communist party headquarters were established, José Díaz, the party general secretary, replied. It *was*, indeed, the party's position that Spain should be neither fascist nor communist. *Mundo Obrero*'s statement that the people would triumph despite capitalism corresponded 'neither to the situation, nor to the policies of our party nor to those of the Comintern. We want the (democratic) states to come to our aid. We believe that in helping us they will be defending their own interests; we try to make them see this and call on them for aid . . .'[2]

No more was heard on the matter. While reaffirming that 'we shall continue with the men of the petty bourgeoisie until the end', the communist party reacted when their defeatism became too apparent. Early in April, it organized pressure to oust Prieto who, as defence minister, was notoriously 'pessimistic' about ultimate victory. His objectives in the Teruel offensive three months earlier had been too patent: to reinforce the republic's hand in potential peace negotiations.[3]

1. See pp. 331–2.
2. *Frente Rojo* (Barcelona, 29 March 1938).
3. The reformist socialists, under Prieto, were essentially in agreement with Azaña, the republic's president, in believing that a negotiated settlement must be reached on the basis of 'safeguarding republican institutions as far as essentials are concerned'; on this basis, 'a number of concessions' could be made to the enemy. There would be neither bolshevism nor dictatorship in Spain. (M. Azaña, 31 August 1937, see *Obras completas*, vol. IV, Mexico, 1966–8, p. 761.) The communists would certainly count among the 'concessions' to the enemy in a negotiated settlement. Negrín's goals were the same – but his tactics two-pronged: negotiations

On 1 May 1938, Negrín set out the republic's war aims, itemized in 'Thirteen points'. The 'popular republic' which would result from victory would safeguard legally acquired private property 'within the limits of the supreme national interest'; would carry out a profound agrarian reform to create a solid peasant democracy – 'owner of the land it works'; would affirm both liberty of conscience and regional liberties, as well as the maintenance of Spain's political and economic independence.

It was an appeal to the bourgeois democracies to consider Spain's cause their own. It failed, as all such expectations had failed before.

Militancies 17

TOMAS MORA

Socialist commissar-inspector

Commissar-inspector of the army of the east, he was on the point of resigning when he read Negrín's 'Thirteen points'. After what had happened already, who would believe them? Who would believe, for example, that religious freedom was to be permitted in the republican zone? Propaganda! A clergyman rescued from death was worth more than all the propaganda of this sort.

Secretary of the National Federation of Pharmaceutical Assistants and a member, in consequence, of the UGT national committee, he had been one of the first five front-line political commissars appointed in October 1936, when, with the enemy advancing hard on Madrid, the commissariat had been set up. He had set out immediately for the non-existent front to rally the militiamen; then he was sent to Valencia to help sort out the complicated situation that had arisen there. With the creation in 1937 of the army of the east out of two army corps before Teruel, he was named to his present post.

Not that his appointment had been officially ratified by the socialist defence minister, Prieto, who believed – for some reason best known to himself – that he was a supporter of Largo Caballero, the former socialist prime minister. That was how far sectarianism went between the factions of the party. As it was, the defence minister had got it wrong; he was a Prieto supporter, and had been even before the war.

Prieto hated the commissariat – and he was right to do so, he thought. With some honourable exceptions, men who helped build the Popular Army, too many commissars were a liability. They tried to dominate the military commanders which was not a difficult matter if the latter were right-wing career officers. The officers were completely inhibited as a result – and an officer in that state could not effectively command troops. He had been a 'bit totalitarian' in

---

alternated with all-out resistance, depending on the circumstances. As the former failed so resistance became the only hope of linking the civil war into the coming world war and ensuring what had so long been vainly counted on: English and French aid.

this respect on the Teruel front, insisting that his commissars collaborate fully with the military commanders, strengthen and support them. If an officer were suspected of treachery, he must be reported immediately; otherwise he must be left to command his men.

But the major problem lay elsewhere; Prieto was determined to undo the several hundred communist appointments, especially in the army of the centre, which, under the statutes, should have been made only by the Commissar-in-Chief. The defence minister ordered all commissars to hand in their appointments and re-appointed only those he approved of; ordered the members of the Commissariat's secretariat to active duty as commissars at the front, and issued an order designed especially to replace the communist commissar of the army of the centre, Antón, with a socialist. Appointed a brigade commissar on the Teruel front, Antón did not take up the posting.

—Instead, within a short time, he turned up as a civilian attaché to General Rojo, the chief-of-staff. How could you win the war with people behaving in an absolutely undisciplined manner like this – and backed by the communist party? . . .

Charges of communist proselytism in the army, especially in Madrid, had become so widespread that he had been sent on a special mission to investigate. He had informed Antón of the allegations of undue influence in membership recruiting and communist infiltration in other parties' military units. There were complaints that the only newspaper reaching the front was the communist *Mundo Obrero*, and that the distribution of the others, which went through the army's commissar, was being held up.

—As far as the press was concerned, Antón told me that the complaints were justified – but not the cause. 'Here are the number of copies of each paper we receive for distribution. *Mundo Obrero* – 10,000; *El Socialista* – 500; *Castilla Libre* (libertarian) – 800; *Política* (left republican) – 500' Your comrades who complain should send us more copies.' I went to the *Socialista* offices and they said that with the newsprint shortage their regular subscribers had to come first. If that was the case, I replied, they had no cause to complain. Having made inquiries of the other papers, where I ascertained much the same, I wrote an objective report on the newspaper situation. How *Mundo Obrero* got sufficient paper to print its 10,000 copies, I don't know. I, who had really been sent to Madrid to find a cause for sacking Antón, was unable to accuse him of anything, for the other charges were extremely difficult to prove. It was well-known that the communists, using the prestige of Soviet aid – very well-paid aid, as Prieto put it – offered military commands in return for party cards. But because of the aid, the government was always under pressure to tolerate such procedures . . .

Recently Prime Minister Negrín had attended a dinner for the commanders of the armies of the east and manoeuvre, and in a speech afterwards had spoken about the Soviets.

—'I know there are those amongst you who dislike the presence of Soviet advisers,' I recall him saying. That was certainly true. Apart from a couple I knew, who were excellent, the rest were little better than master-armourers. I could never understand how the Soviet government sent such people. 'But,' continued Negrín, 'I want to point out what you all know – the Soviet Union is the only country which is sending us aid. The communist party is the party which is putting the most into the war effort. For these reasons alone I beg you to be tolerant of the advisers.' His speech made me boil with anger. I think he was no more than the tool of the communist party. Whether he was sincerely convinced that the communists were the only real force behind the war effort, I don't know. But he was certainly under their influence . . .

Prieto's measures dealing with the commissars were thus totally justified, he believed. The communists had taken advantage of Caballero when he was premier and war minister. Caballero's leadership had been disastrous, not only during the war but before. The most conservative of working-class leaders, he had become a 'real' revolutionary only with the rise of fascism; in October 1934, and again in the first days of the war, when the Madrid masses prevented the formation of Martínez Barrio's government of conciliation,[1] he had shown how 'real' his revolutionary determination was. Demagogy, pure and simple! Instead of seizing the chance on the latter occasion, using the authority he indisputably enjoyed to prove he was the 'Spanish Lenin', and take power, he did nothing. By the time he was appointed premier six weeks later, it was too late; the republic was already under the influence of, if not dominated by, Soviet aid.

Indeed, he reflected, if the socialist party had not been divided, the UGT divided, the military uprising might have been little more than another abortive coup, like that of August 1932. As he looked back on events, he had to conclude that the major responsibility for what had happened had to be laid at the doors of his party. Prieto, on the other hand, was a pragmatist, a man of realities. Julián Besteiro was the only socialist leader who had a viable long-term vision, but Prieto was the only leader who understood practical politics. He should have become prime minister in 1936 after the Popular Front electoral victory. 'He had more political wisdom in his little finger than the whole of the socialist party.' Not that he was without serious faults.

—His sectarianism, his phobias – as soon as he suspected anyone of supporting Caballero he had him down in his black book – his pessimism. The latter was demoralizing. He believed the war was lost from the moment Germany and Italy intervened. He remained at his post out of personal pride or whatever, but without hope of victory. As he was a man who said what he thought, he demoralized others. It was counter-productive to have a defence minister who thought only of peace . . .

He had accompanied his army commander, Hernández Saravia, to see Prieto to tell him that the capture of Teruel on their front would be a relatively easy objective for the Popular Army. '*Hombre*, you fill me with optimism,' Prieto had said.

Militarily, the offensive had turned out well. Executed with speed, it had taken the small enemy force by surprise. But the initial success had not been followed

1. See pp. 57–8.

up. Was it again the Popular Army's lack of manoeuvrability, he wondered. With the exception of General Rojo, the republic lacked good military strategists, as well as good middle-level commanders – so important in a war of fixed positions. You could teach an illiterate to handle a rifle in a short time, but to teach workers the complexities of commanding a body of men over terrain was a totally different matter. Their lack of education told against them, he thought. The nationalists had the advantage on both scores: trained strategists and army commanders on the one hand, students who formed the bulk of their subalterns on the other[1] . . . But it was for none of these reasons that the Teruel offensive had failed to develop and advance deep into enemy terrain, as he believed was necessary. The explanation lay elsewhere.

—Prieto wanted a military success to show foreign nations that the republic had created an army strong enough to mount major offensives in order to gather support abroad for a negotiated peace. In terms of bringing the war to an end, that was not a mistaken strategy, in my view. It was time, from a humanitarian point of view, that the conflict ended. War – and civil war above all – is the most monstrous experience imaginable. After the fall of the north the previous autumn, I believed there was no hope of our winning; and when the enemy reconquered Teruel and pushed us back to the sea, cutting the republic in two, I knew we were definitely beaten. But as a commissar, I couldn't say what I felt. It would have been ridiculous to have remained at my post only to spread defeatism and gloom . . .

In the midst of the battle, when the nationalist defenders, who had held out in isolated buildings in the town for a fortnight, surrendered, he was ordered to bring the bishop of Teruel, who had been sharing the defenders' fate, out alive. As he drove him away in his car, he asked the prelate if he had not considered advising the military to accept an earlier republican offer of surrender to spare further suffering among the civilian defenders, especially the women and children.

—'Yes, you may be right,' the bishop replied, 'but you must realize that no one resigns himself easily to defeat.' It didn't seem to me a particularly appropriate answer from a man of the church. When we got to the train which had been prepared to receive him and the other prominent prisoners, he was asked at General Rojo's initiative whether he would be prepared to write a statement about the way he had been treated in republican hands. He agreed, and began: 'At the request of his Excellency, General Vicente Rojo, chief-of-staff, I declare that during my transfer from Teruel to – where are we? Mora de Rubielos – I have been treated with every consideration and respect by those responsible for my safe passage – ' When we informed Rojo, the latter was furious, for it made the statement appear to have been written under coercion. The bishop was asked to change it, which he did, eliminating the incriminating first words . . .

1. By September 1938, the Popular Army had 6,444 temporary war-trained officers, according to Alpert, *El ejército de la república*. The nationalist army up to the end of the war, six months later, had trained 22,936 provisional second lieutenants. (Payne, *Politics and the Military in Modern Spain*, p. 389.) Both sides mobilized about 1 million men each in the course of the war. Speaking of the republican officers' training schools, Rojo, the chief of staff, told Azaña that 'they produce very little'. (Azaña, op. cit., vol. IV, p. 840.)

Such a statement, MORA believed, was worth any number of Negrín's points, for world opinion could see that the republic had been at pains to save a bishop's life.[1] The propaganda of action was superior to the rhetoric of wishful thinking any day. What was needed was more actions like this, he thought.

Episodes 12

Crossing the lines

On a cold winter's afternoon, five legionaries made their way to the nationalist front line. Their unit, the 16th *bandera* of the Foreign Legion,[2] had just taken up positions a couple of kilometres in the rear in preparation for the nationalist counter-offensive on Teruel.

The men had bought two bottles of *anís*. In front of them, they knew, a Canaries regiment was manning the line, and when they reached it they told the soldiers that they wanted to buy tobacco. They chatted with the lieutenant and sergeant, telling them that they had taken part in the liberation of the north – Bilbao, Santander, Gijón. From their accents it was clear that two were Basques and one Asturian.

One of the Basques, Eugenio CALVO, asked the sergeant where the 'sons of a whore' had their positions. The sergeant indicated the enemy lines. The legionaries stayed on chatting with the soldiers in their dug-outs, waiting for dark to fall. All of them knew the risk they were running.

CALVO was a twenty-three-year-old communist miner from Ortuella, in Vizcaya. From the first day he had fought the uprising, first in the militias, later in a communist battalion in the Basque army. Encircled in Santander, he had managed to crawl through the Italian lines before the surrender of the city and, in civilian clothes, hitch a lift on an Italian army lorry back to Bilbao. In hiding, he had undergone an interior struggle: should he try to get to the French frontier? 'I thought of my comrades, I thought: one must be consistent with one's political ideals, must fight to the end.' Hungry, exhausted by the ordeal of hiding, he one day came across a Foreign Legion recruiting office in Bilbao. Rather than risk the frontier crossing, he would join the Legion with the express idea of crossing the lines. Having just reached the front after three months' intensive training in Talavera de la Reina and Saragossa, the moment had come.

During the training, he and the four others with him had, little by little, sounded each other out, small things revealing their thoughts. One was a communist comrade from Santander, another a CNT member from Logroño, the Basque was a schoolteacher. All of them from the north were under suspicion as potential deserters. 'When we get to the front,' CALVO remembered

1. Prieto proposed having him escorted to the French frontier and freed. The cabinet opposed the idea, and the bishop was held in prison until the following year when, in the last moments of the retreat from Catalonia, he was assassinated.

2. Despite its name, the Legion had always been composed predominantly of Spaniards.

a sergeant saying with venom, 'we'll have to watch this lot more than the reds.'

Only a few days before, the *bandera* had paraded to witness the execution of five legionaries from the north for trying to cross the lines. Three of them died bravely, shouting *¡Viva la República! ¡Viva el Partido Comunista!*

—We had to march past the corpses. A lot of the old legionaries and falangists spat on the bodies. The schoolteacher reproached me later for not doing the same, for not showing enough caution. But I couldn't – they had been men like me . . .

The bulk of the recruits were peasants from Galicia and Navarre, attracted to the Legion by the higher pay and the excellent food: fish and meat every day. They were men, he observed, without an ounce of political awareness.

—Men who had had it drummed into them by their priests that the reds were the devil incarnate who attacked the church and would rob them of their plots of land and their livestock. That made a big impact on them. I remember more than one saying that if he caught a red he'd cut his ears off as a trophy. They had the mentality of the small peasant – individualistic, egotistical, tied to their land and the church . . .

Night fell. The legionaries told the soldiers they were returning to their unit. Having carefully noted a zone in the barbed wire between sentry posts, they crawled towards it, managed to lift it and get through. The sentries spotted the schoolteacher and shot him in the buttock, but his companion, the Asturian miner, hoisted him on his shoulders and, at the risk of his life, carried him into no-man's-land.

Lost, frightened of wandering back into the nationalist lines, they spent the night in the open; it was several degrees below zero. At dawn, carrying a small Italian hand-grenade in each clenched fist, they moved towards some trenches in front of them. '*Camaradas, ¡Viva la República!*' A soldier appeared, then another.

—But they didn't shout back. They simply gestured to us to approach. We couldn't tell which side they were on. Clutching our grenades, we advanced with our hands up. The soldiers came up to the wire, their rifles at the ready. Still they said nothing. I was trying to make out their insignia. At 30 metres I still couldn't see it properly. Suddenly I couldn't stand it; I started to run forward. I was ready to sell my life dearly. I was looking at those badges. When I was almost up to them I saw we were all right. They were republican troops – Catalan at that. They didn't speak a word of Spanish nor we of Catalan. We handed over the grenades and they found an officer who spoke some Spanish . . .

The 'deserters' were able to inform the republican command of the nationalist troop dispositions. Throughout his time in the Legion, the schoolteacher had taken note of air fields, aeroplanes and other military installations, and CALVO had learnt them by heart. But their ordeal was not yet at an end.

Taken to Madrid, they were interrogated so severely that the communist from Santander nearly lost heart; what was the point of risking their lives crossing the lines to have to face this? 'But I understood; we could have been spies.' It was easier for CALVO; he had been in hiding in Madrid after the October 1934 rising, and could get people to vouch for him. Cleared finally, and after a few days' leave, they were told at the recruiting office in Barcelona that they would be posted to the army of Andalusia which was short of men.

—'We've been caught by the Franquistas once, we're not going to be caught again. Here in Catalonia we can get across the border,' the others said. 'We're fighting for the republic and we've got to defend it wherever we're sent,' I replied. 'We've got to be disciplined.' I was convinced we would win the war, and I took the train to report to my new unit. But the others didn't. I never saw them again . . .

Episodes 13
Execution

The men were drawn up on parade in the main square of Bolea, on the Huesca front. General Urrutia, commander of the nationalist forces, had ordered every man not on duty in the front line to be on parade. The night before, a villager had been arrested, suspected of helping Basque nationalists manning the narrow corridor into Huesca to cross the lines. The number of Basques deserting the Franquista army which they had volunteered or been called up to join after the defeat of Euzkadi was causing the general staff serious concern. Civilians in Bolea must be involved in the nightly desertions, incited by the republicans using loud-hailers from their positions only a couple of kilometres away.

At noon, as the tension grew amongst the men on parade, Lt Juan Ignacio MALZAGA, a Bilbao industrialist who had volunteered for the nationalist army when Bilbao fell, saw the general, accompanied by his staff, gallop into the square on a splendid charger, its mane tressed with the Spanish colours. They came to a halt with a clatter. The officer commanding the parade brought the troops to the general salute. Without dismounting the general ordered the prisoner brought out. The old-looking man, wearing corduroy trousers, was brought from the *guardia civil* barracks. The general bellowed: 'Step out of the ranks the soldier who denounced this man.' The soldier, a Navarrese whose father had been assassinated by the 'reds', had come the previous evening to Lt MALZAGA's unit and reported the villager to his battery commander. The soldier stepped forward. 'At your orders, *mi general.*' The general looked down on the prisoner and the soldier.

—'Soldier, do you believe in God?' 'Yes, *mi general.*' 'Do you swear by God' – all this in a sepulchral silence with the whole parade and the village listening – 'Do you swear by God that what you have said is the truth?' 'I swear, *mi general.*' 'Execute the prisoner.' . . .

A firing squad was drawn up immediately; MALZAGA's battery commander, a falangist captain, commanded it. The procession set off for the cemetery. All the village followed, including the man's relatives. The priest walked beside the prisoner.

—The old man was put up against the white cemetery wall. The firing squad took up position. For the first time, very suddenly, the old man reacted. '*Me cago en dios, ¡Viva la República!*' he shouted. The volley rang out and he fell to the ground. But so great was his strength that four shots from the officer's pistol still did not kill him. He kept struggling to rise. Finally, the captain succeeded.

I couldn't get over the directness of what had happened. On one man's orders another man could be put up against a wall and shot. Then I remembered the body of one of our soldiers who had been killed a couple of days before by an anti-personnel booby-trap; as one soldier picked up the corpse by the arms and another by the legs each was left holding half the body. These were the two visions I had of this war – the incredible impossibility of finding a means whereby the people of this country could understand each other and live together. Civilization is measured by the capacity of compromise, not by the Spanish idea that one must defend one's ideals to the death . . .

A judgement of God by a cavalry general; the desertions ended.

The National-Syndicalist Organization of the State will be inspired by the principles of Unity, Totality and Hierarchy.

The vertical trade union is an instrument at the service of the State . . .

The State recognizes private enterprise as the source of the Nation's economic life . . . All forms of property will be subordinated to the supreme interests of the Nation, as interpreted by the State.

Gradually, unremittingly, the workers' standard of living will be raised in the measure in which the Nation's superior interest permits . . .

Labour Charter (Burgos, March 1938)

Today it is not the government which needs public opinion, but the reverse: public opinion needs the government so as to prevent a return to political parties . . .

The civil governor of Seville
and national councillor of the FET y de las JONS,
Pedro Gamero del Castillo (April 1938)

***Article* 1. The organization, vigilance and control of the national press is the duty of the State . . .**

Press Law (Burgos, April 1938)

After the Italian defeat at Guadalajara, in the spring of 1937, Franco unified and took over the political forces in his zone. It was after another setback, the republican capture of Teruel, that he formed his first regular cabinet. Its composition faithfully reflected the forces in the nationalist zone: four military men, including Franco, four of the new single party (only one of whom came from the pre-war Falange), two monarchists and two technicians who were personally close to the Caudillo. The minister of public order was General Martínez Anido, who had been responsible for the repression of the CNT in Barcelona in the 1920s. The construction of the strong state, on which the bourgeoisie had wagered, was being given a new impetus.

Meanwhile, a national council of the single party had been founded. Its fifty members were all appointed directly by Franco. Its task, under the party's statutes, was to consider 'all the great national questions which the head of the movement may submit to it': the major lines of state and trade union structures, important international questions, etc. Both Dionisio RIDRUEJO, the falangist propaganda chief, and Eugenio VEGAS LATAPIE, the former editor of *Acción Española*, found themselves among the new members.

—It served no purpose. Spain was being run by Franco and his brother-in-law, Serrano Suñer, observed VEGAS LATAPIE. The latter imagined he was going to play Hitler or Mussolini to Franco's Hindenburg or Victor Emmanuel. They thought we were going simply to sit there and applaud whatever was said. I maintained on the contrary that it was necessary to say loyally what I really thought . . .

He put forward a motion which would have restricted all important posts in the nationalist zone to people who had participated ideologically or practically in the uprising's preparation. The motion was aimed at Serrano Suñer, a former

CEDA deputy, who fitted neither category. 'Although I was assured of the vote of some twenty of the fifty councillors, the motion never got that far. I was dimply dismissed.'

Shortly afterwards, VEGAS LATAPIE, whom Serrano Suñer had appointed secretary-general of press and propaganda, resigned that post and enlisted as a private in a Falange *bandera* and later in the Foreign Legion.

After a few formal sessions, the national council began discussion of the labour charter which the new Burgos government proposed to adopt. The original draft was 'so pale and paternalistic' that a commission, of which RIDRUEJO was a member, rejected it and drafted a new one.

—The charter had very concrete origins: the Italians demanded it, maintaining that it was necessary to give the new state a more progressive social look and to remove suspicion that it was simply a reactionary regime. It was one of the very few times that the Italians intervened in the internal politics of the new regime, unlike the Germans.[1]

The latter's main concern was repayment of their aid. I heard Serrano Suñer relate privately how German pressure became so great at one time that Franco said he would renounce German aid entirely and, if need be, fight the war as a guerrilla operation. 'We shall win the war in whatever way we can, for I am not prepared to sell any part of the national territory.'

RIDRUEJO defended a maximalist position on the labour charter, trying to ensure that his syndicalist ideas were put into effect.[2] His proposals were – 'of course' – defeated.

As adopted, the charter clearly delineated the structure of labour relations in the new state, basing them on the maintenance of private property and state intervention in work norms and wages. The business enterprise was to be organized hierarchically under its owner who would be responsible to the state; class trade unions were prohibited; in their place, a corporative-type vertical syndicate, based on the principles of 'Unity, Totality, Hierarchy', and including workers and employers, was set up. Any individual or collective acts that prevented 'normal production' (strikes, go-slows, etc.) would be considered treason. The syndicate – 'an instrument at the service of the state' – was to have as its leadership only militants of the single party.

—As a result of the national council's refusal to accept the original government draft, the council was never again called to meet as a deliberative organ, only to listen . . .

1. Early in 1938, the Italian foreign minister, Ciano, told VEGAS LATAPIE and a visiting Spanish mission in Rome that nationalist Spain must come out of the war with a 'clear and strong ideology, like that of Italy or Germany.' He went on to attack high Franco officials for being anglophile. The war, he insisted, was being waged more against Britain and British influence in Spain than against the Soviet Union or the republic. VEGAS LATAPIE: 'The idea that the main danger to Spain came from Britain and France was fairly common in the nationalist zone. Britain still officially recognized the republican government – as by international law it was obliged to, for it was the nationalists, the military, who were the rebels. In spite of that, many British actions – not least Non-Intervention – helped the nationalist cause. I know that the duke of Alba, who was Franco's unofficial agent in London, was being given information by an officer in the Admiralty on ships carrying arms for republican ports.'

2. See Militancies 10, pp. 313–16.

The following month, the nationalist press was 'redeemed' from its 'capitalist servitude to a reactionary or marxist clientele' and declared 'authentically and solemnly free', by Serrano Suñer's new press law. The latter gave the state the right to determine the number of newspapers and periodicals published, to intervene in the appointment of editors, to oversee everything published and to establish the rules governing the journalistic profession.

Primary school norms were revised. Under the rubrics, *Religion*, *Patriotic Education* and *Civil Education*, the following enjoinders to schoolteachers were circularized:

'Saturate all teaching with a religious spirit. Instil in the children the social catholic doctrine contained in the Encyclicals *Rerum Novarum* and *Quadrésimo Anno* . . . Exalt the Fatherland in the study of History. Permeate the school with a patriotic ambience, with popular songs and patriotic anthems . . . Instil an austere concept of life, which is the art of soldiery. Develop a spirit of brotherhood between all Spaniards. Display without fail the Caudillo's portrait in the classroom. Create, in girls' schools, a very feminine atmosphere, using the work tasks appropriate to the home . . . '[1]

During this Second Triumphal Year (as the new terminology had it), while the state apparatus was being reinforced and the ideological bases of the new state defined, Franco did not capitalize on his recent victories which had taken the nationalist army to the borders of Catalonia. Instead of advancing on Barcelona – and to final victory, as it appeared to many in the nationalist zone – he swung his forces southwards on Valencia. The offensive was thwarted by the heavily fortified XYZ line built into the Sierra de Espadán.[2] The end of the war, which had seemed so close in the spring, receded. There were rumbles of discontent which reached to the top of the nationalist command. At a falangist banquet, General Yagüe, who had led the Army of Africa's advance on Madrid, praised the republicans' fighting qualities, attacked the Germans and Italians as 'beasts of prey' and called for a revision of the repressive policies which were keeping thousands of men in gaol 'for having belonged to a party or to a trade union' – men who could be incorporated into the nationalist movement . . .

There were many, among them RIDRUEJO, who believed that Franco was waging the war with deliberate slowness. In his opinion, Franco knew that a rapid war would not provide him with the means of destroying the enemy totally, or of establishing himself solidly in power.

—A short, rapid war inevitably meant negotiations and concessions to bring it to an end. A long war meant total victory. Franco opted for the more cruel but effective solution from his own point of view. The repression bore testimony to that . . .

Undoubtedly, as Paulino AGUIRRE, the philosophy student who had been caught in no-man's-land at the start of the war, observed, many people in the nationalist zone naïvely believed that the army could advance at will and criticized it for not doing so. As a junior nationalist army officer, he knew that

1. It was now, also, that women's role in the new state was defined. See p. 310.
2. See p. 404 n.

this was impossible.[1] And yet he could not rid himself of the idea that Franco was proceeding with a studied slowness because he did not want to have to absorb too rapidly large areas of newly conquered territory with a large proportion of republican sympathizers. He wanted the republican regime's complete destruction, its unconditional surrender. It suited his inherent caution, his determination always to be on firm ground.

—Moreover, if the nationalist army, whose resources were not unlimited, had suffered any severe reverses, demoralization in the rearguard would have been very great indeed. My view was confirmed by Franco's insistence always on unconditional surrender, by the way the war ended . . .

On the night of 24–25 July, the republican army in Catalonia, which three months before had appeared on the verge of defeat, launched one of the most ambitious offensives of the war. A newly-formed army of the Ebro under communist commands crossed the Ebro river under cover of dark and established a large bridgehead on the western bank. The aim was to divert the enemy from Valencia and, if possible, to re-establish land communication with the central zone.

The nationalists were taken by surprise. Second-lieutenant Juan CRESPO, the monarchist youth from Salamanca, was ordered to lead the van of his Moroccan *regulares* battalion on a forced march to hold back the republican bridgehead at Mequinenza. In the 50 km from Gandesa covered at night, eight of his Moorish troops died of exhaustion. His sergeant lay on the ground unable to get up. CRESPO raised his riding crop. The sergeant rolled over and showed his feet – the hemp soles of his boots were worn through and his feet were a bloody pulp. He lowered the whip; he had never had to use it in battle to make his men get up to advance. As long as you led them from the front where they could clearly see you upright, they would follow. The casualty rate among subalterns was commensurately high; 'after three months you were a veteran.'

His company took up its new positions; he was raising himself off the ground

1. From within, the nationalist army sometimes appeared a less professional fighting force than it was often credited with being. A seventeen-year-old *alférez provisional* (temporary second-lieutenant) who was wounded seven times in the northern campaigns, the Teruel counter-offensive, the break-through to the sea, the Ebro and Catalan offensives, suggested that at the infantry level there was little to choose between either side. Ignacio HERNANDEZ: 'If anything, the republicans had better [Czech] machine-guns and machine rifles; we in the nationalist infantry armed ourselves with them whenever possible. Both armies lacked manoeuvrability; the Nationalist Army had relatively few professional officers in it, and the level of training of those I encountered seemed deplorable. I remember a colonel throwing a map on the ground and, without taking compass bearings, ordering us to take a hill which we knew was in the opposite direction to the enemy lines. I, as a seventeen-year-old, commanded a company; I had had only a few weeks' training; I knew no arms drill at all. The battalion was led by an *alférez provisional* for a long time. The professional officer nominally in charge of the battalion spent long stretches back at the regimental depot. We lacked mobility. We did the whole Catalan campaign on foot . . . What won the war for the Nationalist Army was its superior artillery and bombing capacity. You could almost say that the Condor Legion won the war.' It should be added that the nationalist command was able to move reinforcements to threatened fronts with greater rapidity than the Popular Army; nationalist forces, for example, were transferred in little more than twelve hours from the northern front to Brunete to stem the republican break-through in the summer of 1937.

to start the advance when a bullet hit him in the stomach. It was his second wound in three months.

The Ebro turned into a bloody, four-month battle of attrition.

Episodes 14

Survivor

He had been classified as 'indifferent'; how could anyone in this war be indifferent, he thought, as he reported for service in the republican army. It was just another sign of the regime's naïvety; you were classified as either an 'anti-fascist', a 'fascist' or 'indifferent'. Well, what did it matter if it kept him out of danger? The only thing he was determined to do in this war was to survive.

It had been a close thing to date. The war was barely a month old when Joan MESTRES was arrested in Barcelona. A born monarchist, an admirer of Dollfuss's social Catholicism, a pre-war member of Gil Robles's CEDA, he had been left on the street when the insurance company office, where he was a sub-manager, was taken over by a committee. His arrest followed. Someone denounced him. His hope of surviving, of simply living through whatever happened, vanished before he had time to work out how best his aim could be achieved.

Expecting to be assassinated at any moment, he had hardly been surprised when an FAI militant came to the gaol to demand that he be handed over to him. The man drove MESTRES to the CNT woodworkers' union headquarters, explaining en route that he had seen MESTRES's parents, a modest couple living in a working-class quarter, crying because of his arrest. As a result he had decided to take matters into his own hands.

At union headquarters, the FAI man, who lived in the same part of the city as MESTRES, went up to the union's president and began haranguing him. He had rescued MESTRES because he was born poor and lived in a poor *barrio*.

—'He is a son of the people. He is a special case, and it is unjust that he should be in prison. His only fault was to be taken in by religious propaganda; his only sin was religion. He didn't leave his house on 19 July – '

The president looked at me. 'Get up on this table,' he said. Hesitantly I climbed up. 'Silence,' shouted the president. The noise, the people milling about, the confusion that had met me when we first came in, immediately stilled. The president began addressing them as though he were holding a political meeting. 'This man didn't take up arms against the people. We believe he should be given a chance to live. A chance to purify his life, rid himself of his mistaken religious beliefs.' The crowd shouted agreement, turning immediately to other matters. Ignored, I got down from the table and went out, 'free' . . .

Only a relative freedom, however; a Popular Tribunal wanted him for trial on charges of rebellion. He went into hiding. The only thing that made life bearable to him was *Socorro Blanco* – White Aid – which started as a spontaneous movement among those who felt their lives endangered.[1] In the house where he was hiding, people helped each other in a truly Christian manner.

—There was no question of individual possessions; everything was shared. It was a marvellous example of human solidarity. Everything was heightened by the imminence of death. You became far more sensible to religion, living in a constant state of God's grace. A sort of primitive Christianity at the time of the persecutions. Sin – the sin of ordinary day-to-day life – became irrelevant, if that's the right word. Throughout the war, I never touched a woman; I'm sure there were many believers like me . . .

Survival in Barcelona looked increasingly less assured as the war continued without a decisive nationalist victory; the only course, he thought, was to escape. For 1,000 pesetas a head – half down, the balance payable on reaching safety – smugglers would guide a party of a dozen across the border to France. Each had to make his own way to the rendezvous. From there they set out on foot in the dark. They were already some way towards their destination when they heard the sounds of a patrol: the *carabineros* with dogs. The smuggler-guide insisted they turn back. There was nothing for it but to return to Barcelona; hiding was preferable to capture. He went to see the Basque government's representative, Irujo, brother of the minister in the central government. MESTRES's mother was Basque, and he was able to get a Basque identity card on the strength of it. Irujo gave him an introduction to the manager of an export company in Valencia who needed an assistant to write French and English business letters. Survival in Valencia, where he was not known, would be easier than in Barcelona. He went.

—I bought two English correspondence primers published by Pitmans and Macmillans. French was no problem, but English certainly was. In the mornings I took down the correspondence in Spanish; in the afternoons I sweated over the translations. But, at least, I seemed out of danger . . .

Unexpectedly, the government took over the company. Still wanted by a Barcelona tribunal, he found himself overnight a government civil servant in Valencia. Moreover, he was promoted to head of the export department. He did the job to the best of his ability, believing in being meticulous in all things, and because he was determined to survive. One shock followed on another: the government decided to move to Barcelona. He would have to go too. It was impossible; he risked death if he went. He decided to talk the matter over openly with his boss, a former socialist deputy for whom he had done a favour in the past.

—He looked at me amazed. 'I don't know how to help you. The only thing I can suggest is that you stay here and look for another job' . . .

1. The organization later moved into espionage and sabotage, helped people escape to France, issued doctors' certificates exempting sympathizers from military service, organized secret religious services, etc.

Before long he found work in the state import–export company, dealing with the Russians, all of whom worked under Spanish names. There he saw his first adding machine. The woman added up a long column of figures on it and when she had finished, added them all up again – in her head. He wondered why; it seemed to him that if she were to make two operations of it, it would have been more logical to proceed the other way round.

In 1938, his call-up papers came. He had been a reserve officer in the pre-war army, and was posted, as a lieutenant, to his regimental depot. His attempt to remain a survivor by setting up an NCOs' school at the depot – 'the republican army suffered enormously from a lack of NCOs and sub-lieutenants' – was soon brought to nought by his honesty. Serving as an orderly officer, he discovered that milk due to a batch of recruits had been adulterated. He protested, and it transpired that the milk had been taken by the brigade commissar. The next day he was posted to the front and the commissar disappeared from the brigade.

The chance of survival appeared reduced beyond appeal: his posting was not to an ordinary front line unit but to the newly formed Special I Brigade. The battle of the Ebro had turned against the republic. Refusing, as always, to permit a metre of nationalist territory to remain in enemy hands, Franco had launched a frontal counter-offensive on the bridgeheads across the Ebro. In mid-November, the republicans were forced to withdraw to the east bank, each side having suffered heavy casualties. A republican diversion was considered necessary. In December, Special I Brigade, composed of four battalions of specially selected men, was to land from the sea behind enemy lines at Motril, in Granada, and march on Málaga.

—We embarked in Almería one night after explosions had been set off to frighten the civilian population into their cellars and air raid shelters so no one would see us. We waited, packed in the old boats until 2 a.m. Then suddenly there was a shout. The operation had been called off. We heard that the naval commander in charge of the operation – which was to be supported by combined attacks on the Andalusian fronts – maintained that the landing was too dangerous and he would not support it . . . [1]

Posted to the Granada front, MESTRES had still to survive a republican attack. The wife of the mayor in whose house he was billeted consoled him that everyone who stayed there had always returned alive. It was a small village, and her husband, a peasant, appeared to be a communist.

—'You see,' she cried when she saw me return, 'what did I tell you?' And then she added: 'Lieutenant, the *señoritos* won't return, will they?'

It was his last action; he had achieved his aim . . .

1. Generals Miaja and Matallana refused to support the operation; the republican government had to accept this insubordination. (See H. Thomas, *The Spanish Civil War*, p. 868.)

Episodes 15

Death-watch

—The room looked as though it were a visiting place for prisoners to receive their families on Sundays or something like that. It had high windows, some benches and chairs. There was a statue of Liberty that looked like the one in New York, but perhaps it was the figure of justice carrying scales in her outstretched arms. There were some armed warders in the room. As we came into the prison there were shouts from the guards: '*¡Centinela, alerta!*' '*¡Alerta está!*' I remember all this as vividly as though it were now, although I thought for a long time that I didn't remember, that it was stories my mother and aunt told me. But it isn't so. I've proved my memories correct since then, though I was only five at the time.

We were going to spend his last night on earth with my father. In the morning he was to be shot.

He was a member of the Catholic youth workers' organization JOAC in Valencia. At the start of the war, he was thrown out of his job in the townhall for belonging to a right-wing organization. He managed to get a job in a garage first, and later as a draughtsman in a surveyor's office. My whole family, with one exception, was right-wing.

My father was arrested in January 1938, accused of having attended a clandestine meeting at which a proposal was alleged to have been made to call on the youth of military age not to answer their call-up papers. I've never been able to find out if it was true, or whether the meeting was an attempt on the part of townhall employees who had been thrown out to get some compensation or re-instatement. At most, I believe, there may have been an attempt to establish contact with *Socorro Blanco*. A court martial found him guilty and sentenced him to death. No one expected the sentence to be carried out, not that late in the war; but all appeals were in vain. It was said that there had been a massacre in the nationalist zone and that the republic was determined to show that it could reply in kind.

My first memory in life is of going to the SIM headquarters in the Calle Colón in Valencia to visit him. Then he was transferred to the model prison where I used to visit him alone, taking the parcels my mother sent. I had been taught to give the clenched fist salute to make things easier. The warders laughed: 'Here comes the fascist's son.' One day when someone sneezed, I said, '*¡Jesús!*' and they all laughed: the salute and the exclamation contradicted each other. It's a curious thing, all that time in prison I don't remember his face at all; it's like a shadow. He would tell me that he was engaged on some very difficult, special work, which was why he was there. I didn't even realize he was in prison. I never had any sense of tragedy until that last night.

They let my mother, who was thirty-three, my aunt, two years younger, myself aged five and my brother who wasn't yet two, in to spend the last night with him. As soon as I heard the sentries' shout, as soon as we went through the prison yard, I knew that something terrible was going to happen.

My father was perfectly calm. He embraced us, we sat down, we watched my brother trying to walk, playing, and it made us all laugh a bit. Then my father told me the story of Brother Wolf. Some of the warders started to swear, and he went up to them and said that he was about to die for the things they were blaspheming about, and asked them to keep quiet. Then he told me I must sleep for a while in order to be rested for the morning. 'I am very tired, too, I am going to rest a little, because there is something important I have to say to you and your mother later on, and I want to do so with complete serenity.' He sat on the bench leaning against the wall. I suppose I slept a bit. My mother says she didn't cry at all, but she must have looked so tragic, have been so obviously holding back her tears, that despite my father's sustained confidence throughout the night, I was in a constant state of terrible shock. I felt I understood perfectly what was going to happen. Not only because of my mother but from the sight of the other condemned man in the opposite corner, whose wife and daughter were both hysterical with grief. From their cries and sobs I knew that this was not a farewell such as might take place at the beginning of some ordinary journey.

During the night there was an air raid. As the bombs fell, my mother – she told me later – said to my father: 'If only a bomb would fall and kill us all – ' 'For the Lord's sake, don't think of such a thing. I shall go straight to heaven, and there I shall be able to intercede on your behalf.' His death, he assured her, was a step into the other world, where he would be awaiting her, his death was a passport to a better life.

His serenity was impressive. He had never been a very decisive or determined man; nor unduly religious, going to mass only on Sundays. None of his family expected such resoluteness of him in his last hours.

At last he told us what he wanted us to know: a message of love and fraternity. He said that he was going to die for a better Spain, for a social justice that would be brought about within a framework of order. He said that he was dying not only for us but also for the sons of people like his guards. And because this was the case, he enjoined us never to manifest a spirit of vengeance, never to want to avenge his death, because to do so would be to divide Spain into two opposing camps yet again, and therefore to perpetuate all the ills which the country had been suffering from. 'They believe they are right, and I believe that I am right. It would be tragic if Spain were to be divided again. Never hate, never harbour enmity.'

At five o'clock in the morning they came for him. As he got up to leave, he took his watch off and gave it to me. He was wearing an ordinary jacket over a pyjama jacket, and he took the former off and left that too. He was executed an hour later by firing squad. My mother's brother was serving in the barracks from which the squad was drawn by lot; happily, it did not fall on him to be a member of it.

We took a tram home. The journey seemed to last an eternity. My mother and aunt were completely silent except for their sobs. Once in a while they embraced me. I looked at their faces, saddened and fear-ridden, and the journey stretched on and on. When we got to my grandmother's house, I was put to bed, and my grandmother kept saying, 'Tomorrow father will come, tomorrow – ' And I knew perfectly well what had happened . . .

Until he was fifteen, José Antonio PEREZ believed that he had not lived through that night, that he had been told about it later by his mother and aunt. But in 1949 he had occasion to visit the prison where an uncle was serving as an army officer. The latter did not know the prison well, but José Antonio was able to locate the positions of the sentries, and the room where they had spent the night. 'In that corner was the low bench, there was the corner where my father was, over there the other condemned man. The warders sat at that table, there was the statue of Liberty. All those things had been engraved on my memory; I knew now that I had lived through that night – '

LAW

. . . Whatever concept of local administration inspires future legislation, it is clear that the Catalan Autonomy Statute, unhappily conceived by the republic, lost all Spanish juridical validity from 17 July 1936 . . .

But the entry of our glorious forces on Catalan territory poses the strictly administrative problem of the practical implementation of that abrogation. It is necessary, in consequence, to re-establish a legal system which, in accord with the principle of the Fatherland's unity, restores to those provinces the honour of being governed on an equal footing with their sister provinces of the rest of Spain.

Preamble to law, signed by General Franco, abrogating the Catalan autonomy statute (Burgos, April 1938)

Winter 1938 to Spring 1939

BARCELONA

The Ebro crossing, brilliantly conceived and executed, demonstrated finally the error of a traditional concept of war. In a direct confrontation of military strength, the odds were on the nationalist army ending the day victorious. It was a repeat, on a larger scale, of earlier republican offensives: Brunete, Belchite, Teruel. A breakthrough, exploiting the enemy's surprise; containment of the offensive by rapidly mobilized nationalist reinforcements; finally, the nationalist counter-offensive. The Ebro offensive gained time and lost vast amounts of war matériel which the republic could not replace. Fighting with their back to a river made matters no easier. The battle started at the height of the international crisis over Czechoslovakia when world war seemed imminent – which almost inevitably would have involved the bourgeois democratic powers directly in the republic's fate; it was dealt a political death-blow by the Munich pact at the end of September.[1] By the time it ended six weeks later, France had again closed her border with Spain.

Two days before Christmas, with the promise of a large infusion of German aid, Franco launched his offensive on Catalonia.

Timoteo RUIZ, nineteen-year-old communist peasant from Toledo, had been promoted lieutenant during the Ebro battle; he was now dispatched to Barcelona to raise a company to defend Catalonia. When he saw the men who reported to the Carlos Marx barracks, he was disheartened: they were all men who had been exempted from military service because of specialist skills, most of them married. Their wives and children came to see them off as they set out to hold a line along the Bruch pass. He felt the men hadn't their hearts in fighting. There was a spirit of defeat; people were war-weary.

—'Oh, when this finishes,' peasants said to me, and what they meant was that they didn't care which way it finished, as long as it finished. There was no spirit of defence as there had been in November 1936 in Madrid. The political struggles in Barcelona had sapped the people's spirit, I thought. During the defence of Madrid, ideological differences had played no part . . .

But once he got his men to the front, their combativeness rose; it was in the rearguard that the demoralization was greatest.

Among those in the rearguard called up at this late stage was Tomás ROIG LLOP, the Lliga Catalana member who had remained in Barcelona.[2] He was thirty-six. Reporting to the Francesc Macià school, he found 400 men assembled

1. A month later, the International Brigades (by now in the main manned by Spaniards) were withdrawn, following Soviet suggestions that Russia would be glad to withdraw from Spain. The Non-Intervention committee approved a plan for the withdrawal of all volunteers; some 10,000 Italian 'volunteers' were withdrawn (leaving 12,000 still in Spain). While officially supporting Non-Intervention and the withdrawal of volunteers, Britain negotiated an agreement with Italy which recognized the presence of Italian troops in Spain until the end of the war.

2. See Militancies 16, pp. 443–5.

on the third floor – all heads of families, like himself. They waited and waited, wondering what was going to become of them.

—After three hours of this, one of the men spoke up: 'Do you want to leave here?' 'Of course,' we all chorused. 'Well then, form up in a column of fours. I will act as the commander, and you will keep in step, shouting – "one-two", "one-two" as we march out – ' We formed up, and with the man giving the orders and us shouting as he had told us, we marched out of the building. We marched past the guard, still shouting 'one-two, one-two' until we had gone a short distance around a corner. Then our leader – a man of genius, a man with a real sense of humour – shouted a last 'one-two', and with that we scattered and ran. The army never saw us again . . .

1939 was not 1936, reflected Josep SOLE BARBERA, the Reus communist lawyer, now serving at the front. In Madrid, unknown heights of heroism had been scaled, expressing a true popular unity. The Catalan forces lacked neither morale nor heroism; but the circumstances had changed. The north had been lost, the Non-Intervention committee had played its part in helping the enemy, the political events since May 1937 had had their effect. 'The conditions for a resistance to the death no longer existed.'

In Barcelona, Adolfo BUESO, the POUM printer who had returned from hiding after the May events, saw only a spirit of defeat. No one, he thought, was willing to fight to the death to save the city.

—Everybody was thinking, 'How am I going to escape?' If Barcelona had been besieged in 1936, the people would have reacted as they did in Madrid. But after thirty-two months of war, their spirit had gone. People started leaving a week before the city fell . . .

Stubborn resistance at the front for a fortnight held up the advance; then weight of military strength told, and the nationalists advanced on Barcelona as fast as their columns could march. 'We could have got to the French frontier in a couple of days if anyone had thought of providing us with transport,' thought Ignacio HERNANDEZ, the seventeen-year-old temporary second lieutenant in the nationalist infantry. 'Instead, we did our 30 kilometres foot-slogging a day . . .'

On 26 January, just a month after the start of the offensive, the nationalists entered Barcelona. President Companys telephoned Josep ANDREU ABELLO, president of the Barcelona high court, and told him he wanted to leave the city with him. After dining together in Companys's *torre* in the Horta quarter, they got into ANDREU's car and drove into the centre.

—It was a night I'll never forget. The silence was total, a terrible silence, the sort you can imagine only at the height of a tragedy. We drove into the Plaça de Sant Jaume, said farewell to the Generalitat and to the city. It was 2 a.m. The vanguard of the nationalist army was already on Mount Tibidabo and close to Montjuich. We didn't believe we would return. Alone in the car we set off for Sant Hilario de Sacalm, near Gerona, where we were to spend the next three or four days on a marquess's estate . . .

Eulalia de MASRIBERA, student librarian, who had felt her loyalties divided, who had believed that the 'best day of the week' would be when 'these' left and 'those' hadn't arrived, now watched the mass exodus. The word suddenly went round: 'The people are leaving . . . '

—A tragic procession of people on foot, trudging past our house, carrying their belongings. People in mule carts, even people in cars. It went on all day and through the night. It was like those pictures of the South Vietnamese fleeing with all their possessions . . .

*

At the other end of the city, a liberal republican doctor conscripted into the nationalist army drove in with orders to take over the Clinical hospital. As he pushed open the iron gates, a man in a beret began running away.

—'They're here already,' he shouted. 'Who?' 'The fascists.' 'Yes, that's us,' I shouted. '*¡Viva España!*' he cried. 'Don't go on, I'm fed up with hearing that shout,' I replied. Then we went into the hospital. I was amazed to find a ward with all the beds made, everything in order, spotlessly clean . . .

In addition, he found a great number of right-wingers sheltering there and in the medical faculty. They appeared to have plenty of food: meat, *butifarra* and wine. That night, after a good meal, they held a dance. Dr Antonio TORRES settled down to a pleasant time; the girls were pretty and the military had plenty of food.

Eulalia de MASRIBERA watched the Moorish troops coming in. Suddenly she saw an officer lash one of them with the whip he was carrying. She cringed. 'What a horrifying, depressing sight!'

The streets of the city were littered with paper, torn-up party and union membership cards, documents. In the port the masts of bombed ships stuck out above the water. But at least everything was over, at last, thought Juana ALIER, the mill-owner's wife. The people she knew went mad with joy. 'The happiness was that the war was finished, not that one side or another had won.'

*

Within a fortnight, the nationalist army reached the French border, completing the capture of Catalonia. Nearly half a million civilians and soldiers crossed to exile and confinement in the terrible conditions of French concentration camps.

Timoteo RUIZ fought all the way to the French frontier with his hastily formed unit of men called up only a few weeks before in Barcelona, holding off the enemy by day, retreating to new positions by night. As he crossed the frontier, he and many other militants hid their small arms instead of surrendering them to the French; they were convinced that shortly they would be returning to Spain to continue the struggle. But as he marched to a concentration camp and saw the train-loads of Russian war matériel – aeroplane spare parts, artillery, ammunition, which the French had held up – he was demoralized. For the first time he realized the extent to which the bourgeois democracies had refused to help the republic. Had it not seemed, for so long, in the gathering crisis brought on by fascism, that in their *own interest* they must help? But no, they were blind. And in the light of that refusal, it was necessary to rethink the strategy of war, to learn to find means of depending only on the Spanish people's resources, of fighting to win . . . [1]

Soviet arms, shipped via France and held up on the border, came too late. Some train-loads were sent through at the last moment. Francisco ABAD, communist organizer pre-war of his Madrid regiment's clandestine soldiers' and corporals' movement, found himself, as acting military commandant of the town of Figueras, having to order trains back into France. Had they remained, they would have served only the enemy. Figueras was the last town of any size before the border. At the last minute he and his father-in-law, Lt Col. Díaz-Tendero, made for the frontier at Port Bou where they found more trains on sidings. Searching them they discovered a wagon full of republican defence ministry documentation concerning the Popular Army. With difficulty they managed to destroy it, believing it had been deliberately left there to fall into enemy hands.

The republic's last foreign ministry was set up in a village schoolhouse near the border. José LOPEZ REY, art historian and wartime head of the ministry's political and diplomatic office, and Quero, the sub-secretary, were the last civil servants left. LOPEZ REY had never believed that resistance could be continued – as Negrín publicly maintained – until a Second World War broke out. Hitler and Mussolini would not begin a world war until the Spanish civil war was liquidated; and Britain and France would not move until they were attacked. No, Negrín's other card – negotiations – was the only, if difficult, one to be played. Negotiations, he knew, had begun with the Spanish monarchy in exile sometime the previous May after Negrín announced his Thirteen Points.[2] The monarchy's restoration would go hand-in-hand with attempting to save as much of the republic's progressive legislation as possible. Without knowing the details, he wondered whether Negrín did not have in mind that, once the inevitable Second World War had broken out, it would be possible to restore a republic.

On 1 February, five days after the fall of Barcelona, the prime minister named three conditions for peace: a guarantee of Spanish independence; a guarantee of the Spanish people's right to determine their own government; and freedom from persecution. All who heard his speech to a rump meeting of the Cortes in Figueras knew that the conditions would not be accepted by Franco; thus Negrín was recommending the continuation of the war.

LOPEZ REY put the schoolhouse key in his pocket and, with his companion, walked to the frontier. He was suffering from scurvy; for the last six months in Barcelona he had eaten nothing but rice. A lettuce cost as much as 75 pesetas. It was one of the few times in his life when he had money to spare. Crossing the border without problem on his official pass, he reflected that as soon as Franco's victory looked certain, France and England would recognize the Burgos regime. Non-Intervention had been a farce. The French and English governments were cowardly; so, too, was Hitler, but everything depended on his bluff.

In the Perpignan restaurant he ordered for two. When the meals came, to the waiter's astonishment, he settled down to eat them both.

*

1. See pp. 327–8.

2. See p. 461. Negrín also attempted other avenues of negotiation, including direct contacts with representatives of the Nazi regime (see Thomas, op. cit., p. 848).

The tens of thousands of civilian refugees streaming for a fortnight over the 160 km separating Barcelona from the frontier were not so fortunate; their only concern was to reach safety. Rosa VEGA, the schoolteacher who had returned from the Soviet Union, was among them. With her was a young pregnant woman who, after some days on the road, gave birth in a *masía* without light or water; two days later, holding her baby in her arms, the woman was again struggling towards the border.

At the frontier post she watched the soldiers throw down their arms. They appeared passive, defeated.

—The French had set up big pots in which they were heating milk, and as we filed past we were each given a drink and a bit of bread. It was the saddest day of my life. Everything seemed at an end. We were defeated, we counted for nothing now . . .

The women and children were separated from the men and sent to different concentration camps. For Dr Carlos MARTINEZ, who had escaped from Asturias in a fishing smack, it was the second time in sixteen months that he was fleeing Spain. He had been fortunate to escape an air raid in Figueras which had destroyed the hospital where he was working. At the border, he watched the old men, women and children crossing into exile in the rain, the weight of defeat heavy on their shoulders. There were terrible scenes as families were separated, as they left for unknown fates in concentration camps.

—There was a general feeling that defeat, exile, would last only three or four years. The full dimension of the war seemed to have escaped these optimists. I was sure the enemy was not going to let his triumph be wrested from him that easily, that soon . . .

*

In Barcelona, Dionisio RIDRUEJO, Falange propaganda chief, prepared to put into practice an ambitious programme. Foreseeing Catalonia's fall, he had decided on the need to give the Catalans and syndicalists the impression that they had not been defeated – at least not as Catalans or as syndicalists. His project, which had the approval of the Falange's secretary-general, Fernández Cuesta, included distributing quantities of Catalan language books and manifestos. Having seen the joy on the faces of so many of the Barcelona petty bourgeois who had cheered the entry of the nationalist forces, he felt his decision was justified. Their relief that the war was over, that the hunger which lined their faces was at last to be satisfied, could – he thought – be put to good use.

The Falange was anti-separatist and fought for the unity of Spain. But for him the defeat of separatism did not mean the defeat of Catalonia's cultural autonomy. As for the anarcho-syndicalist working class, he had teams prepared to hold meetings in proletarian *barrios* to explain that the new form of syndicalism was not aimed at burying their syndicalism but of replacing it.

He went to explain his plan to the military commandant, General Alvarez Arenas. The latter barely heard him out.

—'This is a city that has sinned greatly, and it must now be sanctified. Altars should be set up in every street of the city to say masses continually,' he told me. He ordered all my material confiscated, prohibited the speaking of Catalan and forbade the meetings in working-class *barrios*. Soon posters began to appear: 'Speak Castilian, the language of the Empire.' Shopkeepers' signs were changed to Castilian; all foreign names were 'nationalized' . . .

RIDRUEJO remained in the city only a fortnight. Totally disheartened, he suffered a nervous breakdown and was hospitalized.

Barcelona was a conquered city; the Catalan nationalist middle classes would now feel the weight of Franquista Spain's cultural repression.

Article 1. All those persons who, from 1 October 1934, to before 18 July 1936, contributed to creating or aggravating the subversion suffered by Spain; and all those who, from the second above-mentioned date, opposed the National Movement actively or passively, shall be considered answerable for their political activities . . .

Law of Political Responsibilities (Burgos, February 1939)

MADRID

The sudden collapse of Catalonia dismayed the rest of the republican zone, a not inconsiderable area – about one-third of the country – stretching from Madrid to Valencia and south to Almería, and defended by four undefeated armies of about half a million men.

Negrín and some cabinet ministers, accompanied by communist political and military leaders, returned from France to the centre-south zone; but the president of the republic, many government members, the executives of political parties and trade unions, and some of the republic's top military remained in France.

On 12 February, two days after his return, the prime minister met Col. Casado, commander of the army of the centre, in Madrid. The latter said continued resistance was impossible: his army lacked aircraft, artillery and automatic weapons, the troops winter clothing; while the population of Madrid was close to starving. Recognizing the seriousness of the situation, Negrín replied that Soviet arms were in France, that peace negotiations had failed, and that food supplies for Madrid would be forthcoming. Casado asked him to call a meeting of the chiefs of the armed forces to discuss the situation; it was held four days later. The army commanders, all regular officers, were – with one exception – of like mind: the war could not continue. Admiral Buiza reported that the fleet's crews had decided to leave Spanish waters if peace negotiations were not begun. Only General Miaja, the 'hero of Madrid' and now supreme commander, argued for continued resistance. Negrín maintained that there was no other course;[1] for almost a year he had been attempting to secure peace by negotiation – without success. However, he made no concrete proposals about further resistance.

There now began a fortnight of complicated and obscure manoeuvring which was to end in tragedy.

It was abundantly clear to all that the republic could no longer hope to win the war alone; but there were different ways of bringing the war to an end. Knowing Franco's intransigence, Negrín no doubt believed that only resistance could win concessions; the imminence of world war might yet change the situation and, while resistance continued, the maximum number of people could be evacuated. Col. Casado, who became his leading antagonist, believed that Negrín's intransigence and his support by the communists were the major stumbling blocks to winning concessions from the enemy. Both men were determined to save what they could from the war; neither acted resolutely. Negrín never made clear what might be won by continued, if limited, resistance; Casado, who believed he alone could save the situation, offered the republican zone, as well as the enemy, more than he could realistically deliver and thereby allowed the chimera of an 'honourable peace' to transcend momentary ideas of resistance.

The drama was heightened by the population's war-weariness and the increasing anti-communist sentiment.[2] The absence of political mobilization in the rear, essential to a revolutionary war, had begun to tell. The communist party's dominance in the army, the police, the political commissariat, led many non-communists to fear for the future. The bitter struggles of the past were not forgotten in defeat.

While concentrating their efforts on the front, the communists continued implacably to call on a half-starving civilian population for all-out resistance in the rear. 'United we began the struggle, united we must continue until the end,' wrote *Mundo Obrero*, the Madrid communist party organ. 'Prepare for victorious resistance.' 'While an invader remains on Spanish soil, the people will be on a war-footing.'

Despite the hunger and cold, the will to resist was not totally dead. In the 'tunnel', where armaments production continued, Pedro GOMEZ, UGT

1. See Thomas, op. cit., p. 892. See also J. M. Martínez Bande, *Los cien últimos días de la república* (Barcelona, 1973), p. 96. Immediately upon his return, he had left anarcho-syndicalist leaders with a different impression. Lorenzo IÑIGO, secretary-general of the libertarian youth, was one of three members who went to see him in Valencia to determine what the government proposed to do. Military leaders, said IÑIGO, maintained that resistance was possible for no more than two months; had the government the means to organize resistance? If so – and it would require more than verbal assurances – the libertarian movement would put itself at the head of the resistance, he told the prime minister. ' "I congratulate you on your clarity," replied Negrín. "I will now answer with the same clarity and sincerity. The government has come to Valencia to save the moral values of the republic. We consider the war lost. There is no possibility of organizing resistance. I have already given orders to all civil governors to prepare the evacuation of men whose lives are at risk." There was no more to say; we left.'

2. See, for example, M. Tagüeña, *Testimonio de dos guerras* (Mexico, 1973), pp. 306 and 323.

turner, reflected on the situation. They were weary of the war and wanted it to end.

—But not in surrender – even less unconditional surrender. There were rumours of arms stocks in Valencia which would solve everything. We didn't believe we could lose the war completely . . .

Resistance, however, could not be summoned up, as in 1936, by exhortation. There must be a purpose. 'What is the meaning of resistance?' asked *Mundo Obrero*. 'To ensure Spain's peace and independence,' it answered itself. The explanation to many seemed inadequate. Would not peace come sooner without fighting to the bitter end?

—I no longer believed in the communists. Their language, everyday familiar language, was completely stereotyped; they reminded me too much of priests, the same slogans day after day, recalled Alvaro DELGADO . . .

In the past year he had discovered an aptitude for drawing, and, leaving his job as delivery boy in his father's clothes shop, became a student at the school of Fine Arts, one of the few schools to remain open in the capital throughout the war. There, he was offered a scholarship to study in the USSR; his distaste for what he had seen of communism led him to turn it down.

—The ideal of a new Spain in which social justice would reign supreme – that ideal that had moved us at the beginning of the war – no longer seemed clear. After three years, everything had become muddled for moderate left-wingers like us. We were tired of the war and beginning to hope that a right-wing victory would be what the nationalists claimed – not in fact what it turned out to be . . .

Disaffection in the rear was translated into a growing fifth column. 'What is to be in the future has great strength in the present,' thought David JATO, one of the main clandestine Falange militia leaders. As soon as they saw that the repression was no longer serious, people willing to serve the fifth column turned up in the most unexpected places.

—I wouldn't say we had people inside Casado's general staff; I'd say the majority of the staff was willing to help us. So many doctors joined that Madrid's health services were virtually in our hands. The recruiting centres were infiltrated by our men. Even some communist organizations like *Socorro Rojo* ended up in fifth column hands . . .

The clandestine Falange had one important piece of sabotage to its credit: the blowing up of a long section of metro tunnel which was being used as part of the underground munitions factory. But its main task was essentially defensive: the seizure of strategic objectives in the last stages of the war, the undermining of republican morale.

Every day, in soldier's uniforms, three clandestine falangists with forged vouchers were sent by another leader to a barracks to collect bread. 'To raise the morale of our militia we had to provide them with the one thing most of the population was lacking: food.' The youths got the bread and made off, feeling they had accomplished a dangerous mission.

—What they didn't know was that the corporal who handed them the bread was a member of our militias; that the captain in whose office the voucher was made out – amongst other, genuine vouchers – was working with us; that the colonel commanding the barracks was on our side. I had been to see him myself . . .

The Medical and Supply Corps were so full of fifth columnists that they were popularly known in Madrid as the Italian and German embassies.

The capital, reported the Quaker International Commission for the Assistance of Child Refugees, could not support life for more than another two or three months at the existing levels of food supplies.[1] There was no heat, hot water, medicines or surgical dressings. As though to underline the differences, the nationalists bombed the capital with bread.

—It came down in sacks with propaganda wrapped round it saying: 'This bread is being sent you by your nationalist brothers,' recalled Alvaro DELGADO. It was beautiful, fine white bread. Some came through a broken skylight at the Fine Arts school, and when no one was around I and other students ate so much we felt sick . . .

His action was not imitated in the streets, where people trampled the bread with rage.

—I did so myself; we were almost dying of hunger, and yet people were shouting at each other: 'Don't pick it up.' We weren't demoralized, this was proof that our enthusiasm, our support for the cause remained alive, remembered Pablo MOYA, a UGT turner.

*

From before Negrín's return, Col. Casado had had contacts with nationalist agents in Madrid. On 20 February, four days after the army commanders' meeting with the prime minister, an officer under his command appeared as a nationalist agent to give him a statement by Franco offering certain concessions to republican army men who voluntarily laid down their arms. If they had committed no crimes they would be 'generously' treated – all the more so if in the last moments of the war they served The Cause of Spain.[2]

Shortly afterwards, Col. Casado called on Régulo MARTINEZ, left republican leader in Madrid, to travel to Paris to ask Azaña to solicit French government intervention to end the war. MARTINEZ agreed. Casado was a personal friend, an authentic democrat and republican who had sworn loyalty to the republic as an army officer and abided by his oath.

—He had had several confrontations with the communists already, because of their habit of calling black white one day and white black the next, because of

1. Cited Thomas, op. cit., p. 893. 'It was almost impossible to get the peasantry to hand over its wheat in Cuenca, which was a well-known reactionary province,' observed Carmen TUDELA, who had joined the communist party during the war and was possibly the only woman civil governor in Spain at the time. 'Despite rationing, you could see plenty of bread in the villages; but only force would have made the peasantry deliver its wheat – and it wasn't considered politic to use force.'

2. See Martínez Bande, *Los cien últimos días de la república*, pp. 123 and 131.

their servile discipline to party orders. We knew the war was lost; but we republicans feared there would be an armed confrontation between the communists and anarchists before anything was resolved. The former were obsessed with the idea of continuing the war until the future European conflict began. Thanks to Soviet aid, they had been able to infiltrate so many of their members into important army posts that we feared them capable of blowing up Madrid rather than surrendering . . .

Casado wanted to prevent the fight between those who knew the war was lost – anarchists, socialists and republicans – and the communists, MARTINEZ thought. He agreed; it was useless to sacrifice more lives in a struggle so patently lost. The people were war-weary, and while there was willingness up to a point, the material means of continuing the struggle were missing.

He set off for Paris with another party member. By the time he got there, at the end of February, France and Britain had recognized the Franco regime, and Azaña had resigned as president of the republic. They were unable to see him. They talked instead to Martínez Barrio who, as speaker of the Cortes, had succeeded him; he said nothing could be done, and he would inform Casado of this.[1]

The recognition and resignation were further blows to the sinking republic. As far as regular army officers were concerned, what affected them most was, it appeared, the refusal of General Vicente Rojo, architect of the defence of Madrid, the capture of Teruel, the battle of the Ebro, to return to the republican zone. His prestige among regular officers was so great, thought Col. Jaime SOLERA, chief-of-staff of one of the four armies, that they would all have obeyed him.

—Knowing Casado, I was convinced that had Rojo been there he would not have risen. Rojo should have returned. In his absence, Casado felt free to act . . .

Col. Solera believed that surrender was the only solution. His army commander had returned from the meeting with Negrín fully persuaded that peace negotiations were about to begin, and that preparations for surrendering the army must be undertaken.

In this atmosphere of uncertainty and confusion, a curious inertia affected all organizations. Tagüeña, the brilliant young communist corps commander who had returned from France, drew up plans to seize strategic objectives in Madrid and arrest Casado. Cipriano Mera, the anarchist corps commander on the Madrid front, had earlier proposed kidnapping Negrín and forcing him to open peace negotiations. Both plans were quashed by their respective organizations. The libertarians, under instructions from their leaders in France, were preparing to end the war and save as many of their militants as possible. The communists, possibly underestimating Casado's threat – three of the four army corps in his command were led by communist officers and could be expected to quell any

1. MARTINEZ managed to return to Madrid forty-eight hours before the capital fell, having ignored advice to remain in France. 'They would certainly have shot you if they caught you there,' said Mije, the Spanish communist leader, congratulating him on having reached safety. 'One dies when one's hour comes,' he retorted, adding that it was necessary to set an example and return to Spain. However, he had considerable difficulty in getting money from any of the republican government ministers in France to allow him to return.

coup – prepared no pre-emptive move. Popular Front unity must be made to prevail. Communist militants believed the war could and must be continued; the Comintern meanwhile was preparing to liquidate it.[1]

Looking out over the war-torn city from a balcony of the JSU headquarters, Ricardo SALER feared for the first time that the war might be lost. A pre-war communist youth member, now on the JSU executive, he had just received the assignment of going to Valencia to organize student resistance if Madrid fell to the threatening Franquista offensive. Beside him stood his comrade, Azcárate.

—He turned to me and said, very emphatically: 'There's no problem if we lose, it will be for only a very short time.' And then he went on to talk of the need to resist for as long as possible because a world war was inevitably going to break out soon; the longer we held out the more chance there was of linking our cause to the world war. I think at that moment we reflected the thinking of the communist party leadership, and perhaps even of Negrín . . .

Those who 'didn't believe in miracles', like Sócrates GOMEZ, former socialist youth member of the JSU, were convinced that Negrín lacked any policy whatsoever. Symptomatic of this, in GOMEZ's view, was that government ministers in the capital could not locate the prime minister when they needed him. He had come to Madrid, called for resistance, and left immediately for Alicante. When they were able to see him, it was usually hurriedly and without prior planning.

—All this added to the confusion. Moreover, while calling for resistance, Negrín had given instructions for the delivery of passports to be speeded up for anyone who wanted to leave, recalled GOMEZ, whose father was civil governor of Madrid . . .

Negrín promoted Casado to general, and informed him he was to become chief of the central general staff, which would have removed him from Madrid. Two days later, on 3 March, the ministry of defence Official Gazette published the promotions of a series of communist officers to the commands, amongst others, of Alicante and Cartagena, ports which would be vital in any evacuation. Negrín's plans to resist were made manifest by his reliance on his only possible allies, even if both he and they were in fact uncertain about the possible extent of resistance. It was rumoured that even more sweeping changes were imminent.

In Madrid, as Eduardo de GUZMAN, libertarian journalist, recalled, the other parties and organizations reacted out of fear of what might happen next.

—Especially after what *had* happened in May 1937, in Barcelona. If the communists succeeded in monopolizing power, it could only be at the expense of all other organizations. It was impossible to know whether the communists were manipulating Negrín or whether Negrín was manipulating them. Our reaction was designed as a purely defensive movement against a communist take-over . . .

1. 'If the government is willing to continue resistance, the communist party will support it. If, on the other hand, it is determined to negotiate peace terms, the communist party will not put any obstacles in its way,' Negrín was told by a communist party delegation (see D. Ibarruri, *They Shall Not Pass*, London, 1967, p. 335).

—With absolutely no intention of seeking revenge against them, assured Sócrates GOMEZ. But if the communist party succeeded in taking over all key commands, the results would be incalculable. Negrín's appointments speeded up our next move . . .

For two and a half years, the over-riding aim of winning the war had, in the last resort, prevented the break-up of the republican camp. Now, with only defeat ahead, political hostilities broke into a final, confused, bloody conflict. It began in Cartagena where, on the night of 4 March, units of the important republican naval base revolted against the appointment of the new communist commandant; soon the fifth column also rose. Threatened by a shore battery (commanded by an officer who turned out to be a nationalist) and attacked by enemy bombers, the fleet the next morning put out to sea and internment by the French in Bizerta. At one blow, the republic lost the means of evacuating significant numbers of people.

That evening (5 March) in Madrid, Casado formed a national defence council in which socialists, anarchists and republicans were represented. Its leading figure was Julián Besteiro, leader of the socialist right-wing, who had become increasingly anti-communist during the war, which he had spent in the capital as a municipal councillor. The radio broadcast a manifesto. 'As revolutionaries, as proletarians, as Spaniards, as anti-fascists, we cannot any longer endure the imprudence and lack of planning of Dr Negrín's government . . . We cannot tolerate a situation in which bitter resistance is demanded of the population, while preparations for comfortable and profitable flight continue . . . We who oppose the policy of resistance give our assurance that not one of those who ought to remain in Spain shall leave until all who wish to leave have done so.'

—Our aim was to take over from a government which, to all intents and purposes, was inoperative, in order to save the lives of combatants and political militants in a situation where the war was lost and there was very little chance of negotiations succeeding, explained Sócrates GOMEZ, who became a junior member of the new council . . .

In Elda, near Alicante, where Negrín had established his headquarters since his return three weeks earlier, the cabinet was discussing the text of a radio speech the prime minister was to make to the republican zone the following day. Telephone calls from Negrín and other ministers to Casado produced no results. The following dawn, the government decided to leave Spain; but while waiting for his plane, Negrín consulted communist leaders. A communist staff officer, Ricardo RODRIGUEZ, was present.

—There was a great deal of confusion; we all more or less attended the meetings. Togliatti (the Comintern's main representative in Spain) advised Negrín to send a message to Casado's defence council saying that, while the government deplored the disastrous situation, it could and should be discussed in order to avoid a bloody conflict, and to reach a settlement with the common enemy . . .

Negrín drew up a message to this effect, and RODRIGUEZ was sent to find a telex to transmit it to Madrid. He was ordered to wait only a certain time for an answer. Thereafter, he was to return with the copy. No reply came. 'I went back and handed over the telex carbon to Alvarez del Vayo, the foreign minister.'[1]

Fearing that the Casado forces might arrest them, the government flew off to France and North Africa; the newly appointed communist commandant of Alicante, only 40 km away, had already been detained. That evening, the communist party's central committee held its last meeting in Spain for thirty-eight years. Togliatti said that responsibility for ending the war would have to be left to the Casado council which was the only real authority. To wage an armed struggle against it would be to start a civil war within the civil war. The communists, champions of unity, could not engage in such a struggle, he asserted. Was he unaware that since 6 a.m. that day, communist-led forces in Madrid had been successfully attacking Casado? He made no mention of it.[2] That evening and the next day, the communist leaders flew out of the country. Togliatti, Checa, Hernández and Claudín remained behind to organize the evacuation of as many communist militants as possible.

MADRID

A shout went up in the 'tunnel' where he was working. 'The communists are coming!' Almost all the men in Pedro GOMEZ's workshop tried to flee; some of them escaped through the cesspit under the prime minister's office.

—'What's going on here?' the communists asked those of us who remained. 'Nothing.' 'You keep on working. We're up above and nothing will happen.' So while the fighting went on in the streets, we went on working below. We had no difficulty getting to work through the battle . . .

After two days, the communist troops attacking Casado's small forces virtually controlled the city, having besieged their enemy in a number of isolated buildings. General Miaja, once the hero of the communists, and the only senior officer to agree but a fortnight before with Negrín on the need for resistance, switched sides and became president of the defence council. Other officers had already shown that their communist sympathies (and even party membership) had been no more than momentary opportunism. Wherever their opponents were in control, communist militants were rounded up en masse. Under arrest, Julián VAZQUEZ, communist garment workers' union leader, believed that their blind faith in ultimate victory had prevented party members like himself from

1. See p. 494 n. for further details.

2. See M. Tagüeña, *Testimonio de dos guerras*, p. 316. The communist corps commander reflected that the political line was no last-minute improvisation and explained the party's passivity in the face of Casado's well-known plans. Only two days later, in France, did he learn from the newspapers that his comrades were fighting Casado. The initial confusion, however, was very great. Narciso JULIAN, communist armoured brigade commander, found, when he was arrested trying to return to Madrid, that even communists and JSU members had joined the Casado forces at the beginning, on rumours that political-military leaders had fled. (There is some evidence that the party sent orders to some of its units round Madrid to move against the defence council. [See Martínez Bande, op. cit., pp. 181–2.] GUZMAN, who was in gaol after the war with Maj. Ascanio, the communist officer who led the first forces against Casado, maintains that he told him he had received party orders to attack. But nowhere is it clear at what level these orders were given.)

seeing reality. Others, like Miguel NUÑEZ, felt that the Casado supporters had a demented idea of the fate that awaited them.

—They believed that the Popular Army would be combined with the nationalist army; that the republicans would be sent on a short course – those officers who weren't communists, naturally – and then be incorporated in the new, united army, at one rank below their present one . . .

NUÑEZ, the former education militiaman and now a political commissar, told the officers who had ordered his arrest that they were mad. The fascists were not nineteenth-century liberals.[1] He was taken off to prison where he was held until the day the nationalists started to move into Madrid . . .

The fighting lasted a week. To save the situation for the defence council, the anarchist leader Cipriano Mera, who had supported Casado from the beginning, called in reinforcements from his army corps reserves. The news that the government and communist leaders had left the country became widely known; the communist-led troops began to vacillate, then retreat. Throughout the fighting, which caused several hundred casualties, civilian life continued in a state of suspended animation. Amidst the desolation of two simultaneous civil wars, Alvaro DELGADO stood in the Plaza de Colón, discussing Goethe's *Werther* with the girl he had fallen in love with at the school of Fine Arts. A shell exploded, killing a man in front of them, his brains splattering onto a tree. 'We went on with our discussion. Our lack of concern for the war was total; we fled from reality into German romanticism and painting.'

None the less, the fighting gave him a daily excuse to prove his love to Margarita. Every evening, he crossed the lines from her house to his after seeing her home. 'You could tell by the newspapers being sold which zone you were in. The soldiers kneeling in doorways firing down Alcalá at the war ministry in the Plaza de Cibeles gave you an idea of where the shooting began and ended.' Once safely home, he rang up to tell Margarita of his arrival, offering her his 'heroism' as a token of adolescent love.

By 12 March, the fighting was over and Casado's defence council was the only authority in the republican zone. The three communist corps commanders on the Madrid front were dismissed, and one of them executed. Possibly the conflict had been entirely unnecessary.

During the fighting, the communist forces occupied the civil government building and arrested the socialist incumbent, Gómez Ossorio, although he had not supported the defence council. On his release, he returned to his office where his son, Sócrates GOMEZ, watched him rummage in the drawers of his desk. Failing to find what he was looking for, he told his son that two sheets of hand-

1. Historical precedent suggested the idea. The first Carlist civil war ended in 1839 with the Convention of Vergara which safeguarded defeated Carlist officers' pay and promotion in the Spanish army.

On the southern front at this moment some Popular Army units were issued with Spanish army regulation white parade gloves. 'I hadn't had a uniform the whole time I'd been in the army. Multiforms rather than uniforms were what we all wore. And now white gloves! It was as though the commanders expected a glorious reconciliation parade between the two opposing armies . . .' (Joan MESTRES: see Episodes 14, pp. 473–5).

written notes given him by Negrín had disappeared; they were the notes of the broadcast the prime minister intended to make on 6 March, and which he had given Gómez three days before when, on one of his rapid trips to Madrid, he instructed the civil governor to prepare the radio broadcast from his office. Not finding the sheets, Gómez told his son what they contained. Negrín was going to announce that the war was lost.

—The speech contained a number of diatribes against foreign governments, particularly the British and French, for being to blame for the defeat; and great praise for the heroism and spirit of sacrifice of the republican combatants. But, the speech went on, there was no way of continuing the war; it was 'each for himself' now, so to speak . . . [1]

Militancies 18

ANTONIO PEREZ

Socialist youth political commissar

He was fiddling with the knobs of the artillery group's radio trying to get some music. Tuning in to an enemy station broadcasting from Andalusia which, for reasons of morale, he normally wouldn't listen to, he heard the programme interrupted by an announcer giving news of a communist uprising in Madrid. He didn't believe it. Tuning in to Madrid, he heard the news of the Casado coup. He didn't need to think twice to know that the latter meant surrender, and that he was totally opposed. Taking out one of the radio's valves, he hurried to find the head of the SIM, a communist who shared his room. At that moment, he thought, he was probably the only person in the unit who had heard what was going on in Madrid.

—'Look. I'm a member of the socialist party and the JSU. I'm in complete disagreement with my party's position and in agreement with that of the JSU.' The SIM chief told me to lay my hands on as many spare rifles as possible while he called a communist militants' meeting. 'Good,' I said. 'I'd also like to

1. As the speech was never made, and the notes lost, no proof can be adduced for this version, as Sócrates GOMEZ recognized. However, some evidence exists. On 5 March, the cabinet was discussing the radio speech Negrín was due to broadcast the following day when it received news of Casado's coup. The last telexed message sent by Negrín to Casado on 6 March (which, as we have seen, received no reply) stated, among other things, the following: 'If they [the defence council] had waited for the explanation of the present position, which was to have been given tonight in the government's name, it is certain that this unfortunate episode would never have taken place. If contact between the government and those sectors which appear to be in disagreement could have been established in time, there is no doubt whatsoever that all differences would have been removed.' And, finally, a hint that, if peace demanded it, the government was willing to make way for the defence council: 'Inasmuch as it is of interest to Spain, it is of interest to the government that, whatsoever may happen, any transfer of authority should take place in a normal, constitutional manner.' (See text of statement in J. Alvarez del Vayo, *Freedom's Battle*, New York, 1940, pp. 298–9.)

put in my application to join the communist party.' 'All right, you're a member as of now. You can attend the meeting' . . .

At the meeting, it was decided that each should immediately go to different batteries and artillery groups on their sector of the Valencia front to rally the militants. On their return, they began to clean the rifles he had got hold of in preparation for taking over the radio and telephone posts. Suddenly, the door was kicked in and a sergeant, pistol in hand, with soldiers behind him, arrested them. Under protest, he was taken to the commanding officer, who informed him he had just received a teleprinter message to arrest anyone opposed to the government.

—'From what I've heard,' I said, 'it is you rather than I who are opposing the government. I recognize only Dr Negrín.' 'I'm not discussing politics with you,' he replied. He offered me the possibility of remaining in my room on my word of honour not to escape. I refused. So I was held under guard. I was allowed the newspapers, and from these I learnt that my father had been appointed a member of Casado's defence junta on behalf of the UGT . . .

It seemed an eternity since, leaving his father who had to remain in Madrid, he had set off to spend the summer of 1936 in the family house in the mountains. When his father, who was secretary-general of the socialist railwaymen's union, was not in gaol – the Popular Front elections had released him and thousands of others who had been imprisoned since October 1934 – the family could just afford to leave the capital for the cool of the Guadarrama. They lived modestly at all times, for whatever his political fortune, their father exhibited the absolute, even excessive, working-class honesty characteristic of all the socialist leaders. It was, he thought, a very working-class party, formed in the paternalistic image of its founder, Pablo Iglesias. The majority of its leaders had never read a line of Marx.

When the news reached them of the uprising from people fleeing Segovia, they decided it was not safe to stay in the hamlet. People had been shot in the nearest large village, they heard. For five days, their mother, aunt, the two maids and three boys walked over the mountains, guided by shepherds. Going in the opposite direction, they heard, were priests and some nuns. One night, he and his brothers mounted guard inside a shepherd's shack where the women were sleeping; their arms were the catapults they had made during the holiday. He remembered it with a laugh; he had gone from a boy's world of shooting at birds with a catapult to a new world of rifles and killing men.

Reaching Madrid, he volunteered immediately for the militia. He was just sixteen, a student of commerce; his brother, who was a year younger, joined up also. Within a couple of months of service at the front, he was a sergeant in the artillery, having completed a fortnight's course.

He was in the army to fight fascism, to defend the republic, not to make the revolution; though he had no doubt that a victorious republic would be very different to the pre-war regime. Important social conquests had already been won, and the existence of the Popular Army meant that the defence of these conquests was in the hands of the people. The communist party, which from the start had best understood the needs of the war, and had developed a political strategy which corresponded most fully to the reality of the moment, understood very well the importance of controlling the army in as far as it could. Any party with an ounce of political consistency must be thinking not only of the present, but of the future and the links between the two.

The socialist party had been a disappointment. Its decline from its position as the major working-class party at the start of the war could not be hidden by the fact that it had provided the majority of the government and both prime ministers since September 1936. It was due in part to the contradictions between the party's three tendencies, he thought.[1] In peace time the party could continue despite them, but in war – when its decisions affected not just the party but the lives of hundreds of thousands of people who weren't even members – it was a different matter. Largo Caballero had made serious mistakes in the conduct of the war. He seemed to be living in the past, his methods were traditional and bureaucratic. He made ill-judged statements, attacked the communists unnecessarily, lost his temper. He was no longer a guide.

As a Caballero supporter himself, a revolutionary socialist youth close to communist positions, he couldn't help but see that Caballero was failing to live up to the needs of the moment. These could be summed up in a few words.

—The need to defend ourselves, the republic; the need to enlist the active support of the bulk of the population in the struggle – only fascists or insurgent supporters should be kept out; the need to strain every effort to winning the war. People were not fighting to make the revolution, not living the war as a projection of the future; they were fighting to defend the republic . . .

The communist party had understood this, he thought, had analysed Spanish development and realized that the situation was not ripe for a socialist revolution. The party had not 'camouflaged' the revolution, as some liked to say, had not decided to 'appease' the bourgeois democracies. No, the party's strategy responded to a concrete situation, in which support for the socialist revolution would inevitably have jeopardized the alliance with large sectors of the masses who were not prepared for revolution, but were willing to fight the common enemy. Thousands upon thousands of people had joined the communist party without thought of socialism; most of them didn't know what they wanted politically except to be in an efficient and strong party. The fact that the communist party's policy corresponded more closely to reality than the socialist party's in some part explained the latter's decline.

Not that the communist party and the JSU had been immune from mistakes. One of the biggest of these, undoubtedly – its effects were being experienced in the Casado coup – was the lack of mass political work in the rear. It had made them very vulnerable at the front; they had been much too involved in their localized concerns while, behind them, the rearguard had been allowed to disintegrate. Communist and JSU militants had devoted all their efforts to the problems of the military war. In the rear, the average citizen's problems – of which there were plenty – had been dealt with only in global terms by a few

1. The unification, just before the outbreak of war, of the socialist and communist youth movements in the unified socialist youth (JSU) also deprived the socialist party of one of its bases of support. Led by Santiago Carrillo, the JSU swung to communist positions after many of its leaders joined the PCE in November 1936.

political leaders who expressed their party's line. They would have to suffer the consequences of that mistake in the coming weeks.[1]

One error which, happily, had not been made was to split up the JSU into its two constituent parts. He had resisted considerable pressure early in the war to support such a move. A sector of the socialist party argued that the party needed its own youth movement again. Unified socialist youth members, they claimed, tended now to join the communists and not the socialist party.

These arguments, he thought, lacked validity. If the JSU considered the communist party's policy the correct one, then its members – and there were over 1 million by now – should support it. If they thought the communists represented their interests better than the socialists, it was right that they joined the communist party. The party with the correct positions should gain members.

—What would have happened to the masses of youth who had joined without previously belonging to the communist or socialist youth movements if the JSU had split up? Where would they have gone? They had joined the JSU because it was a well-run organization which demanded no previous adherence to any political position other than that of being anti-fascist . . .

After the enemy cut the republic in two the previous spring, he had been made a commissar. As such you did everything: tried to keep up the soldiers' morale, looked after their physical needs, their comfort and security. A sort of personal counsellor, an intermediary between the soldier with his human problems, and the commander with his military requirements and orders.

—You could incur serious tension with the military commander, if he was a man who concerned himself only with military matters or belonged to a different political organization. But, despite that, it was a fascinating and worthwhile job. The level of commissars varied greatly. Some were bureaucrats, others turned themselves into the military commander's personal secretary; others lived entirely without contact with their men, and others again lived so totally with their men that they barely ever appeared at staff HQ, and when they did, turned up dirty and unshaven . . .

As defence minister, Prieto made sweeping new appointments of commissars to eliminate those appointed by the communists. Replacing men much loved by the soldiers, the new commissars tended to be bureaucrats, he observed. In fact, it would have been better if the commissars had been elected by the men themselves. That would have prevented the corps ending up as a fairly mediocre body of men . . .

He read in a paper that his father, labour councillor in the Casado defence council, was shortly to make a trip to Valencia, and he asked his commanding

1. The communist party's Madrid provincial congress, held from 8 to 11 February 1939, 'uncovered the weakness of our work in Madrid at the time when the socialists had increased their activities and were undermining the influence which we had acquired at the cost of so much effort and sacrifice', wrote La Pasionaria. (Ibarruri, *They Shall Not Pass*, p. 332.)

officer to be allowed to see him. The former agreed, taking him in his car to Valencia where he had official business. As they pulled up in front of the hotel, he saw his father emerging. He jumped out and ran towards him; his father's two bodyguards nearly gunned him down.

—'We can't stand here talking,' my father said. 'Get into my car.' As we drove off, I said: 'You've all gone mad; this is monstrous. You've lost everything – dignity, political judgement, rationality. All you're offering is complete surrender of everything we've been fighting for. I'm utterly opposed. I've been under arrest because of it – '

'I'll have Casado send an order immediately to have you released. That's the first thing. Next: have you got any photographs of yourself? No? Get me some quickly so I can get you a passport.'

'A passport? What for?' 'To leave the country, of course.' 'I'm not leaving. What right have you to dispose of my life as a militant and revolutionary?' 'It's not a question of that. One of the things we're attempting to negotiate with the Burgos government is that everyone who wants to leave shall be free to do so. Lists are being drawn up. I don't imagine you will want to stay in Spain once the army has surrendered.'

'That is correct. But I refuse to accept the way this is being settled. We have the capacity to resist another four to six months; by that time, the international situation may have changed. A world war may have broken out.'

'You young people don't understand the first thing about these matters . . . '

'In that case, I think I'm getting sick of adults. You have the wisdom, the experience, the professional qualifications – but it seems to me you are completely blind. Though we lack experience and all the rest, it is the youth who understand the real situation . . . '

My father refused to discuss it further, saying only that the war was lost and that it was preferable to come to an honourable agreement with the enemy.

'How can you expect an honourable agreement with fascists? It's impossible. That's where your theory breaks down.'

'No, we've already established contacts with them – ' and he went on to talk about the English, the world and I don't know what else. Finally, he told me to introduce him to my military commander, and he asked the latter to free me, saying a teleprinter order would come that afternoon from Madrid. I accepted the release, but told him I would give no promise as to my conduct.

'All right,' he said. 'I have done what I could.' We embraced and said farewell . . . [1]

1. It was not the only case of a family divided: Wenceslao Carrillo, socialist supporter of Largo Caballero in the past, served on the Casado defence council. His son, Santiago Carrillo, communist secretary-general of the JSU, who had not returned from France after the fall of Catalonia, remained staunchly opposed. On the other hand, Sócrates Gómez, a junior socialist council member, was elected president of the socialist youth which withdrew from the JSU; at the same time, his father, the civil governor of Madrid, was elected president of the re-organized socialist party executive; father and son thus led the twin socialist organizations for a short time.

I distrust any bargain. Everything will be decided by arms . . . The reds will never accept the conditions which I shall impose. The state I want to erect is the complete antithesis of what they want . . .

**General Franco to Roberto Cantalupo,
Italian ambassador (Spring 1937)**

Whoever desires mediation serves, consciously or unconsciously, the reds and Spain's hidden enemies.

General Franco (Speech, Summer 1938)

The surrender must be unconditional . . . If Madrid accepts we will not fight; otherwise we shall take it by force, it makes no difference to us.

**General Franco, telegram to his staff headquarters
(25 February 1939)**

MADRID

For two weeks, from 12 March, the defence council attempted to negotiate 'an honourable peace' with the Burgos regime. On 15 March, Hitler marched into Prague; at the end of the month, the Anglo-French guarantee to Poland transformed the international situation. Had the republic remained intact even this short time, had it drawn up a realistic last-stand policy to use in negotiations with Burgos, the situation might have changed. As it was, there could be few illusions of success, believed Sócrates GOMEZ. It was naïve to imagine that concessions could be wrung from the enemy when defeat was inevitable, when everyone knew how the nationalists had acted in their own zone.

—What were we to do? Besteiro always believed that we wouldn't succeed, but that we had to try. The council's fundamental aim was to save the lives of combatants and those who, because of their political pasts, were in danger. We couldn't abandon what was left of the republican zone, leave every man to fend for himself. Having heard from my father the details of Negrín's intended broadcast, I felt that the council – so often accused of being liquidationist – was doing nothing other than what he had planned . . .

Franco was adamant, as he had been throughout the war: only unconditional surrender. By 22 March, the defence council had accepted the principle, but was still trying to ensure one condition: the evacuation of those who wanted to leave.

—If we couldn't get that, the only solution was revolutionary war; this was what the libertarian movement proposed, Eduardo de GUZMAN recalled. We were all aware of the fate that awaited us if we fell into enemy hands. Málaga and the north had taught us that. We still held ten provinces, had half a million troops; we could carry out a desperate struggle for several months. A scorched earth policy, if need be, as we fought our way back to Cartagena . . .

But such a threat was not made with full force. Two republican military envoys flew to Burgos to 'negotiate'; to their question as to whether evacuation was possible, their nationalist counterparts replied by demanding that the republican air force surrender the following day, 25 March, and the army two days later. On the defence council, Wenceslao Carrillo, for the socialists, and the libertarian representatives refused to agree to surrender unless Franco signed a document agreeing on terms; the struggle would otherwise continue. On 25 March, the two envoys again flew to Burgos; but this time the talks were cut off by the nationalist High Command: the republican air force had not surrendered, and now it was too late. The final nationalist offensive was planned to start at dawn the next day, Sunday, 26 March.

In Madrid, the libertarians agreed to implement their last-stand policy, according to GUZMAN, who was given the task of drawing up a manifesto calling for all-out struggle, warning of the fate which awaited people if there was unconditional surrender. The libertarian representatives on the council, which was meeting again, assured them that it would support the libertarian stand. They waited; the manifesto was to be broadcast at the end of the meeting.

—Then someone rang. We couldn't believe it. The defence council had voted against, had agreed to the enemy demand that the white flag should be raised by our forces as the nationalist troops advanced . . .

At this late stage, the libertarians' plan was no more than rhetoric, believed Sócrates GOMEZ. There was no certainty that the troops, who were now expecting surrender, were prepared to obey. The defence council's mistake was not to have envisaged such a plan itself much earlier, not to have prepared it properly and executed it. 'But now it was too late.'

When the negotiations collapsed, Casado rang Col. Jaime SOLERA's army headquarters.

—He told me (something that I believe has never been properly reported) that in his opinion it was now necessary to resist at all costs. He himself was prepared to lead the resistance. I don't know whether he was sincere or speaking out of despair. In any case, the order to raise the white flag on all fronts came from him, too . . .

There was little else that could be done, the colonel thought. Everywhere except on the Madrid front the troops, who knew what to expect, had begun to desert.

To organize all-out resistance while unconditional surrender was being negotiated was an evident impossibility. Once again – and now for the last time – the libertarian movement had reacted rather than taken the lead. Nowhere, with the exception of the defence of Madrid two and a half years ago, had total revolutionary war been waged. The fusion of trained combatants and civilians in desperate resistance, scorched earth and sabotage – it was too late for that now. The proletarian revolution had not developed its own revolutionary instruments and strategies of war; it had suffered defeat as a result. The communist democratic revolution had made good the deficiency by concentrating on building a war machine equal to, if not modelled on, the one it faced across the lines. The machine had appeared to many as an instrument of a single party, not proletarian pluralist, rule. The spectre of Stalinist dictatorship haunted Popular Front Spain; the repressed revolution had returned as anti-communism.

—As the white flag was raised, the troops threw down their rifles and abandoned the lines; some fraternized with the enemy . . .

In the lorry he had commandeered, Antonio PEREZ looked at the crowds of soldiers jamming the main Valencia road. There were white flags everywhere, an air of fiesta. They were singing and shouting exultantly, 'the war is over'.

—'All these men are returning to their villages and to certain death,' I said to my companion. I became tremendously depressed. We had to draw our pistols to prevent soldiers climbing onto our lorry. Finally, we were able to reach Valencia . . .

While the young political commissar, newly a communist in the hour of defeat, made for the military government building in Valencia, the nationalists launched offensives around Madrid. The following day, 28 March, amid a desperate last-minute exodus, the end came for the capital: what was left of the army surrendered.

At 8.30 that Tuesday morning, a friend of Pablo MOYA's came to the workshop and called the UGT turner.

—'Pablo. You don't still doubt that the war is over, do you?' 'Marcelino,' I replied, 'do me the favour of leaving immediately. We're friends, and I don't want to have a fight with you.' That was the last day of the war. Imagine how blind, how full of enthusiasm and faith I still was. I thought the defence council still had cards in its hand, I believed the democratic countries would say, 'It is only just that we help smooth the way to negotiations now . . . '

In the embassy where he had been in hiding for two years,[1] Enrique MIRET MAGDALENA was awoken by shouts. '*¡Viva España!*' The Catholic student thought the other refugees had gone mad. During the fighting between the communists and the Casado forces, they had been on the edge of despair, their imprisonment seemingly doomed to continue for ever. He went into the corridor and saw others throwing their sheets in the air. Madrid was free!

—Suddenly everyone started handing out tobacco, I don't know where they had

1. See Episodes 5, pp. 298–300.

kept it hidden for so long. We threw open the shutters. It was the first time I had seen the street for two years and nine days. I leapt out. It was true, there were people shouting '*¡ Viva España!*' . . .

The fifth column was demonstrating in the streets when María DIAZ arrived in an army lorry. It was twenty-eight months since she had left the North Station as a militiawoman alongside her father to meet the enemy at the gates of Madrid; the same length of time that she had been a communist. She heard the demonstrators shouting hysterically that they had been liberated. Running up the stairs of her uncle's house, unable to contain her hysteria, she began screaming: 'Ay! we've been liberated, uncle, liberated.'

—'What's come over you, girl?' My uncle looked at me. Then I broke down and I cried and cried . . .

The scene remained engraved on his mind. The jubilant right-wingers sweeping through the working-class quarter; the workers didn't attack them, didn't shout back. It was the look of hatred and despair on their faces that José VERGARA, the 'neutral' agrarian reform expert, would never forget. 'They knew there was nothing they could do; they had lost the war.'

Soldiers in capes came in from the front. Alvaro DELGADO watched them throwing their rifles down in the streets. The sun was shining brightly. He walked down the street to get away from the gloom that had overtaken his home. His right-wing relatives had just telephoned to share their joy with his mother; but she wasn't to be consoled. She hadn't forgotten her brother, a moderate republican, who had been executed by the nationalists in Andalusia.

The Plaza de España was crammed with demonstrators. A short time before, right-wingers in a lorry had stopped and forced her cousin in his republican military uniform to give the fascist salute. All around her, people were raising their arms outstretched. Her girlfriend and her girlfriend's mother were doing the same. María PLAZA was frightened they would notice. But she was only a child, and no one paid any attention. Daughter of a life-long republican, she couldn't bring herself to give the salute. Everywhere there were blue shirts. She couldn't believe that so many falangists had been hidden in Madrid. The women impressed her most; the *señoritas* of the 'good' families from the Salamanca neighbourhood shouting: 'At last, at last,' and singing *Cara al Sol.*

—On all their faces I saw not joy but hatred and rage. Hatred for the population amongst whom they had been living, the ordinary working people of Madrid . . .

ALICANTE

Fifteen thousand men, women and children were crammed in the port area; many of them had already spent forty-eight hours in the open waiting. Ships, insistent rumour had it, were on their way. Since the fall of Madrid on Tuesday, Alicante had become the last major possibility of escape. The refugees who poured into the chaotic conditions of Valencia from all parts of the republican zone were given only one word of hope: Alicante. A ship was waiting. By Wednesday morning, when the first large contingents reached the port, they found it empty. The ship had sailed, with only a few passengers, at dawn, the captain no doubt fearing that he would be stormed by thousands of anguished refugees determined not to be left to their fate.

Despite efforts made to maintain morale, many were beginning to despair. The republican fleet's desertion proved a bitter blow now. On their first night, the refugees had seen two ships, a few hours apart, approach the docks. The promised relief had at last arrived. Spirits soared. As the ships closed in, each suddenly stopped, put about and inexplicably sailed off. It was more than many could bear. With their backs to the sea and the enemy in front, the refugees felt they had been deliberately trapped in the port to make their capture and death easier. It was the last straw.

—Defeated, we were now being betrayed. I don't believe I could bear to relive such anguish. Seeing those boats arrive and then turn away. Too many emotions for one person to bear . . .

Carmen CAAMAÑO, a librarian, clutched her newborn baby to her. It was another French and English betrayal, she was sure. She had managed to get to Alicante two days before and the captain of an English freighter had promised to take her off. But as he lowered the gangplank, twenty or more people suddenly appeared and wanted to board the ship. The master asked them to leave, he would only take her. They refused, he had pulled up the gangplank and made ready to sail. She stood on the quay watching the freighter leave.

His eyes glued to the horizon, searching for the faintest sign of a ship, Saturnino CAROD imagined the terrible scene that would take place if a ship did finally arrive. Commissions representing all the political parties and organizations had been set up, discussions had gone on endlessly with the local consuls, especially the French, who assured them that the French navy was coming to the rescue. Ships of the Mid-Atlantic Company, which had been responsible for most of the republican maritime transport, refused to help; the company alleged that its contract was with Negrín, not Casado, and that it had not been paid. Lists and more lists of those whose political record put their lives in greatest danger had been drawn up. Each party and organization had its quota, and these would be evacuated first on the French ships. The Aragonese CNT militant and divisional commissar[1] was on the list. But if a ship came that would mean nothing. There would be a bloody battle – the majority of those waiting were armed, military men like himself – because everyone was determined to embark. 'Let's hope the ships don't arrive,' he said to himself, unable to tear his eyes from the horizon and the hope of seeing a ship.

As he stood staring out to sea, the man standing next to him with a cigarette in his mouth slit his own throat and crumpled on to the quay. Almost immediately, word came from the other end of the port that someone he knew had shot himself. Suicides spread like an epidemic; he no sooner turned to look at some people running than he heard it was because someone had thrown himself into the water. A man climbed up a lamppost and began shouting incoherently of the dangers that awaited them. At the end of his speech, he threw himself from the post and crashed on to the quay.

—Everywhere you looked you saw desperation on people's faces. Women were

1. See Militancies II, pp. 363–6.

crying, children were holding on to their mothers' hands; some men looked on the verge of madness . . .

Hardly anywhere was there room to lie down. Some slept standing. María SOLANA and her husband, director of the JSU cadre school in Madrid, hadn't eaten since their precipitate flight from Madrid where, as a leading communist youth member, he had been under arrest; only at the last moment had he managed to escape. Around them were peasants stolidly eating from ample baskets of food, without offering anyone anything. 'But the terror of not knowing what was going to happen was even greater than hunger. No one asked them for food, let alone tried to take it from them.'

Chief commissar of the Estremaduran army, Tomás MORA[1] agreed with Carod that if a ship arrived they would not get off alive. It would end in slaughter. Suicide crossed his mind. When the ship was seen heading for the port, then turning back, he thought of climbing up a dock crane and throwing himself into the sea.

—But then I remembered my mother, my wife and children and I thought: 'Let them see me die rather than that' . . .

The next morning he awoke to find one of his commissars huddled in a pool of blood next to him. A professional pianist, who had returned from South America to fight, he had slashed his wrists. 'I can face the trenches, but not prison or concentration camps,' he had told MORA once.

The only leading member of the Casado defence council to reach Alicante was Antonio Pérez, father.[2] Rumours that Casado and the others, who were seen leaving Valencia on Wednesday, 29 March, in a convoy of cars, had been killed en route began to circulate. In fact, they had made not for Alicante but Gandía, nearer to Valencia, where a British warship was due to take off Italian prisoners of war that day.

The arrival of a warship, which was shortly joined by two more, was certainly known to the republican authorities.[3]

Shortly after noon, while the Italians were being embarked under Royal Marine escort, Casado and other defence council members, with some 200 other refugees and as many armed troops, arrived in the port. British Rear-Admiral Tovey, commanding the First Cruiser Squadron, approved a request for Casado's embarkation, on condition that Casado and his staff 'clearly understood that their final disposal would depend on the decision of H.M. Government'. The admiral, meanwhile, signalled for instructions as to what such 'disposal' should be. Earlier that day, before sailing from Palma de Mallorca,

1. See Militancies 17, pp. 461–5.
2. See Militancies 18, pp. 494–8.
3. The evacuation of the 168 Italians had been agreed to on 26 March by the authorities – on condition that they were not to be taken to a Spanish port; on the night of 28–29 March, the republicans changed their minds and agreed they could be taken to Palma de Mallorca. About forty of the prisoners were due to be exchanged for a similar number of British prisoners in nationalist hands. For this, and subsequent details of the Casado evacuation, see reports by Rear-Admiral Tovey, Captain Hammick, and Captain Lumsden to their superiors, Admiralty records, PRO.

he had been informed by the British consul there that evacuation of republican leaders would cause 'intense resentment' among the nationalists.

Dramatic discussions took place among the council members as to whether to accept the British condition. While Casado hesitated, fifteen members of his 'entourage' embarked. Casado announced that he refused the condition and was leaving for Alicante. Many of the armed men accompanying him moved off. Shortly after, the captain commanding the Royal Marine detachment on the quay received an order to stop Casado from leaving. On the recommendation of members of the International Committee for the Coordination of Assistance to Republican Spain, Casado reconsidered his decision and, some twelve hours after reaching the port, embarked on the British warship *Galatea*.

Earlier, the British consul in Valencia, who was aboard the *Galatea*, had received Foreign Office instructions that only those in 'imminent danger of their lives' could be taken off on British warships. A second Foreign Office signal told him to interpret his earlier instructions 'in as wide and generous a manner as possible'. In accordance with this, he went ashore early the next morning to arrange for a further 143 men, nineteen women and two children to be taken aboard. 'The type of person embarked,' noted the rear-admiral, 'varied from apparently respectable officers and officials of moderate tendencies, to the lowest of criminal types, and included a number of prominent anarchists and members of the SIM.' The refugees were all transferred to the hospital ship *Maine* which set sail for Marseilles. The rear-admiral, meanwhile, prepared to send a warship to Alicante. That afternoon, he received a signal from the Admiralty saying that the latest Foreign Office instructions were meant solely for the British consul and did not imply any change in British government policy. He delayed, and then cancelled, the warship's departure for Alicante.

Some hours before Casado's arrival at the port, Narciso JULIAN, communist armoured brigade commander, and other communist military had reached Gandía. No warship had yet arrived, and they were told – the British port manager, Apfel, was assiduous in this task – that ships were waiting in Alicante, not Gandía. They set off; there were no ships in Alicante either.

It was folly, he thought, to remain in this crowded port. It was a trap. They must escape while they could. Rumours that the Italians were closing in were growing. JULIAN was fortunate to have escaped so far. Arrested by the Casado forces on the Madrid front, released by a tank battalion which by chance was passing through, he reached Valencia only to find that the secret police were already looking for him. His party organized a hide-out in a farmhouse; from there he and some others were dispatched the day before to Gandía where, they were told, a ship was waiting.

One of his men, a mechanic, was trying to make a fishing boat seaworthy; the engines of the many boats in the Alicante docks had all been put out of action before they arrived. Hurriedly, they made a selection of tank corps men who would leave. The boat was plainly visible to the people crowded in the docks; it was going to be a tricky operation to get it out to sea. Unsure of whether the engine would work, the mechanic tried it. It broke into life. At the sound of the engine's steady beat, refugees threw themselves headlong on to the boat which immediately capsized and sank. Though no one was drowned, there was no way of salvaging it.

They would have to return to his original idea: fill their haversacks with whatever they could lay their hands on and set off with short-arms for the mountains. Some of the men had managed to get to the port with their tanks, but these were useless now. If they couldn't remain in the mountains, they'd have to try to make for the Pyrenees and France.

They set off; it was already too late. They no sooner got out on the road than they were surrounded and taken prisoner by Italian troops who had begun to arrive.

Throughout Thursday, the Italian forces took up positions without entering the port. Word had it that their commander, General Gambara, was prepared to convert the docks into a neutral zone. The refugees feared that the Basque surrender to the Italians at Santoña was about to be repeated. By Friday, Gambara was telling the refugees' representatives that it was in everyone's interest that they should be able to leave that day. But the captains of the French cruiser and two merchant ships preparing to put in to Alicante demanded that the refugees first surrender all arms. After much discussion, arms were piled, thrown into the sea or hidden. Three ships had been seen patrolling off the coast; they disappeared, re-appeared, began making for the port. Hearts rose. It was only as the leading warship closed in that the refugees saw it was not a French but a Spanish nationalist minelayer. It broke out a large red and gold Spanish flag. From its deck, laden with soldiers, came the sounds of a nationalist anthem. Soon the order, given by the Spanish military commander, was being passed from mouth to mouth by the refugees: 'Within half an hour we have to be out of the port.'

Three days of hope and despair came to an end. A burst of machine-gun fire broke over the refugees' heads from the Santa Barbara rock rising steeply behind the port. Refugees threw arms, valuables, suitcases over the quay-side; the water turned red, then yellow as cases of saffron, worth a fortune, began to sink. Between ranks of Spanish soldiers, the refugees started to leave the port; there were so many that not all could be got out before nightfall. Saturnino CAROD and other leading anarcho-syndicalist militants from Aragon remained. Two of them proposed that they should commit suicide. Another, Antonio Ejarque, army corps commissar, looked pensive. CAROD replied that it was no solution.

—'I will not deny my enemies the pleasure of shooting me. If I am to die, it will be at their hands. As long as I'm alive, I'll do everything in my power to escape. Our duty is to continue fighting' . . .

None the less, he believed, it was a good thing they hadn't won the war. The struggle between the conflicting forces on the republican side would have been so savage that all would have perished in the end. Even taking into account the privations and sufferings that were certain to be inflicted on the defeated – sufferings which, in the event, were even worse than he could imagine – defeat was preferable to the inevitable internecine conflict that victory would have unleashed. He recalled the communist sweep through Aragon, the attempted communist blackmail to make him accept party membership in return for arms for his men. For too long he had had his eye on the rear for the stab in the back.

His two companions, Mariano Viñuales and Máximo Franco, were not persuaded by his arguments. As the hour approached for the last of the refugees to leave the port, they shot themselves.

*

The refugee-prisoners wound along the road to San Juan. Nationalist soldiers stole what they could from them. A rubbish cart, with a fat, dirty woman sitting on top, came past the column in the opposite direction. Andrés MARQUEZ, Madrid left republican youth leader and brigade commissar, who on the day of the uprising so long ago had watched the crowd threatening bus-loads of insurgent military officers being taken to Madrid prisons, saw the cart approach. As it drew level, the woman, her rolls of fat quivering, shouted at them: 'Assassins! Reds!'

Things hadn't changed, he thought. The hour of the lumpen-proletariat had come with the victory of reaction. The garbage woman could well have been among those who had greeted the return of Ferdinand VII, the last absolute king, a hundred years earlier, with the shout: 'Long live our chains!'

The men were segregated and herded into a large almond orchard, a short distance from Alicante. Within a few hours, the young fruit that was just setting, the leaves of the trees, were being picked and eaten; soon the tender shoots and even the bark were being stripped for food. Then the prisoners were ordered to lay barbed wire around the orchard's perimeter. As they imprisoned themselves, General Franco was penning a communiqué several hundred miles to the north. Suffering from 'flu – the first time in the war that he had been even slightly ill – he crossed out several words, changed another and, satisfied at last, signed what he had written:

Having captured and disarmed the red army, Nationalist troops today took their last objectives. The war is finished.

Burgos, April 1, 1939.

VAE VICTIS!

The war was over. In crowded prisons and concentration camps, the sufferings of the vanquished were just beginning.

From the almond orchard, the prisoners captured in Alicante were shifted to the concentration camp in Albatera. Designed to hold a few hundred, the camp was packed with nearly 10,000 prisoners. Hygiene and shelter were primitive to the point of non-existence, food and water scarce. Falangists, police, civilians, even priests came from different parts of Spain to look for men they wanted; many whom they took away at the beginning never reached their home towns or villages. Some prisoners succeeded in escaping; others were executed in front of the camp inmates for trying. On one occasion, a temporary second lieutenant inspecting the sentry posts turned a machine-gun on the inmates and opened fire.

Narciso JULIAN, communist armoured brigade commander, and three companions dug a hole under their tent in the camp where they hid when visiting groups came looking for men they wanted. After four months, a companion, who had been beaten up, revealed his presence in the camp, and JULIAN surrendered to a man who had come for him. By then, however, unauthorized assassinations of prisoners had ended. JULIAN was taken to Porlier prison in Madrid and court-martialled with sixteen others in a trial that lasted a total of eleven minutes. (Courts martial considered the accused guilty unless otherwise proven.) Sentenced to death, he spent one year and seventeen days awaiting execution.

Every evening the prison inmates were lined up. The prison officer would sometimes be smoking a cigar as he read out the next day's execution list.

—Often he would read out only the first name, Pedro, and pause for several minutes. Everyone with that Christian name went through agony until he read out the first surname. It might be a common one, several people might share it. Agony again. Until finally, he read out the second surname . . .

Most of the men went to their deaths courageously. On the pretence that he was a relative, JULIAN was often able to spend time with friends on their last night before execution. One night, as he entered the condemned men's room, he was amazed to find the prison warders standing against the wall, their faces as white as sheets, and the prisoners roaring with laughter at a parody of a Franquista court martial they were acting out.

—One of them, his cap pulled down over his eyes, was playing the part of the military prosecutor. He was demanding the death sentence because the defendant had a cat called Franco. As I listened, I thought: 'Which of these men are going to their deaths in a few hours? It looks more like the warders.' When the time came for their execution, they went out heads held high, shouting '*¡Viva la República!*' . . .

JULIAN's sentence was commuted to thirty years' imprisonment. He served seven of them and was released. Six years later, in 1952, he was arrested for communist activities, court-martialled twice and sentenced to twenty years, of which he served eighteen.

Keeping faith with his word, Saturnino CAROD escaped after a short time in Albatera camp. After many nights walking over the mountains, he was able to contact his wife who helped get him to the French border. In France, he was again confined in a concentration camp. On his release, he returned clandestinely to Spain to re-organize the CNT, was arrested, court-martialled twice and sentenced to death. The sentence was commuted to thirty years, of which he served eighteen, being released finally in 1960.

Tomás MORA, socialist chief commissar of the Estremadura army, remained nine months under sentence of death, having been found guilty by a summary court martial of having been a 'general in the red army'. In 1944 his life sentence was reduced to twenty years' imprisonment and he was conditionally released under an amnesty which reprieved prisoners with terms of up to twenty years' imprisonment.

Sócrates GOMEZ's father, last socialist civil governor of Madrid, who was in the camp, was executed; his son was court-martialled and sentenced to twenty years. Antonio Pérez, father, Casado defence councillor, was another victim of Franco's firing squads. His son, who had not made for Alicante but for Madrid, reached the capital and went into hiding for two months. Convinced that the republic had suffered only a temporary set-back – 'the country was still basically republican' – and that the fascist victory could last only a year or two at the most, he located former JSU comrades and began clandestine work. Within three months, the group was broken up, most of its members arrested – one of whom died under torture – and Antonio PEREZ was forced to flee Madrid for the provinces. (Later he was to be imprisoned for clandestine communist activities.)

It was not only the leaders who suffered. José MERA, Madrid schoolteacher, who answered his union's call to defend the capital in 1936 and later became a communist, was court-martialled in Alicante for 'aiding the rebellion' – the usual charge. The prosecutor demanded a twelve-year sentence; his defence, whom he had never seen before – which was also customary in these summary courts martial – asked for a reduction to six. The court handed out a twenty-year prison sentence.

—At least I was lucky. I didn't have an extra charge made against me as did a right-wing republican history professor I knew, who was accused, on top of the usual charges, of 'intellectuality' . . .

MERA had been forewarned by his experience with an extreme right-wing doctor and his wife whom he had helped protect during the war. In return, they had offered him every protection if it was ever in their power to help. Now that the moment had come, the couple refused him; as a consoling thought, the doctor said: 'Don't worry, they can't shoot your wife until your son is a year old.'

*

In Madrid, some communist militants who had been arrested during the Casado coup were left in prison to be found there by the enemy. On the day the nationalists occupied the capital, Miguel NUÑEZ, eighteen-year-old communist education militiaman and commissar, managed to persuade the socialist lieutenant, a bricklayer whom he knew, to release him and fifteen others. Like Pérez, he was convinced that the fascist victory would be shortlived, and he set about reorganizing his party. He contacted a JSU comrade, and together they were walking down a Madrid street when they came across a group of right-wingers talking about their hardships during the war. Stopping to listen, his friend, Vicente Goya, suddenly was unable to contain himself.

—'But that's nothing,' he burst out. Everybody turned to him. 'What happened to you, then, *joven*?' one of the men inquired. 'To keep me from the reds and certain death, my father hung me up for three years on a clothes-hanger with an overcoat over me.' The people looked at him, not knowing whether it was serious or a joke. 'Come on, *chico*, let's get out of here before they kill us,' I said . . .

Within three weeks, NUÑEZ was arrested. He was sentenced to thirty years' imprisonment, later reduced to twelve, of which he served four. His friend Goya, who was even younger than he, was sentenced to death. On his return from his court martial, he threw himself out of the police car and, although handcuffed, managed to escape. He made for his grandfather's house in Segovia, reaching it still manacled. The old man, who had spent all the war in the nationalist zone, threw him out to cries of 'Bandit, red – ' Goya made for his roadmender uncle's hut in the mountains; it was an excellent place to hide. His uncle also threw him out. Too exhausted to continue, the youth lay in the road until he was found by the *guardia civil.* Taken back to prison, he was executed not long after . . .

Régulo MARTINEZ, left republican leader in the capital, who returned from France to Madrid forty-eight hours before the city fell, was sentenced to death for being a 'traitor to religion', the 'creator of the Popular Tribunals' and a republican. The Vicar General of the Navy, whom MARTINEZ had saved after his arrest by anarchists in Madrid, moved heaven and earth to save him. 'Now I see that there was a great deal more goodness and generosity on your side than there is on this,' he commented. 'These people are cold, they lack generosity of spirit – ' His pleas, however, were successful; MARTINEZ's sentence was commuted to thirty years and he served five, later being imprisoned again for anti-Franco activities.

On his release after seven years in prison, nine months of which he spent under sentence of death, Francisco SANPEDRO, Popular Army staff officer, took the opportunity of asking the prison chaplain, whom he had got to know while working in the prison offices, a question.

—'You know that I killed no one, robbed no one, committed no crime. Can you tell me, therefore, why I have spent seven years in gaol?'

'That's very simple, I'm glad you asked me that question,' replied the priest. 'I can answer it. You were on the point of being shot, but you weren't; the same could very well have happened to me had things turned out the other way round. Your side lost, and the rest – whether you robbed or killed – matters not a jot. Many who have committed murders are still alive, and many who didn't have been shot. You've been in prison seven years because you lost the war' . . .

A civil war, he might have added. For the objective was not only to castigate the defeated but to crush for all time working-class militancy and the threat of socialist revolution, so that Spanish capitalism could prosper. The worst of the repression continued until 1943.[1]

Many of those who managed to escape from nationalist vengeance to French concentration camps after the fall of Catalonia were to experience the oppression of Nazism. Timoteo RUIZ, the lad who started the war with a lance, was released from a French camp when he volunteered for work in the French coal mines. Caught by the Germans during the invasion of France and thrown into a concentration camp, he was later taken to work on German fortifications at Brest. Aided by communist party members outside, he and three others managed to escape to Bordeaux. There the only job they could find was working for the Germans

1. In 1940, according to official prison statistics, there were 213,000 prisoners, compared to a pre-war average of 10,000, a level which was not again reached until after 1950 (see Tamames, *La república, la era de Franco,* pp. 353–5. The author estimates that 875,000 man-years were lost to the Spanish economy in the first twelve post-war years. The remission of sentences must be seen in this context: the working class was needed to produce surplus value, not to vegetate in prison at the state's expense).

in the submarine pens. A fight with the Nazi foreman led them to escape to the French *maquis*, where they remained fighting the Germans until the end of the war. After an abortive guerrilla invasion of Spain, he became a member of an armed group that was sent by the Spanish communist party to Valencia, clandestinely crossing half of Spain from the French frontier on foot. Once in Valencia, he was summoned by his party to Madrid to participate in the clandestine struggle there. Arrested, he was sentenced to twenty-five years' imprisonment, of which he served just over eleven. Arrested a second time, he served a further seven years.

Josep CERCOS, libertarian youth metalworker, who started the war with a pistol in the streets of Barcelona, was released from a French concentration camp to work in a labour battalion in northern France. He retreated with British and French forces to Dunkirk and, with some Italian international brigaders, set off in a rowing boat after most of the British had been evacuated. Picked up by a British ship as they drifted helplessly in the Channel, they were taken to Dover, then to a prison in London where the warders, believing them to be German prisoners, greeted them as 'bosch'. CERCOS wanted to go to America; the prison governor simply smiled. After a few days, a French captain informed them they would have to return to France because they were working for the French. Paris had not yet fallen. They reached Cherbourg in a Belgian ship. No sooner had they arrived than British troops began embarking; the retreat was in full tide. Left foodless and leaderless, they got on board a Lithuanian collier which took them round the coast to St Nazaire. From there, they joined the flood of refugees pouring south. Finally, CERCOS reached Perpignan and his original concentration camp. After six months, the Germans forced him into a labour brigade which was sent to fortify St Nazaire. Six months later, he escaped and reached Chartres, where false documents were procured, and he went to work as a Frenchman in various factories for the Germans while operating with the French resistance.

*

The victors' fate was kinder, naturally. But not always as kind as might have been supposed. Alberto PASTOR, falangist farmer from Tamariz de Campos, Valladolid, ended the war as a lieutenant, and volunteered for the Blue Division, Franco's contribution to the Nazi cause, which fought the Russians on the eastern front. After the world war, he returned to his life as a farmer, occupying an occasional post in the farmers' vertical union but refusing the bureaucratic benefices and perquisites with which the new regime favoured its petty-bourgeois rural supporters. (Between 1940 and 1950, the bureaucracy doubled in numbers; its one and a half million members were then nearly three times as numerous as in 1930.)

Among the great numbers who welcomed the nationalist victory and prospered from it, the Carlists were not prominent. Antonio IZU, *requeté*, who returned to the family farm for a time, felt that the Carlist cause had been betrayed. First and foremost, by the movement's own leaders – 'out-and-out conservatives who joined to protect their own interests, who manipulated the movement to keep down the ordinary people's real Carlism'. And thereafter, by the new regime, which had no place for authentic Carlism, which had forcibly united it with the Falange, and had instituted a totalitarianism that was anathema to Carlism.

Many radical falangists – a minority amongst the mass of wartime newcomers who, in the post-war, found their security and well-being in the new regime – also felt that their cause had been betrayed. Amongst these was Dionisio RIDRUEJO, Falange propaganda chief, who was disillusioned by the time the war ended. He felt that the repression, aimed almost exclusively at the working class, and the reinforcement of capitalism, was symptomatic of the true nature of the regime. To prevent his lack of active service being used against him later, he joined the Blue Division; on his return from Russia, he resigned all his posts in a letter to Franco which resulted in his being sent into internal exile. His opposition to the regime, which brought imprisonment later, led him politically (unlike many other falangists) to social democracy.

Wounded three times in nine months, Lt Juan CRESPO, monarchist student from Salamanca, was in a military hospital at the end of the war. He had continued to fight at the head of his Moorish troops, but without illusions. The new Spain he had hoped to see rising was not going to be created; the memory of the fate meted out to his uncles did not recede as the war progressed. When he saw the doctors, nurses and orderlies rushing from the hospital to celebrate the victory, he knew that the combatants no longer counted. He sat down and wrote a verse Oration for the Victors. A year later, in Madrid for his final medical to give him a place in the army's Disabled Corps, with its scales of promotion and pay which would have assured him a comfortable future for life, he came across a one-legged bootblack in a café. The latter was shining his shoes. 'Well, lieutenant, I see you've been wounded in the leg. I lost mine in a tank battle in this zone.' They started to talk, exchanging war experiences. 'And what compensation are you getting for your wound?' CRESPO asked, finally. 'None,' replied the republican, 'they give us who fought on this side nothing at all – '

In disgust, CRESPO refused to report for his medical, was never admitted to the Disabled Corps. His later life was spent in poverty. 'What else could I do? If the regime was going to excommunicate one half of Spain for having fought on the other side, how were we ever going to heal our wounds?'

The Republic 1931–6

Points of Rupture

The following sections are intended to provide a summary outline of the major areas of pre-war conflict and thus of the causes of the war. They make no pretence of being exhaustive studies of these problems, which would require a volume to themselves. Like the rest of the book, they are an attempt rather to capture the atmosphere of the times.

A. The land

The dominant problem in a dominantly agrarian country like Spain lay in the land. To 'modernize' Spain it was necessary to reform agriculture: industrialization could not fully develop unless agricultural productivity increased, creating a home market for consumer goods and transferring an increased surplus from the land into industrial investment.

In the southern latifundist region, where a few thousand landowners controlled two thirds of the available land, the exploitation of close on three quarters of a million labourers at subsistence wages, and the estate owners' refusal to invest in their land, impeded this. Instead, low levels of agricultural techniques immobilized half-starving labour on the land, jeopardizing industrial development which could absorb that surplus labour productively in the towns.

Ownership conditioned not only farming techniques but social relationships in the countryside. Wherever large landowners monopolized the land, agrarian unrest and the demand for the take-over of the estates was endemic. Agricultural reform was not only an economic necessity for the development of capitalism, it was a socio-political necessity for the development of liberal democracy, for holding the rural proletariat within the framework of the capitalist system. Agrarian reform was the chosen means.[1]

1. It was, of course, not the only possibility. A different model in the post-war Franquista era had the desired effect, using the mechanisms of repression to ensure low agrarian wages, and the black market to ensure high profits which, via the banking system, were transferred into industrial development. See J. Leal, J. Leguina, J. M. Naredo, L. Tarrafeta, *La agricultura en el desarrollo capitalista español* (Madrid, 1975).

As approved in September 1932, eighteen months after the republic's proclamation, the agrarian reform law was a complex compromise to a series of conflicting interests. It involved little outright expropriation, other than land belonging to the upper nobility, and was based on an individual's holdings in each municipality, not on his or her aggregate ownership throughout the country. Depending on area, landowners would be allowed to retain from between 300 to 600 hectares of grainland in each municipality before being subject to take-over with compensation: in effect, each owner would be left with a *latifundio* or large estate in each township. However, this was not the case if the land had been systematically leased, for all land in this liberally defined category was to be seized in its entirety.

It was widely believed at the time – and even later – that the large estates belonged in the main to a 'semi-feudal' nobility. The bourgeois democratic revolution's historic task had been to abolish feudalism and introduce capitalist relations of production into agriculture. The take-over of the upper nobility's (grandees') estates would, it was thought, achieve this historic aim and open up millions of hectares for the settlement of the landless. Unfortunately, common belief was wrong. The upper nobility, who formed the largest aristocratic landowners (and whose expropriation was, in fact, a late addition to the law, on the pretext of a couple of its members' participation in the abortive Sanjurjo monarchist uprising against the republic in 1932), owned in all just under 600,000 hectares of arable land throughout Spain. By no means a small amount in absolute terms, enough to settle some 60,000 landless labourers; but a very small amount relative to the size of the problem which would, eventually, require some 10 million hectares if 1 million needy landworkers were to be settled. Nine tenths of this land would have to come from the rural bourgeoisie, for it was the latter class which owned 90 per cent of farmland. However primitive, capitalism had been the dominant mode of production on the latifundia since the mid-nineteenth century.[1]

1. See E. Malefakis, *Agrarian Reform and Peasant Revolution in Spain*, pp. 77, 223, 359. Also J. Martínez Alier, '¿Burguesía débil o burguesía fascista?: La España del siglo XX,' *Cuadernos de Ruedo Ibérico* (Paris, January–June 1975).

In 1936, the agrarian reform bulletin referred to the evolution of a 'half-feudal, half-bourgeois agriculture towards a capitalist agriculture'. It quoted thirty-four cases of feudal dues and services which had been abolished over the past three years. J. Maurice, citing this (in his *La reforma agraria en España en el siglo XX*, Madrid, 1975), adds that only one of these cases referred to Andalusia. This is hardly surprising, since historically feudalism had not established itself in Andalusia. The contemporary confusion about the 'semi-feudal' noble character of the latifundia can perhaps best be explained by: (a) the fact that by far the greatest part of the upper nobility's land holdings was concentrated in the latifundist regions; (b) the fact that the rural bourgeoisie adopted seemingly 'aristocratic' (extensive, undercapitalized, unmechanized) *modes* of farming. 'The large domains were managed without initiative or imagination . . . their owners failed to apply modern farming techniques and the rate of capital investment in the land was minimal' (Malefakis, op. cit., p. 78). That the bourgeois landowning class 'displayed little of the enterprising spirit that distinguished its counterparts in north-western Europe', did not prevent its being a capitalist class. The problem lay in the *full development* of capitalist farming, not in the *introduction* of capitalism into farming. (Capitalist economic rationale underlay even the apparently 'backward' extensive system of farming known as '*al tercio*' compared to the more intensive '*año y vez*' which reduced fallows. Without mechanization, the former was more profitable than the latter. See J. Naredo, 'Estudio de las motivaciones del paso del cultivo al tercio al de año y vez', typescript, Madrid, no date.)

The crux of the problem of agrarian reform, in consequence, resided on the one hand in whether the liberal, mainly urban petty bourgeois republicans could oblige the mainly Catholic, conservative rural bourgeoisie to cede large tracts of its private property, to accept 'sacrifices' in the immediate for the long-term gain of forestalling rural revolution.[1] On the other hand, whether it could persuade a large sector of the revolutionary rural proletariat, under anarcho-syndicalist influence, to accept an agrarian reform that did not 'profoundly alter the system of land ownership' and operated to reinforce liberal democracy.

A twenty-five-year-old republican agronomist, a self-styled liberal, who was dispatched to Toledo province, soon discovered a number of inherent contradictions in the reform, the application of which had been delayed for a year after its approval by the Cortes. The agriculture minister, Marcelino Domingo, sent for José VERGARA and told him that the situation in the countryside was very serious: the landless were about to take over all the land, and if they did so the Republic would collapse. He was taking immediate action, sending a delegate with absolute powers to each of the fourteen latifundist provinces covered by the first stage of agrarian reform.[2] Something had to be done immediately, even if the reform were not applied until after next year's harvest was in.

—'Yes, *señor ministro*. But what action am I supposed to take?' The minister pulled an envelope out of his pocket. He took hold of his pen and on the back of the envelope he drew a sketch. 'Here, you see, there's a large area of unemployed. Find estates around there to take over and put the people to work. Do the same wherever there are unemployed. I wish you luck' . . .

VERGARA left immediately for Toledo where he set about taking over land where the right to expropriation was in no doubt: the grandees' lands, and estates voluntarily offered by their absentee owners for temporary occupation which assured them a rent.

Faced with a mass of landless labourers, he soon saw that the grandees' estates – which often included whole villages – were not going to be sufficient.[3] The bulk of these, moreover, were on the poor scrublands of the southern part of the province. The agrarian reform law also spoke of assistance for the newly settled labourers: credit, technical assistance, implements, etc. None of this was put into effect.

1. The problem was expressed in the provisional republican government's first declaration of principles. 'Private property is guaranteed by law and is consequently not expropriable except for public utility with due indemnity. Nevertheless, the government, conscious of the conditions in which the immense mass of peasants live . . . adopts as a norm of policy the recognition that agrarian legislation should correspond to the social function of the land.' (Cited in Malefakis, op. cit., p. 166.)

2. To the thirteen latifundist provinces (see Map, p. 20) had been added Almería, to the east of Granada, as a result of its great poverty rather than because it contained many large estates (see Malefakis, op. cit., p. 217, n. 19).

3. Grandees owned 38,522 hectares in the province (Maurice, op. cit., p. 93) out of a total of 633,000 hectares of farms above 50 hectares in size (C. de Castro, *Al servicio de los campesinos* (Madrid, 1931), cited in Peirats, *La CNT en la revolución española*, vol. 1, p. 273). Between 1933–4, effectively the only period of active agrarian reform until after the Popular Front electoral victory, 33 per cent of the grandees' land was expropriated and 883 land workers settled on the 13,000 hectares (Maurice, op. cit., p. 131).

—It soon became evident that, since the big landowners' estates weren't going to provide enough land, medium-sized estates would have to be taken over also. But how could it be done? What I didn't see, and nor did the republicans, was that agrarian reform without social revolution is impossible – if by reform we mean the modification of existing structures within the existing order. In a predominantly agrarian country, agrarian property – the country's wealth – is in the hands of the rich; those who hold power through their ownership of land are not simply going to give it up. Property in an overwhelmingly rural country – 45 per cent of the working population earned its living from the land, some 60 per cent of the total population lived in the countryside – cannot be expropriated by democratic means; it has to be done by violence. In saying that, I am not condoning violence. I'm simply saying that agrarian reform by democratic legislation is impossible. Agrarian reform comes as a result of revolution, not vice versa. And once the revolution has been made, the problem of agrarian reform is solved, since the landowners, as enemies of the new regime, are automatically expropriated . . .

In any event, the law was never applied because, as the result of a series of a political compromises, it contained internal contradictions which, in his view, prevented it from being applied. The major contradiction was that the law attempted to reconcile the reform to the existing legal structure: each owner was given the legal right to show why his land should not be expropriated. Every estate required its own proceedings, its own dossier. 'The only lands taken over were grandee lands or those voluntarily offered.'

The parcelling out of land did not necessarily satisfy the poor peasantry.[1] In one of the southern Toledo villages, Navalmorales de Pusa, Timoteo RUIZ's father, a smallholder, received two plots.

—The land was so poor that when we calculated how much work we would have to put into it for the small return we would get, we realized we were wasting our time. A lot of the landless and smallholders came to the same conclusion and left the land idle. Without tools, seed or credit, agrarian reform was useless. Moreover, it did nothing to take the land from the big, non-grandee owners . . .

Because of a clause which would have expropriated all lands within 2 km of a village not directly cultivated by owners who held more than 20 hectares of grainland in the municipality, more medium and small owners were potentially affected by the reform (when, later, it would be applied to the rest of Spain) than large bourgeois owners. The latter thus found allies in their struggle against the reform. Faced with losing land for compensation which at best would give

1. Landless labourers, peasants owning less than 10 hectares, tenants and sharecroppers working less than 10 hectares, and legally constituted agricultural workers' societies were entitled to be settled on the land, to which the state retained the property rights. The societies' members could choose whether they would form collectives or work the land in individual plots. 'However, at the end of one article it was explicitly stated that if a workers' society in any municipality demanded that expropriated land be handed over to be worked collectively, the demand had to be met,' recalled VERGARA. But believing that the peasants did not favour this solution, sponsored by the socialist Landworkers' Federation, he ignored it and distributed the land in individual holdings.

them only two thirds its market value,[1] the large bourgeois owners had no interest in paying the cost of consolidating liberal democracy, a political system they had not favoured in the past. Other questions, especially the religious problem, compounded their hostility. Both were attacks on the holders of economic power. Inevitably, as Ernesto CASTAÑO, lawyer and prime mover in mobilizing Catholic agrarian reaction in Salamanca, saw, the defence of one involved the defence of the other.

—The socialist agrarian reform terrified the landowners. Their lands were going to be taken from them – with or without compensation. As soon as the republic was proclaimed, subversive, demagogic propaganda got a ready hearing amongst agricultural labourers. In many villages they were saying, 'The sickles this year aren't going to reap wheat but the farmers' heads' . . .

He helped found the Salamanca Agrarian Bloc which, while declaring its allegiance to the republic, called for the end of class struggle in the countryside, 'the harmony of capital and labour', being convinced that the interests of both on the land were the same. The solution to the land problem was not the redistribution of land but a change in the structures of existing agriculture, a revaluation of its price levels, its consideration by the government as of equal importance to industry and commerce.

The Agrarian Bloc was one of the original nuclei of what was to become the mass Catholic CEDA, although it retained its own identity within it; Gil Robles, the CEDA leader, was a deputy for Salamanca and was supported by the Bloc from the beginning. CASTAÑO, who was elected to parliament for the CEDA in 1933, had gone to gaol the previous year for inciting farmers not to sow land to wheat 'except on the most productive soil, for elsewhere it was entirely uneconomic, given the government's wheat price.' This was seen by the republican government as a landowners' and farmers' boycott.

—The republic needed class war. It made worker fight employer, labourer and tenant fight landowner. And it provided justifications. The right for tenants to have their rents revised, the right for any worker in a given municipality to get agricultural work ahead of a man from outside. It meant that a farmer had to hire an incompetent local labourer, even a non-agricultural worker, before he could take a competent man from outside.[2] If, instead of taking measures like these, the government had reformed the structures of agriculture, the working class would have benefited from the increased profits to be made from farming. Landless labourers were not professionally or psychologically suited to become

1. 'A predominantly rural country does not generate sufficient National Income to repay, in a few years, the capital which has produced that income. This was the nub of another problem' (VERGARA). None the less, despite its backward economy, Spain at the time had the world's fourth largest gold reserves. Obsessed by financial orthodoxy – the first two years of republican regime ended with budget surpluses – the Agrarian Reform Institute (IRA) was allocated only 50 million pesetas a year, little more than 1 per cent of the national budget and less than half of what was spent on the *guardia civil*. To develop capitalist farming was going to require *capital*; agrarian reform did not receive it. After three years of operation, the IRA had managed to spend less than half the budget allocated.

2. A number of socialist-sponsored decrees, including the municipal boundaries law, in the first months of the republic, increased real wages and 'swung the balance of legal rights from the landowners to the rural proletariat' (see Malefakis, op. cit., p. 70).

farmers; they had lived too close to the problems, knew a farmer had to work harder than they as labourers, didn't want his headaches. A farmer has to be born a farmer . . .

In scores of villages across the land, the change of regime had changed the names of the political parties but little else. There was no change in the local power structure when a former monarchist *cacique* became the local leader (or behind-the-scenes manipulator) of a newly formed republican party. Fulgencio DIEZ PASTOR, a radical deputy on the parliamentary agricultural commission in 1933, who came from an Estremaduran village, knew the problem intimately. In each village there would be two or three men who were relatively rich 'given the general poverty that then existed'. They were men whose ownership of some olive groves or pasture land meant that they did not have to work with their hands; they were the *caciques*, the people who ruled the villagers' lives. It was this class which sabotaged the republican regime.

—Not only by their resistance, but by their cleverness – however crude – in being able to infiltrate political parties at the local level. More often than not it would be the same man who organized the different local parties, putting his followers into the committees to run them. It happened in my own party, it happened in the CEDA. It completely falsified the political situation[1] . . .

From their vantage point, as he saw, the rural bourgeoisie fought all reform. Had an attempt been made to expropriate them – as indeed was required under the agrarian reform – it would have had only one effect: 'to bring forward the date of the civil war. For that, at heart, was what the uprising was about: the defence of their property'.

The rural bourgeoisie's hostility to reform was shared by the one capitalist sector which stood to gain most in the long run: the industrial bourgeoisie. The fact that in large part the world depression was initially palliated for the Catalan textile industry by an increase in rural purchasing power (thanks to socialist-decreed rural wage increases) did not evidently outweigh the disadvantages for the Catalan bourgeoisie of breaking its political alliance with Spain's landowning class. (Had the latter been a 'feudal' nobility, rather than a rural bourgeoisie, the alliance might have been less tenable.) The most 'politically advanced' capitalist sector in the peninsula went even further: it prevented a capitalist agrarian reform in its own homeland. The *Llei de contractes de conreu*, passed by the petty bourgeois Esquerra party, attempted to resolve a long-standing peasant dispute by guaranteeing tenant farmers (*rabassaires*) security of tenure and the right to purchase land they had been working for eighteen years. The Lliga Catalana, representing the big bourgeois industrial and agrarian interests, succeeded in having the law overturned as unconstitutional. Paradoxically, it was agrarian reform in industrialized Catalonia (rather than in the latifundist south) which precipitated the greatest political conflict in this area: the blockage of its reform led the Esquerra to clash with – and eventually to rise against – the central government in October 1934.[2]

1. For particular cases of the rural bourgeoisie's political 'shirt-changing' see p. 358; also Fraser, *In Hiding*, p. 112.

2. See Balcells, *Cataluña contemporánea II (1900–1936)*, p. 127 *et seq.*

The CEDA (whose participation in the government was the immediate cause of the October insurrection) revealed the depths of the rural bourgeoisie's opposition to any reform. The CEDA's parliamentary membership blocked its own agriculture minister's attempt to restart agrarian reform and, in particular, a proposed new lease law which would give tenants the right to purchase their land after twelve years of uninterrupted leasing. Gil Robles, the CEDA leader, was later to call such blocking action 'suicidal egoism'; CEDA members at the time labelled their minister a 'white Bolshevik'.

Thus even the most modest changes were blocked. The bourgeois opposition was matched by a part of the agricultural proletariat's refusal to accept agrarian reform. At both its extraordinary congresses under the republic, the CNT came out in opposition to it. In 1931, it stated that the anarcho-syndicalists' task was not to collaborate in land reform but to prepare for the day when the rural masses, in collaboration with the proletariat, would overthrow capitalism and seize the land. Five years later, at the Saragossa congress, a more defensive tone crept into its warning about reform. This was no doubt as a result of the recent large-scale seizure of land by the socialist Landworkers' Federation and the speed-up of agrarian reform under rural pressures after the Popular Front electoral victory. Agrarian reform, the CNT then admitted, presented the anarcho-syndicalist movement with 'a serious problem, namely how not to lose control of the peasant masses'. It then went on to call for the expropriation without compensation of all property over 50 hectares in extent, and the handing over of the land to peasants' unions for their direct and collective exploitation.[1]

Where good arable land was taken over, the new settlers found themselves considerably better off but also facing problems. The duke of Medinaceli, the largest noble landowner in Spain with 79,000 hectares, owned three estates covering just under 3,000 hectares near Espejo on the road from Córdoba to Castro del Río. The smallest of these, La Reina, about 650 hectares, was handed over to the inhabitants of Santa Cruz, a near-by hamlet. Felipe POSADAS, son of a sharecropper and renter in the place, who received no land because he tilled more than the necessary minimum, remembered the moment when the news was announced.

—What joy there was in Santa Cruz that day! Soon sixty-two settlers were in occupation on the *cortijo*. I was very interested in agrarian reform, convinced that the only solution was to work the land collectively, and I often went to La Reina to see how things were going . . .

The agrarian reform institute, IRA (Instituto de Reforma Agraria), decided that the estate should be worked collectively because it was late in the year and the ploughing and sowing had to be got under way rapidly. The IRA delegate selected and bought sixty-two mules from the 400 or more that were brought to the *cortijo* by dealers. The *labradores* (large tenant farmers) who had lost their rented farms were paid compensation for the livestock, straw and crops. 'One of them made enough to put down a part-payment on the purchase of a

1. See Peirats, *La CNT en la revolución española*, vol. 1, pp. 123–4. See also Militancies 3, pp. 94–7, for an Andalusian anarcho-syndicalist day-labourer's reasons for rejecting agrarian reform.

350-hectare farm.' The settlers drew their mules by lot and the price was set down against each. It would have to be paid back to the IRA in due course. To every two settlers the IRA gave a yoke, a plough and a threshing board. Each settler could choose his ploughing team-mate which usually ended up as a family affair between relatives.

—Some of the settlers were happy because they had worked with their mules in the past. But others weren't. Then the ploughing started. Many of the settlers began to say that others' mules were being worked less hard than their own, and that there was favouritism. I went to the estate one day; there was an hour to go before the work day ended. Twenty-five teams were ploughing – if you could call it that. Each was running almost in the furrow of the plough ahead. The mistake, of course, was to have allocated the mules individually and then expect them to work in common . . .

While the land was being worked collectively, each settler got a day-wage from the IRA as an advance on his share of the harvest. Each had been allocated a plot of land which varied slightly in size depending on the quality of the soil. Soon there were complaints that the two *cabezaleros* – foremen or managers of the collectives whom the settlers had elected – weren't working like the rest of the men.

—The complaints were ridiculous. The *cabezalero* worked when he could, but he had to attend to the other duties for which he had been elected: keeping the accounts, reporting to the IRA agronomists who came out once or twice weekly from Córdoba, etc. Moreover, if the settlers didn't like them they could elect other managers. Instead they preferred to grumble. The trouble was that everyone wanted to be a boss . . .

This, the following year, the settlers proceeded to institutionalize; they decided to work their plots individually and the IRA agreed. The settlers now did not get a day-wage. Some had better land than others, some, because of the fallow system, would not be able to sow wheat that year. Others had land which would never support wheat, only barley at the best . . .

—The fact is they were all worse off. Even more ridiculous was the fact that specialists in different agricultural jobs – sowing, livestock, etc. – were now having to do everything on their own plot. 'If you worked in common, each doing what he knows best how to do, you'd all be better off,' I used to say; but there was no convincing them, not in this village at least . . .

La Reina was the only one of the three estates, as POSADAS remembered, which was worked entirely individually. On another, individualists and collectivists co-existed, and on the third, which had been made over to the village of Espejo, it was entirely collective.[1]

—There was little awareness here, in truth. Espejo was much bigger, it had its

1. Of nine estates taken over in Seville province, six were worked collectively; in Toledo province, four out of nine. When the IRA decided that four estates in Espera (Cádiz) should be worked individually rather than collectively because the collective was not making a profit, there were well-publicized clashes between partisans of both solutions. Otherwise the question seems to have been peacefully resolved.

socialist and anarcho-syndicalist organizations. In my village, with its 900 inhabitants, there was only a socialist centre as I remember, but it wasn't of much importance. Remember the lack of education, the backwardness that existed in the countryside then. For all that, and even if La Reina was the worst off of the three, the settlers were a lot better off than they had been. Their houses – if you can call them that, they were shacks really – were bursting with wheat: 1934 was a magnificent year. Some managed to make enough to buy their house and even a bit of land; and that after paying off their share to the IRA for wages, tools, seed-corn, mules . . .

*

Fear of rural unrest pushed the first republican coalition to take action on agrarian reform; when that unrest failed to materialize (or rather built up much more slowly than anticipated), the coalition allowed matters to drag. 'Moderate, defensive-type working-class pressure (even in industry), active employers' resistance, and an uncertain economic conjuncture, explain without doubt the governing coalition's relative disinterest in the agrarian problem.'[1] After two and a half years under left and centre-right republican governments, only 45,000 hectares had changed hands to the benefit of some 6,000–7,000 peasants.

The Popular Front electoral pact promised fiscal and financial help for the smallholding peasantry and renters, whom it considered 'the firmest base' of the necessary national reconstruction, and a new lease law. Hitherto, agrarian reform had done nothing to help the smallholding peasantry: a national agrarian bank, a lease law, redemption rights had been promised under the first coalition government but had never seen the light of day. Thus the 1936 electoral pact attempted to remedy the situation. But as to the urgent problem of the landless, it had virtually nothing to say (see section E).

Within four months of the Popular Front victory, under massive peasant pressure, over 100,000 landworkers were settled on nearly 600,000 hectares. No one, landowner or worker, could be unaware of the difference. The left republican agriculture minister, Mariano Ruiz-Funes, underlined the point in a speech a month before the uprising: 'A class struggle is being waged through agrarian reform . . .'[2]

No por mucho madrugar
Amanece mas temprano,
En España no hay quién sea
Católico y repúblicano

Arise as early as you wish
The dawn will break no earlier,
In Spain no one can be
Catholic and republican

1. J. Maurice, 'Problemas de la reforma agraria en la segunda republica', in *Sociedad, politica y cultura en la España de los siglos XIX–XX* (Madrid, 1973).
2. Cited in Maurice, ibid.

Si los curas y frailes supieran
La paliza que les van a dar,
Suberían al coro cantando
Libertad, libertad, libertad

If the priests and the friars knew
The beating they're going to get,
They'd go to the choir stalls singing,
Liberty, liberty, liberty

Sung to the tune of
the republican national anthem,
Himno de Riego

Yo tenía una bandera,
Hecha de sangre y de sol
Me dicen que no la quiera
Yo ya no soy español

I had a flag
The colour of blood and sun
They tell me I no longer love it
So I am a Spaniard no more

Reference to the red and gold flag of Spain
introduced in the eighteenth century and substituted
under the republic by a red, gold and mauve flag

B. The petty bourgeoisie and the religious question

The urban and provincial petty bourgeoisie – artisans, medium-sized peasantry, shopkeepers, civil servants, small industrialists, professionals – numbered in the 1930s perhaps some 1,300,000 (compared to an urban and rural proletariat of over 3 million). Excluding the north-eastern Mediterranean and sections of the northern Atlantic seaboards, the *provincial* petty bourgeoisie[1] had shown no particular predilection for the republic before its advent.

But it was to develop a considerable 'negative' political weight under the

1. The schematic use of the terms 'provincial' and 'urban' in connection with two sectors of the petty bourgeoisie is patently arbitrary, but is an attempt to differentiate between 'small town' life and that in the major capitals. Obviously, members of each sector could be found in the other's geo-social location, and the usage should be considered descriptive rather than analytic.

republic, withdrawing direct support from, withholding outright opposition to, the liberal republican regime. It formed the electoral support of the conservative republican parties, especially the CEDA from 1933 on, as long as these offered hope of protecting the interests and social positions it had occupied under the monarchy. These interests were, above all, local. The retention of power at the level of township and village was of equal, if not greater, import than national government, which was, moreover, 'centralist'. The provincial bourgeoisie displayed considerable skill in maintaining its local positions despite the change of regime. (See also section A.)

In the 1930s, nearly 60 per cent of the population lived in rural Spain. This could well mean townships with populations of several thousands, usually relatively self-sufficient communities dependent on agriculture, livestock, fishing, and, less frequently, mining. After Madrid and Barcelona, each with just over 1 million inhabitants in 1936, the next largest city, Valencia, had a population of 380,000. A provincial capital like Burgos, for example, had some 45,000 inhabitants. Life in the small towns often seemed closer in style to nineteenth- than twentieth-century models.

—All the profound changes which took place in Europe after the First World War reached Spain, which had not taken part in the conflict, in a mediated, sterile form; life continued much as before . . .

Jesús-Evaristo CASARIEGO, born in 1913, the son of an Asturian dentist, was brought up by his grandparents in the small Asturian coastal town of Luarca. Girls didn't go out alone, women didn't smoke, weddings were arranged, courting – if permission was given – took place with the man in the street, the girl on the balcony. Transportation was by bus, and it took five or six hours to travel the 100 km to the provincial capital, Oviedo. New ideas percolated slowly; it was 'an archaic life – made even more nineteenth-century-like for me by being brought up by grandparents who talked about the last Carlist war, the Franco-Prussian war, the war in Cuba as though they were yesterday . . . '

The petty bourgeoisie from which he came did not correspond in outlook to what, in western Europe, was generally expected of that class.

—In large areas of Spain, the petty bourgeois was still much closer in outlook to the Spanish *hidalgo* or minor nobility – to don Quixote – than to the typical European petty bourgeois of the time. Religion was more important to him than business; and when economic matters concerned him, it was much less to start up a small business and make money on the French model than to keep what money he already had in order to provide for his children. The European petty bourgeois, the shopkeeper or small merchant who defended the values of the French revolution, who was concerned about divorce to resolve his matrimonial problems, but unconcerned about his 'masculinity', did not really have his counterpart on any large scale in provincial Spain . . .

Monarchist until the monarchy fell, this petty bourgeoisie became republican out of convenience, he thought. It was a fluctuating mass, prepared neither to form a solid, liberal republican base nor to confront the republic head-on. This explained the success of Gil Robles and the CEDA which offered to defend the existing social order – and in particular religion – from within the confines of the republic.

A Carlist, CASARIEGO rose with the nationalists. Dr Carlos MARTINEZ, a fellow-Asturian and a radical socialist deputy in the 1931 Constituent Cortes, fought for the republic. But he, too, noted the uneven development which marked a large part of the provincial petty bourgeoisie. In his own party, modelled on the French party of the same name, he found a lack of the class which should have swelled its ranks – lawyers, doctors, engineers, medium-sized businessmen. In their place were small shopkeepers, socialist party and anarcho-syndicalist dissidents. With the exception of Catalonia, the Basque country and Valencia, the petty bourgeoisie very soon withdrew its support from the republic, remaining in a state of neutrality inclining to hostility. The case of Azaña was illustrative.

—Here was an intellectual, liberal democrat of stature, who should have represented the middle-class ideal: democratic freedoms, a liberal social policy, etc. The petty bourgeoisie should have rallied unanimously behind him. Instead, it refused him its support . . .

But if they failed to back Azaña – 'and their failure largely determined his' – then there were conservative Catholic parties to the right of him which a frightened petty bourgeoisie should have joined. On one occasion, given the task of looking for people in Asturias to join just such parties – Miguel Maura's and Alcalá Zamora's – he found himself making very little headway: 'The middle classes were not going to participate.' He often wondered why this was so, and the only explanation he could find was that the anarcho-syndicalist offensive against the republic frightened them.

Dionisio RIDRUEJO[1] was brought up in a provincial town of Old Castile and received the traditional middle-class education of the time: 'Catholic and patriotic', at the hands of Jesuits and Augustinians. Critical of his class's conservatism, but sharing much of its religious values, he found the solution in the Falange which he joined before the war.

For him, the petty bourgeoisie was much more a 'state of being' than a class conscious of itself as a class; it felt itself 'distinct' because it differentiated itself from the working class by a life style which – in very relative terms – brought it closer to the privileged upper bourgeoisie.

—Economically speaking, a schoolteacher, a shopkeeper, a petty civil servant, was much closer to the proletariat than to the upper class; but the fact that he wore shoes and usually a tie, gave him a personal dignity which made him feel close to the upper class. In provincial towns, moreover, there was very little difference in life style between the different strata of the bourgeoisie. It must be admitted that the big bourgeoisie did not exercise its undisputed power in a particularly ostentatious manner . . .

In fact, there were in these small provincial towns really only two classes, he believed: the upper and the lower. *Señoritos* and proletarians. All those who

1. See also Militancies 10, pp. 313–16.

wore ties, who had fixed employment and did not work with their hands, were *señoritos*. The poorer the province, the truer this distinction was.

—This provincial petty bourgeoisie – that large sector of it which had not been influenced by the enlightened bourgeoisie – would objectively have found its proper place within a reformist party under the republic. But its cultural and religious prejudices kept it firmly within traditionalist postures. Religion provided the cement which kept this 'traditionalist' class, as I call it, together. The fact that large sectors of the left were violently hostile to the church resulted in an unnecessarily crude polemic which influenced wide sectors of the petty bourgeoisie, as it did me. Anti-clericalism, of course, was a common antibody to a clericalism that had been a driving force in Spanish history for a long time. Because of these characteristics – its concept of itself, its economic position, its cultural and religious attitudes – the 'traditional' class was very easily manipulated and dominated by the conservative forces representing capitalist, militarist and clerical interests . . .

The provincial petty bourgeoisie was product and victim of the country's weak capitalist development. The urban and nationalist liberal petty bourgeoisie's attempt to introduce a liberal democracy lacked the support of its provincial counterpart. No other class could substitute for it; and when the military rose, it became the civilian base of the insurgent offensive and of the new, Franquista state.[1]

In the gulf between 'urban' and 'provincial' petty bourgeoisie, religion played a seemingly large part. The former stratum was heir to the anti-clerical liberals of the nineteenth century who had failed to carry the bourgeois revolution to its ultimate conclusion. The peculiar form of that revolution, which had concluded with the bourgeoisie's alliance with the landed aristocracy, had meant the acceptance of the oligarchy's dominant ideology; there was no 'rupture', no new bourgeois ideology. The church's ideological dominance – in the 1930s as in the previous century – was the opposite face of the bourgeoisie's failure to make its ideological revolution. From the preceding period of absolutism, the church provided the 'ideological categories to justify the repression and intolerance necessary to maintain the system, and had transposed these on to the religious plane: intolerance assumed the character of sanctity . . . The immobilist defence of the system charged with heresy any reforming attitude.'[2]

1. The question of whether a petty bourgeois base for fascism in Spain existed before the war was posed by Andreu Nin, the POUM leader. Unless the revolution were made, he wrote in February 1936, the petty bourgeoisie, which was unable to resolve its own problems, would 'throw itself into the arms of reaction – and in that case, fascism will have found the social base it has lacked until now'. ('Después de las elecciones del 16 de febrero', in *Los problemas de la revolución española.*) Nin did not pursue the analysis. Theoretically, the absence of a large industrial petty bourgeoisie deeply marked by the contradictions of capitalist development, empirically, the very slow growth of the Falange prior to the 1936 elections, and the mass support for the clerical-conservative CEDA (significantly, the Vatican continued to back the CEDA when it had abandoned the Italian and German Catholic parties for Mussolini and Hitler), suggest the accuracy of Nin's perception that such a base did not exist at that moment. However, a close analysis of the class, for which data is unavailable, would be necessary to confirm his supposition.

2. Elorza, 'La mentalidad absolutista en los orígenes de la España contemporánea', in *La utopía anarquista bajo la segunda república española.*

In taking on the church, the left republican–socialist coalition which had come to power after the republic's advent, confronted an opponent of great strength: 30,000 priests, 20,000 monks and friars, 60,000 nuns gave it the highest proportion of regular and secular clergy per head of population outside Italy. Its wealth was unknown but still large. Yet its real strength lay neither in its size nor wealth, but in its ideological dominance within society. In attempting to break this – especially in the important area of religious education – the urban petty bourgeoisie was attacking the ideological cornerstone of ruling-class domination. Religion was the 'cement' which bound other classes, including the provincial petty bourgeoisie, into acceptance of this power.

The new regime launched headlong into the battle. Religious freedom was proclaimed by decree; the new constitution separated church and state and cleared the path for abolishing state stipends for priests within two years, banning religious orders from engaging in any but religious teaching, making all education laic, dissolving the Jesuits, introducing divorce, civil marriage and burial. The reaction, as could be expected, was not long in coming.

—A great number of Spaniards called themselves Catholics because they had been baptized. Little else in their attitude to life would make one particularly aware that they were Catholic, maintained the monarchist professor and deputy, Pedro SAINZ RODRIGUEZ. Under the monarchy, on the feast day of the Sacred Heart, perhaps seven out of every hundred would display hangings from their balconies. When the republic forbade hangings, suddenly people who believed neither in the Sacred Heart, in Jesus nor in God himself, put out hangings . . .

In the opinion of David JATO, the falangist student leader, the liberal republicans forgot how easy it was to confuse anti-clericalism with anti-Catholicism. People who felt themselves profoundly Catholic, even if they weren't practising Catholics, came to feel that their religious sentiments were gravely threatened by the new regime.

Before any legislation had been introduced, less than a month after the republic's proclamation, an event took place that aroused the right, confirming its suspicions of the republic's anti-clericalism. After monarchists held a private meeting and the Royal March had been played, there was a riot. The next day a number of convents[1] in Madrid were fired, and the burning spread southward, to Málaga and Seville. In the view of a Madrid priest, Father Alejandro MARTINEZ, the republic committed suicide that day.

—Here was a regime which, unbelievable as it may sound, had come in with clerical support, and in less than a month was condoning the burning of convents and churches. The left in Spain had always been anti-clerical, anti-religious . . . It was from that day – 11 May, 1931 – that I realized nothing would be achieved by legal means; sooner or later, to save ourselves, we should have to rise[2] . . .

—The burnings had a tremendous impact on the country at large, recalled

1. Friars' abodes, as opposed to those of monks, are called convents in Spanish, as also are nunneries.

2. See also Militancies 15, pp. 419–21.

Marquess PUEBLA DE PARGA, a monarchist university student. In the face of the republic's disrespect for law and order, we anti-republican students began to organize, forming guards at night to defend the convents . . .

Another student, Enrique MIRET MAGDALENA, who belonged to the Catholic youth organization, saw that from that moment the clergy divided the country into 'Catholic' and 'non-Catholic', right-wing and left.

—Unable to grasp what was new in the world, the clergy shut itself in behind a palisade where it fomented an ideology which would sustain its position in society. They realized that the republic was going to combat clericalism, which was the bane of this country. At that time I shared the clergy's view; it was only later that I came to see things differently,[1] to realize that the average republican was very respectful of religion in fact . . .

Very few people took part in the convent burnings. The new regime acted maladroitly in not preventing the provocation which, after the event, was wholeheartedly condemned by the republican and socialist parties. But the shock-waves which reverberated through the bourgeoisie were tremendous; this was, after all, what it had expected, what modern Spanish history had led it to expect of the anti-clerical liberals.

A left republican youth leader in Madrid, Andrés MARQUEZ, denied that anti-clericalism was the main cause of the burnings. He had passed by the house where the monarchists were meeting the day before.

—What a provocation! Only weeks after the proclamation of the republic, which had happened so peacefully that anyone who wanted to could go to mass! The next day several convents were burnt but not a single priest, friar or nun was killed. Under the monarchy in the last century, not only did convents burn but priests were massacred. No, the fact of the matter was that the Spanish right had its roots in clericalism, was a 'religious' oligarchy; but it was a religion that had nothing to do with Christianity . . .

The real battle, however, was not to be waged over the burning of churches; more vital issues were at stake. Not surprisingly, it was the educational aspects that mobilized traditional opinion.[2]

—The removal of crucifixes from state school classrooms, the suppression of religious education in those schools, divided the country and created a very violent reaction, maintained Marquess PUEBLA DE PARGA. The matter of crucifixes caused the most bitter hatred; they were a symbol of the attempt to tear religious belief from the country's heart . . .

In reaction, believers and their children started to wear black crucifixes on their clothes. The law, however, permitted state schools to remain open on Sundays if sufficient numbers of parents petitioned that their children be taught religion.

1. See Episodes 5, pp. 298–300; also, Fraser, op. cit., pp. 102–3.

2. And also liberal petty bourgeois and proletarian opinion. One of the reasons for the attacks on convents, as much as on churches, was that the regular clergy virtually monopolized secondary education to the benefit of the children of the rich.

—That was a sign of tolerance, it's true. Volunteer schoolteachers and youths like myself would go and teach the children Sunday school. I enjoyed it, I felt I was doing something useful. Afterwards, we'd go into a local bar in the working-class district of Carabanchel bajo, which is where my school was, and have a beer. The workers in their Sunday best would joke with us. They seemed pleased we were teaching their children the catechism. No doubt, they supported parties which, in the Cortes, were voting in favour of these anti-clerical measures. It was a very contradictory, difficult period of Spanish history . . .

Not all left republicans shared their party's views on the religious question. Régulo MARTINEZ, the priest who had given up his parish to become a schoolmaster in a lay school, believed the offensive against the church was an error.

—Exaggerated, mistaken. Not just anti-clericalism, but a phobia against everything ecclesiastical and religious. I was in favour, and said so, of church and state being separated: it was fundamental to the well-being of both. I agreed with the dissolution of the Jesuits – they were the republic's bitterest enemy. One preached a sermon saying that any woman who applied for divorce was no better than a whore. I believed the republic was justified in abolishing bishops' and canons' stipends; but not those of the rural clergy. The republic wanted to expand education but lacked schoolmasters; let the priests help with this task. If the republic allowed them to help it, this rural clergy would be attracted to the republic. They had been deformed, as I had, by a seminary education and, like me, they would have to re-educate themselves . . .

In what was generally acknowledged to be one – if not the – most religious area in the peninsula, the Basque country, the clergy's reaction was more muted.[1] Father José María BASABILOTRA, a Bilbao priest recently ordained and exercising his ministry in a small village of Alava, felt there were even positive aspects to it. It made the Basque clergy work harder, brought them closer to the people.

—Of course, the burning of churches and the clergy's persecution depressed and angered us. This wasn't the republic we wanted, but it didn't make us anti-republican. I was in favour of the separation of church and state. Support of the church should be a matter for the faithful . . .

'Sons of the people who lived with the people', the Basque clergy kept faith with the humble, the ordinary. If the Basques' deep sense of religion was missing elsewhere, he blamed the priests, not the people; in other parts, the majority of the clergy was too close to the powerful and rich. 'Here people went to church to worship God – not to worship images.'

Like Father BASABILOTRA, a supporter of Basque nationalism, Father Luis ECHEBARRIA believed that if the republic had confined its religious legislation to the separation of church and state there would have been few repercussions.

1. Uneven development applied even to the church which had historically developed somewhat differently in the Basque country. It had never been a landowner there, the Inquisition had never held direct jurisdiction and, under the original *fueros* of Vizcaya, the bishop was prohibited from entering his diocese because his appointment by the king of Spain was considered political. Relations with the 'Spanish' hierarchy were never close, since Toledo was considered 'centralist'.

But instead, the republic was really attempting to wipe out religion. In the Basque country and Navarre, where 'religious belief was genuine', such a project was doomed to fail.

—In other parts, it was an official religion; as such it lacked the one thing necessary to prevent persecution being effective – a mass base. That was why elsewhere the clergy opposed the republic totally while we, here, opposed only its religious legislation. Anti-clericalism, in truth, hardly affected us . . .

In Catalonia, homeland of industrial anarcho-syndicalism, no churches or convents had been fired in 1931. Maurici SERRAHIMA, a leading member of Unió Democrática – 'the only Christian Democratic party to have existed in Spain' – felt that Catalan nationalism had been beneficial to the church in Catalonia. For the past fifteen years or so, the Catalan clergy – in response to the defence of Catalan interests which raised the country's general level of culture – concentrated attention on Catalan cultural matters. This had helped to open the church much more to the world. 'One couldn't call it conciliar, but it was authentically pre-conciliar.'

None the less, in the view of Tomás ROIG LLOP, a practising Catholic lawyer and Catalan liberal, this did not mean that the republic had not made a very serious political error in its handling of the religious problem. The evolution of the typical Spanish Catholic had been slow, if evolution had taken place at all. To expect the great mass of Spaniards to confront, simultaneously, a new political and a new religious situation when 'they did not know how to live out their religious beliefs' was expecting too much. The republic should have left the problem alone.

—It was much too delicate to permit radical solutions. That was true of Catalonia and all the more for much of the rest of Spain. At the same time it was necessary to make the church, especially the hierarchy, much more aware of the need to be close to the people as Cardinal Vidal i Barraquer of Tarragona and a few others were managing to do . . .

Although ROIG LLOP did not favour the separation of church and state, this – objectively considered – might have been accepted by Catholics had it not been for the fear that the republic was attacking Catholicism in general and religious education in particular. The church burnings and the subsequent legislation reinforced the fear.[1]

It was no accident that the liberal republicans pressed home their attack on the ruling class with more vigour at the ideological than at the economic level. The republicans were heirs of the nineteenth-century anti-clerical radicals; they had suffered more from ideological-cultural than socio-economic problems; and they had no wish to destroy the capitalist system, but rather to reform it. Their concern for cultural problems was amply demonstrated during the first two years of the republic when great progress was made in schooling.

1. Significantly, separation of church and state figured in General Mola's political programme for the uprising. The Cortes approved separation by a vote of 278 to 41. But on Article 26, which limited the activities of the religious orders and dissolved others, notably the Jesuits, almost half the deputies avoided participating, and the vote was 178 to 59 (see Jackson, *The Spanish Republic and the Civil War*, p. 51).

None the less, in the matter of establishing a parliamentary democracy, the bourgeoisie's two related bases of power could not be separated. Agrarian reform threatened economic power as lay education threatened ideological dominance. The opposition saw this plainly. Ernesto CASTAÑO, one of the prime movers in mobilizing catholic agrarian reaction in Salamanca to the agrarian legislation (see also section A), had no doubts that defence of one involved defence of the other.

—Material and religious interests were, necessarily, intertwined. In the bitter struggle that was taking place, we had to recruit every possible force which was opposed to republican violence. We were in the front line, the trenches. The constitution confirmed the republic's sectarian, anti-religious position, allowed Azaña to say that Spain was no longer catholic,[1] just as other measures plainly showed that the republic wanted to encourage class war on the land . . .

It was only later, during the war, that CASTAÑO began to see the church in a different light, realizing that it had not played a christian, educational role.[2] But before the war, and in particular in the first two years of the republic, defence of religion, defence of the family, defence of property, defence of the social order were the constituent parts of the overall bourgeois counter-offensive which was summed up in the phrase 'At the service of Spain'.

C. Two nationalisms

The problem confronting the petty bourgeois republicans of finding new forms of expressing and legitimizing bourgeois domination under the new regime included the task of satisfying the petty bourgeoisies of Catalonia and the Basque country in their desire for home rule. Success would reinforce these bourgeoisies in their own countries and thereby reinforce the republic in the centre. The republican-dominated coalition understood this in respect of Catalonia, which received an autonomy statute in 1932; but the Basque country had to wait until the war. The difference was not accidental.

—The Catalans got their statute because they were on the left. But we Basque nationalists were neither black nor white, we fitted no definition, we were disliked by everyone . . .

This view, expressed by Juan Manuel EPALZA, member of a leading Bilbao PNV family, pointed to a widely accepted reality. The Catalan petty bourgeoisie and its political party, the Esquerra Republicana de Catalunya, stood firmly to the left of the PNV whose slogan was 'God and the Old Laws'. Members of the future Esquerra had subscribed to the San Sebastián pact of 1930 which laid the political foundations of the new republic; the PNV had not. Francesc Macià,

1. The prime minister said that the religious situation of a country was not constituted by the 'numerical sum of beliefs and believers, but by the creative effort of its spirit, the direction followed by its culture'. In this sense, Spain had been Catholic in the sixteenth century and, despite its millions of believers, no longer was today. (Jackson, op. cit., p. 50.) A statement which was both provocative and bound to be misinterpreted by his enemies.

2. See Militancies 14, pp. 414–16.

the Esquerra's leader, declared the Catalan republic a few hours before the second Spanish republic was proclaimed in Madrid on 14 April, 1931;[1] the PNV did not emulate this dramatic move. It waited three days to welcome the republic and call for an autonomous Basque regime within a federal republic which would recognize the 'freedom and independence of the Catholic church'.[2]

The PNV was a liberal, anti-socialist and Catholic party; the Esquerra was a radical party whose programme included 'the socialization of wealth for the benefit of the collectivity'.

The differences between the two nationalist parties expressed deeper socio-economic differences between the two countries – and between them and the rest of the Spanish state.[3]

Catalan capitalism, based on family-owned enterprises, mainly in textile consumer goods, required a large Spanish market. The agrarian oligarchy under the monarchy consistently prevented the expansion of this market by its failure to 'modernize' agriculture and increase domestic purchasing power. Lacking finance capital with which to penetrate the Spanish economy, the Catalan bourgeoisie retrenched into Catalanism the better to take over and 'renovate' the Spanish state – something it signally failed to do. At crucial moments, when its class interests appeared threatened by the proletariat, it sacrificed nationalism to the central government's intervention.

Unlike its Catalan counterpart, the industrial and financial Basque bourgeoisie did not espouse nationalism. Basque industry, producing mainly capital goods, and finance capital was much less dependent on the Spanish consumer market and much closer to the landed oligarchy. Only one of Spain's major six banks in the first quarter of the twentieth century was not directly or indirectly linked to Vizcayan capital, and two were actually founded in Bilbao. Unlike Catalan enterprise, Vizcayan capital operated in joint-stock companies. Thanks to its resources – the major one, iron ore exports, was totally independent of the

1. It appears that he first proclaimed the Catalan republican *state* and called for a confederation of Iberian peoples. This, however, was shortly changed to the Catalan republic 'as an integral state of an Iberian federation'; and later, on the insistence of representatives of the new republican government in Madrid, he agreed to await the drafting of an autonomy statute (see J. A. González Casanova, 'La proclamació de la república a Catalunya', in *Canigó* (Barcelona, April 1975).

2. Payne, *El nacionalismo vasco*, p. 171.

3. The difference between Catalonia and the state as a whole can be rapidly seen in the following statistic of the percentage distribution of the working population in 1930, the all-Spanish percentage figuring in brackets.

Agriculture	*Industry*	*Services*
26·6 (45·5)	50·7 (26·5)	22·0 (27·9)

Source: Balcells, *Cataluña Contemporánea II (1900–1936)*, pp. 60–61.

The proportions of those engaged in agriculture and industry are approximately reversed. Unfortunately, I have been unable to find a directly comparable statistic for the Basque country. The Basque nationalists claimed in the 1930s that with 5 per cent of the Spanish state's total population they produced 24 per cent of the banking capital, 42 per cent of all bank deposits, 33 per cent of all personal savings, 78 per cent and 74 per cent respectively of all iron and steel production, 71 per cent of all paper and naval industry. (Payne, *El nacionalismo vasco*, p. 163.) Catalonia, with 12 per cent of the state's total population, produced 34 per cent of all personal savings, 31 per cent of all electricity, 19·5 per cent of banking capital and 28 per cent of industrial capital (see J. Alzina, *L'economía de la Catalunya autònoma*, Barcelona, 1933, cited in Balcells, op. cit., pp. 110–11).

Spanish market – the Basque bourgeoisie was better placed to 'cash in' its economic weight in political terms in Madrid. It needed no nationalism to give it weight.[1]

By the 1930s, both the large and petty bourgeoisie in Catalonia was able to sustain separate nationalist, class-based parties, the Lliga Catalana and the Esquerra. In the Basque country, only the inter-class PNV, whose policies were closer to the liberal conservative Lliga than to the Esquerra, represented nationalism.[2]

Politically speaking, both Esquerra and PNV displaced their respective oligarchies under the republic. Both were also supported by broadly the same social class: peasantry and urban petty bourgeoisie – small industrialists and artisans. But there the similarities ended.

Tomás ROIG LLOP, a Catalan nationalist lawyer who joined the Lliga under the republic, believed that the differences could be easily felt. As a member of a Catalan commission invited by the PNV to visit the Basque country in 1933, he was impressed by the intense nationalist and religious feeling he saw there. Intuitive nationalist sentiment in the Basque country was much deeper than in Catalonia.

—I was tremendously impressed to see workers, priests and the middle classes spontaneously mingling together, united by their intense nationalism. What was lacking in Basque nationalism was the cultural element. Catalans live and feel their culture, their traditions, their language in particular, very strongly . . .

Whatever the differences, it was, he felt, a great mistake of the republic not to have granted an autonomy statute to the Basque country at the same time as to Catalonia.

In August 1931, a draft statute was drawn up and approved by 75 per cent of the Catalan electorate. In Barcelona, with 370,000 non-Catalan inhabitants in its population of 1 million, only 3,000 votes were recorded against the draft. The working class had, patently, voted for home rule. The CNT left its members to act as they wished. Josep COSTA, a lifelong CNT militant in the textile industry, sympathized with the concept of Catalan autonomy. Although the libertarian movement maintained that voting was a 'stupidity which would resolve no problems' – a position with which, ideologically, he identified himself – he voted for the draft.

—I wasn't alone. Large sectors of the CNT in Catalonia were more or less Catalanist. Immigrant workers, on the other hand, tended to be hostile. Posters appeared before the war in La Torrasa district of the city saying: 'It is forbidden to speak Catalan here.' It was this type of newly arrived immigrant worker who backed the extremist elements in the CNT . . .

1. See Ortzi, *Historia de Euskadi: el nacionalismo vasco y ETA* (Paris, 1975), p. 145. Significantly, the founder of Catalan nationalism, Prat de la Riba, spoke for big Catalan capital, while his Basque counterpart, Sabino Arana, the son of a shipbuilder whose wood ships had been displaced by iron, was hostile to the Basque oligarchy.

2. A split in the PNV in 1930 led to the creation of Acción Nacionalista Vasca (ANV); but it remained small throughout the republic. See below, pp. 540–41.

But when the statute was granted in September 1932, COSTA got a shock. He realized suddenly that, although Catalonia now had its own government, economic interests remained the same as before.

—My boss was a Catalanist. He went on screwing me and the rest of us workers as he had done before. I realized I had to choose where my real interests lay – and there couldn't be much doubt about that . . .

The autonomy statute approved by the constituent assembly in Madrid did not provide for the 'autonomous state' which three quarters of the Catalan electorate had voted for. Instead, it referred to Catalonia as an 'autonomous region' and conferred a considerably smaller portion of internal tax contributions than had been demanded.[1]

The new statute recognized Catalan as the official language alongside Castilian, and gave the Generalitat – named after the medieval parliament of the kingdom of Aragon–Catalonia – the following major areas of competence: schooling, internal police services, road, rail and water transport, public works, justice and certain tax-collecting.

The Spanish right was up in arms over the statute; and the phrase was no metaphor. The monarcho-militarist rising by General Sanjurjo in Seville in August 1932, was an attempt to prevent parliamentary passage of the bill (see section F, p. 564). Four months earlier, Calvo Sotelo, the monarchist leader, had termed the bill a 'spoliation of sovereignty and a theft of patrimony'.

Underlying this outburst by General Primo de Rivera's former finance minister was a certain economic reality: the Spanish state received just under 19 per cent of its total revenue from Catalonia while spending only 5 per cent of its total budget in Catalonia.[2]

Significantly, opposition in the constituent assembly was not confined to the right but stretched to include liberal republicans. Hostility to 'separatism' was one of the few ideological areas in which the old monarchical ruling class had hegemonized large sectors of other classes, including the working class, outside the advanced Atlantic and Mediterranean seaboards.

In fact the Esquerra was never separatist, although its enemies liked to maintain the myth.

—Separatism was supported by only a small minority in Catalonia and never played a dominant role. But one thing must be remembered, stressed ROIG LLOP: as soon as Catalans of different tendencies begin to group under the banner of Catalan nationalism, people in Spain who previously have shown a lively sympathy for Catalonia start to view our problem with considerable hostility . . .

1. 'In 1933, to ensure that the budget for the services which the state was making over to the Generalitat (the new Catalan government) was the same as the national per capita average, it should have equalled 251·5 million pesetas. That is, 12·1 per cent of the total, since that was the percentage of the Catalan population in the total Spanish population. Instead, the amount (conceded by the central government) was 135 millions' (Balcells, op. cit., p. 25). The lack of finance capital – the Bank of Catalonia crashed in 1931 – now made itself felt, for the Generalitat had no equivalent of the Bank of Spain behind it.

2. According to the calculations of the Catalan economist J. Alzina, cited in Balcells, op. cit., pp. 111–12.

This was explicable by the fear of separatism, something which, in his view, it was impossible to conceive of geographically, economically or 'mentally'. Catalonia was the transit route of Spain to the rest of Europe.

—But as soon as there is the slightest threat of Catalan separatism, then all the factions in Madrid automatically combine to combat the threat; and the army has been the leader in putting down the threat . . .

Victorious in the 1931 municipal elections that led to the republic's proclamation, the Esquerra thereafter was not only the dominant Catalan political party but the majority governing party. Its task, of course, was to resolve the fundamental bourgeois crisis. The autonomy question having received a solution (even if that solution did not satisfy all nationalist aspirations), there remained the working class. The former could help solve the latter, more difficult task. A radical working class required radical social solutions which could be taken within the framework of a self-governing Catalonia.

Given the economic situation, it was not easy to achieve such solutions, however. Although the Catalan textile industry was less affected by the depression for the first two years of the republic than other industrial sectors, the paucity of financial means afforded to the Generalitat by the central government and the absence of Catalan finance capital, made it difficult to re-activate the Catalan economy. The latter, obviously, was an important element in 'incorporating' the working class. Unemployment amongst building workers, an anarcho-syndicalist stronghold, was massive in Barcelona. None the less, they fought a bitter three-and-a-half-month strike in mid-1933, the worst year of the depression. The influence of the FAI 'purists' within the CNT made the petty bourgeois republicans' task even harder. For in fact the Esquerra required working-class votes to remain in power.

Sebastià CLARA, one of the signatories of the *treintista* manifesto which had split the CNT in 1931 (see section D), became an Esquerra supporter, though not a member. Had there been a Catalan socialist party with the same chance of attracting working-class support he would have preferred to work with it.

—But the CNT masses wouldn't have shared my point of view. The CNT was not a-political, it was fundamentally anti-political. And, within that perspective, CNT militants were far more hostile to authoritarian marxist parties which defended the need for a state than they were to a petty bourgeois republican party like the Esquerra. With the support of working-class votes, the Esquerra became and remained the dominant party in Catalonia . . .[1]

1. The question of electoral abstentionism, so often credited – especially by anarcho-syndicalists – with decisive political results, is only now being studied in depth. In the interim, the comment by Molas, in his *El sistema de partidos políticos en Cataluña, 1931–1936*, would appear valid for Catalonia. 'Pure' anarchists of the FAI almost certainly never voted, while moderate anarcho-syndicalists of the *treintista* line, and ordinary CNT union members (who were not necessarily anarcho-syndicalists), might very well vote. Molas's study of a series of elections in Catalonia in the 1930s bears out his view, suggesting that in all probability a majority of the CNT voted for the Esquerra. (For a detailed study of voting patterns in one election in Gerona province, see M. Vilanova, *Revista de Geografía*, University of Barcelona, Jan.–Dec. 1974; also M. V. Goni, *El abstencionismo electoral durante la segunda republica en San Feliu de Guixols*, memoria a la Fundación Juan March (unpublished).

The Esquerra maintained itself in power by an electoral strategy of incorporating elements known for their political and social leftism, including socialists, in order to attract the radicalized petty bourgeoisie and proletariat; independent republicans and representatives of the liberal Catalan bourgeoisie; and peasant leaders to ensure the important support of the *rabassaires*, the Catalan peasant union.[1]

—Progress didn't frighten the Esquerra, recalled Josep ANDREU ABELLO, one of the party's deputies in the Catalan parliament. Though it lacked a clear socialist position, it was a progressive party which included members of the bourgeoisie, left-wing progressives, socialists and even a certain number of CNT members . . .

By 1934, when a centre government with CEDA parliamentary support was in power in Madrid, Catalonia alone in the Spanish state remained under left republican rule. Confrontation was almost inevitable. It arose – paradoxically in an industrial region – over agriculture: the *Llei de contractes de conreu*, the Esquerra's land reform, was opposed by the upper bourgeoisie and judged to be 'unconstitutional' (see section A). This, and the slow transfer of powers under the autonomy statute, provoked the Esquerra into joining the October 1934 uprising.

In the preceding year, one wing of the party had become increasingly nationalistic and proto-fascist. Its leader, Dencàs, Generalitat councillor of public order, and his loyal follower Miquel Badía, Barcelona police chief, harried the CNT, which used this as a pretext for not joining the rising. On the evening of 6 October, Lluis Companys, the Esquerra leader and member of the party's democratic republic wing, declared – once again – the Catalan state within the Federal Spanish republic. Dencàs's green-shirted *escamots* (squads), who had wished for a declaration of independence, took to the streets. Without the CNT, no rising in Barcelona could hope to succeed. Within less than twelve hours, the Generalitat surrendered to a small army force, and the uprising was over. Dencàs fled before the surrender. Companys and the members of the Generalitat government were arrested and sentenced to thirty years' imprisonment. The autonomy statute was suspended.

The defeat had one important effect on the Esquerra. It meant the end, within the party, of the extreme nationalist and proto-fascist Estat Català wing. Henceforth, the democratic republican tendency, which was more closely linked to the petty bourgeoisie, was dominant. As a result, the Esquerra became increasingly moderate and sought a modus vivendi, within the republican regime, with the Lliga Catalana, representative of the large bourgeoisie.[2]

In February 1936, the Esquerra, as the leading member of the Left Front of Catalonia (as the Popular Front was known there), was restored to its dominant political position. The Left Front won 59 per cent of the popular vote against 41 per cent for the right. Companys and his government were released from prison. At the same time the Lliga Catalana adopted a more centralist position than its anti-liberal, anti-autonomy posture of the election campaign and prepared to become a loyal opposition. This, in ROIG LLOP's opinion, was in

1. See Molas, op. cit., p. 83.
2. See Molas, op. cit., p. 82.

accord with middle-class Catalan tradition. 'Coexistence, conciliation, dialogue, a hatred of violence – in short, the English model, which for us represented the political ideal . . .'

Catalonia, despite the weight of the CNT, could arguably be said to be the only area within the Spanish state before the war where an advanced bourgeois democracy was establishing solid roots.

Compared to the Esquerra, the PNV pre-war was a non-governing party in a non-autonomous country confronted by a socialist-led working class strongly influenced by Prieto's centrist line. Nationalism and religion provided the PNV's ideological 'cement'. EPALZA, of the party's youth movement Mendigoixales, likened the PNV to a harlequin's costume.

—It covered everything: upper class, middle class, workers, peasants. United by a deep sense of religion, Basque patriotism and democracy.[1] It had its left and right wings; it was like a resistance movement. When the oppressor had been got rid of and freedom won, the party would almost certainly split into its constituent parts. Meanwhile, it represented the spectrum of a future Basque parliament, for the other parties had excluded themselves by their refusal to espouse the nationalist cause . . .

But what did 'freedom' mean in terms of the future? An independent nation state, or autonomy within the Spanish state? The PNV, in Luis MICHELENA's view, was always ambiguous about its aims. A Basque nationalist party militant from the age of fifteen (and later the leading philologist of the Basque language), he knew that the party avoided coming out in favour simply of home rule.

—But it also avoided defining itself as separatist. In fact, I believe that the bulk of its supporters really wanted an autonomy sufficient to defend the 'personality' of the Basque country . . .

Separatism was born in Madrid, thought EPALZA. The Basque country wanted to be itself, live its own life.

—Was that incompatible with being more or less united with Spain? No more than, say, Canada being part of the Commonwealth. But if Spain acted towards us in the way that the English landlords acted in Ireland, then separatism was inevitable. We became separatists finally because there was no other way of solving the matter. We were Basques, and Euzkadi was our homeland. It was as simple and as complicated as that. To build a wall of China around our country was an absurdity, of course. But if we were forced to by the attitude of others, then we would have to do so. Sentiments, hatreds, can run so high that one would prefer to be united with Alaska rather than with one's neighbour . . .

Jagi-Jagi ('Arise-Arise'), the youth movement which had split from the PNV, was overtly separatist. The split had come, in the words of a Jagi-Jagi member, because the PNV was 'too concerned with Spanish politics' and not radical enough in its social policies. But separatism, in Trifón ETARTE's view,

1. The lower clergy, with its deep roots in local Basque life, was one of nationalism's main bases of support. But priests were not permitted to be members of the PNV.

was not synonymous with isolationism or exclusivity. It meant wanting to be free to create a union of all Basques on both sides of the Pyrenees.

—A union with its own Basque personality which would then join other unions. Once our personality has been recognized, there is no problem involved in reaching agreement with Spain or with a confederation of the peoples of Spain. But first we had to be free – free from the central state which oppressed us . . .

The sense of oppression, beginning with the erosion and final abolition of the foral rights[1] after the last Carlist war in 1876, was felt particularly at the cultural level. There was no Basque university; even to qualify as a nurse a woman had to travel to Valladolid in Old Castile to sit her examination. There was discrimination against Basque-speakers at school.

—We didn't talk Basque at home. Yet my parents knew Basque better than they did Spanish, recalled Asunción CARO, daughter of a merchant navy captain. My father, whose native language was Basque, had to struggle very hard to pass his exams in Spanish. So when it came to us children, he hoped to spare us the same difficulties . . .

Her mother shared this view. She could remember being made to wear 'the ring' on her finger for speaking Basque at school – 'a horrible punishment imposed by the Spanish schoolmistress, who removed the ring only when a pupil denounced another for speaking Basque'. Asunción CARO didn't learn Basque as a child.

—It was considered vulgar, peasant-like to be caught speaking Basque by the majority of Spanish nuns at my school. We couldn't speak our own language in our country . . .[2]

A high proportion of the Bilbao nationalist petty bourgeoisie was indeed – and for the same reason – unable to speak Basque. Reflecting on the cause, when they knew that their grandparents, if not their parents, had spoken the language, reaffirmed their sense of oppression.

From shortly after the republic's proclamation until the outbreak of the war, three projected home rule statutes were presented without becoming law. The first, in 1931, foundered in the constituent assembly because it included a clause guaranteeing the complete autonomy of the 'Basque state's' relations with the church and the right to negotiate an independent concordat with the Vatican. The second, which omitted this clause and referred to a Basque 'autonomous political administration within the Spanish state', was narrowly defeated by Navarre.[3] A third project was presented to a plebiscite in November 1933. While it won nearly 90 per cent of the vote in Vizcaya and Guipúzcoa, the two seaboard provinces, it secured less than 50 per cent of the vote in Alava to the south. The latter was used by the centre-right, which had just come to

1. Relative self-government in fiscal, military and administrative matters via municipally elected delegates to the governing *juntas generales* within the all-Spanish monarchical state.

2. Whereas Catalan for a Spanish-speaker is a relatively easy language to learn, Basque without any common roots is extremely difficult.

3. By a vote of 123 to 109 municipalities. As it was a single statute for the four provinces, it meant that it had to be re-elaborated to cover the remaining three: Vizcaya, Guipúzcoa and Alava. (For the situation of Navarre, see p. 541.)

power in Madrid, to argue against the concession of a statute. Finally, after the Popular Front electoral victory, the third statute was retabled in parliament and was being considered by a parliamentary committee when the war started.

Too right-wing to find support in the republican–socialist coalition of 1931–3,[1] the PNV was too nationalistic and liberal to be supported by the centre-right government which succeeded it until 1935. The right's hostility to home rule had increased, and the Catalan statute was now identified with the left. From 1931 and an electoral alliance with the Carlists, the PNV had moved by 1934 to support of the Esquerra in its conflict with the central government.

Although the PNV followed a line 'which sometimes seemed to take us closer to the right and at other times to the left', it was, in EPALZA's view, 'a line which ran straighter than either right or left'.

A line which consistently pursued the goal of autonomy but which initially, at least, misread the map of political realities in its quest. Such was MICHELENA's view.

—We were ourselves largely responsible for cutting off the possibility of home rule during the constituent assembly. We were too clerical – and the republican regime too anti-clerical. To bring in religious questions, to propose direct relations with the Vatican, as in the first proposed statute, was patently unacceptable to Madrid. The Catalans were more advanced in these matters than we. They knew it too. We were accused – by Prieto – of trying to create a Vaticanist Gibraltar in the north . . .

But the right, which had initially supported home rule, saw that the republic was 'taking root' and that Basque autonomy would only consolidate it. They began to oppose it.

—Under the centre-right regime we clearly saw that we would not be granted autonomy. And so, little by little, we began to move towards the defence of democratic positions, supporting the Esquerra in the conflict over its agrarian reform law . . .

The difference between the PNV and the Esquerra was clearly illustrated in October 1934. Whereas the Esquerra rose, the PNV – while considering that the major danger came from the right – ordered its members to abstain. In this it foreshadowed what many members were to feel should have been the party's attitude at the beginning of the war.[2]

If there was mutual suspicion between the liberal republicans in Madrid and the PNV, there was outright hostility between the working-class parties in the Basque country and the nationalists. Street clashes led to shootings and even

1. It is worth recalling that mutual suspicion between the two had historical roots: the petty bourgeois republicans in the coalition and those in the PNV were the political heirs respectively of the liberals and Carlists who had fought the civil wars of the nineteenth century.

2. Solidaridad de Trabajadores Vascos (STV), the Basque nationalist trade union, did, however, order its members out on strike; in consequence a considerable number of PNV members who belonged to STV were involved. 'But the STV did not order us to support the insurrection. All the factories in the industrial zones of Guipúzcoa and Vizcaya came out on strike, and a number of STV militants were imprisoned afterwards, as were individual PNV members' (MICHELENA). The STV was ordered to be dissolved by the civil governor after the events.

deaths in the first two years of the republic. Ramón RUBIAL, lathe operator and UGT metalworkers' executive member, remembered that the cry *¡Gora Euzkadi!* (Long live the Basque country) was enough to launch socialists into the attack. The Basque nationalists were 'conservative, confessional and racialist'. Mining fortunes had been built on immigrant labour which lived in virtual ghettoes in the mining villages of Las Encartaciones.

—We believed that the liberation of the region had to come with the liberation of all Spain – the liberation from capitalism. When the new republican constitution incorporated the idea of regional autonomy, we accepted it. But our hostility towards the PNV as a party did not cease. The socialist party then, it must be recalled, was resolutely anti-clerical. A member could be expelled from his branch for getting married in church or baptizing his children. The church was allied with the capitalists, and we had a class position to defend . . .[1]

The charge of racialism was supported by a young communist miner, Saturnino CALVO.

—The foremen and supervisors were Basques; the majority of the miners were from other parts of Spain. The PNV supporters had their own insulting word to describe us non-Basques: *maketo*.[2] But the communist party's attitude to the nationalists was, admittedly, pretty sectarian in the first years of the republic . . .

The view that the influx of immigrant workers was a threat and that the left-wing parties were the mortal enemy was widespread among PNV supporters. Pedro BASABILOTRA, the son of a building contractor who had returned from three years at a Catholic school in Scotland to join the party, staunchly believed that the Basques had to defend their heritage.

—The flood of immigrants threatened the purity of the Basque race, our blood. We weren't racialists – no, no! I have nothing against the peoples of any nation, only their governments. Moreover, most of these immigrants joined the socialist party. The left was as sectarian as the right. We were struggling for an independent state. If Britain would have helped us, I for one would have gladly supported joining the Commonwealth . . .[3]

Failure to lead the struggle for the right to self-determination left the

1. Reconciliation between PNV and socialist militants began after the defeat of Euzkadi in the war, when they were imprisoned together and came to know each other.

2. In the vocabulary of Sabino Arana, founder of Basque nationalism, Maketanía was Spain. In his writings, he condemned mixed (Basque-Spanish) marriage, and defended the 'purity' of the Basque race and language as a means of preserving the values and forms of Basque life. For a Spaniard to speak Basque would be the 'ruin' of these values. (It should be added that the Catalan bourgeoisie tended to refer depreciatingly to immigrant southern workers as *Murcianos* – Murcia being one of the provinces from which many migrants came.) In Sabino Arana's view, one of the differences between Catalan and Basque nationalisms was that the former attempted to attract Spaniards to its policies while Basque nationalism consisted in 'spontaneously rejecting Spaniards as foreigners'. (I am indebted to M. Heiberg and M. Escudero for this observation contained in Sabino Arana's 'Minuta: Errores Catalanistas', *Obras completas*, Bayonne, 1965, p. 401.)

3. Ramón de la Sota, one of the few large Bilbao industrialists to support Basque nationalism, refused a Spanish title and accepted a British knighthood for his services after the First World War.

proletarian parties without the means to win over large sectors of the Basque workers and peasants. This was clearly demonstrated in 1936 when the Popular Front espoused home rule and the suspension of rural evictions, and the PNV lost five of the twelve seats it had won in the previous general elections of 1933. The Popular Front now won seven seats to put it level with the PNV. The latter joined neither left- nor right-wing electoral alliances in 1936, standing for a programme which was resumed in its election slogans as : 'For Christian civilization! For Basque liberty! For social justice!'

Unlike the Catalanist petty bourgeoisie, the Basque nationalist movement was able to sustain a trade union.[1] This was Solidaridad de Trabajadores Vascos, a catholic union in its origins. Its president was Manuel ROBLES, a linotype operator, who was elected to his post in 1933, the same year in which he became a PNV deputy to parliament. The union did not believe in the class struggle; the latter was 'society's sickness'.

—We couldn't believe that the history of the world should be reduced to two classes. Certainly, it was the capitalists who were responsible for imposing a system opposed to the workers. But we always remembered Basque history, the time before we lost our freedom, in which the class struggle did not exist . . .

'Communitarianism', a third way between marxist socialism and capitalism, was the solution the STV proposed. The trouble with socialism, ROBLES believed, was that it did little to give the actual worker control over the means of production, which were taken over by the state. As to capitalism, the STV wanted to show the owners, the monopolists, that it was possible to run industry differently, to allow workers' participation so that each would understand the purpose of what he or she was producing.

The STV, which by the 1930s was no longer a confessional union, set up consumer and producer cooperatives and organized the peasantry; in 1936 it claimed 100,000 members.[2]

While being the largest, the PNV was not the only Basque nationalist party. Acción Nacionalista Vasca, the result of a split from the PNV in 1930, declared itself republican from the start and joined the anti-monarchist bloc before the republic. In 1936 it formed part of the Popular Front.

—What differentiated us most from the PNV was our desire to separate politics and religion, explained Gonzalo NARDIZ, one of ANV's founders. We were not separatists. Politically speaking, the existence of a nation with its own rights is compatible with the existence of the Spanish state. We considered separatism an impossibility, and devoted our efforts to finding a means of reaching an understanding with the Spanish state . . .

ANV adopted a socialistic platform which called for the nationalization of basic industries, banking and communications. Recruiting mainly in the urban

1. The CADCI (Centre Autonomista de Dependents del Comerç i de la Indústria) and the *rabassaires*' (peasants) union deserted the Esquerra, going over progressively to working-class political postures during the republic. (See Molas, op. cit., p. 86, and Balcells, op. cit., p. 36.)

2. 'Including more than 9,000 farming families, each of whom might have six to eight members' (ROBLES).

petty bourgeoisie, it did not grow rapidly, evidence of the conservative nationalist milieu in which it had to operate.

The heartland of Basque nationalism lay in Vizcaya and Guipúzcoa, the two industrialized provinces. Basque-speakers were more widespread there than in Alava, the third Basque province, or in Navarre. The latter, as we have seen, narrowly rejected joining Basque home rule in 1931. Use of Basque had been gradually declining in Navarre and was concentrated mainly in the mountainous north where the peasantry supported nationalism. But where the peasantry was self-sufficient or relatively prosperous as in other areas of Navarre, it tended to Carlism. On the extensive estates along the Ebro in south-eastern Navarre, the agricultural workers joined the UGT or CNT.[1]

The Carlists by and large rejected Basque nationalism because it was 'separatist'; regionalists, defenders of their *fueros*,[2] they had no wish to 'dismember' the nation. The PNV had only once won a parliamentary seat in Navarre under the republic, and that had been in 1931.

But there were perhaps other reasons why sectors of the bourgeois Carlist leadership in Navarre did not support Basque home rule.

—We didn't feel sufficiently identified with the Basque country to exchange dependence on Madrid for dependence on Bilbao and San Sebastián, explained Mario OZCOIDI, a Pamplona Carlist . . .

The financial and industrial strength of the two cities to the north might well be seen by a predominantly rural Carlist bourgeoisie as more threatening than that of unindustrialized Madrid to the south. Agrarian Navarre might be defenceless against one of the two most advanced industrial regions in the Spanish state.

That this was not necessarily the view of the Carlist peasantry, however, was suggested by Antonio IZU. He believed that the Carlist leadership, as personified by the Conde de Rodezno, was responsible for the split with the Basque nationalists.

—In the struggle between centralism and regionalism, the leadership always sided with the former. In this case, it argued that the Catholic faith could not be defended by coming to agreement with an anti-Catholic republican government and demanded a statute which would respect religion. We, who weren't of the leadership tendency, would certainly have accepted the autonomy statute had Carlists and nationalists reached agreement . . .

But it was not to be. The division of 1931, and the Carlist rejection of its political heir, Basque nationalism, was to be fought out six years later in the green countryside of Guipúzcoa and Vizcaya.

1. Ortzi, *Historia de Euzkadi: el nacionalismo vasco y ETA*, p. 207, discusses the socio-economic structure and the peasantry's political allegiances in greater detail. Of the 400,000 Basque-speakers in the 1930s, 80,000 were in Navarre, 10,000 in Alava and the rest in Vizcaya and Guipúzcoa. The population of Navarre was 350,000, Vizcaya 500,000, Guipúzcoa 311,000 and Alava 105,000.

2. The Navarrese *fueros*, in terms of self-government, were more extensive than those of the Basque provinces which had been reduced in 1876 to a '*concierto económico*' or the right to negotiate a global tax contribution to the central government and apportion the tax-raising themselves.

D. Libertarians and the republic

Two months after the republic's advent, in which a number of anarcho-syndicalist leaders had unofficially participated, the CNT declared that it remained 'in open war with the state. We are confronted by the Constituent Cortes as we would be by any power that oppresses us.'

The republican–socialist coalition responded with a similar declaration. As a result, though not formally outlawed, the half of the country's working class that was enrolled in the CNT was virtually outside the law. This was a serious situation for a new regime whose political success depended in great part on the incorporation of the working class. It was, if anything, an even more serious situation for the working class to find itself irremediably split at the start of a new revolutionary period.

The split, as is well known, was not new. The introduction of anarchism in the previous century preceded that of socialism in Spain; then, as now, the question of the state and the working-class movement's participation in politics divided them. Until 1932 the CNT, undoubtedly the most revolutionary mass union organization that the European working class had endowed itself with, outnumbered the socialist UGT. Anarcho-syndicalism was deeply rooted in certain areas of Spain – amongst the industrial Catalan working class and the Andalusian rural proletariat; in certain points of Galicia and Asturias, and increasingly in the Levant, Saragossa and Madrid. Its major strength was amongst agricultural labourers, textile, building and wood workers. Almost the only place where it had strength in heavy industry or mining was in Asturias, especially in the steel town of La Felguera.

Outlawed during the dictatorship, the CNT took its stance of open war against the republic at its first congress for twelve years, held in Madrid. The decision represented a victory of the ultra-left 'purists' organized around the FAI, and manifested a division which, from as far back as the 1880s, had marked the movement. On the one hand, those who believed that revolution could be achieved by violent actions which would set the masses in spontaneous movement; on the other, those who thought that revolution required the prior organization and education, within a coherent revolutionary strategy, of the masses.

Both tendencies could agree on the ultimate revolutionary objectives: the abolition of private property, government and state, and the administration of production by the producers themselves: workers' self-management. The proletariat would sweep aside rural and industrial capitalists, the state and politics would disappear, and farms and factories would be run by free associations of producers. How this was to be achieved, and the structure to be given to it once it had been achieved, was where the differences arose.

The two differentiated but linked concepts which comprised anarcho-syndicalism, as its hyphenated name suggested, could by the 1930s be schematically stated in a series of polarities: rural/urban; local/national; artisanal/industrial; spontaneous/organized; autarkic/inter-dependent; anti-intellectual/intellectual.

The first in the series could broadly be categorized as the anarchist view. Libertarian communism and its attainment was characterized by its simplicity:

> There is no need to invent anything, or to create a new organism. The nuclei of the organization around which the future economic life will be organized already exist in the present society: the trade union and the free municipality . . . [The latter] of ancient origin in which, spontaneously, the inhabitants of villages and hamlets gather, offers a way to the solution of all the problems of co-existence in the countryside.[1]

This view, as put forward by Dr Isaac Puente, one of the two most influential Spanish anarchist writers at the time, expressed total confidence in the masses and their spontaneity; the free municipality, which was the sovereign workers' assembly in a small locality, must remain autonomous, for only its proper functioning guaranteed the functioning of the whole. No superstructure must exist over it, except that which exercised special functions that could not be carried out locally. Any form of 'constructive' anarchism must be rejected because it contained the seeds of bureaucracy which would lead to the restoration of the state. The free municipality was the only institution which guaranteed the development of individual freedom.

This vision was based on rural life, rural revolution. The insurrection would start from the villages, readied for war by 'a handful of audacious comrades or a small rural syndicate', while urban workers declared a general strike to hold back the armed forces. 'The major part of the Spanish population lives in small municipalities and their reorganization in a libertarian form is the easiest imaginable thing.'[2] Moreover, if the cities turned out to be an obstacle, a focus of reaction, 'it will be preferable to wipe them off the face of the earth. The rural municipalities will absorb their reactionary plague and purify it.'[3]

This tendency, with its virulent a-politicism, anti-parliamentarianism, anti-militarism, anti-clericalism, its deep hostility to all government and political parties – including (especially) working-class parties[4] – saw as its fundamental methods of action the insurrectional strike, sabotage, boycott and mutiny. The popular dimension of its ideology could be expressed in a series of equations: politics = 'the art of cheating the people'; parties = 'no difference between any of them'; elections = 'swindle'; parliament = 'the place of corruption'; the army = 'the organization of collective crime'; the police = 'paid assassins of the bourgeoisie'.[5]

It was by no means a totally false image of the monarchy. Was it a functional image to deal with the realities of the republic? Most agreed that it was.

Held in tension with this view was the other, the syndicalist. In essence a view shaped by industrialization, it centred on the premise that, in order to

1. I. Puente, *El comunismo libertario*, 1932, re-edited Toulouse, 1947, cited in Mintz, *L'Autogestion dans l'Espagne révolutionnaire*, p. 36.

2. *Tierra y Libertad* (August 1931).

3. *El Libertario* (November 1932). Both cited in Elorza, *La utopía anarquista bajo la segunda república española*, pp. 357 and 376.

4. When they voted, anarcho-syndicalists opted normally for petty bourgeois republican parties like the Esquerra in Catalonia (which depended on their vote to remain in office) or the radical socialists; they would not normally vote for an 'authoritarian marxist' working-class party (see section C).

5. Lorenzo, *Los anarquistas españoles y el poder*, p. 40.

overthrow the bourgeois order, a strong, proletarian organization was needed: the *sindicato*. 'For us the social revolution is not just a matter of rising violently against the organized forces of the state . . . The social revolution consists in taking over factories and mines, the land and the railways, all the means of production, to put them at the people's disposal. It is not sufficient to take over social wealth, it is necessary to know how to use it – *and to use it immediately, without any discontinuity*.'[1]

The crucial role in this revolutionary and post-revolutionary process devolved on the *sindicato*, since the overthrow of capitalism did not signify a rupture with capitalist productive structures but the necessity of ensuring their continuing functioning under trade union management; this, in turn, required organization and discipline.

The trade union had a triple function: under capitalism it (1) acted to defend the proletariat's interests while (2) 'preparing, by its practical and educational activities, the economic framework of a new social, egalitarian order', which (3) after the revolution it would realize by carrying through 'the economic transformations which permit the consolidation of libertarian communism as the first stage of the free commune'.[2]

Because of increasing capitalist concentration and because of the role the unions would be called on to play in the post-revolutionary society, National Industrial Federations would be needed to link local industrial unions, each of the latter being responsible for organizing relations between each factory within its local industry – the factory or workplace having been taken over by its union committee which would administer it.[3]

1. J. Peiró, *Sindicalismo* (April 1933), no. 10; cited in Elorza, op. cit., p. 403. My emphasis.

2. *Les syndicats ouvriers et la révolution sociale*, by Pierre Besnard, the French syndicalist writer whose work in translation was influential in Spain at this time. See Mintz, op. cit., p. 34.

3. The basic CNT structure since 1918 had been the industrial branch union, e.g. each trade working within the building industry had its own section within the overall building workers' union, each section being represented on the union's leadership. (There were no paid union officials, no strike funds and dues were modest.) Each union was represented on a local federation of syndicates which, with the local unions, federated at the regional level in a regional committee. A national committee existed but, with the exception of the secretary, this was composed up to the war of CNT militants in the city where the committee had its seat. There was no direct *organizational* link between the same branch unions in different regions; such links as existed were arranged by the local federations or regional committees, which were the decisive forces in each area. This corresponded to the anarcho-syndicalist concept of local autonomy and federalism, but made coordinated union action at national level more difficult. National Industrial Federations, approved at the 1931 Madrid congress, were combated by the ultra-left 'purists' as potentially bureaucratic organisms which threatened local autonomies, both in the present and in the post-revolutionary future where they would have a large part in the running of the economy. Moreover, they required *industrial* unions as their base. The latter (as set up in the Badalona textile industry early in 1936) included everyone engaged in the industry, from the workers making textile machinery to all those engaged in the wholesale and retail garment trade, and bringing in the technicians and foremen alongside the workers at all levels of the industry. 'The advocates of the old branch unions disliked this new structure because the former could be mobilized much more easily by its central leadership since its members were, in the main, a despairing proletariat. In the industrial union, the membership of technicians and foremen meant there was more likelihood of actions proposed by the specific anarchist groups being blocked,' in the words of Josep Costa, secretary of the new Badalona industrial union, and a militant with a long CNT past. The branch unions continued to dominate the CNT, the industrial union movement having made little headway by the outbreak of war; only a few National Industrial Federations were created.

Common to both tendencies was the idea that the working class 'simply' took over factories and workplaces and ran them collectively but otherwise as before. 'No one supposes that after the revolution the factories will function backwards . . . all workers will have to do the same as they did the day before . . .'[1] Underlying this vision of simple continuity was the anarcho-syndicalist concept of the revolution not as a rupture with, the destruction and replacement of, the bourgeois order but as the latter's *displacement*. The taking over of factories and workplaces, however violently carried out, was not the beginning of the revolution to create a new order but its final goal. This view, in turn, was conditioned by a particular view of the state. Any state (bourgeois or working class) was considered an oppressive power *tout court* – not as the organization of a particular class's coercive power. The 'state', in consequence, rather than the existence of the capitalist mode of production which gave rise to its particular form, often appeared as the major enemy. The state did not have to be taken, crushed and a new – revolutionary – *power* established. No. If it could be swept aside, abolished, everything else, including oppression, disappeared. The capitalist order was simply displaced by the new-won workers' freedom to administer the workplaces they had taken over. Self-organized in autonomous communes or in all-powerful syndicates, the workers, as the primary factor in production, *dispensed* with the bourgeoisie. The consequences of this were seen in the 1936 Barcelona revolution; capitalist production and market relations continued to exist within collectivized industry.

Within two months of the Madrid Congress which declared war on the republic, thirty leading CNT militants signed a manifesto maintaining their adherence to the position that revolution would not be made exclusively by minorities, however audacious, but by the 'overwhelming movement of the working masses. We want a revolution that springs from the people, not a revolution that a few individuals can make . . . ' The ultra-left, concentrated in the FAI, immediately attacked the *treintistas* (as the thirty signers and – by extension – their supporters came to be known) as reformist and counter-revolutionary. The feuding grew excessively bitter and within a year unions with some 70,000 members had been expelled from the CNT. The anarcho-syndicalist confederation, which had just emerged from clandestinity under the dictatorship with a membership of over half a million, split along the line of its major tension.

Sebastià CLARA, a former corkworker and now a reporter on the CNT's major Barcelona paper, *Solidaridad Obrera*, was one of the manifesto's thirty signers. In his view, the manifesto was not counter-revolutionary, but a new formulation of how to achieve revolution in opposition to the FAI's tactics. The mass of CNT members was not at that moment prepared to leap into the unknown of revolution. They had joined the CNT to defend their class interests, and what they wanted was to be able to operate openly as a trade union. 'That was why they had struggled to bring in the republic, and why they welcomed it when it was proclaimed.' What was needed now was political realism and agility to build on this movement for revolutionary ends.

Ricardo SANZ, member of the FAI and the *Nosotros* ('Us') group in Barcelona,

1. García Oliver, interview October 1931, *La Tierra*, cited in *El movimiento libertario español* (Paris, 1974).

which included such leading militants as Durruti, Francisco Ascaso and García Oliver, did not disagree that both the CNT and the working masses were unprepared for revolution. But that fact could lead to radically different conclusions.

—After seven years of clandestinity, the members generally didn't know where they were going or what they wanted. In such a situation, what was needed was practice, exercise, revolutionary gymnastics. We were the motor or spark that could get those gymnastics going . . .

The 'gymnastics' had definite objectives, specific dates: January 1932, January 1933, December 1933 – revolutionary insurrections to inaugurate libertarian communism. The first was practically confined to the mining zone of Catalonia; the second spread into agricultural villages in Levant and Andalusia;[1] the third affected mainly villages in Aragon and La Rioja. While each mobilized more participants than its predecessor, none of them was the spark that set the countryside alight; with a few notable exceptions, the landless day labourers and peasantry failed to respond in strength. But each, more seriously than the last, threatened republican order.

—We weren't unduly disappointed at the failure; from the beginning, given the situation, we doubted whether they could have effective results. But as we were convinced – we, the working class that had been formed under the dictatorship, especially the youth – that such exercises were needed, we carried them out. The working class had to learn to head towards the conquest, not of the state, not of power – we never spoke of these – but of the means of production and consumption . . .

A large sector of the Catalan anarcho-syndicalist movement was in agreement with neither side in the dispute. Anarchists like Andreu Capdevila (see Militancies 6, pp. 213–16) and anarcho-syndicalists like Josep COSTA, of the CNT textile union in Badalona, were hostile to the revolutionary gymnastics. In the latter's view, the mood of the working class was opposed to these insurrectionary uprisings, which, moreover, did great harm to the CNT.

—We lost at least a quarter of our membership in Badalona in that period.[2] A lot of us, who supported neither side, but adopted a 'centrist' position, 'went home to sleep'. Our textile union was virtually paralysed by the dispute . . .

—The FAI wanted to make the libertarian revolution, to attain a society without God or Bosses, without laws or police forces, using human material that wasn't prepared for it, reflected Josep ROBUSTE, a CNT book-keeper. The FAI was acting like a political group within the CNT, taking its own decisions and trying to impose them on the CNT, talking of liberty and acting like dictators . . .

1. This included Casas Viejas where government assault guards assassinated a score of anarcho-syndicalists who resisted. The Azaña government never fully recovered from the scandal which marked the beginning of the end of the republican–socialist coalition.

2. In August 1931, the Catalan regional CNT claimed nearly 400,000 members (58 per cent of the workers of both sexes in Barcelona were affiliated); in March 1933, the figure had dropped to 208,000, and by May 1936, to 142,000. The latter figure still represented 20 per cent of all Catalan workers and 30 per cent of the industrial working class (see Molas, *El sistema de partídos políticos en Cataluña, 1931–1936*, pp. 117, 119).

Some leading militants who shared his views were not only expelled from their unions but thrown out of work. He began to think that what was needed was what the UGT enjoyed – a real political party which could express the CNT's demands and needs at the political level and further awaken the workers' consciousness.

From an anarchist perspective, the FAI was not totally incorrect in understanding that inherent in the *treintista* position was a 'politicization', a 'reformism', nor in seeing the dangers contained in the new republican regime's political need to 'incorporate' the working class. In fact, however, when Angel Pestaña, a *treintista* and former CNT leader, founded the syndicalist party, which ROBUSTE joined, few members, even among the *treintista* unions, could be recruited. Politics remained anathema, loyalty to anarcho-syndicalism high.

The form the split took was not only organizational but generational, often almost personal. Its immediate history lay in the previous decade. After the economic boom of the First World War and increasing proletarian militancy, Catalan employers confronted lean times by attempting to crush the anarcho-syndicalist movement in Barcelona. The crushing took the form of creating 'yellow' unions and, with the authorities' approval and leadership, the hiring of gunmen to assassinate CNT leaders. A spiral of assassination and counter-assassination began: more than 800 criminal assaults on life – 440 against workers, 218 against employers and their subordinates, the rest against the authorities – took place between 1917 and 1923.[1]

The boom had brought new young workers into the city and the CNT. These, formed in this harsh, bloody struggle, became a new type of militant. This was the moment when the *Solidarios* group (forerunner of the *Nosotros* group and with many of the same militants) was formed, expressly to take revenge for workers' assassinations, not on the gunmen who executed them, but on the employers who paid and organized them. When, soon afterwards, the dictatorship outlawed the CNT, scores of militants had to flee to France and elsewhere, to return only when the republic was proclaimed. Sebastià CLARA, the *treintista* signatory, was among them.

—Before the 1920s, the CNT was an organization in which the masses could express themselves democratically. Afterwards, this was no longer the case. Things changed with the creation of the FAI in 1927. It was they who now imposed their decisions . . .

It had to be remembered, he stressed, that the level of revolutionary culture was very low. Militants had, at best, read one or two pamphlets, and Kropotkin's *Conquest of Bread*. They hadn't read Marx, Engels, let alone Hegel. 'The libertarian movement was suspicious of, hostile to, intellectuals – intellectuals who could have helped the movement greatly.'

Although complaint about the FAI's methods, especially in Barcelona, was common, it would be mistaken to suppose that the FAI was a cohesive 'political' grouping throughout Spain. It was a federation of individual anarchist groups (each of which was formed on the principle of personal 'affinity'); there was no general FAI 'line' which all groups had to adhere to. Such would have run counter to the very nature of anarchism.

1. See Balcells, *Cataluña contemporánea II (1900–1936)*, p. 17.

Progreso FERNANDEZ, a Valencian anarchist who had been living and working in France, returned to his native city, on behalf of Spanish anarchist groups in France, to attend the FAI's founding meeting, 'in the large covered yard of a companion's house, on 24 July, 1927'. The next day, the thirty to forty delegates from all over Spain and Portugal met among the pine trees of El Saler where some of the participants were on the alert to bury all the documents in the sand if surprised.

—The purpose of forming a federation of the anarchist groups scattered all over Spain was that they should emerge from their ivory towers to propagate revolutionary anarchist ideals to the working class – inevitably in clandestine forms at that time since we were under the dictatorship and the CNT was outlawed. All the founding members were also CNT members. The allegation that the FAI was set up to manipulate and control the CNT was completely false. There was no fear at that moment that the CNT was going to fall into the trap of revisionism; the only problem was that attempts were being made to legalize the CNT on the model of the UGT.[1] Nor is it true to say that the FAI was created to maintain the CNT's ideological purity. It is, of course, possible that in certain regions like Catalonia the FAI's role was conceived like that; but it was not the case in Valencia . . .

The FAI's specific weight in Catalonia was almost certainly greater than in other regions; and this, in itself, appeared to give it even greater importance since the weight of the Catalan CNT within the Confederation was indisputable. And within the Catalan CNT, it was Barcelona which dominated.[2]

1. The 1931 split had been prefigured under the dictatorship when a group of militants, led by Pestaña, favoured an attempt to legalize the CNT by renouncing its anarchist aims. The FAI founding meetings had on the agenda a discussion of the 'Archinov Platform' – a proposal by Russian anarchists exiled in France to take measures to prevent the possible influence of the communist party in the libertarian movement; this was not discussed at the meetings, however, because the Platform had not been translated. (See the Synthesis of the minutes of the FAI founding meetings, in *El movimiento libertario español*, op. cit., p. 293.) Prior to the FAI's foundation (whose existence as a clandestine organization was not announced for two years), Abad de Santillán was militating in favour of the presence of anarchist groups in the trade union leadership to ensure the permanence of a 'specifically anarchist workers' movement'. The theory of the 'bond' between anarchist groups and the trade union was designed to prevent communist infiltration and anarcho-syndicalism's deviation to reformism or pure syndicalism. (See Elorza, *La utopía anarquista bajo la segunda república española*, p. 413.) These ideas did not go entirely unheeded in Barcelona; but at the same time it is erroneous to conceive of the FAI as an anarchist force exterior to the CNT; it was part of the latter and represented a tendency which, to one degree or another, had existed in the movement virtually since its inception.

2. Attempts to discover a symbiotic relationship between Catalan and Andalusian anarcho-syndicalism, seeing the latter as fuelling the former's revolutionary anarchism with waves of impoverished migrant workers, founder on the facts of migration. Andalusian migration was minimal (see Malefakis, *Agrarian Reform and Peasant Revolution in Spain*, pp. 104–6). In Barcelona (city) in 1930, Andalusians represented only 4·2 per cent of the population, the third group of non-Catalans behind the Levant with 13·2 per cent, and Aragon with 8 per cent (Balcells, op. cit., p. 61). While at times in the past the movement had numerically favoured Andalusia, the leadership had been dominated by Catalans. The failure to sustain a specific day-labourers' and peasants' union is perhaps significant in this respect. This is not to deny the importance of non-Catalan workers in the movement; the members of the small but influential *Nosotros* group were almost all non-Catalans (Durruti, Ascaso, Sanz, Vivancos, etc.), García Oliver being the outstanding exception.

The CNT in other regions of Spain, especially where the UGT was the major union, was not able or willing to afford the voluntarism of revolutionary gymnastics. In Madrid, for example, the small CNT unions had had a different experience under the dictatorship: in place of the violence that reigned in Barcelona, the half-dozen Madrid unions joined the UGT (on an individual member basis) to protect themselves and to attract new members. Miguel GONZALEZ INESTAL, a leading CNT and FAI militant in the capital, believed that this had made an important difference in their trajectory.

—For example, we considered the Catalan FAI's insurrectionary attempts dangerous, while admiring their initiative and combativeness. But there could be no doubt that these revolutionary uprisings and strikes were wearing down the militants' fighting spirit and the organization itself. We could see that difficult times were looming ahead, given the right's attitude, and that combativeness was going to be needed. Considerable sections of the Libertarian movement in Levant, Andalusia and Asturias supported our position . . .

There were, he thought, two major tendencies within the FAI. One which believed it necessary to build up a strong trade union organization, educate the members and prepare the organizational means for revolution. The other was 'formed in the shadow of certain groups which wanted to control the CNT – although this was not part of the FAI's founding principles' – and succeeded to a large extent in its aim in Barcelona. 'Many times one could say it was the Barcelona tendency against the rest of Spain.' Madrid remained solidly in the first tendency, although when the split occurred, it opposed the *treintista* movement as reformist.

—One of the things that most damaged the working-class movement, we believed, was the type of trade unionism which concentrated purely on wage claims and improvements in working conditions. It was necessary to retain the moral, doctrinal and cultural traditions of anarchism, the ideals which could raise the level of the members in human terms . . .

In Asturias, the *treintista* split had no serious repercussions. The Asturian FAI did not share the Catalan posture. Ramón ALVAREZ, secretary of the CNT regional committee, and an FAI militant, explained his members' views to a national CNT plenum in Madrid.

—'Revolution isn't the same as a strike which can be called for a certain day of the month. Revolution is a social phenomenon, which ripens in its own time, which man's consciousness influences, accelerates, retards, but which does not happen simply because someone sets a date – ' In Asturias, we thought that those who believed Spain was ready for revolution were victims of their own enthusiasm – an enthusiasm we shared up to a point – instead of making a calm, lucid analysis of the situation . . .

Not that the theory of revolutionary gymnastics was totally wrong he believed; had the CNT been an organization that simply sat back waiting while its members paid their dues, it would have been caught by surprise by the military on 18 July.

In the general elections of November 1933, the CNT called on its members to abstain; this overtly political move represented the libertarian movement's profound disillusionment with the republic, which had solved few if any of the problems faced by the working class, and had harshly repressed the anarcho-syndicalists who had participated in the insurrections. Allied with other factors (the women's vote for the first time, the disarray of the republican–socialist coalition and the cohesion of the right-wing reaction under CEDA leadership), the CNT's abstention resulted in the right's victory. The CNT had promised to launch a revolution if this happened; their rising in December 1933 was the third in just under two years. The Asturian CNT was in disagreement and put forward a 'political' alternative. An electoral abstentionist policy must be accompanied by something positive. If the CNT was to prove to the socialists, who had just been ejected from government, that successful proletarian conquests were made in the streets, not in the ballot boxes, then the ground for such conquests had to be laid.

—Logically, this meant reaching an understanding with the socialists. Success comes to those who organize beforehand, not to those who improvise. I argued this at the 1933 Madrid plenum which decided on abstention. Our thesis was rejected. Durruti and others claimed that if there was a 50 per cent abstention rate the CNT would make the revolution. But the germ of the Workers' Alliance was already formed in our minds . . .

The December insurrection spread through Aragon and La Rioja, but failed within a few days like the two before it. Durruti was the only one of the *Nosotros* group to take part. However, out of this process came the formidable Asturian alliance with the UGT, initiated by the CNT, and which was sealed between the two unions in March 1934 (see section E).

Compared to the waves of ultra-leftism which swept the CNT nationally, the Asturian CNT had a long history of revolutionary realism. Perhaps because of its minority position within a strongly proletarian mining region dominated by the social-democratic Asturian mineworkers' union; perhaps because of its isolation from the extreme southern rural poverty; but certainly because of the presence of one man, Eleuterio Quintanilla, the most formative single influence in Asturian anarcho-syndicalist development, it had always been willing to join in common action with the socialist proletariat in the struggle against the class enemy.[1]

1. As far back as 1919, Eleuterio Quintanilla, the Asturian anarchist leader, had argued for the unification of the UGT and CNT on equal terms and through a joint Congress which would create a new trade union organization; the CNT had voted instead to 'absorb' the UGT, giving the latter's members three months to join or be declared scabs. At the same congress, Quintanilla argued in favour of creating national industrial federations; the CNT voted against. He went on to propose that the Bolshevik revolution must be defended against its capitalist aggressors although it did not represent the 'dictatorship of the people in arms' but rather the dictatorship of a government, however revolutionary; the CNT voted to join the Third International provisionally. The ultra-leftism of the Catalan movement was already beginning to make itself felt. So opposed was Quintanilla to splitting the working-class movement, that he opposed the creation of a CNT miners' union in Asturias, believing that an opposition to the UGT's reformist policies should remain in the socialist union to capitalize on the miners' revolutionary instincts and to bring the union round to authentic syndicalism. (When a CNT miners' union was formed, it was led for several years by communist militants, also in disagreement with the reformism of the Asturian socialist mineworkers' union.)

After three abortive risings, the CNT outside Asturias – in particular, the Catalan CNT – failed to respond to the challenge of the October 1934 revolution. Catalan libertarian militants had been persecuted by the ultra-nationalist wing of the Esquerra and the CNT saw the rising in Barcelona as a petty bourgeois affair.

—I told Durruti: 'It's a revolutionary's duty to channel such a movement along the right road – ' But the fact of the matter was that they didn't want to have anything to do with the Esquerra which was planning to rise, along with the forces in the Workers' Alliance. Their only excuse – after always saying: 'We'll meet in the streets' – was that the Generalitat had arrested some of their militants. In part those arrests were due to the fact that the CNT had warned the public about the rising . . .

The Asturian CNT, ALVAREZ knew, could have been criticized for signing a pact with the UGT at a regional level without a decision having been taken nationally. José María Martínez (who was killed in the October rising) and he attended a Madrid CNT plenum in June 1934, to explain the Asturian CNT's position. After a great deal of negotiation, a compromise was worked out.

—If, within two months, a CNT national conference met and voted against such an alliance, we would break our pact with the UGT. If, on the other hand, we were able to persuade the national conference of the correctness of our position, the pact would be made national. The conference was never called . . .

The possibility of a national pact with the UGT was not returned to until the CNT's extraordinary congress in Saragossa two months before the start of the war. That congress, which saw the re-incorporation of a large number of the *treintista* opposition unions, consecrated the anarchist tendency within the movement.

The free commune was to be the keystone of the future libertarian society; federations and economic plans, while recognized, were to be created only *if* the communes considered them necessary. Within time, each commune would be given the agricultural and industrial elements necessary for its autonomy, 'in accord with the biological principle which affirms that man – in this case the commune – is freer the less he needs from others', said the resolution on the nature of libertarian communism.

It was not the CNT rural masses who pushed through this bucolic programme; it was the major Barcelona unions, in particular the textile workers. Abad de Santillán, the anarchist writer, who had himself swung from a position of trusting the 'spontaneity of the masses' to that of believing in the need for economic organization, criticized the programme. 'There's talk of the family, delinquency, jealousy, nudism and many other things [the resolution had gone into all of these as part of the future life under libertarian communism] but you hardly find a word about work, workplaces or the organization of production'. It was in this condition that the CNT found itself two months later when faced with the task of establishing a revolutionary economic order in Catalonia.

*

The anarcho-syndicalist insurrections in the first two years of the new regime destabilized the republic; but they expressed also the incipient working-class discontent with the republic which the socialists, whose participation in the government was damping it down, would themselves feel shortly when they moved to the left. The revolutionary drama lay in the fact that – except in Asturias – the two did not coincide. The socialists in government shared the responsibility for placing the militants of the rival union beyond the law; the anarcho-syndicalists refused to see that revolution – if such could be made – required more than the CNT alone, and thus contributed gravely to the lack of unity in the working class.

E. October 1934, the Popular Front, orthodox and dissident communists

In 1934 the first shots of the civil war were fired, and postures were assumed which were to make the conflict virtually inevitable.

Amongst the working-class organizations the socialist party, after two years of junior partnership in the liberal republican–socialist coalition, veered sharply to the left in 1933–4. The rise of fascism, Hitler's accession to power, Dollfuss's corporative social christian dictatorship which seemed to share common aspects with the CEDA, and was shortly to drown the Austrian socialists in blood, were among the international factors. At home, unemployment – 1933 was the worst year of the depression in Spain; the ineffectiveness of agrarian reform; the repression of anarcho-syndicalists in Casas Viejas; the great number of political prisoners; and the increasing resistance being offered by employers, were among the factors that explained the change from reformist collaboration to revolutionary opposition in little more than a year. A month before the socialist ministers left the coalition government in 1933, Largo Caballero, the Labour Minister and UGT secretary-general, said that his conviction that it was impossible to 'carry out socialist tasks within a bourgeois democracy' had been confirmed.[1] The defeat at the 1933 general elections doubtless further served to radicalize sectors of the party. The Landworkers' Federation (now accounting for nearly half the UGT's strength, which had quadrupled in eighteen months) was declaring that without revolution there could be no agrarian reform. The socialist youth declared for revolution and the dictatorship of the proletariat.

—Disappointment at the results of collaboration with the petty bourgeoisie was so great that the party and youth saw revolution as the only way forward. This wasn't surprising, maintained Sócrates GOMEZ, a Madrid socialist youth leader, because the conquest of proletarian power was a fundamental principle of our party, which was the most class-conscious, marxist socialist party in Europe . . .

1. Caballero's shift was no sudden change of attitude, as has been usually assumed. Marta Bizcarrondo has shown that his ideas on collaboration with bourgeois regimes and proletarian revolution were those of thirteen years earlier. This did not prevent them being ambivalent and reformist, however (see M. Bizcarrondo, *Araquistaín y la crisis socialista en la II república. Leviatán*, Madrid, 1975).

Even Prieto, the centrist socialist leader, warned that the party would unleash revolution if the new government attempted a *coup d'état*. Not everyone in the party agreed; nor did all those who did agree have the same reasons for doing so. None the less, with the inevitability of a pendulum's swing, a large sector of the party went from being the unconditional sustaining force of the republican alliance to total rupture with it. This extreme posture was given additional support by the evidence that, sooner or later, the CEDA, the largest single party in the new parliament, would demand direct governmental participation rather than confine itself to parliamentary support. 'Better Vienna than Berlin' became a socialist slogan. The conquest of power – or at least, the denial of power to the CEDA – became an increasingly immediate aim.

The mass catholic party was seen by a large spectrum of republican opinion, ranging from the centre to the left, as an 'enemy of the republic', a fascist threat. Innumerable public statements by party leaders, including Gil Robles, could be adduced to support the latter view.[1] Its counter-revolutionary, anti-socialist policies were undeniable; its initial refusal to declare itself unambiguously republican suspicious; its rhetoric menacingly fascistic on occasions, especially at its youth movement's rallies (El Escorial, April 1934, and Covadonga, Asturias, in August of the same year). Despite the latter, the fact remained that it was a clerical-conservative *parliamentary* party[2] whose ambiguities were those of its mass following: a bourgeoisie frightened of revolution and unsure whether the republican regime would further or contain that threat. Inspired by the social catholicism of Pope Leo XIII, its principles were the defence of Religion, Fatherland, Family, Order, Work and Property. Its determination to smash the left, its aim of revising the constitution to accord with the 'affirmation and defence of the fundamental principles of christian civilization', and its long-term corporativist aims were the principal threat to the left republican and working-class organizations.

During 1934, there was certainly an element of provocation in the CEDA's rhetoric. Sooner or later, it feared, a revolutionary coup would take place; advisable, therefore, to face it from a 'position of power before the enemy was better prepared'.[3]

Nowhere more than in the mining valleys of Asturias had the socialist radicalization, especially amongst the youth, taken firmer root. Many had believed that the seizure of power was the only way forward since General Sanjurjo's abortive monarchist rising in Seville in 1932. At the beginning of 1934 the first defence groups – a euphemism – were formed. This was followed in March by a momentous political agreement: the Asturian UGT and CNT signed a pact agreeing, 'in the face of the economic and political situation under

1. See p. 85; also P. Preston, 'Spain's October Revolution and the Rightist Grasp for Power', *Journal of Contemporary History*, vol. 10 (1975).

2. Its adherence to the parliamentary road, its progressive acceptance of the republic after the 1933 elections, its ultimate unwillingness to embark on extra-parliamentary solutions (especially after October 1934), was what finally lost it its constituency: the bourgeoisie deserted when, after the defeat in the 1936 elections, the parliamentary road no longer appeared a guarantee against revolution.

3. Gil Robles, cited Preston, op. cit., p. 567. The CEDA leader later claimed that he knew his party's participation in the government would provoke a revolutionary movement and that he had joined deliberately so as to be able to smash it from within the government.

the bourgeois regime, to joint action with the exclusive aim of bringing about the social revolution'. The new revolutionary regime would be based on 'socialist federalist principles'. The Workers' Alliance, which had been created in Catalonia by the Bloc Obrer i Camperol (Workers' and Peasants' Bloc, one of the two parties which later founded the POUM), was to reach its culmination in Asturias, where proletarian unity had a long tradition (see section D).

—Socialists and anarcho-syndicalists in Asturias were different to their counterparts in the rest of the country. Relations between the two, though they had been bad at times, were on the whole good, asserted Alberto FERNANDEZ, a prominent socialist youth member. The originality of the Workers' Alliance was that it was initiated by the two trade union organizations. Only after did the political parties join . . .

—We thought collaboration with the UGT was essential, especially as the working class had seen that the republic was not going to satisfy its aspirations, stressed Eladio FANJUL, an FAI steelworker from La Felguera.

Only one proletarian party, the Spanish communist party, initially refused to join the Workers' Alliance which it went so far as to castigate as 'the nerve centre of the counter-revolution'.[1] Barely a fortnight before the October rising, however, the party, whose call for a single front with the socialist party and CNT had gone unanswered, embarked on what it termed an 'audacious tactical turn' and joined. The change marked the breaking out of a self-imposed ghetto and the party's first real entry into working-class politics which was to reap it very considerable gains.

The rising was precipitated when, in the first days of October, Gil Robles withdrew his party's support from the government; the outcome of the crisis was that three CEDA members – although not Gil Robles – joined the radical government. Republican leaders as far to the right as Miguel Maura wrote to the president of the republic and broke all relations with the country's 'existing institutions', maintaining that the president was guilty of handing over the republic to its enemies. The socialist party leadership in Madrid, which had turned down a communist proposal for a general strike, gave the order on its own to launch an armed uprising.

In the small township of Figueredo, just south of Mieres in Asturias, Alberto FERNANDEZ of the socialist youth had been waiting two nights for the signal. At 2 a.m. on 5 October he heard the sound of an old car advancing and jumped out on to the road. It was the *Avance* (the Oviedo socialist newspaper) car. Antonio Llaneza, son of the great mineworkers' leader, was in it.

—He took my hand and said with great feeling: 'This is what we have been waiting for. *A la calle* (Into the streets).' 'To the very limit?' 'Yes.' That meant it was the revolution. The seizure of power. The inauguration of socialism. Not simply to restore the republican regime to what it had been in its first two years, as some later said. We set off . . .

Within forty-eight hours, the miners and metalworkers had captured nearly seventy *guardia civil* posts in the mining valleys, won their first pitched battle

1. M. Grossi, *L'Insurrection des Asturies* (Paris, 1972), p. 36.

against the army on the outskirts of Oviedo and were fighting in the city; to the south, they had pinned down army units sent from León. Foreshadowing what would happen in most parts of Popular Front Spain less than two years later, revolutionary committees were set up in the villages and townships. Each set about making the revolution, instituting forms of war communism. For two weeks in the Nalón and Caudal mining valleys the proletariat held power.

Elsewhere, the rising failed. In Barcelona, the Esquerra, in almost inevitable conflict with the radical government in Madrid, rose on 6 October and was forced to submit by a small army unit six hours later. The CNT, which had refused to join the Workers' Alliance in Barcelona, refused also to join the uprising; without the CNT's support, no rising could succeed in the Catalan capital (see sections C and D).

Indecisively led by Caballero himself, the movement rapidly fizzled out in Madrid. In the countryside, the socialist-led national peasants' strike of the previous June had left the Landworkers' Federation dismantled and the peasantry in considerable disarray: they repaid the industrial proletariat's failure to support their strike by failing to mobilize *en masse* now.[1] In Bilbao, the strike lasted eleven days. Juan IGLESIAS, a shop assistant and treasurer of the Bilbao socialist youth, could not understand why the strikers did not launch an attack on the centre of the city and take it over. Control of the working-class district, centred round the Calle de San Francisco and the *casa del pueblo*, was complete; some arms, stocks of home-made hand grenades were available.

—We waited four days, then we decided to act on our own. Two hours before we planned to set off, we received an order not to move . . .

Ramón RUBIAL, metalworker and president of the socialist youth in Erandio, on the right bank of the estuary, believed that the counter-order was given when it became clear, after the Catalan failure, that the Bilbao working class would be uselessly sacrificed if it rose. The strike continued, but the workers from the heavy industries on the left bank and the iron-ore mines, where the socialist party and UGT were strongest, did not emulate their Asturian comrades' insurrectionary bid for power.

Isolated, the revolution in Asturias could not hold out. In the course of its two weeks, many lessons were offered for future consideration: ammunition, which was in shorter supply than arms, was wasted; the shortage (which the capture of the Oviedo arms factory did little to relieve) afflicted the insurrection. Aerial bombing caused panic amongst the militiamen;[2] military expertise (in the shape of a captured *guardia civil* lieutenant who offered his services) increased the militiamen's fighting ability. In the rearguard, there was the emergence of a lumpen-proletariat, a certain amount of pillaging and a number of unjustifiable assassinations. And, as defeat threatened from 11 October with

1. Caballero argued against staging the peasants' strike in June when, almost certainly, a massive confrontation was looming with the government; to the detriment of October, his advice was not heeded. But the UGT did everything possible to discourage acts of solidarity with the peasantry (see Maurice, *La reforma agraria en España en el siglo XX*, p. 52).

2. 'Ninety per cent of our defeat was due to the aviation which contributed the most to spreading panic and demoralization amongst the revolutionaries who were incapable of effectively combating it' (Grossi, op. cit., p. 127).

the government forces beginning to recapture Oviedo, a number of revolutionary committees took flight.

On the advice of General Franco, the government called in the Foreign Legion and Moroccan troops – the first time these forces had been used militarily in the peninsula. At the end of the fortnight, Belarmino Tomás, the veteran Asturian socialist leader, negotiated the surrender of the mining villages on condition that the Foreign Legion and Moors did not form the vanguard of the occupying forces.

Alberto FERNANDEZ, the socialist youth baker from Figueredo, had been wounded in the fighting and was in hospital in Mieres when the troops entered.

—The Moors took some of the wounded downstairs and shot them. I was lucky. I was saved, thanks to Gen. Burguete, who in 1917 had put down the general insurrectionary strike in Asturias and was now the Red Cross representative. I talked to him while the others were being taken away. Although the revolution had failed, and soon there were 30,000 prisoners in gaol, we thought it had served a positive purpose: it held up the advent of fascism . . .

In hiding for nearly five months before getting to France, Ramón ALVAREZ, secretary of the CNT regional committee, shared this view. There had been only one choice.

—Either we allowed the capitalists and reactionaries time to organize from their positions of power, or we confronted the situation when they weren't prepared. We chose the latter. If we hadn't, there might never have been a civil war. No war victims. Instead, there would have been civil victims of capitalist reaction for hundreds of years . . .

Severely beaten up in prison, like most of those who had taken part in the revolution, José MATA, a socialist miner incarcerated with 2,000 others in Oviedo gaol, came to think that not even Caballero had intended to launch a socialist revolution. But the insurrection was inevitable.

—We had to defend the rights we had won and which the Spanish capitalists were trying to take from us. If we hadn't risen, fascism would have taken over without a struggle – and without a civil war . . .

—The CEDA for us was Dollfuss's corporative social Christian dictatorship. In other words, fascism as we conceived it then, recalled Alberto FERNANDEZ. Perhaps we were wrong. Perhaps it was something else – the old-style Spanish reaction which, like Franco later in justifying his rising, took on a fascist-style ideology because it lacked any other, and that was what was in fashion . . .

Supporters of the centrist socialist leader, Prieto, never had any illusions about making the socialist revolution. The insurrection was to prevent the CEDA entering the government, nothing else, thought Ramón RUBIAL in Bilbao. Prieto hoped that the president of the republic, rather than face the consequences of armed confrontation, would not allow the CEDA to join the government.

—From a purely insurrectional point of view, the uprising was a mistake; it couldn't succeed. But politically speaking, thanks to the sacrifice of a great number of socialists, the Republic was 'reconquered' as a result. Because of the repression after October – not only in Asturias but in Bilbao and elsewhere – widespread support was gained for the creation and electoral victory of the Popular Front. This, although not really damaging to the ruling class's interests, gave the latter and its agents the pretext for staging various actions which they and the army then used to justify the need for a rising because of the republic's so-called 'inability to maintain law and order.' Thus, if October led to the reconquest of the republic due to the Popular Front victory, it also led to the civil war . . .

*

The rising made a deep impression on the right. But, in the view of a prominent falangist, Dionisio RIDRUEJO, this was subjectively transformed into more optimistic perspectives. At first, the bourgeoisie was very frightened by Asturias.

—But then, believing that a revolution could be put down with relative ease, they became over-confident. They did not have the means, however, of effecting what their confidence led them to believe they could do. It meant relying as always on the only force available to them – the army . . .

*

On the left, the aftermath of October favoured the communist party rather more than the socialists, most of whose leaders were in gaol and who were racked by polemic over the outcome of the insurrection and future aims.

Claiming a membership of about 20,000 at the time of the October insurrection, the communist party had grown very considerably under the republic, which, at its inauguration three years before, had found it with only 800 members. However, it was still no match for the 70,000-strong socialist party, which controlled more than 1 million members in the UGT, nor for the CNT which had a similarly large membership. Although the party had joined the Workers' Alliance only at the last moment, its militants had played a significant role in Asturias. Raising the banner of October in the months thereafter, while the socialist party carried it furled, the communist party's influence increased. Six years of extreme ultra-left sectarianism during the Comintern's 'third period', in which no collaboration with social democratic leaderships was possible and the latter were labelled 'social fascists', were drawing to a close. Nationally, they had led the Spanish party into an impasse, while internationally they had led to Hitler's rise to power in January 1933.

Under a new leadership since 1932, the PCE was one of the first communist parties to herald a shift in line when, in March 1933 – 'against the opinion of many members and of the Comintern delegate', according to José SANDOVAL (see below) – the party proposed an anti-fascist front to the socialists and anarcho-syndicalists which both rejected. In May 1934, the Comintern gave the signal that its national sections could propose united action to the socialist leaders; pacts were rapidly sealed in France and Italy, and in Spain – the proposal having been rejected by the socialist party – the PCE joined the Workers' Alliance despite the presence of trotskyists in it.[1] On the eve of the October rising it declared: 'When the struggle begins, the Workers' Alliance

1. See Claudin, *The Communist Movement: From Comintern to Cominform*, p. 174.

will take the leadership into their hands; they are the fundamental organism in the struggle for power.'

José SANDOVAL, communist militant (who later belonged to the commission that wrote the party's official history of the civil war, and a member of the party's central and executive committees), recalled the communist party's position at that moment. It was not, like that of the left-wing of the socialist party, to struggle for the socialist revolution but rather to complete the bourgeois democratic revolution.

—Capitalism was the dominant mode of production in Spain; the dominant contradiction was thus between the proletariat and the bourgeoisie. But there were still strong feudal vestiges remaining in the countryside which were holding back the full development of capitalism. The bourgeois democratic revolution, which could abolish these, could not be completed unless it was led by the working class and peasantry – precisely because no other class interests were as closely concerned with achieving such a revolution. It was Lenin's position of 1905 in Russia, and it went back virtually to the founding moments of the PCE . . .

A timid start, in the party's view, had been made to initiating the bourgeois democratic revolution under the republic. But it had not reached half-way to its final objectives. In believing that this revolution must be completed, the party by no means discounted the fact that in the course of carrying through this first stage of the revolution, higher aims could be posited and achieved. 'That is to say, that the bourgeois-democratic revolution could transform itself into the socialist revolution.'

—But there was one thing that differentiated the 1905 strategy from the new situation: the rise of fascism. From 1933 on, the major problem which informed the communist party's strategy and tactics was this threat, the need for working-class unity and the need for that unity to seek alliance with all anti-fascist social classes and strata who were willing to seek a democratic solution to the country's problems . . .

In June 1935, following the French example, the PCE proposed the formation of a Popular Anti-Fascist Bloc. In a speech, José Díaz, the party's secretary-general, put forward a minimum programme for all anti-fascists: the confiscation of large landowners' and church lands which should be given over immediately to the poor; the return of the right of self-determination to Catalonia (which had lost its autonomy statute as a result of the abortive October rising), and its application to Euzkadi, Galicia, etc.; general improvement in working-class living standards; amnesty for political prisoners and the formation of a provisional revolutionary government to put this programme into practice. At the same time, he said: 'The proletariat must be the leadership ('*fuerza dirigente*') of this anti-fascist concentration. This is the best guarantee that this programme of struggle will be carried through.'[1]

1. Speech in the Monumental Cinema, Madrid, 2 June 1935. (García-Nieto, 'La segunda república II' (*Bases documentales de la España contemporánea*, vol. 9, p. 317.) The five-point programme was a reduced version of a thirteen-point programme launched the previous month calling for the formation of a new Workers' and Peasants' Alliance. Among the points

The following month, the Seventh Congress of the Comintern set its official seal on this new line of collaboration with sectors of the bourgeoisie and called for the formation of Popular Fronts to meet the threat of fascism. The nucleus of this new type of alliance was to be the united front of all proletarian parties. 'The entire political activity of our party must revolve around the task of organizing Workers' and Peasants' Alliances. We must give these alliances a revolutionary programme, turn them in practice into the mainspring of the entire united front movement of the workers and peasants . . . transform [them] into live organs of the struggle for the immediate demands of the labouring masses and for preparing the seizure of power,' said *Ventura* (Jesús Hernández) on behalf of the Spanish communist party.[1]

The post-October repression by the centre-right government made not only the proletarian parties receptive to the need for unity of action,[2] but also the left republicans: Manuel Azaña had been imprisoned and viciously attacked by the right on the unsubstantiated charge of having taken part in the uprising in Barcelona. With the prospect of general elections, the Popular Front became a reality within six months of its being mooted. However, it was not the pact that the communist party had proposed. The concept of a united front within it was watered down by the socialist party, which remained the dominant left-wing force, to a commission to negotiate terms with the liberal republicans; gone – as the 'mainspring of the entire united front movement' – were the Workers' and Peasants' Alliances; and soon to go in the negotiations were all but two of the PCE's minimal programme points of six months earlier: the concession of an amnesty and autonomy statutes for the nationalities.

The workers' organizations represented on the negotiating commission in Madrid were the socialist party, UGT and socialist youth, the communist and syndicalist parties and the POUM. Juan ANDRADE represented the latter. In the commission it was the socialists who dominated and Largo Caballero who dominated them.

—Everything he suggested was approved. He was given too much latitude. One has to understand the feeling of the time: Caballero was like a god, he could do what he wanted – and what he wanted was to reach agreement, whatever the difficulties, in order to fight the elections united. He was prepared to compromise to do so. A man of goodwill, he was fundamentally a trade union bureaucrat and not very intelligent at that . . .

---

dropped were: the dissolution of the armed forces and the arming of the workers and peasants in a Red guard; the nationalization of major industries, finance, transport and communications; immediate and unconditional liberation of northern Morocco and all other Spanish colonial territories; the radical reduction of taxes on small businessmen and smallholders (see S. Payne, *The Spanish Revolution*, London, 1970, p. 168).

1. D. T. Cattell, *Communism and the Spanish Civil War* (Berkeley, 1955), p. 219.

2. In the period 1934–6, one of the most marked phenomena on the left was the grouping of forces; the Workers' Alliances, the fusion of the socialist and communist youth, the incorporation of the communist CGTU (Confederación General del Trabajo Unitaria) into the UGT, the return of the bulk of the *treintista* opposition unions to the CNT, the fusion of the *Izquierda Comunista* (trotskyist) with the Bloc Obrer i Camperol to form the dissident communist POUM, and the negotiations for the fusion of the four Catalan parties which were to form the PSUC in the first days of the war.

It was useless, ANDRADE soon saw, to try to object to the terms of the pact, to attempt to achieve working-class political leadership within it.

—The socialist party was bent on suicide. And the rest of us, as we say in Spanish, were no more than poor relations; we were there thanks to the socialists. Caballero said he wanted to exclude no working-class tendency; the POUM was represented due to him. At the first meeting, the communist party representative, Jesús Hernández, posed the problem of the POUM's exclusion. Making considerable play of the fact that his attitude had nothing to do with me personally, he said it was motivated by my party's policies. Caballero put an end to the matter with a 'No one is being expelled from here.' Hernández didn't return to the charge.

Reading the pact now one can see that it was a mistake; personally, I wasn't in favour of signing it. The final agreement was delayed while I spoke by phone to the POUM's executive in Barcelona who told me to sign. In fact, there was no alternative; we had to go into the elections united, the POUM would have split if we hadn't signed. Moreover, it gave our newly created party a magnificent opportunity to make itself known at electoral meetings which, as part of the Popular Front programme, reached hundreds of thousands of people. Once the point had been made of the need to support the Popular Front at the polls, each party was free to develop its own policies at these meetings.

The POUM was allocated four candidates on the Popular Front lists. But only Maurín could stand in Barcelona. The three other candidates, who included Nin and Gorkín, were rejected by the communists in the provinces where they were due to stand . . .

The pact – 'a common political plan which will serve as basis and programme for the coalition in the coming elections and as the norm of government' in case of victory – was essentially a statement of the liberal republicans' position and their refusal of socialist demands.[1] On the burning problem of agrarian reform it said only that it would stimulate cooperation and the collective exploitation of the land and 'carry out a policy of settling peasants and providing them with the necessary technical and financial resources'. Thus it promised more help to the smallholding peasantry than to the landless, considering the former the 'firmest base' of national reconstruction and offering them fiscal and financial help, as well as a new lease law. A decent minimum agricultural wage was to be established.

In the industrial sector, it proposed protecting small industry and commerce, and setting in motion a large public works programme, which would include rural areas, and would serve to absorb unemployment. The catalogue of socialist demands, including nationalization of the land and banking, and unemployment benefits was explicitly rejected.

This could hardly be called a large step forward to completing the bourgeois democratic revolution under the leadership of the working class and peasantry. But the 'struggle of democracy against fascism', in the communist party's eyes, now overrode all other objectives.

—The task of creating an anti-fascist alliance occupied the strategic foreground,

1. See Prologue, p. 44.

imprinting its particular mark on the situation and the party's policies, asserted José SANDOVAL. It was necessary to make every possible concession to the petty bourgeoisie and sectors of the bourgeoisie to attract them to the anti-fascist camp; they had to be given the widest scope for participation, even the leadership of the struggle. It was this that modified the Leninist strategy of 1905; it made it impossible to dispute the petty bourgeoisie's leadership of the government, and it altered the fundamental strategy of the phases of the bourgeois democratic revolution. It meant that the subsequent socialist revolution would now be pursued as far as possible in conjunction with all those sectors involved in the anti-fascist struggle; en route, some of them would drop out and others would continue – and we would continue with them, giving them participation in the whole process of democratic transformation.

The Popular Front alliance, I am convinced, contained within it enormous possibilities of social transformation. The role of the working class within it after the 1936 elections was growing stronger day by day. And though it sounds paradoxical, since the outcome was a civil war, the Popular Front contained the possibility of a peaceful development, the strengthening of the democratic revolution and even its transformation into a socialist revolution . . .

The party's strategy of six months earlier – not to mention the Comintern's pronouncements – had been fundamentally altered. Not the working class and peasantry but the petty bourgeois liberal republicans were to lead the struggle between 'democracy and fascism'.

It was this concept that the dissident communist POUM attacked. Fascism was the 'last and desperate attempt' by the bourgeoisie to resolve the internal contradictions of the capitalist system and to ensure its continued dominance as a class.

At a moment when capitalism was living an unparalleled crisis, fascism could not be fought by subordinating the working class to the bourgeoisie, socialism to the 'rebirth of a form of capitalist domination that is already transcended – bourgeois democracy'.[1] To hold back the democratic-socialist revolution, to deny demands that went beyond bourgeois-democratic freedoms in order to attract the petty bourgeoisie to the anti-fascist camp, was to invite the victory of fascism. When, as was inevitable, the petty bourgeoisie's own political parties would once again fail to satisfy their needs and resolve their problems, they would, in their disappointment, become the social base which fascism in Spain had lacked. Only the democratic-socialist revolution could solve these problems, could swing over the petty bourgeoisie and popular masses.[2] Implicit in the POUM's view was that the failure to make the revolution would provide the conditions for the successful fascist counter-revolution. If this was the case, why had the POUM signed the Popular Front pact?

1. *Qué es y qué quiere el Partido Obrero de Unificación Marxista*, POUM pamphlet (Barcelona, 1936, republished Paris, 1972). The democratic-socialist revolution was defined as 'bourgeois and socialist at the same time'. Bourgeois for the peasantry to whom the slogan 'The land for him who works it' would be applied, the nationalized land being given to the peasantry in usufruct; socialist elsewhere with big industry, mining, commerce and the banking system being nationalized.

2. See section B, p. 525, n.1, for Andreu Nin's formulation of this problematic.

—We joined because it was simply an electoral bloc which, in Catalonia where our major strength was, had no written platform and was called the Left Front of Catalonia. Given the electoral system that then existed, a bloc was necessary to win. We wanted no Popular Front as organization; indeed, the communist party was the only one to use the expression. We wanted the unity of the working class, to free political prisoners and to set the revolutionary process in motion again . . .

This position, put by Wilebaldo SOLANO, later to become the secretary of the POUM's youth movement, had to be understood in terms of electoral strategy which the working class knew required electoral pacts.

—Trotsky attacked us very violently for joining. He maintained that the workers would reproach the POUM for having compromised itself. The contrary was the case: the workers would have reproached us if we hadn't joined. There was a tremendous feeling of working-class unity in the face of the need to overthrow the right; the working class knew that the system obliged the POUM to join if it wanted to make any headway. But the workers equally well understood that tactical conditions could dictate elections one day and armed struggle the next, as indeed happened: the essential task – the seizure of power and the destruction of the bourgeois state – might require the use of a variety of tactics. If the situation we were living through had been properly explained to Trotsky, he would have understood. But living in Mexico, where communications were slow, and going through the worst period of his life, he was inevitably out of touch . . .

The POUM's position after the elections was that the working class should strive for the leadership of the struggle. But for the communists and many socialists, the perspective was not that: 'it was simply for the establishment of the Popular Front'.

In Asturias, Ignacio IGLESIAS, a POUM veteran of the October rising, saw the consolidation of the Popular Front policy as an extreme mistake. Rather than prepare the proletariat for revolution, the communist party's policy and actions gave the petty bourgeois republicans a role which they had lost.[1] 'Their failure in the first two-year period of the republic was notorious; there was no reason for allowing them to retain the leadership.' It was not, however, the communist party's fault, he thought.

—The blame lay with the Comintern, and in particular the Soviet Union which, in the face of the very real threat of fascism, was attempting to reach alliances with the bourgeois democracies, England and France. This explained their policy in relation to the indigenous bourgeoisie . . .

The Comintern Seventh Congress had defined the central slogan for the communist parties as 'the fight for peace and for the defence of the USSR'.

1. The liberal republicans' dominance in the Popular Front electoral results – they seated 162 deputies (including the Esquerra's 36) to 99 socialists and 17 communists – represented their *political bargaining strength* in determining the candidates' slates rather than their social force in the country. This was seen as soon as the war started when the proletarian organizations were revealed as the real strength – as they had been since the elections.

The idea, however, that the Popular Front solely served the needs of the Soviet Union's foreign policy was 'tendentious' in José SANDOVAL's view.

—The Soviet Union's needs and those of the Spanish democratic revolution were complementary, not contradictory. Logically, all communist parties at the time had the theoretical duty to defend the Soviet Union; but this duty was best carried out by engaging in the revolutionary struggle in one's own country. The Seventh Congress and the new line certainly served the interests of the Soviet Union; but this determination to create as wide an alliance as possible against fascism did not contradict the interests of the working classes of each specific country. Concretely, we in Spain saw the need for such a Popular Front and neither thought of nor considered the Soviet Union's interests . . .

In fact, the USSR's need to seek anti-fascist alliances with the bourgeois democracies found a perfect 'fit' in the need, at the national level, for alliances between the Comintern's national sections and the bourgeois parties which could be brought into the anti-fascist struggle. This was clearly perceived by a Madrid socialist youth member, Antonio PEREZ. However necessary to the Soviet Union's foreign policy, the Popular Front was an absolute necessity in Spain. 'The example of Austria and the slaughter of the social democrats had alerted us to the necessity of combating fascism . . . '

—The radicalization which we of the socialist youth had undergone, recalled another member, Sócrates GOMEZ, did not prevent us from believing that it was necessary to renew our experience of collaborating with the bourgeoisie. Without for a moment denying our hopes of repeating – successfully this time – October 1934 . . .

The socialist youth, in PEREZ's opinion, lacked theoretical preparation, knew very little of marxism, and by and large were unable to answer the communists with positions of their own.

—When the communists talked about completing the bourgeois democratic revolution before being able to pass on to the socialist revolution we didn't know what to reply. Our political education was virtually nil, 98 per cent of us had never read a word of Marx. The communist youth, which carried out the policies of its parent party, were better prepared than us; they were also more dogmatic and virulent. And what was true of us was true of our parent party: the majority of its leaders had never read a word of Marx either . . .

The radicalization of Spain in the last months before the war was illustrated by the communist party's rapid growth. Its claimed membership rose from 20,000 in October 1934, to 35,000 in February 1936, 102,000 in May and 117,000 on the eve of the war.[1]

1. Both Cattell, op. cit., and Hermet (*Les Communistes en Espagne*) have made much lower estimates: 3,000 members in 1934, 10,000 in February 1936, 50,000 at the outbreak of the war. The importance is less in the absolute numbers than in the relative increase in the space of less than two years.

F. The army

On the advent of the republic, the Spanish army had one officer for every eleven soldiers, one active general for every 1,266 men.[1] This top-heavy structure was nothing new. It stemmed from the first half of the nineteenth century when first guerrilla leaders of the anti-Napoleonic wars and later Carlist officers were allowed to join the army as career officers. Needless to say, it did not lead overall to an efficient fighting force.

The army's successes in the field in the late nineteenth and the first quarter of the twentieth centuries were limited. The loss of Cuba, the Philippines and all Spanish possessions in the Pacific in 1898 was followed by the long and costly 'pacification' of the Riff tribesmen in Spanish Morocco. Begun in 1908, this led to a disastrous defeat in 1921 at Annual where over 8,000 Spanish troops were slaughtered in a single battle. When pacification was finally achieved in 1925, it was as much due to French as to Spanish military might.

Over-staffed, the army was under-equipped. Although in 1931 defence (army and navy) took 18 per cent of the national budget,[2] the military had only 300 machine-guns that did not date from the Moroccan wars. The majority of its rifles were of an 1893 model; and the greater part of the artillery was inadequate.[3] In short, the army was better suited to its role as domestic policeman than to fighting international or colonial wars.

Several schemes for reducing the strength of the officer corps had been put forward in the past, but none had been implemented. The Alfonsine monarchy was close to the army. The army, however, having borne the onus of the Primo de Rivera dictatorship,[4] was not prepared to support the burden of Alfonso XIII against the will of the urban vote in 1931. Its passivity permitted the bloodless proclamation of the republic.

'The attitude of most of the military toward the new republic was passive and expectant,' an historian of the Spanish army has written.[5] This by no means meant that the army was 'republican'. It was with the memory of the military's long history of political interventionism that the liberal republicans – in particular Azaña – saw the army's reform as an urgent task of an advanced bourgeois democracy. As war minister in the provisional republican government of 1931, Azaña set about the task without delay. Within a fortnight of the republic's proclamation, he issued a decree which allowed virtually all officers to choose complete retirement on full pay. His plan was that the new army

1. There were 190 generals and 20,303 other officers for 240,564 men (see R. Salas Larrazábal, *Historia del ejército popular de la república*, Madrid, 1974, vol. 1, p. 8). I wish to thank Dr M. Alpert, author of *El ejército de la república en la guerra civil* (Barcelona, 1978), for his help in interpreting these and subsequent figures.

2. See Tamames, *La república, la era de Franco*, p. 128.

3. E. Mola, *Obras completas* (Valladolid, 1940), pp. 1096–8, cited in Payne, *Politics and the Military in Modern Spain*, p. 274.

4. The dictator's appointment of officers to oversee local government, his abolition of the staff corps and of promotion by strict seniority (the closed scale – see pp. 565–6 below) were among the main causes of friction with certain sections of the army. Artillery officers' resistance to the promotion measure led to the dictator dissolving the corps for a time. There were abortive military conspiracies against him in 1925 and 1926.

5. Payne, *Politics and the Military*, p. 266.

should consist of about 7,600 officers and 100,000 troops on the mainland, and 1,700 officers and 40,000 native and European troops in Morocco.

Within a year, between 5,000 and 6,000 officers had chosen to retire.[1] The figure was in itself eloquent testimony to the corps' acceptance of this aspect of Azaña's reforms.

—It was the best possible solution to the problem, reflected the Marquess de MARCHELINA, a Carlist artillery officer who retired under the law. Azaña's decree respected officers' rights and political opinions. He realized that career officers who felt themselves monarchists could not serve the republic . . .

The reduction in the size of the officer corps was not what mainly concerned many right-wing officers.

—If the nation considered a smaller army necessary, then so be it. We officers had always been made to bear the burden, stressed Pedro SALAZAR, a monarchist infantry officer from Burgos. But what we really objected to was that the republic deprived us of our flag. I cried like a child when the republican flag was hoisted in place of the flag of Spain. We had to swear allegiance to the republic. Many of us had private reservations about that; but we took the oath . . .

Azaña's intention of creating a republican army by allowing the regime's opponents to leave did not turn out the way he intended, the Marquess de MARCHELINA observed.

—What happened, in fact, was that great numbers of republican army officers took advantage of the reform to leave the army! They felt that they would have greater possibilities in civilian life now that their regime was in power. At the same time they were assured of their officers' pay . . .[2]

Azaña's other reforms included reducing the number of mainland divisions from sixteen to eight; opening 60 per cent of the enrolment in military academies to outstanding NCOs; requiring that all candidates for academies had six months' prior active service; and abolishing three military institutions: the Saragossa military academy, under Brigadier General Franco; accelerated promotion by combat merits; and separate military jurisdiction.

The abolition of the first of these was a reform which even liberal officers believed might have been better achieved by sweeping changes of the academy's staff, composed mainly of *africanistas* (as those who had served in Morocco were known). The second revived a long-standing dispute between the peninsular and African armies. The former, by and large, stood resolutely for promotion by strict seniority; the latter, which demanded compensation for active

1. According to M. Alpert's computation.

2. A general view substantiated, if for other reasons, by a republican army officer, Antonio Cordón. At the time a member of Azaña's Acción Republicana party (and later a distinguished communist party member), he wrote: 'We saw that the army was going to continue to be led in large part by ex-legionary officers, by the most reactionary generals . . . This was the reason why so many officers who had welcomed the republic left the army in disillusion.' Azaña's reforms, in Cordón's view, evinced an almost total blindness, a 'suicidal legalism' in respect to democratizing the high command (see A. Cordón, *Trayectoria*, Paris, 1971, pp. 192–7).

service, defended accelerated combat promotions.[1] The third abolished a law which, since 1906, had given military courts the right to try all 'crimes against the Fatherland and the army'.

These moves aroused the suspicion of right-wing officers, especially the *africanistas*. Fatherland and army shared an identity. To attack one was to attack the other. 'Where a government by its actions brought the nation to dishonour in the eyes of the world, either by proving itself unable to maintain order, or by placing it under the control however remote of a foreign power, then it was the bounden duty of the army officer to rise in defence of the country against the government: for however lawfully instituted, it had ceased to be lawful by its bringing dishonour to the nation.' These words, by a biographer of Franco, discussing the nature of the officer corps' training which Franco underwent, succinctly describe the attitudinal relationship of officers to Fatherland.[2] The concept took precedence over an oath of loyalty to a particular regime.

Suspicion was further aroused when Azaña, with his particular gift for presenting his enemies with phrases to use against the regime, spoke of 'pulverizing' the army.[3]

—The republic wanted to crush the army. The regime was determined to build a new, stronger army, as does every communistic state, thought Lt Carlos BRAVO, an infantry officer who had joined the *guardia civil* in Morocco. For most of us, Azaña was a pervert, a moral disaster. If we hadn't been Christians, we officers would have hanged him by a rope – a rope which would slowly have throttled him for a week . . .

Right-wing officers, especially in Morocco where civilian rule had replaced military government, felt that the officer corps was being denigrated. But it was other issues – the very issues that began to arouse civilians of the same class origins – which focused their hostility to the new regime. These were law and order, 'separatism', and (to a lesser extent perhaps) attacks on the church. There was nothing surprising about this. The uneven development of Spain had its reflection in the officer corps which was manned not by personnel from the advanced industrial regions but by Castilians and Andalusians in the main. The latter came principally from the 'provincial' petty bourgeoisie (see

1. In the peninsular army, the officer viewed his rank 'as his permanent bureaucratic status, unrelated to merit, ability, activity or competition . . .' according to Payne, op. cit., p. 127. The *africanistas*, on the other hand, tended to 'look with scorn on those of their colleagues (*peninsulares*) who had not volunteered for the imperial adventure . . . [They] were an offensive elite, romantically moved by having "written a glorious page" in history . . .' (Thomas, *The Spanish Civil War*, p. 93). Among the *africanistas* who had benefited from accelerated combat promotion was Franco, who became in quick succession the army's youngest captain, major, colonel and brigadier general. Other *africanista* generals – Mola, Goded, Queipo de Llano, Sanjurjo – were to be the prime movers of the 1936 uprising.

2. See G. Hills, *Franco* (London, 1967), p. 66.

3. During the election campaign in June 1931, Azaña spoke of putting all his energy into pulverizing the 'tyrannic forces' threatening Spain as he had already done to 'pulverize [*triturar*] other, no less threatening forces . . .' (cited in Tamames, op. cit., p. 191). The allusion was as obvious as it was inaccurate, although Azaña later said that he had been referring to *caciquismo* and not the army (see Azaña, *Obras completas*, vol. II, pp. 38–9).

section B) and shared most of its assumptions. Added to which was their particular sense of defending the nation's honour.

—We accepted the republic until disorder started, explained Lt BRAVO. I had some regrets for the monarchy, perhaps, but the change of regime was acceptable in itself. Would have been, I should say, if outrages hadn't almost immediately got the upper hand . . .

People had the right to demonstrate and demand what they considered their rights, he believed. But they must do so in a disciplined, orderly way. Instead, now the republic had come, they thought they were the 'bosses'.

'Disorder', as Lt BRAVO envisaged it, broke out in Morocco almost as soon as the republic was declared. A major strike in Tetuán at the beginning of May 1931 was met by a declaration of martial law and the calling out of a company of *regulares*.[1] Left-wing activity was discovered in several army bases. General Sanjurjo, then head of the *guardia civil*, was ordered to Morocco to restore order. Army officers, however, continued to be insulted in the streets, according to Lt BRAVO, who had decided to join the *guardia civil* because it was a corps which still enjoyed some respect.

—I could see that sooner or later it was going to be necessary to restore order – and the armed forces would have to do it. Let me give you an example. I was walking down a street in Ceuta when some building workers sat down on the pavement in front of me so that I couldn't pass. They expected me to step into the street or walk over them. Had I done so they would have protested that I had stepped on them. I wasn't having any of this. I pulled out my pistol and said: 'Clear the pavement.' With their heads hanging, they did as I ordered . . .

It was, of course, the *guardia civil* which was the bourgeois state's first line of police defence. Founded in the mid-nineteenth century as a rural police force to combat banditry, it had soon become an efficient, well-armed para-military force for repressing 'trouble' in the countryside. Patrolling always in pairs, the *guardia* in their tricorne patent-leather hats became a symbol of oppression for the landless labourers of the south. If the need arose, the *guardia civil* could always be called into the major cities. Under the republic, the strength of the force was about 25,000 men; its officers came almost without exception (and its commander always) from the army officer corps.

As a counterweight, the republic created the assault guards. This national republican police force was to be used for the suppression of demonstrations in the towns and to avoid the need for recourse to either the army or the *guardia civil*. It was, of course, also hoped that it would be a loyal republican force. Its fate in this respect has been seen in the pages devoted to the 1936 uprising in this book. After Sanjurjo's abortive rising (see below), the size of the force was doubled to 10,000; and by July 1936, it stood at a nominal 18,000.[2]

The army's initial lack of willingness to rise against the republic was demonstrated in August 1932, when General Sanjurjo, who had made his name in

1. Moroccan troops so called in contrast to the *irregular* tribesmen they were recruited to fight. The *regulares* were led by Spanish officers.

2. Payne, *Politics and the Military in Modern Spain*, p. 347.

Morocco, attempted a rising. Only 5 per cent of the officer corps directly backed the plot.[1] The rising succeeded for a day in Seville where a general strike and the dispatch of loyal troops put Sanjurjo to flight. In Madrid, only one under-manned cavalry battalion supported the rising, of which the government was well-informed. The monarchist plotters had had to assure other conspirators that there would be no immediate attempt to restore the monarchy; and some units in Seville refused further support when the word spread that the rising was aimed at bringing back the king.

Sanjurjo had a few months earlier clearly expressed the right-wing officer corps' attitude to the republic. 'We shall loyally serve the existing government; but if by chance the trend to the left should lead Spain to anarchy, we will rapidly assume full responsibility for the re-establishment of order. Our first duty is the maintenance of public order and we shall perform it at all costs. No revolutionary government shall be established in Madrid.'[2]

In the opinion of the monarchist deputy, Pedro SAINZ RODRIGUEZ, who arranged a meeting between Sanjurjo and Franco prior to the rising, the latter was precipitated by the attempt to prevent the Catalan autonomy statute being approved by parliament.[3]

—That was why the rising failed. It had to take place in August, rather than, say, the following January by which time it might have been well-prepared. Separatism was a burning issue in the army, as elsewhere. Franco told Sanjurjo clearly that he would not support the rising. I think he was well aware that it was poorly planned . . .

Sanjurjo was condemned to death, but the sentence was commuted to life imprisonment. About 300 other officers were purged. The ease with which the rising had been crushed led to an exaggerated sense of triumph among republicans, for which later they were to pay dearly.[4] It led also to rapid parliamentary approval of the agrarian reform bill and the Catalan statute.

While Azaña's reforms reduced the army's strength in numbers, it did little, in experts' opinion, to increase its effective combat strength.

Under the centre-right government of 1933-5, the army received satisfaction on a number of scores. Sanjurjo and those who had risen with him were amnestied. When Gil Robles became war minister in May 1935, he appointed Franco chief-of-staff, General Mola c-in-c Morocco, and General Goded to head a special army inspection under the war ministry. Promotions by merit were again authorized. Gil Robles and Franco carried out a purge of liberal republican officers, and a start was made to re-equipping the artillery and raising cartridge production.

1. Payne, ibid., p. 288. Lt Bravo was one of those to rise, being then in Seville. But many other officers who might have joined were unaware of the conspiracy or of its aims.

2. Payne, ibid., pp. 282–3.

3. Even liberal republican officers were not immune to anti-Catalan sentiment and believed the statute was 'contrary to national unity.' (See Cordón, op. cit., p. 201.) A socialist artillery captain, Urbano ORAD DE LA TORRE, affirmed that Catalan autonomy and religious persecution were at this time the two major mobilizing areas of the right-wing in the army.

4. Republicans and left-wingers in Seville credit Queipo de Llano's easy seizure of the city in July 1936 in large part to the false sense of security which Sanjurjo's defeat there four years earlier had created among them.

The Asturian rising of October 1934 was put down by Foreign Legion and Moroccan troops from the Army of Africa. Franco played a leading coordinating role in the operation. The rising also gave impetus to a clandestine right-wing organization within the army: UME (Unión Militar Española). This was composed in the main of middle-rank and junior officers, and after Asturias its leaders held talks with the Falange.

In early November 1934, Calvo Sotelo, the monarchist leader, encouraged parliament to consider the army's position.

'It is necessary to affirm Spain's need for a powerful army and to restore moral satisfaction and spiritual dignity to the leaders of that army,' he said. 'It is necessary, in a word, that the honour of the army be the very honour of Spain.' Refuting Azaña's statement that the army was the arm of the fatherland, he continued: 'It is now obvious that the army is much more than the arm of the fatherland. I shall not say that it is its head, for it ought not to be that; but it is much more than the arm. It is the spinal column – and if it breaks, bends or cracks, it is Spain that is bent or broken.'

At the other end of the political spectrum, the communist party fully understood the importance of organizing within the army. It had for several years published *La Voz del Cuartel* (Voice of the Barracks) as an outlet for soldiers' views and complaints. After October 1934, Franco attempted to crush the left inside the army.[1]

It was at this moment that Francisco ABAD, an Andalusian communist, joined the army as a regular. Having been thrown out of work as a barrel-maker in his native Almería, he hoped to be able to pursue his ambition of becoming a musician in the army. He joined the No. 6 infantry regiment in Madrid, where he found that the clandestine organization which had previously existed had been wound up. He set about recreating it. By March 1935, a clandestine newspaper called *Soldado Rojo* (Red Soldier) began to appear.

—It was the organ of the soldiers' and corporals' organization, and was published by the communist party. Above all, it expressed the need to defend democratic liberties, the republic, and warned constantly of the necessity to be alert to the possibility of a military coup. By December 1935, about 175 soldiers and corporals from my regiment were members of the organization. Hardly any of them were members of the PCE, nor did they know that the organization was led by the communist party . . .

In October 1935, his regiment took part in manoeuvres in the Guadarrama mountains. His organization issued a leaflet denouncing these as a 'fascist try-out' for the seizure of Madrid. The barracks committee which he had organized, and which controlled the soldiers' and corporals' organization, consisted of only two or three men. A soldier was detailed by the regiment's Lt Colonel to keep a watch on ABAD. Unknown to the colonel, the man belonged to ABAD's

1. In the experience of Narciso JULIAN, communist railwayman, anyone who had been to gaol for political offences was now not called up to do his military service. Other left-wingers had the experience of being called up but of not being issued with uniforms or arms and, after a few months, of being sent on extended leave.

organization and was in charge of smuggling in propaganda. Unknown to his company captain, ABAD kept all propaganda hidden in the officer's room.

When, in December 1935, a new government was appointed to prepare for the 1936 general elections, Gil Robles, in one of his last acts as war minister, asked Generals Franco, Goded and Fanjul to sound out support in the army for a declaration of martial law. The response was not encouraging. Senior officers were unwilling to act against a constitutional government as long as it remained in the hands of moderates. After the Popular Front electoral victory, Gil Robles asked the prime minister, and Franco requested the war minister, to declare a state of war (martial law); both turned down the request.

The liberal republican government now posted the generals it most feared to what it considered geographically peripheral posts: Franco to the Canary Islands, Goded to the Balearic Islands, Mola to Pamplona. Before leaving, these and other generals met in Madrid. No precise plans were laid, but it was apparently agreed that all would act if any one of the following occurred: dissolution of the *guardia civil*, dismissal of army recruits, disbanding of the officer corps, armed rebellion by the left or a premature coup by a single garrison.[1]

Most of the active army leadership, however, was not outright anti-republican, militarist or favourable to authoritarian solutions. Franco, with his habitual caution, was apparently willing to allow the liberal republican regime time to see if it could 'contain' the situation arising from the Popular Front victory. Some other generals, who for the most part had retired under Azaña's reform, were less sanguine, and attempted to organize risings in April and May 1936. Neither got off the ground. It was after the first of these that Mola took over the planning of the definitive rising.

It was not by chance that an *africanista* should be responsible for masterminding the operation. After years spent pacifying Riff tribesmen, officers of the Army of Africa tended to look on Spain itself 'as a Moroccan problem of a new kind: infested by rebellious tribes masquerading as political parties and demanding an iron, if fatherly, hand'.[2]

Even if Mola's political plans for the post-rising regime were somewhat more sophisticated than this description allows (see below), the young officer in Morocco could easily see the need for pacifying the mainland.

—Things couldn't be allowed to continue as they were. The burning of churches, armed hold-ups, censorship of the press, surveillance of private mail. And if that wasn't enough, there was separatism. Not only in Catalonia and the Basque country, for by now regions which had never before considered it, like Andalusia and Castile, were infected . . .

This viewpoint, expressed by Lt Julio de la TORRE of the Foreign Legion, was shared by many young officers; it was among them that the determination to rise was the strongest. 'The senior officers, the old men, were prepared to put

1. See Payne, *Politics and the Military in Modern Spain*, p. 315. The strength of the army and security forces in 1936, as computed by M. Alpert, was as follows: 103 generals, 15,728 officers, 120,286 soldiers, 32,869 civil guards, 17,660 assault guards, 14,113 *carabineros* (frontier guards), for a total of 15,831 officers and 184,928 men.

2. Thomas, op. cit., p. 94.

up with the situation, to see what would happen.' Many of the junior officers felt sympathetic to the Falange.

—We saw there the principles of discipline and order, the sense of the Fatherland. Although I wasn't a member, I felt that the Falange represented my ideals. It was evident after the Popular Front elections that the influence of communists and masons was increasing daily – even in the Army of Africa! In order to get a decent posting you had to be a mason – most of the people who held high civil and military posts were members . . .

Another threat faced the Army of Africa, according to Lt de la TORRE: a sergeants' revolution. Communist organization among legionary NCOs was having its effect; cells already existed.

—We feared they were going to stage a rising. There was a moment in March or April 1936, when *regulares* had to be brought in to surround certain legionary units. The sergeants had been promised by the communists that they would be promoted to officers . . . [1]

The Popular Front victory served to increase the strength of the soldiers' and corporals' organization in Madrid. In ABAD's No. 6 infantry regiment, the number enrolled rose to about 300. Popular Front committees, in which soldiers of all anti-fascist parties and organizations participated, were also set up. ABAD attended the first conference of the anti-militarist organization of the Madrid garrison, under communist party auspices, on 1 January 1936. During the threatened uprising that spring, the soldiers' and corporals' organization was on full alert, taking over the barracks' main entrances and the armoury.

It was not only communist party members who organized among the troops. Revolutionary workers of other organizations formed barracks committees when called up for military service. Such was the case of Ramón FERNANDEZ, a POUM carpenter from Barcelona, who was posted in October 1935 to an infantry regiment in Jaca, Aragon. It was the regiment which Capt. Fermín Galán and Lt García Hernández had led out on an abortive attempt to overthrow the monarchy in December 1930; both were executed as a result. FERNANDEZ became one of an eight-member barracks committee which 'controlled' one of the companies and the detachment in charge of the artillery accompaniment.

—We knew that a major and a lieutenant were the head of the UME in the barracks. We managed to lay our hands on documents they were circulating about the need for an uprising. When we took these documents to republicans and socialists in the town they simply laughed. They didn't believe any of it . . .

His barracks committee laid plans in case the regimental officers attempted to rise. The men would seize the armoury, then harangue the troops and open fire on 'anyone wearing an officer's hat'. One night the men were awoken by the sound of firing. They took over the armoury – a corporal member of the committee had the key – only to find that the noise came from a sandal factory

1. Despite its name, the Foreign Legion was almost entirely Spanish. It consisted at the time of two *tercios* comprising a total of about 4,200 men.

in town which had caught fire: the asbestos sheeting on the roof was exploding from the heat.[1]

During the spring of 1936, the UME grew rapidly, claiming some 3,400 officers on active service and 1,800 reserve or retired officers.[2] Most of the groups, however, functioned more or less in isolation. Its opposite number, the republican military anti-fascist union, UMRA (Unión Militar de Republicanos Anti-fascistas), was smaller. Capt. ORAD DE LA TORRE, who was a member, estimated that at best it had something like 200 officers, most of them in Madrid.

—But if there were few officers, there was a greater number of warrant officers and sergeants, for UMRA was open to other ranks. In about 1933 we received an anonymous letter threatening all UMRA officers with death. We took no notice. But on 9 May 1936, Capt. Carlos Faraudo, a member officer, was gunned down in the street as he was walking with his five-year-old daughter. The reason for his assassination was that he had been training the socialist militia – as though that were a reason. It was then that we drew up a statement saying that we would not reply in kind on our brother officers, but rather on a politician if such an assassination were repeated . . .[3]

As the pre-revolutionary ferment grew throughout the spring, attitudes in the officer corps began to harden, as they did amongst their civilian counterparts. Violence between left-wingers and officers increased. Socialists and anarchists were resolutely anti-militarist; and the left was in no doubt as to the threat of a military rising. The slogan of a red army had been raised in the May day parade in Madrid. The rumours of a communist plot to establish a soviet in Spain were widely believed by right-wing officers. And yet the bulk of the peninsular officer corps was not prepared to rise.

Officers were now jeered at by the middle classes for their refusal to take action. Invited to a military dance in Madrid, middle-class women threw chicken feed on the floor to show their disgust at the officers' 'cowardice'.[4] The bourgeoisie looked to the army to defend it yet again. When Laura KELLER, who was pregnant, went to a clinic in Madrid for a check-up, the gynaecologist looked at her officer husband.

—'And you officers – what are you doing?' he asked my husband as we went up in the lift. The gynaecologist was very right-wing, had attended the queen in the past. But ever since the Popular Front elections, people had been saying things like that to my husband, thinking that because he was an officer he must be right-wing . . .

Mola hoped to be able to stage the rising by the end of June. In one of his

1. FERNANDEZ left the army a fortnight before the uprising in July. As far as he was able to learn later, the committee was unable to prevent the regiment rising to the cry of '*¡ Viva la república!*' The corporal who was the committee's moving spirit was a 'brave but naïve man, and he paid for his naïvety with his life'. In Madrid, on the other hand, ABAD's infantry regiment did not rise. See p. 117.

2. See Payne, *Politics and the Military in Modern Spain*, p. 317.

3. See p. 103.

4. See J. Pérez Salas, *Guerra en España 1936–1939* (Mexico, 1947), p. 80, cited in Payne, op. cit., p. 327.

first directives, he made explicit the means and ends of the operation: 'It will be borne in mind that the action, in order to crush as soon as possible a strong and well-organized enemy, will have to be very violent. Hence, all directors of political parties, societies, or unions not pledged to the movement will be imprisoned: such people will be administered exemplary punishments so that movements of rebellion or strike will be strangled.'[1]

Mola planned to retain a republican regime – but under a five-man directorate which would exercise power 'in all its amplitude'. The 1931 Constitution would be suspended, the president of the republic and the government dismissed, and all laws not in accord 'with the new organic system of the state' abrogated. All political and social organizations and sects which were 'inspired from abroad' would be outlawed. Among Mola's 'social' points were: the separation of church and state and freedom of worship; unemployment pay; the abolition of illiteracy; a public works and irrigation programme, and a solution to the agrarian problem based on smallholdings and collective farming where possible. All the directorate's decrees would be approved in the future by a constituent parliament 'elected in a manner to be determined'.[2]

Sanjurjo, now in exile in Lisbon, would be president of the directorate. The difficulties of organizing the rising when only a minority of the officer corps in the peninsula was willing actively to participate led to the postponement at the end of June. Despite protestations to the contrary, the Madrid government was aware that something was afoot. In June two cavalry regiments were transferred from Madrid because of doubts about their loyalty. On 29 June the director of the security forces travelled in person from Madrid to Pamplona with a large police escort, ostensibly in search of contraband arms. Mola had been warned the day before by his contact, the Madrid chief of police, and had taken precautions.[3]

Well aware that the rising could not be a *pronunciamiento* in the old military style, Mola had sought civilian support: in his plan a twin military–civilian structure to the rising was envisaged. However, this led to imbroglios with the Carlists and, to a lesser extent, with the Falange. The Carlist leadership broke off relations with him because they were not assured of being in charge of the new state's 'organic and corporative' reconstruction and because the rising was to take place under the republican, not monarchist flag.[4] Agreement was reached only two days before the rising in Morocco, on the basis of an anodyne compromise suggested by Sanjurjo. Meanwhile José Antonio Primo de Rivera, leader of the Falange, was both suspicious of military conspirators and

1. Cited in Thomas, op. cit., p. 174.
2. The full programme is contained in del Burgo, *Conspiración y guerra civil*, p. 534.
3. See Maíz, *Mola, aquél hombre*, pp. 214–17.
4. In March 1934, a commission of Carlists and monarchists had visited Mussolini to put forward a plan for overthrowing the republic. The Italian dictator agreed to provide 20,000 rifles, 20,000 grenades, 200 machine-guns and 1,500,000 pesetas. Only the financial part of the agreement was met. It was the only material assistance afforded to conspirators against the republic by a fascist government before the war started. A number of *requetés* went to Italy for military training in the guise of Peruvian officers. The Carlists later organized the dispatch of a ship-load of arms from private sources in Europe, but the cargo was embargoed by the Belgian authorities. See A. Lizarza, *Memorias de la conspiración* (Pamplona), 1953, p. 48, and del Burgo, op. cit., pp. 516 and 520.

concerned by the postponement of the rising. From his prison in Alicante he demanded that a firm date be fixed. Mola set a new date: 12 July.

During June, Mola had sent four messages to Franco; none of them had received an answer. On 23 June, Franco wrote a letter to the premier and war minister, Casares Quiroga, in which he suggested that the left's anti-military campaign was sapping the army's spirit, and protested against the removal of right-wing officers. He warned the premier of the peril involved 'for the discipline of the army'. This letter, as Hugh Thomas observes, 'was a final statement by Franco "before history", that he had done his best to secure peace, though he must have known that little could be done at that late hour'.[1]

Preparations were still not completed by 12 July. The dispute between the Carlists and Mola was still unsettled. On 14 July, Mola received a coded message from Madrid that Franco was not going to participate. By then Mola had sent a message to the Army of Africa to prepare for the rising from 1700 hours on 17 July. On 15 July a new message was received rectifying the previous one concerning Franco.[2] While the error was no doubt due to garbled communications, it was certain that Franco had not finally made up his mind to join the rising until a few days before.

The assassination of Calvo Sotelo in reply for the murder of Lt Castillo in Madrid ensured that, whatever the outcome, the rising could be postponed no longer. But even then, only two days before the event, Eugenio VEGAS LATAPIE, editor of the monarchist *Acción Española*, discovered that the officers of the artillery academy in Segovia had received no instructions. Nor had his brother who was an officer in the signals regiment stationed at El Pardo outside Madrid.

—It was the day after Calvo Sotelo's funeral. I was talking to an artillery major in Segovia when his father, a retired colonel, insulted his son in front of me for not having risen yet. 'If I were a young officer I wouldn't tolerate this situation a moment longer.' It impressed me that an old man, who would normally be concerned only to lead a quiet life, should be inciting his son to action like that . . .

1. Thomas, op. cit., p. 199.

2. See Maíz, *Mola, aquél hombre*, pp. 219, 271 and 281 for details of the communications between Mola and Franco.

Appendix

A. Collectivization and foreign capital
B. Non-libertarian collectivization

A. Collectivization and foreign capital

The Catalan collectivization decree mentioned compensation for owners of expropriated enterprises without spelling out the conditions. An original draft clause – in which the industrial credit fund would have been responsible for eventual compensation – was dropped from the published decree.[1] The result of this ambiguity was that pressure of foreign capital on the compensation question became a major problem.

—A sort of cat-and-mouse game, in which we were the mouse, recalled PEREZ-BARO. There wasn't anything that we could do, because the legal conditions under which compensation would be paid had not been agreed on . . .

There was nothing to offer foreign companies since the industrial credit fund had not been set up; moreover, these companies might not have accepted long-term government bonds – 'they were always demanding compensation in foreign currency' – had it been offered them. But at least, he thought, such an offer might have shut them up.

Claims were made on behalf of just over 100 foreign firms, half of them French, sixteen British, five North American, nine Argentinian. PEREZ-BARO received the representatives.

—The British consul was certainly the worst. When he came to lodge a complaint on behalf of a British firm – Fabra & Coats was demanding £1 million, for example – he acted as though he were in his own office, and always came accompanied by a stenographer to record every word said. The Belgian and Argentinian consuls needed careful handling, but at least they acted with a certain amount of respect . . .

Many foreign companies with interests in Catalonia reached agreement to boycott the republican economy, he explained. The directors of the Bank of Spain were in the nationalist zone and, naturally, they used their influence abroad to ensure that international capital sabotaged the collectivized economy. 'We found that the few exports we could make were embargoed as soon as they arrived at foreign ports.'

1. Albert PEREZ-BARO, secretary of the decree's application commission, was never able to get to the bottom of why this happened. 'But I believe that the PSUC representation on the Economics Council, which was drafting the decree, managed to persuade the CNT members that compensation should, in certain circumstances, be paid; and that in the Generalitat, Nin, the POUM leader, persuaded the CNT ministers to reject the compensation clause. If my interpretation is correct, it shows again that the CNT lacked consistency, allowing itself in this case to be led in opposite directions by two people who didn't belong to its organization.'

To avoid undue trouble, the Economics Council decided that firms with foreign capital which, in principle, fell under the collectivization decree would be collectivized only if the workers in the firm themselves agreed to it. Some twenty foreign companies were thus not collectivized. But even when they were, the subsequent offer to 'de-collectivize' an enterprise would not necessarily satisfy foreign owners, as Joan FERRER, secretary of the CNT commercial employees' union, discovered.

He had been asked by the potash miners of Sallent, who had collectivized their Franco-Belgian company, to become the collective's administrator. Potash was an important Catalan export, 165,000 tons having been produced in 1935. Although the foreign technicians and engineers had disappeared, the mines were rapidly got working again. Then came the task of finding markets. One week's production satisfied the annual domestic demand; export markets were vital. Spain at that time had a quota within an international cartel, and through the Generalitat's good offices, the collective was soon able to find foreign buyers, most of them in Asia. As the collectivization decree had legalized Catalan collectives, there appeared to FERRER no reason why potash should not be exported.

—But as soon as our freighters reached the high seas, they were seized by the Non-Intervention committee forces and the cargo embargoed on the orders of the original owners. We tried getting freighters out under different flags, but it made no difference. After this had happened about a dozen times, we took the case to the International Court in The Hague. It found against us, at the beginning of 1937, for one reason and one alone: the collectivization decree was a regional, not a national law . . .

Before the hearings, he and other members of the collective made several trips to Valencia to put their case to Negrín, then finance minister in the central government.

—He refused to recognize the collectivization decree. He, and the majority of the central government along with him, were determined not to accept it, nor allow the CNT in particular to control any part of the economy. We explained that there was a difference between a foreign-owned factory, built with foreign capital, and a mining concession. Throughout the world, the sub-soil is state property, and mining companies only hold concessions from the state for a fixed number of years to exploit the mineral resources: they do not own the sub-soil. We attempted to persuade him that the concession be withdrawn from the foreign holders and made over to the collective, against state compensation for the loss of the concessionary rights. Negrín refused even this, the only legal way out. He would have nothing to do with Catalan collectivization . . .[1]

Having lost their case, they decided to approach the concession owners, Potasas Ibéricas, the Franco-Belgian company. The important thing, in

1. Shortly before the CNT withdrew from the central government following the May events in Barcelona, Joan Peiró, the CNT industry minister, issued an order for the state take-over of the mines which in turn were to be handed over to the miners for the purposes of interior sales, while a state organism would handle exports. The order, in effect, remained a dead letter. See Peirats, *La CNT en la revolución española*, vol. 2, pp. 205–6.

FERRER's view, was to keep the 700 miners at work and, by exporting, to earn much-needed foreign currency for the war effort. Accompanied by two miners' delegates and a Generalitat representative, he went to Paris to negotiate with the owners.

—I had to do all the talking since the company chairman spoke French, and I was the only one on our side with some command of the language. Our proposal was simple: the company should resume control of the mines and run them as before with only two conditions: the Works Council should continue in existence, and a number of improved working conditions be recognized. The company had been particularly exploitative before the war. In effect, we were offering to 'de-collectivize' the mines and to allow the company to make and retain its profits as before.

They categorically refused to listen to our proposals. They said – literally – that they would prefer to lose two, three or four years' Spanish production, knowing that sooner or later they would re-assume control. 'You will be swept away, and the mines will be ours again,' they said. We broke off relations and returned to Barcelona . . .

At the anecdotal level, one event impressed FERRER. At the end, the chairman took his leave of the delegation in perfect Spanish. Throughout, he had spoken only in French, even though he saw that FERRER was not entirely fluent. Moreover, FERRER had to translate for his mining companions; their answers were pretty rough, and included some harsh language for the chairman. The latter, who for three days of negotiations had retained an impassive exterior, revealed at the end that he had understood everything.

—And not only that: the company was perfectly informed of our movements. We had arrived two days before the talks started, and the chairman, during one of the intervals, had told me exactly what we had been doing. Their information service out of Catalonia was excellent; they knew each time a ship loaded with potash was preparing to sail. I never found out how they organized it, but I suppose it must have been one of the technicians . . .

The mines had to close. The miners were sent by the Generalitat to construct roads. Not a gram of potash was mined from Sallent thereafter throughout the war.

*

Finally, a special tribunal within the Catalan Appeals Court was set up by the Generalitat finance councillor, Josep Tarradellas, of the Esquerra, in the second half of 1938, to hear foreign claims. This, in the view of Joan GRIJALBO, UGT representative on the Economics Council, might well have been a double-edged instrument as far as collectivization was concerned.

—As it happened, the tribunal never operated fully. But if it had, a demand for compensation could have raised the constitutionality of the collectivization decree – which might have been declared unconstitutional. We considered this tribunal a cover-up to ward off foreign capital; but it was really an attempt by the Esquerra to create the possibility of reversing the revolution in Catalonia . . .

B. Non-libertarian collectivization

While the PSUC's view of the Catalan revolution was summed up by its secretary-general, Joan Comorera, in March 1937, as 'seven months of grave errors, adventures, lamentable and dangerous experiments . . . which have ended as all such experiments inevitably do',[1] the PSUC did not propose to abolish collectivization. Indeed, a number of UGT collectives existed; and few, if any, large properties appear to have been returned to their bourgeois owners. In contradistinction to the PCE, which stood for the nationalization of large industry, the PSUC, faced still with a militant CNT working class, attempted rather to centralize the collectives under Generalitat (or PSUC) control from June 1937, when Comorera became economics councillor. In this, he was much aided by the fact that many collectives had mortgaged themselves to the Generalitat's 'pawn bank' to pay their workers' wages.[2] In the course of this centralization, Comorera inevitably modified many essential aspects of the collectivization decree, including the role of the Economics Council, which was turned from an executive into an advisory organ. Such modifications could have paved the way for a later move from centralization to nationalization. The latter was, in any case, to a large extent achieved in August 1938, when the central government took over the Catalan war industries, which included not only engineering and chemical plants, but also cloth and tanning factories. In the last months of the war, partly because of foreign capital's and central government's hostility to Catalan collectivization, PSUC proposals were made in support of the petty bourgeoisie's determination to transform collectives into cooperatives.[3] But by this time, the collectives were in sharp decline, and the war appeared unlikely to last much longer.

The Catalan UGT was not opposed to collectivization; indeed, it advocated extending the system to the whole of Spain. But it was – like its political counterpart, the PSUC – resolutely opposed to trade union (or autonomous working-class) power.

The experiences of a PSUC worker in a UGT-led collective reveal some of the complexities of the problem. Antonio RIBAS worked in the maintenance section of an enterprise manufacturing oxy-acetylene gas, vital for the engineering industry and the war effort. His plant had eighty workers only, but the company had plants in Berga (Catalonia) and Valencia (as well as in other towns which were now in the nationalist zone). The two Catalan plants together numbered more than 100 workers, and were thus subject to collectivization under the decree. Until the latter came into force, the plant was not collectivized.

—It would have weighed on our consciences to have taken over the firm just like that. The management hadn't treated us badly in the past. Moreover, none of the plant managers had fled Barcelona after 19 July. Our reluctance didn't

1. Report to the Plenum of the Amplified Central Committee of the PCE, Valencia, cited in Bricall, *Política econòmica de la Generalitat*, p. 317. Comorera said that on the day Málaga fell (7 February 1937) the Generalitat, the political parties, the unions and the press had been concerned with only one problem: the collectivization of dairies.

2. See p. 211 n.

3. See Pérez-Baró, *Trenta mesos de col·lectivisme a Catalunya*, especially chapters 4 and 5; also Bricall, op. cit., pp. 314–22.

stem from the fact that the UGT was the majority union – the UGT wasn't opposed to collectivization – but it didn't believe there was any great hurry about it. We expected the war to end fairly soon in our favour, and we thought that we should wait until victory to lay the basis of the future economic regime, otherwise it was bound to be a haphazard affair . . .

He realized as soon as he saw the figures in the company accounts, 'and my head began to spin', that to run the plant it was necessary to retain the old managers who knew the company's business. 'I knew I wouldn't personally be capable of running the enterprise, and I think most of the workers felt like that.' But he was all in favour of a workers' control committee, as were the other workers. They liked the idea of participating in the plant's running.

—They would come and say, 'Look, why don't we do this, why don't we try that?' They had ideas about what should be done, how things could be improved . . .

Participation was one thing: full-scale collectivization another. He believed the workers weren't prepared for the latter. Too much time and energy was spent in Catalonia on collectivizing and not enough on the necessary groundwork to ensure the experiment's success. All energies had to be bent first to winning the war.

When they were obliged to collectivize under the decree, they formed one collective of the three plants.

—The most immediate problem of collectivization was that each factory thought of itself as an independent unit. We wanted to avoid that. If the workers in the Berga plant, where they produced carbide, were autonomous, they might start to do business on their own . . .

Three workers from each plant, an accountant and the plant managers formed the works council. While the workers were in an indisputable majority, they left technical matters as a rule in the hands of the former management. Work conditions were a different matter, however. The works council met once a week, the representatives from Valencia and Berga travelling to Barcelona. The nine worker-members, who included two CNT members, continued to work at their normal jobs when there were no meetings.

—Although there were one or two cases of workers who thought that the new situation meant they could do what they wanted, the majority reacted well, understanding from the start that it was necessary to work hard. In fact, an intensive work rhythm had always existed in the plant, but we worked even harder now, for we imagined that when the war ended in a republican victory, the gains we had made would be consolidated . . .

The collective made no profits, as far as he knew. But none of the work force went hungry either. The collective set up its own store and had a lorry which went round the countryside collecting food. The collective negotiated direct exchanges of carbide for olive oil. If it had a surplus of oil, it would exchange it for soap, and some of the latter would be used in barter with peasants for rabbit and kid meat. 'We ran our own economy, you might say; a small one, but our own . . .'

*

The polemic about the Aragonese collectives sometimes obscures the extent of the rural collectivization movement in other regions, and the degree to which the UGT participated in, or initiated, collectives which differed little in some respects from those of the anarcho-syndicalists.

One such was in the village of Cardenete, with a population of under 2,000, in the province of Cuenca. It was started on the initiative of the thirty-four-year-old socialist mayor, José MILLAN, who had read books on the Soviet experience, as well as books by Joaquín Costa, the Spanish social reformer and polymath. Son of a medium-holding peasant in a village dominated by large landholdings which, in some cases, included as much as 1,000 hectares of hill and mountain land rich in pine forests, he had been moved in his youth by his father's account of how all the forests, the village's two olive mills and two bakeries had been communally owned until taken over by feudal landlords. He came to believe that collectivization, which would make possible mechanization, was the only answer to the agrarian problem.

A brief demonstration of force by local right-wing landlords on 19 July subsided rapidly when it became apparent that Madrid had not risen. But four days later, when CNT militiamen came from Cuenca to collect arms in the village they were met by fire and their leader was mortally wounded. More militia arrived and the right-wingers surrendered: thirty-eight of them were taken to Cuenca and approximately a dozen were shot. This was to have an important effect because, with the exception of two brothers, all the large landlords had either fled or been taken by the militia.

MILLAN sent trustworthy labourers to look after their livestock; the harvest continued to be brought in by hired hands.

—Nothing much changed, in fact. The day-labourers simply went on doing what they would have done anyway. These landlords had never worked on their land. As it was harvested, the grain was stored in their houses . . .

Founder of the UGT locally, and a moderate socialist, MILLAN had been swept aside, his power as mayor reduced to nothing, by the revolutionary village committee made up of leading UGT members. (The CNT did not exist in the village pre-war.) In September 1936, the communist agricultural minister's decree appointing mayors as the local delegates of the Agrarian Reform Institute to take charge of all abandoned farms, gave him some renewed administrative power. It was then that he began to think that what once had belonged to the village, and was now in the hands of four or five large landowners, could be restored to the villagers 'so that they could again be free'.

—We had heard that collectives were being set up in other places, although not in Cuenca province which was one of the most reactionary in Spain. Most of the landlords had not risen with the military and, camouflaging themselves as best they could, remained in possession of their lands. But things had turned out differently in my village. The landowners' farms, which I had to administer, could form the basis of a collective. I knew the agrarian reform delegate in Cuenca, and I went to see him. He said it was an excellent idea, and so we simply went ahead. We had no proper legal basis for doing so . . .

The collective was established in January 1937. Of the 160 villagers who joined, the great majority were landless labourers; only about twenty smallholders joined – about 5 per cent of the village total. They put in their land, livestock, tools, etc., but not their private savings. Including families, some 500 people, or just over one quarter of the village, were in the collective, which farmed nearly 300 hectares of arable land and several thousand hectares of mountain and woodland. The founding capital was the land, the grain produced the previous harvest and the seizure of two shops belonging to the rich who had fled. The latter had fairly extensive stocks of clothes and food, as well as cash reserves.

Money was abolished as currency within the collective, membership of which was entirely voluntary. MILLAN, who put in his olive mill, grocer's shop and his father's 25 hectares of land, became the collective's assistant secretary.

—Abolishing money caused some complications, but not that many. It prevented the individual collectivist from misusing the product of his labour on unnecessary things. In the collective stores, with his family ration card, he could get all the vital necessities that he and his family required. And that was his major wish at the time: to have enough for him and his family to eat. Later, had the experiment continued, other needs, new aspirations would have arisen . . .

To draw his rations, the collectivist had to show that he had fulfilled his tasks as a producer: the foreman of each work group stamped his card at the end of the day with the single word '*trabajó*' – he worked.

The collective grew everything that the people needed in the way of food. It was able to fatten up at least 120 pigs in the collective's styes, for rearing a pig was the basis of peasant domestic economy at the time.

—People's tastes weren't exotic, the peasantry was used to a simple, hard life. They preferred what was locally grown. There were no food shortages – indeed, there was always a surplus which mainly we sold, although occasionally we exchanged produce directly with a neighbouring village. This was something that had been done in the past, privately, and the collective continued the practice. In fact, the collective was like a big household, a large family . . .

A portion of the money received from the sale of the collective's produce was distributed to the collectivists; the remainder was reserved in a fund to permit the collective to purchase agricultural machinery in due course. In the first instance, a flour mill was built; agricultural machinery was unavailable – 'in fact barely known in these parts then'.

—The money distributions were simply to allow the collectivists to have some small reserves to satisfy their individual whims. It was my hope that in the end, once the collective had raised a permanent fund, we could distribute all the surplus among the collectivists. But, of course, the experiment didn't continue long enough for that.

We were able to sell all that we produced; we didn't have to send supplies to the front. Occasionally, militiamen would come round and ask for produce, but we never had to deliver a regular quota. In fact, as the collective had money, it led a fairly autonomous existence. Governmental authority barely reached us; official organisms functioned, but in a way that hardly led to their presence being felt. We carried on as we thought best . . .

Culture was not forgotten; a small library was set up and schooling for collectivists' children organized with school teachers evacuated from places close to the front. Unforced, untroubled by conflicts with government or unwilling peasants, the collective lived on in its own world until the end of the war.

*

The spirit, if not the practice, which moved the socialist peasantry to collectivize was little different to that of the libertarians. But the practical differences between the Aragonese collectives we have observed and this socialist experience are obvious enough: the latter was entirely voluntary, did not attempt to include other village occupations (although some socialist collectives might include shoemakers or barbers), and was not part of a regional economic system, operating an exchange system, with its own regulatory body or government, like the Council of Aragon.

With some important modifications, it was this type of socialist collective which communist party militants were prepared to support and promote.

In Toledo province, for example, the communist party's provincial secretary, Trinidad GARCIA, told the local peasantry that they had the right to work the land as they wished, but encouraged the day-labourers to form collectives. State credits, fertilizers, agricultural machinery, seeds would all be easier to obtain that way, he stressed.

—'The agricultural ministry can't provide each of you with a loan, or a tractor, *compañero*; whereas it can provide the collective with these. You'll see that the day-labourer in a collective lives better than someone working their own plot, earns more. If you stay out, your whole family will have to slave to earn as much – and in the end you'll want to join the collective. Alone you're not going to be able to sell your produce in the village. Think about it, *compañero*' . . .

Collectives, GARCIA was convinced, were a higher form of social organization than cooperatives. In the latter, the means of production remained the personal property of each member; each peasant continued to work his own land. But it was evident to him that, in the present stage, this was the only solution for the small peasant who was reluctant to hand over his plot and his livestock. 'Why should we have to put in everything we own when the day-labourers put in nothing,' was their attitude. It even took a great deal of work, in his experience, to persuade labourers, who wanted their own plots, to change their minds in favour of forming collectives. There he did what he could; but for the smallholding peasantry he favoured cooperatives for the time being – 'cooperatives which, in the long run, would be replaced by collectives; that was the direction the agricultural ministry, supported by the communist party, was heading'.

Meanwhile, in any village without a collective there was, in his experience, nothing but trouble.

—The people said: 'Yesterday, it was don José and today it's don committee.' They understood very well what was going on. Where the committee simply controlled things and worked the land in place of the former landowner, people knew they were no better – indeed, sometimes worse – off. This happened in Corral de Almaguer, one of the richest villages in Toledo. The *cacique* mentality continued to operate. We had to go there and tell the committee members, who included socialists and communists, that the government's agrarian reform decree had got to be applied. As we got no concrete reply, we summoned a village assembly. As soon as we explained the situation, the villagers solved the problem immediately – they went out and took over the land themselves . . .

The village committee complained to the Popular Front provincial committee that GARCIA had stirred up the villagers against it. He and fellow party members were called to task. 'I told them we had done what they should have been doing.' The villagers didn't want a committee whose members ate meat they had 'expropriated' while the rest had none; didn't want to work and get whatever wage the committee happened to decide to pay; didn't want a committee that rendered no accounts. 'The people have got to be told the truth. We are at war. If there is only bread – then by bread alone; but they have got to know the truth . . .'

The communists did not support 'total' collectivization; they favoured only the collectivization of production, not consumption. Similarly, they did not support the abolition of money or an egalitarian wage. GARCIA found it necessary to explain to the collectivists that they needed foremen and specialists, as in the past, and that these would have to receive a higher wage.

—The difference with the past was that these foremen and specialists must be elected by the collectivists and that they would have to work longer hours than the rest. Because of that, and their extra responsibility, it was only right that they should receive 25 *céntimos* a day more for their work. The collectivists understood this when it was explained . . .

These, and all the other political differences between communists and anarchists, led to bitter clashes over collectivization in GARCIA's province. He maintained that the CNT's rapid growth was in large measure due to its admitting right-wingers. On the other hand, CNT militants were killed by troops attempting to break up collectives, as Eduardo de GUZMAN, editor of the CNT paper *Castilla Libre*, recalled. More than once, GARCIA was attacked by the paper for his work in the province. But he continued, firm in his belief that the agrarian reform decree was a gigantic leap forward towards socialism.

—I always said that we wanted the revolution and, while it might not be the moment for the inauguration of the dictatorship of the proletariat, that under Popular Front pluralism we were inevitably heading towards socialism . . .

Wounded in the retreat to Madrid in November 1936, Timoteo RUIZ, the youth who started the war with a lance, spent some time convalescing in Los

Navalmorales de Pusa, his native village in Toledo. There he found that the land belonging to the half-dozen large owners had been taken over and a collective, of which his father, a smallholder, was one of the founding members, was flourishing.

—'Never have I seen the country women looking so pretty,' my father said to me, and I knew what he meant: never before had the country women eaten so well, nor been better off . . .

The proposal to form a collective of all the village lands had run into the opposition of many of the village's 500 smallholders; they wanted to retain their plots. The organizers of the collective respected their wishes and agreed, moreover, that the collective would help them with tools, seeds, fertilizers, etc.

—And not only that: each was given extra land from the expropriated estates so that his plot was large enough to keep him in work all year round, but never larger than he could till with help only from his family. He could not hire labour . . .

RUIZ, who was a JSU member and would soon join the communist party, attended a collective assembly. Socialists still outnumbered communists in the village, but it appeared to him that the communists had the clearest ideas. A section of the assembly, a group of some twenty CNT members, argued that smallholders should be forced to join, accusing them of egoism.

—The local communist secretary argued that this was wrong, they had to be convinced by example. It would be the collective's own development and progress which would make these smallholders join. 'If we force them, we shall make enemies of them – and not only that, they may well try to sabotage the collective,' I remember him saying. He succeeded in persuading the assembly of his point of view . . .

On entering the collective, RUIZ's father had put in his smallholding, 'one of those to set an example'. By the end of the war, he told his son later, only 5 per cent of the smallholders who had started out working their own plots remained outside the collective.

—The reason was simple: they saw it worked well, was able to buy machinery, new tools, fertilizers which had never previously been known. They saw that people worked more enthusiastically but with less worries than before. A ploughman, for example, did not have to stable and feed the mules after work. That was taken care of by others and he could go straight home. A smallholder had all those additional tasks to do at the end of the day . . .

The CNT had not existed in the village pre-war. Having failed in their effort to oblige the smallholders to join, the twenty or so members decided to form their own collective, accusing the village collective of reformism 'since to wait for the smallholders to make up their minds was to delay the revolution', in RUIZ's words.

—The CNT made a tremendous mistake in opening its doors to anyone who wanted to join. The most reactionary falangist elements in my village became members, as I know from personal experience, because it was they who persecuted the workers with the greatest hatred after the war.

Nor, I know, was the communist party exempt from this error. Obviously, the party wanted to attract as many new members as possible, draw in the best elements. But not all those who were allowed to join were good elements by any means. People in my village who lacked the faintest communist feelings – and who, by their condition, could never hope to aspire to them – were admitted to party membership . . .

Chronology

	SPAIN	INTERNATIONAL
1875–1923	Constitutional monarchy.	
1898	Spanish-American war, loss of Cuba, Philippines, Puerto Rico, etc.	
1917	Socialist-led revolutionary general strike, beginning of monarchical crisis.	
1921	Spanish army defeat by tribesmen at Annual, Morocco.	
1917–23	Employers attempt to crush CNT in Barcelona; spiral of repression and terrorism.	
1923	Gen. Primo de Rivera becomes dictator.	
1930		
January	Primo de Rivera dismissed.	
August	Republican leaders agree on political objectives in San Sebastián pact.	
December	Abortive republican military rising at Jaca, accompanied by general strikes in many cities. Capts Fermín Galán and García Hernández executed for leading rising.	
1931		
12 April	Municipal elections.	
14 April	Republic proclaimed, king's departure.	
25 April	Azaña's army reform decrees.	
10–11 May	Convent burnings.	
28 June	Elections to Constituent Cortes.	
August	Publication of *treintista* manifesto heralding split in CNT.	
October	Alcalá Zamora resigns as prime minister after debate on Art. 26 of constitution (forbidding religious orders from teaching, etc.). Azaña becomes prime minister.	
December	Alcalá Zamora becomes president of republic. Castilblanco: peasants murder civil guards. JONS formed in Valladolid. First issue of monarchist review *Acción Española*.	
1932		
January	Arnedo: civil guards shoot down demonstrators. First FAI-inspired rising in Catalonia. CNT general strikes. Dissolution of Jesuits.	Dollfuss becomes Austrian chancellor (May).
10 August	Gen. Sanjurjo's abortive rising against the republic.	
September	Parliamentary approval of Catalan statute and agrarian reform law.	
October	CEDA founded.	
1933		
January	Second FAI-inspired rising. Murder of anarchists in Casas Viejas by police forces.	New fascist-type constitution, inspired by Salazar, in Portugal (February).
August	Largo Caballero declares that 'socialist tasks' cannot be carried out in a bourgeois democracy.	
October	New Cabinet under Martínez Barrio to prepare for general elections. Founding of Falange Español in Madrid by José Antonio Primo de Rivera.	Hitler takes power in Germany (March).
November	Right-wing electoral victory; Lerroux (radical) prime minister.	
December	Third anarcho-syndicalist rising, epicentre in Aragon.	

	SPAIN	INTERNATIONAL
1934		
February	Falange–JONS unification in Valladolid.	Dollfuss crushes socialist insurrection and outlaws all political parties (February).
March	Workers' Alliance pact signed in Asturias.	
April	Monarchist–Carlist agreement with Mussolini in Rome to provide aid for an uprising. Creation of left republican party under Azaña. Sanjurjo and companions amnestied.	
June	Socialist-led agricultural workers' strike. Esquerra's agrarian reform law for Catalonia declared unconstitutional.	Comintern signals that CPs can propose united action with socialist leaders (May).
September	PCE joins Workers' Alliance, socialist party having refused pact with communists.	
4 October	New government with three CEDA ministers.	
5 October	Revolution begins in Asturias, lasting a fortnight and crushed by Army of Africa units.	CP–socialist party pacts signed in France (July) Italy (August).
6 October	Esquerra-led rising in Barcelona collapses.	
November	Governmental repression of insurgents.	
1935		
May	CEDA opposition to its own minister's agrarian reform projects. Gil Robles becomes war minister. Franco appointed chief of staff.	Soviet–French mutual assistance treaty (May).
June	Formation of Popular Front proposed by José Díaz, PCE secretary-general. Companys and Generalitat ministers sentenced to thirty years' imprisonment for October rising.	Comintern's 7th Congress approves tactic of Popular Fronts (July–August).
September	Unification Congress of BOC and IC to form POUM.	Nuremberg anti-semitic laws (September).
October	Azaña mass meeting at Comillas outside Madrid.	
December	Formation of new government to prepare for general elections.	Italian invasion of Abyssinia (October).
1936		
15 January	Popular Front pact signed by left republican, socialist, communist parties, UGT, socialist youth, syndicalist party and POUM.	
16 February	Popular Front wins general elections.	
19 February	Azaña government. October 1934 prisoners freed.	
26 February	Generalitat restored.	
14–15 March	Falange outlawed, J. A. Primo de Rivera arrested.	
25 March	Mass socialist-led land invasions in Estremadura.	
1 April	Socialist and communist youths fuse in JSU.	
1 May	Opening of CNT Saragossa Congress. Prieto's Cuenca speech warning of dangers of violence.	
10 May	Azaña president of the republic after Alcalá Zamora's destitution by Cortes. Casares Quiroga (left republican) new prime minister after socialist party refused post for Prieto.	
June	Madrid building strike.	Popular Front government in France. Mass strikes and factory occupations (June).
12 July	Assassination of Lt José del Castillo (UMRA member).	
13 July	Assassination of Calvo Sotelo, monarchist leader.	
17–20 July	Military rising in Morocco and peninsula.	
18 July	Casares Quiroga resigns as prime minister. Rising successful in Seville.	

	SPAIN	INTERNATIONAL
19 July	Martínez Barrio resigns as prime minister. José Giral (left republican) new prime minister. The people are armed. Rising defeated in Barcelona.	
20 July	Rising defeated in Madrid. Army of Africa airlift starts. Gen. Sanjurjo killed in air accident. Libertarian leaders in Barcelona reject power. Anti-fascist militia committee formed.	

	REPUBLICAN ZONE	NATIONALIST ZONE	INTERNATIONAL
1936 *24 July*	Catalan columns head for Aragon.		
25 July			Hitler agrees to Franco request for aid.
30 July		Italian planes reach Spanish Morocco.	
4 August		Army of Africa columns begin advance from Seville towards Madrid.	
6 August		Joint bishops' pastoral to Basques.	
8 August			France closes border with Spain; unilateral start of Non-Intervention.
14 August		Insurgents take Badajoz.	
24 August			Italy, Germany, Portugal accept 'in principle' Non-Intervention proposed by Anglo-French statement (1 August).
26 August	Popular Front tribunals created.		
29 August	Soviet ambassador presents credentials in Madrid.		
3 September		Insurgents enter Talavera.	Start of Stalin's purges: Zinoviev and Kamenev executed.
4 September	Fall of Giral government. Largo Caballero forms government of socialists, communists and republicans.		
5 September		Insurgents take Irún and seal off Basque/French border.	
9 September			Non-Intervention Committee meets for first time in London.

	REPUBLICAN ZONE	NATIONALIST ZONE	INTERNATIONAL
13 September		Insurgents take San Sebastián.	
25 September		Decree forbidding all political and trade union activities.	
26 September	CNT joins new Generalitat council (government).		
27 September		Insurgents take Toledo, relieve Alcázar.	
29 September		Franco appointed head of government of Spanish state and Generalissimo of the armies.	
30 September	Decree 'militarizing' the militias, creating Popular Army.		
1 October	Basque autonomy approved by parliament.		
4 October	Offensive on Oviedo begins.		
6 October			USSR states it will not be more bound by Non-Intervention than Germany–Italy–Portugal.
7 October	State expropriation of insurgent supporters' lands decreed. Aguirre sworn in as Basque president in Guernica.		
12 October	Arrival of first Russian aid.	Unamuno attacks nationalists in speech in Salamanca.	
17 October		Nationalist army takes Illescas, 37 km from Madrid.	Texas Oil Co. assures Franco of availability of oil supplies on credit for duration of war.
24 October	Catalan collectivization decree. First Russian tanks in action on Madrid front.		
2 November	Russian fighter planes in action.		
4 November	Anarcho-syndicalists join central government.		
6 November	Government leaves Madrid for Valencia.		
7 November	Madrid defence junta under Gen. Miaja formed.	Offensive on Madrid starts.	

	REPUBLICAN ZONE	NATIONALIST ZONE	INTERNATIONAL
8 November	Madrid defenders, reinforced by first (XI) International Brigade, hold off offensive in Casa de Campo.		
15 November		Legionaries and Moors break through to University City.	
15–17 November	Heavy air raids on Madrid.	Nazi Condor Legion in action.	
18 November			Germany and Italy recognize Burgos regime.
20 November	Durruti dies in Madrid. J. A. Primo de Rivera executed in Alicante.		
23 November	End of Madrid battle with lines stabilized.		
December	Organization of mixed brigades of new Popular Army.		
17 December	POUM ousted from Generalitat government.		
22 December		First Italian black shirt units arrive in Cádiz.	
23 December	Council of Aragon recognized by central government.		
1937			
5–24 February	Battle of the Jarama – nationalist attempt to encircle Madrid held off by Popular Army.		
7–8 February		Málaga captured with participation of Italian forces.	
8–18 March	Battle of Guadalajara – Italian forces routed by Popular Army in last nationalist attempt to take Madrid until end of the war.		
31 March	Durango (Vizcaya) bombed by Condor Legion.	Beginning of nationalist offensive on Vizcaya.	
19 April		Unification of Falange and Carlist movements under Franco.	Non-Intervention land and sea patrol inaugurated.
25 April		Hedilla, Falange leader, arrested, sentenced to death (9 June).	
26 April	Guernica bombing.		
3–7 May	Civil war within the war: anarchists and POUM confront communist and Generalitat forces in streets of Barcelona.		
17 May	New government under Dr Juan Negrín.		

	REPUBLICAN ZONE	NATIONALIST ZONE	INTERNATIONAL
3 June		Mola killed in air crash.	
12 June			Soviet Marshal Tukachevsky sentenced to death. Bukharin and Rykov on trial in Soviet Union.
16 June	POUM dissolved, leaders arrested.		
19 June		Bilbao captured by nationalist army.	
21 June			Blum government in France falls.
1 July		Bishops' collective letter.	
6–26 July	Popular Army offensive on Madrid front; Brunete captured; recaptured by nationalists on 24 July.		
8 July			Sino-Japanese war. Peking occupied by Japanese.
10 August	Council of Aragon dissolved; Lister's sweep through Aragon.		
15 August	SIM (Servicio de Investigación Militar) created.		
24 August	Popular Army offensive on Aragon front: Belchite captured but offensive contained, ends on 15 September.		
26 August		Santander captured by nationalist army.	
1 September		Nationalist offensive on Asturias begins.	
19 October		With fall of Gijón, nationalists complete their capture of the north.	
31 November	Government moves to Barcelona.		
14 December	Popular Army launches offensive on Teruel; last resistance in city overcome on 8 January. Nationalists re-take city 22 February.		
1938			
30 January		Franco forms first government.	
22 February		Recapture of Teruel.	
9 March		Fuero del Trabajo promulgated.	Hitler occupies Austria.
10 March		Nationalist offensive on Aragon begins.	
18 March			Blum again premier, frontier opened but government falls four weeks later.

	REPUBLICAN ZONE	NATIONALIST ZONE	INTERNATIONAL
16–18 March	Barcelona bombed by Italians day and night.		
3 April		Nationalist army reaches border of Catalonia. Catalan autonomy statute abrogated (8 April).	
5 April	Prime Minister Negrín relieves Prieto and takes over his post as defence minister.		
14 April		Army reaches Mediterranean at Vinaroz, cutting republican zone in two.	
21 April		Offensive on Valencia begins, continuing until 23 July but without major breakthrough.	
1 May	Negrín's thirteen-point declaration of republic's war aims.		
5 July			Non-Intervention Committee approves plan for withdrawal of volunteers.
24 July	Popular Army launches Ebro offensive; start of the war's greatest battle lasting until mid-November.		
30 September			Munich pact between Hitler, Mussolini, Chamberlain and Daladier.
28 October	International brigaders' farewell parade in Barcelona.		
30 October	POUM leaders' trial.		French Popular Front breaks up.
16 November	End of Ebro battle with the Popular Army's orderly retreat across the river.		
8 December	Proposed sea-landing by Popular Army in Andalusia called off.		
23 December		Start of offensive on Catalonia.	
1939			
5 January	Last major Popular Army offensive bogs down on Estremadura front.		
15 January		Tarragona captured.	
26 January		Barcelona captured.	
5 February	Azaña, Companys, Aguirre leave Spain for France. Mass exodus across French–Catalan border.		

	REPUBLICAN ZONE	NATIONALIST ZONE	INTERNATIONAL
9 February		Law of Political Responsibilities.	
10 February	Some government ministers, including Negrín, return to central Spain.	Army completes conquest of Catalonia, reaching French frontier.	
27 February	Azaña resigns presidency of republic.		Britain and France recognize Burgos regime.
2 March	Negrín's military promotions.		
4 March	Anti-Negrín rising in Cartagena.		
5 March	Council of National Defence formed by socialists, anarcho-syndicalists and republicans in Madrid to replace Negrín government.		
6 March	Negrín and cabinet fly to France and N. Africa.		
6–12 March	Fighting between communist and Defence Council forces in Madrid.		
15 March			Hitler marches into Prague.
24 March	Council representatives fly to Burgos to negotiate surrender.		
25 March		Franco breaks off surrender negotiations.	
27 March		Burgos regime joins Anti-Comintern pact (Germany–Italy–Japan). Army occupies Madrid.	
28 March	Flight from Madrid.		
29–31 March	Refugees seek to escape from Alicante port.		
31 March			Anglo-French guarantees to Poland.
1 April		Franco declares end of war.	US recognizes Burgos regime.

Bibliography

The following list of books and articles, comprising only a small portion of the literature on the republic and civil war, includes those works which I have referred to in footnotes or have found of use in writing this book. Where a work has been republished I have tended to give the later publication date.

ABAD DE SANTILLAN, DIEGO, *Por qué perdimos la guerra* (Madrid, 1975).

ABELLA, RAFAEL, *La vida cotidiana durante la guerra civil, La España nacional* (Barcelona, 1973); *La vida cotidiana durante la guerra civil, La España republicana* (Barcelona, 1975).

AGUIRRE, JOSE ANTONIO DE, *Report on the Civil War* (first 95 pp., Bolloten collection, typescript, no date).

ALBA, VICTOR, *Historia del POUM* (Barcelona, 1974).

ALPERT, MICHAEL, *El ejército de la república en la guerra civil* (Barcelona, 1978).

ALVAREZ, RAMON, *Eleuterio Quintanilla* (Mexico, 1973).

ALVAREZ DEL VAYO, JULIO, *Freedom's Battle* (New York, 1940).

ARANA, SABINO, 'Minuta: Errores Catalanistas', *Obras completas* (Bayonne, 1965).

AUB, MAX, *Campo cerrado* (Mexico, 1943); *Campo del Moro* (Mexico, 1963); *Campo de los almendros* (Mexico, 1968).

AZAÑA, MANUEL, *Obras completas*, 4 vols (Mexico, 1966–8).

Balances para la historia (mimeograph, Barcelona, no date).

BALCELLS, ALBERTO, *Cataluña contemporánea II (1900–1936)* (Madrid, 1974).

BALEZTENA, DOLORES, *Veinticinco años al volante, Memorias de una chofer* (unpublished).

BAREA, ARTURO, *The Forging of a Rebel* (London, 1972).

BIZCARRONDO, MARTA, *Araquistain y la crisis socialista en la II república. Leviatán (1934–1936)* (Madrid, 1975).

BLINKHORN, MARTIN, 'Carlism and the Spanish Crisis of the 1930s', *Journal of Contemporary History*, vol. 7 (July–October, 1972).

BOLLOTEN, BURNETT, *The Grand Camouflage* (London, 1968).

BORKENAU, FRANZ, *The Spanish Cockpit* (Ann Arbor, 1963).

BRADEMAS, JOHN, *Anarcosindicalismo y revolución en España (1930–1937)* (Barcelona, 1974).

BRENAN, GERALD, *The Spanish Labyrinth* (Cambridge, 1943).

BRICALL, JOSEP MARIA, *Política econòmica de la Generalitat (1936–1939)* (Barcelona, 1970).

BROUE, PIERRE, *La Révolution espagnole* (Paris, 1973); (and TEMIME, EMILE), *La Révolution et la guerre d'Espagne* (Paris, 1961).

BURGO, JAIME DEL, *Conspiración y guerra civil* (Madrid, 1970); *Requetés en Navarra antes del alzamiento* (San Sebastián, 1939).

CABEZAS, JUAN ANTONIO, *Asturias: catorce meses de guerra civil* (Madrid, 1975).

CARR, RAYMOND, *Spain 1808–1939* (Oxford, 1966); (ed.), *The Republic and the Civil War in Spain* (London, 1971).

CASARES, FRANCISCO, *La CEDA va a gobernar* (Madrid, 1934).

CASTILLO, ALBERTO DEL, *La Maquinista Terrestre Marítima, personaje histórico* (Barcelona, 1955).

CATTELL, DAVID, *Communism and the Spanish Civil War* (Berkeley, 1955).

CLAUDIN, FERNANDO, *The Communist Movement: From Comintern to Cominform* (Harmondsworth, 1975).

COLODNY, ROBERT, *The Struggle for Madrid* (New York, 1958).

COMIN COLOMER, EDUARDO, *Historia del partido comunista de España*, 3 vols (Madrid, 1973).

Contestacions al questionaria que ens ha estat adrecat per la Generalitat relacionat amb la requisa dels nostres talleres . . . (mimeograph, Barcelona, May 1938).

CORDON, ANTONIO, *Trayectoria* (Paris, 1971).

CORES FERNANDEZ DE CANETE, A., *El sitio de Oviedo* (Madrid, 1975).

CRUELLS, MANUEL, *Mayo sangriento: Barcelona 1937* (Barcelona, 1970).

De Companys a Prieto, documentos sobre las industrias de guerra de Cataluña (Buenos Aires, 1939).

DIAZ, JOSE, *Tres años de lucha* (Paris, 1970).

DIAZ DEL MORAL, JUAN, *Historia de las agitaciones campesinas andaluzas-Córdoba* (Madrid, 1967).

DURAN DE VELILLA, MARCELINO (and GARCIA PRIETO, MANUEL), *18 de julio – episodios del glorioso movimiento nacional en Córdoba* (Córdoba, 1938).

ELORZA, ANTONIO, *La utopía anarquista bajo la segunda república española* (Madrid, 1973).

ESCOBAR, JOSE IGNACIO, *Asi empezó . . .* (Madrid, 1974).

ESCOFET, FREDERIC, *Al servei de Catalunya i de la república* (Paris, 1973).

FERNANDEZ, ALBERTO, *Procès à Madrid* (Paris, 1973).

FERNANDEZ CLEMENTE, ELOY, *Aragón contemporáneo (1833–1936)* (Madrid, 1975).

FRANCO SALGADO-ARAUJO, FRANCISCO, *Mis conversaciones privadas con Franco* (Barcelona, 1976).

FRASER, RONALD, *In Hiding, The Life of Manuel Cortes* (London, New York, 1972).

GALLO, MAX, *Spain under Franco* (London, 1973).

GARATE, RAFAEL DE, *Diario de un condenado a muerte* (Bayonne, 1974).

GARCIA-NIETO, MARIA CARMEN (and DONEZAR, JAVIER M.), 'La dictadura' (*Bases documentales de la España contemporánea*, vol. 7) (Madrid, 1973); 'La segunda república I' (*Bases* . . ., vol. 8) (Madrid, 1974); 'La segunda república II' (*Bases* . . ., vol. 9) (Madrid, 1974); 'La guerra de España, 1936–1939' (*Bases* . . ., vol. 10) (Madrid, 1975).

GARCIA VENERO, MAXIMINIANO, *Falange en la guerra de España: la unificación y Hedilla* (Paris, 1967); *Madrid, julio 1936* (Madrid, 1973).

GIBSON, IAN, *The Death of Lorca* (London, 1973).

GIRON, JOSE, 'Un estudio de sociología electoral: la ciudad de Oviedo y su contorno en las elecciones generales de 1933', *Sociedad, política y cultura . . .* (Madrid, 1973).

GOÑI, MARIA VICTORIA, *El abstencionismo electoral durante la segunda república en San Feliú de Guixols*, memoria a la Fundación Juan March (unpublished).

GROSSI, MANUEL, *L'Insurrection des Asturies* (Paris, 1972).

GUARNER, VICENTE, *Cataluña en la guerra de España* (Madrid, 1975).

GUZMAN, EDUARDO DE, *El año de la victoria* (Madrid, 1974); *La muerte de la esperanza* (Madrid, 1973); *Nosotros, los asesinos* (Madrid, 1976).

HERMET, GUY, *Les Communistes en Espagne* (Paris, 1971).

HILLS, GEORGE, *Franco: the Man and his Nation* (London, 1967).

IBARRURI, DOLORES, *et al.*, *Guerra y revolución en España 1936–1939*, 3 vols (Moscow, 1967–71); *They Shall Not Pass: the autobiography of La Pasionaria* (trans. of *El único camino*, London, 1967).

IRUJO, MANUEL DE, *La guerra civil en Euzkadi antes del estatuto* (typescript), (Bayonne, 1938).

ITURRALDE, JUAN DE, *El catolicismo y la cruzada de Franco*, 3 vols (Bayonne, 1955, and Toulouse, 1965).

JACKSON, GABRIEL, *The Spanish Republic and the Civil War 1931–1936* (Princeton, 1965); *A Concise History of the Spanish Civil War* (New York, 1974).

JELLINEK, FRANK, *The Civil War in Spain* (London, 1938).

KAMINSKI, HANS, *Ceux de Barcelone* (Paris, 1937).

KAPLAN, TEMMA, *Anarchists of Andalusia, 1868–1903* (Princeton, 1977); 'Spanish Anarchism and Women's Liberation', *Journal of Contemporary History*, vol. 6 (1971).

KOLTSOV, MIKHAIL, *Diario de la guerra de España* (Paris, 1963).

LEAL, JOSE LUIS, *et al.*, *La agricultura en el desarrollo capitalista español (1940–1970)* (Madrid, 1975).

LEVAL, GASTON, *Collectives in the Spanish Revolution* (London, 1975).

LIZARZA, ANTONIO, *Memorias de la conspiración* (Pamplona, 1953).

LORENZO, CESAR, *Los anarquistas españoles y el poder* (Paris, 1972).

MAIZ, FELIX B., *Alzamiento en España, de un diario de la conspiración* (Pamplona, 1952); *Mola, aquél hombre* (Barcelona, 1976).

MALEFAKIS, EDWARD, *Agrarian Reform and Peasant Revolution in Spain* (New Haven, 1970).

MARTINEZ ALIER, JUAN, *Labourers and Landowners in Southern Spain* (London, 1971); '¿Burguesía débil o burguesía fascista?: La España del siglo XX', *Cuadernos de Ruedo Ibérico* (Paris, January–June, 1975).

MARTINEZ BANDE, JOSE MANUEL, *La guerra en el norte* (Madrid, 1969); *La campaña de Andalucía* (Madrid, 1969); *La marcha sobre Madrid* (Madrid, 1968); *Los cien últimos días de la república* (Barcelona, 1972).

MASIP, ANTONIO, 'Apunte para un estudio sobre la guerra civil en Asturias', in *Sociedad, política y cultura . . .* (Madrid, 1973).

MAURA, MIGUEL, *Asi cayó Alfonso XIII . . .* (Mexico, 1962).

MAURICE, JACQUES, *La reforma agraria en España en el siglo XX* (Madrid, 1975); 'Problemas de la reforma agraria en la segunda república', *Sociedad, política y cultura . . .* (Madrid, 1973).

MAURIN, JOAQUIN, *Revolución y contrarrevolución en España* (Paris, 1966).

MEDINA, RAFAEL DE (DUQUE DE MEDINACELI), *Tiempo pasado* (Seville, 1971).

MERA, CIPRIANO, *Guerra, exilio y cárcel de un anarcosindicalista* (Paris, 1976).

MINTZ, FRANK, *L'Autogestion dans l'Espagne révolutionnaire* (Paris, 1970).

MIRAVITLLES, JAUME, *Episodis de la guerra civil espanyola* (Barcelona, 1972).

MITCHELL, SIR PETER CHALMERS, *My House in Málaga* (London, 1938).

MODESTO, JUAN, *Soy del quinto regimiento* (Paris, 1969).

MOLAS, ISIDRE, *El sistema de partidos políticos en Cataluña, 1931–1936* (Barcelona, 1974).

MORROW, FELIX, *Revolution and Counter-revolution in Spain* (New York, 1974).

Movimiento libertario espanol, El (Paris, 1974).

MUNIS, GRANDIZO, *Jalones de derrota: promesa de victoria, España 1930–1939* (Mexico, 1948).

NAREDO, JOSE, 'Estudio de las motivaciones del paso del cultivo al tercio al de año y vez' (typescript, Madrid, no date).

NATIONAL FEDERATION OF SOCIALIST YOUTH, *Octubre* (Madrid, no date).

NIN, ANDREU, *Los problemas de la revolución española* (Paris, 1971).

ONAINDIA, ALBERTO DE, *Hombre de paz en la guerra* (Buenos Aires, 1973).

ORTZI (F. LETAMENDIA), *Historia de Euzkadi: el nacionalismo vasco y ETA* (Paris, 1975).

ORWELL, GEORGE, *Homage to Catalonia* (Boston, 1959).

PASTOR, MANUEL, *Los orígenes del fascismo en España* (Madrid, 1975).

PAYNE, STANLEY, *Falange* (Stanford, 1961); *Politics and the Military in Modern Spain* (Stanford, 1967); *The Spanish Revolution* (London, 1970); *El nacionalismo vasco* (Barcelona, 1974).

PEIRATS, JOSE, *La CNT en la revolución española*, 3 vols (Paris, 1971); *Los anarquistas en la crisis política española* (Buenos Aires, 1964).

PEIRO, JOAN, *Perill a la reraguarda* (Mataró, 1936).

PEREZ-BARO, ALBERT, *Trenta mesos de col·lectivisme a Catalunya* (Barcelona, 1970).
PEREZ SALAS, JESUS, *Guerra en España 1936–1939* (Mexico, 1947).
PEREZ SOLIS, OSCAR, *Sitio y defensa de Oviedo* (Valladolid, 1938).
PONS PRADES, EDUARDO, *Un soldado de la república* (Madrid, 1974).
Preliminary report on atrocities by communist forces in S. Spain, 1936–1937 (London, 1936).
PRESTON, PAUL, 'Alfonsist Monarchism and the Coming of the Spanish Civil War', *Journal of Contemporary History*, vol. 7 (July–October 1972); 'Spain's October Revolution and the Rightist Grasp for Power', *Journal of Contemporary History*, vol. 10, no. 4 (1975); 'The Origins of the Socialist Schism in Spain, 1917–1931', *Journal of Contemporary History*, vol. 12 (January 1977).
PRIETO, INDALECIO, *Convulsiones de España*, 3 vols (Mexico, 1967–9); *Palabras al viento* (Mexico, 1942).
PRIMO DE RIVERA, JOSE ANTONIO, *Antología* (Madrid, 1942).
Qué es y qué quiere el Partido Obrero de Unificación Marxista (POUM pamphlet, Barcelona, 1936; republished Paris, 1972).
RAMON-LACA, JULIO DE, *Cómo fué gobernada Andalucía* (Seville, 1939).
Revolución de octubre en España, La (Madrid, 1935).
RICHARDS, VERNON, *Lessons of the Spanish Revolution (1936–1939)* (London, 1972).
RIDRUEJO, DIONISIO, *Escrito en España* (Buenos Aires, 1962).
ROBINSON, RICHARD, 'The parties of the Right and the Republic', in (ed. R. Carr), *The Republic and the Civil War in Spain* (London, 1971).
ROMERO, LUIS, *Tres días de julio* (Barcelona, 1967).
RUIZ, DAVID, *Asturias contemporánea (1808–1936)* (Madrid, 1975); *El Movimiento obrero en Asturias* (Oviedo, 1968); 'Aproximación a octubre de 1934', *Sociedad, política y cultura . . .* (Madrid, 1973).
SALAS LARRAZABAL, RAMON, *Historia del ejército popular de la república*, 4 vols (Madrid, 1974).
SALCEDO, EMILIO, *Vida de don Miguel* (Salamanca, 1964).
SANCHEZ DEL ARCO, MANUEL, *El sur de España en la reconquista de Madrid* (Seville, 1937).
SANZ, RICARDO, *El sindicalismo y la política* (Toulouse, 1966); *Los que fuimos a Madrid, Columna Durruti, 26 division* (Toulouse, 1969).
SEMPRUN-MAURA, CARLOS, *Revolució i contrarevolució a Catalunya (1936–1937)* (Barcelona, 1975).
SERRANO SUÑER, RAMON, *Entre Hendaya y Gibraltar* (Madrid, 1947).
SOUCHY, AGUSTIN (and FOLGARE, PAUL), *Colectivizaciones. La obra constructiva de la revolución española* (Barcelona, 1937); (and BAUER), *Entre los campesinos de Aragón* (Valencia, 1937).
SOUTHWORTH, HERBERT, *Antifalange* (Paris, 1967); *El mito de la cruzada de Franco* (Paris, 1963); *La destruction de Guernica* (Paris, 1975).
TAGUENA, MANUEL, *Testimonio de dos guerras* (Mexico, 1973).
TAMAMES, RAMON, *Estructura económica de España* (Madrid, 1969); *La república, la era de Franco* (Madrid, 1973).
THOMAS, HUGH, *The Spanish Civil War* (3rd edition) (Harmondsworth, 1977).
TROTSKY, LEON, *The Spanish Revolution (1931–1939)* (New York, 1973).
TRUETA, JOSEP, *Reflections on the Past and Present Treatment of War Wounds and Fractures* (mimeograph, Barcelona, no date).
TUNON DE LARA, MANUEL, *La España del siglo XIX* (Barcelona, 1973); *La España del siglo XX*, 3 vols (Barcelona, 1974); *El movimiento obrero en la historia de España* (Madrid, 1972); *et al.*, *Sociedad, política y cultura en la España de los siglos XIX–XX* (Madrid, 1973).
TUSELL, JAVIER, *Las elecciones del Frente Popular* (Madrid, 1971).

VICENS VIVES, JAIME, *Historia económica de España* (Barcelona, 1967).

VILANOVA, MERCE, 'Un estudio de geografía electoral: la provincia de Girona en noviembre de 1932', *Revista de Geografía* (Barcelona, 1974).

VILAR, PIERRE, *Historia de España* (Paris, 1963); 'La guerra civil en la historia contemporánea de España', *Historia Internacional*, no. 13 (Madrid, 1976).

VINAS, ANGEL, *La Alemania nazi y el 18 de julio* (Madrid, 1974).

WHEALEY, ROBERT, 'How Franco Financed his War – Reconsidered', *Journal of Contemporary History*, vol. 12 (January 1977).

WILLIS, LIS, 'Women in the Spanish Revolution', *Solidarity* pamphlet 48 (London, 1975).

ZUGAZAGOITIA, JULIAN, *Guerra y vicisitudes de los españoles*, 2 vols (Paris, 1968).

NEWSPAPERS AND REVIEWS

ABC, Seville.
Azul, Córdoba.
Butletti oficial de la Generalitat de Catalunya.
Correo de Andalucía, Seville.
Cuadernos de Ruedo Iberico, Paris.
Defensor de Córdoba.
Diario de Burgos.
Diario de Córdoba.
El Norte de Castilla, Valladolid.
El Popular, Málaga.
Guión, Córdoba.
Historia 16, Madrid.
Historia Internacional, Madrid.
Historia y Vida, Barcelona.
La Vanguardia Española, Barcelona.
Libertad, Valladolid.
Nova Iberia, Barcelona.
Nueva Historia, Madrid.
Revista de Estudios Históricos de la Guardia Civil, no. 9 (1972).
Revista de Geografía (January–December 1974), Barcelona University.
Solidaridad Obrera, Barcelona.
Tiempo de Historia, Madrid.
Treball, Barcelona.

Name Index

Notes

* — pseudonym
[M] — Militancies

Professional occupations are those at the start of the war; political and trade union memberships are those before and during the war.

JSU–S, JSU–C indicates membership of the JSU (unified socialist youth) with prior membership respectively of the socialist youth and communist youth.

PSUC–S indicates prior membership of either the Unió Socialista de Catalunya (USC) or the Catalan Federation of the PSOE; PSUC–C prior membership of either the Partit Català Proletari or Partit Comunista de Catalunya.

A colon between party memberships indicates a change of party in the course of the war. Thus JSU–S: PCE indicates a unified socialist youth member, previously of the socialist youth, who later joins the communist party.

Place names indicate the regions in which the people concerned appear in the book.

General Index